J. Hillyard, James Robinson

Queen's bench and practice court reports

J. Hillyard, James Robinson

Queen's bench and practice court reports

ISBN/EAN: 9783742815682

Manufactured in Europe, USA, Canada, Australia, Japa

Cover: Foto ©ninafisch / pixelio.de

Manufactured and distributed by brebook publishing software (www.brebook.com)

J. Hillyard, James Robinson

Queen's bench and practice court reports

QUEEN'S BENCH

AND

PRACTICE COURT

REPORTS.

BY

JAMES LUKIN ROBINSON, ESQ.,

BARRISTER-AT-LAW, AND REPORTER TO THE COURT.

VOL. III.

CONTAINING THE CASES DETERMINED
FROM HILARY TERM 9 VICT., TO HILARY TERM, 10 VICT.,
WITH A TABLE OF THE NAMES OF CASES ARGUED
AND DIGEST OF THE PRINCIPAL MATTERS.

SECOND EDITION.

TORONTO:
ROWELL & CO., LAW PUBLISHERS.

1881.

JUDGES

OF

THE COURT OF QUEEN'S BENCH

DURING THE PERIOD OF THESE REPORTS:

THE HON. JOHN BEVERLEY ROBINSON, C. J.
" JAMES BUCHANAN MACAULAY.
" JONAS JONES.
" ARCHIBALD McLEAN,
" CHRISTOPHER A. HAGERMAN.

Attorney General:
WILLIAM HENRY DRAPER.

Solicitors General:
HENRY SHERWOOD.
JOHN HILLYARD CAMERON.

A

TABLE

OF THE

NAMES OF CASES REPORTED IN THIS VOLUME.

A.

	PAGE
Ainslie v. Rapelje, Sheriff &c....	275
Ambridge v. Foster................	157
Anderson v. Todd.................	16
Armstrong v. Somerville..........	472

B.

Baby v. Davenport................	13
" v. "	54
Bacon v. McBean	305
Baldwin q. t. v. Henderson......	287
Ballard v. Pope...................	317
Bank of Montreal v. Grover....	27
" v. Dennison.......	136
" v. Humphries et al.	463
" v. Burritt.........	375
Bank of Upper Canada v. Street..	29
" v. Lewis..	325
" v. Parsons et al....	383
" v. Smith...	358
Barry v. Eccles	112
Barton v. Fisher..................	75
Bates v. O'Donohoe...............	178
Beekman v. Jarvis.................	280
Bell v. Flintoft...................	122
Biggar, In re.....................	144
Black v. Stephenson...............	160
Bleeker v. Colman	172
Boulton v. Shields................	21
Boulton et al. v. Weller..........	372
Brock et al. v. Bond..............	349
Brown v. Allen	57
" v. Palmer.................	110
" v. Ross et al..............	158
Burger v. Beamer et al............	179

C.

Cameron v. Playter et al.......	138
" v. Lount............	453
Campbell v. Elliott.............	167
Cayley and McMullen, In the matter of Award.............	124
" v. "	241
Coates v. Lloyd.................	51
Commercial Bank v. Culross et al.	176
" v. Newman et al..	176
" v. Reynolds et al..	360
" v. J. L. Hughes..	361
" v. Cameron et al.	363
Cook et al v. Mair.............	478
Cramer v. Hodgson.............	174
Cronkhite v. Somerville.........	129
Crouse v. Park...................	458
Curtis v. Flindall...............	323
Cuvillier et al vs. Browne.......	353

D.

Darby v. Earls	6
Davis v. Inland Marine Insurance Company..............	18
Davidson, Administrator, v. Raddish........................	82
Decatur v. Jarvis, Sheriff.......	133
Doe ex dem. Crooks v. Cumming.	65
" " Wood et al v. Fox et al...........	134
" " McLean v. McDonald	126
" " Hunter v. Roe......	127
" " Flanders et al. v. Roe	127
" " Anderson et al. v. Fairfield.........	140

Doe ex dem. Harris and Wife v.
Benson 164
" " Wheeler v. McWilliam 165
" " Trustees Presbyterian Church, Galt, v. Bain 198
" " Vancott v. Read 244
" " Sullivan v. " 293
" " Dissett v. McLeod ... 297
" " Stevens and Wife v. Ford 352
" " Yeigh v. Roe. 377
" " Smith v. Leavens.... 411
" " Malloch v. H. M. Ordnance 387
" " Ausman et al. v. Minthorne 423
" " Talbot v. Paterson .. 431
" " Perry et al. v. Henderson 486
Downs v. Macnamara et al. 276
Dowling v. Eastwood et al. 376
Drennan v. Boulton, one, &c.... 72

E.

Easton et al. v. Longchamp 475
Eberts et al. v. Smyth et al 189
Evans v. Kingsmill, Sheriff 118
Eldridge v. Richardson 149
Ewing et al. v. Lockhart 248

F.

Forrester v. Clarke 151
Fowler v. McDonald 385
Fralick v. Lafferty 159
Furniss v. Sawers 76

G.

Gallagher v. Brown et al. 350
Gates v. Tinning 295
Geddes v. Culver 162
Gillespie et al. v. Cameron 45
" v. Grant 400
Glen v. Box 182
Good et al. v. Harper 67
Gould et al. v. Freeman 270
Graham v. Quinn 183
" v. Newton 249
Grantham v. The City of Toronto 212

H.

Hancock v. Bethune 47
" v. Gibson 41
Henderson v. Moodie 348
" v. Perry et al. 252
Hobson v. Stroud 74
Hodgkinson et al. v. Brown 461
Hornby v. Hornby 274
Hurbert v. Thomas 258

I.

Ireland's Clerk,&c., v. Guess et al. 220
" " v. Noble 235
Irving v. Merygold 272
Ives v. Calvin 464

J

Jones v. Hamilton 170
" v. Ross et al 328

K.

Keesor v. McMartin 327
Kingston Marine Railway Company v. Gunn 368

L.

Lancey v. Spencer 169
Lemesurier v. Willard 285
Lee v. McClure 39
Leslie v. Davidson 459
Logan v. The Cobourg Harbour Company 55

M.

Manly v. Corry 380
Masecar v. Chambers et al 186
Monaghan v. Ferguson et al 484
Murphy v. Boulton 177

Mc.

MacDonell v. Weeks et al 441
McGrath v. Cox 332
McLachlin, In re 331
McLaren v. Cook et al. 285
" v. Muirhead 59
McLeod v. Bell 61
" v. Boulton 84
" v. " 89
" v. Torrence 146
" v. " 174
McNab, Duncan et al., In re 135
McNairn et al., In re 153
Mcpherson et al. v. McMillan .. 30
" " v. " .. 34

TABLE OF CASES.

N.
Nugent v. Campbell............ 301

O.
O'Hara v. Foley............... 216
O'Neill et al. v. Leight......... 70
O'Reilly v. Moodie, Sheriff..... 382

P.
Parker et al. v. Roberts........ 114
Petrie v. Taylors............... 457
Playter v. Cameron............ 129
Powell v. Boulton............. 19
    " v. " 53
Prentiss v. Beemer............. 270
Price v. Brown................ 127
    " v. Lloyd................ 120

Q.
Queen, The v. Land........... 277
    "   " v. " 279
    "   " v. Jarvis........... 125
    "   " v. Jagger et al...... 255
    "   " v. Kerr............. 247

R.
Rainville v. Powell, in the mat-
  of Complaint................ 128
Rattray v. McDonald et al...... 354
Registrar, County of York, In re. 188
Reynolds v. Shuter et al........ 377
Ross v. Merritt................ 60
    " v. Calder................ 180

S.
Sanderson et al. v. Kingston Ma-
  rine Railway Company...... 168
Seaton v. Taylor............... 303
Sherwood v. O'Reilly.......... 4
    " v. Moore............. 468
Slack v. McEathron............ 184
Small v. Beasley............... 40
    " v. " 141
    " v. Stanton.............. 148
Spalding v. Parker............. 66
Smith v. Hall.................. 315
    " v. Collins.............. 1

T.
Tait v. Atkinson............... 152
Tanner v. D'Everado et al...... 154
Taylor v. Carr................. 306
The Board of Police, London, v.
  Talbot..................... 311
Thompson v. Armstrong........ 153
Tylden v. Bullen............... 10

V.
Vincent v. Sprague............ 283

W.
West v. Brown (R.R.).......... 290
    " v. " (J. Y.).......... 291
Wheeler v. Sime & Bain........ 143
    " v. " " 265
Wood et al. v. Moodie et al..... 79
    " " v. Campbell........ 269
Wright et al. v. McPherson et al. 145

REPORTS OF CASES

IN THE

QUEEN'S BENCH AND PRACTICE COURTS.

Hilary Term, 9 Victoria.

SMITH V. COLLINS.

It is actionable to charge a man with having committed a felony in a foreign country.

Case for defamation. The declaration alleged in the first count, that the defendant, maticiously intending to injure the plaintiff, and to cause it to be believed that he was guilty of theft and larceny, and to subject him to the penalties by the laws of this province provided against persons guilty thereof; and to subject him to the pains and penalties of the laws of the *United States*, or some of them, made and provided against, and inflicted upon, persons guilty thereof; and to cause, and make him liable to be arrested and imprisoned on the said charge; and to cause and make him liable to be arrested, imprisoned, and delivered up, upon requisition, to the authorities of the United States of America, for and upon the said charge; and to be thereupon tried and punished for the said offence so charged upon him, &c. In a discourse which the defendant had concerning the said theft and larceny, in the presence of divers persons, he maliciously spoke the following false and scandalous words of and concerning the said theft and larceny, &c., viz.: "old Smith over the way" (meaning the plaintiff), "is a d—d thief, he stole a cow in the States," (meaning the United States of America), &c., thereby meaning that the plaintiff was a thief, and had been and was guilty of feloniously stealing a certain cow in the *United States* of *America*. In the third count of the declaration, the plaintiff complained of the following scandalous words, "you never keep any other but a w——e house, " and a parcel of w——s about you," meaning *that the plaintiff's house was a w——e house, and that the plaintiff was guilty of keeping a common bawdy house, and disorderly house, to wit in the said Home District.*

The defendant pleaded the general issue. The words as laid in both counts were proved. It was objected that the slander charged in the first count was not actionable, because it did not impute any offences for which the plaintiff could be indicted in this province; moreover, that stealing a cow was not shewn to be a crime in the United States of America, and if it were, yet it was not such an offence that the plaintiff could be surrendered under it, according to the treaty. The objections were over-ruled, and the jury gave a verdict for the plaintiff, with £3 damages.

Hagarty, for the defendant, obtained a rule nisi, for a new trial for misdirection, or to arrest the judgment.

Durand shewed cause.

ROBINSON, C. J.—We are of opinion that the plaintiff was entitled to recover upon both counts, if the jury were satisfied that the slander was maliciously uttered; and that this rule must, therefore, be discharged. Without going into an examination of the multitude of decisions in actions of slander, many of which (among the older cases,) are directly opposed to each other, we take it not to be at this day necessary to an action for slander, that it should impute some crime for which the plaintiff would be still liable to be punished or harassed, if the charge were believed to be true. No doubt it was at one time held, that the words to be actionable in themselves must charge a crime, for which a party might, in consequence of the charge made, be still in danger of being *indicted*, and upon conviction punished by loss of life or limb, or at least by some infamous corporal punishment. And several cases have been decided on this principle and a remedy denied, because the person slandered could not be brought in danger; as when a person said to have been murdered by the plaintiff, was shown to be living; but the law is not so now, it is sufficient if the words maliciously impute a crime to the plaintiff of *that nature* that it would, considered merely with respect to the legal character of the offence, subject any one who should commit it to corporal punishment. (*a*) It is not indispensable that the person slandered should by reason of the words, actually stand in danger of being so punished. Thus in Gainford v. Tuke (*b*) an action was held to lie for saying "*thou wast burnt in the hand for coining*." And to say of a man that he was a thief and had had a narrow escape " by having a friend on "the jury," or that "he was whipped for stealing," or that he had murdered a person, who can be shown to be still living, have been held to be actionable without any proof of special damage, though they all charge offences for which the person culminated is in no danger of any future punishment. In some late cases the language used seems to imply that the courts still adhere to the older doctrine that there must be a present danger in consequence of the words. As in Carslake v. Mapeldoram, (*c*) Mr. Justice Ashurst says "charging a person with having committed "a crime is actionable, because the person charged may *still be punished; it affects him in his liberty;* but charging another with *having had a "contagious disorder is not actionable.*" No doubt the decision in the case itself was in accordance with sound principles, but the allusion to the state of the law as regards words charging offences is either inaccurately reported, or his lordship did not reflect carefully before he made it. So Mr. Selwyn in a note to the late edition of his work, (*d*) says "the charging another with a crime of which he cannot by any possibility "be guilty, as killing a person who is then living, is not actionable, "because the plaintiff cannot be in any jeopardy from such a charge."

(*a*) Bac.; Abr.; Slander.   (*b*) Cro. Jac., 536.
(*c*) 2 T. R. 474.   (*d*) Selwyn's Nisi Prius, 1268, note 4.

This is delivering the doctrine laid down in the old case of Snagg v. Gee (a), is being still law, but it clearly is not; the contrary has been held in a multitude of cases, and as the law is now settled, I conceive that what is meant by the principle that the words must impute an offence is, that they must obtain some charge of a definite crime known to our law, for which a person committing it might be punished in a temporal court by death, banishment, imprisonment, or other corporal punishment (admitting that the punishment must be of this description), taking this standard merely as characterizing the gravity of the imputation. It ought to be no objection to this action that for the theft committed abroad the plaintiff could not be tried and punished here, because he could as little be punished for any offence for which he had already been tried and acquitted, or convicted and punished, or for which before the speaking of the words he was convicted and pardoned, as was the case in Cuddington v. Wilkins (b), where the action was nevertheless sustained. So also in Boston v. Tatham (c), where the court said "it is a great slan-" der to be once a thief; for though a pardon may discharge him of the " punishment, yet the scandal of the offence remains." I find only one case in which a question was raised upon words imputing an offence committed abroad, in which it was held, that to charge a person with high treason committed in the " Low Countries," is actionable. The reason given would make against the plaintiff in this case, (upon the general principle), for the judgment was rested upon the fact, that under the statute of Henry VIII. he could be tried for the offence in England ; but that case was at a period when it used to be held that to make the words actionable per se., they must actually place the person slandered in danger of punishment. I have a strong impression that this question is not new in our own court, and that it has been held that an action lies in such a case, though I cannot call to mind at what time, or between what parties, such a decision was made. It is true that we do not recognize the criminal law of foreign countries, and, therefore, it is argued that we cannot be certain that by the law of the United States, a man who has stolen a cow (which is what this plaintiff has been charged with), would be liable to any corporal punishment. The same might be said of words imputing murder, forgery, arson. But surely we may infer that in any civilized community which has laws and property to protect, to steal must be an offence of a very grave character. How they may punish it we may not precisely know. But I think the good sense of the rule as now maintained is that the charging a man with committing abroad such a crime as would subject him to the punishment of felony here, by the common law fixes with equal certainty the character of the imputation, and places the man in fully as degraded a position in society. Indeed to charge a man with committing, in another country, an offence so disgraceful and pernicious that it must be an offence every where, may be more injurious to his character than it would be to impute to him the having committed a similar offence here, for the having left the country in which he had once lived and removed to this, gives some color of probability to the charge. People would be apt to think that he had found it convenient to fly from justice, and the accusation could not be so readily

---

(a) 4 Co. 16.   (b) 1 Hob. 81.   (c) Cro. Jac. 622—see East. 96

refuted, if it were false. A circumstantial story deliberately told of a man having committed forgery, or theft, or murder, in a foreign country, would be to the full as prejudicial to the person slandered, as if the scene of the supposed offence was laid here, and it would be in general quite as readily believed. In my opinion, therefore, the words which impute theft committed in the United States are actionable, independently of the consideration that either under the treaty between Great Britain and the United States, or under our statute 3 Wm. IV., ch. 6, they might expose the plaintiff to be arrested and transferred to the United States for trial.

As to the third count, I am of opinion that the words as stated in it, and as proved, were actionable in themselves as conveying to common apprehension the charge of keeping a disorderly house in this province, for which the plaintiff might be indicted and punished by imprisonment, and which is moreover disgraceful to the plaintiff's character. I think that the inuendos in that count do not unwarrantably extend the meaning, or bring the case within the principle of the decision in Day v. Robinson (a).

Rule discharged.

Sherwood v. O'Reilly.

In an action for a malicious arrest without any probable cause of action, it is not sufficient to establish a prima facie case, that the plaintiff puts in at the trial the exemplification of the judgment in the former case, by which it appears that a verdict was rendered for the defendant in that action.

Case for malicious arrest. Plea, general issue.

The plaintiff had been arrested by the defendant in a civil action, for £108.

Upon the trial of this cause, it was proved that the defendant, when he was arrested, gave bail, and acknowledged that he was indebted to the plaintiff, and had offered him some goods on account, but had not admitted that he owed any particular amount. The plaintiff then put in evidence the judgment roll in the original cause, which shewed, that upon the general issue and a set-off pleaded, a verdict had been rendered for the defendant, and he had judgment to recover his costs.

Mr. Justice Hagerman, before whom the cause was tried, held that the mere production of the record of acquittal, without some further evidence to shew a want of probable cause, was not sufficient to warrant a verdict for the plaintiff; and the jury, under that direction, found for the defendant.

Becher, for the plaintiff, having obtained a rule nisi for a new trial on the ground of misdirection,

G. Duggan shewed cause.

Robinson, C. J.—I was inclined to think, upon the argument, that the record of acquittal, while wholly unexplained, might, in an action for malicious arrest, be held to supply prima facie want of probable cause and malice, so as to call upon the defendant to shew that he had some ground for the arrest; because in such cases the plaintiff in the original cause must be supposed to be cognizant of the facts relating to the debt claimed by him, though persons prosecuting in a criminal case are often obliged to proceed upon the relations of others, and upon mere circumstances of

---

(a) Ad. & Ell., 554.

suspicion. The idea has some appearance of authority to support it. In Willes' Reports, Hunter v. French (a), which indeed was an action for malicious prosecution, and therefore a stronger case in favor of the plaintiff, Mr. Justice Bennett held, "that when a person is acquitted by "a jury, malice need not be proved at first on the part of the plaintiff; "but it is incumbent on the defendent to shew on the other side, that "there was a probable cause." Lord Chief Justice Willes, who gives a very careful report of the case, though he was absent from indisposition when judgment was given, intimates no disapprobation of this opinion; and Mr. Selwyn, in his work on Nisi Prius (b) cites it without controverting it. In a case of Hamilton v. Reddell, cited by Mr. Roscoe in his Treatise on Evidence (c), Chief Justice Pratt held that the defendant's suffering the former action to be non prossed, was sufficient evidence of malice. He said "I hold most clearly, that the affidavit, arrest, bail and "non pros, make up sufficient prima facie evidence to call for a defence." Nicholson v. Coghill (d), gives some support to the ruling of Chief Justice Pratt; but if it were consistently maintained, as a general principle, which it is not by any means, that the plaintiff in the first cause suffering himself to be non prossed, or discontinuing, afforded prima facie evidence of want of probable cause, yet it would not by any means follow, that a judgment of acquittal upon a trial should have the same effect. Upon examining into the question, I have now no doubt that actions for malicious prosecutions, and for malicious arrest, stand on the same footing, as regards the onus of proof of want of probable cause and malice; and, that the weight of authority is against the position that a mere acquittal by the jury, with nothing more shewn, supplies any proof of want of probable cause; something besides that must be shewn, tending to lead to a conclusion that the plaintiff was not proceeding in good faith, and with a sincere conviction that he had a legal cause of action, though very slight evidence might be received, for the purpose of putting the other party on his defence. In Sinclair v. Eldred (e), the court held that the fact of the plaintiff not going on with his action, was not, alone, any proof of want of probable cause; and it need hardly be said, that there would be much less reason in inferring a want of probable cause from the mere fact of acquittal, where the plaintiff took his cause to trial without wavering, and for all we know, struggled to the last in the conviction that he was entitled to recover; though the jury, for some cause unknown to him, rejected his demand. In Hadden v. Mills (f), it is expressly said by Tindal, C. J., that a judgment alone in favor of the defendant in the original action, would not be sufficient. Understanding that in this case nothing whatever was given in evidence but the mere record of the judgment, we find the ruling of the learned judge to have been clearly right, and discharge the rule.

Rule discharged.

(a) Page 517. (b) P. 1080. (c) P. 390, 6th ed. (d) 4 B. & C. 21
(e) 4 Taunt. 7. (f) 4 Car. & P. 486.

Darby v. Earl.

Under the Common School Act 7 Vic., ch 39, the trustees of any school district might make a valid agreement with the teachers of the school for the district, to give him the whole allowance appointed for such school district for the year when the act came into force, if the teacher served for three months.

This was on action for a false return to a mandamus nisi issued from the Court of Queen's Bench directed to the defendants, and commanding him to join with the other trustees for common schools named in the writ, in giving an order upon the city superintendent of common schools for the City of Toronto, directing him to pay to this plaintiff the sum of £82 0s. 5¼d., being the balance coming to the plaintiff of the school fund apportioned for the school district number ten in the said city, as the school teacher for that district. The writ was grounded on an alleged contract set forth in the recital, as being made by the trustees, whereby they agreed to pay to this plaintiff, as such school teacher, "*during the "continuance of his office, the whole of the public allowance which should be "apportioned to the said school*, besides certain other rates and allowances;" and the grievance complained of was, that although the trustees contracted with the plaintiff on 1st August, 1844, upon those terms to teach the school, and although he continued to teach from that time till after the close of that year ; and although under the provisions of the school act, the sum of £104 10s. 5¼d. was duly apportioned as the public allowance for the said district for the year 1844, and came into the hands of the city superintendent to be so applied ; and although the city superintendent, during a delay which occurred in making the apportionment, paid the plaintiff £22 10s., on account of the said public allowance, yet that this defendant refused afterwards to join with the other trustees in making an order upon the city superintendent to pay him £82 0s. 5¼d., being the balance of the said public allowance, as appeared when the same was afterwards ascertained ; by reason whereof the plaintiff was prevented from receiving the money due to him upon his contract. The object of the court was to compel the defendant to join the other trustees in making such an order, or to shew cause why he did not. The defendant made a return to the writ, denying that the trustees had made any such contract with the plaintiff as he alleged, but that, on the contrary, it was expressly agreed that he was to receive for his services during the year 1844, only such an amount of the aggregate school fund to be apportioned to the school district number ten, for the year 1844, as should be proportioned to the period of his teaching, together with the whole of such monthly dues as should be collected from the scholars attending the school during that period. And for this sum the defendant stated he had been always ready to give the plaintiff an order upon the city superintendent from the time that the amount could be ascertained. The plaintiff complained of this return to the mandamus as false, affirming that the trustees did make such contract with him as that set out in the mandamus ; and that they did not contract with him in manner and form stated in the defendant's return.

Upon the trial of this issue, the jury found for the plaintiff, giving him a verdict for the amount claimed as the balance remaining in the city superintendent's hands, of the public allowance for common schools apportioned under the statute 7 Vic. ch. 29, to district number ten, for the year 1844.

The Solicitor General moved to arrest the judgment, on the ground that no valid contract, such as the plaintiff alleged, could have been made by the school trustees; that it would have been contrary to the statute, and illegal upon the face of it, and therefore such as the court ought not by their judgment to carry into effect.

Baldwin shewed cause.

ROBINSON, C. J.—The question is one wholly between the plaintiff and the trustees; or, rather between the plaintiff and his defendant, as one of the trustees, for the others do not seem to have objected to the payment, and it is the opposition of the defendant alone that has created the difficulty. The money is in the mean time in the city superintendent's hands, to be drawn out upon the order of the trustees, whenever they may concur in giving it.

To determine whether if the trustees did really make the contract, which the plaintiff alleges, and which *we must now* (since the verdict), assume they did make, such contract would be illegal and void, it has been necessary for us to look carefully into all the provisions of the statute 7 Vic. ch. 29.

According to these provisions, supposing all to have been done which the act directs, and confined as we are upon this motion to the record, we have no grounds for imagining the contrary, then the following are the steps which we must suppose have been taken. On or soon after 1st March, 1844, the superintendent must have apportioned the school money of each township, city, &c., assigning to the city of Toronto its portion; on 1st August, 1844, such money must have been paid to the *county superintendent :* the county superintendent must have given notice forthwith (that is directly after the 1st August, 1844), to the city superintendent, of the amount for the city in his hands, and must have held the same subject to the city superintendent's order: he must also have sent *at the same time* to the city clerk notice of the sum assigned to the city: the city clerk must at once have laid that information before the city council, and they must *without delay* have assessed at least an equal sum, through the city collector, to be paid by him to the city superintendent of common schools; the city council must also have appointed a city superintendent of schools for the city, who may have divided the city into school districts and applied for the school money, and fixed the proportions to be paid to each, for he is not to apportion the allowance alone of the aggregate *school fund*, that is of the public allowance and the rate: and the city superintendent must, within twenty days after forming the school districts, have appointed a time in each for a district school meeting: at such meeting the trustees must have been chosen, who might at once " contract with and employ teachers," and who might draw from the *city superintendent* the amounts due them for their salaries, " so far as the *monies in his hands applicable to their district shall* " *be sufficient for that purpose*," and who might *collect* and pay over the salary: that is, if the public allowance and the sum assessed should not be as much as they had contracted to give to the teacher, they might levy the deficiency from the parents of the children taught. The condition that a school shall be kept in the school district for at least three months, to entitle the trustees to receive the public allowance, cannot, I think, be applied to the first year, 1844. The 19th, 25th, and 68th clauses sufficiently shew that. But if it could, the condition appears in this case, by the statement in the record, to have been complied with. On receiving notice of the sum which the chief superintendent had allotted to the City of Toronto, the city superintendent should at once have informed the city council, as we must suppose he did, of the sum allotted for their schools, and the city council should then have forthwith levied by assessment at least an equal sum, which being paid by the collector into the hands of the superintendent, would form part of the school fund; the other part, namely, the allotted portion from the provincial revenue, remaining in the hands of the county superintendent, subject to the order of the city superintendent. Both these amounts, when received, would form in the hands of the city superintendent the *aggregate school fund*, which school fund (and not the allowance alone,) he is to apportion among the several districts, according to the number of children between five and sixteen years of age, residing within the division. Now for all that appears before us in these pleadings, the statute has been regularly acted upon, and a school fund formed for the district number ten, being the aggregate of the public allowance for this district, and of the rates levied to be added to it; and the plaintiff was engaged as teacher by the trustees for that district, not for any definite period of service, and has actually served from August, 1844, to the end of the year; and the trustees did, as is stated in the record, contract to pay him, "during the continuance of his office, the "whole of the public allowance which should be apportioned to that "school district, besides certain other rates and allowances." Waiving any question as to "the other rates and allowances," about which no difficulty has arisen, the plaintiff claims under this contract £104 10s. being the whole of the public allowance paid in 1844, as the school money for the district number ten, for that year. And the questions are, first, what does the agreement as set out by the plaintiff really import? and secondly, is the agreement, according to what we must hold to be its import, a legal agreement by which the trustees are bound; or, is it illegal and void as being contrary to the statute, and one which the trustees could not lawfully make? The defendants evidently understand and admit that such a contract as the plaintiff has set out would assure to him that which he claims, namely, the whole allowance *for the year*. They put the same construction as he does on the words of the contract which he sets out. For my own part I have been strongly inclined to doubt whether that would be the fair effect of the words. The contract, as the plaintiff himself states it, is not that the trustees were to pay him the whole public allowance *for the year* 1844, or "for the year," but that "*during his continuance in office they would pay him the whole public* "*allowance apportioned to his district;* not the allowance apportioned for the year. And the first question we have to ask ourselves is, whether this really means anything more than that for the period of his service they would pay him *the whole public allowance*, that is the public allowance received for that period, paying him pro rata; as for instance, if a salary of £100 per annum were by act of parliament attached to a particular office, and on the 1st July a person should be appointed to such office, and he should serve to the 1st January following, if he were then to receive £50, he would receive the whole public salary allotted to the situation *during his continuance in office.* He does not in that case receive the whole salary *for the year;* but this contract, as the plaintiff sets it out in his declaration, does not express that the plaintiff is to receive the whole allowance for 1844, or, for the year, but that "*during his continu-* " *ance in office, he should receive the whole of the public allowance which* "*should be apportioned to the said school district.*" I have had a good deal of doubt whether, consistently with the language used, the plaintiff's contract as he himself states it, would assure to him anything more than a full proportion of the public allowance, during his period of service, taking £104 10s. as the money for the year, in other words the whole public allowance during the period of his service; and if that were the construction which we must give to the agreement on which he himself relies, then the return which these defendants have made to the mandamus would be the same in effect, though in different words, and would not be a false return on which he could ground a right of action, and the plaintiff would be claiming under the agreement set out a sum to which he would not be entitled. But both plaintiff and defendant seem clearly to admit and understand that the contract according to which the plaintiff claims, would cover the whole £104 10s.; and my brothers, I believe, take the same view of the legal construction of the words used. It is perhaps the more natural and sound one. "The whole of the public allowance "*which shall be apportioned to the district*" may well have been meant to extend to the whole specific sum allotted by the chief superintendent which would be the £104 10s., and both parties have seemed to admit that if such were the words used, that would be their effect. As my brothers are also of that opinion, it is of no moment to dwell further on the doubt which I have had on that point. Now admitting (as the jury have found), that such an agreement was made, would it be illegal and invalid? At first view it would seem to be an unreasonable agreement, unjust towards the public, and inconsistent with the spirit of the act, for the contract set out does not make it a condition that he should serve for any certain period, and such a system would afford no assurance that the service and compensation should bear a just proportion to each other. But though it might be an unreasonable and incautious contract for the trustees to make, it does not of course follow that it must be invalid under the act, and still less that we have any arbitrary discretion to pronounce it void. The best security against injury to the public would have been in the trustees being furnished under the 6th clause of the act, with a suitable form of contract and suitable instructions or regulations for their guidance. When we come to consider, which I have done very carefully all the provisions of this statute, reading them over repeatedly in order to discover their connection and effect, I do not feel that we have authority to say that the trustees, under the very general power given to them by the 44th section to make contracts with the teachers, could not legally engage to give to any one of them the whole public allowance and the whole of the rates for that particular district, without requiring that he must serve the whole year. It would be absurd, I think, and wrong to do so, or at least to promise him the allowance without making it a condition that he should serve some certain period, and without guarding against the contingency of the teacher ceasing to serve during the year, or for such a portion of it as they might consent to accept as sufficient.

The statute seems to admit a claim to the whole allowance being founded on a service of three months, or any period above that, if the trustees shall consent. The contract set out here did not bind the teacher to any certain term of service, but it is averred on the record, and not denied, that he did in fact serve from the 1st August to the end of the year, which was as large a portion of the year as he could well have served, allowing for the time at which the act could be brought into operation; that for such a service he could not legally receive by agreement with the trustees the whole of the public allowance for 1844, considering that it embraced all that part of the year in which a school could be taught under the act, and also extended beyond three months, is what I think we can on no very clear ground hold; though to have made such a contract, even under the very general authority given to the trustees, might be imprudent and improper. The power given to the trustees by the 44th clause of the act, to contract with and employ teachers, is very general in its terms, and we have no authority to place it within restrictions which the legislature has not prescribed. As the trustees seem not to have had the means of knowing, when they made the contract, what amount of money would fall to their district in the general apportionment throughout the province, it is not improbable that they believed they might safely engage to pay to this teacher the whole allowance, and that it would form no extravagant recompense. There can be no doubt that the proper and just mode of proceedings would be to assure a certain sum according to the period of service; but we can neither make any law to that effect, nor do we find in the statute that the trustees were placed under any actual legal necessity for entering into that description of contract. And as we cannot on any legal principal hold that the contract under which the plaintiff claims is void, admitting it to assure to him for five months' service only the whole allowance for the year, we are of opinion that the rule for arresting the judgment must be discharged.

Rule discharged.

Tylden v. Bullen.

In order to dispense with the production of the subscribing witnesses to a deed, it must be shewn that every reasonable inquiry has been made for them in the place where they were most likely to be found, and that they cannot be discovered.

Where in trespass quare clausum fregit, the plaintiff proved admissions of the defendant as to the title of the lane in question, which should have been left to the jury, but the case rested upon the want of sufficient evidence to admit the testimony of the handwriting of the subscribing witness to the deed, under which the plaintiff claimed, which the court decided against him, a new trial was granted with costs to abide the event.

Trespass quare clausum fregit, and for cutting trees and taking away the timber. Pleas the general issue; secondly, that neither the close, nor the trees, were the property of the plaintiff; thirdly, that the plaintiff was not possessed of the close; fourthly, that the close was the soil and freehold of the defendant; wherefore he committed the several trespasses in the declaration mentioned. The plaintiff joined issue. It was proved that Roswell Mount, deceased, was the grantee of the crown of this land, and that he executed a deed in 1826, conveying it to Charles Duncombe, and the plaintiff produced, and endeavoured to prove, a conveyance from Charles Duncombe to him, dated in August, 1836. There were two witnesses to this deed named, J. W. Deane, and Mary L. Deane, neither of whom was produced on the trial. The deed was dated at Burford, and all the account given of the subscribing witnesses was, that one person swore that he knew *a family* of the name of Deane who lived, before the rebellion (in 1837), in the township of Norwich, or near it, and that he believed they went away about that time. Norwich is an adjoining township to Burford, but whether the family spoken of had any person in it of the same name ss those witnesses was not shewn. Then another witness swore that he had inquired for "the Deanes," but could not hear of them; that he had heard of the family referred to by the last witness; that he had inquired of persons acquainted with all the township of Burford, but could hear nothing more of them, except that he was told they lived in Erie, in the state of Pennsylvania. The handwriting of Duncombe, the grantor, was proved. This conveyance had never been registered, nor the one from Mount to Duncombe; and the defendant, ignorant, for all that appeared, of the title having passed from Roswell Mount, had purchased from his eldest son and heir, and had placed his deed on record. A nonsuit was moved at the trial, on the ground that the deed from Duncombe to the lessor of the plaintiff was not proved; and the question whether there was, under the circumstances, any legal evidence of its execution to go to the jury, was reserved. There was also evidence of admissions made by the defendant, tending to establish the plaintiff's title to the land. A verdict was found for the plaintiff with £3 15s. damages.

Becher, for the defendant, having obtained a rule nisi, moved according to the leave reserved.

J. Hillyard Cameron shewed cause.

ROBINSON, C. J.—The result of this motion depends upon the question, whether such efforts were shewn to have been made for procuring a satisfactory account of the subscribing witnesses, as entitled the plaintiff to have the deed from Duncombe to the plaintiff read, upon proof given of Duncombe's hand writing. The law is not unreasonably rigid in this respect, but we are all of opinion that *it* clearly requires more to be done than was done in this case. The case cited from the Law Journal (a) is very much in point. It really cannot be said here that the parties made any serious effort to find out even who the witnesses were. Inquiring in London of such persons acquainted with the township of Burford, as they might happen to meet there, is not sufficient. Search should have been made in the neighbourhood in which this family of Deane resided, since the plaintiff supposed it to be the one to which the subscribing witnesses belonged. And upon that point whether the subscribing witnesses were of that family or not, which was the first step in the enquiry, no pains seem to have been taken. The plaintiff, or some agent of his, should have gone to the former place of residence of those Deanes, and ascertained whether J. W. Deane and Mary L. Deane, were of that family. It is only necessary to look at the signatures to see that they are persons who might be easily traced, if they had been living in Norwich. The

(a) 7 Page 96.

signature of J. W. Deane is a very peculiar one. Then if it could not be learned with certainty whether the witnesses were of that family, or where they had gone to, the obvious step remained of going to the last or present place of residence of one or both of the parties to the deed, and making enquiry there. That was considered necessary in the case of Cunliffe et al. v. Sefton (a), and there is no reason to doubt that if the attorney had done so, he could not have been uncertain who the witnesses were, and what had become of them. All that he has shewn is that some persons of the same surname once lived somewhere in that part of the country, and have now gone out of it. If the plaintiff, or his guardian, had become possessed of a promissory note against J. W. Deane, for a sum of money, he would have made a very different kind of enquiry after him, before he gave up the debt as lost. There may be no doubt whatever, that the deed in question was really executed by Duncombe, in the presence of persons who have attested it by their signatures, and the objection here may seem a mere formal impediment in the administration of justice, but the defendant is entitled to have the subscribing witnesses produced, if they are not shewn to have been inaccessible, for he may desire to inquire of them about the circumstances attending the execution of the deed, and it is important that the rules of evidence should be fixed and adhered to. Another point was made in the argument, namely, that the plaintiff was entitled to recover without proving the execution of the deeds, because it is contended that it was proved on the trial, that the defendant, on a complaint being made to him that he had been cutting timber on the lot, admitted the plaintiff's right and promised to make compensation. The case of Doe dem Loudon v. Watson (b), was cited, but it is not in point ; for that was an admission by the plaintiff himself, in an action of ejectment, that he had no right to the possession, and the court held that he could not recover in the face of that admission. The admission of the defendant in this action of trespass to the freehold, if it amounted only to an admission, qualified or unqualified, that he had himself no right would not be sufficient to support the plaintiff's case, unless it went farther, and admitted that the plaintiff was the person entitled to ; and we do not think that the evidence was express to that effect. It was not the plaintiff, but his father, who conversed with the defendant and charged him with taking timber off the lot, producing the titles to the land, whereupon the defendant did not deny having taken the timber, and said he would settle with the plaintiff's father for it. But that admission, it is probable, was nothing more than a declaration, that if Mr. Mount had really conveyed the estate to Duncombe before he, the defendant, bought it, he must of course pay for any injury he had done to the place, to the person who claimed under Duncombe. The plaintiff's council evidently did not consider upon the trial that any thing had passed, which relieved him from the necessity of proving the deeds, in order to shew that the plaintiff was really the person entitled to compensation for the alleged trespass, for he commenced by giving such evidence as he could of the execution of the deeds ; and, upon the sufficiency of that evidence the question was raised which, by consent, was made the ground of motion for a nonsuit in term. To make the alleged

---

(a) 2 E. R., 182.   (b) 2 Stark N. P. C., 230.

admission sufficient to maintain the action, the jury should have been satisfied from the evidence that it was an unqualified admission, extending to the right of this plaintiff, the infant, and not to any supposed right of the father; and that it was not contingent upon his being satisfied of the genuineness of the deeds. The discussion and questions raised upon the proof of the execution of the deeds, seems to have called attention from the precise extent of these admissions, &c. We think, therefore, that the deeds not having been sufficiently proved, the proper course is to grant a new trial, with costs to abide the event.

New trial, costs to abide the event.

BABY v. HORACE DAVENPORT.
BABY v. LEWIS DAVENPORT.

Where in debt on award, the plaintiff declared reciting a submission by bond, and that under the bond the arbitrators had made an award upon one of the matters in difference, the other matters submitted having been by the consent of the parties withdrawn from their consideration, and that afterwards the other matters having been again submitted, the arbitrators made an award in favor of the plaintiff, and the defendants pleaded no such submission, and never indebted, and at the trial the plaintiff proved the parol submission, but did not produce the bond, and a point was reserved to the defendant to move upon that objection the court, on motion for a *new trial,* (the verdict being in accordance with the justice of the case) refused to interfere.

Debt on award. The declaration set out a submission by bond, an award made upon a certain claim respecting the repair of the ferry-boat wharf at Windsor, &c , and a refaining of the arbitrators by the desire of both parties to the suit to make any award upon other matters in controversy, though all were submitted by the bond set out, which was on the face of it a general submission, and that, after this first award had been made, the parties submitted by parol their other differences which had not been awarded upon, to the same arbitrators; the declaration then set out an award made that the defendants should pay the plaintiff £41 15s. 1d. for which this action was brought. The defendant pleaded two pleas, which were demurred to; thirdly, he denied the parol submission on which the latter award was made; and fourthly, he pleaded nunquam indebitatus. In each action the pleadings were precisely similar. The submission set out in both was by the plaintiff on the one side, and Lewis Davenport, and Horace Davenport, on the other; and the award was that both should pay to the plaintiff £41 15s. 1d. They had been sued in separate actions, from a difficulty in serving process upon one of them, who resided out of the country at the time the other was served. The case was a peculiar one; the parties had submitted all their difference by bond to three arbitrators, on the usual condition that the award was to be made by a certain day. Before that day the arbitrators and parties met, for the purpose merely of deciding, on that occasion, what amount the plaintiff ought to receive from the defendants for repairing and putting in a tenantable condition a certain ferry wharf, which they had rented from him. They awarded to the plaintiff on that account £37 10s. 1d.; and they stated in this award, that as the bond authorized them to arbitrate on all matters depending between the parties, they had, at their request, waived going into any matter, except as to the wharf, at that time, and that, in the event of the parties disagreeing on other matters respecting the occupancy, they (the arbitrators) would be prepared to resume the arbitration and to decide the same. This award was made under the hands and seals of the arbitrators on the 18th day of April, 1843; and on the 29th day of April, which was still within the time limited by the bond for making the award, the arbitrators met again, and with the consent of all the parties, and, indeed, as it was proved, at their express desire, investigated whatever matters were in difference between them; and, upon hearing the parties and their witnesses, they made on that day another award under their hands and seals: in which they stated, that at an adjourned sitting of the arbitrators appointed to determine between the parties, who had been bound in a bond in the sum of £1,000 to abide by their decision, they determined that the two Davenports should pay to the plaintiff the sum of £41 15s. 1d. in discharge of all claims whatsoever, in addition to the sum of £37 10s. before awarded. This action was brought to recover the sum last awarded. At the trial it was objected by the defendant that the plaintiff had not sufficiently proved the submission declared on. The learned judge declined to nonsuit the plaintiff, but reserved leave to move on the legal objection.

Harrison, Q. C. for the defendant, then moved to set aside the verdict, not strictly upon the legal objection, but on the general ground that it was rendered against law and evidence.

(In each case the same evidence was given, and the same course had been taken in moving against the verdict.)

J. Hillyard Cameron shewed cause.—In these cases the court cannot but see that the verdict of the jury is strictly in accordance with the justice of the claim, and the defendants are not entitled to prevail upon the form of motion that they have adopted. The objection taken at the trial was a strictly legal one, and upon which a right was reserved to the defendants to move, but they have not availed themselves of that right; they have come before the court, to set aside the verdict as having been rendered contrary to law and evidence, and as their rule cannot be sustained in that shape, it must be discharged.

Harrison, in reply.—The plaintiff sets out a bond of submission in his declaration of which he gives no proof at the trial, and consequently his action fails; but that point is reserved by the judge, and it can be considered as reserved, only because in law without the production of the bond the evidence of submission was incomplete. The defendants, therefore, had the option of insisting upon the legal point taken at the trial, or moving their rule in its present shape; and if the bond be considered as forming a necessary part of the plaintiff's case, the defendants are entitled to prevail on this motion.

ROBERTSON, C. J.—The verdict is evidently consistent with the justice of the case, for the award is not impeached; and the fact of the parties having freely submitted to the reference is not disputed. For the sake of the parties, therefore, we should sustain the verdict if possible, for in another proceeding the sum could, without doubt be recovered. It is then to be considered that the defendant has not moved upon any strictly legal exception, but generally against the verdict, as being contrary to law and evidence. The declaration certainly alleges a submission by bond, in the first instance, and an award upon that submission; but it does not treat the award sued upon as having been made under the same submission: on the contrary, it alleges that a particular subject of difference having been awarded upon under that submission, the parties determined, afterwards, to leave all other things to the same arbitrators, apparently referring to the first submission and award, for no other purpose than for shewing that the latter submission excluded one matter which had already been settled. Then although it may be true, as I think it is, and as the court intimated, when giving judgment on demurrer between these same parties, that the arbitrators might properly, on the second occasion, have taken up the unsettled matters in the original submission, and that the two awards might be taken as one settlement of all matters in difference, though made at different times, the first award being upon the face of it not a complete execution of the arbitrator's authority, nor intended to be so; yet the parties were not compelled so to regard it. They might suppose it to be at least more safe and proper to agree, afterwards, expressly to submit their other matters, and that is the kind of submission which the declaration sets out. There is no impropriety in bringing debt on the award, rather than suing on the bonds, even if the bonds would undoubtedly have extended to the second award, under the peculiar circumstances of this case, as I think they would. It is recommended, for good reason, in general to sue in debt on the award as is done in this case, and not on the bond. The question of evidence, at the trial on the issue on the second plea, was, whether the parties did submit, as the declaration averred; that is, whether after the first award was made they did agree that the same arbitrators should determine their other differences. I think it was clearly proved that they did. They requested the arbitrators to investigate and award upon the other matters, and they went before them, and were heard. That proof was of a submission such as was declared upon, and although the plaintiff may have known that the former submission by bonds was still in existence, and could be made use of for enforcing this latter award, yet he was not obliged to sue or to rely upon the bond. The parties had not the less agreed, on the 29th April, to submit their differences, because they had agreed before. It is the latter submission the plaintiff proceeds upon, as I think he may, and he sufficiently proved such a submission. If he had sued upon the submission as being by bond, he must have proved it as he had laid it; but he did not so lay it. There is no question here as to a remedy upon a submission by parol merging in a remedy of a higher kind in consequence of the bond; for it is the common practice to sue in debt on the award, which is not a speciality, when the parties have submitted by bond. It is merely a question of evidence. The substance of the issue is, whether they submitted or not; and it was proved they did. As to all that is said in the declaration about the manner in which the amount due for repairs of the ferry wharf had been settled, it is merely an explanation given, as it seems to me without any necessity, of a matter about which the parties were no longer in difference. I do not see why the record need have been encumbered with it. If the parties had settled that one matter by means of a trial and judgment at law, or, by compromise between themselves, that fact need not have been alluded to in the declaration; and if it had been, I do not conceive that proof of such unnecessary statements need have been given; and that in my opinion is the case with the pleadings as they stand. We can put aside all mention of the award about the ferry wharf, without prejudice to the statement of the cause of action sued upon. It is quite true that, in one respect, such a submission as that sued upon was not proved. It is averred that the parties submitted on the condition that an award should be made on or before the 29th April; there was no proof of such a condition. But the variance was not material to the defence on the merits, and as no objection was taken on that precise ground at the trial, we should not do well to give effect to it now, because if it had been made a defence at the trial, the plaintiff might have moved to amend.

Rule refused.

ANDERSON V. TODD AND BLOOMFIELD.

Where in trespass for mesne profits, there were several issues joined, and at the trial a verdict was found for the defendants upon one issue clearly against evidence, the court granted a new trial to the plaintiff, unless the defendants consented to allow a verdict to be entered for the plaintiff upon that issue.

Trespass for mesne profits. The plaintiff declared that the defendants, on the 6th January, 1843, brake and entered into certain closes of the plaintiff, being Lot No. 15 in the 3rd concession west of Hurontario Street, in the Township of Toronto, and ejected and expelled the plaintiff, and kept him out *from the day aforesaid* to the 21st June, 1845, and during that time received the rents and profits, and caused great waste, damage and injury to the premises, and put the plaintiff to cost in recovering possession. The defendants pleaded, first, as to all the trespasses except the breaking and entering the close and continuing thereon till the 21st June, 1845, that they were not guilty thereof; secondly, as to the breaking and entering the close *before* the 20th day of June, 1845, and continuing therein, and keeping the plaintiff out *until the 20th June*, 1845, the defendants pleaded, that long before the alleged trespasses, and before the plaintiff had any interest in the premises, viz., *on the 18th May*, 1842, one Robert Anderson, being seised in fee of the premises by his will, sealed with his seal, and bearing that date, and of which they make profert, gave and granted to the defendants leave and license to enter upon the premises after his death, and to take the rents and profits until the 20th June, 1845; that he died on the 3rd of June, 1842; wherefore the defendants *in their own right*, after his death, broke and entered the close, &c.; and continued therein, and kept the plaintiff out until the said 20th June, 1845, as they lawfully might, which were the same trespasses, &c.; thirdly, as to the breaking and entering the close, and continuing therein until the 21st June, 1845, they paid one shilling into court. The plaintiff replied to the second plea, that Robert Anderson did not make and publish the will and testament in that plea mentioned in manner and form, &c. And to the third plea, that he had sustained greater damages than one shilling. Verdict for the plaintiff on the general issue, and one shilling damages; and for the defendants on the second and third issues,

R. B. Sullivan, for the plaintiff, having obtained a rule nisi for a new trial on the law and evidence, and for misdirection, and for the reception of improper evidence in mitigation of damages;

Bell and *D. G. Miller*, shewed cause,

ROBINSON, C. J.—The defendant was not, in my opinion, entitled to succeed on the second issue. The devise under which he endeavours to vindicate his possession up to the 20th day of June last, has been, in the action (a) which preceded this suit, adjudged void, as being prohibited by the English statute 9 Geo. II. ch. 36, called The Statute of Charitable Uses, which, upon the grounds then stated by us, we considered to be in force in Upper Canada. Then, holding it to be void, as prohibited by that statute, it follows that it is void " to all intents and purposes ;" and we should not be acting in conformity with the statute, if we were to give it the partial effect of a license to hold the possession, though it cannot pass the estate. But independently of this objection, it is impossible to hold what was intended to be a devise in fee, to be merely a license to hold possession till the certain day named in the plea. The will either passes an interest in the estate, or it does nothing. It clearly gives no license that can operate after the testator's death, and for a certain time and no longer. The verdict, therefore, on the second issue, ought, I think, to have been rendered for the plaintiff, and not for the defendants. Upon the third plea the jury were not misdirected, for they were told that they ought to find substantial damages for the plaintiff. Making allowance, however, as I suppose they did, for improvements sworn to have beeen made during the occupation, and considering the peculiar circumstances under which the defendants took possession, upon a supposition that under the will it was their right and duty to do so, they chose to award no substantial damages ; I think there was no injustice in their view of this matter, and that the plaintiff should have been content with gaining possession in such a case ; and, at all events, this, I think, is not a case in which we ought to set aside the verdict, at the plaintiff's instance, for smallness of damages. Upon the finding on of the several issues, the case stands thus : the general issue does not deny the breaking and entering the close and continuing therein *till the* 21st June, 1845, but it does deny the expelling and keeping the plaintiff out, the receiving the rents " and profits, and committing waste." Upon the general issue the plaintiff has recovered a verdict with one shilling damages ; which is not moved against by the defendants. The question, therefore, is only whether we shall at the plaintiff's instance grant a new trial, on account of any thing wrong in the ruling of the court, or in the finding of the jury on the special pleas, or either of them. The issue on the second plea, ought, I think, to have been found for the plaintiff, because the alleged license was not made out, but it only bars the recovery for the breaking and entering before the 20th June, and continuing thereon and keeping the plaintiff out *until the 20th June*. It does not bar the plaintiff's right to recover for any other injury complained of, and therefore leaves unanswered the trespass in entering on the 20th or 21st June, and continuing in possession, and keeping the plaintiff out on those two days, which the declaration clearly alleges. The verdict, therefore, if wrong upon that issue, does not interfere with the plaintiff's right to recover the nominal damages which alone the jury have given him ; but it is a verdict against evidence, and so clearly so, that we cannot properly refuse to grant a new trial, though the costs of the issue only are concerned, unless the defendants

---

(a) 2 Cameron, 82.

will consent that the plaintiff may enter a verdict in his favour, or will waive the costs of that issue. Though there seems in the opinion of the learned judge who tried the cause, to have been a misapprehension in his mind in respect of the effect of the evidence upon this issue, there was no such misapprehension in regard to the issue on the third plea; and we do not think that we can properly interpose, because the jury, on a view of all the facts, did not choose to give substantial damages when it was left to them to do so or not, as they thought right upon the facts.

Rule absolute for a new trial.

DAVIS v. THE ST. LAWRENCE INLAND MARINE ASSURANCE COMPANY.

Where in an action on a marine policy, the plaintiff recovered as for a total loss, the facts only shewing the partial loss, which, however, were not so distinctly left to the jury, the court granted a new trial, without costs.

This was an action upon a policy of insurance upon a barge navigating the waters between Kingston and Montreal, and the plaintiff recovered a verdict as for a total loss, the evidence not being quite distinct and clear that the loss was total, and the case not having been left to the jury for any expression of opinion by them on that point.

Blake, for the defendant, obtained a rule nisi for a new trial for misdirection, and urged several legal objections to the recovery of the plaintiff, in addition to the question as to the amount of damage which the plaintiff was entitled to recover; but as the court expressed no opinion upon those objections the argument is omitted. He contended that the evidence established only a partial loss, and as the case went to the jury as a constructive total loss, the defendants were entitled to a new trial.

J. Hillyard Cameron, for the plaintiff, admitted that the evidence did not sustain the verdict as for a total loss in fact, nor could the verdict be sustained as for a constructive total loss; but contended that the other legal objections raised by the defendants were not entitled to prevail.

ROBINSON, C. J.—We need not hesitate to grant a new trial in this case, because the plaintiff's counsel fairly concedes that the verdict cannot be sustained. He admits that, upon the evidence, he was entitled to recover as for a partial loss only, therefore the application for a new trial cannot be resisted. It must, under the circumstances, be granted without costs; because, although there were one or more issues in the case which were left to the determination of the jury, yet upon the question of partial or total loss, I gave the jury such a direction upon the trial as no doubt led to the present verdict; and, if that was wrong, it was a misdirection of which the defendants had a right to complain. The case was tried before me, at Kingston, and I remember that at its conclusion the attorney-general, who was counsel for the plaintiff, observed, that upon the declaration the plaintiff might recover either for a total or a partial loss, according as his right might appear upon the evidence, which no doubt he might. The defendant's counsel contended very strenuously that the evidence did not shew a total loss in fact, and that the plaintiff could recover only for the damage done to the boat, which was afterwards got off and repaired; and that if, under the circumstances, it could be made a constructive total loss by abandonment and notice, yet that there was not proof of such an abandonment. Whether the plaintiff's counsel means to admit that now, I am not sure. If he does, then the verdict is for an amount much too large. I was under a different impression at the trial. When the barge was sunk and stranded in the St. Lawrence, in consequence of the accident she met with, the master and crew, before they abandoned her, stripped off her sails, and anything that could be saved from her, and deposited them in a barn near where the barge remained stranded. It was contended that at least the plaintiff could not recover the sum insured, without making a deduction for the value of those things saved from the wreck; but as there was no evidence that the sails, after being deposited in the barn, had ever been removed from thence by the plaintiff, or that he had exercised any act of ownership over them since, I considered that they ought, for all that appeared, to be regarded as merely secured for the benefit of the insurers, if they should appear to be liable for a total loss. An express clause in the policy provides, that at the time of the accident, the owner or master of the barge should be at liberty to make every effort for saving or recovering the property, without prejudicing his claim. I think so still; but in any such case it must always be a question on the evidence, whether the conduct of the insured has been such as to make the goods saved his own or not. Upon the other points which have been raised in the case, we think it better not to express our opinion, as there is to be another trial; and whatever may seem doubtful can be more advantageously discussed after a full extent of the evidence is known, and the opinion of the jury ascertained upon the facts.

Rule absolute for new trial, without costs.

POWELL v. BOULTON.

Where in debt on bond conditioned to save the plaintiff harmless from all demands or suits regarding a certain sum of money, and to discharge all damages, costs and charges that might be recovered in respect thereof, the defendant pleaded non damnificatus, and the plaintiff assigned two breaches, setting out a judgment for the said sum of money in the condition mentioned, not specifying any particular sum for which judgment had been recovered; held on motion in arrest of judgment that the breaches were sufficiently assigned.

This was an action on a bond given by the defendant to save the plaintiff harmless against any action brought against him by McLeod in regard to a certain transaction. The defendant pleaded that to whatever extent the plaintiff had been damnified, he was so damnified of his own wrong. The plaintiff then replied, setting out breach of the condition, which was, that after the making of the bond, McLeod recovered judgment against him upon the cause of action referred to in the bond. Verdict for the plaintiff (a).

J. Hillyard Cameron, for the defendant, moved in arrest of judgment, objecting to the sufficiency of the replications, on two grounds: first, that there was no sum of money mentioned for which judgment was recovered;

(a) 2 Cameron, 487.

secondly, that there was no damage specified such as constituted a breach of the bond. The condition was that the defendant should save the plaintiff harmless *in all things*, from " all *demands* or *suits*, either in law or " equity, *regarding a certain sum of money*, stated to have been advanced " by one George W. Buller to the said plaintiff, through the agency of " James Boulton, Esq., and which said sum of money was also claimed to " have been paid to E. Powell, by and on account of one Alexander " McLeod, and to be then due and owing to him ;" and should " well and " truly *discharge* all *damages, costs,* and charges recovered or *awarded in* "*law* or equity, regarding the said sum of money, or any part thereof, "*without* damage or *prejudice* to the said Edward Powell," &c. In assigning the first breach the plaintiff averred that, after the making of the bond, McLeod commenced a suit in B. R., against Powell *for the money* in the said condition mentioned, &c., and on the 8th April, 1843. " did recover judgment in the said suit, and such proceedings were there- " *upon* afterwards had, that McLeod caused to be sued out of the said " court a fi. fa. against the plaintiff's lands, indorsed to levy £229 0s. 11d. " being the sum of money in the condition of the said bond mentioned, " with costs, together with his fees and expenses ; and that the sheriff " under that writ *had* seized, and *then held*, the lands of the plaintiff, of " all which proceedings the defendant on the day and year aforesaid had " notice." For a second breach the plaintiff assigned in his replication the bringing of the action as before ; and " that McLeod did, afterwards, " viz., recover judgment in the said suit *for a large sum, to wit, for* " £229 0s. 11d., being the sum of money in the condition of the said bond " mentioned, and damages and costs ; *and that such proceedings were* " *afterwards thereupon had, in due course of law, that the lands of the* "*plaintiff were afterwards seized and were then held by the sheriff of the* " *District of Brock ;*" of all which proceedings the defendant had due notice, yet that the defendant had not discharged all damages, costs and charges recovered and awarded in the above mentioned suit, or any part thereof, without damage or prejudice to the plaintiff.

ROBINSON, C. J.—I can see no ground for arresting the judgment, for it cannot be denied that a good cause of action is stated in the record. Whether the averments are such as would support a verdict for the amount of damages which has been given is not the question upon this motion. As to the first breach : clearly the defendant has not saved the plaintiff harmless from " all demands or suits respecting the money," if McLeod has sued the plaintiff, as the replication avers, for that money, and has recovered judgment, and taken out execution on that judgment for £229 0s. 11d. ; and if his lands have been thereupon seized, and are still held in execution. As to the 2nd breach, the same may be said. We can not arrest the judgment if any breach is well assigned in the replication to which the evidence applies. The second breach avers a recovery for £229, being the money mentioned in the bond ; and if such proceedings were thereupon had that the plaintiff's lands were seized and are now held by the sheriff, and if the defendant, having notice, has not paid the damages recovered in such action, which is what he undertook to do, the bond is forfeited. Rule refused.

BOULTON ET AL. v. SHIELDS.

An action for slander of title cannot be maintained, where the alleged slander is spoken bona fide and in assertion of right.

The plaintiffs declare in case. For that whereas the plaintiffs, before and at the time of committing the grievances hereinafter mentioned, were entitled to and possessed of certain goods, chattels, fixtures and effects, then in the possession of the said plaintiffs; and that the plaintiffs, before and at the time of the committing the grievances hereinafter mentioned, to wit, on the 14th March, 1845, caused the said goods, chattels, fixtures and effects to be, and the same then were put up and exposed to sale by public auction by one Robert McClure, as auctioneer and agent of the plaintiffs, in order that the same might be then sold for the plaintiffs; yet the defendant, well knowing the premises, but contriving, and falsely and maliciously intending to injure the plaintiffs, and to cause it to be suspected and believed that the plaintiffs had no title or interest of, in, or to the said goods, chattels, fixtures and effects, and to hinder and prevent the plaintiffs from selling or disposing of the same, and to cause and procure the plaintiffs to sustain and be put to divers great expenses attending the said exposure to sale; and to vex, harass, oppress, impoverish and wholly ruin the plaintiffs, heretofore, to wit, on the day and year last aforesaid, and before the said goods, chattels, fixtures and effects had been sold and disposed of, wrongfully, injuriously, and maliciously, published a libel of and concerning the title of the plaintiffs to the said goods, chattels, fixtures and effects, and of and concerning their right to sell and dispose of the same, in the form of a notice in the following words and figures: " Toronto, March 12th, 1845. Sir, I hereby give you notice that " all the fixtures (meaning the said goods, chattels, fixtures and effects of " the plaintiffs), in and about the North American Hotel, formerly rented " to Mr. William Deering, and afterwards occupied by Mr. Thomas Pearson, " are my property, and I hereby forbid you selling the same or any part " thereof, as I shall not permit any person to remove them or any of them, " and shall treat all persons as trespassers who shall take down, remove, " injure or destroy any of them. Scott Shields. To Robert McClure, auc- " tioneer, Toronto (meaning the auctioneer and agent of the plaintiffs " above mentioned). List of articles (meaning the said goods, chattels, " fixtures and effects of the plaintiffs): gas fittings and fixtures, bells and " fittings, bar and counter and show case, iron door, dumb waiters, cornices " over windows, chimney boards, signs outside of house, labels on door, bell " and frame on roof, water fittings, verandah in front of house, posts and " awning frame, rails and pins, lamp pulleys in halls."

And whereas also the defendant afterwards, to wit, on the 14th day of March aforesaid, immediately upon the said exposure to sale of the said goods, chattels, fixtures and effects in the first count mentioned, further intending and contriving as aforesaid, wrongfully, injuriously, falsely and maliciously attended and was present at and upon such exposure to sale, and thereat, and before the said goods, chattels, fixtures and effects had been sold and disposed of, falsely and maliciously did speak and publish, in the presence and hearing of divers liege subjects of our lady the Queen, then present at and upon such exposure to sale as aforesaid, the false and malicious words following, that is to say: "I forbid you (meaning the "said auctioneer of the plaintiffs) to sell them (meaning the said goods, "chattels, fixtures and effects of the plaintiffs); they shall not be removed;" (meaning that the plaintiffs were not the owners of the said goods, chattels, fixtures and effects, and had no right to sell or dispose thereof, and that he the defendant would prevent any bidder at the said auction who might be declared the purchaser of the same taking possession of or removing the same).

And whereas also heretofore, to wit, on the 3rd day of March, 1845, and before the committing of the grievances in this count mentioned, the plaintiffs being lawfully possessed of and entitled to a certain house and appurtenances situate in Front Street in the city of Toronto, and known as the North American Hotel, wherein certain goods, chattels, fixtures, and effects of the plaintiffs were then being, as tenants thereof to the defendant for a certain term then unexpired, it was agreed between the plaintiffs and the defendant, that the plaintiffs should then deliver up the possession of the said house to the defendant, and that the defendant would thereafter, to wit, upon the 14th day of March, in the year aforesaid, permit and suffer the plaintiffs to enter into and upon the said house and appurtenances, and there to hold a public auction in the same, for the purpose of selling and disposing of the said goods, chattels, fixtures and effects, and to continue holding the said sale until the whole of the said goods, chattels, fixtures and effects were sold; and whereas afterwards, to wit, upon the day and year first in this count mentioned, being the time in that behalf agreed upon, the plaintiffs did deliver up the possession of the said house and appurtenances to the defendant, upon the terms aforesaid, who then accepted the same, and it then became and was the duty of the defendant to permit and suffer the plaintiffs to enter into and upon the said house and appurtenances, and to hold a public auction therein, at the time and for the purposes hereinbefore in that behalf mentioned, as agreed upon; and the plaintiffs in fact say, that afterwards, to wit, upon the 14th day of March aforesaid, being the day and time in that behalf agreed upon, they, the plaintiffs, did, by permission of the defendant, enter into and upon the said house and appurtenances, and did peaceably and lawfully, and according to the said agreement, proceed to hold a public auction therein, for the sale of the said goods, chattels, fixtures and effects, before divers liege subjects, of our lady the Queen, who were there present and desirous of bidding for and purchasing the same, and did in fact sell and dispose of a considerable part of the said goods, chattels, fixtures and effects, and were then lawfully and peaceably as aforesaid continuing to sell the same, yet the defendant, although the plaintiffs fulfilled their agreement in all things as aforesaid, contriving and intending to injure the plaintiffs in this behalf, and disregarding his said duty, did falsely, fraudulently, wrongfully and maliciously obstruct, hinder and prevent the plaintiffs from so selling and disposing of their said goods, chattels, fixtures and effects. Concluding with a statement of special damage.

Pleas: 1st, Not guilty to the whole declaration.

2nd, That the plaintiffs were not at the time when, &c., *entitled to* or *possessed* of the goods, chattels, fixtures, and effects in the declaration mentioned.

3rd, That the plaintiffs at the said time, when, &c., were not possessed of or entitled to the house and appurtenances called the North American Hotel, as *tenants thereof* to the defendant in manner and form as the plaintiffs in their last count have alleged.

4th, That the defendant did not make any such agreement with the plaintiffs as in the last count mentioned, in manner and form as the plaintiffs have in that count alleged.

On the trial, a lease was put in, dated 18th April, 1842, from the defendant to William Deering, for five years, from 1st May, 1842, of the North American Hotel. Secondly, a mortgage from Wm. Deering to Wm. Campbell, dated 25th April, 1842, to secure £1,490, embracing a great variety of things, and amongst the rest the fixtures in question. Thirdly, a deed of assignment from Wm. Deering to Thorne and Sutherland, of all his property, including the lease of the premises, and the fixtures in dispute, in trust for creditors, dated 11th July, 1843. Fourthly, assignment from Thorne and Sutherland to Thomas Pearson of the leasehold, dated 1st August, 1843. Fifthly, assignment from Thomas Pearson to the plaintiffs of the leasehold and furniture, including fixtures, to secure them against certain amounts for which they had given promissory notes for Thos. Pearson.

It appeared also, that Pearson having failed to save the plaintiffs harmless by the payment of the monies for which they had become his sureties, the plaintiffs entered the premises to sell the property mentioned in Pearson's assignment; that after the sale was advertised, the defendant persuaded Pearson to surrender possession of the house to him, which he did in writing, giving the defendant at the same time liberty to advertise the premises to be let. This surrender is dated 24th February, 1845. Pearson remained in the house and did not give up the possession of the keys to the defendant though the defendant came into the house a few days after the assignment. When the defendant came to Pearson about the surrender, he was told by Pearson that he must remain in possession till the house was cleared of the effect, till the property was all sold, and the house cleared of everything after the auction, and the defendant then said "he would not interfere with that." Pearson further stated, that at the time of the surrender he had assigned all to the plaintiffs as trustees, and that he had no existing interest. The defendant entered the house the second day after the date of the surrender, remained there two or three days, and then went away, and his son came and remained three or four days. One of them remained till the date of a paper shewn, to wit, a lease from the defendant to Turner, one of the plaintiffs, subsequently put in evidence. Some of the fixtures claimed by the defendant were put up by Campbell, a former tenant, by whom they were assigned to Deering; the defendant making no objection and asserting no claim to them.

The gas fittings were paid for, by Deering, to the gas company, though not put up by his order or with the assent of the defendant, his landlord. The publication of the libel complained of in the first count, and the verbal slander charged in the second count in reference to the fixtures were proved.

Boulton, Q. C., for the defendant, moved for a non-suit, on the ground that the claim of the defendant being bona fide and no malice being shewn on his part, the first and second counts could not be sustained, and as to the third count, that there was no evidence of such an agreement, as was stated therein, and that there was no proof of any actual obstruction made to the sale, and that if there had been such an agreement, the remedy was assumpsit and not case, and that the plaintiffs were not proved to be, as laid, the lessees or owners of the property. The case went to the jury by consent, with leave to the defendant to move a nonsuit on the plaintiffs' case as it stood at its close, if the evidence were insufficient to support the plaintiffs' case, and the jury found a verdict for the plaintiffs.

Boulton, Q. C., for the defendant, moved to set aside the verdict for the plaintiff, and to enter a nonsuit on the above points, or for a new trial for misdirection, and the verdict being contrary to law and evidence, or to arrest judgment.

Blake and *J. Hillyard Cameron* shewed cause.

McLEAN, J., pronounced the judgment of the court.—To entitle the plaintiff to maintain the verdict on the first two counts, it appears to me that it must appear by the evidence, that the defendant was influenced by malicious motives in the publication of the alleged libel, or in making use of the words charged. If the statements were wholly untrue, and the title of the plaintiff to the property undisputed before and since the sale of the goods, then malice might be inferred, and the action maintained; but when the evidence shews, as I think it does pretty clearly, that the claim of the defendant to the fixtures in dispute was put forth in good faith, and as to part, if not the whole, well founded, the presumption of malice, which is the foundation of this action on the first and second counts, wholly fails. It may be admitted that most of the fixtures in dispute were such as the out-going tenant had a right to remove before the expiration of his term, or to assign to an in-coming tenant; but some of them, as appears by the evidence, were not erected at the expense of any tenant, and, being attached to the freehold, would belong to the landlord. The gas fittings, which were valued in the assignment to Pearson, as he states, at £58 10s., were put up by the gas company while Mr. Campbell was the tenant and keeper of the North American Hotel; he declined having them put up to be paid for by him; but the gas company proceeded with them nevertheless, and had them put up, depending upon the owner or some future occupant to pay for them. These were up when Deering obtained his lease from the defendant, and were not valued to Deering by Mr. Campbell, the out-going tenant; they were therefore included in the lease as part of the premises and appurtenances leased to Deering; and if Deering afterwards chose to pay the gas company the value of these fittings, he did what he was under no obligation to do, and what could not give him any right to these fittings, or any authority to include them as his property in any assignment made by him. As to these gas fittings, therefore, it is clear that the defendant was not only asserting a claim which he conceived to be well founded, but one which was actually and clearly correct in law, though in equity he ought to pay for these fittings, if of any value to his house, and he desired to retain them. Then, as to the other fixtures which are in controversy, there seems to be no doubt that they might have been removed during the continuance of the term, by any person entitled to them. They were assigned by Thorne and Sutherland (the assignees of Deering) to Pearson, with the assent of Campbell, who had originally placed them in the house, and had during his term sold them to Deering, and who held a mortgage on them for their value. Campbell's claim being arranged by the plaintiffs, as sureties of Pearson, Pearson, during the term, assigned them to the plaintiffs, his sureties, with authority to sell if he failed to make certain payments to Campbell and others, for which they had become responsible. Pearson failed in his payments, and the whole property, as well the leasehold term as the personal property and fixtures, were given up to the plaintiffs and advertised to be sold. Before the sale, the defendant was let into possession of the house, by Pearson, who had previously assigned to the plaintiffs, and being thus in possession, whether rightfully or wrongfully it is not necessary to inquire, he was in a position to prevent the sale from taking place in the house, and to retain the fixtures, unless dispossessed by the plaintiffs under the assignment of the term to them by Pearson. They could no doubt have dispossessed the defendant of the premises, as they held the assignment before Pearson's surrender to the defendant; but had they done so, they must have become responsible, as the assignees of the term, for the rent, and this they had no desire apparently to assume. They could of course have claimed and removed all the property assigned to them, which did not come properly under the designation of fixtures, and if the defendant had refused to allow its removal, he would have been responsible for its value; but the fixtures could only be claimed by them, as belonging to the freehold which they were entitled to hold during the remainder of Pearson's, or rather Deering's term, if they chose to assert their right and to accept of the assignment with all its liabilities. After the surrender by Pearson and while the defendant was in possession, one of the plaintiffs, probably with a view to obviate the necessity of removing a large quantity of furniture which had been offered for sale, and possibly thinking thereby to put an end to all difficulty with the defendant, took another lease from the defendant, and under that lease the plaintiffs were in possession of the house at the time of the sale of the goods, and when the defendant in writing and verbally, forbade the sale of certain fixtures, and gave notice that he would treat as a trespasser any person who should attempt to remove them. This last mentioned lease to Turner, acted upon and accepted by the plaintiffs, must be regarded as a waiver on their part of any interest which they were entitled to assert under the assignment of the term, and as a declaration on their part not to accept of or avail themselves of such assignment. Then in taking a new lease, they took the premises as they were, and acknowledged the defendant's right to these premises with all the fixtures belonging to them, and precluded themselves from setting up a claim under the assignment from Pearson, which they had repudiated by the acceptance of the new lease. If so, the fixtures at the time of the sale belonged to the defendant, as a part of his freehold demised to the plaintiffs; and he had an undoubted right to forbid their sale, and to give notice that he would oppose their removal; and his doing so in good faith in the assertion of his right, whether in writing or verbally, could not subject him to an action. With respect to the third court, it is alleged that the plaintiffs were in possession of a certain house of the defendant, as his tenants, in which they had divers goods and chattels, fixtures and effects, and that in consideration that the plaintiffs would give up possession of the house, the defendant agreed to allow them to sell in the house the goods, chattels and fixtures which they had there ; but intending to injure the plaintiffs, though they had given him up possession, that the defendant permitted them to enter and sell a considerable part of their effects, but afterwards, during the sale, did *falsely, fraudulently, wrongfully and maliciously obstruct, hinder and prevent* the plaintiffs from selling their goods, chattels, fixtures and effects, &c. Now it does not appear to me that any such agreement as the plaintiffs have set out has been proved on the trial, unless indeed the statement of the defendant to Pearson, that he would not interfere with the sale can be considered to amount to such an agreement. It will be recollected, that after this conversation with Pearson, Turner, one of the plaintiffs, had taken a lease from the defendant, and that at the time of the sale he and the plaintiffs were in undisputed possession of the house, and entitled to hold an auction there if they chose. The defendant, therefore, supposing him to have made such an agreement as that referred to, was not in a position to permit and suffer, or to hinder and prevent their holding the auction. But supposing such an agreement to have been established by evidence, has the defendant been guilty of any violation of it ? When he agreed to allow them to hold an auction in his house, of their own effects, he was not bound to allow them to sell property which belonged to himself, without objection ; and the assertion of claim to any article exposed to sale which he honestly believed to belong to him, could scarcely be tortured into such a hindrance and interruption of the plaintiffs, in carrying on their sale, as would subject the defendant to an action for a breach of his agreement. With the exception of the gas fittings, the other fixtures seem to have belonged to the tenants, and might be assigned with the term, or removed at any time during the term, doing no injury to the freehold. Some of these fixtures may have been so put in as to be removable at any time without injury to the house, and if so, the cases of Davis et al. v. Jones et al. (*a*), and Penton v. Robart (*b*), would seem to establish the right of the plaintiffs to recover their value in trover. That remedy is of course still open to the plaintiffs, if any portion of the property retained is so situated ; but they cannot recover in an action for a malicious libel or verbal slander of their title, when no malice appears, nor can they recover for an alleged breach of an agreement, which is not shewn to have existed, and which if it had existed, is not shewn to have been violated by the defendant ; and which, moreover, if it ever did exist, is shewn to have been superseded by the subsequent taking of a lease of the premises by one of the plaintiffs. Under all these circumstances, I am of opinion that the rule should be made absolute to set aside the verdict for the plaintiffs, and enter a nonsuit.

Rule absolute for nonsuit.

(*a*) 2 B. & Al. 265.   (*b*) 2 E. 88

The Bank of Montreal v. Grover.

The following notice of dishonour was held to be insufficient, the note having been indorsed by the defendant in his own name, and not in the name of the partners to whom the notice was addressed, although the defendant was one of the firm; "Messrs. P. M. Grover & Co.—Gentlemen, Take notice, that the promissory note of J. R. Benson, for £46 0s. 11d., on which you are indorser, due this day, remains unpaid; therefore the holders look to you for payment thereof, as such indorser."

The plaintiff declared against the defendant, Grover, as indorser of a promissory note, made by John R. Benson, payable to Thomas Benson, or order, and indorsed by Grover. The note was made on 3rd February, 1845, and payable on 1st June then next. It was not made payable at any bank or other particular place. The defendant pleaded that he had no notice of dishonour, and non presentment to the maker.

The evidence of notice to this defendant as indorser, was, that on 1st June, 1845, a note was sent to him, addressed "Messrs. P. M. Grover & Co." as follows: Gentlemen,—" Take notice that the promissory note of John R. Benson, for £46 0s. 11d., on which you are indorser. due this day remains unpaid; therefore the holders look to you for payment thereof, as such indorser." This was signed by one Nicholls, agent for the holders.

It was objected at the trial that the notice was insufficient to charge Grover, as indorser, because it described a note indorsed not by himself, individually, but by the firm, and was given not to him but to the firm, of which he was a member; and secondly, because it did not state or show that the note had been presented to the maker, and dishonoured. A nonsuit was moved by

Crooks, for the defendant, on these objections, upon leave reserved at the trial.

D. E. Boulton shewed cause.

ROBINSON, C. J.—This latter objection we take to be the more formidable one; and it is not without some regret that we consider ourselves bound to give way to it. This subject of the form of the notice to be given by the holder of a promissory note, to the indorser, was brought particularly under our consideration some years ago, in a case of the Bank of Upper Canada v. Street(*a*). The notice in that case did not state in terms that the note had been presented, or dishonoured; but the grounds on which we held it nevertheless to be sufficient, were, that the note was made payable at the bank; the effect of which is, that the maker of such a note engages that there shall be funds there to meet it when it falls due. It is not necessary that the bank should present it to themselves, nor that any one should attend there to present it to them. The notice stated that the note which fell due on such a day remained at the bank unpaid; and upon a review of the various cases on this subject, we held that to be sufficient, as it implied a presentment and dishonour. We think that decision was correct. But in regard to this note, there are not such circumstances on which to build an implication that the note had been presented to the maker, and dishonoured. The note is not

---

(*a*) Reported the next case.

made payable at any particular place, there is nothing therefore to relieve the holder from the necessity of resorting to the drawer : there is nothing that we can hold equivalent to a presentment. And the notice merely states that the note (which is particularly enough described), remains unpaid ; and that the holder looks to the indorser for payment. This is in no degree inconsistent with its being possibly the fact, that the holder had, up to the time of sending the notice, kept the note in his desk, and never taken any step to obtain payment from the person primarily liable. In Tindal v. Brown(a), it does not seem to have been considered that anything more was essential than to let the indorser know in due season that the note or bill had not been paid, and that the holder looked to him. There had up to that time been no critical nicity as to the form of the notice; and it is remarkable, that Mr. Justice Bayley, in his Treatise on Bills, contented himself with laying it down, "that the "notice (although there is no prescribed form for it) ought to import that " the person to whom it is given is considered liable, and that payment "from him is expected." His vast experience in the administration of the law would therefore have led him to exact nothing more than the notice in this case clearly imports. But since that time, objections which have been taken to the form of the notice, have produced a series of decisions which, whether they have created new law, or have revived forgotten law, have placed the matter on a ground admitted to be strange to commercial men ; and I believe we are bound to say, now, that we are not permitted, in the face of these decisions, to understand from such notices as that before us, what men of business would in general infer from it, and what used to be considered all that it was material for an indorser to know.—I need hardly say that I refer to the modern cases of Solarte v. Palmer, adjudged upon a writ of error in the Exchequer Chamber (b) ; Hartley v. Case (c) ; Boulton v. Welsh (d) ; in which latter case it was freely admitted by the court, that no mercantile or ordinary man, could misunderstand the notice ; Hedger v. Stevenson (e) ; Grugeon v. Smith (f) ; Nordditch v. Cantry (g). In these and many other cases, though the courts seem to have felt the embarrassment which has been produced by the introduction of an inconvenient strictness in regard to the form of these notices, yet they treat the rule, to the extent to which I have stated it, as being too firmly fixed by authority to admit of their disregarding it ; and the present notice is unfortunately destitute of anything that we could allow, under the most liberal construction, to take the case out of the reach of those authorities. I think it is to be regretted that the law has been so settled. There must, I dare say, have appeared to have been good reasons for the decisions, but they do not strike me. Even the strictest of them require no more than that the holder of the note should tell the indorser that it has been presented, or something from which *that* may be implied ; as, that it has been dishonoured, or returned protested, or returned noted, or with charges, &c. He need not say when, where, or how, the note was presented ; though on all these points there may be something material to be considered, before the presentment can be determined to be good. And, after all, the notice is the

---

(a) 1 T. R. 167. (b) 7 Bing. 530. (c) 4 B. & C. 339.
(d) 3 Bing. N.C. 688. (e) 2 M. & W. 799. (f) 6 Ad. & Ell. 499.
(g) 6 Scott, 209.

mere assertion of an interested party, which may be true or untrue; it is no proof of the fact for any purpose. If the indorser should desire, as indorsers too often do, to evade his responsibility by taking some rigid objection to the presentment, he would not content himself with what the holder of the note has been pleased to tell him, but would inquire, and if he saw any ground, he would dispute the fact; and then, when the case comes to be tried upon that point, it is not what the holder may have stated in his notice that the jury will have to find, but what he did in fact do. When the holder of the note has, without delay, informed the indorser that the note is unpaid, and that he expects him to pay it, he places him at once in a position to be aware of his liability, and to make whatever inquiries, and take whatever measures may seem essential to his security. It would seem reasonable, then, to hold that such a notice was enough, but we can clearly not determine that it is sufficient, without going against many deliberate decisions of the several courts in England, by which we hold ourselves in general bound. It is clear that nothing that took place here can be taken to have waived the necessity of shewing notice of presentment.

The Bank of Upper Canada v. Street.

Sufficiency of notice of dishonour of a promissory note.

The question in this case was, whether a notice of dishonour in the following form, was sufficient to charge the indorser of a promissory note made payable at the Bank of Upper Canada, ninety days from date.

No.   Bank of Upper Canada.

Toronto, 22nd April, 1841.

Sir,—The note of A. B. for £50, at 90 days from 20th January, 1841, indorsed by you, and due this day, remains unpaid. You are therefore hereby notified that this Bank looks to you for payment.

Yours, &c.

For the Cashier.

To Mr. J. Street.

J. Hillyard Cameron, for the defendant, relied upon Hartley v. Case (a), Solarte v. Palmer (b), and Boulton v. Welsh (c).

R. E. Burns shewed cause.

Robinson, C. J.—We have considered this point, and have no doubt that the notice was sufficient, and that the postea must be delivered to the plaintiffs. It would have been better, because more unquestionable in appearance as well as reality, if the notice had said, your note "remains 'here' unpaid;" and you are therefore hereby notified that this bank "as the holders thereof" look to you for payment; but the notice as it stands is, in our opinion, sufficient. Supposing all the cases relied upon by the defendant to be free from doubt and wholly unshaken, which can hardly be said respecting Boulton v. Welsh, the one mainly relied on, still they are very far from being decisive of this case. In Hartley v. Case, the notice was simply a call upon Case to pay the bill; it was not

---

(a) 4 B. & C. 839.   (b) 1 C. & J. 417.   (c) 3 Bing. N. C. 688.

stated to be due, nor to have been accepted or presented for acceptance, or in any way dishonoured. In Boulton v. Welsh, there was no statement of the bills being dishonoured, nor any averment of presentment, or anything equivalent to a presentment. In Solarte v. Palmer, the note was only a demand upon the defendant for payment; there was no statement that the bill had been dishonoured, or was over due. In all these cases the maker had assigned no place where he undertook to pay, and where, consequently, he was bound to have the money at the day, or the bill would be at once dishonoured; there was nothing to relieve the holder from the necessity of taking the bill to the maker, or at least to his place of business, and there demanding payment. But this is a note made payable at the Bank of Upper Canada, and admitted to have been indorsed to the bank. The bank thus being the holders, were not to present it to themselves—2 H. Bl. 510. It was enough for them to turn to the account of the maker of the note, and to see that he had no balance in their hands to cover it. If the payee had still held the note, he might have called at the bank and presented it, or might have made a demand anywhere on the maker in person. This notice describes the note exactly, and the bank, writing on the day when the note was to be paid, and from the place where it was appointed to be paid, informed the indorser that it remained unpaid, and that they looked to him for payment. Its remaining unpaid *there* on that day was conclusive as to its being dishonoured. It was presented as much as in the nature of circumstances it need be, and the call on the indorser to pay it was certainly explicit. No one conversant with mercantile affairs of this nature could doubt for a moment what it implied, viz., that the bank had discounted the note, and the maker not having called to pay it, they now looked to the indorser. If the cases which the defendant had cited had not been considered in later authorities, and explained so as not to touch this case, I should still not have thought that they extended to show such a notice as this to be insufficient, for they are all widely different in their circumstances. But after considering the cases in 6 Ad. & E. 500; 8 C. & P. 355; and 2 M. & W. 804, we think it clear that the notice is sufficient. The language of the court in these latter cases is just and reasonable. We are bound to understand such notices as the rest of mankind understand them, and certainly no one could fail to understand what is meant by the one given in this case.

Rule discharged.

McPHERSON ET AL. v. McMILLAN.

In debt on a judgment of the Court of Queen's Bench at Montreal in Lower Canada, the defendant pleaded that the said court had no jurisdiction in the matter in which the judgment was rendered, and also that the defendant was never served with any process whereby he could be or was notified or apprized that the action was commenced or was depending, and that the judgment was obtained without his knowledge, and contrary to reason and justice, the court held that both pleas were bad on demurrer.

The plaintiffs declare in debt, for that whereas heretofore, to wit, at a supreme court of judicature, of our Sovereign Lady the Queen, called the Court of Queen's Bench, holden at the City of Montreal, in and for the

District of Montreal, in that part of the Province of Canada, formerly called Lower Canada, and within the jurisdiction of the said court, to wit on the 16th day of January, in the year of our Lord, 1845, before the Honourable Chief Justice Vallieres de St. Real, chief justice of the said court, and the Honourable Mr. Justice Day, then sitting judges of the same court, by the consideration and judgment of the same court, a certain judgment was rendered in and by the said court, in a certain cause then depending in the same court, wherein the said John McPherson and Samuel Crane were plaintiffs, and the said Alexander McMillan was defendant, wherein and whereby, after reciting as is therein recited, the said court did order and adjudge that the said defendant should, within fifteen days after the last of two notifications which the said court did thereby order and adjudge to be given of the rendering of the judgment in the said cause by publishing the same twice in some newspaper published in the English language, in the City of Montreal, and twice in some newspaper published in the French language, in the said City of Montreal, transfer, assign, and set over to the said plaintiffs, their heirs and assigns to and in favour of them the said plaintiffs, their heirs and assigns, execute a good, sufficient and formal deed of assignment and transfer, without the payment from the plaintiffs of any other consideration save and except the nominal consideration of five shillings currency, with warranty by him the said defendant against his the said defendant's acts or deeds, of, in and to the undivided third part, share and portion of the two lots of land and premises thereinbefore described, with all the buildings thereon erected, and all the members and appurtenances thereunto belonging; and in default of his the said defendant's executing such transfer and assignment as aforesaid, that the said judgment should be taken, held and considered to be and should be a good and valid transfer and assignment, and as a title to and in favour of the plaintiffs, their heirs and assigns, and to the said undivided third part or portion of the said two lots of lands thereinbefore described, with warranty against the acts and deeds of him the said defendant. And the said court did further condemn the defendant to pay the costs of the then present suit. And the plaintiffs aver that afterwards, and after fifteen days from the last of two notifications had been given of the rendering of the said judgment in the said cause, by publishing the same twice in a certain newspaper called the " Montreal Gazette," published in the English language, in the City of Montreal, and twice in a certain newspaper called " Aurore de Canadas," published in the French language, in the said City of Montreal, as in and by the said judgment ordered and directed as aforesaid, to wit, on the 7th day of March, in the year of our Lord 1845, the said costs of the said suit which the said court did, in and by the said judgment, condemn the defendant to pay as aforesaid, were taxed by the prothonotary, then being the proper officer of the said court, due to the plaintiffs on the said judgment so rendered as aforesaid, at £35 14s. 1d. currency; which said judgment still remains in that behalf in full force and effect, not in any wise satisfied, reversed or annulled. Usual conclusion and breach.

The defendant pleaded first, that the supreme court of judicature in the declaration mentioned, in which, &c., had no jurisdiction in the matter for which the said supposed judgment was rendered and given. Verification.

Secondly, That *the cause of action*, if any, on which the said judgment in the said supreme court of judicature in the declaration mentioned was rendered, *accrued to the plaintiffs* in that part of this province formerly called *Upper Canada;* that the defendant, before and at the time when the said cause of action, if any, accrued to the plaintiffs, resided, and ever since hath resided, and still continues to reside in that part of this province formerly called *Upper Canada;* that he the defendant was never, from the time the said cause of action, if any, accrued to the plaintiffs, *served with any process*, or copy of process, or other paper in the said cause in the declaration mentioned, *whereby* he could be, or was notified or appraised that the said cause had been commenced or was depending, or that judgment had been rendered in it; and the defendant says that the said supposed judgment in the said declaration mentioned, was had and obtained without his knowledge, and contrary to reason and justice. Verification.

The plaintiffs demurred specially to the first plea, alleging for cause, that although the defendant has indeed by his said third plea alleged that the said supreme court of judicature in which, &c., had no jurisdiction in the matter for which the said judgment was rendered, yet he hath not shewn any where in or by his said third plea, why or wherefore or for what reason the said court had no jurisdiction, nor in any manner shewn to this court any facts or reasons from whence or whereby they could judge or determine whether or not the said supreme court had such jurisdiction as aforesaid; that the said want of jurisdiction if true should have been pleaded before the said supreme court; that it is not anywhere shewn in or by the said third plea that the said defendant denied the jurisdiction of the said supreme court, or that the question of the jurisdiction of the said supreme court in the subject matter of the said judgment had been ever raised or mooted by the defendant before the said court, or that he had taken any steps or measures whatever to reverse the said judgment for want of jurisdiction as aforesaid; that it is not stated or shewn in or by the said third plea that the said judgment had been reversed, but on the contrary it is stated in the declaration, and not denied by the said third plea, that the said judgment still remains in full force and effect, not in anywise satisfied, reversed, or annulled; that the said judgment is admitted to have been rendered by a supreme court of judicature in that part of this province formerly called Lower Canada; that it is not in or by the said third plea denied that by the laws of said Lower Canada the said supreme court had jurisdiction in the matter upon which the said judgment was rendered, nor is it therein or thereby denied that the said matter was cognizable by the laws of the country, or consonant to the justice of the case, nor is it therein or thereby denied that by the laws of said Lower Canada the said judgment was conclusive between the parties thereto. And yet the defendant hath attempted in and by the said third plea to put in issue a matter namely, the jurisdiction of the said supreme court, in the matter of the said judgment, which without such denials or some of them was not properly issuable. And also for that the defendant hath in and by his said third plea inartificially and improperly attempted to put in issue a matter of law to be inferred from facts which are not stated, and not the facts themselves, from which the law is to be inferred. And also for that the said defendant hath in and by his said third plea denied the jurisdiction of the said supreme court in the said matter, but hath not shewn what other court, if any, had jurisdiction in the same.

The plaintiffs demurred specially to the second plea, because the several matters and facts by him in that plea pleaded are insufficient to bar the plaintiffs from recovering in this action upon the said judgment, in this that the defendant hath not in or by his said fourth plea shewn, that the cause of action upon which the said judgment was rendered was not properly cognizable by the said supreme court of judicature, nor hath he therein or thereby shewn that he was not at or during the time the said cause was commenced or pending subject to the laws of the country wherein the said judgment was rendered, nor hath he therein or thereby in any manner denied his possession or ownership of property, real or personal, heritable or otherwise, within the time aforesaid, within the jurisdiction of the said supreme court, or that he had at any time before resided within such jurisdiction. And that although the defendant hath in and by his said fourth plea pleaded that before and at the time when the said cause of action accrued he resided and still continues to reside in that part of this province formerly called Upper Canada, yet it doth not appear but that at some time or times, at or during the time aforesaid he may have been and was within the limits of, and subject to, the jurisdiction of the said supreme court, and answerable to its process. And for that although the defendant hath therein pleaded that he was never from the time the said cause of action accrued served with any process or copy of process, or other paper, in the said cause, whereby he could be or was notified or apprised that the said cause had been commenced or was depending, or that judgment had been rendered in it, yet it doth not appear but that the defendant may have been and was notified of such matters in some other lawful way, so that he might have defended himself in the said suit. And although the defendant hath in his said fourth plea averred that said judgment was had and obtained without his knowledge, yet he hath not shewn that the proceedings anterior to the said judgment were had without his knowlenge. And also for that the defendant hath attempted to put in issue a mere matter of law, and inference from facts, namely, that the said judgment was contrary to reason and justice. Joinder in demurrer.

J Hillyard Cameron and *S. M. Jarvis* for the demurrer.

Sherwood, Sol. Gen., contra.

ROBINSON, C. J.—The third plea is clearly bad, because this Court of Queen's Bench for the District of Montreal is a superior court of record, in fact the supreme court of judicature, within its jurisdiction; and therefore must have jurisdiction of all matters of contract, and other matters arising out of jurisdiction, as well as those arising within it. It is not an inferior court, in regard to which it must in general be shewn that the cause of action, on which it has proceeded, arose within the locality over which its authority extends. There may be causes of action not of a transitory nature, over which the court of Queen's Bench of Montreal has not jurisdiction, because they arose abroad and are not transitory; but this does not appear to have been such a case; and, if it were so, that should have been shewn. The merely pleading that the cause of action arose out of the limits of the jurisdiction is not a defence. Then the third plea is a general assertion merely, that this supreme court of judicature "had no jurisdiction in the matter for which the judgment was given;" not stating why it had not, nor whether any and what other court had jurisdiction over the case. But we know that the Court of Queen's Bench of Montreal is one of the Queen's courts of supreme jurisdiction, and it is so allowed to be in this record; we must, therefore, take it that it has jurisdiction when the contrary does not appear, which it does not here. And if the cause of action be indeed one of which, for any cause, that court had not jurisdiction, then that should have been explicitly shewn. I mean the fact or facts should have been pleaded which disable this supreme court from entertaining the cause; and it should have been pointed out in what other tribunal the plaintiff could have brought his action. (a)

The fourth plea, in my opinion, is insufficient; for it merely asserts that the defendant was never *served with any process* whereby he could be or was notified or apprised that the action was commenced, or *was depending;* and that the *judgment was obtained without his knowledge, and contrary to reason and justice.* For all that is stated in that plea, the defendant may have agreed to accept a declaration, as is often done in cases in our own courts, and may have waived any service of process. It is not pleaded that he did not know that the suit was brought and was pending, but only that he was not apprised of the fact by *the service of process*, which is not a matter of necessity; then, if he knew the action was pending, and omitted to defend it, which, for all that is averred, may have been the case, it would be of no consequence whether he knew of the judgment being rendered or not. The plea, then, is double and uncertain. If it shewed that he was not served with process, and if that were indispensable, then it would signify nothing whether he merely knew of the judgment being rendered or not; and, when the defendant pleads that the judgment was "had and obtained without his knowledge, and "contrary to reason and justice," we cannot tell whether he means to assert merely that it was contrary to reason and justice that the judgment should have been obtained without his knowledge, or that the judgment was, on other grounds, and upon the merits, contrary to reason and justice It is, besides, a substantial objection to this plea, that it does not state such facts as would shew that the case is not one in which judgment could have been obtained without actual service of process, under the provisions of our statute 7 Vic. ch. 16, sec. 54; which statute is binding upon us, and enables plaintiffs to obtain judgments, in certain cases, without service of process, substituting a particular notification instead.

Judgment for plaintiff.

McPHERSON ET AL. V. McMILLAN.

In assumpsit on a foreign judgment, the judgment cannot be impeached for any alleged defect in the proceedings prior to the judgment, under the general issue. The statute 7 Vic. ch. 16, is binding on the courts in Upper Canada, as much as upon the courts in Lower Canada.

(a) Rex v. Johnson, 6 E. R. 596.
(b) See the other pleadings in this case on demurrer, ante, page 30.

Plaintiffs proved their cause by putting in,

1st. An exemplification of a Lower Canada judgment, which also contained a certificate of the amount at which costs were taxed.

2nd. The original bill as taxed by the prothonotary, and under their certificate, £35. 14s. 1d.

3rd. Mr. Rose, a practising advocate of Montreal, and who conducted the cause there for McPherson & Crane, was called, who proved the signatures of the Chief Justice and prothonotaries, that the court was that mentioned in statute of 1843, 7 Vic. c. 16, s. 54. He also proved the signatures of the prothonotaries and judge to the bill; that by the practice of the court judgment is simply entered for the cause of action, and the party is condemned to pay the costs, which are afterwards taxed, but not ascertained in the judgment certified by the prothonotary and judge; the bill put in was the identical bill in the cause, and he proved it was taxed and certified according to the course and practice of the court, and that execution would issue upon it without any further entry of record. He further proved the receipt of a letter from defendant in reply to one from witness calling upon him for a conveyance of the property in question, in which defendant says *he never will convey the Montreal property without* plaintiffs come forward and settle all matters to his satisfaction. He further proved the judgment was founded upon a writing or memorandum in plaintiffs' blotter, proved to the satisfaction of the court below by the subscribing witness as signed, agreeing to convey to plaintiffs the *McCord property in Montreal* (the property in question), and proved a copy of such writing, and that the original entry was lost. He further proved that the McCord property mentioned in the *memorandum*, the *judgment*, and alluded to in *defendant's letter*, is a piece of property in Montreal. Defendant's handwriting was proved. And upon this evidence the plaintiffs rested their case.

G. *Sherwood*, for defendant, then moved for a nonsuit on these grounds:—

1st. That the judgment was on the face of it bad, contrary to reason and justice, the defendant having never been served with process or notice of action, and it appearing he was a resident in Upper Canada.

2nd. That even admitting the statute of 1843 authorized the proceedings had in this case, yet there was no sufficient evidence of defendant having real estate in Lower Canada.

3rd. That the bill proved did not appear to be between the same parties, inasmuch as it was headed John McPherson et al. v. McMillan, instead of the parties' names in full.

The learned judge thought that such a defence was not open to the defendants under the general issue, since the New Rules; but that admitting it was, he thought the case came within the provisions of 7 Vic. ch. 16, s. 54; that the judgment was therefore regular; though if that statute had not been passed, he would have been inclined to rule against the plaintiffs.

A verdict was taken for the plaintiffs, subject to the opinion of the court on the objections taken at Nisi Prius.

J. *Hillyard Cameron*, for plaintiffs.—That case hardly admits of an argument in the face of the statute the plaintiffs rely on, 7 Vic. ch. 16, s. 54, "That in any suit or action to be brought against any person who "shall have left his domicile in Lower Canada, or against any person who shall have had no domicile in Lower Canada, but shall have personal or real estate in the same, it shall be lawful for the plaintiff, if no curator be appointed in the ordinary course of law to represent such person, to summon and implead such person by a writ issued in the usual way out of the Court of Queen's Bench, or out of any of the circuit courts in and for the district or circuit wherein such person may have had his domicile, or where such property may be situate; and that upon the return of the sheriff or the bailiff to the writ that the defendant cannot be found in the district or circuit, it shall be lawful for the court to order that the defendant shall by an advertisement, to be twice inserted in the English language in any newspaper published in that language, and twice in the French language in any newspaper published in that language in Lower Canada, be notified to appear and answer such suit or action within two months after the last insertion of such advertisement, and that upon the neglect of the defendant to appear and answer such suit or action within the period aforesaid, it shall be lawful for the plaintiff to proceed to trial and judgment as in a case by default." Now the judgment on the face of it comes in every way within this statute. It purports to be a judgment of the Court of Queen's Bench, Lower Canada, District of Montreal, in favour of plaintiffs against A. McMillan, now residing in Prescott, in that part of the Province of Canada heretofore known as Upper Canada, gentleman, thereby shewing the non-residence of defendant in Lower Canada; it then recites the sheriff's return of Non est; the defendant's subsequent double notification in the Montreal Gazette and Minerve, and defendant's neglect to appear within two months; and then the consideration of the court that the defendant had bound himself in writing to convey all his right, &c., of and in one undivided third of a certain real estate called the McCord property, in Montreal, and after minutely describing the land, proceeds, "the said undivided third part or portion of which said above described two lots of land he the defendant acquired under and by virtue of a certain deed of sale from said John McPherson, passed before Griffin and his colleagues, notaries public, at the city of Montreal, 19th May, 1828, and the value of which share to the defendant, he the defendant did receive on the dissolution of co-partnership," thereby shewing clearly that it was in evidence before the court that the defendant had real estate in Lower Canada, which he had agreed to convey to the plaintiffs, and that the course pointed out by the statute had been taken; viz., the sheriff's return of non est, and the newspaper notifications, and the defendant's neglect to appear and answer. The court then pronounces judgment in rem., and condemns the defendant in the costs. In addition to the evidence on the face of the judgment of the defendant's possession of real estate in Lower Canada, to justify this procedure, there was his own letter impliedly admitting his possession of such property, by a refusal to convey it, and the copy of his agreement to convey such property, which was sworn to have been proved before the court below by the subscribing witness. The defendant however contends under his first point, that though this judgment be all regular enough in Lower Canada, yet it cannot be enforced in Upper Canada, as it is contrary to reason and justice, &c., that a man should be condemned without notice, and he relies strongly on Ferguson v. Mahon, 11 Ad. & Ellis, which was the case of an Irish judgment, to which the defendant pleaded that he had not been served with process, and had never appeared, and the court decided the plea was good, and that the judgment could not be upheld; the defendant urges this as a similar case, the two Canadas being no more united than Great Britain and Ireland, but in the case cited it was not shewn that even in Ireland such a judgment was regular, nor that there was any law of Great Britain authorizing such a course.

Our courts must take judicial cognizance of the Acts of Canada—they are the Acts of Upper as well as Lower Canada; and it would be absurd in us to say that the very course we have authorized by a solemn legal enactment is contrary to reason and justice, and therefore refuse to enforce it. If it be so, let the law be repealed; but while it stands on the statute book, our courts must give effect to it. The case of Cowan v. Braidwood, 5 Man. & Gran., is in favour of the plaintiffs. The old process of horning, in Scotland, (a certain procedure against absentees), was abolished in the reign of George the Fourth, and another form of proceeding substituted, still permitting the courts to proceed in a party's absence. This case sought to enforce a claim for costs upon a Scotch decree, prosecuted and pronounced in defendant's absence. He pleaded he was not served with process or notified; but the court held the plea insufficient, inasmuch as he had not negatived the existence of every circumstance which could have justified the Scotch court proceeding against him in his absence. This case is very similar to the present, and under it the plaintiffs are entitled to the postea,

Sherwood, Sol. Gen., shewed cause.

ROBINSON, C. J.—The statute of this province, 7 Vic. ch. 16, sec. 54, in my opinion, is binding upon us as much as upon the courts in Lower Canada. It is a law of our own legislature, to which all the inhabitants of Upper Canada, including the defendant, have assented, and we cannot say on any sufficient ground that it shall not have effect. We must suppose, then, while the case is being tried upon the general issue, which merely denies the fact of the recovery by the foreign judgment, that all was regularly done in the foreign court, till the contrary is shewn. There was sufficient evidence given in the case, I think, to shew prima facie that the defendant had land in the district of Montreal, where the judgment was rendered, and so was amenable to the jurisdiction of the court under the provision of the statute referred to, though he might not have been personally served, (if that appeared). And besides this, I think the general issue only opened to the defendant the defence that no such judgment was in fact rendered against him. Until the regularity of the judgment is impeached, it must be assumed to have been duly obtained; and as it is particularly set out in the declaration, and is not impeached by the plea, I think nothing more is denied on the record than the fact of such a judgment having been rendered against him, this defendant. If, however, the defence was open on non-assumpsit, that the defendant had not been summoned, yet I do not see in this case any proof to that effect, and it was certainly no part of the plaintiff's case to shew in the first instance that the defendant was summoned, since the presumption would be in support of the judgment. The case of Buchanan v. Rucker(a)

(a) 9 E. R. 192.

throws no difficulty in the way of these plaintiffs' recovery, because there the court remarked that the legislature of Tobago, were assuming by their act to bind the whole world ; and the defendant, Rucker, was a person described in the record as of London, and formerly of Dunkirk ; and there was nothing to shew that he had ever been in Tobago, or had property there. The defendant, it appears, had land in Montreal ; and land, too, about which the very contest settled by this judgment arose. In such a case, the statute law of this province dispenses with the necessity of personal service, and substitutes for it a certain printed notice in the newspapers. If there is any thing unjust, or incautious, in allowing a judgment to be thus obtained, we must leave it to the legislature to make better provision ; and, in the mean time, must give effect to the law as it stands, which is the law, not of any foreign country, but of this province We do not stand to Lower Canada in such a relation as England does to Tobago. Montreal, where this judgment was rendered, is within this province where the defendant resides, and subject to the same government and legislature to which we ourselves are subject. The case is the same as if an act were passed allowing a judgment to be obtained in any of the district courts in this province, against a person living in another district, substituting notice in a newspaper for actual service of process. We could not refuse to carry into effect the provisions of such a statute. And as we must presume, until the contrary is shewn, that all was regularly done in this superior court, we must hold this judgment to be regular, as it may have been, and as the contrary is not shewn. The bill of costs was shewn to be the bill taxed in the cause, and sufficiently identified with the judgment. We are to suppose that the mode of proceeding is agreeably to the law there, and indeed it was proved to be so.

Rule discharged.

PROUT v. HOWARD.

A Plea to a declaration on a promissory note, and account stated that the defendant did not make the note in the first count mentioned, is bad on special demurrer, as attempting to offer an answer to the whole declaration.

Demurrer. The plaintiff declares in the first count upon a promissory note made by the defendant to the plaintiff, and in the second count upon an account stated.

The defendant pleads "that he did not make the promissory note in the first count mentioned," concluding to the contrary.

The plaintiff demurs specially, because the plea is pleaded to the whole declaration, although it is an answer only to the first count.

Joinder in demurrer.

H. *Eccles* for the demurrer.

G. *Duggan* contra.

ROBINSON, C. J.—The objection urged to this plea is, that it is no defence whatever to the second count ; and yet it is so pleaded, that it can be not otherwise considered than as an intended answer to the whole declaration. This plea would undoubtedly be good on general demurrer ; for it is quite clear what is meant, and what is in substance asserted.

though informally (a). But the plaintiff has demurred specially. The plea is precisely like that in Worley v. Harrison (b), which Patterson and Littledale, judges, seemed to think informal, though they did not decide the point. In 5 Nev. & Man. 173, the same case is reported, and Lord Denman is there stated to have given his opinion that the demurrer must be sustained. The courts in England seem to hold that any plea which is not in terms limited to a partial defence, must in point of form be regarded as a plea to the whole declaration or count to which it is pleaded. I should think that our 41st rule was decisive upon this objection; but the similar rule in England has been otherwise explained.

Judgment for the plaintiff on demurrer.

LEE ET AL. V. M'CLURE.

The conclusion of the affidavit of debt, negativing any vexatious or malicious motive, required by the statute 2 Geo. IV. ch. 1, sec. 8, is not necessary since the statute 8 Vic. ch. 48. sec. 44.

This was a motion to set aside an arrest on a capias ad respondendum, on account of the affidavit to hold to bail not containing the declaration that the deponent did not sue out the process from any vexatious or malicious motive, as required by 2 Geo. IV. ch. 1, sec. 8.

The question was whether the provision in the statute 8 Vic. ch. 48, sec. 44, is cumulative in regard to the form of the affidavit; or, whether it must be taken to be the only subsisting legislative provision on that point.

Blake moved for a rule nisi to set aside the arrest, for irregularity in the affidavit of debt, which did not contain any statement negativing any vexatious or malicious motive, according to the form given in 2 Geo. IV. ch. 1, sec. 8.

ROBINSON, C. J.—We are of opinion that the provision in the 8th Vic., ch. 48, sec. 44, is not cumulative, but is to be looked upon as substituting a form of affidavit in the place of the one given by the former act. That undoubtedly is the most convenient footing for the matter to rest upon, and such a construction is the most reasonable one to give to the clause last referred to, for if it were intended only to prescribe some addition to the other form, or an alteration in some part of it, then it would have been unnecessary that the new form should have expressed anything about the cause of action, and the amount due, because that had been required by the previous statute. It would seem not reasonable either, after the legislature had so far altered the other form of affidavit, as to compel the plaintiff to swear that he verily believes his debtor is immediately about to leave Upper Canada, with intent to defraud him of his debt, to suppose that they would require him, at the same time, to disclaim any malicious motive in arresting him. When the form of affidavit only expressed an apprehension in very general terms, there might appear to be some reason for the additional clause. There is another

---

(a) Harvey v. Graham et al. 5 Ad. & Ell. 61.
(b) 3 Ad. & Ell. 674.

consideration which seems conclusive. The 8 Vic., ch. 48, sec. 44, expressly provides that an affidavit of the same form *as that act requires* shall be sufficient for taking out a writ of capias ad satisfaciendum; a provision of the same kind as is contained in the 15th section of the 2nd Geo. IV. ch. 1, and certainly it is not expressly required by the 8th Vic., that the deponent should disclaim any malicious motive.

Rule refused.

SMALL V. BEASLEY.

If an objection to a pleading is taken on special demurrer, it must distinctly point out the defect objected to.

Where the condition of a bond was to account for monies received once in every six months, and the defendant pleaded that he did account, &c., according to the terms and true intent and meaning of the condition; the plea was held bad on special demurrer, because it did not expressly allege that the defendant accounted once every six months.

Declaration in debt on bond. The defendant sets out the condition on oyer, in these words: "Whereas the said Charles Coxwell Small has "been required by an act passed in the second year of the reign of his "late Majesty King George the Fourth, to have in each and every dis-"trict of the province formerly known as Upper Canada, an office, the "duties of which shall be discharged by deputy, and for the due and "faithful performance of the office the said Charles Coxwell Small requires "that security shall be given; and whereas the said Charles Coxwell "Small has appointed Arthur Gifford, Esquire, to be the deputy clerk of "the crown in and for the district of Gore; now the condition of this "obligation is such, that if the said Arthur Gifford shall well, truly and "faithfully fulfil, perform and discharge all and every the duties of his "said office, and shall duly and regularly keep and render all accounts "which ought to be kept and rendered by him, and shall account for and "pay over to the said Charles Coxwell Small, his heirs, executors and "administrators or assigns, all and every such sum or sums of money as "shall come into his hands as deputy clerk of the crown, *at least once in* "*six months*, then this obligation to be null and void, otherwise to remain "in full force, virtue and effect," which being read and heard, the defendant, Henry Beasley, says that the said Arthur Gifford did from time to time, and at all times, after the making of the said writing obligatory, and the said condition thereof, well, truly and faithfully fulfil, perform and discharge all and every the duties of his said office, and did duly and regularly keep and render all accounts which ought to have been kept and rendered by him, *and did account for and pay over to the said plaintiff* all and every such sum and sums of money as came into his hands as deputy clerk of the crown, according to the terms, true intent, meaning and effect of the said condition of the said writing obligatory, and this he, the said Henry Beasley, is ready to verify, &c.

The plaintiff demurs specially because it is not averred in the said plea, nor does the said plea in any manner state in what manner or how the said Arthur Gifford kept and rendered the accounts, which ought to have been kept and rendered by him; nor does the said plea state or shew in manner, except inferentially, how or *in what manner the said Arthur*

Gifford did account for the moneys that came to his hands as Deputy Clerk of the Crown ; nor does the said plea allege, or shew, or give the court to understand how, in what mode, *at what times*, or by what means the said Arthur Gifford *paid over to* the said plaintiff all and every such sum and sums of money as came into his hands as Deputy Clerk of the Crown.

Grant for the plaintiff.

Eccles for the defendant.

ROBINSON, C. J.—The plea should have stated that the defendant did once in every six months account for and pay all moneys received, or should have confessed and avoided a breach. It is objected that the defect is one of form only, and the demurrer does not clearly point it out. If we could say so satisfactorily, we should be inclined to do it, for demurrers of this kind are not to be favoured, there being often difficulty in assigning or answering a breach specifically without going inconveniently into detail (a). The defendant in this case binds himself to account for and pay over "all such moneys as shall "come into his hands once in six months," &c., and he pleads that "he did "account and pay over to the plaintiff all such moneys, &c., according to the "terms, true intent, meaning and effect of the condition." The plaintiff objects that he does not shew "in *what* mode, or *at what times*, or by *what* "*means* he paid over the money," &c. Now as to that part, I incline to think the demurrer does not hit the defect ; for it was not necessary to state *in what mode* he paid the money, nor *at what time*, that is, on what particular days, for they might have been very numerous, and the defendant was not bound to specify the days, nor need he shew by *what means* he paid the money ; and I confess I do not very well know what may have been meant by that. But as to the breach in not accounting for moneys received, the demurrer must be taken, I think, to be sufficiently specific, in objecting that it was not shewn by the plea *how or in what manner* the defendant accounted for the money ; except by stating generally that it was according to the condition, &c.; whereas he should have pleaded expressly that he accounted at least every six months, which is the manner of accounting for which he undertook.

Judgment for plaintiff.

HANCOCK V. GIBSON.

In *assumpsit* for the non-delivery of a quantity of hams, which were to be delivered at the opening of the navigation in the spring, the defendant pleaded that he was ready and willing to deliver the hams at the opening of the navigation in the spring, but that the plaintiff refused to accept or pay for them, on which issue was joined, and there was no proof of any offer or readiness to accept them at the opening of navigation, although some evidence was given of a readiness to receive them at a subsequent period, and the jury found for the defendant, the court refused to grant a new trial.

Assumpsit for not delivering a quantity of hams and bacon sold by the defendant to the plaintiff, to be delivered at or before the opening of the navigation in the spring of 1845. The defendant pleaded, first, *non-assumpsit;*

(a) 1 B. & P. 644.

secondly, to the first count (relating to the hams), that he was able, and ready and willing, until and at the opening of the navigation to deliver the hams according to the agreement, but that the plaintiff refused to accept *or to pay for them*, and discharged and prevented the plaintiff from delivering them; with a special traverse that the plaintiff was ready and willing at the opening of the navigation to accept and pay for the remainder. And he pleaded a similar plea to the second count, which was for non-delivery of a quantity of bacon. It appeared that in March, 1845, the plaintiff bought of the defendant hams and bacon, to be delivered (but not shewn where) at the opening of the navigation. After the opening of the navigation the defendant wished the plaintiff to come for them, but he begged that they might be allowed to remain for some time, as he had not room for them, and the defendant assented. The navigation opened about the last of April. On the 22nd May, the defendant came to the plaintiff and said the hams were ready if he would send for them. About an hour after, the plaintiff sent a man with a note, to inform him that if he would send the hams and bacon to the city scales to be weighed, he (the plaintiff) would be ready to take them. The defendant refused to send them. About the 14th May, it appeared that the plaintiff was in treaty with one Davis, for selling to him a great part of the hams and bacon, and there was some difficulty between them about the payment. On the 13th or 14th May he sent Davis to get a part of them, and intimated that he would take the remainder. The defendant had all ready for weighing, but when Davis came with an order for his portion, the defendant declined letting them go till he had got the money, and Davis did not get them. The plaintiff attended the same day, but did not get the hams, because he could not then pay the money as the defendant required. It was left to the jury to say whether the plaintiff was acting *bona fide* when he sent word he would take the hams, or whether he was making a demand without actual readiness to pay, in order to make a case, as the defendant had objected to let the hams go without being recompensed for a loss in the weight (which it was proved would have been considerable), while the hams were left in his hands, which was for three weeks or more. The jury found a verdict for the defendant, and

Blake, for the plaintiff, obtained a rule *nisi* for a new trial on the law and evidence, and for misdirection.

J. L. Robinson shewed cause.

ROBINSON, C. J.—There are two points in this case; first, whether the plaintiff gave such evidence upon the issue of his being ready to pay for the goods purchased, as to entitle him to a verdict, so that there was nothing for the jury to consider in connection with that issue which could warrant the jury in finding for the defendant; and secondly, whether, admitting that to be so, the plaintiff's right to recover was not repelled on other grounds. Upon the first point, the cases of Wilks v. Atkinson (*a*), and of Squier v. Hunt (*b*), fully establish the principle for which they were cited, namely, that when A. sells goods to B., either to be delivered when called for, or on a certain day, upon an agreement express or implied, that they are to be paid for on delivery, then if B. demands the goods, and they are withheld from him, and he brings such an action as is brought here, averring that he was ready to pay for the

---

(*a*) 6 Taunt. 11.   (*b*) 3 Price, 69.

goods, the fact of his going and demanding them is sufficient evidence *prima facie* that he was ready to pay for them; and it must be inferred that he was ready, unless the vendor proves the contrary. Lord Kenyon, in Rawson et al. v. Johnson (a) had held otherwise, and stated it to be clearly his opinion that in such a case the vendee must prove that he was prepared to tender and pay the money. It is not material to the decision of this case, to consider which of these opinions appears to be the more reasonable, for the authority of the two later cases is not doubted; and in' Levy v. Lord Herbert (b), the law is held to be as is there laid down. The inference which is sustained by them would no doubt be in general correct, and therefore it is perhaps safe, and reasonable, in the first instance, to entertain it. Punctuality in commercial transactions is so necessary, that it is commonly expected as a matter of course, and it is natural to assume that the parties to such transactions intend to be punctual on their part, especially when they come to exact performance on the other side. If, therefore, this plaintiff had gone to the defendant to demand the goods purchased, at a time when he was entitled to insist upon their delivery under the contract, it would seem reasonable to presume, when there was no evidence to lead us to think otherwise, that he went expecting and prepared to pay for them; and that the very fact of his demanding the goods, was evidence of his readiness to pay for them. His sending for the goods by another, instead of going in person to demand them, would not place him in a different position (c). But after all that occurred here, I think the learned judge was fully warranted in leaving it as a question to the jury, whether the plaintiff was sincere and in earnest in his demand of the goods, being prepared to pay for them; or, whether he was not rather making a demand as a matter of form, in order to enable him to maintain an action if the delivery should be refused, as he had much reason to expect it would be. On the 13th or 14th May, after a good deal of latitude had already been allowed to him by the defendant, who might have held him strictly to his contract, he sent Davis for part of the hams, having agreed to sell them to him at a small profit: but as he did not supply him with money to pay for them, and Davis had it not of his own, the defendant declined letting the hams go. Then the defendant, being informed at the same time that the plaintiff would call for such portion of the hams and bacon as he had not agreed to part with to Davis, got them out to be weighed, and was evidently willing and prepared in good faith to complete the sale and delivery; but he was disappointed, for though the plaintiff came to demand them, he proved that in his case at least the inference did not hold that he must of course be prepared to pay for them, and as the defendant would not let the hams go without the money, the plaintiff went away promising to call and close the matter the next day; he failed in this however, and nothing more is heard of him till the 22nd May, when the defendant went to him, and they had some dispute about the transaction. The defendant had been reasonable and accommodating so far; he had, to suit the plaintiff's convenience, and with some trouble to himself, kept the hams on hand a month after the time when he might have insisted on their being taken away, but he was not bound to extend this indulgence indefinitely. After the failure on the 14th May, and when the plaintiff did not come for

---

(a) 1 East. 203.   (b) 7 Taunton, 818.   (c) 3 Price, 69.

some days, while the season was advancing when it is desirable to dispose of articles of this kind without delay, the defendant was at liberty, I think, to have done what he pleased with the hams, and might have considered himself no longer bound to observe a contract of which the terms had been so little regarded on the other side. We may gather from the evidence, that although he would have done what he could not have been compelled to do, and was still willing to let the plaintiff have the hams at the price they had agreed upon, yet that he had refused to do so, unless the plaintiff would make him an allowance for what the hams had lost in weight since the time when the plaintiff was to have accepted them, according to his contract. It was proved that this loss was considerable; not less, perhaps, than from £10 to £12. The defendant had a right to annex such a condition, for though he had once or twice before waived strictness as to time, there was nothing to bind him to any delay beyond the 14th May; nor, indeed, till that day; though the defendant, as it appears, was then willing to have delivered the goods. Now what was the position of the parties? The defendant had agreed to sell to the plaintiff a large quantity of hams and bacon, both articles perishable in their nature, and liable from various causes to suffer from keeping; the goods to be delivered at the opening of the navigation, and to be paid for on delivery. When the navigation opened, the plaintiff was not prepared to accept them; but he was nevertheless selling them in portions to others, and was evidently endeavouring to make a profit of the defendant's hams by thus disposing of them, while he was apparently not in a situation to fulfil his own part of the contract. Some difficulty arose between him and Davis, to whom he had agreed to sell a large portion. Davis could neither pay him nor the defendant for that portion, unless the plaintiff would join him in a note to be discounted, which the latter declined; and it was while matters stood in this position, on the 13th or 14th May, that the defendant very reasonably declined to allow either the one or the other to take any part of the hams until they could pay for them; though he was clearly willing to have acted fairly, and, under the circumstances, liberally by both, if he had been paid then what he was entitled to have claimed by his contract a considerable time before. Then as the plaintiff had, after previous delays, presented himself on that occasion without the money, and as there is not evidence that should have led the jury to find that the defendant had agreed to let the plaintiff stand in the same position on any other day, I do not consider that when the plaintiff is found, on the 22nd May, to have written the note which he did to the defendant, the jury were driven to conclude that he was then ready to pay; or that the court could hold, that if he were ready, the defendant was bound to deliver the goods according to the very terms of the original contract, so that he had no discretion, but must comply. The case, in my opinion, was put properly to the jury under the circumstances of the plaintiff's conduct, and there could be little justice in disturbing the verdict which they have given. There was evidence from which the jury might reasonably conclude that the defendant had not agreed to let the plaintiff have the hams, after his failure to take them on the 14th May, unless he would compensate him for the loss in weight. If the defendant did refuse on that or any other ground which warranted him in refusing, then it would not signify whether the plaintiff was or was not ready with the money. The necessity for a tender would of course be dispensed with; but if the jury did not believe that the plaintiff was prepared to pay for the goods, that would of itself be a good reason for refusing to give him damages as for a breach of the contract. But if the justice of the case had not appeared so clearly to be with the defendant, still the pleadings would not seem to admit of any other verdict than has been given, for the issues raised in regard to both counts by the special traverses are, whether the plaintiff was ready to pay for the hams and bacon before or at the opening of the navigation; and it was proved that he was not then ready. If being ready some weeks afterwards to pay for the hams, &c., would entitle him to demand them, it could only be under a different contract from that which is set out upon the record.

Rule discharged.

GILLESPIE, MOFFATT ET AL. V. CAMERON.

Where the plaintiffs commenced separate actions against the acceptor and endorsers of a bill of exchange, and the acceptor paid the amount of the claim against him, but without the costs, and judgment was entered, and execution issued against him for their amount, and the costs of the suit against the endorsers, the court ordered the writ to be restrained to the costs against the acceptor alone.

This was an application made by *Blake*, for the defendant, to restrain the plaintiffs from levying more than a certain amount of costs, and that the plaintiffs' attorney should pay the costs of the application. The facts out of which the application arose are fully stated in the judgment of the court.

Crooks shewed cause.

ROBINSON, C. J.—It seems difficult to understand how the plaintiffs' attorney, in this case, could have supposed himself warranted by anything that had occurred, or by any principle or practice, in suing out an execution against the defendant's goods, endorsed to levy the amount of the plaintiffs' costs in this suit, and also the costs in their suit against McGregor and McDiarmid. The defendant, being acceptor of the bill to which McGregor and McDiarmid were also parties, as payee and endorsers, was of course the person to whom the plaintiffs were entitled to look as primarily liable to them; and it has been considered that in such cases, when the holder of a bill takes his remedy, as he has a right to do, against the several parties to the bill, he has so far an equitable claim to look to the acceptor for saving him against all charges incurred through his failure to pay his acceptance, that the court may and should decline to interpose and stay proceedings in an action against the acceptor, unless he will pay the costs of any actions that may have been instituted on the same bill against other parties, as well as the costs of the action against himself.—Smith v. Woodcock (*a*). A modern rule of court in England (*b*), which we are not at liberty by our constitution and practice to regard as binding upon us, has changed the course that had constantly been

---

(*a*) 4 T. R. 691.   (*b*) T. T. 1 Vic.

observed there in this respect; but as we had not made a similar rule, it was not thought proper to refuse to the plaintiffs any advantage which they might suppose they could derive from the court declining to stay proceedings in their action against this defendant, till they had complied with the equitable condition (as it was considered) which the general practice in England, before the late rule, authorized the courts there to exact. The plaintiffs therefore were left at liberty to proceed against the defendant, the acceptor, though he had paid the bill, on which alone he was sued, together with interest and charges. All they could expect to gain by proceeding, however, was the costs in this action, if the defendant should persevere in his resolution not to pay the costs of the suit against the endorsers. And this shews that the courts in England have not without reason changed the former course; for if, when the action proceeds, the holder of the bill cannot recover more than the debt and costs in that action (as it is certain he cannot), it seems hardly sensible to refuse to stay the proceedings, upon the defendant's submitting voluntarily to all the law can in that suit enforce. Sometimes, perhaps, where the suit against the other parties has not proceeded far, and the costs are therefore trifling, or where the person primarily liable is made to feel, upon reflection, that he ought to save the party who has trusted to his acceptance from all loss, the refusal to stay proceedings may have had a good effect; but when the acceptor is determined not to pay the costs of other actions, the holder of the bill has no means of compelling him, and he can gain nothing (though his attorney may) by declining to stop proceedings on payment of the debt and costs in the action as soon as they are tendered. It is not surprising in this case, that the acceptor was unwilling to pay the costs of the action against McGregor and McDiarmid, because they were not endorsers for *his* accommodation; and whatever might be the justice of the case as between him and these plaintiffs. he might naturally enough feel that the endorsers had at least no claim on him to relieve them from costs, considering the nature of the transaction out of which the bill had arisen. But it is strange that the plaintiffs' attorney should have imagined that he could, as a consequence of the court declining to stop proceedings summarily, do anything more than go on with his action, till it should be brought formally to a conclusion, when the same consequences only must follow as in other cases, namely, that he could enforce payment of the debt and costs in that action, and nothing more. The debt was paid in August, 1845, by the defendant in this action, that is, the bill with interest and all charges upon it; yet the plaintiffs went on to compute damages before the Master and sign judgment. Under the circumstances detailed in the affidavits, and not denied, there was clearly no necessity for taking out execution for the costs in this action, because it was well known that the defendant's attorney was ready and desirous to pay them, and had offered to do so; waiting only till the plaintiffs' attorney should let him know the amount. There was therefore no fair pretence for suing out execution for anything; but the adding, in the sum directed to be paid under the *fi. fa.*, the costs of the other suit against the endorsers, which could not possibly have been recovered by the judgment in which the *fi. fa.* issued, was wholly unauthorized. The manner in which this was done does not alter the effect, and cannot support the step taken. The plaintiffs, it seems, had been advised, that having an equitable claim upon this defendant for the costs of the other action against other parties, and this defendant, as the plaintiffs allege, having engaged to pay them, they could apply part of the money paid to them in August, expressly in discharge of the *bill* and interest, in covering the costs of the action against the endorsers, and could then endorse their *fi. fa.* for so much money, as being still due upon the bill in addition to the costs proper to this action. But they had certainly no right to do that. The person paying his creditor a sum of money, has a right when he pays it to direct how it shall be applied. If he omits to do so, then the person receiving the money has in general a discretion to apply it to such claims of his upon the person paying it, as he may prefer. This discretion, however, is limited in particular cases by circumstances; but here nothing was left to the plaintiff's choice, for the debtor, when he paid his money, applied it expressly to the discharge of the whole debt due upon the bill. He was sued for that and for nothing else, and he paid it upon the computation of the amount made by the plaintiffs themselves, who can only be understood as accepting the money in discharge of the claim on account of which they had demanded it. There was no debt due by the defendant to these plaintiffs on account of the costs of the other action. If they had, under the circumstances of the payment, any choice to exercise, they could not apply part of the money to pay a debt not due; and if we could act upon the statement, of which we have no proof, that the defendant had verbally agreed with the plaintiffs to pay these costs, and if such an undertaking was binding, still more clearly the plaintiffs could not issue execution for that money when it was not, and could not be, embraced in the judgment. The only consequence would be, that if the promise to pay these other costs was binding, it could be enforced as in other cases. We are of opinion that the first part of the rule obtained should be made absolute, restraining the levy under the *fi. fa.*, to the amount of costs taxed in this cause; and that the plaintiffs' attorney should pay the defendant's costs of this application, and of the applications made in chambers for relief against any proceedings taken by the plaintiffs after the costs had been taxed, together with any costs in the shape of poundage or mileage, provided the defendant will undertake to bring no action of the wrong complained of.

Rule accordingly.

Hancock v. Bethune.

Quære.—If in *assumpsit* on a contract to carry goods safely, with an averment of total loss, and a plea that the goods were carried safely, and delivered in like good order as they were received, and no evidence is given to shew that any of the goods were lost, but only that the cask in which they were packed was injured, and some of the goods damaged, the plaintiff is entitled to recover anything, or more than nominal damages?

The plaintiff declared against the defendant, not as common carriers, but on a contract to carry from Kingston to Toronto, in a steamer, a cask containing a quantity of brushes; and he charged that the defendant did not deliver *the said goods and merchandise safely*, as he agreed to do, but so carelessly conducted himself, that by reason thereof the said goods and merchandise *became and was entirely lost.* The defendant pleaded, first, *non-assumpsit;* and secondly, *that he did deliver the goods and merchandise to* the plaintiff "*in like good order as he received the same.*" It was left to the jury to find what was the whole value of the brushes in the cask, assuming a certain paper which the plaintiff produced to be a correct list of them; but the plaintiff gave no evidence whatever respecting any invoice, further than by producing the list; and the jury was told by the learned judge to find the extent to which the brushes were damaged, if at all, and for the brushes lost, if any were lost. They found the value of all the brushes to be £19 5s. 6d., and they gave the plaintiff a verdict, with £5 damages; and leave was reserved to the plaintiff to move to increase the verdict to £19 5s. 6d., if the court should think he had a right to recover. No counsel attended for the defendant at the trial.

Sherwood, Sol.-Gen., for the defendant, moved to set aside the verdict, as being against law and evidence, and for misdirection.

Blake shewed cause.

ROBINSON, C. J.—The plaintiff in his particulars claims damages for the loss of the cask and the brushes contained in it. The jury, on very unsatisfactory evidence of loss, or rather, as I think, without any evidence, gave a verdict for the plaintiff, with £5 damages. Nothing is claimed in the declaration for damage suffered by the cask or brushes, either by wet or any other cause. It is simply the non-delivery, and consequent *loss* of the *goods* and *merchandise*, that is complained of in the declaration; and supposing these words to include the cask in which the goods were packed, still it is a loss by non-delivery that is alone complained of. Now it is clear that the cask was delivered without delay, but not in good order (as it was received), the head being loose, so that some of the brushes *might have* dropped out, or *might have been taken* out; but there is really no proof, so far as I can see from the judge's note, that any were missing. We are not asked by the plaintiff to increase the verdict, but the defendant has moved to set it aside, as being against law and evidence, and for misdirection. I really cannot see that the plaintiff shewed a right to recover for anything; he did not complain of damage done either to the cask or goods, and so could not properly recover for either; and if he could, still he proved no damage done to the goods, but only that the head of the cask was loose, which in packages of this sort is very slightly secured. Upon the record, the jury had only to inquire whether there were any brushes not delivered. I do not see evidence that a single brush was missing; there was no proof how many were in the cask, nor that any were taken out. It seems to me that the jury had no ground for awarding £5, or any sum to be paid by the defendant. If it was worth the plaintiff's while to bring this action, it was incumbent on him to give some proof of his loss. It is clear on the face of his declaration, that he was suing for the non-delivery of his merchandise, not for the trifling injury to the cask which contained it. He could hardly have been so unreasonable as to bring an action in this court against the owners of a steamboat, because the head of a hardware cask had become loose. He might as well have brought it because a hoop had come off, or a nail dropped out; and if he had been so absurd as to complain of that as a breach of contract, the defendant could probably have protested himself by paying sixpence or a shilling into court. But it was not in fact for any injury of that kind that he sought redress, nor even for the more substantial cause that his goods had been damaged. What he complained of was, that in consequence of not being delivered, they were lost to him; and that, in my opinion, was the cause of action which he was bound to prove. He had narrowed his breach of contract to that. It has been argued that, because the defendant in his plea alleged that he had delivered the goods safely, and in like good order as he received them, he has subjected himself to damages for an injury of this kind, however trifling, although the plaintiff had not complained of such an injury. This would be giving to his plea the effect of enlarging the breach which the plaintiff had set forth; but I think we cannot legally, or justly, allow that effect to the plea. If we could, then, upon the same principle, if a plaintiff were suing upon a bond to pay money by instalments, and were to assign as a breach the non-payment of a certain instalment, for instance, the third, and if the defendant should plead that he had well and truly paid that instalment, and all the other instalments mentioned in the bond, the plaintiff should be allowed, though the third instalment should be proved to have been paid, to recover for some other instalment which had not been alleged to be due. The defendant, in this case, when he pleaded that he had safely delivered the goods in like good order, &c., only desired to meet the terms of his undertaking specifically, but the question upon the issue was not merely what he averred he had done, but what the plaintiff had charged him with not doing; for I take it to be a clear principle of law, that a plaintiff cannot recover for any injury which he had not complained of, whatever the facts may be; he can only recover *secundum allegata et probata*. If the defendant had been present by counsel at the trial, as he ought to have been, I do not see how the plaintiff could have been allowed to recover for brushes lost and not delivered, without either proving directly that some were taken away, or proving the loss indirectly, by shewing how many had been in the cask when shipped, and how many were in it when he received it. He shewed neither; and yet the jury gave a verdict for £5, on an idea, I think, that they could allow something for possible damages, which were neither alleged nor proved. The amount to be sure is small, and that occasions us to doubt whether we should grant a new trial; but it is important to persons engaged in business of this kind, and inevitably exposed in the course of it to daily risks, that they should receive such protection as the law entitles them to. The costs of an action in this court are not inconsiderable, and the evidence ought at least to shew, when uncontradicted, some right of action, such as the plaintiff has declared upon. The verdict besides seems to have proceeded upon the jury being inadvertently told that they might give damages for any deterioration of the goods, though no such injury was charged. I think there should be a new trial, without costs. The only doubt I have had has been on account of the smallness of the damages; but that cannot weigh under all circumstances, though it generally influences the court when it is the plaintiff who has failed, or when the evidence has been conflicting.

MACAULAY, J.—It appears that I was in error in leaving the determination of the injury to the jury, as matter of damage on this record, the declaration being for a total loss, and not a partial injury. No counsel appeared at the trial, and no defence was made, and my attention was not sufficiently directed to the precise nature of the loss alleged, or in the course of the trial I lost sight of it owing to the examination of a witness on the subject of partial damage. But under the evidence applied to the issue as joined, which asserts full performance on the defendant's part, I still think the plaintiff was entitled to a verdict for some damages. I should have been better satisfied with a verdict for one shilling or five shillings in compensation for the injury proved to the head of the cask containing the brushes, which alone was clearly established; although there was some evidence, not very definite, from which the actual loss of some few of the brushes might be inferred. The verdict being, however, only £5, though more than the loss actually proved, I cannot satisfy myself that it should be set aside, if the plaintiff is entitled to recover anything, as I think he is. The amount of damages may in some measure be attributed to the absence of any defence; and I do not see that any objection to the charge for misdirection or error in law not going to the whole cause of action should, when the sum is so small, be admitted as a sufficient ground for a new trial. It would be making a precedent not advisable to be established. I therefore think the rule should be discharged.

JONES, J.—It is contended for the defendant that there was no evidence of any loss, and that the learned judge should have so told the jury, and directed them to find for the defendant. I should have been much better satisfied if the jury could have so found, the action being one which should never have been brought; but I cannot say that the defendant safely carried and delivered the cask in the like good order in which he received it, and therefore strictly speaking the plaintiff would be entitled to nominal damages; and in such cases a carrier would at all times be liable if a hoop had fallen off a barrel or cask which he had undertaken to carry safely. The protection of the defendant in this, as in many other cases, rests with the court, by exercising the right of restraining the plaintiff from costs. In this case, if a certificate was not obtained at the trial, the plaintiff will only have District Court costs, and the defendant will be entitled to Queen's Bench costs for his defence. The plaintiff being entitled to nominal damages, and the verdict being only £5, I do not think the court can properly grant a new trial. If the defendant had allowed judgment to go by default upon this declaration, and the plaintiff had given no evidence upon the assessment, or if the defendant had merely pleaded the general issue, and the plaintiff, as he did here, had proved the agreement and delivery of the goods to the defendant, he would have been entitled to nominal damages. And in either case, upon proof of the value of the goods, he would have recovered the amount. The second plea was a plea of performance, and the onus was upon the defendant to prove as he alleged, that the goods were delivered in the like good order in which he received them.. In this he failed, giving no evidence; but it appearing by the evidence of the plaintiff that the cask containing the brushes had been injured, the action being one upon a breach of contract, and the agreement being proved by the plaintiff, he had a right of action; upon proof of the special damage laid, to substantial damages, and wanting such proof, to nominal damages, the defendant having failed to establish his pleas. This point was determined during the last term in the case of McLeod v. Boulton.

MCLEAN, J.—It does not appear that the plaintiff is entitled to any damages upon the breach that he has himself set out in his declaration, as he has not proved any loss; and the description of injury that he is shewn to have sustained, he has not made the ground of complaint in this action.

The court being equally divided,

Verdict stands.

QUEEN'S BENCH.

SITTINGS AFTER HILARY TERM, 9 VICTORIA.

Present,—THE CHIEF JUSTICE,
MR. JUSTICE MACAULAY,
MR. JUSTICE JONES,
MR. JUSTICE MCLEAN.

COATES V. LLOYD.

Where in *assumpsit* for money had and received, the defendant pleaded that he had received the money as the agent of the plaintiff, and had paid it over by his directions to a person to whom the plaintiff was indebted, and the plaintiff replied, that he countermanded the direction before the payment, to which the defendant rejoined, that before the countermand, or any notice thereof, he had given notice to the plaintiff's creditor that he held the money for his use, and the creditor had assented thereto, the rejoinder was held a good answer on demurrer.

Assumpsit for money had and received.

The defendant pleads, that the said sum of money in the declaration mentioned, was received by him as the agent and servant of the plaintiff, and for his use, and by his permission to be kept by the defendant as such agent and servant in his possession and custody for the plaintiff, until he the said plaintiff should direct the defendant how to dispose of and appropriate the same; and the defendant further says, that after he had so received the said sum of money as such agent and servant as aforesaid, and before the same or any part thereof was demanded from him by the plaintiff, and while the same was so in the defendant's custody and possession as such agent and servant as aforesaid, and before the commencement of this suit, to wit, on the 1st day of July, in the year of our Lord, 1845, the plaintiff directed the defendant to dispose of and appropriate the said sum of money, by paying the same to one Alexander

Murray and one Lewis Moffatt, in payment of a certain debt then due from the plaintiff to the said Murray and Moffatt, and the defendant afterwards, to wit, on the day and year last aforesaid, did pay the said sum of money to the said Murray and Moffatt, in payment of the said debt so due to them by the plaintiff, in compliance with the said direction of the plaintiff for the disposal and appropriation of the same as aforesaid, and this the defendant is ready to verify, &c.

The plaintiff replies, that the said direction by the said plaintiff to the said defendant, to dispose of and appropriate the said money in the said second plea mentioned, by paying the same to the said Alexander Murray and Lewis Moffatt, in payment of their said debt as in the said second plea mentioned, was countermanded, recalled and revoked by the said plaintiff, and notice thereof given to the said defendant by him the said plaintiff, previous to the payment by the said defendant of the said money in his the said defendant's second plea alleged, and this the said plaintiff is ready to verify, &c.

The defendant rejoins, that before the said direction of the said plaintiff to the said defendant was countermanded, revoked or recalled, or any notice thereof given to the defendant, he, the defendant, to wit, on the first day of July, in the year of our Lord, 1845, had given notice to the said Alexander Murray and Lewis Moffatt, that he held the said money for their use and benefit, and for the purposes in the said plea mentioned, and the said Alexander Murray and Lewis Moffatt then agreed to accept the same, and informed the said defendant that they did accept of the said sum of money in the said plea mentioned, in payment of the said debt of the said plaintiff to the said Alexander Murray and Lewis Moffatt, and this the said defendant is ready to verify, &c.

The plaintiff demurs generally to this rejoinder.

J. Duggan for plaintiff.

J. Hillyard Cameron for defendant.

ROBINSON, C. J.—The first question is, whether the answer to the replication is good in substance. Was it a sufficient reason for not regarding the plaintiff's countermand of his order to pay Messrs. Murray and Moffatt, that the defendant, before he received notice of that countermand, had acquainted Murray and Moffatt that he had received the money, and held it to their use, by the instruction of the plaintiff, and that Messrs. Murray and Moffatt had thereupon informed the defendant that they agreed to the arrangement, and accepted it in payment of the plaintiff's debt? The principle is, that an agent, receiving money to be paid over to a third person, is accountable to his principal until he has entered into some binding engagement to hold the money to the use of such person. What is set out here constitutes such an engagement, under the authority of several adjudged cases (*a*). An authority to an agent to pay money over cannot be revoked after the agent has acted upon it, so as to incur a liability to a third party (*b*). But then it is objected that, admitting the defence to be sufficient, the defendant cannot plead it, because it is a departure from his first defence. This is founded on a misconception

---

(*a*) Williams v. Everett, 14 E. R. 582; 1 C. & J. 83; Baron v. Husband, 4 B. & Ad. 612; 1 M. & W. 365.

(*b*) 1 H. Bl. 242; 7 Taunt. 339.

of the effect of the pleadings. The defendant is not in any manner shifting his ground by the rejoinder. He had pleaded as his defence to the plaintiff's action, that by his desire he had paid over the money to a third party. The plaintiff replies that he had no right to pay it over, because before he made the payment (which admits that he did make it), he, the plaintiff, had countermanded his instructions. The defendant rejoins, that he nevertheless did right in paying the money, because before the countermand came he had informed the third party that he held the money to his use. It seems to have been assumed in the argument, that these latter pleadings involved a statement that the money was still in the hands of the defendant; and that in his rejoinder he had relied upon his having pledged himself to Messrs. Murray and Moffatt, as being tantamount to actual payment; in other words, the plaintiff treats the rejoinder as if the defendant had by it withdrawn his first assertion of actual payment, and was setting up an obligation to pay as equivalent to it. If that were really the effect of the rejoinder, it would, I think, be a departure; but whatever the fact may really be (of which we can take no notice on this question of pleading), it is plain that the rejoinder does nothing more than fortify the original defence, without in any degree abandoning it. All it professes to do is to maintain that the payment already pleaded, and not denied by the other side, was rightfully made, notwithstanding the plaintiff's revocation, because the revocation came too late to enable the defendant to withhold the money.

Judgment for the defendant.

POWELL v. BOULTON.

Where a case had been pending for several terms on a motion for a new trial after a verdict for the plaintiff, the court refused, after discharging the rule for a new trial, to allow the plaintiff to enter judgment as of the term in which the motion was made, in order that he might obtain interest on his verdict, while the proceedings had been stated by the motion for the new trial.

Blake moved to enter judgment *nunc pro tunc*, in order that the plaintiff might have interest for the time that the rule for a new trial was under the consideration of the court.

Boulton, Q. C., shewed cause.

ROBINSON, C. J.—We think we cannot properly comply with this application. It is quite true that in England, to prevent the inconvenience which would otherwise arise from the death of parties while the verdict is suspended in consequence of some application pending in the court, the party is allowed to enter his judgment *nunc pro tunc*, so as to give it, for some purposes at least, a retrospective effect; and the courts have done so sometimes to avoid other inconveniences. But this application is made on a ground quite new here, and for which we cannot look for a precedent in England. The object is to extend the effect of an express statutory provision (a), which allows legal interest on the sum recovered in an action "*from the time of entering the judgment.*" We shall always regret any considerable delay in disposing of any motion before

(a) 2 Geo. IV. ch. 1, sec. 19.

the court, whether the interest be small or great, and we do whatever we can to avoid it, but some delay is inevitable; and if we were to accede to this application to give a fictitious date to this judgment, in order that the party may receive a few months' interest, we may be asked to do the same in almost every case, and must either, in most instances of motions for new trials, make the records of the court inconsistent with the truth, at the risk of injuries to third parties from some inadvertence, or must enter into needless discussions of the comparative circumstances of particular cases, when we could not, after all, draw any line that would appear to be just. As no precedent for such a rule has, that we are aware of, hitherto been made, though there have been many cases which must have seemed as strongly to call for it, we think we should not begin the practice now.

Rule refused.

Baby v. Horace Davenport.

One of two partners cannot execute an arbitration bond in the partnership name, without the authority or consent of the other partner, so as to bind the other partner.

Debt on submission bond.

Plea, *non est factum.*

The bond was between this plaintiff on the one side, and Louis Davenport and Horace Davenport on the other, and was executed thus:

L. & H. Davenport,
By H. Davenport. } One seal.

It was objected that there was no proof of the execution of the bond by the defendant, Horace Davenport. It was proved that the two were co-partners. No evidence was given that Louis Davenport had been authorized by the defendant to execute the bond for him, and the defendant was not present when the bond was executed. But both Louis and Horace Davenport attended before the arbitrators, and were fully assenting to their differences with the plaintiff being awarded upon. The award directed that the two Davenports should pay £37 10s. to the plaintiff. The objection made by the defendant was overruled at the trial, and

Harrison, Q. C., afterwards moved to set aside the verdict, as being contrary to law and evidence, without costs.

J. Hillyard Cameron shewed cause.

Robinson, C. J.—We are of opinion that the defendant was entitled to succeed on the issue of *non est factum.* The bond was not executed by himself, nor by any one in his presence, in such a manner as that his authority could be presumed, nor by any one having authority to bind him by deed. If it is true that he was present at the investigation before the arbitrators, his conduct would be proof of his submission to the reference, and enable the plaintiff to sustain an action upon the award, as being made under a parol submission.

Rule absolute.

LOGAN V. THE COBOURG HARBOUR COMPANY.

The Cobourg Harbour Company are not wharfingers, because they have erected piers and wharves according to their charter, and are not therefore responsible for loss or damage sustained by persons whose goods have been left upon their wharves unstored.

The plaintiff sued in case, charging the defendants as wharfingers.

The first count stated that the defendants, on the first May, 1845, received *from a certain steamer* upon a wharf or pier of the defendants, at Cobourg, two hogsheads of sugar, to be by them safely kept on the said wharf for and to be delivered to the plaintiff, for certain tolls and reward, to be paid by the plaintiff to the defendants, whereby it became the duty of the defendants safely to keep the said goods, and to deliver them to the plaintiff. Then it alleged that the defendants, not regarding their duty, were guilty of such negligence that the goods were damaged and spoiled.

The second count charged that the plaintiff had delivered to the defendants the said sugars, *to be by the defendants unladen and landed* from the steamboat *City of Toronto*, for the plaintiff, upon a wharf or pier of the defendants; to be taken care of, and delivered in a reasonable time to the plaintiff. It then stated the duty, and charged the breach of it as in the first count.

The third count charged that the defendants, at their request, had the care of the sugars for the plaintiff (as upon a gratuitous bailment); that it therefore became their duty to take care of them for the plaintiff, and it charged a breach of duty, and damage to the sugars from the negligence.

The defendants pleaded first, that the goods were not delivered to, nor received by the defendants for the purpose in the declaration mentioned.

Secondly, not guilty.

It was proved at the trial that Mr. Kitson was toll-collector for the Harbour Company, and usually attended on the pier to check the goods landed; that the company had no warehouse, and carried on no business as wharfingers, and received no tolls or fees, except those allowed by the statute for harbour duties. These two hogsheads of sugar were landed from the steamer *City of Toronto*, for the plaintiff, at eleven o'clock at night, with many other articles of goods for other persons. The clerk of the toll collector was present when the goods were landed, and some days afterwards gave to the master of the steamer a receipt, on behalf of Kitson, for all the goods then landed. It was proved that Mr. Kitson had a storehouse of his own, in which any goods landed might be and sometimes were stored when the consignees desired it, or when for any reason it might be necessary; but that the merchants of Cobourg, and this plaintiff among the rest, were constantly in the habit of receiving their goods from carters, who attended at any time of the day or night to take them from the wharf, without any specific direction from the owner of the goods, or from the company's agent, the desire being to avoid any charge for storage. The carter who usually drew up the plaintiff's goods was not on the watch that night, and so it happened that the sugars were not drawn up immediately, as the other goods were; and these being left near the end of the pier, and a heavy wind rising in the night, the water dashed over the hogsheads, and did great injury to the sugars.

It was objected by the defendants that they were not chargeable as wharfingers; that all their agent did was to allow the sugar to be landed, which was subject of course to harbour dues, on which account only he attended at the delivery upon the wharf; that the Cobourg Harbour Company was incorporated for no other purpose than to make and keep in repair the harbour, and not to do business as wharfingers; and that they could not be charged in any action alleging a duty, independent of the purpose for which they are chartered.

Leave was reserved to move for a nonsuit in *banc* on these objections, and the jury gave the plaintiff a verdict for £33 11s. 6d., which was proved to be the amount of damage sustained from the sugar being left exposed to the weather.

D. E. Boulton obtained a rule *nisi* to enter a nonsuit upon the leave reserved.

Sullivan shewed cause.

ROBINSON, C. J.—We are of opinion that a nonsuit should be entered. The Cobourg Harbour Company was incorporated for the purpose of making a harbour "and all necessary piers, wharves, buildings and erections proper for "the protection of the harbour, and for the accommodation and convenience "of vessels entering, lying, loading and unloading within the same." There is certainly nothing here to give them by necessary implication the power of carrying on business as *wharfingers;* and if they desired to do so, it would become a question whether they could legally make that use of their charter. That would bring up several considerations which we need not go into, because it is clear, that whether they could transact such business or not, they are not obliged to do so, but may, if they please, confine themselves to the single object of affording the public a good harbour, with all needful piers, wharves and erections, for the accommodation of vessels. They are not bound to find shelter for the protection of goods after they are landed. The evidence in the case clearly proves that Mr. Kitson was not there as agent for the company in any other sense than that he was there as harbour master; he could not refuse to let the master of the steamer land the goods on the wharf; he attended only to check the goods, with a view to the receipt of the harbour dues established by law. None others were claimed by the company. The owners of the other goods, landed at the same time, got their goods at once upon sending for them, and so would this plaintiff (as he had often done before), but his carter happened not to be on the watch. The company had nothing to do with that. It is an unfair pretence to say that they were detaining the sugars for their tolls, and therefore were bound to keep them safely. It is manifest from the evidence that they did not take possession of the casks in any such spirit, or for any such purpose, and the defendant had no reason from the course of business at the harbour to suppose they had. I see nothing in the whole evidence that afforded any ground for contending that the company had incurred, either by contract or by their duty, any liability as wharfingers. The duty of the carrier, on such occasions, with regard to delivery, is well settled; and where goods are lost or damaged on a wharf, when there is no warehouse keeper or wharfinger in charge, the loss will either fall upon the owner, or on the carrier who should have delivered them, according to the facts of each case. This is an attempt to bring in a third party to bear the loss, without any adequate ground being shewn for it. Rule absolute.

BROWN V. ALLEN.

Where in trover for a schooner there was a great deal of evidence of an unsatisfactory character, as to the plaintiff's right to the vessel, and the defendant was not proved to have used or employed, but merely to have allowed the person who left her with him to take her away and the jury found a verdict for the defendant, the court refused to grant a new trial.

Trover for a schooner, in two counts, and one count in trover for her rigging, &c.

The defendant pleaded, first, the general issue to the declaration.

Secondly, that the schooner, &c., was not the property of the plaintiff; pleaded to the whole.

Thirdly, that the plaintiff was not possessed of the schooner, rigging, &c., as of his own property, as alleged, &c.

The fourth and fifth pleas were demurred to.

Sixthly, the defendant claimed a lien for £12 10s., due by the plaintiff to him for wharfage and moorage of the vessel, in the first and second counts mentioned, and refusal to deliver on account of the lien.

The plaintiff took issue on the pleas, denying property and possession; and replied to the sixth plea that the defendant did not deliver the schooner on account of the lien mentioned in the plea.

In August, 1843, the plaintiff Brown was shewn to have been the sole registered owner of the schooner, in the proper office in Detroit. On the 8th December, 1842, Robert Ardross made a bill of sale of the schooner to one Prevost; and the 24th May, 1843, Prevost, for one dollar, assigned his interest under that assignment to Brown the plaintiff. The same Robert Ardross, by an instrument bearing no date, assigned one-third of the schooner to the plaintiff on certain conditions, giving him the control of the schooner. On the 8th August, 1843, one Grodavant made a bill of sale of the same schooner for one dollar to the plaintiff Brown; and his interest in her anchors, chains and furniture, which he said in the writing was two-thirds. The schooner was demanded by the plaintiff, but the defendant refused to give her up without an indemnity, as she had been left in his possession by the person who had been sailing her; the plaintiff then tendered him an indemnity bond but he refused to accept it, and determined that he would not give up the vessel, and Ardross afterwards took her away.

The learned judge thought the evidence of property was unsatisfactory; and that, under the circumstances, the refusal to give up the vessel without adequate indemnity, was not tantamount to a conversion. He left the case, however, open to the jury, who found for the defendant a general verdict. Judgment had been given in favour of the plaintiff upon the fourth and fifth pleas demurred to.

J. Hillyard Cameron, for the plaintiff, moved for a new trial, on the law and evidence, and for misdirection.

Vankoughnet shewed cause.

ROBINSON, C. J.—We are of opinion that this rule must be discharged. It cannot be said that there was a clear misdirection, because the learned judge did leave the fact of conversion to the jury, though with strong remarks as to the probable unfairness of considering the defendant's refusal to deliver up the vessel under the circumstances, without good security, as equivalent to a conversion. I think one can hardly read the evidence in the cause and be satisfied what the facts really were, as to Brown's exclusive ownership of the schooner. It appeared that the plaintiff and one Ardross, both inhabitants of a foreign country, had had various transactions there together in regard to this schooner, the exact nature of which it is impossible to understand clearly without more explanation than was given upon the trial. I dare say the papers which the plaintiff produced to shew his exclusive right were not quite intelligible to the jury, and it is possible that the circumstances apparent in them may have excited some suspicion that all was not even as fair as it appeared to be. Ardross, who had been for some time sailing the schooner as master, brought her over to this side and left her in the defendant's charge, with directions to take care of her. The plaintiff went to him, when Ardross was absent, and demanded her. The defendant, knowing nothing of the real facts of the case, would not give her up, in the absence of the person who had left her with him, unless indemnified by the plaintiff, with some good person as surety. Ardross afterwards took her away, not, as it appears, with any active interference of the defendant, but rather without his assistance ; and, for all that we see, the schooner, which cannot be easily concealed, is again in the country to which these parties belong, where they may contest their right with the advantage of better means of proving all the facts. The papers advanced by Brown upon the trial, were certainly anything but clear. First, Brown had a conveyance from one person, Prevost, (whose right did not appear,) of the whole schooner, for a consideration expressed of five shillings ; then, he took another transfer from one Grodavant, of the whole property in the schooner, for five shillings ; then, being thus already possessed of the whole schooner, by a double conveyance for a nominal consideration, the motives to which were unexplained, he took from Ardross a conveyance of one-third of the schooner, therby acknowledging a right in him ; and this last instrument, which is a security rather than a sale, contains such conditions as seem to imply that Ardross still retained a property in the schooner besides this third ; for they would be idle and unnecessary, if Ardross had no such interest in her as those conditions are apparently intended to protect. What led to these shiftings of the property, upon nominal considerations is not shewn ; but considering that this defendant made no use of the schooner, and did her no injury, and did not presume to dispose of her, but merely kept her in charge for a person who, for all he might know, had her lawfully in his possession, till that person who brought her took her away again ; and considering also these dealings that the plaintiff and Ardross had certainly had together respecting this vessel, which they might understand though strangers could not, nothing would seem harder, I think, than to make this defendant pay five or six hundred pounds for the value of the schooner, merely because in such a case he had not unhesitatingly given her up when Brown came and claimed her as owner.

As to the objection that was raised about Woods' competency as a witness, it is immaterial, for he was the plaintiff's witness, and the defendant got a verdict; and he was rightly admitted, I think. The plaintiff did give evidence of title to the boat sufficient to support his claim, if it satisfied the jury; but the proof on that point cannot be said to have been conclusive, for it was not shewn what right either Grodavant or Prevost had to make the assignments to him which they assumed to make; and as they seem to have made these transfers for a nominal consideration only, though the schooner was sworn to be worth six or seven hundred pounds, the jury were left to conjecture where the real ownership may have vested at that time. These might have been mere re-assignments from persons to whom Brown had conveyed the schooner in security for some debt due, or in order to place her out of the reach of persons who had claims upon him; and if so, these several assignments at a nominal consideration may be accounted for. But then, when Brown is found taking a transfer from Ardross of a partial interest in the schooner, without its being shewn how he retained any interest, or what the extent of it might be, that might well perplex the jury in regard to Brown's right to exclusive possession. The defendant certainly did not prove any such lien as he set up in one of his pleas; but still it was necessary for the plaintiff to prove what the law would deem equivalent to a conversion; and he did, I think, do this sufficiently in a legal sense, and if the jury had given a verdict in his favour, we should probably not have interfered; but we think it not a case for granting a new trial on any satisfactory view which we can take of the merits.

Rule discharged.

McLaren v. Muirhead, Cornell & Camp.

In a joint action against the maker and endorsers of a promissory note under the statute, the maker is a good witness against the endorsers.

Where the defence intended to be urged by the endorsers of a note was forgery, and they defended on that ground at the trial, and the plaintiff recovered, the court refused to grant a new trial.

Assumpsit against the maker and endorsers of a promissory note. The maker allowed judgment to go by default, and the endorsers pleaded that they did not endorse. At the trial the maker was admitted as a witness for the plaintiff, to prove the handwriting of the endorsers, and the endorsers endeavoured to defend on the ground that the endorsements were forgeries, but the plaintiff recovered.

Freeman, for the defendants (the endorsers), moved for a new trial on the admission of improper evidence and on affidavits.

R. O. Duggan shewed cause, and filed affidavits in answer.

ROBINSON, C. J.—There is no legal ground of exception against the verdict which has been rendered for the plaintiff. The defendant Muirhead, though sued jointly with the other parties to the note sued on under the statute, is clearly as admissible as a witness as he would have been if the parties had been sued in separate actions; that has been always recognized as the effect of the provisions of the statute. It all, therefore, rests on the affidavits of Cornell and Camp. They knew that they had placed their defence on the denial of the endorsement, and they give no reason for not having brought, at the trial, all the evidence they could at any time bring, to disprove the genuineness of the signatures ascribed to them. They did bring such evidence as they chose on that point, and the jury, upon testimony which supports their verdict, found in favour of the plaintiff. Under these circumstances, and considering how these defendants' affidavits are repelled by those filed on behalf of the plaintiff, we cannot properly do otherwise than discharge the rule.

Rule discharged.

Ross v. Merritt.

In trespass for seduction, the jury gave a verdict for the plaintiff, with £200 damages, and the court refused to grant a new trial for excessive damages.

Trespass *quare clausum fregit*, and for debauching the plaintiff's daughter.

Second count, for assault and debauching the daughter, not charging trespass to the close.

The defendant pleads first, as to coming with force and arms, and whatever else is against the peace, &c., not guilty.

Secondly, to the breaking the close in the first count mentioned, that he entered by the plaintiff's license; to which the plaintiff replies *de injuria*.

Thirdly, to the same trespass in the first count mentioned, he pleads the license of the daughter.

Fourthly, to the second count, the defendant pleads the license of the daughter. The last two pleas are demurred to. The jury found for the plaintiff, with £200 damages.

Sullivan, for the defendant, moved for a new trial on the law and evidence, and for misdirection, and also for excessive damages.

J. Hillyard Cameron shewed cause.

ROBINSON, C. J.—The evidence of the seduction was clear and unimpeached; the plaintiff is in a moderate station in life, the defendant in good circumstances; he promised marriage before the seduction, but afterwards refused. No point was reserved or objection taken at the trial; the defendant, therefore, is not in a situation to claim the benefit of any strict legal objection not going to the merits of the action. The verdict is general, so we must infer that the jury did not find that the defendant had license from the plaintiff to commit all that is charged as a trespass. The debauching the daughter, as stated in the declaration, is a trespass, and it cannot be pretended that there was any evidence of the plaintiff's having given license to commit that injury. The defendant relied, in his argument, on what was said of the nature of this action by Mr. Justice Buller, in Bennett v. Alcott (a), where he treated the action as one of case, and not trespass, except as regards the illegal entry into the plaintiff's close; but this doctrine was contrary to many former authorities, as was shewn in the case of Woodward v. Walton (b), where the opinion given in Bennett and Alcott was reviewed, and it was held in opposition to it, that independently of any trespass to the freehold, the action is one of trespass. Tullidge v. Wade (c) is precisely this case; and the point was determined in this court in Cavan v. Walsh (d).

(a) 2 T. R. 167.   (b) 2 New Rep. 476.   (c) 3 Wils. 18.   (d) Mich. 1 Will. IV.

I am of opinion that the learned judge at the trial could not, upon the evidence, have directed the jury to find for the defendant on the second count; and if he could have done so, yet that view of the case was not submitted to him. It stands, therefore, on the too common footing of other cases, where a party admitted into the house as a visitor abuses the privilege of a guest, and commits an injury which the law recognizes as being itself a substantial trespass, where loss of service in consequence is proved, or which is now the same thing, alleged, and for which he cannot pretend he had the license of the owner of the house. No license, besides, was pleaded in this action to the second count. We do not think we can properly set aside the verdict for excessive damages, on anything that has been laid before us.

Rule discharged.

McLeod v. Bell.

Where in trespass the plaintiff declared for an assault and battery and striking blows, whereby the plaintiff was greatly hurt, bruised and wounded, and the defendant justified the hurting, bruising and wounding, concluding "which "are the same trespasses, &c.," the plea was held good on special demurrer.

The plaintiff declared in the second count for an assault and battery, and beating, bruising and wounding, and the defendant justified the assault and battery by a plea of *molliter manus imposuit*: Held, sufficient.

Trespass for false imprisonment, the declaration containing two counts as follows: Alexander McLeod complains of James Bell, for that the defendant on the 1st day of February in the year of our Lord 1844, with force and arms, &c., assaulted the plaintiff, and then seized and laid hold of him, and with great force and violence pulled and dragged him about, and gave and struck him a great many blows and strokes, and also then forced and compelled him to go in and along divers public streets and highways to the common gaol of the said Home District, and then imprisoned the plaintiff, and kept and detained him in prison, without any reasonable or probable cause whatsoever, for a long time, to wit, for the space of twelve hours then next following, contrary to law and against the will of the plaintiff, whereby the plaintiff was then not only greatly hurt, bruised and wounded, but was also thereby then greatly exposed and injured in his credit and circumstances. And also for that the defendant, on the day and year last aforesaid, with force and arms, &c., assaulted the plaintiff, and then beat, bruised, wounded and ill-treated him, and other wrongs to the plaintiff then did, against the peace of our Lady the now Queen, and to the damage of the plaintiff of £200, and therefore he brings his suit, &c.

The defendant pleads in his first plea, as to the said several supposed trespasses in the first count of the declaration mentioned, that the plaintiff ought not to maintain his aforesaid action thereof against him, because he says that one Charles T. Gardner, before the said time when, &c., to wit, on the 1st day of December, in the year of our Lord 1843, sued and prosecuted out of Her Majesty's Court of Queen's Bench in and for the province of Upper Canada, a certain writ of our said Lady the now Queen called a *capias ad satisfaciendum*, against the said plaintiff, directed to the sheriff of the Home District, by which said writ our said Lady the Queen commanded the said sheriff that he should take the said plaintiff if he should be found in his district, and him safely keep so that he might have his body before our said Lady the Queen at Toronto on the first day of Easter Term then next, to satisfy the said Charles T. Gardner or £102 7s. 2d., which in the court of our said Lady the now Queen before the Queen herself at Toronto aforesaid, were awarded to the said Charles T. Gardner, for his damages which he had sustained as well on occasion of the not performing certain promises and undertakings made by the said plaintiff to the said Charles T. Gardner, as for his costs and charges by him about his suit in that behalf expended, whereof the said plaintiff was convicted as appeared to our said Lady the now Queen, of record, and that the said sheriff should have then there that writ, which said writ was afterwards, and before the return thereof, and also before the said time when, &c., to wit, on the first day of December, in the year of our Lord 1843, at Toronto, aforesaid, delivered to one William Botsford Jarvis, Esquire, who then and from thenceforth, until, at and after the said time when, &c., was sheriff of the Home District aforesaid, to be executed in due form of law, whereupon the said William Botsford Jarvis, so being such sheriff of the Home District as aforesaid, afterwards, and before the return of the said writ, and also before the said time when, &c., to wit, on the day and year last aforesaid, for having execution of the said writ, made his warrant in writing, sealed with the seal of his said office of sheriff of the Home District aforesaid, and then and there directed the same to the keeper of the gaol of the said district, and also to the defendant and one James Severs who then and there, and at and after the said time when, &c., were bailiffs of the said sheriff of the Home District, and the said sheriff of the Home District, by the said warrant, commanded them and every of them, jointly and severally, that they or one of them should take the said plaintiff if he should be found in his said sheriff's district, and him safely keep, so that he the said sheriff might have his body before the judges of the court of Queen's Bench, at the city of Toronto aforesaid, on the first day of Easter Term next after, to satisfy the said Charles T. Gardner, for his damages aforesaid, by him in form aforesaid recovered according to the exigency of the said writ, which said warrant afterwards, and before the return of the said writ, and also before the said time when, &c., to wit, on the day and year last aforesaid, was delivered to the said defendant to be executed in due form of law, by virtue of which said warrant the said defendant as such sheriff's officer as aforesaid, afterwards and before the return of the said writ, to wit, on the same day and year last aforesaid, being the said time when, &c., within the bailiwick of the said then sheriff of the Home District aforesaid, in execution of the said warrant gently laid his hands upon the said plaintiff to take and arrest him by virtue of the said writ and warrant, and did then and there arrest and take him into custody by virtue of the said writ and warrant, for the causes therein mentioned, and in the said writ specified, as he lawfully might, for the causes aforesaid ; and the said defendant further saith that afterwards. to wit, on the day and year last aforesaid, and while the said plaintiff was in the custody of the said defendant, under and by virtue of the said writ and warrant, he the said plaintiff then and there unlawfully, and against the will of the said defendant, escaped rom and out of the custody of him the said defendant, whereupon the said defendant, the said judgment, writ and warrant being then and there in full 'force, immediately pursued the said plaintiff, and retook and arrested him again by his body, and kept and detained him in custody, at the suit of the said Charles T. Gardner, under and by virtue of the said writ and warrant, and forced and compelled him to go along the said streets and highways to the common gaol of the said Home District, and there imprisoned him for the said time in the said declaration mentioned, as he lawfully might, for the cause aforesaid. And because the said plaintiff, on the occasion of the said last mentioned retaking and arrest, then and there resisted the said retaking and arrest, and endeavoured again to escape from the custody of the said defendant, he the said defendant then and there necessarily gave and struck the said plaintiff a few blows and strokes, in struggling with the said plaintiff to prevent his escape, and in so doing unavoidably a little hurt, bruised and wounded the said plaintiff, as in the first count mentioned, doing as little damage to the plaintiff as he possibly could on these occasions, which are the said supposed trespasses in the introductory part of this plea mentioned, and whereof the said plaintiff hath above in his said first count thereof complained against him, and this the defendant is ready to verify, wherefore he prays judgment if the said plaintiff ought to have or maintain his aforesaid action against him, &c.

In the second plea the defendant pleads as to the said assaulting and beating of the said plaintiff, in the second count of the said declaration mentioned, the said defendant saith that one Charles T. Gardner, before the said time when, &c., to wit, on the first day of December, in the year of our Lord 1843, sued and prosecuted out of Her Majesty's said court of Queen's Bench, in and for the Province of Upper Canada, a certain other writ of our said Lady the Queen, called a *capias ad satisfaciendum*, against the said plaintiff, directed to the sheriff of the Home District, by which said last mentioned writ our said Lady the Queen commanded the said sheriff that he should take the said plaintiff if he should be found in his district, and him safely keep, so that he might have his body before our said Lady the Queen at Toronto, on the first day of Easter Term then next, to satisfy the said Charles T. Gardner, for £102 7s. 2d., which in the court of our said Lady the now Queen before the Queen herself at Toronto aforesaid, were awarded to the said Charles T. Gardner for his damages which he had sustained, as well on occasion of not performing certain promises and undertakings made by the said plaintiff to the said Charles T. Gardner, as for his costs and charges by him about his suit in that behalf expended, whereof the said plaintiff was convicted, as appeared to our said Lady the now Queen of record, and that the said sheriff should have then there that writ, which last mentioned writ was afterwards, and before the return thereof, and also before the said time when, &c., to wit, on the first day of December, in the year of our Lord 1843, at Toronto aforesaid, delivered to the said William Botsford Jarvis, Esquire, who then and thenceforth, until at and after the said time when, &c., was sheriff of the Home District aforesaid, to be executed in due form of law; whereupon the said William Botsford Jarvis, so being such sheriff of the Home District as aforesaid, afterwards and before the return of the said last mentioned writ, and also before the said time when, &c., to wit, on the day and year last aforesaid, for having execution of the said last mentioned writ, made his certain other warrant in writing, sealed with the seal of his said office of sheriff of the Home District aforesaid, and then and there directed the same to the keeper of the gaol of the said district, and also to the defendant and one James Severs, who then and there, and until and at and after the said time when, &c., were bailiffs of the said sheriff of the Home District, and the said sheriff of the Home District, by the said last mentioned warrant, commanded them and every of them jointly and severally, that they should take the said plaintiff if he should be found in his district, and him safely keep, so that he the said sheriff might have his body before the judges of the court of Queen's Bench, at the city of Toronto aforesaid, on the said first day of Easter Term next after, to satisfy the said Charles T. Gardner for his damages aforesaid, by him in form aforesaid recovered, according to the exigency of the last mentioned writ, which said last mentioned warrant afterwards and before the return of the said last mentioned writ, and also before the said time when, &c., to wit on the day and year last aforesaid, was delivered to the said defendant to be executed in due form of law, by virtue of which said last-mentioned warrant the said defendant as such sheriff's officer as aforesaid, afterwards and before the return of the said last mentioned writ, to wit, on the same day and year last aforesaid, being the said time when, &c., within the bailiwick of the said then sheriff of the Home District aforesaid, in execution of the said last mentioned warrant, gently laid hands upon the said plaintiff to take and arrest him by virtue of the said last mentioned writ and warrant, and did then and there arrest and take him into custody by virtue of the said last mentioned writ and warrant, which are the said supposed trespasses in the introductory part of this plea mentioned, and whereof the said plaintiff hath in his said second count thereof complained against him, and this the defendant is ready to verify, wherefore he prays judgment, if the said plaintiff ought to have or maintain his aforesaid action thereof against him, &c.

The plaintiff demurs specially to the first plea; because in the commencement of the said plea it professes to answer the trespasses in the first count of the declaration mentioned, but it does in fact answer more, to wit, the hurting, bruising and wounding the plaintiff, which is not in the first count complained of, and yet the said plea untruly alleges the hurting, bruising and wounding to be mentioned in the said first count ; and further in and by the said plea it is averred, that the defendant arrested the plaintiff within the bailiwick of the sheriff, without shewing whether such bailiwick was within the Home District. And for that also it is untruly alleged in the said plea that the several trespasses so justified are those mentioned in the introductory part of the same plea, and whereof the plaintiff hath in the said first count complained, whereas in truth they are not the same.

The plaintiff also demurs specially to the second plea, because in the commencement thereof it professes to answer the assaulting and beating of the plaintiff, as in the second count mentioned, but does in fact answer and justify only the assaulting the plaintiff, and that the said plea shews no cause of justification for the beating the plaintiff, as in the introductory part of the said plea mentioned ; and for that it untruly alleges the said assaulting to be the same supposed trespasses in the introductory part of that plea mentioned ; and for that in and by the said plea it is alleged that the defendant arrested the plaintiff within the bailiwick of the sheriff, without shewing that the said bailiwick was within the Home District.

The defendant joins in the demurrer to both pleas.

H. *Eccles*, for plaintiff.

S. B. *Campbell* and *Sullivan*, for defendant.

ROBINSON, C. J.—The first plea is objected to on the ground that it justifies injuries not complained of in the first count, viz., the hurting, bruising and wounding of the plaintiff: but it is averred in the first count that the plaintiff was greatly hurt, bruised and wounded by the blows of which he complains. The defendant shews how he came to give him the blows which the plaintiff declares had occasioned the wounds and bruises, and then concludes in the common form, "which are the same supposed trespasses, &c.;" not that the hurts and wounds are the same trespasses, but the blows, &c., which occasioned them; for it is the blows which he justifies.

The plea to the second count does not profess to justify anything more than such a battery as *molliter manus imposuit* will justify. The plaintiff had charged the defendant with assaulting, *beating*, *bruising*, and *wounding* him. The defendant, having denied by the general issue all the trespasses complained of, only answers by this plea an assault and battery of the common kind; and he confesses a battery by saying that he laid his hands quietly on the plaintiff to arrest him, which is at the same time his justification. If the plea had assumed thus to answer the wounding, it would not have been good, but it sufficiently justifies all that it professes to answer.

Judgment for defendant.

DOE DEM. CROOKS V. CUMMING.

In a local action, it is irregular for the plaintiff, if he desires to try the cause in another district, to obtain an order to change the venue. The application should be to enter a suggestion on the roll to try the cause in another district.

J. *Hillyard Cameron* moved to make absolute a rule *nisi* of this court for rescinding an order made by a judge in chambers, upon summons to change the venue in this cause, upon application of the plaintiff. He contended it was irregular; that the plaintiff, desiring to amend, should have moved to amend his declaration for that purpose, and that the defendant would then have been entitled to plead again; or should have applied for leave to enter a suggestion upon the roll, that an impartial trial could not be had in the proper district.

Crooks, for the lessor of the plaintiff, filed affidavits in answer, applying wholly to the merits, and setting forth that he could not have an impartial trial by a jury of the District of Niagara, as the defendant was a member of the Legislative Assembly for one of the counties in the district, and had great influence with the persons who were likely to be jurymen on the trial of the cause.

ROBINSON, C. J.—It is certainly not regular to move to change the venue as has been done here by the plaintiff. If the action were one transitory in its nature, so that the plaintiff might at first have laid it in any district, and he desired afterwards to change it from the one in which he had laid it, his motion should be to amend his declaration for that purpose. But when the action is local, as it is in this case, it is not a change of venue that is wanted, for that would remain on the record as it was, but the plaintiff should move to enter a suggestion on the roll that an impartial trial could not be had in the district where the venue was of necessity laid; and if the court are satisfied on the ground, and direct the suggestion to be entered, it is conclusive and cannot be traversed. In Rex v. Harris et al. (a), Lord Mansfield says: "No two things "can be more distinct than changing the venue, and continuing it as it was "with a suggestion on the roll that the cause cannot be impartially tried in "the proper county." The order in this case, it appears, was granted by the learned judge to whom the application was made, no cause having been shewn by the defendant to the contrary. It is explained in the affidavits filed, that the defendant's attorney did intend to oppose it, but accidentally, and perhaps from want of due vigilance, lost the opportunity, and the plaintiff's attorney would not consent to open the matter again in order that his objection might be heard. Considering that the order that was thus obtained is irregular, we rescind the informal order which has been made for changing the venue, without costs, and leave it to the lessor of the plaintiff to make, if he thinks fit, the proper application for leave to enter a suggestion which may enable him (without changing the venue), to try the cause in an adjoining district. The judge before whom the application may be made will then consider, upon cause shewn, whether the grounds that may be laid are sufficient to authorize such an order.

Rule discharged.

SPALDING V. PARKER.

A statement by a defendant, "that he did not think that he owed the money, "and that if he did, the Statute of Limitations would prevent the recovery, "but that he would give the plaintiff fifty dollars rather than have any "trouble about it," is not sufficient to take a case out of the Statute of Limitations.

Assumpsit on a foreign judgment, and on an account stated. Pleas, general issue and *actio non accrevit infra sex annos:* and issue thereon.

The defendant had brought an action against the plaintiff in the supreme court of the State of New York, but failed to recover, and this plaintiff had judgment for costs of the defence, which was entered in December, 1838. After six years had expired, an agent of the plaintiff's attorney asked the defendant for payment, and he said that he would give an answer in a few days, and afterwards said "he did not think he owed the money, and that if "he did, the Statute of Limitations would prevent the recovery, but that he "would give the plaintiff fifty dollars rather than have any trouble about it." But he paid nothing. The plaintiff obtained a verdict with leave to the defendant to enter a nonsuit, if the court should be of opinion that the evidence was insufficient to take the case out of the Statute of Limitations.

Crooks having accordingly obtained a rule *nisi*,

J. *Hillyard Cameron* shewed cause.

ROBINSON, C. J.—It was objected at the trial which took place before me that this was not an acknowledgment on which a promise could be implied to

(a) Burr. 1333.

take the case out of the statute, and I thought so, but saved the point in order that the plaintiff, if his action could be supported, might have the benefit of the opinion of the court. It might, perhaps, at one time, have been held that a recovery could be supported, upon such a conversation, but not, I think, of late years, nor even before any change whatever had been made in the law of England by the passing of Lord Tenterden's Act. In A'Court v. Cross, (a) the defendant said "*I know I do owe the money*, but the bill I gave "is upon *a three-penny stamp, and I will never pay it.*" It was held that when the defendant so distinctly and expressly declared that he would not pay, a promise could not be raised by implication that he would. Now, if when a defendant said that he did owe the money, but would never pay it, a promise could not be implied, it would be strange to imply it from his declaration that he did not think he did owe the debt, but at any rate he would not pay it, because the statute protected him (b). This leaves the case, then, to rest only on the offer to pay £12 10s., if the plaintiff would take it, rather than have any trouble about it. It was upon that, I think, the plaintiff chiefly relied; and the question is, whether that ought to prevail against the defence under the statute, either as to the whole debt, or as to so much of it as the defendant thus offered to pay. That offer was no admission of any certain amount being due, nor, indeed, an acknowledgment of anything, but it was strictly an offer made in order to buy peace, and avoid an action; and it was accompanied by a declaration, at the time, that the defendant thought he owed nothing. This case comes clearly within the principle laid down by Mr. Justice Buller, in his treatise on *nisi prius* (c), where he says, "if the terms, '*buy peace*,' are "attended to, they will resolve all doubt on this head of evidence; but for an "example, I will add one case. If A. sue B. for £100, and B. offer to pay him "£20, it shall not be received as evidence, for this neither admits, nor ascer- "tains, any debt, and it is no more than saying he would give £20 to get rid "of the action." Now this in fact is what this defendant did in terms say, that he would give £12 10s. rather than have further trouble. In Black v. Buchanan (d), Lord Kenyon affirms the same principle. The debt in this case may be honestly due, but as the law is now administered, the recovery is barred.

Rule discharged.

GOOD, ARMSTRONG & BEATTY, v. HARPER.

Where the defendant had ordered the plaintiffs to make for him some iron castings for a shop front, of specified thickness, and the plaintiffs made them much thicker than the order, but the defendant allowed them to be put up in the building for which they had been made, without objection, on a verdict for the plaintiffs for their full value, the court refused to grant a new trial.

The plaintiffs sued in *assumpsit* on the common counts. The defendant pleaded *non-assumpsit* to the whole declaration, except as to £15 10s. Secondly, as to £13, part of the said £15 10s., he pleaded a set-off to the amount of £100. Thirdly, as to £2 10s. residue of the said £15 10s., the defendant

---

(a) 3 Bing. 129. (b) 3 Taunt. 380.
(c) Page 236. (d) Peake's N. P. C. 5.

paid that amount into court, and averred that the plaintiffs have not sustained damage to a greater amount than the sum of £2 10s., in respect of the cause of action in the introductory part of this plea mentioned, (in other words, that they have not sustained greater damage in respect to this £2 10s., part of the £15 10s., which he acknowledges to have been due by him when the action was brought, than £2 10s., that is, nothing in addition on that account.) The plaintiffs replied, denying the set-off, and to the third plea, that they had sustained damages to a greater amount than the said sum of £2 10s. in respect of the causes of action in the declaration mentioned, as to the said sum of £2 10s., residue, &c. The case at the trial turned chiefly on the point whether the plaintiffs had not unwarrantably departed from their instructions in making cast-iron pillars, which the defendant had ordered, much thicker and heavier than they were told to do. The plaintiff had furnished these castings to the defendant for the front of a shop. The patterns and moulds were made from drawings furnished by the defendant, which shewed the castings were to be of a certain thickness—their value being according to their weight—and being estimated at about £30 by the defendant; but as the castings were made much thicker, their whole value when the plaintiffs' account was rendered, amounted to about £140. The defendant knew that the castings were thicker than those ordered; but he nevertheless allowed them to be put up in the building. The drawings given by the defendant to the plaintiffs were not produced at the trial. The learned judge left it to the jury to determine whether there was a limit as to price; and if they thought that there was not, directed them to find for the plaintiffs for the actual value of the work, less the payment and set-off proved by the defendant. The defendant objected also, that the issue as to the £2 10s., was insensible and absurd; and that the plaintiffs' claim for the residue could only be supported, if at all, under the general issue. A verdict was found for the plaintiffs on the first and third issue, in £115 17s. 0½d.; and for the defendant on the second issue.

J. Hillyard Cameron, for the defendant, having obtained a rule *nisi* for a new trial on the law and evidence, and for misdirection, without costs, and on grounds disclosed in affidavits,

G. Duggan, jun., shewed cause.

ROBINSON, C. J.—We have considered the facts of this case carefully, for as the iron pillars in question have been finished by the plaintiffs and set in the defendant's house, or rather in a house which he was building for a third party, it is either right that the defendant should pay for them according to their actual value, or we must be able to say that by law, under the facts proved, the defendant has a right to keep for £30 what appears to be really worth more than £100. The evidence, I think, would warrant the plaintiffs in having made the cast-iron pillars as much as three-eighths of an inch in thickness, although some suspicion may certainly arise from the fact of the plaintiffs' having either destroyed, or being unwilling to produce the board on which the defendant had made the working draft of the pillars. It is evident that the defendant had abundant opportunity to see and judge of the castings before he accepted them; he was aware that they weighed a great deal more than he had supposed they would, on account of their having been made thicker, and he had made objections to this variation from the design. The circumstances of such a case require that the conduct of the party for whom the article is furnished should be unequivocal. The defendant knew that the plaintiffs expected to be paid for the work according to the weight of iron, otherwise they must have been great losers by the work; and if he meant to refuse paying for them he should positively have rejected them. It is not objected that the work is ill done, or that the materials are bad, and I do not wonder that it seemed reasonable to the jury to conclude that as the defendant had allowed the plaintiffs to place such pillars as he has done in his building, he must pay for them, unless he could show clearly that he had been deceived into accepting the pillars. As to the question of evidence that was raised in regard to the proof formerly given of the state of the partnership between these plaintiffs and others, we think it was properly determined at the trial, but it was in reality immaterial, for it was of no moment what was attempted to be proved on that point at the former trial, and, besides, the verdict has not been moved against on the ground of rejection of evidence. Upon the evidence that was given, the plaintiffs' right to sue appeared to be plain. In regard to the issue upon the third plea, the plaintiffs do not dispute that the defendant was entitled to succeed upon it, and have, therefore, consented that the verdict may be so entered, or that the costs of that issue may be taxed against them. The plea only concerns the sum of £2 10s. parcel of the demand, and does not affect the plaintiffs' right to the damages given on the general issue. Upon the whole case, if the difference between what the defendant may at first have expected to pay for these pillars, and the charge which the plaintiffs have made for them, had not been so great, we should have had no hesitation in disposing of this rule. The amount in question is considerable; not less than £80 or £90; but on a review of the whole evidence, we cannot say that the pillars were not in themselves worth what the plaintiffs charge for them; and having been put up in the building with the knowledge of the latter, and with his knowledge also of the price intended to be charged for them, if the defendant could retain for £30 an article really worth £115, it could only be because his conduct was unequivocal in giving the plaintiffs to understand that he would take the pillars on no other terms. We do not think that the evidence entitles us to say this. Nothing is more easy than for people to protect themselves in these transactions by putting their agreement in writing; and where they omit to do this, and a jury is in consequence left to judge, as well as they are able, from the conflicting testimony of witnesses, it is not in the power of the court any more than of the jury to say which party is certainly in the right.

Rule discharged.

O'NEILL ET AL. V. LEIGHT.

Where in *assumpsit* the defendant pleaded that the plaintiff had impleaded him in a former action on the same promises, and that the defendant had in that action recovered judgment, to which the plaintiff replied that the action in which the judgment was recovered was not on the same promises, it was held that the issue was on the defendant, and that he must prove the record of the former recovery.

The plaintiff sued in *assumpsit* on a special agreement, by which the defendant, being hired by the plaintiff to work for him at certain wages in making pianofortes, engaged that he would not, during the term, make pianofortes for other persons, or for himself. And the breaches averred were, that the defendant wrongfully absented himself from the plaintiffs' service, and also, that he did, during the term, manufacture and do work at the said pianoforte business for himself, and for one Charles Romaine, and also for one Charles March, to a large amount, to wit, £200, stating a special damage.

The defendant pleaded a former action brought by the plaintiffs against him for not performing the same promises, &c., among others, in the declaration in the cause mentioned, and that in that suit the defendant had judgment that the plaintiffs should take nothing by their writ, &c.

The plaintiffs replied that "the promises, &c., were not the same as those "declared on this action."

(The plaintiffs declared in the first action in March, 1845, for making pianofortes and selling them to other persons, before that time, not naming the parties, &c.)

Upon the production of the agreement, it appeared that the plaintiffs had the power of withholding a portion of the defendant's salary weekly, until the end of the period of service (two years), and it was contended for the defendant, that the issue on the plea of judgment recovered was on the plaintiffs, and that they should produce the record; and the learned judge having ruled the contrary, the defendant's counsel then offered to give evidence of the former recovery from office papers, not examined copies; and this having been rejected, he contended that the amount of the defendant's salary retained by the plaintiffs should be allowed against any amount of damage to which the plaintiffs might be entitled. The judge, however, charged the jury that no such allowance should be made; and a verdict having been rendered for the plaintiff for £30 damages,

J. Hillyard Cameron, for the defendant, obtained a rule *nisi* for a new trial for misdirection, the rejection of evidence, and on affidavits.

G. Duggan, jun., shewed cause.

ROBINSON, C. J.—The plaintiffs here should, I think, rather have replied that this action was brought for a different breach of contract from that in which the judgment pleaded had been obtained by the defendant; then the inquiry would have been, what evidence of claim had been given on the former trial, on a declaration admitted to be on the same undertaking (or at least not denied to be so); but the plaintiffs' form of pleading here raises this issue, in which the defendant has joined, viz., that the record in the former action was not on the same *promises and undertakings* as in the present; and whether it was or was not, the record itself could best prove. We cannot but see that the declaration in the present action is one special count framed on a certain agreement, limited as to time and objects, and not admitting of evidence of a variety of promises, like the common counts in *assumpsit*. When it is alleged that another action spoken of was not on the same special promises, the party who asserts that it is, has only to produce his pleading to shew it; and he *must* shew it, for any variance in the terms of the contract would be fatal, and would necessarily appear on the record, if they were not for the same cause of action. It seems to me that to plead thus in a special action of this kind, is an informal mode of denying the record, in the same sense as is done by a plea of *nul tiel* record, in which case the party pleading the record must shew it. I do not find anything express on the point made at the trial in this case, namely, on whom the burthen of the proof rested in such case; but I cannot think that the question admits of doubt. In Lord Bagot v. Williams (a), Lord Chief Justice Abbott says, in a case similar to this, "The issue raised by the pleadings is, whether "the causes of action mentioned in the declaration are the same identical "causes of action as those mentioned in the second plea, and in respect whereof "the judgment was recovered. It appears from the authorities cited, that "*when the declaration in the second action is framed in such a manner that the* "causes of action may be the same as those in the first suit, *it is incumbent on* "*the party bringing* the second action to shew that they are not the same;" and he adds, "It does not distinctly appear in this case what was the form " of action in the inferior court." That was from the peculiar nature of the proceeding in the inferior court, which is explained in the judgment. Now, in this case, if the first record were before the court, we must be certain, considering the special contract on which this declaration is framed, that it would at once be seen from it whether the promises declared on, and under which the plaintiffs could have recovered, were or were not the same identical promises (not breaches), which are declared on in this action. But how can we tell, till we see what promises were declared on in the first suit, whether those last declared on are identical or not. It seems to me, then, that the defendant, on whom the affirmative of the issue lies, should have first shewn a judgment upon a record, in which the declaration was so framed that it might have covered these causes of action; and then it would be incumbent on the plaintiffs to shew, that in fact the recovery was not for the same cause of action, though *prima facie* it might appear to be. I think it most probable, that the evidence given in the case of Lord Bagot v. Williams, to prove that the causes of action were the same, came from the defendant's witness, and that as he proved that the recovery might have included the same demand, the court held that the plaintiff was then driven to shew that the demand was in fact not the same, and that as he did not shew that, they held the plea proved. In another case cited, of Sedden v. Tutop (b), Lawrence, J., remarks: " The parties went into evidence to see whether the former verdict was for the " same cause of action; but there would have been no occasion to have gone " into that evidence if the defendant *could have contented himself with shewing* " *that there had been a former verdict*, and that the demand for which the " second action was brought, existed prior to the first action. This seems to " imply that upon such an issue something is to be shewn by the defendant,

---

(a) 3 B. & C. 239.   (b) 6 T. R. 610.

"or it would be insensible to have observed upon what he might content "himself with shewing." I am of opinion that it lay on the defendant in this case to shew that so far at least as the pleadings were concerned, the causes of action were identical, and therefore that the plaintiff apparently sued in the first for the same injuries that he had sued in the second; and then, the plaintiff would be called upon to shew the difference from the evidence given on the former trial. This being so (as I think it is), the next point is clear, that parol evidence of the nature of the former recovery, and, indeed, of the fact of such a recovery, was properly rejected. Upon the evidence and affidavits, I do not think we can properly interfere on the ground that injustice is done by the verdict, for we know that some breaches were proved on this trial which could not have been given in evidence on the former trial, because they occurred afterwards. The money that may have been in the plaintiffs' hands as a proportion of wages, withheld under the agreement, could not have been legally made the ground of reducing the damages in this case, for there is no plea of payment, or set-off, on the record; even if it could have come under either, which I think it clearly could not, being a matter wholly collateral and independent of the breaches sued on; and a set-off being out of the question, indeed, in such an action. The defendant seems to have acted unfaithfully, and in disregard of his agreement; and has no particular claim to relief on the ground of excessive damages, if on this motion we could properly grant a new trial on that ground.

Rule discharged.

DRENNAN V. BOULTON, ONE, &C.

Where a promissory note was given to an attorney to get the amount of it secured, and the attorney subsequently said that he would pay the amount in a few days, and an action was subsequently brought against him for negligence in not *suing* the note, with a count for money had and received, the court held that neither count was supported by the evidence, and a verdict having been rendered for the plaintiff, a new trial was ordered without costs.

Assumpsit. First count alleges that in consideration that plaintiff at request of defendant had retained him as an attorney of this court, to prosecute or conduct a certain action in the District Court of the Newcastle District, at plaintiff's suit against one Steele for the recovery of sixteen pounds twelve shillings and three pence, due plaintiff from said Steele for reward in that behalf, defendant promised plaintiff to use due care, skill and diligence, in bringing, prosecuting, and conducting said action, and to bring that action against said Steele, within a reasonable and proper time in that behalf. The plaintiff then avers that although a reasonable time hath elapsed, yet defendant, though requested, did not, nor would bring or prosecute the said action, but neglected and refused—by means whereof the plaintiff hath wholly lost the said sum of money, and is otherwise injured.

Second count. £100 money had and received, £100 interest, and £100 on the account stated.

Pleas. First, *non-assumpsit.*

Second, That the defendant did use due care, skill and diligence in and about bringing, prosecuting and conducting the said action, and did bring the same within reasonable time, &c., &c.

To support the first count, a copy of receipt for a promissory note given by Steele to the plaintiff for £16 12s. 3d., dated 30th March, 1842, payable at four months, was proved. The plaintiff would not produce the receipt in notice, and the copy is received in evidence, and is as follows:—2nd June, 1843. Received of the plaintiff a note of Steele for collection, for £16 12s. 3d., being interest from 3rd August, 1842; which amount I will secure *(if I can)*, with other claims of my own, for the plaintiff. The words "if I can" are said to have been in the receipt, but have been erased since. The plaintiff also offered evidence to show that the defendant admitted having received the money, by once promising to pay it in a few days. On this head a witness represented, that having called upon the defendant at the plaintiff's request, in April or May, 1844, to ask for the money for the plaintiff, the defendant said he had not the money then, but would let the plaintiff have it in two or three weeks; afterwards the defendant, on another occasion, said he did not know whether he would pay it, and the plaintiff might do what he could. The jury found a verdict for the plaintiff for the amount of the note and interest, and

Sullivan, for the defendant, obtained a rule *nisi* for a new trial, on the ground that the verdict was contrary to law and evidence.

H. Eccles shewed cause.

MACAULAY, J., delivered the judgment of the court.

It cannot be inferred, from the defendant's answer, that he had received the money previous to the time he gave such answer. And there is no proof of its subsequent receipt, farther than the promise, that the plaintiff should have the money in a few weeks, expressed by the defendant, and the lapse of time since, afford ground for its presumption. Against which there seems to be equal ground for inferring, that in point of fact it has not been received. The count for money had and received does not therefore seem to be satisfactorily suppported.

Then as to the first count, the receipt for the note shews that it was to be collected by being secured with the other claims, not by an action in the District Court. And the proof does not establish the contract as laid. The breach of duty on the defendant's part, if any, would seem to be (not a neglect to prosecute the debt in the District Court, according to instructions,) but rather not securing it according to promise. It was received in the expectation held out to the plaintiff that it would be secured. And I cannot on the evidence discover very clearly whether it has been secured or not. If it has been secured, as promised, the plaintiff must await its collection under the securities, if no delay or neglect has occurred therein. If not secured, then I should think the defendant ought to have apprised his client of his inability to accomplish that object, that he might exercise his discretion in prosecuting the note, or adopting other measures to enforce its payment; instead of this, nothing would seem to have been done for upwards of two years; and so far from any notice to the plaintiff of inability to secure the debt, the only evidence on the subject represents, that nearly a year after the note was placed in the defendant's hands, and before which period it must have been known whether it could be secured or not, the defendant being called upon, held out the hope that the money would be forthcoming. It is said Steele is insolvent, and therefore the damages are not necessarily to be the full amount of the plaintiff's demand; nor is it at all clear that the note has been or could be secured. The evidence on this head is obscure. And at all events the money is not shewn to have been received. Under these circumstances, neither count is supported by proof; nor is a clear right of action in another form shewn, though it may exist. And I therefore have no objection to a new trial, on payment of costs.

JONES, J., and McLEAN, J., concurring with the judgment of Mr. Justice Macaulay, that there should be a new trial, but conceiving that there was no ground for the verdict, the rule for a new trial was made absolute without costs.

Rule absolute without costs.

HOBSON v. SHAND.

Where the plaintiff had obtained judgment against the defendant ten years ago, and two or three years afterwards fled from the province charged with a criminal offence, and a writ of execution was issued on the judgment without any leave of the court, or notice to the party, the court made a rule absolute to stay the proceedings.

Blake obtained a rule *nisi* to set aside a writ of *fieri facias*, for irregularity, the judgment having been entered after a long lapse of time since the verdict was rendered, without leave of the court, or notice to the defendant, or any other step; and the *fi. fa.* being issued without authority from the plaintiff; or to shew cause why the judgment of William Leys, or so much thereof as may be necessary, should not be set off against this judgment; or why all proceedings on this judgment should not be stayed till the return of John Leys. It appeared by the affidavits filed, that the plaintiff had fled from the province seven or eight years ago, charged with some crime, and had not since been heard of; and that there had been an agreement that the judgment in this cause should be set off against a judgment against William Leys, which had never been enforced in consequence. It did not appear upon what authority these proceedings had been instituted, or the writ of *fieri facias* issued. A verdict was rendered in this action in the autumn of 1835, for the plaintiff, for £35, and judgment was entered thereon in July, 1845, and goods seized under a *fi. fa.*, a few days ago.

Richards shewed cause.

ROBINSON, C. J.—On the affidavits it appears to us, that the proceedings on the *fi. fa.*, should certainly be stayed as regards the debt; the plaintiff is stated to have agreed to set off (as he should have done,) the judgment in one case against the other. He has fled for crime, he has not been heard of for seven or eight years. For all that appears, he may be dead. I think we should stay further proceedings wholly, till the plaintiff's attorney produces proof that the plaintiff is living, and of his authority to enter judgment; or at all events till we have some information before us to show that there is good reason for moving, at this late day, in a cause which, under very peculiar circumstances, had been apparently abandoned for many years. If the costs are unpaid, and the defendant's goods have been seized on that account, that should be shewn, and perhaps on a view of all the facts, when they are stated, we might find it right to let the execution proceed, on the plaintiff's attorney undertaking to accept a return of *nulla bona* for the amount beyond the costs, or in any other way to limit the execution of the writ to that extent.

Rule absolute.

BARTON V. FISHER.

The plaintiff sued in *assumpsit* for work and labour, and at the trial put in a sealed instrument under which he had agreed to perform the work, by which it appeared that the defendant was bound to pay the price of the work at certain stated periods. The work was not done according to the contract, and the plaintiff consequently sued in *assumpsit*; but having been nonsuited at the trial, on the ground that the covenants in the sealed instruments were independent, and that he could sue for the money although the work was not performed, the court set the nonsuit aside.

Assumpsit on the common counts for work and labour, and materials, and on an account stated.

Pleas: *non-assumpsit*, and payment of the whole demand.

The particulars delivered claimed £618 18s. 9d. for building a mill, and for machinery and materials, on which £200 was acknowledged to have been paid.

Upon the trial, an agreement under seal was produced, dated 8th April, 1843, between this plaintiff of the one part, and Michael Fisher and the defendant, Joseph Fisher, of the other part: by which the plaintiff covenanted that he would, on or before the 1st October, 1843, in consideration of £550, to be paid by M. & J. Fisher, and of the covenants to be performed by them, build gearing for a grist mill on their farm, according to a specification annexed. The defendants bound themselves to pay the plaintiff said £550, viz., £150 on the execution of the agreement, £125 on the 1st October next, and the remaining £275 in two equal annual payments of £137 10s., *from 29th December last past*. M. & J. Fisher bound themselves to put up the building, to receive the machinery by the 1st August, 1843, and to find all the lumber that might be required for the plaintiff's job by the 1st June, and to board him and his hands. The plaintiff engaged that the machinery should be of the best quality, and done in a workmanlike manner; all to be ready for running on the 1st October. And the plaintiff further agreed, that if he should delay or neglect the work, or absent himself, the other party might, after giving him ten days' notice, employ workmen to go on with the work, and to alter, amend and finish the same, deducting the costs from the money then due to the plaintiff. It was objected, on the trial, that the plaintiff could only sue upon this sealed agreement; that the covenant to pay the money was an independent covenant, and an action could therefore be sustained upon it whether the plaintiff had performed his part or not; and consequently, that as the remedy on the sealed instrument was open to him, he could take no other; although it was admitted that the plaintiff had not performed the work according to the agreement. The learned judge so held, that the plaintiff, on that ruling, declining to claim on extra work alone, took a nonsuit, which

Blake moved to set aside, as being contrary to law.

J. Hillyard Cameron shewed cause.

ROBINSON, C. J.—I understand it to have been fully admitted, at the trial, as it was upon the argument here, that the work contracted for was not so done by the plaintiff in conformity with the agreement that he could have sustained an action on the covenant for the money, if performance on his part was necessary to be shewn. Then, if that be the case, the plaintiff must be allowed to sue in *assumpsit*, or lose all recompense for the mill he has built; unless the undertaking to do the work on the one side, and to pay the money on the other, were such independent covenants in the written agreement, that this plaintiff could enforce the payment of all the price he was to receive without doing any part of the work by which he was to earn it; in which case, it is true, he would have a clear action on the deed as his higher remedy. My opinion is, that the covenants are not independent. That question does not turn wholly on the language of such a deed, nor on the order in which the stipulations may happen to have been set down, but upon the reason of the thing, considering the nature of the transaction. Then the building the mill, or the machinery, was the whole consideration for the money which the defendant was to pay. Part of the money was paid down; a further part was to be paid on the very day when the work was by the plaintiff completed, and the remainder not until days long after. In such a case, I take it to be clear, that the party engaging to do the work is not in a condition to sue for his money under the instrument till he has performed his part. I take this point to be well settled by such a number of decisions that it is unnecessary to cite them particularly. And indeed if we consider a little, it is clear, I think, that there could be no room for the objection which the defendant took to this action; for if no such mill as that contracted for was actually built, but a different kind of one, either much larger, for instance, or smaller, or essentially different in any way, then how could it be held that the plaintiff could be estopped for recovering in *assumpsit* for a mill which he had built on a verbal agreement, because the same party had covenanted by deed to pay him a certain sum for building a different description of mill, which he never did build. The two sums of money have no necessary relation to each other, or connection with each other; and, if in this case the plaintiff could recover under the covenant the £550 which were to be paid to him though he did not build the mill contemplated, then it must follow, as I conceive, that he must also be allowed to recover in *assumpsit* for the work which he actually did, and which was not done under the agreement. This injustice and absurdity is avoided by holding, and I think the books compel us to do so, that the conditions in the first agreement are dependent, so that the plaintiff, being unable to recover under the deed, must be allowed to sue for all he is entitled to in *assumpsit*.

Rule absolute.

FURNISS V. SAWERS.

Where at a sale by auction the defendant purchased goods on the condition of furnishing endorsed notes for their amount, with the option of obtaining a discount of 10 per cent. for cash, and that if the conditions were not complied with, the goods were to be resold at the risk of the purchaser, and after the sale the defendant paid £15 on account, but performed no other part of the conditions, and the plaintiff resold the goods at a loss : *Held* that the part payment took the case out of the Statute of Frauds, so as to dispense with the necessity of proof of a written contract, and that such part payment could not be considered to deprive the plaintiff of the right to resell, and make the defendant responsible for the loss on the re-sale.

Special *assumpsit* to recover an amount said to be lost by the plaintiff on a re-sale of goods that had been sold to the defendant at an auction.

The first count stated that on the 15th September, 1843, the plaintiff exposed to sale a large quantity of goods, on the conditions that purchasers to an amount above £2 10s. should have six months' credit on furnishing good endorsed notes; that the goods should be taken away and thus paid for as soon as the accounts were made out, otherwise to be resold and the first purchaser to be charged with the difference. It was further averred that the plaintiff agreed in case this defendant should buy at the sale to a larger amount than £100, and should pay promptly, that a discount of ten per cent. should be allowed to him; and that the defendant undertook to comply with these conditions of sale, and to pay for the goods accordingly; that is, if over £100, either in cash, deducting ten per cent. discount, or the full amount in good endorsed notes, payable in six months; that the defendant bought at the auction to the amount of £225 10s. 10d. ; that the plaintiff, on the day of sale, furnished him an account in writing, but that the defendant had never paid for the goods either in cash, deducting the discount, or by furnishing an endorsed note, though he did pay the sum of £15 on account thereof. The declaration then set forth a re-sale on the 1st October, 1843, at a loss of £70, besides charges of sale amounting in all to £85, which the defendant was liable to pay.

In a second count, the plaintiff set out the first sale and re-sale, as before, omitting any mention of a condition to allow a discount on principal payment, and omitting the statement that the defendant had paid £15 on account.

The third count was for goods sold and delivered.

The defendant pleaded the general issue; and five special pleas to each count, setting up various defences, as that the defendant had no notice of re-sale ; that the second sale was negligently conducted, whereby the goods were needlessly sold under their value ; that they had been damaged by the plaintiff's carelessness before the re-sale, &c. All of which the plaintiff took issue upon.

To the second count the defendant also pleaded that after the defendant's failure of performance, and after the plaintiff became entitled to rescind the contract, he received from the defendant £15 on account, and then agreed to give the defendant a further reasonable time to pay the residue, (not averring that such reasonable time had not elapsed before the re-sale.)

The plaintiff replied, denying that he made any such agreement.

It appeared on the trial, that the auctioneer having died since the sale, the plaintiff had been unable to produce any of the printed conditions of sale ; but the clerk who attended at the first auction, swore that the conditions of sale were as stated in the second count, *i. e.*, sales not over £2 10s., to be paid for in cash; over £2 10s., in good endorsed notes at six months; that the defendant during the sale, asked the clerk whether, if he should purchase to a larger amount than £100, he might not be allowed a discount of ten per cent. on paying cash; and the clerk engaged that he should. The clerk produced the sales book, in which he had written during the sale the defendant's name opposite to each lot of goods knocked down to him. The goods were packed up for the defendant, and an account furnished, and a few trifling articles were delivered to him; and about five weeks after the sale he paid the auctioneer £15 on account. He did not comply any further with the conditions of sale, and in January the goods were advertised to be resold, and were sold on or after the 15th February. It was clearly proved that the defendant had ample notice of the re-sale; that the goods were not damaged, that the auction was well attended, and that the sale was fair and open. A loss was incurred of £67 6s. 4d., besides £10 12s. 5d., charges.

The defendant's counsel objected that the conditions of sale were not legally proved, there being no written evidence of them whatever.

Secondly, That the plaintiff, after receiving the £15, could not resell the goods; but was bound to look to the defendant, as purchaser, for the residue of the money, having a lien on the goods.

Thirdly, That, at all events, the £15 paid should have been tendered back to the defendant before the goods were resold.

Fourthly, That the plaintiff could not recover on the count for goods sold, having rescinded the first sale by selling again.

The learned judge overruled the objections, leaving the party to move, if he should choose, in *banc*, and a verdict was rendered for the plaintiff for the exact amount of the loss on the re-sale, with the charge, giving the defendant credit for the £15 paid.

Baldwin having accordingly obtained a rule *nisi* for a new trial, on the ground that the verdict was against law and evidence, and for misdirection, and also in arrest of judgment,

R. B. Sullivan shewed cause.

ROBINSON, C. J.—We agree that the plaintiff cannot recover on the count for goods sold, because that would be affirming the first sale as conclusive; whereas the plaintiff has repudiated it by the re-sale, as he had a right to do. But we see no objection to the plaintiff recovering on special counts. As regards the sufficiency of those counts—the first, it is objected, ought to have shewn a return of the £15; but we do not think that was necessary. Even if under the facts the defendant would have a clear right to receive that sum back, upon making good to the plaintiff any loss upon a re-sale, still we could not hold, upon any legal principle, that the return of the £15 must form a condition precedent to the plaintiff's right to sue on the special contract. And with regard to the second count, the objection to the plaintiff's recovering upon that is, that the contract there stated varied from that proved, inasmuch as that count omits any statement of that part of the agreement which respected the allowance of discount if prompt payment should be made; but as that is stated in the first count, and as it was proved upon the trial, that was no part of the general conditions of this sale. It could do no harm to state it, as it is stated in the first count, because it is true, (if we assume, as I suppose we may, that the agent had authority to make the concession which the defendant requested); but as the defendant did not avail himself of the privilege which he might have claimed, and never did pay the money, it became wholly immaterial.

The contract was not that the defendant should pay in cash, receiving ten per cent. discount, or in bills at six months; all that he engaged to do was to pay in bills, and under that contract he asked to be allowed a certain privilege if he should pay at once; but as he did not pay at once, this privilege, which was nothing binding on him, became unimportant.

As to the evidence, I think we must hold that the payment of £15 on account of the bargain (to say nothing of the delivery of part of the goods), made the contract binding, and took the case out of the statute. Then the contract, being thus rendered binding, written evidence of it is not required; and we are to hear what the terms of this parol contract were. It seems to have been such as was set out; it is a contract of a very common kind, and the plaintiff seems to have acted under it, as he had a right to do. It would be unreasonable to hold that the plaintiff, by accepting £15, must abide by his first sale; he took that of course, in the confidence that the remaining conditions would be fulfilled, and unless they were fulfilled, he had a right to resell; for he could not be compelled to accept of a part performance as a fulfilment of the contract. The defendant could never have forced him to give up the goods, so long as the conditions of the sale were unperformed, and the plaintiff's right under the agreement to resell them and make the defendant pay any loss, is a mere extension of his right to keep them, or sell them in any way he might choose. The verdict seems to be a just one, and should not be set aside, except on some clear ground, and we see none.

Rule discharged.

Wood v. Moodie and Selden.

Where in trespass to personal property, and several pleas pleaded, a verdict was taken for the plaintiff by consent, subject to be reduced or a verdict entered for the defendants, by the award of arbitrators, and the arbitrators made their award determining the cause "in favour of the plaintiff, and that "the verdict should be reduced to £7 10s.;" the court, after a lapse of two terms, refused to set aside the judgment entered on the award, on the ground that the award was void, as it did not dispose of the issues in the cause, and also held that the application was made too late.

Crawford, for the defendants, moved to set aside the judgment and execution in this cause for irregularity.

The cause was referred at *nisi prius*, and "a verdict was taken, by consent, "for the plaintiff for £100, subject to be reduced, or a verdict rendered for "the defendants by the award of arbitrators."

(*All matters in difference in the cause* were not in terms referred, as is done in some cases, and which it has been contended impose the necessity of expressly awarding upon all the issues in the cause.) The costs of the cause and of the reference were "to abide the event of the award."

The award was, "I do hereby award, order, and finally determine the said "cause in favour of the said plaintiff, and that the verdict taken for the plain- "tiff in this cause as aforesaid, be reduced to the sum of £7 15s."

The action was trespass to personal property.

Pleas.—First, Not guilty.

Secondly, That the goods were the defendants', and that they had bailed them to one Allen, who delivered them to the plaintiff, from whom the defendants took them.

Thirdly, That the defendant, Moodie, as sheriff, seized the goods under a *fi. fa.* against Allen's goods, they being his property at the time.

Fourthly, Denying the plaintiff's property in the goods.

The plaintiff took issue on all the pleas.

The cause was referred on the 6th October—the award made on the 9th October—Judgment entered on the 22nd December, 1845; and the defendants' goods seized in execution thereon on the 17th January, 1846.

The defendants objected that the award was not final, as it did not dispose of the several issues, and was therefore bad, and the judgment entered on it void.

The defendants swore that they had no copy or notice of the award, though one of the defendants requested it; but it was not stated when such request was made.

Read shewed cause.

ROBINSON, C. J.—So far as the rule is in question, which makes it necessary to move against an award in the following term (even when the reference is by order of *nisi prius*), or to move within the first four days of the term, when a verdict has been taken subject to the reference, there is not sufficient shewn by these affidavits to overcome the objection that the motion is not in time. The defendants, or one of them, may, notwithstanding what is sworn to, have been well aware that an award was made; and if up to the term they had in vain demanded a copy, they could still have moved the court in the following term, shaping their application according to the circumstances.

If it can be properly considered that the objection here is on the face of the award, then, perhaps, the defendants could move at this late day. It is so far apparent on the award, that the submission being recited in the award, we can see that if there were several issues in the cause, the award does not specifically dispose of those issues as it ought to do. But in order to see how that is, we must look at the record, and, therefore, out of the award. This being a motion against the judgment, and not merely against the award, it is contended that the objection of delay in moving against the award has not been held in such cases to apply. It is not easy to reconcile the different decisions on this point; but my impression on the whole is, that the defendants come too late in the second term after verdict, to insist on it as a matter of right that we must set aside the judgment for this supposed defect in the award. If, however, delay were not an answer to the application, and granting (which seems not clear amidst the various decisions on the point) that the award in this case must be held void as not being final, still we ought not, in my opinion, to make this rule absolute for setting aside the judgment upon motion, which the court are not in any such case bound to do, but should rather follow the reasonable course taken in the case of England v. Davidson (a) where the court discharged the rule, on the party, in whose favour the award was, undertaking

---

(a) 9 Dowl. 1052.

to allow the costs on the issues not formally disposed of to be taxed for the other party. This would be a more just cause, for it cannot be denied that the arbitrators in this case, when they found for the plaintiff, must have intended to determine, and must have determined in fact, that none of the defences pleaded were true; for any one of them would have barred the action necessarily, if it had been proved.

The search which we have had occasion to make again into the various decisions on this point, confirms me in the opinion I expressed in Bernard v. Strachan (a), that the judges in England seem to have been rather rigid in holding the arbitrators to the necessity of disposing formally of all the issues on the record. The courts seem, indeed, to have been much perplexed by the question as it presented itself under different aspects, and sometimes to have laboured to reconcile decisions upon the point, which I cannot consider to be reconcilable. The cases which have arisen in this court are Townsend v. Morton (b), and Bernard v. Strachan (a), both decided in Easter Term, 8 and 9 Vic., and in accordance with what I find to be the current of authority. The latter case of Bernard v. Strachan, was referred to in the argument in support of this motion, and cited as a case precisely in point; but in that case no verdict has been taken as in this case; the question was not before the court upon a motion to set aside an award or judgment, but upon demurrer to the pleadings, when the court has no discretion to impose conditions, but must dispose of the bare legal question whether the pleading is sufficient. The replication, in that case, was clearly bad upon other grounds noticed in the judgment, independent of the question of the finality of the award; and if we had decided differently on the point now referred to, still the judgment in that case must have been the same. But we could not have determined otherwise than we did as regards this question, without directly overruling the case of Bourke v. Lloyd (c), on which our judgment was founded, as well as on the elaborate judgment of Mr. Justice Coleridge, in England v. Davidson (d), and other cases which were cited by me at the time.

If the case of Cooper v. Langdon (e), could only be regarded as being directly in opposition to the decision of Bourke v. Lloyd, and were undistinguishable from it in its facts, we should still have adhered to the later decision of the two made in the same court, especially as it is in accordance with the general bearing of the authorities. In the case of Bourke v. Lloyd, the defendant had pleaded the general issue and payment, and the arbitrators awarded a sum to be paid to the plaintiff. This surely was finding in effect that the debt had not been paid, and was therefore as much a virtual finding for the plaintiff upon both the issues as there could be in any case; and there, as in Bernard v. Strachan, no verdict had been taken. In Cooper v. Langdon, the defendant's pleas were equally such as would bar the action, if found for him, and it was therefore contended in that case, as in Bourke v. Lloyd, that the awarding in favour of the plaintiff necessarily disposed of the issues upon the pleas; and so the court held, and, I think, reasonably; though in Bourke v. Lloyd, they afterwards determined otherwise. There was, to be sure, this difference

---

(a) 2 Cameron, 128.   (b) 2 Cameron. 100.   (c) 10 M. & W. 550.
(d) 9 Dowl. 1052.   (e) 9 M. & W. 60.

between the cases, that in the former there had been a verdict taken for the plaintiff as in the case now before us, and in the latter, as in Bernard v. Strachan, no verdict had been taken. That may, in the opinion of the court which decided both cases, have afforded a reason for disposing of them differently, though I confess the reason does not strike me.

Where a record is ready for trial on several issues, the case may be either determined by verdict of a jury or by arbitration, if the parties prefer it. If arbitrators are substituted for a jury, to pronounce upon the facts, it seems to me that the effect of their finding should be the same; and if when a jury says, "We find £100 for the plaintiff," adding nothing more, that can be taken as determining in effect that all the defences pleaded were untrue, I do not understand why when the arbitrators, who by consent of the parties have been put in the place of the jury, say the same thing, they should not be taken to mean the same thing. The Court of Exchequer, nevertheless, have made the distinction, and in the somewhat uncertain state of the question, as noticed by the Queen's Bench in a late case, it will be safer for parties, whether a verdict is taken or not, to have it expressed in the terms of their reference, that the costs of the several issues shall abide the general event of the award as it may be, for the one party or the other, and that the arbitrators need not find specially on each issue. For the reasons which I have already given, this rule should, in my opinion, be discharged. We need not exceed the strictness observed in England on this point, and as the case is precisely similar to that of Cooper v. Langdon, verdicts having been taken in both, we may follow the authority of that case, and hold the award sufficiently final. If it were otherwise, I am inclined to think that this motion ought to be held too late; and at any rate, we would not have given effect to it without giving the plaintiff the option of conceding the costs of the special issues, as was done in England v. Davidson.

Rule discharged.

WM. DAVIDSON, ADMINISTRATOR OF JOHN DAVIDSON, V. RADDICK.

The defendant, after a verdict in detinue for the plaintiff, and one shilling damages, was granted a rule *nisi* for a new trial, but having obtained a certificate to deprive the plaintiff of costs under 43 Eliz., he served a written notice on the plaintiff's attorney, that he did not intend to proceed upon the rule *nisi*, which accordingly was never taken out or served; afterwards, the certificate to deprive the plaintiff of costs was rescinded, and the defendant then obtained a rule *nisi* to revive the rule *nisi* that he had abandoned, but the court refused to make the rule absolute.

The plaintiff sued the defendant in detinue, setting forth that the defendant, in the lifetime of the intestate, received from him a note made by one Gilchrist to the intestate, for £62 10s., to be redelivered to the intestate on his request; but that he had refused to redeliver the same, though requested by John Davidson in his lifetime, and by the plaintiff since his decease. The defendant pleaded several pleas, on which the defendant took issue; among others, one denying that he had detained the note. It was proved at the trial that the note was for £57 17s., and had been placed by John Davidson and one Gilchrist in the defendant's hands, upon the express understanding that he was not to part with it to either, unless both should be present, there being some matters yet unsettled between Gilchrist and Davidson. After the death of Davidson, his son went to demand the note of the defendant, who referred him to Gilchrist, and the latter objected that no one had yet administered to the estate of John Davidson. The plaintiff then obtained letters of administration, and demanded the note, but the defendant said he was bound to do as he had promised, and could not give him the note till Gilchrist came with him. According to Gilchrist's evidence on the trial, the defendant had never wrongfully detained the note, which he brought into court and gave to the plaintiff. The jury found a general verdict for the plaintiff, and one shilling damages. Last term the defendant obtained a rule *nisi* to set aside the verdict as being contrary to law and evidence; but the learned judge having, at the defendant's instance, certified under the 43rd Eliz., to deprive the plaintiff of his costs, the defendant served the plaintiff's attorney with a written notice that he did not intend to take out his rule for a new trial, and it was never taken out or served. It being afterwards considered that this was not a case in which a certificate could properly be granted, the certificate was rescinded, and

Crawford, for the defendant, moved to revive the rule *nisi* for a new trial, on the ground that it had been allowed to lapse through a misapprehension.

Read shewed cause.

ROBINSON, C. J.—The defendant, to whom he had granted a rule *nisi* for a new trial, which we might perhaps have made absolute on cause shewn, not only forbore to take it out, but formally abandoned it. It is true he did this under the impression that the learned judge who tried the cause would certify under the statute of Eliz. to deprive the plaintiff of costs, as the action was certainly very groundless; and such a certificate was granted, but upon reflection it was found right to rescind it, for the learned judge had not adverted to the circumstance that the action was in detinue, where the damages might well be nominal, because the article itself was the real subject of the action, and it was given up after action brought. It is to be regretted that the misapprehension occurred; but it was incumbent on the defendant's attorney to look into and consider the point, before he relied upon the certificate; and at any rate, we cannot, because the mistake has happened, revive a rule which was never issued, and therefore never existed, which is what we are asked to do. On looking at the record I am inclined to think that, on the pleadings, the plaintiff was strictly entitled to nominal damages; and this is all he has recovered besides the note itself; for the defendant has not pleaded, as he ought to have done (considering what the facts were), that he did not undertake to deliver up the note to John Davidson on request; for in truth his agreement was to deliver it to him only in case Dr. Gilchrist and he should come together and desire him to give it up; but he rested his defence on denying that he had ever detained the note from the plaintiff, though in fact he did detain it, but not in breach of his agreement.

Rule discharged.

McLeod v. James Boulton.

Where an attorney was retained to make an application to the court to relieve a sheriff from an attachment, and the jury in an action against the attorney for negligence in conducting the application, found that he was in fault: *Held* that he was liable to nominal damages for such negligence, although all the grounds of special damage laid by the plaintiff failed.

This is an action on the case, brought by the plaintiff against the defendant, for negligence as an attorney.

The first count of the declaration recites, that heretofore, to wit, on the 7th November, 1838, and before committing the grievances, &c., Alexander Hamilton was sheriff of the District of Niagara, and so continued till his death; and that the plaintiff was his deputy, and under-sheriff of said district; and that Wilson, as his surety, became bound under hand and seal, to save and keep harmless and indemnified the said Alex. Hamilton, his heirs, executors, &c., touching the return and execution of all process, writs and warrants directed to said sheriff, and which should come to plaintiff's hands to be executed; that one John Hamilton was surety for said sheriff and for the plaintiff as such deputy, pursuant to the statute; that while the plaintiff was deputy, to wit, on, &c., a writ of *fi. fa.* issued out of this court to the said sheriff, at the suit of James Smilie, against the goods, &c., of Balfour & Drysdale, endorsed to levy £310 11s. 4d., and directed to the plaintiff during the said sheriff's life to be executed, and that under it the plaintiff seized the goods, &c., of the said Balfour & Drysdale; that the said Smilie, after said seizure, directed the plaintiff to stay the execution of said writ, and not to sell the goods of the said Balfour & Drysdale thereunder, unless other writs against the said goods, &c., should afterwards be delivered to the plaintiff to be executed; and that afterwards, to wit, on the 22nd November, in the year aforesaid, while the said writ was so stayed, and before the return day thereof, another writ of *fi. fa.* was delivered to the plaintiff, at the suit of Ross & McLeod, against the goods of the said Balfour & Drysdale, endorsed to levy £70 11s. 1½d. ; and that afterwards, to wit, on the 16th day of February, 1839, the plaintiff sold the goods, &c., of the said Balfour & Drysdale, and made thereout a large sum, and that after deducting prior claims, sheriff's fees, &c., there remained a sum of money, to wit, £126, applicable to the said writs of Smilie and Ross & McLeod, but insufficient to discharge the sums endorsed on the writs ; that from the time of staying proceedings, the said Smilie gave no further instructions to the plaintiff; and afterwards, to wit, on the 19th February, in the year last aforesaid, the said Alex. Hamilton died, and the plaintiff became liable to conduct the business of the sheriff's office, &c., pursuant to the statute; that the said Ross & McLeod, before the said writs of *fi. fa.* had been returned, forbade the plaintiff paying the said sum of £128 to Smilie, claiming a priority, on the ground that Smilie's writ was fraudulent as against them, and threatened an action for false return if their writ was returned *nulla bona;* that having received Smilie's writ first, and deeming it entitled to priority, the plaintiff afterwards, to wit, on the 10th of April, in the year aforesaid, returned the writ of Ross & McLeod *nulla bona;* that afterwards, to wit, on the 19th of April aforesaid, Ross & McLeod brought an action in this court against the said John Hamilton as such surety of said Alexander Hamilton as sheriff as aforesaid ; that the plaintiff being unable to decide which of the aforesaid writs of *fi. fa.* was entitled to preference, and being desirous of applying to this court in order that the said sum of £70 11s. 1½d. should be retained, and the return to the said Smilie's writ be stayed till the result of such action should have been determined, afterwards, to wit, on the 1st May, in the year aforesaid, in consideration that the plaintiff, at the request of the defendant, then retained the defendant as an attorney of this court, to manage and conduct the said application to this court in order that the said sum of £70 11s. 1½d. might be retained until the result of the said suit of Ross & McLeod against the said John Hamilton should have been known for fees and reward to the defendant in that behalf. The defendant being an attorney of this court, it became the defendant's duty as such an attorney to manage the said application with due skill, care and diligence, and to retain counsel in that behalf ; yet the defendant not regarding his said duty, did not nor would conduct the said application with due care, &c., but on the contrary, by reason of the defendant's conducting it in a careless, unskilful and improper manner, and neglecting to retain counsel to appear in that behalf, and for want of due care, &c., in that behalf, afterwards, to wit, on the 12th November, in the year aforesaid, an alias writ of *habeas corpus* issued out of this court against the plaintiff, for not returning the said writ of *fi. fa.* of the said Smilie, and the plaintiff, by means of the premises, was, on the day and year last aforesaid, obliged to pay the said sum of £125 upon the said writ of the said Smilie, and afterwards, to wit, on the 8th day of February, 1840, the said Ross & McLeod recovered in said action against the said John Hamilton the sum of £74 4s. for damages, and £35 0s. 3d. costs ; and that afterwards, to wit, on the 29th March, 1842, H. O. Hamilton, executor of the said Alex. Hamilton, having been obliged to pay the said John Hamilton the said sum of £74 4s. and costs aforesaid, brought an action against the said Wilson in this court for the same, by means whereof the plaintiff became liable and bound to pay the said sum of £74 4s. and £35 0s. 3d., and hath been put to great costs and inconvenience in the premises, and been greatly injured.

Second count: Whereas also heretofore, to wit, on the 7th November, 1838, and before, &c., Alex. Hamilton was sheriff of the District of Niagara, and so continued till his death, and the plaintiff then and until and at his death was his deputy sheriff, and under sheriff of the said District of Niagara; that while the plaintiff was such deputy sheriff as aforesaid, to wit, on the day and year aforesaid, a writ of *fi. fa.* was sued out of this court to the said sheriff of Niagara, at the suit of one Smilie, against the goods, &c., of Balfour & Drysdale, within the said district, endorsed to levy £310 11s. 4d., and delivered to the plaintiff as such deputy sheriff, during the life of the said Alex. Hamilton, to be executed, and that under the said writ the plaintiff seized the goods and chattels of the said Balfour & Drysdale ; that the said Smilie, after such seizure directed the plaintiff to stay proceedings on said writ, and not sell the said goods of the said Balfour & Drysdale thereunder, unless other writs against the said goods, &c., should be directed to him, &c. ; that afterwards, to wit, on the 22nd November, in the year aforesaid, while the said writ was so stayed, and before the return day thereof, a writ of *fi. fa.*, at the suit of Ross & McLeod, issued out of this court against the goods, &c, of the said Balfour & Drysdale, and directed to the Niagara sheriff, was delivered to him the plaintiff as such deputy sheriff as aforesaid to be executed, endorsed to levy £70 11s. 1½d. : and that afterwards, to wit, on the 16th February, 1839, by virtue of said writs, the plaintiff, as such deputy sheriff as aforesaid, sold the goods, &c., of the said Balfour & Drysdale, and made thereout a large sum of money, and after deducting prior claims, expenses, &c., there remained, to wit, £125, applicable to the said writs, which sum was insufficient to discharge both ; that after giving directions to stay as aforesaid, said Smilie gave no further directions to the plaintiff touching the said writ ; that afterwards, to wit, on the 19th February, in the year aforesaid, the said Alex. Hamilton died, and the plaintiff became and was liable to conduct the business of the said sheriff's office, and accountable for the execution of his duty as deputy sheriff as aforesaid, pursuant to the statute ; and which said Ross & McLeod afterwards, and before the said writs of *fi. fa.* had been returned, to wit, on the 10th March, in the year last aforesaid, forbade the plaintiff paying the said £125 to Smilie, claiming a preference on the ground that Smilie's writ was fraudulent as against them, and threatened an action for a false return if the plaintiff returned their writ *nulla bona:* and that the plaintiff being unable to decide which writ was entitled to priority, desired to apply to this court, in order that the sum of £70 11s. 1½d., part of the sum levied as aforesaid, should be retained, and the return of said Smilie's writ be stayed until it should be determined which of the said writs should be first paid ; and that afterwards, to wit, on the first May, in the year aforesaid, in consideration that the plaintiff, at the request of the defendant, had retained the defendant as an attorney of this court to manage and conduct the said application to the said court (in order that the said sum of £70 11s. 1½d. might be retained till the priority of the said writs should have been determined as aforesaid), for fees and reward to the defendant in that behalf, it became the defendant's duty, as such attorney, to conduct and manage the said application with due and proper skill, care and diligence, and to retain counsel in that behalf; yet the defendant, not regarding his said duty, did not nor would conduct the said application with due and proper care, skill and diligence, or retain counsel in that behalf, but on the contrary, by reason of the defendant's conducting and managing the said application in a careless and unskilful and improper manner, and neglecting to retain counsel to appear in that behalf, and for want of due care, &c., in this behalf (afterwards, to wit, on the 20th November, in the year last aforesaid), the plaintiff, through the carelessness, negligence and unskilfulness of the defendant, was obliged to pay the said Smilie the said sum of £125, and was also compelled to pay the said sum of £70 11s. 1½d. so endorsed on said writ of Ross & McLeod, and also a large sum, to wit, £40 for costs in that behalf expended, and also by reason of the premises the plaintiff was and is otherwise greatly injured, to the plaintiff's damage of £500.

Pleas: First, General issue.

Secondly, That the plaintiff did not retain or employ the defendant in manner and form in the declaration alleged, and issue thereon.

The cause was tried before Mr. Justice Macaulay, at the Home District autumn assizes in October, 1845, when the following evidence was given on behalf of the plaintiff.

1st. The exemplification of a judgment recovered by Ross & McLeod against John Hamilton.

2nd. Exemplification of a judgment of John Hamilton v. Hannah Owen Hamilton, executrix of Alex. Hamilton.

3rd. Exemplification of a judgment of Joseph Hamilton v. Hannah Owen Hamilton.

4th. H. O. Hamilton, executrix of Alex. Hamilton, v. John White.

5th. A bond from Wilson to Alex. Hamilton.

6th. A motion paper, entitled in this court in the Queen v. Alexander McLeod, late deputy sheriff of the District of Niagara, in the suit of James Smilie v. John Balfour & Adam Drysdale, for a rule returnable the second Monday, to shew cause why the writ of *habeas corpus* against the above defendant should not be set aside on grounds disclosed in affidavits filed, and why the defendant should not have time to return the writ of *fi. fa.* in the suit of Smilie v. Balfour & Drysdale, and why, in the meantime, all further proceedings should not be stayed, on motion of W. H. Blake; name endorsed, J. Boulton; all in Mr. Blake's handwriting.

7th. An affidavit of the plaintiff, Alex. McLeod, sworn the 17th August, 1839, entitled like the above motion paper, setting forth that the sale of Balfour & Drysdale's goods, at the suit of Smilie, commenced on the 16th February, 1839, also at the suit of Ross & McLeod, and at the suits of R. Armour and A. & R. Laidlaw, all against the same parties, defendants; that the execution of the said Laidlaw was first received in the sheriff's office; that the said Smilie's was next, and received on the 7th November, 1838; that about a week after it was delivered to the plaintiff, he received written instructions to delay proceedings until further orders; that on the 22nd November, the execution at the suit of Ross & McLeod was placed in the plaintiff's hands as such deputy sheriff; that he never received any further instructions in Smilie's cause; that the goods of Balfour & Drysdale were never removed from the shop in which they were sold; that the sale of the said goods lasted six days; that the sheriff died while the sale was going on, to wit, 19th February, 1839; that the plaintiff paid the full amount of Laidlaw's execution, exceeding £300; that £75 was withheld for rent; that the plaintiff, early in March, paid over to the said Smilie £125, being all the money then received from the said sale, except as aforesaid; that immediately after such payment, the plaintiff received notice from Ross & McLeod not to pay over any further sum to the said Smilie, as they claimed to be entitled to be first paid, owing to the stay of his execution; that in consequence of such notice, the plaintiff made the return in the writ now filed; that Smilie's execution was returnable on the last day of last Hilary Term, and that of Ross & McLeod on the first day of Easter Term then last. This affidavit is marked filed the 17th August, 1839, and is drawn in the handwriting of the defendant. It is endorsed, J. Boulton, for defendant, apparently in Mr. Blake's handwriting. The office fees in both were charged to be paid by the defendant, but it might have been done without his having previously known it, as he was accustomed to keep an account with the office, and to pay the same by accepting quarterly drafts therefor before recognizing a statement of the details.

8th. A rule *nisi*, dated 17th August, 1839, entitled as the above affidavit and motion paper, calling on the plaintiff, Smilie, to shew cause on the second

Monday in vacation, before the presiding judge in chambers, why the writ of *habeas corpus* against the plaintiff, McLeod, should not be set aside on grounds disclosed in the said affidavit, and why he should not have time to return the writ of *fi. fa.* in the suit of Smilie v. Balfour & Drysdale, and that in the meantime all further proceedings against him be stayed, on payment of costs; on motion of Mr. Blake. Endorsed, and copy served on Mr. Cameron, 19th August, 1839. J. B. L. The defendant's name endorsed in the handwriting of Mr. Lewis, who had been a clerk of the defendant's. On this rule is endorsed as follows :

"26th August, enlarged by consent to Monday next, noon. J. J." And, "Rule absolute to stay proceedings on the writ of *habeas corpus* until the first "day of Hilary Term next, on payment of costs, and paying the balance of debt "and costs and interest in Smilie v. Balfour & Drysdale into court, in a fort- "night from this date. September 5th, 1859.

"(Signed)   A. McLean, J."

The former in the handwriting of Mr. Justice Jones, and the latter in that of Mr. Cameron.

9th. A motion paper, entitled in this court in the cause of The Queen v. Alex. McLeod, late deputy sheriff of the District of Niagara, in the suit of James Smilie v. John Balfour & Adam Drysdale, for a rule to shew cause why the sheriff of the District of Niagara, or the attorney for James Smilie above named, or John H. Cameron, his agent in this suit, should not pay into court the money paid on the writ of *habeas corpus* in this matter, there to remain to await the decision of this court in the cause of Ross & McLeod v. John Hamilton, and why the said McLeod should not be set at liberty, his retaking by the said sheriff being illegal. On motion of J. Boulton, counsel for Alex. McLeod above named, (&c.) The "&c." is inserted at the end of the line, between the words "counsel" and "McLeod," and may follow either. It probably was intended to follow the word "counsel," &c. Returnable the first day of next term; endorsed, filed 16th November, 1839. Mr. Dempsey proved that a rule *nisi* issued thereon, and that the fees were charged to the defendant, as of course, as counsel or attorney, no other name appearing.

10th. The affidavit of the plaintiff, McLeod, on which the last-named rule was moved, entitled like the last-mentioned motion paper. It is in the handwriting of the defendant, and was sworn and filed the 16th November, 1839. It states that he, the plaintiff, had not yet been able to collect the amount of the money arising from the sale of the goods of Balfour & Drysdale, at the suit of the said Smilie and others, and consequently failed in being able to pay the money into court, pursuant to the order of this court, several of the purchasers at sheriff's sale not having paid for the goods bought, but that he had raised the money from other sources, and had paid it to the sheriff of the Niagara District, in whose custody he was brought into this court upon the writ of *habeas corpus*, endorsed to discharge the plaintiff if he should pay to him £124 17s. 5d.; also, that he did, on the 15th of November instant, pay the said sheriff the sum of £125 in discharge of the writ of *habeas corpus*, less the sheriff's fees, to be paid when the account thereof is furnished; that after the payment of the said sum, the said sheriff was informed by his (McLeod's) counsel, that an application would be at once made to stop the money in the hands of the said sheriff, or to pay it into court to await the decision of this court in the case of Ross & McLeod v. John Hamilton, bail for the late sheriff, and that since the said sheriff had been so informed of the intention of the said plaintiff, he informed him that he had paid over the money to John H. Cameron, Esq., agent for the plaintiff's attorney, and that the same was stated to have been paid that day to the said John H. Cameron ; also, that immediately upon the payment of the said sum of £125 to the said sheriff, the plaintiff was permitted to go at large, and has been at large and out of custody of the said sheriff until this day, when he was again taken into custody by the said sheriff, upon the said writ of *habeas corpus*, and brought into court by him ; that the plaintiff told the sheriff he considered himself discharged from the said writ, though liable to pay the sheriff's fees upon the said writ ; and that as he had paid the amount endorsed, and had been at liberty, he considered it in the light of a *ca. sa.*, and objected to be taken into custody again. No search or proof that the rule *nisi* was made absolute.

An attachment tested 5th of August, 3 Vic.—the names of the Queen omitted in the beginning of it—directed to the Niagara sheriff, to take the plaintiff (late deputy sheriff of the said district), returnable the second Wednesday of that term, marked In re James Smilie v. John Balfour & Adam Drysdale, for not making return to a writ of *fi. fa.;* endorsed to attach for £158 debt, and £6 10s. costs, &c.; signed C. Hall, attorney for Smilie. Returned *cepi corpus*, by K. Cameron, sheriff of Niagara, and filed 16th of August, 1839.

An *alias habeas corpus* tested 4th November, 3 Vic., to the Niagara sheriff, returnable last day of said term, to bring in the plaintiff upon the aforesaid attachment, issued 12th November, 1839. Charles L. Hall, plaintiff's attorney, endorsed to discharge him on his paying £124 1s. 2d., and 14s. 3d. for that writ and fees. Returned, body brought up, also that plaintiff was in his custody in his district, on the limits, on a writ of *ca. ad sa.*, &c.

Mr. Blake proved that he made the motion in August, 1839, at the request of the defendant, who handed him the affidavit for that purpose, and that after he had opened the matter to the court, the defendant, who was present, interfered and took it out of his hands, and that he had nothing further to do with it. That he advised and brought the action of Ross & McLeod against John Hamilton. That the facts were proved or admitted at the trial, and a case made for the court above. That he was not here when it was decided, but understood it was for plaintiffs on the ground of fraud. Mr. Blake also stated that he defended the suit of H. O. Hamilton, executrix, v. Wilson, and that the recovery of Ross & McLeod was one of the breaches suggested, and on which she recovered.

Mr. Cameron proved that Ross & McLeod recovered against John Hamilton on the ground that a prior execution of Smilie v. Balfour & Drysdale was restrained till other writs came ; that the goods had been seized, and then allowed to remain in the debtor's hands, who were merchants in Niagara, and went on selling as usual. Also, that £125 was paid to him on the 19th November, 1839, by the sheriff of Niagara, being the last day of term, in the attachment against McLeod for not returning Smilie's writ, which was paid over to Smilie or his attorney ; that it was so paid over after the judgment of the court in the case of Ross & McLeod v. John Hamilton, in February or

March, 1840; that the Niagara sheriff had plaintiff here on a *habeas corpus*, and was anxious, fearing an escape ; that plaintiff paid the money after dark, and wished it to be retained in his hands. Plaintiff went to defendant, and presently he or Mr. H. Boulton moved to stay the money in attorney's hands ; that the order of 5th of September, 1839, in chambers, was complied with ; wherefore an *alias habeas corpus* issued, and on the 16th November the second motion was made ; that a rule *nisi* was issued and served, returnable the first day of the following term, and the money in fact withheld for some time after the decision of the case of Ross & McLeod v. John Hamilton, so that the event mentioned in the rule had occurred ; that witness was an arbitrator between Mrs. Hamilton, executrix, and defendant; that no charge was made by defendant for fees in this matter ; witness understood it to be a final settlement between plaintiff and defendant.

Mr. Mowatt was called, and proved that he was attorney for the Hamiltons in relation to McLeod's matters, and had received £231, insufficient to satisfy all claims ; none was paid in or specifically applied to settle this matter. Is in receipt of rents and profits of property held in security for the balance. The sums received are disputed as to amount.

Dr. Hamilton stated, that in February, 1839, he had a conversation with the defendant about the suit of Ross & McLeod, on which occasion the defendant said the plaintiff McLeod was acting exceedingly corruptly in regard to the sheriff's office and his deceased brother's estate, and gave as a reason, that he was losing or had lost a sum of money, £120 or £125, which he had saved him from losing the previous summer, alluding to the matter of Smilie and Ross & McLeod, who were quarrelling about it. Witness said to him he understood he had been employed to attend to it, or to look after it ; to which the defendant replied that he had been, but that when the plaintiff chose to commence an action against him (meaning an action of Mrs. H. O. Hamilton, executrix, against the defendant), he did not consider himself bound to look after his interests any longer ; adding, that he was not the man to hold up one cheek when he had got a slap on the other. The witness stated that the defendant admitted he had been employed to look after the money that had been paid into court, that is, after the plaintiff's interest, and to see that the money in question was applied to the right execution. That ill-feeling existed between the plaintiff and the defendant, though they had formerly been on good terms. Witness thought that the defendant spoke to him by way of caution. Witness and the defendant were not then on bad terms. It is probable the defendant told witness that the plaintiff had taken his business out of his hands, and that it is probable he did when the suit of Mrs. H. was brought. That an award was made in the defendant's favour. Amount not yet paid. The defendant did not express whether he had been employed as attorney or counsel; but repeated that the defendant admitted his employment in that matter, *i.e.* Smilie and Ross & McLeod v. Balfour & Drysdale.

The writ of *fi. fa.* in Smilie's suit was put in, and it shewed on the face of it that it was returnable before the *fi. fa* at the suit of Ross & McLeod against Balfour & Drysdale issued. Also, the insufficient return made thereto by the plaintiff, in consequence of which the attachment was ordered.

On the defence, it was objected by *Boulton*, Q. C.,

1st, That Ross & McLeod could not have legally recovered against John Hamilton as the surety of the deceased sheriff, and that therefore it cannot be made the foundation of damages against the defendant in its consequences.

2nd, That no proof could be given of the grounds in which H. O. Hamilton, executrix, recovered against Wilson.

3rd, That Dr. Hamilton could not be asked whether the defendant stated to him for what purposes he had been employed by the plaintiff.

4th, That the retainer was not proved as laid; and that as far as proved, it was shewn to have been complied with, the money being *retained* till the *event* desired by the plaintiff.

5th, That it was proved that the money was stayed till the case was decided, and long after; and that there was no charge of the defendant's being employed to move afterwards anything that could properly be moved when the result of Ross & McLeod's case was known.

6th, That there was no proof of damage, or of the payment of the money by the plaintiff.

7th, That the plaintiff became liable and had to pay by reason of his own default, in not complying with the judge's order, and not by reason of the defendant's default.

Blake, for the plaintiff, relied on all the evidence to support both or either counts.

1st, As to the first, the learned judge admitted the judgment as incontrovertible proof of such judgments, with its consequences.

2nd, He overruled.

3rd, He overruled. As to the whole, it was ultimately agreed that it should go to the jury to decide on the evidence, first, whether the defendant was retained as alleged; secondly, if so, whether he was guilty of negligence, and if so, thirdly, the damages, with leave to the plaintiff to move a nonsuit, if there is not sufficient evidence to go to a jury to support either count as respects the *retainer* and *negligence* as laid; or, if sufficient, why damages should not be nominal, and the verdict be reduced accordingly.

The learned judge told the jury the retainer depended upon the consideration whether the defendant was employed in this matter, and continued so employed till the last rule *nisi* was returnable, and at that time; that if his services were gratuitous, or his employment was revoked, or the plaintiff had withdrawn his business, the retainer would cease; and that he thought this the doubtful and nice point of the case. As to negligence, the learned judge thought there was evidence of it, inasmuch as the rule *nisi* was not followed up, nor any steps taken to protect the plaintiff when the result of Ross & McLeod's case against J. Hamilton was known; that he thought the rule *nisi* should have been followed up—a step the more urgently required, owing to the decision of Ross & McLeod's case on the first day of the term, the day it was returnable; and that if the defendant was *then* charged with the obligation to attend to it on the plaintiff's behalf, the omission to do so was negligence. As to damages, relying on what Mr. Justice Jones was reported to have held, the learned judge left it to the jury to find the whole claim or loss, in their discretion.

Verdict for the plaintiff, £100 damages, being the principal and interest on

£70 11s., recovered by Ross & McLeod against J. Hamilton. The jury found a retainer and negligence.

In Michaelmas Term last the defendant's counsel, Mr. H. J. Boulton, obtained a rule *nisi*, and cause was shewn during the term. The rule was to shew cause why the verdict should not be set aside and a nonsuit be entered as being contrary to law and evidence, or why the verdict should not be set aside for misdirection and a new trial be granted, or why the judgment should not be arrested. At the argument, Mr. Boulton stated the grounds on which he moved in arrest of judgment to be,

1st, That there was no allegation that the plaintiff had paid in any money, only,

2nd, A judgment against another person.

3rd, That there is no ground of action on the record; that it appeared that the plaintiff had levied £125, and decided for himself to return *nulla bona* to the writ of Ross & McLeod, and consequently there was nothing he could be relieved from or against.

4th, No allegation that the plaintiff would have succeeded, or had a right to succeed on his rule *nisi*, and that there was no such right.

5th, No averment of the acceptance of any retainer.

6th, That the judgment against John Hamilton does not bind the defendant, and that Ross & McLeod had no right to recover against him after the death of the principal.

7th, Negligence not sufficiently alleged.

Blake contended for the plaintiff—That under the first count he was only bound to prove the retainer and neglect; that the payments alleged were not denied; that the rule *nisi* secondly obtained was not equivalent to a rule absolute, the money not being paid into court, or placed under its control; that no misdirection is pointed out; and that if moving the rule absolute would have been of no use, the defendant should have proved it or have pleaded it; that John Hamilton, the deceased sheriff's surety, was liable, as seen by a reference to the statute 3 Will. IV. ch. 8, s. 23; that if the recovery was not strictly legal it was of no consequence, because it damaged him and Mrs. Hamilton, executrix. He referred to the case of Hamilton, executrix, v. Wilson, on demurrer, as establishing the plaintiff's ultimate liability; that the second count is good, payment being alleged and not denied.

H. J. Boulton, in reply, contended—

1st, That Mr. J. Hamilton was not liable; that if so, then suitors would have two remedies: one against the deceased sheriff's sureties, and another against the plaintiff's sureties; which could not have been intended.

2nd, That the recovery was wrong, because the surety, J. Hamilton, could not have recovered against plaintiff, as the deceased sheriff might if living; that plaintiff at his decease was no longer his deputy, but appointed by the statute to execute the office in the name of the principal as quasi-principal; that although he was under or deputy sheriff, he was no longer the deceased's deputy.

3rd, That defendant, being a stranger, is not bound by the judgment against J. Hamilton; that although the latter acquiesced in the wrong, defendant is not bound, the judgment being illegal, and therefore not evidence of damage against defendant.

4th. That defendant as a stranger may impeach it as void on the face of it, though it may be good till reversed against the parties and privies, as the defendant therein, his heirs or executors, or a purchaser under it; that this defect in the judgment constitutes a good ground of objection for a nonsuit, for misdirection, or in arrest of judgment.

5th. That it is not averred or proved that the object of the rule was, could, or would have been attained, or would have been of any use, or could have availed; that the plaintiff had already made a return which concludes him, and no relief could have been had; that it was adjudged that Ross & McLeod should recover, and that delay could only be of use in relation to Smilie's writ; as to which no relief could be granted, because the money was confessedly made, and Ross & McLeod's writ returned no goods, a return conclusive on plaintiff; that had the plaintiff obtained leave to return Smilie's writ no goods, quoad the amount recovered by Ross & McLeod, he would be sure to recover against the plaintiff, because he had estopped himself by returning Ross & McLeod's writ *nulla bona* also; and no relief or amendment of the latter could be now granted, or at any time after they had commenced their action for a false return; that the defendant did fulfil all he was called upon to do; that an attorney is not liable for not doing what is useless or improper, and that the money was not in fact paid over by Mr. Cameron till after the decision of Ross & McLeod's writ; that the allegation in the plaintiff's declaration is, that "the money should be retained till the "suit of Ross & McLeod was decided." The motion was to pay the *money* into *court*—the allegation is that he was to *retain* it till that case was decided; that the alleged object of the defendant's retainer was to apply that the money should be retained till Ross & McLeod's case was decided, and that in fact it was retained till afterwards, and there is no charge of neglect in not following it up; in not making a further motion consequent thereon, which, if any, is the neglect proved; that the plaintiff cannot apply the evidence to both or either count at his election; that the evidence cannot amplify the duty laid in the declaration; that no sufficient cause of action is laid; no benefit or advantage to result from the motion is shewn; that the breach is too large as to damages, alleging a liability to pay Ross & McLeod £75, and Smilie £125. Mr. Boulton also objected to Mr. Blake's evidence as to the ground of recovery in Hamilton, executrix's case against Wilson, also to the evidence of Mowatt and Dr. Hamilton that plaintiff had made payments. He cited in the course of his arguments, Peake, N. P. C., 161, Aitcheson v. Maclock ; *Ib.*, 218; 4 T. R., 611, Alexander v. Macaulay ; 2 Chitty, R. 731 (n.), Rybot v. Peckham, 11 A. & E. 439, and 10 A. & E., 477; 2 C. & P. 356; 1 Wilson, 44; 1 Dowl. N. S. 626; 5 Price, 547; Watson's Sheriff, p. 72; Stat. 3 Geo. I., c. 15, s. 8; Ba. Ab. Authority, E. (*a*).

The Chief Justice gave no judgment.

MACAULAY, J., delivered the judgment of the court.—The first thing to be considered under the first branch of the rule is, what material allegations in the declaration are in issue, and what stand admitted, not being traversed.

(*a*) See also 1 T. R. 287; 3 T. R. 374, Duffield v. Scott; 4 M. & S. 20, Tarleton v. Tarleton; 6 Bing. 500, Adams v. Dansey; 1 Stra. 407-8; 5 Vin. Ab. Za. 172, pl. 6 (u); 11 E. 297; 6 M. & S. 42.

The pleas are, not retained *modo et forma*, and not guilty *modo et forma*, and issues. Upon these pleas, under the new rules, the matters of inducement, so far as material, are not in issue, but admitted; such as, that plaintiff was deputy sheriff of the deceased Niagara sheriff, and bound with sureties to him, as alleged; that John Hamilton was surety for the said deceased sheriff; that execution issued; that Smilie's writ was stayed, and other proceedings afterwards had, as alleged. Consequently the first material allegation requiring proof, is, that defendant was retained *modo et forma*.

Now, the objects of the plaintiff, in relation to which the defendant's retainer is alleged, as set forth in the declaration, are as follows: The first count states that the plaintiff, being unable to decide which of the two writs of *fi. fa.* were entitled to preference, and being desirous of applying to this court, in order that the sum of £70 11s. 0½d. should be retained, and the return of Smilie's writ be stayed till the suit of Ross & McLeod (then pending) should be determined, the defendant was retained to manage and conduct such application, in order that the said sum of £70 11s. 0½d. might be retained until the result of such suit of Ross & McLeod against John Hamilton should be known.

The second count states the plaintiff's perplexity and inability to decide upon the priority of the writs, and his desire to apply to this court, in order that the said sum of £70 11s. 0½d., part of the sum of £125 levied as aforesaid, should be retained, and the return of Smilie's writ be stayed until it should be determined which of the said writs should be first paid; and that defendant was retained to manage and conduct the said application, in order that the said sum of £70 11s. 0½d. might be retained till the priority of such writs should be determined, as aforesaid.

Then, was there evidence to go to the jury in proof of such retainer? I think there was. Indeed, the argument for the defendant has not been rested upon the ground that there was no retainer at all, but rather upon the nature, duration and extent of such retainer. No express retainer or instructions are shewn. It rests upon the defendant's conduct and acknowledgment, and upon the contents of the two affidavits made by the plaintiff in August and November, and the motions founded thereon. These shew that the defendant was retained in relation to the subject-matter, as well as what he did in pursuance thereof; and the circumstances of the plaintiff's situation assist in explaining what must have been his object, and therefore the purpose for which the defendant was employed. It would seem that in August the plaintiff, having been previously attached for not returning Smilie's writ, was brought up under a writ of *habeas corpus;* that he had previously returned Ross & McLeod's writ *nulla bona;* and that an action had been brought by them against Mr. J. Hamilton, one of the deceased sheriff's sureties, as stated in the declaration; although the affidavit made by him in August merely mentioned their having given him notice not to pay over to Smilie the balance of the amount levied. This affidavit, however, relates briefly the proceedings that had taken place; and the motion then made was for him *to return Smilie's writ*. A rule *nisi* was granted accordingly, returnable in chambers, and afterwards ordered to be made absolute, to stay proceedings on the *habeas corpus* till the next term, on plaintiff's paying into court the balance on Smilie's writ.

This was not done; and plaintiff was again brought up upon an *alias habeas corpus* late in the ensuing term, when he paid to or deposited with Mr. Sheriff Cameron (in whose custody he was) the £125, which the said sheriff handed over to the agent of Smilie's attorney.

After this the second affidavit was made, in which it is stated that the said sheriff had been notified by the plaintiff's counsel (meaning the defendant), but after the money had been paid over to the agent of Smilie's attorney, that an application would be made to stop the money in his hands, or that it should be paid into court, to await the decision of the case of Ross & McLeod v. John Hamilton, &c. The latter suit is thus briefly referred to, owing perhaps to the fact that it had been argued during the same term, as shewn by the evidence of Mr. Blake and Cameron, and the state of it therefore well known to and fresh in the memory of the court, or to the hurry of the moment. On this affidavit the defendant moved the rule *nisi* on the Niagara sheriff, Smilie's attorney or agent to the cause, why they or one of them should not pay into court the money paid on the writ of *habeas corpus*, there to remain to await the decision of the case of Ross & McLeod v. John Hamilton; and a rule to this cause was granted, returnable the first day of the next term, being the 3rd February, 1840.

Nothing is here moved for suspending the return of Smilie's writ, as on the former occasion; and the question is, whether it is a fair and proper inference from the whole that it was the plaintiff's object, and that the defendant was on the last occasion retained to resolicit a stay of the return to Smilie's writ in addition to what he did move, as alleged in the declaration.

It is evident he was professionally employed to assist the plaintiff, and to try and obtain for him the relief that the exigencies of his situation required; and it was of course his duty, under the facts and circumstances of the case, to advise the course to be taken. The only course he did take was, to move to retain the money; but it does not thence follow that such was the only and full extent of his retainers and duty. The plaintiff was in custody for not returning Smilie's writ; he had paid or deposited the amount due thereon; and then not only desired to be discharged from custody under the attachment, but that the money should be controlled by the court, and of course leave and time to be given to return Smilie's writ, notwithstanding what he had done; for, without the latter indulgence, no other step could be of any ultimate avail to him. Smilie had a right to exact the return of his writ, or to be paid the money. The latter the plaintiff desired to avoid, and the former could only be deferred by leave of the court; and, without such leave, the plaintiff could not be effectually relieved from the attachment and discharged. The plaintiff required time to return Smilie's writ, to be of any use to him, until the suit of Ross & McLeod v. J. Hamilton was decided—the event of that suit determining as between plaintiff and them whether this writ had a right to precedence or not; and it seems to me to be the reasonable inference from the plaintiff's previous defaults, their present position and manifest objects in seeking the intervention of the court, that time to return Smilie's writ—in other words, that the return of his writ should be stayed, with leave afterwards to return it according to the result of the other case then pending—was included in, and formed one part of the defendant's retainer, as alleged.

The next inquiry is, what it became his duty to do under such retainer; and whether he discharged such duty with due care, skill and diligence?

It is charged in the second count that defendant did not conduct the application with due care, skill and diligence, or retain counsel on that behalf; but, on the contrary, by reason of his conducting and managing the said application in a careless, unskilful, undue and improper manner, and neglecting to retain counsel to appear on that behalf, and for want of due care, &c., on defendant's part in that behalf, the plaintiff, through the neglect of defendant, was obliged to pay Smilie the said sum of £125, and also Ross & McLeod the £70 11s. 0½d., &c. To this alleged negligence the plea is, not guilty of the supposed grievance or any part thereof.

1. Did the defendant move enough. This has not been made a specific point; but I think he did not. I think he should have renewed the former motion in addition to what he did move on the last occasion.

2. Was it his duty to have followed up the motion? This is relied upon as the actionable neglect. The jury have found that the professional duty of defendant continued at the time the rule *nisi* became returnable, viz., 3rd February, 1840; and I think there was sufficient to go to them to warrant such finding. The conversation related by Dr. Hamilton must obviously have occurred after that day. The nature of it clearly shews this. It also shews a knowledge on defendant's part that the matter had not been attended to as it required to have been, with his admission that he had been employed to see to it, but paid no attention to it for reasons which he gave; which reasons, however, did not satisfy the jury that his retainer had ceased, nor in law excuse his neglect if it continued. It shews this also, that the defendant's inattention to the case on the first day of Easter Term, 1840, was not because it was useless, or that his profession would not have required it, but because he considered his retainer at an end owing to subsequent occurrences. Considering, also, the way the defendant appears to have been engaged and concerned in these proceedings in August and November, 1839, which, in determining the nature of his retainer and duty, are to be taken together, and the imperfect nature of the last step taken by him, together with the importance of ulterior steps to accomplish the plaintiff's objects, and for which the defendant had been retained, it seems to me nothing but the fair and reasonable inference that his professional obligations towards the plaintiff in relation to this particular matter did continue; for, without doing more, all he had done must necessarily have proved abortive and useless. So far, therefore, as the verdict finds that the defendant was retained for the purposes alleged in the declaration, and that such retainer continued and subsisted at the time the last rule *nisi* was returnable, I think it warranted by sufficient evidence.

Then it is argued for the defendant, that the declaration does not charge that it was his duty to have moved the rule absolute, or to have taken any ulterior measures upon the result of Ross & McLeod's case being known, and that in point of fact, so far as retaining the money went, it remained in the hands of Mr. Cameron, where it was when the rule *nisi* was served in November, and until long after the decision in the case of Ross & McLeod v. J. Hamilton, so that the object was in effect attained; that the event had arrived, and that no further steps would have been of any use; and that nothing is stated in the declaration, or was at the trial complained of, except the neglect imputed to the defendant in not pursuing this rule *nisi*. On referring to the declaration, it will be found, worded in more comprehensive terms; and at the trial I certainly took the main point to be, whether the evidence shewed a neglect of duty in all or any respect within the terms and scope of the declaration. Now the alleged failure to retain counsel points at the neglect to move the rule absolute; it may also point to a neglect to procure sound advice. Besides, the defendant's neglect, mismanagement and carelessness, are laid in very general terms; and the nature of the plaintiff's situation, and the circumstances of the case (which need not be here repeated) shew, I think, that not only did the defendant fail to move enough, but that having moved what he did, the result of Ross & McLeod's case, on the return of his rule *nisi* (a), instead of terminating his duty, and putting an end to the application, only rendered it the more incumbent upon him to have immediately moved that rule absolute, that if possible the money might be placed under the control of the court, and leave be then obtained to the plaintiff to return Smilie's writ. I think it was his clear duty to have pursued the rule, and followed it up by the application the plaintiff wished, in relation to the return of Smilie's writ; and that this neglect or breach of duty is sufficiently included within the terms of the declaration to entitle the plaintiff to urge it as a ground of action at the trial; nor do I consider, as contended in the argument, that the professional duty of the defendant was narrowed to the mere object of procuring the money to be withheld, or not to be paid over to Smilie till the event of Ross & McLeod's suit was known; by reason of that part of the declaration following the alleged retainer of the defendant, which says that he was retained to conduct and manage the said application, in order that the said sum of £70 11s. might be retained till the priority of the said writ should have been determined as aforesaid, not merely till the case of Ross & McLeod should be decided, as assumed in the argument, but till it should be determined which of the writs was entitled to priority. The whole statement in the declaration must be taken together; and when it is clearly seen that the plaintiff alleges a desire to apply to the court with a twofold object, and that the defendant was retained to conduct and manage such application, the passage above quoted may be rejected as surplusage; if not rejected, it only expresses distinctly one of the plaintiff's objects, and one of itself useless without the other; for the retention of the money till the event in question was known, could be of no effectual service to the plaintiff, unless he also had leave to return Smilie's writ of execution. And as the declaration proceeds, the breach of duty alleged is, in relation to the said application, referring back to the whole previous matters, and the damages consequently sustained are alleged to be, that the plaintiff was obliged to pay Smilie the £125, which he would not have been had he the opportunity to have returned his writ *nulla bona* as to the £70 11s. 0½d., for which he became liable to others by reason of the event of Ross & McLeod's suit.

Thus far I consider the case established in favour of the plaintiff. But it is further objected, that under the circumstances, neither the application the defendant did make, nor any application which, according to the allegations

---

(a) 3rd Feb. 40.

in the declaration, he was bound to have made, could have been of any avail to the plaintiff; and that therefore the special damage as laid cannot be ascribed to the defendant's negligence, since no diligence of his could have prevented it, and that no other damage did or could have accrued from the negligence complained of. The grounds of this part of the case are, that the evidence shews that the plaintiff had returned Ross & McLeod's writ *nulla bona;* the effect of which was to declare, that in point of fact the sale had been made under and the proceeds applied to Smilie's writ; that he had nevertheless failed to return Smilie's writ, and was attached; that he could not have returned it otherwise than *fieri feci,* for if he had he would have immediately become liable to an action at Smilie's suit for a false return, and having clearly levied the money, and being estopped by his return to Ross & McLeod's writ from applying any part of it to their use, or from disputing Smilie's right to the whole, the latter must inevitably have recovered (a): also, that the payment to Ross & McLeod is not proved as alleged. To this it was answered, that the special damages, in other words, the alleged consequences of the defendant's neglect were admitted on the record, and if meant to be disputed ought to have been traversed. The argument for the defendant is conclusive as respects the claim for special damages, if we can see that no relief could have been afforded to the plaintiff by the court. If the court could have directed the money to be paid into court under the rule *nisi,* and could afterwards have controlled its application; and could, after delivering judgment in Ross & McLeod's case, have then allowed the plaintiff to have returned Smilie's writ no goods quoad the £70 11s. 0½d., and to withdraw that sum out of court, or to direct its payment to Ross & McLeod, with the residue only to Smilie; it would have been what the plaintiff desired, and the disappointment constitutes the breach and damages for which this action is brought. These forming questions of law on points that the court alone would have decided had the rule *nisi* been moved absolute, may now be considered by the court, as they would have been had they been called upon to consider them when the case of Ross & McLeod was first decided. Then first, clearly the court could not have allowed the return of Ross & McLeod's writ to have been amended to their prejudice after they had successfully prosecuted for a false return, but after their recovery the alteration would have made it a true return, and the only argument against it would be, that it would falsify such recovery on the face of the records of the court; and the cases in 2 C. & P. 356, 5 Price, 547, are pointed to shew the conclusiveness of the return being once made; and there are many cases wherein relief has been refused, unless the application was prompt, and none that I have met with, where it has been granted at so late a stage as the one in question; that is, after a recovery for a false return. Still I do not see that the court might not in their discretion have allowed it, though it would certainly be going a great way to relieve the plaintiff, and perhaps exceeding what any case in the books could be found to warrant (b). Nor am I at all satisfied that the return of *nulla bona* to Ross & McLeod's writ is conclusive upon the plaintiff, except in the case in which it issued, or that Smilie, not being thereby estopped, the plaintiff would, on the principles

---

(a) 2 C. & P. 356.
(b) 10 A. & E., and 2 P. & D. 455; Jackson v. Hill, 7 M. & W. 288.

of reciprocity applicable to estoppels, be estopped as against Smilie in the collateral proceedings.

But supposing the returns to Ross & McLeod's case could have been altered, and granting that in ordinary cases a sheriff may be allowed to return a writ of *fi. fa. nulla bona,* after being attached for not returning it, still would it have been allowed in Smilie's case had leave been applied for early in Easter Term, 1840. The arguments against it are, that the plaintiff, before applying to the court, and after notice from Ross & McLeod, had elected to decide for himself, and had returned Ross & McLeod's writ no goods, thereby impliedly indicating that he had sold under, and applied the amount levied to Smilie's writ. That if doubtful, the plaintiff should have applied to Smilie for an indemnity, and if refused, should then have applied promptly to the court for time to return his writ, till he gave an indemnity, or till the suit of Ross & McLeod against J. Hamilton was decided. That he however neglected to do anything, or to return the execution, and was attached after Ross & McLeod had sued the deceased sheriff's sureties for a false return to their writ. That during the pendency of the latter suit, the court would not, if asked, have allowed an amendment of the return to their writ, at least not without payment of costs, and bringing the money into court; and that if it could have done so, the application should have been made promptly. That pending such suit, the court, if moved, would not have allowed the plaintiff to return Smilie's writ no goods as to the £70 11s. 0½d., for it would have been inconsistent with the return already made in Ross & McLeod's case; therefore the prior right of Ross & McLeod, either by the plaintiff's voluntary concession, or by the result of their suit, and the amendment of their writ, were conditions precedent to any application for relief against Smilie's attachment, or to the permission of the court to return his writ *nulla bona.* Ross & McLeod's right to priority the plaintiff wished to depend upon the result of their action; but in the meantime, his situation became worse; not only had he been attached for not returning Smilie's writ, but had been brought up in August, on *hab. corp.*, when, for the first time, he applied to the court for relief; and although delay of the proceedings was afterwards ordered in chambers on terms, he did not comply therewith; and the application fell to the ground. In the ensuing term he was again brought up on *alias hab. corp.*, and then, before any renewed application to the court, he paid the amount to the sheriff in whose custody he was, who paid it over to the agent of the plaintiff's attorney; and this before the event of Ross & McLeod's case was known.

It is material here to look back; and doing so, we find that the *alias hab. corp.* was endorsed to discharge the plaintiff on his paying £124 1s. 2d., and 14s. 3d. for that writ, and sheriff's fees, &c.; *alias hab. corp.* to Niagara sheriff, dated 4th November, 1839, returnable the last day of same term, issued 12th November, 1839, endorsed, "Mr. Sheriff,—If Mr. McLeod satis- "fies you the sum of £124 1s. 2d., with 14s. 3d. for this writ, besides your "own fees, you will discharge him therefrom. Yours, &c., signed Charles L. "Hall, plaintiff's attorney;" return, brought up, on attachment for not returning writ in Smilie *et al.* v. Balfour *et al.*; and in the plaintiff's affidavit of 16th Nov. 1839, he states his inability to comply with the terms prescribed in chambers, but that he had raised the money from other sources, and had paid it the sheriff of the Niagara District, in whose custody he was brought to this court upon the writ of *hab. corp.* (a). On this affidavit the last motion was founded for two purposes. By the foregoing affidavit and motion, the plaintiff alleges that he paid the money in discharge of the writ, and that in point of fact he was discharged, but was afterwards again taken into custody, which he considered was illegal; in short, on the one hand he wished the payment to be regarded as a payment in discharge of the writ of *hab. corp.*, to entitle him to the benefit thereof as against the sheriff, and on the other to have it regarded, not as an absolute payment in discharge, but a deposit only which he wished to be paid into court without prejudice, to abide its future orders. But the application to pay into court should have preceded the payment, not followed it; having paid the sheriff the amount endorsed on the writ, and in discharge of it, as he admits, the sheriff paid it over to the agent of Smilie's attorney.

Now as to the strict legal course of proceeding in such matters, I think that in ordinary cases, payment to the sheriff does not purge the contempt and entitle the party attached to his unqualified discharge; as was in truth decided in this very matter, and as is shewn by the cases of Good v. Wilkes, 6 M. & Sel. 413; Lewis v. Morland, 2 B. & A. 56; and Pitt v. Coombs, 3 N. & M. 212 (b). And I think, also, a sheriff had no strict right to receive payment of the sum endorsed, any more than upon a writ of *ca. ad. sa.*, unless specially authorized. The case in 3 Dowl. P. C. 10, seems to decide that if he does receive it, the court will not compel him to pay the amount into court; the rule *nisi* was there offered with a view that he should be ordered to retain it. The case of Pitt v. Coombs also shews, that such payment to the sheriff does not exonerate the party paying (c); a sheriff's officer has no right to receive the amount of debt and costs endorsed on process to arrest; but if he does, the sheriff is liable for the amount. This shews that the plaintiff may adopt the payment; and if the money, being paid to the sheriff, is by him handed over to the agent of the plaintiff's attorney, the plaintiff may adopt such payment, though not valid without adoption, or a previous authority (d). The case of Slackford v. Austin is material to the present case, in this, that Lord Ellenborough there says, "that the sheriff under a *ca. sa.* is only agent for the "plaintiff for the limited purpose of executing the writ, and he must pur-"sue the writ, and be ready at the day not with the money but with the body, "unless the party himself who sued out the writ interfere and agree to the "liberation of the person upon receipt of the money which has been paid to "the sheriff." And it may be equally said, that when he previously interferes and authorizes the discharge by the sheriff on receipt of the amount endorsed, the sheriff becomes his agent to receive the money; and in the present case the plaintiff's attorney endorsed the *alias habeas corpus* with a direction to the sheriff of Niagara to discharge the present plaintiff on his paying

---

(a) See the affidavit referred to, ante p. 88.

(b) Rex v. Stokes, Cow. 137; Pitt v. Coombs, 3 N. & M. 212; 2 East. 411; and R. v. Sheriff of Devon, 3 Dowl. 10; 11 Ves. 170; Attorney General v. Mills, 1 Coop. Ch. Ca. 261; Collard v. Hare, 5 Sim. 10.

(c) 8 C. & P. 213, Woodman v. Gist. See also 3 Tyr. 237.

(d) 12 Mod. 230; Tidd, 1069; 14 East. 468, Slackford v. Austin; 2 D. & Ry. 6, Moodie v. Spencer; Douglas, 203, Yates v. Frickleton; 14 East. 532.

£124 1s. 2d., &c. After such payment I should think Smilie could not have proceeded against the sheriff for an escape, or against McLeod as not having so far satisfied the exigency of the writ; and if not, I do not see how the court could afterwards interfere to control it in the hands of the sheriff or of the agent of the plaintiff's attorney. The effect was, that the sheriff immediately became debtor, and liable to Smilie for the money. And if a right of action once vested, the court could not by any future order divest that right. The effect of the plaintiff's payment to the sheriff, instead of to the party under the endorsement on a writ of *habeas corpus*, may be tested by supposing judgment had been afterwards given against Ross & McLeod, in which event the plaintiff would have desired to adhere to the payment as made ; but that the sheriff had failed or refused to pay over the amount to Smilie, his attorney or agent, could Smilie have renewed proceedings against the plaintiff to enforce payment over again from him, as he might do if the payment to the sheriff had been made without authority, and Smilie had not recognized or adopted it? would he (in such an event) have been estopped from disavowing the agency of the sheriff to receive the money by reason of his attorney expressly authorizing it by his endorsement upon the writ? I should think he would, unless he could shew collusion between his attorney and the sheriff, and that he was insolvent. If so, as the payment made would enure to the plaintiff's benefit to discharge him, it ought to enure to Smilie's benefit to charge the sheriff as his agent, and to entitle him to the money when paid. This seems to put an end to the plaintiff's claim for special damages, if not admitted but to be proved by him. It does not seem to be well settled yet to what extent special damages are admitted by the plea of not guilty in case. The new rules provide that such plea shall operate as a denial only of the breach of duty or wrongful act alleged to have been committed by the defendant, and not of the facts stated in the inducement ; and no other defence than such denial shall be admitted under that plea ; all other pleas in denial shall take issue in some particular matter of fact alleged in the declaration. Several cases are reported as to what constitutes matter of inducement within this rule, that must, if intended to be denied, be specially traversed. But the effect of the plea as to special damage is not well settled ; though much may no doubt depend upon the form of the declaration, and the way in which the breach and damages are respectively alleged. When special damage is the gist of the action, as in slander for words not otherwise actionable, it is supposed it may be specially denied, not that it must be, unless a clear line can be drawn on the face of the declaration between the breach and the damages (a).

The declaration in the first count avers that the defendant did not conduct the application with due care, skill and diligence, but on the contrary thereof, by reason of his conducting it in a careless and improper manner, and neglecting to retain counsel in that behalf, an *alias habeas corpus* issued for not returning Smilie's writ, and that the plaintiff, by means of the premises, was obliged to pay the said sum of £125 upon the said writ of the said Smilie, and that afterwards Ross & McLeod recovered in the said action against the said John Hamilton, £74 4s., and £35 for costs, and H. O. Hamilton, executrix, having been obliged to pay him the said sum, sued Wilson, the plaintiff's surety, for

---

(a) 2 Big. N. S. 732; 4 Dowl. 333; 2 M. & Rob. 5; 7 Jurist, 623; 4 A. & E., N. S. 580; 6 Jurist, 958.

the amount thereof, by *means whereof* the plaintiff became liable and bound to pay the said sum of £74 4s., and £35, and *hath* been put to great costs and inconvenience in the premises and been greatly injured.

In the second count it is alleged that the defendant did not conduct the application with due care, skill and diligence, but *on the contrary*, by *reason* of the defendant's conducting and managing the same in a careless and unskilful manner, and neglecting to retain counsel to appear in that behalf, plaintiff, through the carelessness, negligence and unskilfulness of defendant, was obliged to pay the said Smilie the said sum of £125, and was *also* compelled to pay the said sum of £70 11s., so endorsed on said writ of Ross & McLeod, and *also* £40 costs; and *also by reason of the premises*, the plaintiff was otherwise greatly injured, &c., to his damage of £500.

To both counts the plaintiff pleads not guilty of the said supposed grievances or any part thereof *modo et forma*, the effect of which plea under the new rule is to deny only the breach of duty alleged to have been committed by him. And it appears to me that the breach of duty alleged in each count begins at the words "*but on the contrary*," (a) and that it is thereby narrowed to what follows.

The plea of not guilty is not applicable to what goes before, viz., that the defendant *did not* conduct the application with due care, &c., for it would be one negative opposed to another; to that part of the declaration *per se*, the proper answer would be affirmative (b)—that he did conduct the said application with due care, &c.

As pleaded, the general issue traverses negatively the affirmative matter following the words "*on the contrary*," and if amplified it would in terms assert that it was not by reason of defendant's conducting the application in a careless manner, &c., that the said plaintiff was damnified, as alleged by him, or that the defendant did not so conduct it, by means whereof the plaintiff sustained the damages alleged, or any part thereof. Such I take to be its effect, and I cannot separate the misconduct imputed to the defendant from the injurious consequences alleged to have been occasioned thereby, as to limit the plea of not guilty to the mere charge of negligence in the abstract, and separated from the damages as following therefrom. Adopting this view, it appears to me it was incumbent on the plaintiff to shew that he had sustained the special damage alleged by reason of the defendant's negligence, and this I do not think he has done.

Besides, if an action be maintainable without proof of special damage, that constitutes a conclusive reason against the defendant's right to traverse the special damage, because it would not meet the whole cause of action; and as the defendant would not be at liberty to traverse the special damage suggested as a substantive ground of defence, he can resist it, and the plaintiff must prove it as a suggestion of damage consequential upon the defendant's misconduct (c). Restricted to the special damage, the first count fails; because it appears on the face of the plaintiff's evidence, that it was not owing to any

---

(a) 3 T. R. 307, Harris v. Mantle.

(b) See the declaration and plea, Hancock v. Bethune, reported in Upper Canada Jurist, No. 2, Vol. III., July, 1846.

(c) 3 Bing. N. S. 372; 4 Dowl. P. C. 333, Smith v. Thomas; 2 Moo. & Rob. 5; 4 A. & E., N. S. 565; 7 Jurist. 626.

neglect of the defendant that the plaintiff was brought up upon an *alias habeas corpus*, either in August or November, 1839, and compelled to pay *upon* Smilie's writ the £125 ; it was owing to his own laches, in not in the first place having well returned Smilie's writ, and in the second place in not paying the money into court according to the conditional order of Mr. Justice McLean ; the defendant's neglect was afterwards. Both the counts fail so far as respects the alleged payment *upon* Smilie's writ as in the first count, or *to* Smilie himself as in the second count ; because it does not appear that the payment was made by the defendant's advice; wherefore it must be looked upon as made by the plaintiff of his own accord; and it was so made, before the defendant was employed to make the application in relation to which he afterwards incurred the charge of negligence; and this I look upon as the gist of the case on the head of special damage.

Much was said in argument of the proceedings by Ross & McLeod, against J. Hamilton, the deceased sheriff's executrix, and Mr. Wilson ; so far as material, the facts alleged in relation thereto in the first count were proved ; the payment to Ross & McLeod, as alleged in the second count, was not proved. I do not consider the general evidence of payments by McLeod as proof sufficient to establish that particular payment as averred ; a payment expressly for that particular object by the defendant, or the application of unappropriated payments by the executrix, or the deceased sheriff's sureties, should be shewn to render it a discharge of that particular demand, and this was not done. But the matters connected with Ross & McLeod have been treated in the argument as if they constituted the damage complained of, whereas it is clearly not so; no application made or that could have been made by the defendant on the plaintiff's behalf, could have relieved him from liability to Ross & McLeod, nor was such the object. The damage of the plaintiff is, being compelled to satisfy Smilie's writ in full, notwithstanding the result of the case of Ross & McLeod, and the object of the application was to be protected as respected Smilie's writ. If Ross & McLeod failed in their suit, then Smilie of course was entitled to payment; but if they succeeded, as they did, and if (as has been decided in other suits) the plaintiff was liable to answer the consequences, it matters not whether he has paid Ross & McLeod, or the executrix, or the sureties of either himself or the deceased sheriff. His grievance is, that he is liable to do so in consequence of the adverse result of their suit, which established as against the plaintiff, that they were entitled to precedence; and being so liable, has also been compelled to pay Smilie in full, although he wished to have obtained leave to defer the return of his writ until that result was known, with leave to return it *nulla bona quoad* the amount of Ross & McLeod's recovery, not as conclusive upon Smilie, but in order that he might contest with Smilie his right to priority, as it had been contested with Ross & McLeod, though unsuccessfully. The loss of opportunity and the actual payment of Smilie in full is the real ground of the special damage laid in this action. There is no other ground of special damage but this, and it fails him, because we now see in the facts before us what it must (being matter of legal information) be supposed the court would have seen in Easter Term, 1840, had the last rule to shew cause been moved absolute, that the application could not be granted because the plaintiff had concluded himself by voluntarily paying the amount claimed by Smilie to the sheriff of Niagara, who was *authorized to receive it* in discharge so far of the attachment, and the benefit of which payment he in that respect obtained; and this without a previous application to the court to pay it in, subject to future order according to the result of Ross & McLeod's case. No diligence of the defendant could have averted the consequences, under the facts and circumstances of the case; and therefore I think the plaintiff not entitled to the special damage laid. The claim to special damage might fail on another ground, viz., the plaintiff could not obtain effectual relief unless allowed to amend the return to Ross & McLeod's writ from *nulla bona* to *fieri feci*. As to this, it is uncertain whether it could have been granted or not; or, if refused, it is uncertain whether it would estop the plaintiff in an action by Smilie for a false return to his writ of no goods. If Smilie could not be estopped by the return, the argument is strong that the plaintiff should not be estopped thereby as against Smilie. I have no fixed opinion on these points, but am quite as much inclined to the plaintiff's favour on both as against him. It does fail, because, without leave to return Smilie's writ *nulla bona*, the former could be of no avail to him; and the payment made by him in November concluded him.

It is to be considered whether the plaintiff is entitled to nominal damages. Apart from the special damage, the declaration would read thus: "That the "defendant did not conduct the said application with due and proper care, "skill and diligence, or retain counsel in that behalf, and by reason of the "premises, the plaintiff was and is greatly injured, &c." Upon the best consideration I can give the question, I think the plaintiff is entitled to nominal damages, although I have come to this conclusion slowly and with much doubt. The ground on which I think he is entitled to recover is, that though an action of tort, it is founded on contract. The contract and the breach of it are found on sufficient evidence; and, although it is now certain that no diligence on the defendant's part would have attained the result desired, still the failure would not have been owing to any new matter of fact, but only in law as applied to the facts. The application on the plaintiff's part was *bona fide* in a matter in which he was materially interested, and upon a question doubtful in law, and upon which he had a right to obtain the decision of the court. This application upon a doubtful question in law the defendant undertook to make, in his professional capacity; the defendant had a right to his services, and he was not justified in abandoning the case at the most critical part of it, upon collateral and insufficient grounds, and now to resist an action for the negligence by shewing that the application, if persevered in, would have failed in point of law. I do not see that an attorney who undertakes to prosecute before the court a motion doubtful in law in which his client is interested, and has a right to his services, and a right to the decision of the court on the facts laid before it, is at liberty to abandon or neglect the proceedings whenever he pleases without notice to the client, and without any valid excuse, and then to urge the unfavourable result that would have followed as an answer to an action for such misconduct. Herein I think I perceive that legal damage which is sufficient to sustain it.

The plaintiff had a right to the defendant's services; for these services the defendant would have had a right to remuneration. The plaintiff had a right to know the opinion of the court upon a doubtful question, whether he could be relieved or not; the defendant, having engaged to obtain such opinion, abandoned the application without cause, and thereby frustrated the plaintiff's object and violated his right. I do not see how this can be held not actionable, unless in any action or proceeding of which the result is doubtful in law upon the facts of the case; the attorney of the party knowing this can, after engaging to obtain a judicial decision on the point, abandon the proceeding at any stage, and then set up as a bar to an action for negligence (not that he did not break his contract, but) that the law was against his client, and that if he had gone on he would have failed; and as a bar to the suit, call upon the court to determine in this action for negligence what would have been the legal result, however intricate the matter might be, or however important to the client. The defendant knew all the facts before he undertook to make the application; if he knew the law was against his client, he should have so advised him; but he did not consider the law against him, he thought there was good grounds for the application, and there were probable grounds, though insufficient by reason of one circumstance peculiar to this case and already mentioned. The defendant did not afterwards neglect the matter because he thought the law against the plaintiff and the effect useless, but for other reasons entirely foreign to this case, and without notice.

I have felt a difficulty in reconciling this view with all the cases in the books, or with the breach of duty alleged in the declaration. One set of cases imply (especially before the new rules) that an attorney, sued for negligence, might, under the general issue, shew as a defence, that the neglect complained of was in relation to what would have been useless or ineffectual, or something that no diligence could have accomplished (a). While others, distinguishing between actions of tort founded on mere wrong, or on the mere obligations of duty imposed by law, as upon a sheriff in the execution of process, and herein again distinguishing between cases arising under *mesne* and final process, and like actions of tort founded on contract as the present is, lay down in very broad and general terms that there is no distinction between actions of tort or of *assumpsit* founded on an agreement, nor between agreements expressed or implied; but that whenever there is established a contract and a breach of such contract, the plaintiff is entitled to nominal damages; in other words, that the breach of the contract constitutes legal damage, &c. (b). Others again determine, that for a breach of duty, in which an action for neglect would lie, the Statute of Limitations begins to run from the period of such breach, and not from the time any special damage may be afterwards caused thereby (c).

The breach of duty alleged in the declaration is blended with the damages. It is thereby asserted that by reason of the defendant's conducting the application in a careless and improper manner, the plaintiff was put to great inconvenience and greatly injured. This separates the general or legal damage from the

---

(a) Johnston v. Alston, 1 Cam. 176; Bowne v. Diggly, 2 Chitty Rep. 311.
(b) 1 B. & Adol. 415, Marzetti v. Williams; 7 Bing. 413, Godefroy v. Jay; 3 B. & C. 448, and 1 M. & M. 520, Vanwart v. Woolly; 3 Moor, Cleghorn v. Dessange; 4 M. & W. 945, Williams v. Mostyn; 7 Jurist, 626; 4 A. & E. 566; 4 G. & D. 629, Wylie v. Birch; 8 Jurist, 958, Clifton v. Hooper; 2 N. & M. 831, Bales v. Wingfield; 12 A. & E. 491.
(c) 3 B. & A. 626; 5 B. & C. 268.

special damage, and the objection to plaintiff's right to recover is, that the court see in the face of the evidence that he could not have succeeded, and therefore sustained no damage, actual or implied. But upon the best consideration, I think the court must perceive legal damage in the fact, that through defendant's wilful neglect the plaintiff's object in desiring the judgment of the court upon his application was frustrated, and that defendant had no right to desert him, after having contracted to assist him.

It may further be remarked, that although the court could not control the money paid to the Niagara sheriff, it might have allowed Smilie's writ to be returned *nulla bona*, leaving Smilie to his election to proceed against the sheriff or his own attorney for the money paid, or against the plaintiff or whoever was liable, as for a false return. In the latter event the plaintiff would have been enabled to urge that he was not as against Smilie concluded by the return of no goods to Ross & McLeod's suit; perhaps it might have been so urged with success, in which event he would be let in to dispute Smilie's right to precedence, and if with effect, he would become entitled to restitution of the money paid to the sheriff. It is probable that Smilie would have proceeded against those who had received the money in preference; in which event the plaintiff would be without remedy; but under possible circumstances, as it might have been otherwise, and though the court might have allowed him to return Smilie's writ no goods, in case it would be of any contingent advantage to him, the defendant omitted to ask the indulgence. I do not conceal from myself that the legal effect of the whole evidence on the face of it is to rebut the claims for special damage, and that it is difficult to point out any tangible injury or damage that the plaintiff has sustained independently of it; and therefore I rely much upon the adjudged cases (in which, however, a damage in law is probably more perceptible), that this action being founded on a contract, and the contract being broken, the plaintiff is entitled to nominal or legal damages for such breach of contract.

I have tested the case by supposing the action to have been *assumpsit* on the agreement instead of case, and in doing so it seems to me that the evidence, including the defendant's admissions to Dr. Hamilton, shews an express contract on the defendant's part to assist the plaintiff in the application, and that it is not left to be implied from circumstances alone. The defendant admitted that he was employed to attend to the matter, and knowingly neglected it, for insufficient reasons, so far as proved to the satisfaction of the jury. The plea of *non-assumpsit* would deny the contract, but admit the breach, as the plea of not guilty denies the latter but concedes the former, and the contract being distinctly proved, the breach would, under a plea of *non-assumpsit*, stand admitted, and the plaintiff would be entitled to his damages of course. If the promise could only be implied, it might then be contended that the law would not imply such promise, or impose a duty to attempt to render services in trying to accomplish what the law sees must be unsuccessful. But the case does not appear to me reduced to this, and if it were, I apprehend, that while on the one hand the law would imply a promise on plaintiff's part to pay the defendant his legal fees for prosecuting an application of the kind in question, though doubtful in law as to the result, still only doubtful, and one which he had a fair right to submit to the court; so, on the other hand, if the defendant professionally undertook the services, the law would imply a promise on his part diligently to pursue it to the end, for the satisfaction of his client, unless exonerated by some lawful excuse from the obligation. Besides, legal damages could not strictly be negatived by the jury (a), and in this case they have, if warranted in law, found damages. The misconduct of the defendant is the gist of the action, and that is also found (b).

From the best attention, therefore, that I have been able to give this case, it appears to me that,—taking the whole evidence together, and considering the facts stated in the inducement to the declaration, which are not denied, the circumstances in which the plaintiff was placed, the affidavits and motions made in August and November, together with the conduct and acknowledgments of the defendant,—

1. That there was sufficient evidence to go to the jury to warrant them in finding that the defendant was retained in manner and form alleged in the declaration, and that such retainer continued down to and subsisted at the day on which the second rule to shew cause was returnable.

2. That it was his duty, under such retainer, to make the application which the plaintiff in his declaration represents that he wished to have made.

3. That the second motion was deficient in compliance with such wish, because it did not solicit anew to defer the return of Smilie's writ, or for leave to the plaintiff to return it after the result of Ross & McLeod's suit should be known, without which an order upon the motion to pay the money into court to await the result of that case could be of no possible benefit to the plaintiff; his object was to deprive Smilie of a *prima facie* right to it in the event of Ross & McLeod's suit terminating adversely to the plaintiff's interest, which could only be done through the medium of a return to his writ.

4. That there was evidence to go to the jury to warrant their finding negligence in the defendant, by reason of his abandoning the proceedings without notice to the plaintiff, and without an apparent justifiable cause. It appears to me it is a fallacy to say, that the event desired had arrived. It has always appeared to me that the decision of Ross & McLeod's case in their favour, on the 3rd of February, 1840, on which day the second rule *nisi* was returnable, only rendered it the more incumbent on the defendant promptly to have moved it absolute, and to have solicited leave to the plaintiff to return Smilie's writ according to that result.

5. That the special damage alleged is not admitted on the record, the action being maintainable without proof of special damage, wherefore such special damage could not be alone traversed by a distinct plea. It stands, therefore, like damages suggested to be proved by the plaintiff, and the special damage laid is the payment to Smilie, not the liability to answer for the result of Ross & McLeod's suit against J. Hamilton.

6. I do not think such damages are proved, for a reason peculiarly distinguishing this case. As a general rule, the sheriff or coroner is not entitled to accept the amount for which a party is attached, any more than upon a *ca. sa.*; but in this case an express authority to receive the amount claimed by Smilie, was by his attorney endorsed on a writ of *habeas corpus*, and the

---

(a) 8 Jurist, 958.　　　(b) 8 D. & R. 14; 5 B. & C. 259.

plaintiff paid him the amount, of his own accord, to produce his discharge before any renewed application to the court—such payment operated as a discharge of the plaintiff's liability to Smilie, and reciprocally conferred a right upon Smilie to call upon the sheriff for the amount; and of such vested right the court could not deprive him by any subsequent order; the allegation therefore fails, that the plaintiff was obliged to pay Smilie by reason of defendant's misconduct. On this special ground it is that I overrule the claim for special damage; because I am of opinion, that had the court been moved to order the sheriff, or the agent of Smilie's-attorney, to pay the money into court, it could not have been made consistently with a due respect to the vested rights of Smilie, acquired through the plaintiff's voluntary payment, without the privity or advice of the defendant.

7. I think the plaintiff is entitled to nominal damages, because the defendant being retained to apply to the court on his behalf for relief in a matter in which he was interested, but upon the facts doubtful in law, and the defendant, having undertaken the service, was bound diligently to pursue it, and was not at liberty to abandon the proceedings at the most critical stage without notice to the plaintiff, and for reasons foreign to the subject-matter and insufficient to justify it. The plaintiff had a right to the opinion of the court upon his application for relief, and it was the defendant's duty to have obtained it. Being disappointed in this object, through the defendant's neglect, I think him liable to this action, and that the plaintiff is entitled to some damages, although it now appears to me that he would not have succeeded had the motion been persevered in. The defendant broke a contract which the plaintiff had a right to have had performed. The plaintiff was liable to remunerate him for the services rendered, though unsuccessful, and reciprocally the plaintiff was entitled to those services; looked upon in the light of an action of *assumpsit*, the promises would be mutual and reciprocal, and the defendant therefore liable for a breach of the agreement on his part.

8. Upon the motion to arrest judgment, I consider both counts good, all the facts alleged being held proven, and those facts shewing in each count a good and sufficient cause of action.

9. The special damage consisting in the plaintiff's having been forced to pay Smilie in full, the recovery by Ross & McLeod against John Hamilton, and the judgments obtained by him against the executrix, and her proceeding against Wilson, are only important as shewing that the plaintiff is liable indirectly to answer for the event of Ross & McLeod's suit, and *therefore* prejudiced by being compelled to pay Smilie, without the opportunity of contesting his right upon a return of *nulla bona*. Payment of Ross & McLeod's recovery is immaterial; the *liability* is sufficient. Although the court could not take the money out of the sheriff's hands, or those of Smilie's agent, without his consent, still they might have allowed the plaintiff to alter the return of Ross & McLeod's writ to *fieri feci*, and to return Smilie's *nulla bona quoad* the amount of Ross & McLeod's verdict; and if that were done, it might, under possible circumstances, have been of advantage to the plaintiff, and would to a certain (though not to a full) extent, have realized his wishes. I think substantial or special damage is not proved, but disproved on the face of the evidence, but that by reason of the breach of duty and contract on defendant's part, there is legal

damage sufficient to entitle the plaintiff to a nominal sum, and that the verdict should be reduced accordingly (a).

The CHIEF JUSTICE gave no judgment.

JONES, J., and McLEAN, J., concurred with Mr. Justice Macaulay.

(a) ROSS & McLEOD V. JOHN HAMILTON.

Michaelmas Term. 3rd Victoria.

Declaration. Recites the defendant's covenant, dated 21st Oct., 1837, that Alex. Hamilton, then sheriff of Niagara, and now deceased, should not within four years from date wilfully misconduct himself in his said office, to the damage of any person being a party to any legal proceeding. Also recites the recovery of a judgment by the plaintiff against Wm. Clark, Balfour, Drysdale, and Chas. Richardson, for £70 11s. 0½d. The issue of a $fi. fa.$ 17th Nov., 2nd Vict., to the Niagara sheriff, returnable first Easter next, endorsed and delivered to the said Alex. Hamilton, who then and from thence, and until and at and after the said writ, was sheriff, to be executed. Then alleges that the said sheriff seized the goods of the defendant on the writ, and levied the amount thereout, but had not the same at the return of the said writ, but made default; and at the return of the said writ, to wit, on the 4th February aforesaid, he falsely returned *nulla bona* as to all of the defendants, as by the writ appeared. Then avers the death of Alex. Hamilton, after the return of this writ, and before this suit, to wit, 1st January last, whereby, &c.

2nd count. Recites the defendant's covenant, as above, the judgment, $fi. fa.$, &c., as in first count; then avers, that although there were goods of the defendant within his district whereof he might have levied the amount, and of which he had notice, yet he neglected to levy the sum, and at the return of the writ, to wit, 4th February aforesaid, falsely returned *nulla bona;* avers the death of the said Alex. Hamilton, after the return as in first count, wherefore, &c.

Plea as to 1st count. Admits his being sheriff from 17th November, 1838, till and after the 4th February, 1839, and the receipt of the writ, but denies having seized any goods under it, and that the defendant, from the delivery till the return of the writ, had no goods whereof he could have levied the amount, or any part; concluding to the country.

Plea to 2nd count. Admits his being sheriff as aforesaid, and the receipt of the writ, but that the defendant had no goods whereof he could levy any part from its receipt until its return; and concludes to the country.

The postea is for the plaintiff, as upon a plea of *non est factum* only. The jury found the covenant to be the defendant's deed, no such plea on the roll, and assess the damages at £70 11s. But this might be amended, if the judgment is erroneous or void as it stands. The judgment of John Hamilton v. H. O. Hamilton, executrix, is upon an account stated of money paid by him as surety of Alex. Hamilton, the deceased sheriff, for default of McLeod, exceeding £800, and judgment confessed. The judgment of H. O. Hamilton, executrix, against Wilson, is on his bond to the deceased sheriff, Alex. Hamilton, as surety for McLeod, as deputy sheriff. The bond alone is declared on.

Plea. Oyer of condition; and 1st, *non damnificatus;* 2nd, damnified in plaintiff's own wrong.

Replication. Suggests various breaches, and among others, that the $fi. fa.$ of Ross & McLeod against Clark, Balfour, Drysdale and Richardson, 17th Nov., 1838, its delivery to McLeod, deputy sheriff, before return day, and within the four years of John Hamilton's covenant; that McLeod levied and made the amount, but did not return said writ, or pay over the amount to the plaintiffs, wherefore they, Ross & McLeod, sued John Hamilton, on his covenant touching McLeod's conduct in relation to the said writ and the return thereof, and the execution thereof, and recovered against him £109 4s. 3d., which he was forced to pay, and incurred £25 costs of defence, of all which McLeod had notice; and that the said John Hamilton then sued the plaintiff, H. O. Hamilton, as executrix, and recovered against her as such. A second breach on the same matter, alleging a default in McLeod to levy, though the debtor, defendants on the writ, had goods, &c.

The judgment in Ross & McLeod v. J. Hamilton has not been correctly

BROWN v. PALMER.

Where there is a cause pending, the affidavit to hold to bail must be entitled in that cause, otherwise the arrest will be set aside; and where more than one debt is mentioned in the affidavit, and the debts are not combined and the aggregate stated, the affidavit must clearly express plaintiff's apprehension that defendant will leave the province with intent to defraud plaintiff of the *several* debts mentioned; any uncertainty as to which of the debts plaintiff apprehends he will be defrauded of will be fatal.

Motion by *Phillpotts* to rescind so much of an order made by Mr. Justice Hagerman as relates to leave granted to the defendant to plead in this cause, final judgment having been signed.

Bell moved to set aside the *ca. re.* and arrest for various defects: 1st, Because the affidavit of debt, and the alias writ, were not entitled in this cause entered up, but it might, I suppose, be amended on motion. A perusal of the declaration shews that it is perfectly good as against the defendant. If erroneous in point of law, it may perhaps be reversed in error; but while it stands, I still regard it conclusive as a judgment, with the consequences. 1 Stark Ev. pages 183-7, expresses what I have always supposed to be the rule on this subject. Admitting that the deceased sheriff's sureties are not liable for the misconduct of the under sheriff after the death of the principal, still it is by no means clear upon the evidence in the present case that they were not strictly liable to Ross & McLeod. The writs of *fi. fa.* of both Smilie and Ross & McLeod were issued, delivered and returnable during the lifetime of the deceased sheriff (1 M. & W. 728), consequently, the seizure or levy must have been made by him under both. He therefore commenced the execution of those writs, and had the goods in hand at the return day; and not only so, but the sale thereof commenced in his lifetime, and continued several days before he died. To what extent the goods had been then sold does not appear, but for all done up to this period his sureties were clearly liable. It may have been proved at the trial that he seized goods to the value endorsed on the writ, and levied the amount thereout before he died; or, that there were goods on which he might have levied but did not. It is then alleged that he falsely returned no goods. This return was in point of fact made by the under sheriff, in his name, after his death; but it has relation to the return day, when he was alive, and on the record imports to have been made at that time; such false return is made the foundation of the action of Ross & McLeod v. J. Hamilton, but its falsity is proved by shewing a receipt of the debt before the return day, or a neglect to levy though there were goods.—3 M. & W., 188-90; 6 Dowl. 389. A levy having been made, and Ross & McLeod entitled to priority, as established by the result of that case, the return ought to have been *fieri feci;* and had the writ been so returned, though after his death, I apprehend his sureties would be liable for the amount of the debt levied. For moneys levied an action lies at the suit of the creditor against the sheriff or executor, and so against his surety, though not returned.—Watson's Sheriff, page 202; Cro. Car. 539; W. Jo. 430; 1 Sal. 265; Pl. 9 & 10. They would also be liable if there were goods, and yet the sheriff neglected to levy before the return day; the liability was in some shape really incurred in his lifetime. If goods were levied to the amount, he became responsible; if he sold and made the money, equally so; or if there were goods which he did not seize, or seized under other writs not entitled to priority, he would be answerable accordingly. It signifies not that all was done by the present plaintiff. He was, until the sheriff's decease, his deputy; and he alone was answerable to the suitors or parties to the writs.

There is much room to argue that in matters of record relating to a period when he was alive, his sureties would be estopped by the record, as ostensibly the acts of their principal; although I am disposed to think they are not responsible for any acts of the under sheriff after his death, and for which the sureties of the deputy would be liable under the statute in their turn. It is laid down (arrest in a cause pending). 2nd, Variance in names of parties between this writ and the preceding writs. 3rd, The writ not being properly endorsed. 4th, Affidavit uncertain as to which debt the plaintiff apprehends the defendant will defraud him of. 5th, Does not state the £25 was due *before the commencement of the suit*. 6th, Should have been a pluries writ. 7th, Because the aggregate amount of the several demands stated is not sworn to be due. 8th, Does not state that the plaintiff in this cause has good reason to believe that the defendant in this cause is immediately about to leave Upper Canada.

Bell also moves a rule to set aside the final judgment entered in this cause, and all proceedings thereon, first because the summons for order to compute does not appear in the files, or in the judgment roll.

The judge's order, made 29th January, 1846, is this: "That it be referred "to the master to compute principal and interest due on the promissory note "declared upon, and let judgment be entered in favour of the plaintiff for "the amount, and costs to be taxed, &c. ; which judgment is nevertheless not "to be acted upon if the defendant shall forthwith pay into court not less than "the sum of £25, and plead issuably on or before Monday next; and if upon "trial of such issue, a verdict shall be rendered for the plaintiff for a sum "greater than the amount paid into court, then the judgment to be confirmed "for such excess, and all additional costs ; the defendant to pay *the cost of this "rule.*" The £25 was paid in under this order, and taken out by the plaintiff, and costs taxed on appointment, and costs tendered to the plaintiff's attorney on 31st January, and pleas filed and served. The variance in name is in the plaintiff's name, called Abraham W. Brown in the first process, Abraham Wing Brown in the latter. The declaration is on a note for £7 12s. 6d., and on another for £50. The order as to *entering judgment* was so framed at the request of the *plaintiff's attorney*. Judgment entered 31st January, 1846, on the two notes, and *fi. fa.* issued the same day. Two or three days after, the defendant was arrested on the *alias ca. re.* The defendant is now in custody

---

that a sheriff is not liable to an action for not making a return (2 Inst. 452), or before making a return, when the action is founded on a default of duty in executing the writ ; but as observed by Alderson, B., in 3 M. & W., 190, the falsity of the return is the conclusion of law, if the facts stated in the inducement are true ; and here all the facts so stated in Ross & McLeod's declaration may have occurred and existed in the sheriff's lifetime. I am far, therefore, from being satisfied that the action could have been effectually defended on the grounds suggested. At all events, the plaintiff was liable, *directly* or *indirectly* for the false return made, and not having prevented a recovery against Jno. Hamilton, is answerable for the consequences, as has in effect been already decided by this court in the case of H. O. H., executrix, v. Wilson, his surety; and being so liable, I do not see that it is competent to the defendant to resist an action against him for negligence as his attorney in other proceedings. by impeaching a judgment which is binding upon his client, and the foreseeing which induced the employment of such attorney, to assist him in guarding against a twofold liability for one and the same sum of money.

The judgments set out in the first count and proved at the trial, are conclusive to shew, that in fact Ross & McLeod did recover against J. Hamilton—Jno. Hamilton against the executrix—and that the executrix recovered against Wilson, the plaintiff's surety. They are conclusive on the plaintiff, right or wrong, and the defendant, who was his professional agent in collateral proceedings, cannot, that I can see, contend the contrary.—3 T. R. 374 ; 4 M. & S. 20 ; 5 B. & Adol. 715 ; 8 D. & R. 14.

thereon. The precipe for *alias ca. re.* and affidavit of debt was entitled Abraham Wing Brown, plaintiff, &c., there being no such cause pending. The judgment is signed Abraham Wing Brown, plaintiff, under judge's order, entitled in a cause Abraham W. Brown.

ROBINSON, C. J.—Though the judgment may have been irregularly entered in an action of Abraham Wing Brown, plaintiff, upon a judge's order, entitled Abraham W. Brown, plaintiff, and therefore in a different cause, and may have been irregular also on other grounds, yet we ought not to set it aside with costs, because what was done by the judge in chambers seems to have been a matter of arrangement in which both parties concurred; but it is fit the judgment should be set aside, though without costs, in order that the defendant may be able to plead as was intended. The rule for setting aside the arrest we also think must be made absolute, the affidavit being made in a cause pending, and not rightly entitled; and also because it does not swear to the plaintiff's apprehension that the defendant will leave the province with intent to defraud him of the several debts mentioned. If he had combined two debts, and stated the aggregate, then of course the objection would not have applied. It is unnecessary to speak of the other grounds. The defendant to bring no action of trespass.

The rule moved by Mr. Phillpotts, on behalf of the plaintiff, cannot be granted; for it would be unjust to rescind with costs the judge's order giving the defendant leave to plead, on the ground that final judgment has been entered, when the entry of final judgment was allowed at his own request, and for the security of his client (a).

We set aside the judgment, and the order to compute. The defendant's plea stands. Arrest set aside with costs.

BARRY v. ECCLES.

A defendant discharged from an arrest, cannot be detained in prison at the suit of the same plaintiff, upon a second writ issued upon an affidavit sworn while the defendant was in custody upon the first writ.

Crawford moved to rescind an order of Mr. Justice Hagerman, setting aside the writ of *ca. re.* issued in this cause, and discharging defendant (made on 16th December last), and that defendant be recommitted to the custody of the sheriff of the District of Victoria upon the *ca. re.*, on the ground that the proceedings were not irregular, or if they were, that the irregularity was waived by lapse of time and laches of defendant, and that no irregularity existed in regard to the writ set aside. The grounds on which the summons before the judge was moved were, 1st, that when the affidavit for arrest was made, defendant was actually a prisoner in the gaol of the District of Victoria, as plaintiff well knew; 2nd, that plaintiff had before assigned all his interest in the bond and award upon which the arrest was founded, to J. Ross, Esq.; 3rd, that the sheriff, on 13th November preceding, had been served with an order to discharge the defendant since his detention on this writ; 4th, the return of *ca. re.* being irregular, viz., "on the last day of this present Mich. Term next;" 5th,

---

(a) 7 T. R. 207, note.

that the affidavit is uncertain whether it is meant by it to arrest on the bond or the award, and how much was due on the award; 6th, not shewn that anything was due on the writing obligatory, or award when affidavit was made; 7th, that affidavit does not shew what was the condition of the bond, but merely refers to it; 8th, does not state that the submission was not revoked; 9th, nor state nor shew that the time was limited and award made within it; 10th, because the bond was executed by the defendant while he was in prison on an illegal arrest by plaintiff, from which he was afterwards ordered to be discharged; 11th, because this writ was placed in the sheriff's hands while the defendant was unlawfully in his custody in another action at suit of this plaintiff, and that defendant was entitled to have been freely discharged from the first arrest, as ordered, and not detained under this writ; 12th, because the defendant departs from the statute in swearing that the plaintiff apprehended that the defendant is immediately about to leave that part of the province of Canada formerly constituting Upper Canada, with intent, &c.

On the 10th November, 1845, plaintiff's attorney ordered sheriff to discharge defendant from the first process (before the judge's order was made), but at the same time told him that another writ in the same suit was coming, and not to discharge the prisoner. The sheriff accordingly waited till the new writ came to him, which was on the same day, and then told the defendant that he was free on the first writ, but that he detained him on the second.

The discharge from first writ was on account of irregularity in the affidavit.

It appears from the affidavits, that on the 8th of August, 1845, plaintiff arrested the defendant on an affidavit of debt for upwards of £600, on a bill of exchange and other demands. This arrest was held to be illegal for defects in the affidavits to hold to bail, and on another ground; and on the 13th of November, 1845, Mr. Justice Hagerman made an order for discharging the defendant from custody, with costs.

On the 4th September, while defendant was in custody on the *ca. re.* he referred his differences to arbitration by bond. And on the 25th October, the arbitrators made an award directing defendant to pay plaintiff £140 forthwith, and one of the grounds of his discharge was that this submission and award put an end to the cause of action on which he had been arrested. On the 10th of November the plaintiff made affidavit for arrest for £140 on this award, and put the *capias* into the sheriff's hands. The prisoner remained in the cells, and was never set at liberty, but was told through the door of his cell that he was discharged from the first process, but held on the other. On the 26th December the Judge's order of 16th December, discharging defendant, was made a rule of Queen's Bench.

ROBINSON, C. J.—There were, in our opinion, such substantial and clear objections to the plaintiff's proceedings after the order for the defendant's discharge from the first arrest, that we cannot do otherwise than allow the order which has been made for his second discharge to stand, and this without expressing any opinion on the sufficiency of the objections to the second affidavit in point of form. The power of arrest given by the law was in this case abused. The court had ordered the prisoner to be discharged, and he was entitled to the immediate benefit of that order as soon as it was made known to the plaintiff's attorney, or to the sheriff: both seems to have combined to defeat all effect of that order. The plaintiff's attorney, while the application was pending, allows his client to make an affidavit grounded on a new cause of action growing out of the award, while he allowed defendant to continue in custody on an action which was virtually at an end by the award, and in this affidavit the client swears that he was apprehensive the defendant was immediately about to depart the province, while he must have known that he was then a close prisoner at his suit, and could not immediately depart. The clear duty of the sheriff on the order for discharge coming to him was to have discharged the party and given him his liberty *bona fide*, and not detained him in illegal custody until another writ could be brought against him (a). The second arrest resting on such grounds, we shall certainly not rescind the order made by the judge in chambers, and as to any objection urged against that order on the ground of delay in the application, that is matter for the consideration of the court or judge when the application is before him, and on all the circumstances of the case. We should not overrule the exercise of the judge's discretion in that respect, except under very particular circumstances.

Rule discharged.

PARKER, DUNBAR & COMPANY v. HENRY C. ROBERTS.

A plaintiff giving time of payment to the defendant by accepting several promissory notes to become due at distant days, may at the same time, as an additional security, take a cognovit for the whole amount of his debt, with power to issue execution thereon at any moment in his discretion.

A verbal agreement, however, entered into between the parties at the time of the cognovit being given, restricting such a power, will be acted upon by the court.

The fact that none of the notes had become due at the time of the cognovit being put in force, will not affect the judgment or execution on such cognovit.

When the plaintiffs are styled in the proceedings taken upon a cognovit in the same manner as they are named in the cognovit itself, the defendant, having recognized the plaintiffs' name in his cognovit, cannot object that the Christian and surname of the plaintiffs have not been used in the proceedings.

This was a motion to set aside the judgment entered in this cause on a cognovit; or the writ of *fieri facias* thereon; or the levy, as being irregular or void, for that the proceedings were against good faith and the terms on which the cognovit was given; or because *the names of the plaintiffs* were not set forth in the proceedings.

The proceedings were entitled "Parker, Dunbar & Company, v. Henry C. "Roberts."

Sullivan for the plaintiff.

Eccles for the defendant.

ROBINSON, C. J.—The defendant applies to set aside this judgment, or at least the execution, on two grounds. First, because the cognovit has been acted upon in a manner contrary to good faith and the understanding of parties; secondly, because the plaintiffs are not designated, as the law and practice require, by their Christian and surnames, and some of them, as it would appear, not named at all.

(a) 4 M. & W. 592.

The first ground was the one mainly relied on; and in support of it, on moving for the rule, it was alleged that the cognovit had been wrongfully altered after its execution, contrary to the express understanding of the parties, and in such a manner as to make its conditions more stringent upon the defendant. This was indeed making a grave imputation upon the attorney who acted for the plaintiffs; and if the charge had been persisted in, and had not been denied in terms as direct and positive as it was made, there could have been no question with us as to the propriety of vacating whatever had been done under the cognovit. But the allegation has been in direct terms repelled, not only by the affidavit of the plaintiff's attorney, but also by the affidavits of two of his clerks who were present when the cognovit was given, and whose statements are circumstantial and positive. The account given by them is confirmed by the entry of the terms of the cognovit, sworn by one of the clerks to have been made by himself in the docket at the time. And, upon reflection, the accusation, without any reference to personal character, appeared to be most improbable on the face of it, because the effect of the cognovit, without that word in it which was alleged to have been added, would have been exactly the same as it is now; and there would, therefore, have been no inducement to an act which would have been so manifestly improper. The defendant's counsel, indeed, abandoned that ground of his motion; but he contended that the taking out execution at the time at which it was done was irregular, as being contrary to an express verbal understanding of the parties; or, at least, contrary to the understanding that must be considered to be implied from the very nature of the transaction. As to any express understanding, the cognovit is a plain confession of debt in the common form, with a consent that judgment may be entered forthwith, and without any restraint or stipulation in regard to execution.

The effect of course is, that execution might issue whenever judgment should be entered. No condition or understanding to the contrary was shewn to have been entered into, either at the time or afterwards, as was the case in Hatton v. Young (a); and admitting that a verbal agreement, if entered into at the time, would be equally acted upon by the court, and relief granted, on motion, to the party, yet we can exercise no such supposition in this case; because the alleged verbal agreement, which the defendant and his attorney swear to on the one side, is as positively denied on oath by three affidavits on the other side, and the court has no discretion to believe what is asserted on one side, in opposition to what is asserted on the other, and thus assume the existence of a verbal understanding which is expressly denied, and which would be in opposition to the language of the writing. But the defendant maintains that, notwithstanding any express agreement or understanding is denied on oath, yet that the cognovit must be taken to have been acted upon illegally, on account of the very nature of the transaction. The defendant, it appears, was a shoemaker by trade, and had become indebted in nearly £300 to the plaintiffs, who are traders residing in a foreign country. His creditors followed him, with the view of enforcing payment of their debt, which was then due, and for which they held two promissory notes of the defendant. They found him carrying on business in Cobourg, having a shop open in his

---

(a) 2 W. Bl. 943.

line of trade; and, as he could not pay, they commenced proceedings under the Bankruptcy Act; but at his solicitation they agreed not to persist in this course, which might have ruined him, but to divide their debt into sixteen equal monthly instalments, and allow him to pay it off thus gradually, taking notes accordingly. This was shewing very liberal indulgence; and certainly it would not be strange or unreasonable if a creditor, voluntarily postponing the receipt of his money in such a manner from kindness to his debtor, and relinquishing proceedings which he had begun, should take care to guard against the possibility of another and perhaps a later creditor stepping in while he was thus waiting, and sweeping off all the debtor's effects; he might, also, naturally resolve to secure himself against the contingency of losing his debt by the fraud or imprudence of his debtor, or by any change of circumstances that might occur while his remedy was suspended. The plaintiffs could not otherwise do this effectually than by taking such a confession of judgment as would authorize a prompt proceeding, and which they might be at liberty to use in their discretion, according to circumstances. Even that would not be a perfect security, because they might be deceived by appearances, and not act as vigilantly as circumstances unknown to them might call for; but without such security the debtor might at any moment, while the first or any of the subsequent notes were yet running, give a preference to some other creditor, or other creditors might gain the preference, and leave these plaintiffs without remedy for a large debt, honestly due, and which they need not have placed in so uncertain a situation. With a view, then, as we must suppose, to what was no more than a reasonable security for the one to exact and the other to grant, this cognovit was taken, giving a right to immediate judgment and execution on the face of it, and which is sworn not to have been executed upon any other understanding. So far from there being anything inconsistent, or out of the way, in such a cognovit taken under such circumstances, I have known it done in other cases, where certainly nothing unjust was contemplated; and I believe it to be a course not at all uncommon among men of business to give time by taking notes payable at future periods, and at the same time to take a confession of debt for security; with power to act upon it without restriction, in case of any change of circumstances.

An attorney losing a large debt of his client's by neglect of such precaution, while he was granting indulgence, would hardly be excused. We cannot, therefore, hold that there is anything manifestly unfair or contrary to good faith in such an arrangement; for it is a reasonable supposition that, if the debtor had not acceded to it, the creditors would have taken promptly such measures as they could for securing themselves, and would have refused the indulgence. That the insisting upon having a judgment, with power to act according to circumstances, was only a prudent precaution, is proved by the event, unless we are to discredit all the statements on the part of the plaintiffs, which we are not at liberty to do; for, according to these, it was not till the debtor had taken very sudden and decisive measures for breaking up his business, and placing himself and his property out of the reach of these creditors, and that, too, with the avowed intention of making the most ungrateful return for their indulgence, that the execution was taken out. The language of the court in 7 Mod. 48, in a case in which, by the very terms of the warrant of attorney itself, the plaintiff was under a restriction which he disregarded, would apply with much force to the present case. There the plaintiff was bound expressly not to sue out execution before the 16th July, but he took out a *fi. fa.* on the 15th June, and put it into the sheriff's hands, though he did not get it executed before the 16th July—his object no doubt being to secure a priority by binding the property in the meantime. Broderick moved to set it aside, for that the plaintiff, by breaking his agreement, had incapacitated the defendant to perform his promise, since he could not sell his property while it was thus bound by the writ. But the court say, "Since it is for a just debt "and judgment executed, we will not now undo anything, for, perhaps, that "would be a means to frustrate the judgment; and, besides, you have no oath "that any purchaser was deterred by reason of taking out and delivering the "writ; and here Reed had a good remedy by action of covenant." And they all said, "The rule was, that where a mischief was on either side, and a remedy "on the one and none on the other, they would suffer that to continue against "which there was a remedy."

There can, of course, be no inflexible rule laid down as to the interposition proper to be exercised in such cases. The court must consider in each what the ends of justice require, on a view of all the circumstances. Here, there is nothing for us to weigh, as regards any charge of fraud or bad faith; because the terms of the cognovit, and the denial on oath of any agreement to the contrary, disable us from interfering on any such ground upon this motion.

With regard to the legal effect of the sixteen small notes for the debt being outstanding, and none of them due when the judgment was entered, that is a fact which cannot, in my opinion, be held to either affect the judgment or execution. Those notes may be assumed to have put an end to the defendant's liability on the two old notes which had been given for the same debt; but they are only connected with the cause of action confessed in the judgment by parol evidence, proving (what is not denied) that they are for the same debt. Whether the notes were signed before the cognovit or afterwards, I am not sure; but the same description of evidence which shews their connection with the debt in the cognovit shews also that the notes were not to be allowed to interfere with any remedy which the plaintiffs might wish to take upon the cognovit and judgment. And, though the statements on that point are conflicting, the only effect of that is, that we cannot change the situation of the parties by preferring one set of affidavits to another, when both are positive.

Upon the question of irregularity in not naming all the plaintiffs in the proceedings, and by their Christian and surnames, as the law requires, it certainly is not competent to the members of a mercantile firm not incorporated to sue by the name of their firm merely, as is done here—"Parker, Dunbar & Com-"pany;" and in a case intended to be contested, the true plaintiffs could not possibly recover in that form; but when the defendant, instead of questioning the right, has voluntarily confessed judgment in favour of persons suing in that form, we ought not (unless bound to do so) to throw upon the plaintiffs the loss of their debt in consequence of an informality not excepted to, but acquiesced in. The case of the Dutch West India Company v. Van Moses (a) is in point against the objection being urged now as ground for setting the judgment aside.

(a) Str. 612; Lord Raym. 1533.

If error would lie for that cause, we should leave the party to that remedy; and if the terms of his confession would prevent his bringing error, that would be a strong reason against giving him the same advantage in another manner. According to the doctrine of the court in the case I have cited, we may intend that there is such a company incorporated, and entitled to sue by the name which the defendant has recognized; or that they have, by their course of dealing, acquired a known name of business by which they may sue and be sued, and which the defendant is estopped from questioning. In a case reported in 1 Salk. 400, when a feme covert, acting as a feme sole, gave a warrant of attorney to confess a judgment, and afterwards moved to set aside the judgment because she was covert, the court would not relieve her, but put her to her writ of error.

We cannot properly, in my opinion, set aside the judgment or execution on this ground or on the other.   Rule refused.

EVANS V. KINGSMILL, SHERIFF OF NIAGARA.

Neither the declaration nor replication in an action of trespass *quare clausum fregit* against a sheriff charged as an injury "*the breaking of the outer door,*" and the plea justifying the trespass under a writ of *fi. fa.*, on grounds sustained at the trial, contained no allegation "*that the outer door was open,*" the plaintiff cannot, because the plea does not contain such allegation, move for judgment *non obstante veredicto.*

Trespass *quare clausum fregit,* for breaking and entering a dwelling house and shop of the plaintiff, making a great noise and disturbance therein; forcing, breaking open, breaking to pieces and damaging doors, to wit, six doors of the plaintiff belonging to the said dwelling house and shop, breaking the locks, hinges, &c., wherewith the same were fastened, and taking divers goods and chattels, &c., of the plaintiff.

The defendant pleaded, first, the general issue.

Secondly, as to the breaking and entering the dwelling house and shop and making a disturbance therein, as alleged in the declaration, the defendant justified as sheriff, entering to levy a *fi. fa.* against the goods of one Dray ats. Sewell, from the Queen's Bench, by virtue of which "he peaceably and quietly "entered" into the said dwelling house and shop, in order to seize and take, and that he did then seize and take, the goods and chattels of Dray in the said dwelling house and shop for the purpose of levying the moneys; and that in so doing he unavoidably remained therein, and made a little noise and disturbance, &c., doing no unnecessary damage, which were the same trespasses in the introductory part of the plea mentioned; and, thirdly, as to the taking the goods in the declaration mentioned, the defendant denied that they were the plaintiff's goods. The plaintiff replied to the second plea, that at the said time when, &c., there were no goods of Dray in the dwelling house or shop, &c.; and that the defendant of his own wrong, *and without such cause as he had alleged,* broke and entered, &c. It was proved at the trial that the defendant entered in the daytime, the door of the shop being open, and seized many goods of the debtor Dray which he found therein. The jury being satisfied that the goods were the goods of Dray (except a stove of the value of thirty shillings) found a verdict for the plaintiff, with thirty shillings damages. The issue on the second plea was found for the defendant. The plaintiff moved for judgment *non obstante veredicto*, on the ground that the second plea was no defence, because it did not contain an allegation that the outer door was open.

ROBINSON, C. J.—Whether these goods were in fact the goods of Dray, or another person who claimed them, was the question at the trial, and the jury were satisfied, and I think on very sufficient evidence, that all that was seized was his, except perhaps a stove of the value of thirty shillings, in respect of which the facts were different. For my own part, I had little doubt at the trial that this stove was his also, but the jury not being clear on that point, properly found for the plaintiff thirty shillings damages, which was hard too in its effect if this motion must prevail, for the sheriff no doubt acted for the best and discreetly; and as to the entry into the freehold, which was the gist of the action, he was clearly justified, as he was also in regard to the goods, with the exception perhaps of the stove, of which he could not tell all the particulars, and might well doubt what the parties told him, who were evidently trying to deceive him and prevent him doing his duty. The justification in the second plea being made out, inasmuch as there were goods of Dray's on the premises, and the defendant therefore rightfully entered, the issue on that plea was found for the defendant and barred the action, there being but one count in the declaration; which was for breaking into the plaintiff's close and taking his goods, and no new assignment. Now, however, the plaintiff moves for judgment *non obstante veredicto*, on the ground that the second plea is no defence, because it does not contain an allegation that the outer door was open. The case of Buckingham v. Francis (a) is cited, but in that case the plaintiff had charged as an injury *the breaking of the outer door;* here no such wrong is complained of. For all that is stated in the declaration, the outer door may have been open. It is proved, indeed, that it was; and the sheriff entered in the daytime. But granting that the plea should nevertheless have concluded the statement that the sheriff entered, the outer door being open, as necessary to the defence, yet the plaintiff raising no exception to the plea, passes by any objection on that head, and rests his defence on the fact which would have constituted the real and only merits of his case, viz., that the debtor had no goods on his premises. That was what the parties went down to try, and the defendant on that point shewed himself entitled to succeed and get a verdict. To give the plaintiff, nevertheless, judgment *non obstante*, because the defendant said nothing about the outer door, when the plaintiff neither in his declaration nor replication had raised a question upon that, and when the evidence shewed that there was in truth no grievance of the kind, would be an entire perversion of the intention of judgment *non obstante*, which is not to give effect to technical objections to pleadings not raised in the proper time, but to enable a plaintiff, by the discretionary interposition of the court, to have the benefit of a recovery which *upon the merits* he is entitled to, notwithstanding he would otherwise be precluded by a defence true in point of fact, but substantially inapplicable in point of law. All that can be said here is, that the plea for the defect alluded to might have been demurred to; whether

---

(a) 11 Moore, 40.

such demurrer must not have been special seems a question, but the plaintiff neither new assigning, nor objecting to the plea, places his defence upon what he knew to be the real merits, and he failed. A judgment *non obstante veridicto*, we are told is always upon the merits, and never granted but in a very clear case (a); and besides, it is to be remarked, that the defendant's plea does aver that he entered peaceably and quietly, which the plaintiff does not deny, but takes issue on the ownership of the goods.

PRICE V. LLOYD.

In an action for use and occupation, the plaintiff proving a *legal title* to the premises, and a mere naked possession by defendant, is entitled to a verdict. He need not go further, and prove an attornment or contract between himself and the defendant.

The plaintiff declared in *indebitatus assumpsit* for the use and occupation of certain premises, and on an account stated. The defendant pleaded the general issue. The plaintiff by his particulars of demand delivered claimed £26 5s. for nine months' rent, at £35 a year, from 1st September, 1844, to 1st June, 1845. The plaintiff had recovered judgment in ejectment for these same premises, in an action against one Cullen, laying the demise on the 1st December, 1844, to hold for seven years. On the trial, the plaintiff recovered a verdict for £8 15s., being for three months' occupation before the day of demise laid in the ejectment. The facts were these:—Price owned the fee. In 1844 he leased to one Armstrong for ten years, which would expire on the 1st September, 1854; Armstrong, while his term was current (having by agreement with Price an option to purchase within the term), demised the estate to Cullen for the whole residue of the ten years, with a like option to purchase; and Cullen, in April, 1845, leased to Lloyd the defendant, for three years, viz., till April, 1848. The plaintiff brought his ejectment, under which Cullen defended as landlord, and the plaintiff recovered possession on the 24th June, 1845. The defendant knew, when he took the lease, the circumstances under which the estate had been held as between Price, Armstrong and Cullen, and when the ejectment was brought, he voluntarily went out of possession. It was objected by Mr. Eccles, the defendant's counsel on the trial of this cause, that the defendant's occupation was not shewn to be by the permission of this plaintiff, that there was no privity between them; but that the defendant was shewn to be holding under Cullen, and no attornment to Armstrong or Price. Leave was given to move for a nonsuit upon these objections.

J. Lukin Robinson for plaintiff.

H. Eccles for defendant.

ROBINSON, C. J.—The case of Birch v. Wright (b), fully supports this action. Mr. Justice Buller in his judgment in that case, maintains that the real question in such actions is whether the plaintiff was landlord, and whether the defendant stood in that situation that he might if he chose consider him as a tenant, which the learned judge held he could not do in regard to any period of his occupation during which he had already treated him as a trespasser.

(a) 2 Smith's Reports, 9; Bac. Abr. Verdict, K. L.   (b) 1 T. R. 378.

There appeared to be no more privity between the plaintiff and the defendant in that case than between the parties in this, nor indeed, I believe, so much, for it was admitted here that the defendant knew all the circumstances of the plaintiff's, Armstrong's and Cullen's respective interests in the premises; while it would seem that in the case of Birch v. Wright, the defendant had not knowledge of the arrangement by which the premises, which he had taken from Bowes, had been transferred to the plaintiff. But Mr. Justice Buller founded his judgment in favour of the plaintiff to recover on these general propositions; which certainly may as well be applied to the case before us. "The plaintiff," he says, "was the landlord of the defendant; he had a clear "legal title which he could support in pleading, either in an action of covenant "or in an avowry; and the tenant was answerable in his action (for use and "occupation), unless he could allege some legal bar in his defence; and which "I think he could only do by shewing payment to the grantor (that is, to the "person who had assigned to the plaintiff Birch) before notice." "The "defendant," Mr. Justice Buller says, "under his first demise, continued "*rightful tenant to some one* till the time when the ejectment was brought; "and now I say that *that some one*, during all the time that the rent accrued, was "the plaintiff; consequently, the plaintiff is entitled to maintain an action for "use and occupation against the defendant for all that is due and unpaid, as "rent, during the time that the plaintiff was landlord, and the defendant had "his premises as his tenant." The plaintiff, in that case, had already brought an action of ejectment against the defendant, and turned him out of possession; but the court held the only consequence of that to be, that for the time covered by the demise in the ejectment he could not recover for use and occupation, because that would be blowing hot and cold—treating him as being a trespasser and a tenant at the same moment; but that though he was equally liable to have been treated as a trespasser for a period antecedent to the demise, yet the landlord might, if he pleased, as to that time, waive the tort, and, treating him as being in by his permission, sue him for use and occupation. Now Birch, in that case, like the plaintiff in this, was no otherwise the landlord of the defendant than that he was real owner of the premises, which the defendant, upon no contract or undertaking with him, had been occupying. No attornment to the plaintiff was necessary since the statute of Anne, and the defendant had notice of the plaintiff's title; though that is immaterial, for he had not paid rent for this period to any other person. The principles laid down in Birch v. Wright, are in accordance with what was held in Doe v. Ballen (a). The case of Cripps v. Blank (b) was cited by the defendant, and it does seem in some measure opposed to the doctrine laid down in Birch v. Wright. The report is not satisfactory, and I confess I do not understand clearly its bearing. Mr. Starkie, in his Treatise on Evidence, as well as Mr. Roscoe, seems to have taken no notice of it; perhaps for the reason that they either doubted its authority, and could not rely upon it as overruling Birch v. Wright, and that class of cases, or because they did not think the note of it satisfactory and consistent. However, it cannot be considered as advisedly determining anything in opposition to Birch v. Wright; for Lord Tenterden is careful to say in his judgment: "I think we are not

---

(a) Cooper, 246. (b) 9 D. & R. 480.

" called upon in this case to decide the great abstract question, whether it is
" competent for the owner of the land to bring an action for use and occupa-
" tion, instead of trespass, against a person who has entered upon the land
" without any communication with the owner of the land." Perhaps the
circumstances of the case took it out of the doctrine which Lord Tenterden
professed to leave untouched, but as they are stated, I do not clearly see that
they do. And Mr. Justice Bayley is reported in the same case to have said,
" Here the defendant did not receive possession from the plaintiff, and there-
" fore the evidence produced could not support use and occupation." I think
his lordship could hardly have meant to lay that down as a principle, for it
would be in opposition to all authority on the subject. In that case it was
proved that the defendant had said to the plaintiff, " I do not consider the
" land as yours, but prove your right and I'll pay you for it." The plaintiff
let him remain a long time in possession after this declaration, and then brought
use and occupation, and proved his title. It may have been considered that
this manifestation of a denial of the plaintiff's right, made it incumbent on
the plaintiff to take other measures at once, and by shewing his right at the
time, to have given the defendant clearly to understand that he treated him
as holding (if he stayed after that) by his permission; for it is held that *assumpsit*
for use and occupation is not a fit action for trying the title. The defendant
there, it also appears, had entered under no one, but had merely gone upon
land that another trespasser, I take it, had abandoned. Here, the landlord
was known by all to be the legal owner of the fee. Armstrong and Cullen had
been tenants for ten years with an option to purchase, and Cullen presuming,
perhaps, on his own intention to act upon this option by buying the land, had
ventured to lease to this defendant for three years, which overlapped the ten
years' term. Then the case is this: the plaintiff has a clear right as landlord;
the defendant knew it, but held possession for a time not covered by the
demise which the plaintiff had granted, and having paid rent to no one else,
and not having been treated by the plaintiff as a trespasser for the period in
question, is now called upon to pay rent to him. I think the principles, that
there is an indirect and implied permission in such a case arising out of the
plaintiff's title, and that the tort may be waived, are not prevented from
applying to this case by anything that has been shewn: and that the plaintiff
has a right to recover.

MACAULAY, J., JONES, J., and MCLEAN, J., concurred.

Rule discharged.

JOHN BELL, SURVIVING PARTNER OF WILLIAM BELL v. FLINTOFT.

There must be four clear days' notice of striking a special jury; therefore, a
notice given after 11 o'clock A. M. on Saturday, to strike a special jury at
11 A. M. on Tuesday, is not sufficient; but in this case, the verdict being for
more than £300, and the defendant not having made any defence, because
the judge at *nisi prius* would not try the cause by a special jury, considering
the notice too late, the court granted a new trial, the defendant having
made a strong affidavit of merits, and the amount of the verdict being
ordered to be paid into court to stand as a security for the plaintiff.

Assumpsit on the common counts. Plea, general issue. Verdict for the
plaintiff, £306 18s. 5d.

Boulton, for the defendant, moved to set aside the verdict for irregularity, the cause having been tried by a common jury, after a special jury had been struck, on grounds disclosed in affidavit filed. It appeared by the affidavit filed, that the notice to strike a special jury was served on the 18th October, a little before noon, on the plaintiff's attorney, to attend at the sheriff's office at 11 o'clock A. M. on Tuesday, the 21st October. It is sworn that the defendant, believing both days to be inclusive by the practice, served the notice accordingly, which the plaintiff's attorney retained, giving no notice of any objection, though he did not attend at the striking. The special jury attended, but the sufficiency being objected to, the learned judge directed the cause to be tried by a common jury; and the defendant's counsel believing, as he swore, that this was irregular, though he considered that he had a good defence on the merits, did not enter upon his defence, having been instructed by the defendant that he had particular reasons for desiring a special jury.

The Attorney-General shewed cause.

ROBINSON, C. J.—We are of opinion that a notice served after 11 o'clock A. M. on Saturday, to attend at the striking of a special jury at 11 o'clock on Tuesday, is not sufficient; and the jury therefore was irregularly struck, and the plaintiff was entitled to have his cause tried by a common jury. The question then is, whether he should, as a matter of indulgence, be allowed a new trial on paying costs, as he abstained from entering into his defence at the last trial, insisting upon his right to have the special jury, and under the advice, as it seems, of his counsel. The amount in dispute exceeds £300. The defendant swears, in very positive terms, to merits; and though upon the evidence which the plaintiff produced at the trial, and on the affidavit filed in answer to this application, the plaintiff's right to recover would seem hardly capable of being resisted, yet we are unwilling to hold him concluded by the verdict under the circumstances, but we must take care that the plaintiff runs no risk of losing his debt from our interposition. We will grant a new trial on the condition that the defendant pays the amount of the last verdict into the court, or secures it to the satisfaction of the Master, by the first of April next. A similar course was taken in the case of Farren et al. v. Richards et al. (*a*), under circumstances nearly the same.

PRACTICE COURT.
EASTER TERM, 9 VICTORIA.

Before Mr. Justice Hagerman.

IN THE MATTER OF AWARD, CAYLEY AND MCMULLEN.

Where arbitrators disagree on some of the items of account referred to them, and during the investigation call in an umpire to give his opinion on *such items*, and subsequently adopt that opinion as their own, it is not necessary that the umpire should sign the award.

Application was made on behalf of Cayley, by Mr. *J. Lukin Robinson*, to set aside the award of the arbitrators on several grounds, but the only one relied on in argument was, that the arbitrators in the course of the investigation called in an umpire, to whom they referred several points upon which they could not agree, and that having obtained his decision on these points, they adopted it as their own judgment, and made their award accordingly, the umpire not joining in it.

Mr. *Duggan* shewed cause.

HAGERMAN, J.—It is contended that the award so conducted and made is not the award of the arbitrators but of the umpire, who ought to have been a party to it; and that it should therefore be declared void. There is no affidavit that the award made by the arbitrators was unjust, or that they acted correctly; and it was further sworn by McMullen that, in pursuance of one part of the award, he surrendered up to Cayley a lease he held from him of a wharf and store in this city, and that there has therefore been a partial performance of the award and acceptance of it by Cayley.

Beekman (one of the arbitrators), in an affidavit made by him on the 14th November last, when the rule to shew cause was moved and obtained, states that Peter Paterson was appointed umpire, under the submission; that he was present during the examination of witnesses by the arbitrators; that he (Beekman) and the other arbitrator (McDonell) differed upon several items of count in controversy between Cayley and McMullen; and that upon such difference and disagreement they referred the contested points to Paterson, and abided by his decision; that such decision of Paterson was taken by the arbitrators as their decision, and they awarded accordingly. Paterson himself swears that he was appointed umpire by Beekman and, as he understood, with the consent of McDonell, the other arbitrator; that he was present as umpire during the investigation; that the arbitration was conducted by Beekman and McDonell in the following manner : the accounts between the parties were gone through item by item; that upon most of them the arbitrators agreed ; and that although he gave his opinion occasionally, but only when the arbitrators disagreed, which was the case three or four times, when the item in dispute was referred to him as umpire, and decided on by him, which decision the arbitrators adopted and made part of their award.

In answer to these statements, a second affidavit of Beekman, made on the 10th February, is put in and read by McMullen's counsel (Mr. Duggan) on shewing cause to the rule granted. In this affidavit he states that the suggestions of Paterson were in no instance adopted by himself and co-arbitrator unless they were considered just to the parties ; that he believes the award to be just ; that the award made is that of himself and his co-arbitrator, and that Paterson had nothing to do with the making of it, except being consulted on some points, as mentioned ; and that he did not intend to convey any other meaning in his affidavit of the 14th November.

McDonell (the other arbitrator) makes a similar affidavit, although in terms somewhat stronger than those used by Beekman. He says the award was made solely by him and Beekman ; that it was intended that Paterson should be umpire if he and Beekman could not agree ; that they had some conversation with Paterson on some items, but that he and Beekman did fully and entirely agree to the determination and award made ; that in consequence, Paterson was not called upon to make any award ; that as a business man, his opinion was asked on some points, which, after consideration, were adopted by him and Beekman, not because they were the opinion of Paterson, but because they considered them right ; and that the award was made after a full consideration of all the evidence between the parties. I think that upon these affidavits I cannot disturb this award, putting out of view the further answer that the award has been acquiesced in and partly performed.

The case cited by Mr. Robinson (a) does not sustain his motion. There the arbitrators chose an umpire to decide between *them*, not between the parties in controversy, and then made their award on the matters upon which they agreed, and the umpire made a *second* award upon the residue of the subjects in dispute. It was, of course, held by the court that either the arbitrators or the umpire should decide upon the whole controversy, and that separate awards could not be made. The course adopted by the arbitrators here was such as to enable them to determine satisfactorily upon all the questions submitted, and they declare on oath that the award they made was the result of a full investigation and careful consideration of the claims of the respective parties. Rule discharged.

THE QUEEN V. JARVIS.

The sheriff cannot be served with a rule to return a writ until the return day has passed. When an attachment has been issued on such an irregular rule, the proper course is to move to set aside the attachment, and not the irregular rule upon which the attachment has been founded.

Crooks moved to set aside the attachment issued for irregularity. The rule to return the *fi. fa.* had been taken out and sued prior to the return of the writ.

Duggan shewed cause, contending 1st, that a rule to return a writ might be taken out and served as had been done in this case ; and 2ndly, that at all

---

(a) 9th Price, 612.

events the rule was not void, but at most irregular; and that the motion should have been to set it aside in the first instance, and then the attachment.

HAGERMAN, J.—The attachment is founded on a supposed contempt of the sheriff; that officer was not in contempt until he had disobeyed an order of the court regularly made and served. The rule issued in this cause was irregular, if not void, having been taken out and served before the return of the *fi. fa.;* and the motion to set aside the attachment is therefore the proper motion. The King v. The Sheriff of Cornwall (a), The King v. The Sheriff of London (b), and Hutchings v. Hurd (c), are all authorities on this point. Upon referring to the rule, it appears it issued on the 29th January, and was served on the same day; it commands the sheriff to return the writ of *fi. fa. within* four days after notice of the rule; the first day of term was the 2nd of February, which was the fifth day after service; the fourth day would be Sunday, and if the words of the rule be strictly interpreted, it requires the return of the writ on the third day after service, which would be before the return day of the writ.

DOE EX DEM. MCLEAN v. MCDONALD.

The plaintiff accepting a plea, and giving notice of trial, cannot afterwards object that an appearance has not been entered by the defendant.

A motion was made to set aside the *rule for judgment* as in case of nonsuit, granted in Michaelmas Term, 8th Vic., on the ground that the defendant was styled therein "*McDonell,*" instead of "*McDonald,*" having entered into the consent rule and pleaded by the latter name; and because no common bail was ever entered or filed.

In answer to this rule it was sworn in affidavits filed, that in the declaration the defendant's name is in one place spelt *McDonell,* in another *McDonald;* and that in the notice to appear he is called *McDonell;* and that these different spellings are in the handwriting of the attorney for the plaintiff. It is further sworn, that in the notice of trial served the defendant is called *McDonell.* With respect to the second point, a clerk in the crown office swears that he finds by an entry in a book kept there, that on the 26th June, 1843, the agent of the plaintiff's attorney filed consent, appearance and plea for the defendant by the name of *McDonell,* and paid for the same; and that he has no doubt such appearance was then entered.

HAGERMAN, J.—I am of opinion, that upon those affidavits this rule must be discharged; without saying that McDonald and McDonell are not distinct names, or that they are (from the manner in which they are spelt) *idem sonans,* most persons must be aware that those names, so familiar to us, are in common conversation usually pronounced alike; but independently of this, the plaintiff has himself shewn, that he regarded the right spelling as a matter of indifference. It is not stated by which of the names the judgment was entered; all that is complained of is, that the *rule* for judgment was taken out in a wrong name.

(a) 1 T. R. 552.   (b) 2 East. 240.   (c) 5 T. R. 479.

With respect to the second point, independently of the affidavit of the clerk, that he has no doubt, from the facts he states, that an appearance was entered, I think the plaintiff cannot object, at this late period, to the want of an appearance, and it is certain he considered the defendant had done all that was necessary to entitle him to defend the action. The usual consent rule was entered into, and the plaintiff accepted a plea, and having joined issue, gave notice of trial; all previous irregularities (if there were any) were in consequence waived.

Rule discharged, with costs.

DOE EX HUNTER ET AL. V. ROE.

The service of a declaration in ejectment on the son of a tenant on the premises, will not be allowed, unless it be shewn by affidavit that before the first day of term the tenant had knowledge of such service.

It was moved that the service of declaration should be allowed, upon an affidavit that service was made on the son of the tenant, about fifteen years of age, on the premises, on the Saturday preceding the first day of term, which was on the following Monday.

HAGERMAN, J.—There is no proof that the service of the declaration came to the knowledge of the tenant before the first day of term, and therefore it cannot be allowed (*a*).

DOE FLANDERS ET AL. V. ROE.

Where a party fails in his first action of ejectment, and then brings a second, the defendant cannot apply for the payment of costs of first action till he has entered his appearance.

Application was made to stay proceedings until costs of a former action, brought in respect of the same premises, and upon the same title, were paid. Upon return of the summons it was objected that the application was premature, having been made before appearance entered.

HAGERMAN, J.—Mr. Sergeant Adams, in his Treatise on Ejectment, 2nd Edition, p. 320, says, that a motion of this kind may be made even before appearance; but Mr. Justice Coleridge, in Doe Crocket v. Roe, 1 H. & W. 351, ruled otherwise, and this decision is adopted in late books of practice; Chitty's Archbold, Vol. II., p. 993, 7th Ed. The reason assigned is, that the defendant Roe being a fictitious person, the party purposing to defend has no interest in the suit until he has appeared (*b*).

Summons discharged.

PRICE V. BROWN.

In an application for judgment as in case of a nonsuit, for not proceeding to trial pursuant to notice, the affidavit on which such motion is made must shew that issue had been joined; or the record must be produced to shew that the *similiter* had been added by the officer of the court.

Vankoughnet moved for judgment as in case of nonsuit, for not proceeding to trial pursuant to notice.

Crawford, contra, objected to the sufficiency of the affidavit.

(*a*) Chitty's Archbold, 739, and cases there cited.   (*b*) Doe Mudd. v. Roe, 8 Dow. 444.

HAGERMAN, J.—The affidavit on which this motion is made is defective; it contains no statement that issue has been joined; and no record or papers are produced (a). In addition to this objection, an affidavit has been put in, stating that it does not appear, by the papers filed, that a *similiter* has been added to one of the defendant's pleas. By the New Rules of Court, under the head "Practice in Pleading," page 19, it is ordered that it shall not be necessary to furnish issue books or paper books in any case; and in all special pleadings, where the plaintiff takes issue on the defendant's pleading, "the plaintiff may proceed as if the cause were at issue, and *the clerk shall* enter the *similiter* as of course." As this is a direction to the officer of the court, it may be a question whether it be not sufficient for him to enter the *similiter* on the record, without any addition to the plea filed; and being directed to do this, whether it is not to be assumed that it was done, until the contrary appeared. My impression is that upon a motion for judgment as in case of a nonsuit, it would be sufficient to shew that the *similiter* was added in the record; but this must be done either by affidavit or producing the record (b).

IN MATTER OF COMPLAINT, RAINVILLE V. POWELL, A WITNESS MAKING DEFAULT.

When a witness is subpœnaed to attend the assize *on a particular day*, and not from *day to day*, he cannot be attached for disobedience to subpœna, if he was present on that day, but went away afterwards.

In this case a rule *nisi* was taken out, to attach the defendant for making default as a witness served with a subpœna to attend on a particular day.

HAGERMAN, J.—I think I ought to discharge this rule for an attachment, but without costs. The subpœna requires the witness to appear on a particular day of the assizes; and it also states that the cause in which he was required to give evidence would be tried on that day. He did appear on that day, and was present in court the following day also, but the cause did not come on, and he went away; the trial would have taken place the day he left, but being absent, and a material witness, the record was withdrawn. If the plaintiff wished to secure the attendance of the witness from day to day during the assizes, he should have so summoned him; and if commanded to appear on a particular day, he did so. It appears by the judgment of Mr. Justice Pattison, 9 Dow. 179, that he is not liable to be attached for disobedience of the subpœna. I think also, it is at least very doubtful whether the sum paid the witness can reasonably be considered as covering his expenses beyond the first day of the assizes; he swears he resides upwards of fifty miles from the assize town, and that he received thirty shillings. Now calculating, as is usual in taxes here, five shillings a day, and twenty miles travel as a day, the thirty shillings would extend no further than the first day of the assizes. No attachment is ever granted unless the witness has been paid or offered his reasonable, by which I

(a) See Chitty's General Practice, Vol. III. p. 786, and the cases there cited.
(b) Chitty's Archbd. 1075, and note a, and cases there cited; Corbyn v. Heyworth, 5 Scott, 335; 6 Dow. 181; Smith v. Rigby, 3 Dow. 705.

infer (at the least) his taxable, expenses. Still he ought, in fairness, to have demanded a further sum before going away from the court; and therefore I discharge this rule without costs.

PLAYTER V. CAMERON.

Qu.—Has not a party eight days to reply to *amended pleas?*

Brooks moved to set aside the judgment of *non pros.* for irregularity on several grounds.

HAGERMAN, J.—This judgment must be set aside. The amended plea was delivered, and replication demanded on the 28th January, and judgment signed on the 31st. Now, if the 5th rule of court, which directs that no judgment of *non pros.* shall be signed for want of a declaration, replication, &c., until *eight* days next after a demand thereof, does not apply to amended pleadings, still, according to the old practice, the plaintiff had until the fifth day after service of rule or demand to declare in reply, whereas this judgment was signed on the fourth day (a). I do not know what the opinion of the court might be on the question, but I incline to think that a party has, under our rule, eight days to reply to amended pleas, as well as to those first delivered.

Rule discharged, with costs.

QUEEN'S BENCH.
EASTER TERM, 9 VICTORIA.

CROUKHITE V. SOMMERVILE.

Under the statute 1 Vic. chap. 21, it is illegal in a magistrate to cause the arrest of a party *in the first instance;* he must be first *summoned* before him.

In the notice of the causes of action required to be served upon a magistrate, the place where the plaintiff was imprisoned must be correctly stated; the fact that the injury complained of took place in the same district, though not at the exact place named in the notice, will not make the variance less fatal.

Action of trespass and false imprisonment.

First count, for an assault and false imprisonment in the township of Whitby, detaining the plaintiff six hours, on 25th March, 1845.

In the second count the plaintiff complains of an assault in the township of Pickering, on the 26th April, 1845, and an illegal detention there for six hours.

(a) Tidd's Prac., 9th Ed., p. 676.

The defendant, being sued as a justice of the peace, pleads the general issue by statute.

The notice required by the statute charged the grounds of action to be, for that the defendant, on the 25th March, 1845, caused an assault to be made on *the plaintiff, at the township of Whitby*, and caused him to be apprehended and forced to go through the public streets to the defendant's office in the township of Whitby, and to be detained there for six hours. And also, for that the defendant, on the 26th April, 1845, caused an assault to be made on the plaintiff in the township of *Pickering*, and to be imprisoned *there for six days*. No sum is stated in the notice as being claimed by the plaintiff for his damages. The plaintiff, it appeared, was charged before the defendant by the pathmaster of the division in which he was then resident, with having failed to perform his statute labour, and was convicted under statute 1 Vic. chap. 21, sec. 20. A warrant was issued against his goods, and was returned *nulla bona;* whereupon the defendant issued a warrant against his body, and a constable arrested the plaintiff upon it' in Pickering, and took him to the defendant's house in Whitby, where he was tried and convicted. On the 26th April, 1845, the constable arrested the plaintiff in Whitby on the warrant of commitment which followed the conviction, and carried him through Pickering to Toronto, where he was lodged in gaol, and continued there for six days.

Crooks, counsel for the plaintiff.

Hagarty, counsel for the defendant.

ROBINSON, C. J.—The plaintiff's alleged grievance was, that he had in fact performed his statute labour for the year in another division, from which he had recently removed, and that he was improperly convicted, although he gave proof of that to the defendant. The learned judge, however, could not allow the conviction to be impeached on this ground at the trial.

It was then contended that the defendant was liable as a trespasser on several grounds:

1st. Because he had caused the plaintiff to be arrested in the first instance to answer to the complaint, instead of being merely summoned, as the law requires.

2ndly. Because the defendant made the warrant to commit him after conviction, without reciting in it more than that he had not paid the fine, and without shewing on the face of the warrant that process had issued against the plaintiff's goods, and had been duly returned. In fact there had been a warrant against the goods issued, and returned *nulla bona*, before the warrant against the person was made; so that all was in that respect regularly done, though it was not made to appear in the warrant upon which the plaintiff was committed. To remedy this, if it could be done, the defendant, long afterwards, and just before the trial, made out a proper warrant, and sealed it as of the same date in which the other was dated; but the plaintiff was not in fact in custody on any other than the first warrant.

The defendant contended at the trial that the plaintiff must at any rate fail:

1. Because the notice of action was defective, in not stating any amount of damages claimed.

2ndly. That it did not charge any imprisonment at Toronto, and therefore the plaintiff could not legally give evidence of imprisonment there.

3rdly. That the imprisonment for which alone the plaintiff could recover, was that which took place upon the final commitment; that the only part of the notice under which the plaintiff could endeavour to bring that grievance states the arrest and imprisonment to have been at Pickering; whereas upon that warrant the plaintiff was arrested at Whitby, and brought through Pickering to Toronto, where he was actually imprisoned for six days.

4thly. He contends that it is not material that the writ against goods, and return, were not recited in the last writ, since it was shewn to be the fact that such process did issue and was returned.

This is one of those cases in which a magistrate, probably intending nothing wrong, has exposed himself to an action, either from mistaking the extent of his authority, or from not being aware of the strict regularity required in the proceedings in cases of summary convictions. Where there has been a malicious design in the magistrate to use his powers oppressively, there can be no just reason why the law should afford him protection against the consequences which ought to follow such deliberate misconduct ; but I confess it does seem to be a hard measure of justice, by which judges in inferior jurisdictions are occasionally made to pay a severe penalty for mere errors, which, if they had been committed in tribunals of a higher order, would have entailed no such consequences upon those committing them. The privilege which is in any case extended to the judicial office, would seem to be more reasonably due in those quarters where the least degree of skill and legal knowledge is to be looked for. The legislature has indeed not left justices of the peace without protection, to a very considerable extent; and considering the difficulties which embarrass them, even in their best endeavours to apply correctly the ever varying provisions of a multitude of statutes, I conceive it to be the duty of this court to take care, that in all cases brought before them they shall have the full benefit of that protection to which the law entitles them. Now in the case before us, the defendant, a justice of the peace, in proceeding to enforce the provision of the statute 1 Vic. ch. 21, sec. 27, against the plaintiff, who was charged with neglecting to perform his statute labour on the highways, fell into the error of issuing a warrant to apprehend the party complained of, in the first instance, instead of merely summoning him to answer. There is nothing in that statute to authorize that mode of proceeding, and it is contrary to law, except in those cases where it is permitted by express provision, as in some statutes it is. The general course is, to summon the party to answer the complaint ; and our statute 2 Will. IV. ch. 4, which regards summary convictions generally, is in accordance with this understood course.

There was, then, an illegal arrest of this plaintiff when he was arrested in the township of Pickering, by the defendant's authority, and brought before him in Whitby to answer the complaint, and for the five hours that he was then in custody, he would be entitled to some damages ; though a jury might think fit to give but trifling damages, if they believed it to be a mere error, and the arrest was attended with no circumstances of aggravation.

The notice of action, as it regards this cause of action, was not correct ; for it states the arrest to have been made in Whitby, and not in Pickering, as the fact was; but as the plaintiff was taken immediately to the defendant's office in Whitby, he was for a short time illegally in custody there; and the injury comes, as we think, under the terms of the notice as it regards what is stated to have been done on the 25th March, 1845; the assault and imprisonment being, in contemplation of law, one continued act.

But the substantial injury for which the plaintiff claimed damages, was that stated as an independent cause of action in the same notice, and laid as having taken place on the 26th April, 1845; this is described as an assault made by the defendant on the plaintiff, in the *township of Pickering*, and causing him to be imprisoned *there*, for *six days;* the fact which the plaintiff proved as the ground of this complaint was, the arresting him in the township of Whitby, not of Pickering, after his conviction upon a warrant or execution against his body, for default of payment of the fine imposed, by distress or otherwise; and the bringing him under that warrant to Toronto, and imprisoning him in the common gaol there for *six days*. Supposing that to have been illegal, as it is contended it was on several grounds, it was a substantial cause of complaint, certainly, and was so treated by the jury, for they gave £25 damages on account of it; but it was objected at the trial, and we think rightly, that evidence of that cause of action could not properly be received, because it was not complained of in the notice. Complaint of an illegal arrest and imprisonment for six days in the township of Pickering, is a very different thing from an imprisonment in the common gaol at Toronto.

It is true that both are within the same district, and would therefore have been always held to be sufficiently identical, if the question had related to the mere formal statement of a venue; but the object of the notice is, to apprise the justice of the precise injury complained of, so that he may be governed by it in tendering amends, or in preparing for his defence.

We have held in case of Madden v. Shewell, following the authority of Martin v. Upsher, 3 Q. B. Rep. 66, that it is indispensable to state in such notices the place where the jury was committed: and if this be necessary, then it must follow that the place should be correctly stated, otherwise it might have the effect of misleading the party. The authority of Martin v. Upsher, has been recognized in England in the more recent case of Breece v. Jordan (a).

As evidence of the imprisonment in Toronto was improperly received, and as that was the injury for which damages were given, we are of opinion that there should be a new trial without costs, unless the plaintiff will consent to a verdict being entered for nominal damages.

MACAULAY, J., JONES, J., and McLEAN, J., concurred.

Rule absolute.

(a) 4 Q. B. Rep. 585; 2 G. & D. 720; 13 M. & W. 361; 14 M. & W. 381.

DECATUR V. JARVIS, SHERIFF, &C.

Where an execution creditor has placed his writ of *fi. fa.* in the sheriff's hands, and afterwards, and before any actual seizure by the sheriff under the *fi. fa.*, and before the return day of the writ, the goods of the debtor are seized under a commission of bankruptcy, and *nulla bona* returned to the *fi. fa.*, the sheriff is liable on such return, to an action at the suit of the execution creditor.

A. McLean moved for a new trial. Decatur had obtained judgment and execution against the goods of Messrs. Goessman and Henderson, insolvents, and on the 23rd June, 1845, he placed the execution in the sheriff's hands, returnable in the following term (August). When the sheriff went to levy on the writ, he was told that the goods had been all assigned to certain creditors of the defendants, in trust, for the satisfaction of all the creditors who would sign the deed of assignment, by which they were to agree to accept a certain composition upon the amount of their debts. This deed, which professed to assign everything, household furniture, &c., was only signed by Goessman and Henderson themselves—neither trustees nor creditors had executed it. The sheriff, however, without (so far as appeared) apprising the plaintiff of this assignment, which was set up, and giving him an opportunity to exercise his judgment upon it, forbore in consequence of it to do anything under the writ; a few days afterwards, Goessman and Henderson became bankrupts, and on 3rd July, the *fi. fa.* being still current, a commission of bankruptcy was put in the sheriff's hands. Then one of the trustees named in the assignment who was also a creditor, requested of the sheriff to seize all the goods under the commission, as being still the goods of the bankrupts, preferring to relinquish all claims under the assignment; the sheriff did as he was requested. and afterwards returned *nulla bona* on this plaintiff's writ. The assignment had been made on 7th April, 1845, but Goessman and Henderson continued on the premises, selling the goods as before, and were bartering some of them with one of the trustees for other goods. The trustee, who had acted in some degree under the assignment, swore, that having found many false entries in the books, and one of the parties having absconded, giving no security as he had promised for paying the rate per pound at which they had compounded, he thought it better to abandon the assignment and place the estate in bankruptcy,

J. H. Cameron shewed cause.

ROBINSON, C. J.—I told the jury that I thought they could hardly treat the assignment, imperfect as it was, and attended with such circumstances, as a valid sale to put the goods out of the reach of the execution creditor, but that at any rate, when the parties to whom the goods had been pretended to be assigned, agreed to consider the assignment as not existing (no re-assignment having been made,) that the sheriff should have remembered, when he agreed to act as if no such assignment had been made, that he had had all the time in his hands this plaintiff's *fi. fa.*, which was entitled to be satisfied if the goods were really the property of Goessman and Henderson, while it was current, and before the commission of bankruptcy came to him. His return of *nulla bona* amounted to a declaration, that after that writ came to his hands, and while it was current, the debtors had no goods on which he could levy ;

but this was not the case, if the goods (as he consented to consider them), were till the commission came to him, the goods of the debtor.

I thought that the sheriff, having seized the goods under the commission, amounted to an admission on his part, that they were the goods of Goessman and Henderson all the time, for they had never been re-transferred. The jury found for the plaintiff £65 10s. 11d., the amount to be levied on the writ. I see no ground for a new trial.

The case of Cooper v. Chitty, 1 Bur. 20, and another case in the same volume, have been cited by the defendant's counsel, for the purpose of establishing, that as the sheriff did not make his return to the *fi. fa.* until after he had seized under the commission, which was entitled to attach on the goods as there had been no seizure under the writ, his return was true when it was made, and not false, and therefore he is not liable. But those cases have no application to a case like this. There the sheriff had seized goods under a *fi. fa.*, but before he sold them a commission of bankruptcy came, and as the law then stood, the right of property was affected retrospectively from the time of the act of bankruptcy; and the court held, that as the sheriff could not foresee the issuing of a commission, and had rightly seized at the time, yet that he was justified by what afterwards happened in forbearing to sell, and could properly return *nulla bona;* for that return would become the true return in consequence of the bankruptcy, though there had been goods at one time liable to the writ.

There are more modern cases, proceeding on the same principle; Brydges v. Walford (a), Clutterbuck v. Jones (b). It is true, that the usual return of *nulla bona* is, that the party *hath* not any goods or chattels whereof the sheriff can make the debt, &c.; that is, that he hath not goods at the time of his return being made, which is supposed to be at the return day of the writ; and in this case the fact was so, because the sheriff had suffered the commission of bankruptcy to attach, in consequence of his not having seized between the 23rd June and 3rd July. But so, also, if there had been no bankruptcy, and he had allowed the debtor to sell all the goods (as they did many of them); it might have been equally true, that they had no goods at the return of the writ. The grievance in all such cases is, that the party had goods which the sheriff might have seized; that he did not seize them, but falsely and deceitfully returned that the debtor had no goods, which implies that he had no means of levying under the writ.

MACAULAY, J., JONES, J., and McLEAN, J., concurred.

Rule refused.

DOE DEM. WOOD ET AL. V. FOX ET AL.

Where the granting part of a deed of assignment transfers the *indenture* simply and the *habendum* the *estate in the indenture,* the estate passes under the assignment.

On the 14th March, 1840, the defendants, Fox and his wife, made a mortgage of the premises in fee to Ralph M. Clement, to secure an unpaid portion of the purchase-money, upon a sale of the land from Clement to Fox. This mortgage contained, as is usual, a precise description of the estate mortgaged.

(a) 6 M. & S. 43.   (b) 15 E. R. 78.

On the 31st of August, 1842, Clement assigned this mortgage to the lessors of the plaintiff, by an instrument under seal, on a separate paper, which is annexed to the mortgage, and which is in these terms: "For and in considera-"tion of £315, to me paid, I, Ralph M. Clement, of, &c., do hereby grant, "bargain, sell, assign, and set over unto Ross, Wyman, Wood, &c., a certain "indenture of mortgage, executed by George Fox, of, &c., yeoman, bearing "date the 14th day of March, 1840, to the said Ralph M. Clement, on certain "lands in the township of Saltfleet, aforesaid, together with the bond therein "referred to, and which said mortgage is recorded in Liber II, on page 251 ; "memorial No. 88, in the office of the registrar of the county of Wentworth ; "to have and to hold the said bond and mortgage, and the debt thereby "secured, and all the interest thereby conveyed by the mortgage in and to the "lands therein described to the said Ross, Wyman, Wood, &c., their heirs, "&c., for them and their use and benefit."

It was objected at the trial that no interest in the land passed by this assignment.

A verdict was given for the plaintiffs, with leave to the defendant to move for a nonsuit on that ground.

Jones, counsel for defendant, moved accordingly.

Vankoughnet, contra.

ROBINSON, C. J., delivered the judgment of the court.—We think the land clearly passes. If the premises granted Lot A., and the *habendum* was of Lot *A. & B.*, that would not pass B., because that would be a simple addition to the granting part, not an explanation or qualification of it ; but this is different (a). We must look at all parts of a deed, to see what was intended *by each;* and the *habendum* here shews, that when Clement granted the mortgage he meant the estate mortgaged : there is no repugnancy.

Rule refused.

IN RE DUNCAN MCNAB, LANDLORD, AND NATHANIEL DUNLOP AND LUCRETIA MCKEEVER.

The 53rd and other clauses of the statute 4 Will. IV. ch. 1, giving a summary remedy against overholding tenants, apply only to the cases of tenants whose terms have expired by lapse of time, not to those who by alleged breaches of covenant have forfeited their terms.

An application was made for McNab, as landlord, under the 53rd and following clauses of our statute 4 Will. IV. ch. 1, for a writ, in order to dispossess Dunlop and McKeever, as overholding tenants.

The term was created by one Power, from whom McNab derives title, by lease dated 1st of August, 1845, to hold for three years, and so has not expired ; but under a clause in the lease the landlord has a right to re-enter, and the lease becomes void, if any part of the rent shall be in arrear for twenty-one days. The landlord has made affidavit, that a quarter's rent being due, and remaining twenty-one days unpaid, he entered on the premises, and demanded payment ; and the default continuing, he has served the tenants with a written notice under the statute, calling upon them to give up possession.

(a) Shep. Touch., 75; Cruise's Digest, Vol. IV., pp. 434-5, secs. 55, 64.

ROBINSON, C. J., delivered the judgment of the court.—We are clear that the provisions of this statute are only applicable to the cases of tenants whose terms have expired by lapse of time; and that a landlord, claiming a right to possession upon an alleged forfeiture of the term, cannot avail himself of this proceeding. It is not reasonable to suppose that the legislature intended cases of forfeiture to be thus summarily dealt with; and clearly the preamble to this part of the Act, and the enactments themselves, can be applied only to tenants whose terms *have expired*, not to those whose terms may have been otherwise determined.   Writ refused.

BANK OF MONTREAL V. DENISON.

The notice of motion to set aside a writ of trial under the 54th clause of 8 Vic. ch. 13, must specify the day on which the party will apply.

A motion to set aside *proceedings under a writ of trial* in the District Court, where the irregularity is in the writ itself, and not in the subsequent proceedings, is bad.

Under the statute 8 Vic. ch. 13, secs. 51-55, this was taken down to be tried in the Home District Court, in April, 1846.

The defendant was sued as maker of a promissory note for £78 10s., to H. G. Bernard, or order.

He pleaded that Bernard did not endorse and deliver the said promissory note to the plaintiffs, and that the plaintiffs were not at the commencement of the action the holders or endorsers of the said promissory note ("and that he "the defendant did not become liable to pay the amount of the said promis- "sory note") to the plaintiffs, according to the tenor and effect thereof, as in the said declaration is alleged, &c.

In transcribing the pleadings into the writ of trial, the words in the parenthesis were omitted.

On the 9th April, 1846, (being within six days after the verdict was rendered in the District Court,) the defendant gave notice under the 55th clause of the Act, that he would apply to this court, or a judge thereof, to *set aside the writ of trial and all the proceedings under it.*

On the 17th April the defendant obtained a judge's summons, from a judge of this court, calling upon the plaintiffs to shew cause, in the next (Easter) Term, why all the *proceedings had upon the writ of trial* should not be set aside, and a new trial had between the parties for irregularity, the writ of trial not comprising the issue as joined between the parties and on grounds disclosed on papers filed. Moved without costs.

Crawford, counsel for plaintiffs.

Denison, counsel for defendant.

ROBINSON, C. J.—The ground shewn for this rule, besides the alleged irregularity, was, that the plaintiffs had taken the cause to trial on the second day of the court, while the defendant was absent, and in consequence no defence was made; though the plaintiffs were themselves not ready on the first day of court, when the cause stood first in the list, and the defendant was in attendance and urged its being called on.

The defence intended to have been set up was, that this note, having been merely left in the Bank of Montreal, for collection, was improperly sued in the name of the bank, as endorsers of Bernard, the payee, the property of the note being still in Bernard, notwithstanding he had endorsed the note in blank.

But this allegation is now met by affidavits filed on the other side, shewing that Bernard is concurring in the action being brought in the name of the bank, having left the note there in order that the proceeds when collected might be placed to his credit at the bank. The defence has really no merit, and ought not to have defeated the plaintiff's recovery if it had been made at the trial. It could be of no consequence to the defendant, for anything shewn to us, whether he pays the note to these plaintiffs or to Bernard. It is very common for persons to whom notes have been endorsed, under such circumstances, to sue on them as endorsees. As to the variance in transcribing the pleadings, it is a mere clerical error, not altering the sense or effect of the plea; and it must not be supposed that for any mistake of this kind all the proceedings in a cause carried down as this has been must necessarily be set aside. If it were so, the facility given by the Act, for the purpose of avoiding delay and expense, would lead in many cases to an increase of both. And besides, the rule obtained is not to set aside the writ itself in which the error exists, but the proceedings under it, which are regular.

If the irregularity was intended to be relied on, it has been waived, by moving, not against the writ, but against the subsequent proceedings. The rule therefore should, I think, be discharged; and I should have considered that it would be right to discharge it with costs, but the affidavits, I think, do charge on the one side, and leave unrepelled on the other, a taking the defendant by surprise in the way in which the cause was brought on, after the manner in which it had been *allowed to stand over the preceding day.*

As to the proper mode of proceeding in such applications under the 55th clause of 8 Vic. ch. 13, the notice, it seems to me, is merely intended to prevent the entry of the judgment until after the eight days were out; and when the party who failed at the trial goes before a judge to move against the proceedings, he is in the same situation as if he were moving in court for a rule *nisi* after a verdict. He is heard *ex parte*, as is usual in applications for new trials; and if, upon what he shews, the judge thinks there is ground for interposing, then upon his order a fiat is allowed to issue, which is to be afterwards disposed of as other rules *nisi* granted by the court. The legislature did not think it right to allow the delay till next term, as a matter of course, by merely giving a notice to the party; but required that he should at least make out to the satisfaction of a judge a *prima facie* ground for interposing. I do not consider that they meant to exact more—to have in effect two rules *nisi*, by obliging the party to obtain a judge's summons to shew cause against a rule to shew cause; there might be no evil in such a course, but rather the contrary; still the question is, does the statute direct it? I incline to the opinion that it does not; but it is immaterial for the purpose of disposing of this rule, because we discharge the rule on the merits of the application itself.

My brothers are disposed to take a different view of the effect of the statute, as a point of general practice; and I think that we may and ought to hold that the notice, under the 54th clause, must specify a day on which the party will apply in order that the application may be met in the first instance, if it is decreed, and this may sometimes be the means of preventing the plaintiff being tied up by a groundless application. It will be understood, therefore, that the court takes this view of the provisions in question.

CAMERON V. PLAYTER AND PLAYTER.

Where a debt is due to A. and B., and A. makes an affidavit to arrest the debtor, B. is not liable to an action for a malicious arrest, unless it can be shewn that he participated in the malicious act, either by instructing or authorizing A. to do it, or by having some knowledge that it was done or intended, or by having afterwards adopted it by giving his assent thereto: though a writ of *capias* be set aside for irregularity, an action on the case will lie against the parties *suing out the same* maliciously. Trespass would be the proper form of action against the party *making the arrest*.

Case for malicious arrest. The declaration charges that the defendants, *or either* of them, not then having good reason to believe, and not believing that the plaintiff was about to leave Upper Canada, with intent to defraud the defendants of a debt of £100 then alleged to be due and owing from the plaintiff to John Playter the elder, the defendant, J. Playter the elder, falsely and maliciously procured the defendant, John Playter the younger, as his agent to make, and the defendant, John Playter the younger, as agent of and with the knowledge, consent and procurement of J. Playter the elder, falsely and maliciously made affidavit before, &c., that he had good reason to believe, and did believe that the plaintiff was immediately about to leave Upper Canada with intent to defraud the said J. Playter the elder of the said debt. It then charges that the two defendants falsely and maliciously sued out a writ of *capias* upon this affidavit, and delivered it to the sheriff, and caused the plaintiff to be arrested thereon.

The second count charges a malicious arrest by the defendants for £100, when they both well knew that the plaintiff did not owe to the defendant, J. Playter the elder, a debt of £100; and that after the plaintiff was arrested, the writ was by order of a judge of this court set aside with costs, and the plaintiff discharged from custody; and that the said action was and is by means of the premises, and according to the course and practice of the court, thereby wholly discharged and determined.

The defendants pleaded the general issue.

Miller, counsel for the plaintiff.

J. *Duggan* and *Brooks*, counsel for the defendants.

ROBINSON, C. J., delivered the judgment of the court.—At the trial, very slight evidence, if any, was given to shew that John Playter the elder had any knowledge of what his son, the other defendant, had done in his name, any further than that he had, at the request of his son, lent £50 to the plaintiff, for which his son had, for some reason not clearly made out, but to serve a purpose of his own, taken a note for £100, intending probably to cover some claim of his own, upon transactions which he had had with Henry Cameron, the plaintiff, and in which the defendant, his father, was in no manner concerned. There was no evidence to shew that J. Playter the elder either instructed or authorized his son to make the affidavit, or sue out the writ, or had any knowledge that it was done or intended, until some time after the writ and proceedings under it were set aside, when he was called upon to pay the costs of setting aside the writ, which was ordered on the ground of some irregularity; and he then said that it was a sad business, and that he must speak to his son about it. It appeared to me that the defendant, John Playter the elder, could not be made liable for a malicious act done by his son in his name, which he was not shewn to have authorized, or been in any way privy to, and which he had not adopted afterwards by any assent given to it; and more especially when the wrong done, in swearing to a debt of £100 when £50 only was due, was evidently done neither for the benefit nor at the desire of his father, but entirely to serve an end of his own; on which account there could be less pretence to justice in holding the father responsible for it, as upon a presumed authority, when none in fact was shewn.

I intimated to the jury that I considered the evidence not sufficient to charge the father in an action of this nature; but the jury, after being long out, brought in a verdict for the plaintiff £30 against both defendants; probably under an impression that the plaintiff would have little chance of obtaining satisfaction of any damages they might give, if their verdict was confined to the son; and considering that the plaintiff had been clearly ill-treated in the matter; they may have inferred also, from the intimate relationship between the defendants, that it was very unlikely that the son acted in the arrest without the knowledge of the father.

Upon a consideration of the evidence, we are all of opinion that the verdict against the defendant, John Playter, sen., was not warranted by the evidence. There was not in the whole case as proved, anything shewn that fairly connects him with the wrong complained of. For all that appears he may, until after the arrest, have known nothing more of the transaction than that he had, at the request of his son, lent £50 to Henry Cameron. It is not shewn that he even knew that his son had taken a note for anything more than the £50 lent.

The paper by which he is made to declare, when the note was taken, that it was given only to secure £50, was wholly written by the son, and was signed by him, though in his father's name. There was really nothing before the jury to shew, that when the son improperly arrested in the father's name for £100, the latter was in any manner aware that the son had any note in his name for that amount, or had any intention, much less any instruction from him, to take such a step. And when it is considered that the inducement which prompted the son to do it was to cover an alleged claim of his own, of which it is not shewn that his father had any knowledge, there is the less pretence for imputing malice to the father, as arising from the general inference that he was pursuing knowingly his own design through the agency of the son; for in fact, in all beyond the £50 honestly due, the son was attempting to answer a purpose of his own, and not of his father.

The slight evidence given of anything like an adoption or recognition by the father, was insufficient to found the verdict upon. When the fact of the illegal arrest was made known to him, which for all that appears was the first intimation he had received of what had taken place, he said it was a sad business, and he must speak to his son about it. This is what any one would naturally say under such circumstances, if he had been as far as possible from any participation in the wrong complained of.

As to the objection urged for the defendants, that the writ having been set aside, the action against these defendants should have been trespass and not case, that might have been so in an action against the person who actually made the arrest, but not in the action against these parties, in which malice is a necessary ingredient (a).

New trial granted against both defendants, on payment of costs: the plaintiff not objecting, on account of his verdict against J. Playter, jun.

DOE EX. DEM. ANDERSON ET AL. V. FAIRFIELD.

A testator devises certain land to his daughter, to hold during her life, and afterwards to her heirs forever; and then adds, "should *it so happen* that "my daughter shall not have heirs, then," &c. *Held*, that under these additional words, the daughter takes only an estate tail.

Ejectment, on the several demises of John Anderson and Mary Anne his wife, Michael Wenep and Eleanor his wife, and Thomas Howard, to recover possession of parts of Lots 13 and 14, in the 1st concession north front in the township of Amherst Island.

Thomas Jackson was seized of the premises in question, and died in 1816, having made his will in 1813, whereby he devised these and other lands to his wife for life, and "to his daughter, Margaret Jackson, after the death of his "said wife, he devised the same lands to hold during her life, and afterwards "to her heirs for ever;" then follows these words, "and also the whole of my "freehold estate at her mother's death; and should it so happen that my "daughter shall not have heirs, then at her death the whole of the freehold "estate to be divided as follows: one fourth part to John and Thomas Howard, "eldest sons of John and Anne Howard; one fourth part to the two eldest sons "of John and Caty George; and the remaining half to be equally divided "between the daughters of sister Anne Howard and sister Catharine George, "be there few or many alive at that time."

These lessors of the plaintiff claim shares respectively under the will, Mary Anne Anderson being one of the daughters of Anne and John Howard—Eleanor Wenep being one of the daughters of Catherine George, and Thomas Howard being the eldest and surviving son of John and Anne Howard; Margaret Jackson, having been married to William Fairfield, the defendant in this action, died in 1837, leaving no issue.

The defendant objected to the plaintiff's title, contending that the words in the will, "and should it so happen that my daughter shall not have heirs," were not confined to heirs of her body; and, that as the testator describes Margaret Jackson as his daughter in the will, these devisees making title under the will are precluded from disputing her legitimacy, and that the estate must be taken to have devolved upon her heirs on the part of the father.

The learned judge held at the trial, that the clear effect of the will was to devise the estate over, in case Margaret Jackson should die without issue; and

---

(a) 2 T. R. 255; 6 T. R. 315.

that if it could be so construed as to let in her heirs generally, still, being proved to be illegitimate, she could have left none such; and that the lessors of the plaintiff were therefore entitled to take their respective interests under the will.

It was proved at the trial, that Margaret Jackson had joined with her husband, this defendant, in making a deed of this land to one Denny, in 1837, which was registered on the 9th February, 1846. The will has never been registered.

Kirkpatrick, counsel for the plaintiff.

McKenzie, counsel for the defendant.

ROBINSON, C. J., delivered the judgment of the court.

It is only necessary to state the case, to be convinced that there is no room for doubt. The daughter was proved to be illegitimate; when, therefore, the testator directed what should become of the estate "if it should *so happen* that "his daughter should *not have any heirs*," he could only mean, if she had no issue. The very form of expression shews that he meant this; and as all parts of the will must be looked at upon a question of this nature, in order to decide whether the testator intended to create an estate tail or to devise a fee simple, we cannot help seeing that he must have meant the former; for as was observed upon the argument, he never could have meant by the word "heirs" her right heirs, in the full extent of the term, for then the devise over could never have effect upon the contingency mentioned, for the very persons he devises to would have been her heirs if there had been none nearer, and if she was capable of having any collateral kindred. With regard to the non-registration of the will, no such objection seems to have been taken at the trial. The title was not shewn to have been a registered title at the time of the will being made or taking effect. And besides, the daughter being illegitimate, had no estate independent of the will; and if she had, it was evident that the deed which she and her husband made to Denny was not made to him as a *bona fide* purchaser for value, which would be necessary to enable the defendants to avail themselves of any advantage, by reason of the omission to register the will.   Rule discharged.

SMALL V. BEASLEY.

A defendant having appeared, and examined evidence on an assessment of damages which had been carried down to the District Court, by a writ of trial issued from the Queen's Bench, under our statute, 8 Vic. c. 13, s. 55, has by such appearance waived any irregularity in the prior proceedings in the Queen's Bench.

In this case a rule *nisi* was granted in vacation, upon application to a judge of this court, under our statute 8 Vic. ch. 13, sec. 55, to shew cause why the verdict rendered in the District Court, upon a writ of trial proceeding from this court, should not be set aside and damages again assessed for the admission of improper evidence on the trial, and because the verdict is contrary to law and evidence, and for misdirection, and on points reserved at the trial; or why the writ of trial, or the proceedings thereon, should not be set aside for irregularity, with costs, on the ground that no entry of the proceedings had in this court were first made of record in this court to warrant the writ of inquiry, or because the writ does not sufficiently set forth the proceedings in this court, or because no copy was served on the defendant ; or why the judgment should not be arrested, or other relief granted.

The declaration is in debt on bond, given by the defendant as surety for the late Arthur Gifford, in the office of deputy to the plaintiff, as clerk of the crown and pleas. The defendant sets out the condition on oyer, and pleads performance, but not with sufficient precision ; wherefore the plaintiff demurred to this plea and had judgment, and the case was sent down by writ to the District Court of the Home District, to have damages assessed under the 54th sec. of 8 Vic. ch. 13; the plaintiff having suggested as a breach under the statute, that although A. Gifford did, as such deputy, receive divers sums of money, viz. amounting in the whole to £50, between the 1st January and the 1st July, 1844, being six months' time next after the said 1st day of January, and which sums of money he should once in six months have accounted for and paid over to the plaintiff according to the condition, yet the said A. Gifford did not at any time account for and pay over all or any such sum or sums of money as came to his hands as deputy clerk of the crown, between the 1st of January and the 1st of July.

The defendant appeared at the trial by his counsel, and cross-examined the plaintiff's witnesses, and addressed the jury. The plaintiff's evidence was exceedingly vague and inconclusive, not shewing that any money had been received by Gifford, but that a good deal of business must have been done within the six months in question, from the state of proceedings in causes in which business was done by his successor.

The judge, doubting the sufficiency of the evidence, left it to the jury as it was, directing them to assess such damages as they might think it probable from the evidence the plaintiff ought to recover, as being the amount which Mr. Gifford either did receive or should have received during the six months ; in order that if this court should think the evidence sufficient, they might confirm the finding, or otherwise direct a verdict to be entered for nominal damages.

The jury assessed damages at £27.

Grant, counsel for the plaintiff.

Galt for the defendant.

ROBINSON, C. J., delivered the judgment of the court.

We know judicially, for the case has been before us in this same term, and has been adverted to in the argument on this rule, that the plaintiff suing another surety on this same bond has, upon a trial, recovered £31 and upwards, as being the amount of fees which Mr. Gifford ought to have received within the same six months, and for which he had rendered no account.

In that case, however, the pleadings were different, and did not call for proof of money received, as the breach suggested here does, a distinct breach being laid in the words of the condition, for not rendering an account, whereas the breach here is narrowed to the not having paid over such moneys as he had actually received.

We do not see any ground of objection to the assessment for irregularity, considering that the defendant appeared at the trial, and entered into the examination of the evidence in regard to the damages. And with regard to the evidence in support of the breach, it was not precise and conclusive certainly, in regard to any amount of business done; and it may be truly urged, as it has been, that there was no direct evidence of any sum of money having been actually received by Mr. Gifford; but in many cases of this kind, that may be presumed by the jury from the facts shewn; as, for instance, in the cases of persons employed to sell goods upon commission. The account for the preceding period, which had been furnished by Mr. Gifford, contained a note on the face of it that he was not then keeping any account with the attorneys; in other words, that he made them pay the fees for business done as they went. This is the regular course, and when the presumption that it was followed is strengthened by this declaration of the deputy, it was no unwarrantable stretch in the jury to conclude that he had received fees commensurate with the business done; as to what the amount of that business was, we certainly cannot say it was by any means clearly made out; but there was some evidence of it, as good perhaps as could be given, considering that it was proved that Mr. Gifford's books had not been handed over to his successor. And when we are asked to set aside the verdict in a matter of this small account, for this cause, we cannot avoid considering that in the same term in which this rule has been argued, we have had before us the record and evidence upon the trial of an action against the other surety in this same bond, for an alleged default in accounting during the very same period, and that in that action the plaintiff received rather a larger amount than this verdict, and, as we think, upon sufficient evidence.   Rule discharged, with costs.

Wheeler v. Sime and Bain.

To an avowry under a distress for rent, the plaintiff replied *rien* in arrear, and also set out specially an agreement to be allowed to make certain repairs, and to deduct the amount thereof from the rent, which he averred he had done; this answer to the avowry is good, under either of the above pleas.

Replevin. Defendants avow under a distress for rent—Sime as landlord, and Bain as bailiff—setting forth that the plaintiff had occupied a saw-mill and dwelling-house of Sime's for a year and a quarter, ending 25th June, 1845, at a yearly rent of £75, payable quarterly, on the 25th June, September, December and March: the last two quarters' rent, £37 10s., being in arrear.

Plaintiff replies—1st, that Bain was not the bailiff of Simes; 2ndly, *non tenuit*; 3rdly, *rien* in arrear; 4thly, plaintiff pleads an agreement entered into on 6*th February*, 1845, between him and Sime, that plaintiff should make certain repairs to the saw-mill, and that, when finished, plaintiff should deduct one-half of the expense of making such repairs out of the rent then accruing for the said saw-mill, dwelling-house and premises, and pay and bear the other half of the same himself; that he did make such repairs while the rent was accruing, and before it became payable, and that the whole of the expense of making and finishing such repairs amounted to £60 18s. 8d., the one-half of which so to be deducted is £30 9s. 4d.; and that before the said rent became due he paid the several sums of money to Simes on account of the rent, amounting, with the said half of the sum due for repairs, to £40 4s. 4d., and exceeding the said rent.

The defendants deny that there was any such agreement in respect to repairs, and take issue upon plaintiff's other pleas to their avowry.

The jury found a verdict for the plaintiff on the last issue, and damages one shilling, and for the defendants on all the other issues. And the defendants move for a new trial on the law and evidence, and on grounds disclosed in affidavits filed; or to arrest the judgment; or that judgment be entered for the defendants on the fourth issue, *non obstante veredicto*.

Read, counsel for plaintiffs.

J. H. Cameron, counsel for defendants.

ROBINSON, C. J., delivered the judgment of the court.

The only doubt with us is, whether the verdict can be considered satisfactory upon the evidence. The evidence given was properly received under the last issue, and was besides evidence on the plea of no rent in arrear. As to awarding judgment *non obstante veredicto*, we should do that to forward the substantial justice of the case, if the fourth plea appeared to us to be no good answer to the avowry; but there can be no question that, if it really was agreed between the parties that the tenant should be allowed to make certain repairs and deduct the amount from the rent, and if he has made them according to the spirit of the agreement, we should not do right in granting this rule; for, according to the facts pleaded, his answer to the avowry would be good under the fourth plea, and clearly good under the third plea, (*a*).

Rule discharged.

IN RE BIGGAR.

An information in the nature of a *quo warranto* may issue, to shew cause by what authority a municipal councillor for any district in the province claims to be a member of such council.

A rule *nisi* was moved by *Sullivan*, to shew cause why an information in the nature of a *quo warranto* should not be exhibited against Herbert Biggar, to shew by what authority he claims to be a member of the municipal council of the District of Gore, for the township of Brantford.

Affidavits stated that Biggar, on the 10th February, took his seat as a member of the municipal council elected for the township of Brantford. In December, 1845, Clement, town clerk of Brantford for that year, gave notice of a town meeting to be held in the township on the 5th January, 1846, for choosing township officers. At 9 o'clock the inhabitants assembled, and it was required of the town clerk that a chairman should be chosen before they proceeded to the election of a councillor, and one David Christie was nominated (and seconded) to be the chairman. But the clerk insisted on holding himself the election for district councillor before any chairman was chosen, and, contrary to the wish of the inhabitants, he received the nomination of Mr. Biggar for municipal councillor, and declared him duly elected about eleven o'clock on that day, three o'clock being the hour for closing the poll. Afterwards a

---

(*a*) See Chamber's Landlord and Tenant, pp. 645-6; 3 B. & P. 353.

chairman was appointed, and a candidate for district councillor was proposed and seconded; but the chairman declined proceeding in such election after the difficulty that had arisen.

It was sworn in affidavits filed in opposition to this rule that the township clerk, believing it to be his duty to preside at the election of district councillor, went before a magistrate and took the oath required by 4 & 5 Vic. chap. 10, to be taken by the person presiding at the election of a district councillor. It was contended on behalf of Herbert Biggar, that the intent and effect of the 4 & 5 Vic. chap. 10, and of the Township Officers' Act, is, that the member shall be chosen for the municipal council before a chairman is appointed to the meeting, the clerk presiding.

ROBINSON, C. J.—Upon the view which we at present take of the intention and effect of the statute, we think it right to make the rule absolute for the information. Rule absolute.

WRIGHT v. McPHERSON ET AL.

Where a defendant obtains time to plead, on condition of taking short *notice of trial*, this condition does not compel him to take short notice of assessment; this further condition should be inserted in the rule.

The defendant had obtained time to plead, on condition of taking *short notice of trial;* he did not plead, and the plaintiff signed judgment by default, and gave notice of assessment; conceiving that the condition to take short notice of trial, extended, under such circumstances, to taking short notice of assessment, if the defendant did not choose to plead.

Bell, counsel for the plaintiff, contended that the defendant, by obtaining this indulgence, might throw the plaintiff over the assizes, by neglecting to plead after he has asked for time; and he could lose nothing by the contrivance where he has no defence to make.

Campbell, counsel for the defendant.—It has been determined in England, that an undertaking to accept short notice of trial, does not bind a party to accept short notice of assessment; and as to any unfair practice, the plaintiff can easily in such cases provide against it, by having the condition inserted in the rule for time to plead drawn up in the alternative; that is, binding the defendant to accept short notice of trial, or of assessment of damages, where such notice may be necessary.

ROBINSON, C. J., delivered the judgment of the court.

The defendants in this case have made a very strong and precise affidavit of merits; but we are of opinion that the rule should be made absolute, upon the strict ground of irregularity, but without costs; and that the defendants shall have leave to plead, if they desire it, provided they plead within two days; the interlocutory judgment to be set aside for that purpose. I cannot say, for my own part, that I am prepared to extend to this case the decision that has been made in England, in the case of a plaintiff demurring to the defendant's plea, after such terms as to notice of trial have been entered into.

I think the decision was unreasonable; and though we should be bound by it, in precisely such a case, I feel a hesitation in carrying it further; but my brothers see no clear ground for distinction, and it is desirable to have a rule to guide the profession in this respect; it is therefore to be understood, that in future the defendant coming under terms to accept short notice of trial, on obtaining time to plead, will not be bound to take short notice of assessment of damages, if by omitting to plead he has judgment by default signed against him. They will see, therefore, the necessity of having the further condition inserted in the rule, "or of assessment of damages, in case such notice shall be necessary."   Rule absolute without costs.

McLEOD v. TORRANCE.

Semble: That an affidavit stating that *a commission* was duly taken, and not that *the evidence* was duly taken in accordance with the literal wording of the statute, will nevertheless entitle the commission to be read.

Semble, also: That the affidavit need not be entitled in the cause.

The plaintiff sues in *assumpsit* on a promissory note, made by the defendant on the 1st day of January, 1835, payable to the plaintiff (not negotiable) in ten years, for £274 12s. 11d., not on interest; with a count on an account stated.

The defendant pleads the general issue to the second count; and

2ndly, That he did not make the note declared on in the first count; and

3rdly, That the defendant being insolvent on the 6th day of August, 1834, he compounded with the plaintiff and his other creditors, at 10s. in the pound, in full discharge of his debts; that it was at that time agreed between the plaintiff and the defendant, that the defendant should give, and that he did then give to the plaintiff, an undertaking in writing, post-dated as of the 1st day of January, 1835, which is made in this action as a promissory note, and is in the following words:

"Quebec, 1st January, 1835.

"MR. McLEOD. Sir,—In order to make settlement of the balance of account "due you by me, I hereby promise and oblige myself to pay you the sum of "£274 12s. 11d. c'y at the expiration of ten years from this date, without "interest. I am, &c.,   BENJAMIN TORRANCE."

That the plaintiff refused to enter, with the other creditors, into the agreement to accept 10s. in the pound, unless the defendant would make this undertaking; and the defendant avers that he did afterwards pay to the plaintiff and his other creditors the 10s. in the pound; and that the note was given without the knowledge of the other creditors, and is a fraud upon them.

The plaintiff replies *de injuria.*

To prove the composition which took place between Torrance and his creditors at Quebec, in 1834, the evidence of the notary before whom the business was transacted was taken under a commission. It was objected, when the commission was opened, that the evidence could not be read, because the affidavit of the due execution of the commission was not entitled in any cause; and it stated "that the *examination of the witness* (Archibald Campbell, "Esq.) thereunto annexed, was duly taken before the commissioners named "on the annexed commission, in presence of the deponent;" whereas the statute requires that the affidavit shall state that "*the commission* was duly taken," not that the evidence was duly taken.

The evidence was read, subject to these objections; and it established very clearly the facts of the composition made by Torrance with his creditors, at 10s. in the pound; that McLeod executed the deed with the others, on the 6th day of August, 1834, agreeing, for all that appeared, like the rest, to give a full discharge on receiving the 10s. in the pound on the amount of their claims.

Besides this evidence, a witness was examined at the trial, who proved that he had been in the defendant's service in 1834; that the defendant, in 1833 or 1834, became insolvent, and agreed to pay his creditors 10s. in the pound; that this plaintiff declined to come into the arrangement unless Torrance would agree to pay him the remainder of his demand in ten years; that the witness paid him the 10s. in the pound, and took from him an undertaking to that effect, which McLeod objected to because it was dated at the time of the transaction ; *i. e.*, truly, wishing it to bear a date some time subsequent; and it was accordingly dated the 1st day of January, 1835, at McLeod's dictation, though in fact signed and delivered in August, 1834. The witness, as Torrance's clerk, paid McLeod and the other creditors the 10s. in the pound ; and he swore that he was certain the other creditors had no knowledge of the secret understanding between these parties, or they would not have agreed to the composition.

The jury gave a verdict for the plaintiff, by consent, for £286 16s. 11d., subject to leave reserved to move that a verdict be entered for the defendant, if the court should think that the evidence under the commission was admissible, and that in connection with the other evidence it established the defence: or if they should think that the other evidence, without resorting to that under the commission, entitled the defendant to a verdict. And if the court should think that the evidence taken under the commission could not properly be received, and that without it the defence was not established, then the court were to consider whether a new trial should be granted, in order to enable the defendant to repair the defect in regard to the commission.

J. Hillyard Cameron, counsel for plaintiff.

Blake and *Crooks*, counsel for defendant.

ROBINSON, C. J., delivered the judgment of the court.

We have no hesitation in agreeing that a verdict must be entered for the defendant; considering the evidence of the witness at the trial alone clearly sufficient to bar the plaintiff's recovery.

But we wish it at the same time to be understood, that we do not decide that the evidence under the commission could not be received by reason of either of the objections taken. It is better and safer to comply closely with all that the statute directs; but I do not, for my own part, hold that a literal compliance with the direction is indispensable, and that any deviation must be fatal. It would expose parties sometimes to most inconvenient consequences, if it were so; and the 18th section of our Queen's Bench Act seems wisely framed so as to guard against the consequences of unnecessary strictness in what may be non-essential; for it provides only negatively, that the evidence shall not be read, "*if it shall be made appear to the court that the same has or* "*have not been duly taken.*"

Verdict to be entered for the defendant.

SMALL V. STANTON.

In an action on a bond for the breach of a condition assigned in the words used in the bond, "in not having duly rendered all accounts which ought to have "been rendered," the plaintiff may recover whatever moneys the defendant ought to have received, though no money was in fact received by him.

The plaintiff sues on a bond of the defendant, in a penalty of £50, dated the 5th day of February, 1844. The condition is set out in oyer: it recites that one Arthur Gifford, deceased, had been appointed by the plaintiff to be his deputy for the District of Gore, in the office of the clerk of the crown and pleas; and the condition is, "that if the said Arthur Gifford shall well, truly "and faithfully fulfil, perform and discharge all the duties of his said office, "and shall duly and regularly keep and render all accounts which ought to be "kept and rendered by him; and shall account for, and pay over to the said "Charles C. Small, Esquire, all and every such sum or sums of money as shall "come into his hands as deputy clerk of the crown, at least once in six months, "then this obligation to be void," &c.

The defendant pleads, that Gifford did at all times faithfully perform his duty, and did regularly keep and render all accounts which ought to be kept and rendered by him, and did once in every six months account for and pay over to the plaintiff all such sums of money as came into his hands as deputy clerk of the crown, according to the tenor and effect of the said condition.

The plaintiff replies, as to so much of the plea as avers that Gifford did duly and regularly keep and render all accounts which ought to be kept and rendered by him, that Gifford did not duly keep and render all accounts which ought to have been kept and rendered by him, according to the condition; and assigns for a further breach, that he did not once in every six months account for and pay over to the plaintiff all such sums as came into his hands; for that although he received divers sums of money, amounting to £50, between the 1st day of January and the 1st of July, 1844, yet that he did not at any time account for and pay over all or any such sums, &c.

The defendant rejoins as to the first breach, that Gifford did duly keep and render all accounts, &c.; and to the second breach, that he did not receive divers sums of money in manner and form as the plaintiff has alleged.

It was proved at the trial, that Gifford died in August, 1844, and that from the 1st day of January preceding, the business done in the office amounted to £31 16s. 2d.; that he had been in the habit of giving credit to the attorneys, though not as it appeared by the leave of Mr. Small, and had only received during the period £3 2s. 8d.—the defendant, who is an attorney, being himself indebted to the office in £1 3s. 8d. No account had been rendered after 1st of January.

Galt, counsel for plaintiff.

Grant, counsel for defendant.

ROBINSON, C. J., delivered the judgment of the court.

The case was tried before me at Toronto, and I considered that the plaintiff could recover on the pleadings for all the fees which ought to have been received for the business done under the breach for not accounting; but leave was reserved to the defendant to move the court to reduce the verdict to the amount of money actually received, if it should be thought that more could not properly be received on this record.

We are of opinion that the verdict may be sustained upon the evidence given, to the full amount. In this case there is a breach distinctly assigned, in Gifford's not having "duly rendered all accounts which ought to have been rendered;" besides the breach in not accounting for and paying over all moneys received. This breach, though charged in general terms, is in the very words of the condition, and the defendant has taken issue upon it. The plaintiff proved the breach clearly, the damages rested with the jury, and we think they were warranted by the evidence in finding the full amount which they did; for it was clearly proved that business was done in the office which ought to have produced that sum in fees, and the plaintiff had received nothing.

Rule discharged.

ELVIDGE V. RICHARDSON.

To support the common count for goods *bargained and sold*, the plaintiff must prove a certain price agreed upon; when this cannot be done, the declaration should contain a special count for not accepting.

Assumpsit on common counts for goods *bargained* and *sold*, work done and materials found, and on account stated.

Plea, general issue.

This case was tried before the Chief Justice at the last assizes in Toronto. The defendant had employed the plaintiff to make him a thrashing machine of rather a peculiar construction, in some respects wishing it to be lighter than the thrashing machines placed in farmers' barns usually are, as he intended to move it about, and work with it for others in the neighbourhood.

When it was completed it was taken home by the maker, but upon the first trial an important part of the machinery gave way, and the plaintiff took it back to his shop, declaring that he thought he could make it answer; though it was proved on the trial that he spoke of it at other times as if it was a doubt with him whether it was not too slight in some parts to answer the purpose. There was evidence, on the other hand, that the defendant, before he would positively authorize the plaintiff to make a machine for him, asked him whether he would undertake to make a good one, and that he replied he would engage to do so.

After the machine had been made whole again, and some parts improved, it was taken to the defendant to be again tried. For some cause, a delay of a month or more took place before the machine was again set in motion, and which was done by the defendant and his servants without any notice being given to the plaintiff to be present. It was not long in motion on this second occasion when it broke again in such a manner as to make it useless, and the defendant immediately took it in his waggon to the plaintiff's shop, and insisted on leaving it on his hands. The plaintiff helped him to take it out of the waggon, but insisted that the machine was his, and he must pay for it. The evidence was not precise as to the price that the defendant had agreed to give: several witnesses swore that it was somewhere about 110 dollars, depending upon the weight of the castings, which it did not appear had been ever ascertained.

Ewart, counsel for plaintiff.
Bell, counsel for defendant.

ROBINSON, C, J., delivered the judgment of the court.

At the trial, the endeavour of the plaintiff was to satisfy the jury that it was no fault of his that the machine had not held together upon the trial; that the materials and workmanship were good, but that, by the express desire of the defendant, the most important part had been made too light, and that the risk of the experiment should therefore be his, and not the plaintiff's; and further, that the failure upon the second trial was owing to the unskilful and negligent management of the defendant, who had suffered snow and water to become frozen in the bed in which the wheel turned, and also to collect about the logs, which occasioned the mischief; and further, that the machine was not properly fed while it was in motion. On the other hand, the defendant endeavoured to satisfy the jury, that there had been no such fault or negligence on his part, and that as to anything peculiar in the construction of the machine, he had merely stated his wish, and relied on the plaintiff's assurances that he could make a sound and good machine, such as he desired; that he had it on both occasions on trial only, and was not bound to take it unless it proved to be such as had been promised.

It was upon this kind of evidence that the case went to the jury; the object of the one party being to shew, that under the circumstances the defendant was bound to keep and pay for the machine, while the other party hoped to convince the jury that he was not bound to keep it, but was at liberty to throw it back on the plaintiff's hands.

Unfortunately, however, the declaration did not contain a special count for not accepting the machine, which is really the only form of declaring suited to such a case.

The defendant's counsel objected, that the plaintiff could not recover on the count for "*goods bargained and sold*," because there was not evidence that a certain fixed price had been agreed upon, which is a necessary condition to being allowed to recover on that count. I did not think at the trial the objection entitled to prevail, and was less inclined to give way to it, because the evidence went very near to establishing a certain price—namely, 110 dollars, subject however to be affected one way or the other to a small extent, according as the actual weight of the castings when furnished agreed with what they had been estimated at.

Upon the conflicting evidence which was given as to the original bargain and the conduct of the parties afterwards, it was left to the jury to determine whether the cause of failure was the plaintiff's want of skill, or defect in the workmanship or materials; or whether it was well made, according to the instructions given, and failed only on account of the unsuitableness of the proportions which the defendant had insisted upon, or from his improper management of the machine when he started it on the last occasion. I submitted also to the jury whether, from the length of time the defendant had kept the machine on the second occasion, and his manner of trying it at last, as it appeared on the whole evidence, they could infer that the defendant had waived any right to return it, and treated it as his own. The jury found a verdict for the plaintiff, and £22 10s. damages.

It is now objected, that to enable the plaintiff to recover for goods bargained and sold, it is indispensable that there should have been an acceptance of the goods as well as a certain price agreed upon. I think the counsel (Mr. Bell) was right in the point taken by him at the trial, that it was necessary to shew a certain price agreed upon, which if it had been left to the jury, they could scarcely have found upon the evidence. With respect to the point of acceptance, it was not submitted formally to the jury as a point to be decided by them in favour of the plaintiff, before they could allow him to recover. I have no note of any objection to the charge on that ground, and do not recollect that I was requested to leave the case to the jury specially on that point; and if I could say now, that it is quite clear upon the evidence that the jury must have found an acceptance if they had been asked to express an opinion on that point, then I should be against setting aside the verdict. I consider the defendant ought to have a new trial, if he desires it, and without costs, though it is doubtful whether he will mend his situation by taking it, for I think we should give the plaintiff leave to add a special count to his declaration, suited to the case, in order that the merits may be fairly tried, which they can hardly be on the present record. Rule absolute without costs.

FORRESTER V. CLARKE.

Where a man is himself assaulted by a person disturbing the peace in a public street, he may arrest the offender and take him to a peace officer to answer for the breach of the peace.

It need not be averred or proved that the party was taken to the nearest justice.

The plaintiff, in the first and second counts, charges a false imprisonment. The defendant in his third plea justifies the imprisonment, by pleading that just before the said time when, &c., the plaintiff was making a great noise and disturbance in a public street, and behaving in a riotous manner, and made an assault upon the defendant, and that *thereupon* the defendant, in order to preserve the peace, took the plaintiff to a police station close at hand, on the line of the public works at Williamsburg in the Eastern District, before a justice of the peace there, for examination concerning the premises, and to be dealt with according to law, &c.

The plaintiff demurs to this, because it is not stated that the defendant was a peace officer; or, that the riotous conduct was likely to continue; or, that there was any necessity for arresting the plaintiff and taking him to the police station in order to preserve the peace.

Hagarty, counsel for plaintiff.
John Duggan, counsel for defendant.

ROBINSON, C. J., delivered the judgment of the court.

We are of opinion that the plea is not bad for any of the reasons assigned. We consider that a man who is himself assaulted by a person who is disturbing the peace in the public street, may arrest the offender and take him to a peace officer and give him in charge, to answer for the breach of the peace. This plea makes out that defence, assuming that the original plea filed states the arrest to have been made "*thereupon*" and not "*therefore*," as has been erroneously copied in the books before us.

It does not appear to be necessary to aver that the party was taken before the nearest justice—the precedents are not so; and it would tend to great inconvenience if that were an averment necessary to be made and proved.

Judgment for defendant on demurrer.

TAIT ET AL. V. ATKINSON.

Where a plaintiff has been awarded a certain sum of money in accordance with the terms of an instrument under seal, for the non-payment of such award the plaintiff should sue in covenant; he cannot sue in *assumpsit*, unless some new consideration apart from the written instrument can be proved.

The fact that a valuation took place on a day later than at first agreed upon in the written instrument, makes no difference in the form of action that should be brought.

The plaintiffs declare specially in *assumpsit*, for the non-payment by the defendant of a certain sum of money awarded to the plaintiffs; the award was given, as averred, in accordance with the terms of a written instrument under seal, recited at length in the declaration; no new consideration apart from the deed to support the promise was alleged.

The defendant demurs, on the ground that the action should have been covenant, and not *assumpsit*.

Campbell, counsel for plaintiff.

T. Kirkpatrick, counsel for defendant,

ROBINSON, C. J., delivered the judgment of the court.

We are of opinion that this action is strictly founded on the covenant; upon which therefore the plaintiffs should have sued, and not in *assumpsit*. The case of Barber v. Harris (*a*), is much in point. No new consideration is stated for supporting an *assumpsit*, apart from the deed. What the parties had stipulated for in that instrument was, that the house should be paid for to the tenant at the expiration of the term, after being valued by persons appointed by them respectively; they did appoint persons to value, and the valuation was made by those persons, and adopted and assented to as the value, as the plaintiff's statement of his case shews. All, therefore, had taken place which was necessary to enable the plaintiffs to sue under the covenant; and we see no difficulty on account of the valuation having been made on a later day than had been at first agreed on. It would not have been necessary to state any day in the declaration when the appraisers were to determine the value; and it became immaterial, as the value had been ascertained by referees, with the consent of both parties, and subsequently adopted as the value.

Judgment for defendant on demurrer.

(a) 1 P & D. 360.

THOMPSON V. ARMSTRONG.

To a declaration consisting of several common counts, claiming, under *one promise* upon all the counts, the sum of £500, and laying the damages at £200, the defendant pleads a plea of payment "of £250 in full satisfaction "and discharge of the *said promise in the said declaration mentioned*, and also "*of all damages* sustained by the plaintiff by reason of the *non-performance* "*of such promise.*"

Held, Plea bad on special demurrer.

The plaintiff declares on the common counts for goods sold, work done, &c., &c.

The defendant pleads, as his third plea, the following plea of payment: That, after the making of the said promise in the declaration mentioned, and before the commencement of this suit, to wit, on the 1st day of December, in the year of our Lord, 1845, he the defendant paid to the plaintiff, and the plaintiff then accepted and received of and from the defendant a large sum of money, to wit, the sum of £250, in full satisfaction and discharge of the said promise in the declaration mentioned, and also of all damages sustained by the plaintiff by reason of the non-performance of such promise; and this the defendant is ready to verify, &c.

The plaintiff demurs, for that the said third plea, in the introductory part thereof, professes to be a plea in bar of the whole action, whereas the plea itself only contains matter in answer to one count or promise of the declaration, without applying the same to any particular count or promise of the declaration, and leaves it altogether a matter of uncertainty to which promise or count the said plea is to be applied; neither does the said plea in any manner confess or avoid the residue of the causes of action in the declaration mentioned; and the said plea is in other respects uncertain, informal and insufficient.

J. *Hillyard Cameron* and *Vankoughnet*, counsel for plaintiff.

H. *Eccles*, counsel for defendant.

ROBINSON, C. J., delivered the judgment of the court.

We are of opinion that the third plea is bad, being pleaded to the whole declaration, which consists of several counts, and yet averring that the defendant paid £250 in discharge of the promise in the declaration mentioned, whereas we must intend a distinct promise in regard to each count; and then £250 is pleaded in discharge of £500 claimed in the five counts, and of £200 damages.

The plea cannot be maintained against this objection, on the ground that it is in bar of the damages only; for unless it had been pleaded in discharge of the promises also, it would be bad.—1 D. & R. 546; 3 E. R. 256; Str. 23, 573.

Judgment for demurrer.

IN RE McNAIRN AND COMMISSIONERS FOR THE ST. LAWRENCE CANAL.

Mandamus nisi awarded to the Commissioners of the St. Lawrence Canal to appoint an arbitrator to join in awarding upon an unsettled claim. (See this case again in the next term, where it appeared that the statute passed this year, and in force since this rule was issued, prevented any further proceeding upon this application.)

Mandamus, moved by *Vankoughnet* in Michaelmas Term last to the Commissioners, to appoint one of their number an arbitrator to meet an arbitrator who had been appointed on behalf of McNairn, to award upon his claim.

Phillpotts shewed cause.

ROBINSON, C. J., delivered the judgment of the court.

The rule issued in this case is not in accordance with the motion—being merely to shew cause why they should not appoint an arbitrator; but notwithstanding this, we can, of course, if we see cause, award a *mandamus nisi.*

In one respect the applicant, McNairn, does certainly not stand in a favourable position before the court. In the affidavit on which he moved, he withheld information, as to the first claim made by him, for property taken, which was satisfied by the Board, and a formal release of damage taken. He may have thought his claim, for a subsequent injury, to be so distinct, as to require no reference to what had taken place before, but he should certainly have laid his whole case before us. In the many papers however which have since been filed, we see how the matter stands, and without going at this stage into an examination of the merits, we feel bound to award a writ of *mandamus nisi*, which will bring the whole merits before us, upon the return.

The second clause of the 4 & 5 Vic. chap. 28, throws it upon the Commissioners to proceed still, in whatever the previous law required of them, for ascertaining the damages due to claimants, upon any ground, in respect of which they had preferred a claim, before the passing of that Act. Whatever may really be the merits of Mr. McNairn's claim, it is clear that he had preferred it in 1839, and so before the passing of the Act referred to. The Commissioners had determined that they would not, upon their own judgment, pay him more than £3 5s. 7d. on account of that claim. He claimed £500; the Commissioners offered him at one time £200, and he, as they shew us, was willing to reduce his claim to £350; they seem to have approached no nearer, and thus to have let the matter stand open. If the Commissioners had shewn us, or if they will now shew, that they had closed with the offer of £350, then there would be no occasion to go to arbitration; but as it is, we must see that the law takes its course for bringing the matter to a final settlement.

It is objected, that under the new system for managing the public works, the Commissioners have no means of satisfying any award against them; but that is a consideration which we are not at liberty to entertain. The applicant is not asking us to compel the Board to pay him money, but to compel them to put him in a way for having his claim determined, in regard to amount, as the law directs.

Rule for *mandamus nisi.*

TANNER v. D'EVERADO ET AL.

Where payment is to be a condition precedent, or a concurrent act, and is to be made in a certain manner, the plaintiff must aver a readiness to pay in the precise manner stipulated.

The plaintiff declares in covenant—

For that whereas, on the 7th May, 1844, by certain articles of agreement then made between the plaintiff and defendants, which said agreement, sealed with the seals of the said defendants, the said plaintiff now brings here into

court, it was agreed by and between the plaintiff and defendants as follows:—
That for and in consideration of the covenants and promises thereinafter contained, by and on the part of the said plaintiff, the said defendants did covenant and agree to sell and deliver to the said plaintiff, in the city of Buffalo, in the state of New York, on or before the 1st day of September, in the year of our Lord, 1844, 500,000 feet of pine lumber, in assorted thicknesses and qualities, at the following prices: that is to say, number one should be delivered and paid for at the rate of $18 per 1,000 feet; number two, at the rate of $15 per 1,000 feet; number three, at the rate of $13 per 1,000 feet; and common, or number four, at the rate of $8 per 1,000 feet. The inspection of which should be as follows, to wit, number one should be and mean a perfect board in every way; number two should have one perfect side, and on the other side one inch of sap should be allowed, and not to exceed two knots, meaning sound knots; number three should be allowed three sound knots in size not larger than a two-shilling piece, and two inches of sap on each side and edge; all the balance of the said lumber should be considered number four or common, as aforesaid, but should not include rotten boards, boards with unsound knots, or shaky boards; none of which three last descriptions are within the meaning of this agreement. And the said defendants did further agree, that they would deliver the said lumber to the said plaintiff in manner and at the times hereinafter mentioned; that is to say, 100,000 feet during the then present month of May; 200,000 feet during the succeeding month of June; and the remaining 200,000 feet on or before the said 1st day of September, in the year of our Lord, 1844. And the said plaintiff did thereby covenant and agree to and with the said defendants, that he would receive the said quantity of lumber, if delivered as aforesaid, and that he would pay the said defendants at the rates aforesaid, upon the delivery of each load or cargo; which payment should be in the following manner, that is to say, two-fifths of the value of each load should be paid in goods of such description as the said defendants should order, at New York bills, adding transportation and five per centum profits; and three-fifths of the value of each load aforesaid should be paid in cash, lawful money of the State of New York, on delivery of the lumber as aforesaid, until the whole sum so paid should amount to $5,000; and if the said 500,000 feet of lumber should amount to more than $5,000, at the rates aforesaid, then for such excess the payment should be at the same rates, but in goods in manner as aforesaid, until the total sum should amount to $6,000; and for any excess above $6,000, the payment should be at the same rates in money, as aforesaid. And it was thereby understood and agreed, that the said defendants should give to the said plaintiff at least thirty days' notice of the description of goods which they might require under the said agreement; and they might have the privilege of delivering the said 500,000 feet of lumber as much sooner than the time mentioned herein as might suit their convenience. It was also understood and agreed, that the measurement mentioned in the agreement meant "inch measure." And for the faithful performance and fulfilment of the several conditions of the said agreement, the said plaintiff and defendants bound themselves severally each, his heirs, executors, administrators and assigns, to the other, his heirs, executors, administrators and assigns, firmly by these presents. And the plaintiff avers that although, after the making of the said articles of agreement, he has

been always ready and willing to perform and fulfil everything in the said agreement on his part to be performed and fulfilled; yet the defendants did not, nor would, although requested so to do, deliver or cause to be delivered to the plaintiff 100,000 feet of pine lumber, of any or either of the descriptions in the said articles of agreement mentioned, during the said month of May, in the year of our Lord, 1844, or at any time before or since, but therein wholly failed and made default.

And for assigning a further breach, according to the form of the statute, the plaintiff avers that the said defendants did not, nor would, although requested so to do, deliver or cause to be delivered to the plaintiff 200,000 feet of the pine lumber, of any or either of the descriptions in the said articles of agreement mentioned, during the said month of June in the year last aforesaid, or at any time before or since, but therein wholly failed and made default.

And for assigning a further breach, according to the form of the statute, the plaintiff avers that the said defendants did not, nor would, although requested so to do, deliver or cause to be delivered to the plaintiff the remaining 200,000 feet of pine lumber, of any or either of the descriptions in the said articles of agreement mentioned, on or before the said 1st day of September, in the year last aforesaid, or at any time since, but therein wholly failed and made default, to the damage of the plaintiff of £500; and therefore he brings his suit, &c.

The defendant demurs to the declaration on these grounds: That it is not alleged when the said articles of agreement bore date; that it is not alleged with sufficient certainty, that the plaintiff was ready and willing to pay the money or deliver the goods in payment for the said lumber, or to give the goods at five per centum profits on New York bills, as in the declaration mentioned, or, if he were so ready and willing, that the defendants had notice thereof; nor is it alleged at what time the plaintiff requested the defendants to perform their covenant; and for that the allegation that the said agreement was sealed with the seal of the defendants, shews that there was no legal covenant in this, that the said two defendants do not in any way appear to have a joint or corporate seal; and for that the said declaration is, in other respects, insufficient.

J. Hillyard Cameron, counsel for plaintiff.

W. Eccles, counsel for defendants.

ROBINSON, C. J., delivered the judgment of the court.

We are of opinion that, according to the course of pleading, the delivery of the timber and the payment for it, being intended to be concurrent acts, it was necessary for the plaintiff in his declaration, to make his averment of readiness to perform his part more precise than he has done. Instead of alleging that he was ready at all times to perform the agreement on his part, he should have averred expressly that he was ready to pay for the timber in the manner he undertook to do. There does not seem to be much value in the distinction, but the case of Kemble v. Miles, 1 M. & G. 757, and many other authorities, require such an averment, and the objection is taken here on special demurrer.

Judgment for defendants on demurrer.

AMBRIDGE V. FOSTER.

The plaintiff declares on *two* distinct causes of action—the defendant pleads "not guilty of the said supposed grievances:" *Held*, Plea bad on special demurrer.

The plaintiff sues on two distinct causes of action; in one count for a libel, and in another for a verbal slander of a different character.

The defendant pleads that "he is not guilty of the said supposed grievances."

The plaintiff demurs, on the ground that, in and by the said declaration, the plaintiff claims against the defendant for two several causes of action, or two several and distinct grievances, of either one of which the defendant may be guilty, although not of both; while in and by the said first plea the defendant denies being guilty of the said grievances only, but does not deny being guilty of any or either of them.

J. Hillyard Cameron, counsel for plaintiff.

Harrison Q. C., counsel for defendant.

ROBINSON, C. J., delivered the judgment of the court.

If a party, charged with cutting down 100 trees, should plead that he did not cut down the said trees, that would be bad on special demurrer at least as too large a traverse. It could not be applied distributively; and it would be said, that for all that is denied by such a plea, he might have cut down 99 of them. I can see no good ground of distinction between such a plea and the general issue that is pleaded here. The case cited (a) seems to me to turn on a different question; the principle recognized from an early time in regard to replications and subsequent pleadings seems to be, that where the manner of traversing is not such as would prevent the plaintiff from recovering *pro tanto*, then it can be taken distributively, and is well enough. The forms as regards the general issue are certainly without exception, that the defendant did not commit the said grievances or any or either of them. If to a declaration containing a number of separate counts upon as many promissory notes, the defendant was to plead that he did not make the said notes, it would seem certainly a very informal plea, since the question is not whether he made all, but whether he made any of them. This declaration must come within the same principle; and yet it is true that if in any such case the plaintiff were to go to trial on such an issue, he could recover *pro tanto*, from which it should follow that the plea may be taken distributively. On the whole, my inclination is to hold the plea bad, in the absence of any authority to support such a form of general issue, though I must say that I do not see any good reason for not applying to the general issue the principle which in many cases has been applied to other pleadings; that where the plaintiff can recover *pro tanto*, the plea may be taken distributively. The defendant abandons his special pleas, which are demurred to, and as he will probably desire to amend them he may amend this also, and make it conform to the usual course.

Judgment for demurrer.

(a) 13 M. & W. 30.

BROWN ET AL. V. ROSS ET AL.

Where a defendant having stated his defence to part of a declaration, then pleads to another part "and as to the said, &c., that," without using the words "he says:" *Held*, Good on demurrer.

Where a plea of payment of a certain sum is pleaded to two counts, without alleging how much of the said sum is to be paid on each count: *Held*, Good on demurrer.

The plaintiffs declare in *assumpsit* on the common counts.

In their second plea the defendants plead: And as to the said supposed promises in the fifth and sixth counts of the said declaration mentioned, except as to the sum of £36 7s., parcel of the said several sums of money in these counts mentioned, say that they did not promise in manner and form as the plaintiffs have above thereof complained against them; and of this they put themselves upon the country, &c.

And as to the said sum of £36 7s., parcel, &c., the defendants say that the plaintiffs ought not to have or maintain their aforesaid action thereof against them, because they say that after the making the promises in the said fifth and sixth counts mentioned, as to the said sum of £36 7s., and before the commencement of this suit, to wit, on the 27th day of January, 1846, they the said defendants paid to the plaintiffs a certain large sum of money, to wit, the sum of £36 7s., in full satisfaction and discharge of the said sum of £36 7s., parcel, &c., and of the said promises in the said fifth and sixth counts mentioned in respect of that sum, and of all damages sustained by the plaintiffs by reason of the non-performance of such promises as to that sum; and this the defendants are ready to verify, &c.

Demurrer: That the said second plea is nonsensical and absurd, inasmuch as it does not state who it is that denies the promises in the fifth and sixth counts of the declaration; and that the said plea is uncertain and insufficient, in not specifying particularly whether the said sum of £36 7s. was paid upon promises in the fifth or sixth counts, or which or what was paid upon each, or how much; or on which count, the defendants admit the promises to have been made, or whether on both or not specifically, and that the said second plea is in other respects uncertain, informal and insufficient.

Phillpotts, counsel for plaintiffs.

Blake, counsel for defendants.

ROBINSON, C. J., delivered the judgment of the court.

We are of opinion that the plea is good. The defendants are to be regarded as if they were in court, answering *ore tenus* the plaintiffs' declaration. They would be then seen, and understood to be the same persons speaking throughout; and after taking their defence as to one part, they would proceed: "And as to "the other;" &c. It would be no defect that they did not repeat the words, "we say." The record in stating the whole defence made, states that the defendants, as to some of the counts, plead a certain plea; "And as to the "fifth and sixth counts, say." There is no want of sense or grammar in this, although the nominative case to the word say is not repeated as it commonly is.

With regard to the plea of payment, the objection rests on the case of Mee v. Tomlinson, 4 A. & E. 262, which is overruled in the case cited of

Mitchell v. Townley, 7 A. & E. 164; and subsequent decisions support the mode of pleading which has been followed here. The plea being good, in our opinion, it is not material to consider whether the demurrer has not been in fact put in to the wrong plea. I think it has been, for there are in fact three pleas in all, and the demurrer is to the second plea, when the objection is to the third.   Judgment for defendants on demurrer.

Fralick v. Lafferty.

To an action on the common counts, the defendant, A., pleads that it was agreed between the plaintiff, B., and the defendant, A., and a third party, C., that C. should sell to B. all the claim, title and right of pre-emption which C. had to certain land, and that C. should execute a deed at B.'s request to D., in satisfaction of B.'s claim; and then avers that C. did, by the procurement of A., at B.'s request, execute a deed to D. of *all* the title C. had to the land: *Held*, Plea bad on demurrer, in not averring that the defendant, A., had a certain right and interest in the land, and of a certain value, and that his conveyance to D. was *accepted* in satisfaction.

The plaintiff declares in *assumpsit* on the common counts.

The defendant pleads: That after the making the promises in the said declaration mentioned, and before the commencement of this suit, to wit, on the first day of June, in the year of our Lord one thousand eight hundred and forty-four, it was agreed between the plaintiff and the defendant, and one Alexander S. Lafferty, that in full satisfaction and discharge of the promise aforesaid, the said Alexander S. Lafferty by the procurement and at the request of the defendant, should, *and did then and there* SELL, and the plaintiff should, *and did*, then and there *purchase* all the claim, title, and right of pre-emption, which the said Alexander S. Lafferty then had or *would or might have* in or to lots number forty-seven and forty-eight, situate and being on the Grand River, in the Gore District; and that the said Alexander S. Lafferty, should by deed, executed under his hand and seal, convey, assign, and assure unto one Barnabas Crane, to whom the said plaintiff was desirous of selling such claim, title, and right of pre-emption of the said Alexander S. Lafferty as aforesaid. And the defendant further saith, that afterwards, to wit, on the day and year aforesaid, the said Alexander S. Lafferty, did in pursuance of the said agreement, and by the procurement of the defendant, by deed executed under his hand and seal, convey, assign, and assure unto the said Barnabas Crane, at the said plaintiff's request, *all the claim, title, and right of pre-emption of the said Alexander S. Lafferty, in and to the lots numbers forty-seven and forty-eight* as aforesaid; and this the defendant is ready to verify, &c.

Demurrer: For that it is not averred that the plaintiff accepted the conveyance therein mentioned in satisfaction, but merely that he agreed to accept. That it is not averred that the said Lafferty ever had or *would or might* have any claim, title, or right of pre-emption to the said lots. That the value of said land, or of the said right of the said Lafferty thereto, is not shewn, so that it does not appear to the court whether it was equivalent to the plaintiff's claim. That it is not averred that the plaintiff agreed that the conveyance should be made to the said Crane therein named, or that he consented to such conveyance, or that the said Crane agreed to accept, or did accept the same. That it is not averred that the said agreement was in writing signed by the plaintiff, or in any manner binding upon him. That the said plea shews no legal answer to the declaration.

Vankoughnet, counsel for plaintiff.

H. Eccles, counsel for defendant.

ROBINSON, C. J., delivered the judgment of the court.

The plea in our opinion is bad, in not averring that the defendant had a certain right and interest in the land, and of a certain value, and that his conveyance to Crane was *accepted* in satisfaction.—4 M. & W. 658; 3 E. R. 256; 1 Str. 573.

It would of course have been unnecessary to aver that there had been any agreement in writing on the subject, because the defence rests not on an executory but an executed agreement.

For the objections mentioned, the judgment must be for the plaintiff on the demurrer.

BLACK V. STEVENSON.

The plaintiff, in an action of covenant against the father of an apprentice, alleges as a breach, that the apprentice unlawfully absented himself on a certain day, and from thence hitherto *remained and continued* absent from the service of the plaintiff. Plea, that the apprentice did absent and depart from the service of the plaintiff, by his leave and license: *Held*, Sufficient, without pleading a license to *continue* absent, as the plea only professed to answer the absenting himself from the plaintiff's service. *Held*, also, That the plea need not shew that the license to be absent was given by deed or in writing.

Plaintiff declares in covenant, for that whereas heretofore to wit, on the 7th day of October, in the year of our Lord, 1840, by a certain indenture of apprenticeship then made, one part of which said indenture, sealed with the seal of the defendant, the plaintiff now brings here into court, the date whereof is the same day and year aforesaid; one Robert Stevenson did put himself apprentice to the plaintiff to learn his art, trade and mystery of a wheelwright, and with him, after the manner of an apprentice, to serve from the date thereof until the full end and term of five years from thence next following, to be fully complete and ended; during which term it was thereby covenanted and agreed, that the said apprentice his said master faithfully should serve, his secrets keep, his lawful commands gladly do, and that he should not haunt taverns, nor play at cards, dice or any other unlawful game or games, nor absent himself from the service of his said master unlawfully, but in all things as a faithful apprentice should behave himself towards his said master during the said term; and for the true performance of the said Robert Stevenson, of all and every the covenants and agreements therein contained, on the part and behalf of the said Robert Stevenson to be performed and fulfilled, the defendant thereby bound himself unto the plaintiff; as by the said indenture, reference being thereunto had, will amongst other things more fully and at large appear, by virtue of which said indenture the said Robert Stevenson afterwards, to wit, on the said 7th day of October, in the year of our Lord, 1840, entered, and was received into the service of the said plaintiff as such apprentice as aforesaid, and remained and continued in such service, under and by virtue of the said indenture for a long space of time, to wit, from the day and year last aforesaid, until and upon the twenty-first day of February, in the year of our Lord, 1843. And although the plaintiff had always, from the time of the making of the said indenture, hitherto well and truly performed, fulfilled, and kept all things therein mentioned and contained on his part and behalf to be performed, fulfilled, and kept according to the tenor and effect, true intent and meaning thereof; yet the plaintiff in fact saith, that the said Robert Stevenson did not nor would faithfully serve the plaintiff according to the tenor and effect, true intent and meaning of the said indenture; but on the contrary thereto, the said Robert Stevenson, during the said term, to wit, on the twenty-first day of February, in the year of our Lord, 1843, aforesaid, did unlawfully absent himself, and from thence hitherto hath remained and continued absent from the service of the plaintiff, contrary to the tenor and effect of the said indenture, and of the said covenant of the said defendant in that behalf made as aforesaid; and so the plaintiff in fact saith that the defendant, although often requested so to do, hath not kept the said covenant so by him made as aforesaid, but hath broken the same, and to keep the same with the plaintiff hath hitherto wholly neglected and refused, and still doth neglect and refuse, to the damage of the plaintiff of one hundred pounds, and therefore he brings his suit, &c.

The defendant in his third plea, as to the said Robert absenting himself from the service of the plaintiff saith, that he the said Robert Stevenson did absent himself and depart from the service of the said plaintiff in the manner and at the time when, &c., aforesaid, by the leave, license, and permission of the said plaintiff to the said Robert Stevenson for that purpose first given and granted, and this the said defendant is ready to verify, &c.

Demurrer to the third plea, on the ground that it does not show a leave and license from the plaintiff to the said Robert Stevenson to *continue* absent from the said plaintiff's service.

To fourth plea, that the plaintiff caused the illegal imprisonment of the defendant Stevenson, which was the absenting complained of, the plaintiff new assigns, that the apprentice absented himself at a different time, and on another occasion.

The defendant pleads to the new assignment, that the said Robert Stevenson, the said apprentice, at the said time when, &c., absented himself by the leave and license of the plaintiff.

To this plea plaintiff demurs, on the ground that the said plea does not shew in what manner the leave and license was given by the plaintiff to the said Robert Stevenson to absent himself.

Brook for the demurrer.
Durand contra.

ROBINSON, C. J., delivered the judgment of the court.

The defendant is, in our opinion, entitled to judgment on both demurrers. The third plea, on which the first demurrer arises, only professes to answer the absenting and departing *from* service as laid in the declaration, not the continuing absent till the *commencement* of the action; either that is to be taken as including the *continued* absence, or it is not; if it does include it, then the leave pleaded is co-extensive with it, for it is pleaded in the same words, "did absent himself from the service of the plaintiff, with the *leave* and license "of the plaintiff," &c. If the *continued* absence is not included in the words, "did absent from and depart," but only the act of departing, then the plea does not undertake to answer more, and is therefore not faulty in that respect.

As to the plea to the new assignment in the replication to the fourth plea, there is clearly nothing objectionable in it. The cases cited in the argument, from 8 Taunt. 31 and 3 E. R. 344, are inapplicable. There the defendant was endeavouring to shew himself discharged from an obligation under seal by a subsequent parol agreement; what he desired to shew was, that he had been allowed by parol agreement to do something inconsistent with his contract under seal. It is not so here; the covenant is not that the apprentice shall never absent himself, but that he shall not absent himself without *his master's leave*, and the complaint in the declaration is, that the apprentice absented himself unlawfully. To shew a breach of this covenant, therefore, the plaintiff must shew a wrongful absenting, that is, without leave; and if the plaintiff gave leave there is no breach. By comparing this case with Sillers v. Beckford, 8 Taunt. 31, the difference is evident. The defendant here is seeking no discharge from the condition of his deed; he shews that he has performed it. It is not required by the covenant that the master must give his leave in writing or under seal, and it would be an absurdly inconvenient stipulation to enter into. Judgment for the defendant on demurrer.

GEDDES V. CULVER ET AL.

A *bona fide* endorser without notice, who takes a bill of exchange or note in payment of an *antecedent debt*, and not upon a *new consideration* given at the time by discount or otherwise, is not protected against the defence of usury, by our Provincial Act, 7 Will. IV. ch. 5. There is no distinction, in this respect, between the effect of our Act, and of the British Act, 58 Geo. III. ch. 93.

Assumpsit: Second endorser of a promissory note against the makers.

Plea: Usury between the first endorser and the makers.

Replication: That the said promissory note, in the said first count mentioned, was endorsed to the plaintiff before the said note became due, to wit, on the day and year in the said declaration in that behalf mentioned, for valuable consideration, that is to say, for and in consideration of the plaintiff discounting the same, and paying therefor to the said John McFarland, being then the holder thereof, a large sum of money, to wit, the amount of the said sum of money in the said promissory note, less the legal interest thereon, for the time which the said note then had to run; and that he, the plaintiff, had not at the time when the said note was so endorsed to the plaintiff as aforesaid, or at the time of so discounting the same, or paying such consideration for the said promissory note as aforesaid, or at any time before actual or any notice that the said promissory note had been made, endorsed or given, for the usurious consideration, or upon the usurious contract in the said plea to the said first count in that behalf mentioned, or upon any usurious consideration, or upon any usurious contract whatsoever; and this the plaintiff is ready to verify, &c.

Rejoinder: That the said promissory note was endorsed to the plaintiff by the said John McFarland, to secure the payment of a certain debt, to wit, £150, due from the said John McFarland, to the plaintiff long before the said day when the said note was endorsed to the plaintiff, *without this* that the said plaintiff discounted the said note, or paid the said sum of money in the said replication mentioned, in manner and form as the plaintiff has alleged; and of this they put themselves upon the country, &c.

Demurrer to rejoinder: For that the defendants have not in and by the inducement in their special traverse, by way of rejoinder, denied, confessed or avoided the substantial matter in the said replication above alleged, in this, that while the plaintiff in his replication to the said first plea of the defendants, averred that the said note in the said declaration mentioned was endorsed to him for valuable consideration, and without notice of the usury alleged by the defendants in their said first plea, to have been committed, they the said defendants, in their said rejoinder, have not denied, confessed or avoided the endorsement to the plaintiff for valuable consideration, but have denied that the consideration for the endorsement to plaintiff was in its particulars such as is mentioned in the said replication, the said particulars of consideration stated in the replication being mere surplusage, and wholly immaterial to the merits of the case.

J. Lukin Robinson for the demurrer.

W. Eccles contra.

ROBINSON, C. J., delivered the judgment of the court.

It seems clear that, under the English statute 58 Geo. III. chap. 93, it has been held that an endorsee who took the note or bill in payment of an antecedent debt, and who did not pay a consideration for the note at the time he took it by discounting it or otherwise, would not be protected against the defence of usury.—Vallance v. Siddell (a). The holders of such negotiable securities are now put on a better footing by the 5 & 6 Will. IV. chap. 41; and such a distinction as was in Vallance v. Siddel, founded on the words of 58 Geo. III. chap. 93, now no longer exists. The court, it is evident, gave way to it in that case with reluctance. The question then here is, whether our statute 7 Will. IV. ch. 5, which, in the main, closely follows the British statute 58 Geo. III. ch. 93, can be differently applied, by reason of the difference in their language, which has been relied on. Our statute differs in extending the provisions in express terms to bearers—the British Act being limited to endorsers; and, in respect to bearers, it uses the words "who shall have *acquired* the same "for valuable consideration:" thereby not limiting its operation as to bearers, to persons who had *paid* a consideration for the bill. A party taking a bill payable to bearer, in payment of a prior debt, *acquires it for a valuable consideration;* but the concluding words of our statute bring the case even as to bearers under the same construction as the British statute received in Vallance v.

(a) 6 A. & E. 933.

Siddell, and on the same reasoning, for it makes it material to ascertain whether the *bona fide* holder knew of the usury, when he discounted or paid such consideration for the bill, thereby connecting the enacting clause with the preamble, which is *verbatim* the same as in the British statute.

Upon the same pleadings, therefore, we are driven to the same decison upon this point as in Vallance v. Siddell. The question still remains, whether the rejoinder is informal, traversing the particular mode of acquiring the note set out in the replication, namely, by discounting, and thereby raising an immaterial issue; since if the plaintiff purchased the bill by giving any new consideration for it, and did not discount it, he would equally be protected by the statute. That depends on whether the rejoinder, concluding as it does to the country, places the matter of inducement in issue. Our 36th rule, Easter Term, 5 Vic., allows the party to plead to the inducement, when the traverse is immaterial, notwithstanding the conclusion to the country; but the traverse here is not immaterial—it denies all that the replication asserts; and, if it did not sufficiently answer it, then the plaintiff might have pleaded to the matter of the inducement.

Judgment for defendants on demurrer.

DOE EX DEM. HARRIS & WIFE V. BENSON.

The court, under particular circumstances, declined to grant a third new trial in ejectment, though they thought the evidence strongly preponderated against the verdict.

Ejectment for part of Lot No. 5, in the 1st concession of Thurlow, which the defendant defends for, as being Lot No. 35, on the west side of Rear Street, in the town of Belleville.

The plaintiffs had succeeded in two former trials, and shewing no disposition to take their case to trial a third time, the defendant, who had obtained a rule for a new trial, took the case down by proviso. The learned judge, agreeing in the view taken by the court at the former trials, of the evidence given, which did not materially differ from that given on the last trial, directed the jury that, although the decision of the boundary commissioners had established that according to the true division line between Lots 4 & 5 in the 1st concession of Thurlow, the land claimed formed part of Lot 5, of which lot the plaintiffs are seised in fee, yet that there had been a discontinuance of possession by the plaintiffs, and those under whom they claimed, for more than twenty years, which extinguished their title. The ground being considered by the government to form part of Lot No. 4, had been, so long ago as in 1817, laid out by public authority as part of the town of Belleville, and was soon after granted by patent as a town lot; and since that period, and indeed long before, the plaintiffs, and those under whom they claim, had excluded it from their enclosure.

The jury, contrary to the charge of the judge, gave a third verdict for the plaintiffs.

Hon. *R. B. Sullivan* moved to set aside this verdict, as being contrary to law and evidence and the judge's charge.

Hon. *R. Baldwin* shewed cause.

ROBINSON, C. J., delivered the judgment of the court.
Considering the circumstances, we think that we ought not to grant a third new trial in this case. The question upon which three juries have successively determined, is purely one of fact; and upon a former trial, I recollect that the evidence, though it appeared to preponderate much in favour of the defendant, was certainly contradictory. The plaintiffs, it now appears by the affidavit filed, were willing, as the value of the land in question is trifling, to have forborne all further contest about it, and had proposed to the defendant that each party should pay his own costs; but the defendant insisted on proceeding, and took the record down to trial by proviso. He had it tried also, by a special jury of his own choosing; for it is sworn that the plaintiff waived his privilege of striking off the names of any of the jurors drawn. He ought now, we think, when there has been no misdirection, to abide by the result, so far as this action is concerned. He can, of course, become the plaintiff in ejectment, if he wishes to contest the matter further. Granting three new trials in ejectment would be a very unusual course; and we think it right to consider that upon this last trial the defendant did not shew that he had any title whatever to the property, or any interest in it; he contented himself with endeavouring to satisfy the jury that, whatever right the plaintiffs might otherwise have had, they had lost by the effect of the Statute of Limitations. Having already had three opportunities of satisfying a jury that the plaintiffs had lost their right by mere discontinuance of possession, we think we ought not to grant him a fourth, especially considering the circumstances under which he went before the last jury.

Rule discharged.

DOE DEM. WHEELER V. MCWILLIAMS.

Where a marriage in fact has been proved, evidence of reputation and cohabitation is not sufficient to establish a prior marriage.

Where the losing party has been wanting in diligence to make out his case at the trial, the court will not, as a matter of course, relieve against the verdict though it may appear to be contrary to evidence.

Ejectment for Lot No. 12 in the 3rd concession of the township of King.

The verdict, which was for the plaintiff, affirmed the title of the lessor of the plaintiff to inherit as brother and heir of the grantee of the crown, Hephzibat McWilliams (formerly Wheeler), in opposition to the defendant claiming under her son and heir by the alleged marriage with Caleb McWilliams.

Vankoughnet moved for a new trial on the law and evidence, and on affidavits.

H. Eccles shewed cause.

ROBINSON, C. J., delivered the judgment of the court.
It all turns on the question whether a marriage in fact between the patentee and Caleb McWilliams in 1801, by a magistrate, Col. Baldwin, having been proved, the evidence which was given of a prior marriage of Hephzibat

Wheeler to Burton, was such as ought to have been received and held sufficient to disprove the legality of the second marriage.

This evidence of the first marriage was not in our opinion sufficient, because it was only that evidence of marriage by reputation and cohabitation of the parties which would be admissible for the purpose, if no subsequent marriage had taken place, destroying the presumption which would otherwise have arisen from this description of evidence.

It is unnecessary to repeat the grounds of this opinion, which were fully expressed upon the occasion of our granting the new trial after the first verdict.

But now a new consideration has arisen; the plaintiff, who obtained a verdict at the last trial, which in effect affirms the fact of the first marriage in the opinion of the jury, has, in opposition to this motion, filed an affidavit declaring in express terms that his sister, Hephzibat Wheeler, was legally married on a certain day in the Eastern District, by the Rev. Mr. Bethune, a Presbyterian clergyman, and that he was himself present at the ceremony. It is true that the lessor of the plaintiff, who makes this affidavit, cannot be admitted to prove this on a trial, on account of his interest in the cause; but when he made this affidavit, in Michaelmas Term last, he afforded to the defendant full opportunity to inform himself of the truth of this statement; for it must be presumed that Mr. Bethune, as the known resident minister of a congregation, preserved the usual record of the marriage, if it really was solemnized. Before, therefore, we put these parties to further costs, in a litigation which must turn upon that point, we desired the defendant to avail himself of the source of information thus disclosed to him, and ascertain whether he could, upon another trial, if it were granted to him, successfully meet the evidence of the marriage which he is now told exists.

The defendant, while he strenuously urges a new trial, declines to take the obvious means of learning whether a new trial can be of any advantage or not. We do not feel we are compelled, under such circumstances, to grant a new trial on the point of *summum jus*, because the first marriage was not conclusively proved, when the defendant will give himself no trouble to shew us that he can repel the proof of the alleged first marriage upon another trial.

But there is another point in the case; the defendant intends that he gave or could have given some evidence of a will made by his mother, Hephzibat McWilliams (so called), in favour of his brother, under which he claims; which will, if the first marriage were established, would prove to be valid, being made by the widow of Barton, when she could not be held to be the wife of McWilliams. We do not find, in the notes of the learned judge who presided at the trial, any such clear testimony in regard to such a devise, as to shew satisfactorily how the case might turn out to be upon any evidence that can be given of that will; but to allow that fact to be cleared up before the possession is changed, we will grant to the defendant a new trial, on the condition that the costs shall abide the event; which will be but just, because if the defendant, after what is now disclosed, shall protract an expensive litigation without an object, it will be right that the plaintiff, who now has the verdict, should not be needlessly exposed to the cost of a second trial, if it must have the same result.

Rule made absolute, costs to abide the event of a new trial.

CAMPBELL V. ELLIOTT ET AL.

To a declaration upon a special count for dismissing the plaintiff, a schoolmaster, from his situation, before the end of his term, without probable cause, the defendant, A., pleads, justifying the dismissal, but at the same time averring that B., another defendant, made the contract with the plaintiff, and that he, A., *specially approved* the same : *Held*, Plea bad, in not confessing the cause of action, and as amounting to the general issue, and for being double.

The plaintiff declares specially in *assumpsit*, upon a retainer of him by the defendants for a year as schoolmaster, and assigns as a breach the dismissing him, without any reasonable cause, before the expiration of the term.

The defendant, Elliott, pleads to this special count that the said school in the said count mentioned, was a county model school in and for the District of London, pursuant to the statute in that case made and provided—of which model school the defendants, Henry Black, Martial T. Moore and George Southwick, were trustees ; that the said Henry Black, Martial T. Moore and George Southwick, as such trustees, at the said time when, &c., appointed the said plaintiff teacher of the said model school, to wit, for the term of one year from the said time when, &c., subject to the provisions of the statute, with the special approval of the said William Elliott, who before and at the said time when, &c., was, and from thence hitherto hath been, and still is, the county superintendent of common schools for the said District of London ; and the said William Elliott, as such county superintendent, afterwards, to wit, on the 18th day of September, in the year aforesaid, considered it was necessary to dismiss, and did then actually dismiss, the said plaintiff as such teacher of the said model school, as it was lawful for him to do under and by virtue of the said statute ; of all which the plaintiff afterwards, to wit, on the day and year last aforesaid, had notice ; which is the said supposed non-performance, by the said William Elliott, in the said first count mentioned ; and this the said William Elliott is ready to verify, &c.

The plaintiff demurs to this plea on the following grounds : For that the averments in the commencement of the said plea, that the said school was a county model school, and that the other defendants were trustees thereof, are important averments, and should have been laid each of them at and with some specified time or day ; that the term "pursuant," or "according to the "statute," throughout the said plea is not sufficiently explicit ; that the said plea, professing to be a plea in confession and avoidance, is bad in this, that it does not sufficiently, or indeed at all, confess the cause of action, to which it is pleaded, merely acknowledging a "special approval" (and that not in writing) of the appointment of the plaintiff by the other defendants, and not acknowledging any liability originally or at all from the defendant William Elliott to the plaintiff ; that the said plea amounts only to *non-assumpsit*, and is one on which issue cannot be taken, and is otherwise informal and insufficient ; and that the second plea is bad, for the special causes in the demurrer set forth ; and also that it is bad, as not shewing some ground or reasonable cause for the dismissal of the plaintiff by the county superintendent Elliott, who pleads.

Blake and *Becher* for the demurrer.

Hagarty, contra.

ROBINSON, C. J., delivered the judgment of the court.

We think the objection to this plea of the defendant Elliott is well founded ; it denies, rather than confesses and avoids, the alleged promise by the defendant Elliott. What is shewn is apparently advanced as a good ground for not retaining the plaintiff the whole year in service ; but it shews, at the same time, that the defendant was not a contracting party at all, and therefore not interested in avoiding the contract. It amounts to the general issue—a special *non-assumpsit*,—and it is a double defence, for it seems to rely upon a legal dismissal of the plaintiff as putting an end to the contract, while it denies also in substance and effect that any contract had been made by the defendant who pleads to this plea.

Judgment for the plaintiff on demurrer.

SANDERSON & MURRAY V. THE KINGSTON MARINE RAILWAY COMPANY.

Where a wharf has been leased, "with all the privileges thereto belonging," a vessel attached to the wharf by the usual fastenings cannot be distrained upon for rent.

The plaintiffs sue in replevin, for that the defendants on the 1st of September, 1845, "at the premises of the plaintiffs at the foot of Gore Street, in the town "of Kingston, then there lying and being adjacent to a wharf, part of the "premises aforesaid, took the goods and chattels of the plaintiffs," &c.

The defendants avow under a distress for rent, setting forth that the plaintiffs, for a certain sum specified, "held and enjoyed the said premises in "which," &c., with the appurtenances, as tenants thereof to the defendants, at a certain rent ; that a year and one quarter's rent was in arrear ; wherefore the defendants avow the taking of the said goods, "at the said premises, in "which," &c., as a distress.

The plaintiffs, in reply to this plea, say that the defendants ought not to avow the taking of the said goods and chattels, at the said place in which, &c., because they say that the plaintiffs did not hold "the said premises in which, "&c., with the appurtenances, as tenants thereof, to the said defendants, "under the alleged demise, in manner and form," &c., and conclude to the country (the ordinary plea of *non tenuit*).

The defendants pleaded also a plea, denying the plaintiffs' property in the goods upon which issue was joined.

The defendants had by indenture demised to the plaintiffs "the stone ware-"house and the wharf on which it stands, and the frame warehouse and the "wharf on which it stands, both situated at the foot of Gore Street, in the "town of Kingston, together with a right of way twelve feet wide from Gore "Street to each of the above mentioned premises, as shewn in a plan annexed "to the lease, *and all the privileges thereto belonging.*" And there being rent in arrear, the defendants distrained on a steamer and propeller and four barges of the plaintiffs', which were lying in the water of the harbour, attached to the frame wharf by the usual fastenings. It was contended that they were not liable to be distrained, not being on the premises demised.

The jury found for the defendants at the trial, upon a direction from the learned judge that, as the *privilege* of mooring the boats in the basin, by the side of the wharf, was included in the demise, the distress was legal. A new trial was moved for upon the law and evidence, and for misdirection.

Alexander Campbell, counsel for plaintiffs.

Thomas Kirkpatrick, counsel for defendants.

ROBINSON, C. J., delivered the judgment of the court.

Part of the goods, it is admitted, were clearly liable to distress; that is, the rigging, sails, &c., which were seized in the warehouse, but that is of no moment; for, if the plaintiffs failed to recover damages on account of the steamers being illegally distrained, when they ought to have recovered such damages, there should be a new trial to correct that error.

It seems quite clear that, as the rent issues out of the land demised, it can only be distrained for on the land demised (unless in case of clandestine removal, under the statute). The land covered with the water in which these boats were lying, was not included in the demise. It would not pass under the term "privileges," or appurtenances, for the reasons stated in the case cited in the argument (a), and no rent could issue out of the mere privilege or easement. That case, indeed, contains all the reasoning and authority that must decide the present case, unless we can find a substantial distinction in the facts, which we do not think we can. When it came before the Common Pleas (b), it was determined that the vessel, being attached to a wharf that had been demised, might be distrained upon for the rent issuing out of the wharf, being as much upon the premises as in the nature of things she could be; and to me, I confess, that seemed a reasonable decision, but it was reversed in error (c); and upon the same facts, between the same parties, being found in a special verdict, the Court of King's Bench held the vessel not liable to distress, as not being upon the premises demised. It is true that the jury there found expressly that the ground over which the vessels had been moored was not *demised;* but it is quite clear, upon authority, that we must also hold in this case that the water and the land it covered, being outside of the wharf, were not included in the demise before us. The special verdict in Buzzard v. Capel, expressly found that the vessel or barge was attached to the "wharf by ropes, head and stern," and yet the court held that she was not liable where she lay to be distrained upon, not being in or upon the premises demised. We are of opinion that there must be a new trial, without costs.

LACEY V. SPENCER.

To an action of covenant on a deed, the fraud, covin and misrepresentation of the plaintiff may be pleaded in general terms.

Qu.—Can a misrepresentation avoid a contract, without its being fraudulently made?

The plaintiff declared for a breach of covenant in a deed.

Plea: That the deed was obtained from the defendant by the fraud, covin and misrepresentation of the plaintiff.

(a) Buzzard v. Capel, 8 B. & C. 141 (Man. & Ry. 197).
(b) 4 Bing. 139.   (c) 6 Bing. 153.

Demurrer: For that the plea does not state what the fraud was.
H. Eccles for the demurrer.
J. Hillyard Cameron, contra.

ROBINSON, C. J., delivered the judgment of the court.

The plea is not more general than the form always used (a). In Robson v. Luscombe (b), there is an intimation that a plea in these terms might not be held good if specially demurred to, on account of "misrepresentation" being relied upon, when only alleged in such general terms. The judge there added, that it ought to have been averred that the misrepresentation was fraudulently made. As neither of these points was adjudged in that case, we are not warranted in taking it as an authority for holding a form of pleading to be bad, which has been sanctioned by so long a usage under the observation of eminent pleaders and judges.

We shall abide by the general form of pleading adopted in making this defence from the time of Lord Coke, until it has been adjudged insufficient, and especially since it is not solely upon the ground that fraud and covin are supposed to lie only within the knowledge of the party practising it, that the general form of pleading has been allowed; that ground would not apply to misrepresentation, but another reason would, which has led the courts to permit this general method of pleading, namely, to avoid prolixity and the risk of failure from variances in stating minute particulars. I apprehend whenever it comes to be maturely considered, whether misrepresentation may not avoid a contract without its having been fraudulently made, it will be determined that fraud is not indispensable to such a defence.

Judgment for defendant on demurrer.

JONES V. HAMILTON.

The plaintiff in his declaration charges the defendant with the non-performance of a certain contract; the defendant pleads, that the said contract was not duly performed by the said parties, to wit, the plaintiff and the defendant, respectively, in manner, &c.: *Held,* Plea bad, in leaving it uncertain which of the said parties had not performed the contract, and in what particular it had not been performed.

The plaintiff declared specially in *assumpsit,* for that whereas heretofore and before the making of the promise and undertakings by the defendant hereinafter in this count mentioned, to wit, on the first day of April, in the year of our Lord, 1838, the said plaintiff owned and was possessed of certain steamboats, to wit, the steamboats *William IV.* and *Sir Robert Peel,* then navigating Lake Ontario and the River St. Lawrence; and the defendant also owned and was possessed of certain other steamboats, to wit, six other steamboats, also navigating the said lake and river aforesaid. And whereas Her Majesty's Government, before that time, to wit, on the first day of March, in the year aforesaid, had advertised and given public notice to receive from the owners and masters of steamboats navigating as aforesaid, tenders for contracts, for

---

(a) 2 Chit. Pl. page 176; 2 M. & S., 378; 9 Co. 110.
(b) 2 D. & L., 859.

the transport, carrying and conveying of all descriptions of munitions of war and store, and for the conveyance of troops of all kinds and description, and other persons connected with the said government; and for other purposes in the said tenders to be more particularly described and set forth, for the year aforesaid. And whereas it was thereupon agreed, by and between the plaintiff and the defendant, that he the defendant should tender for the said government transport for the said year, with the said steamboats aforesaid of the defendant, and include in his said tender the said steamboats, *William IV.* and *Sir Robert Peel*, so belonging to the said plaintiff as aforesaid; and that the whole of the business done in the said contract, shall be divided into eight shares; and that the said two steamboats, *William IV.* and *Sir Robert Peel*, should receive two-eighths of the whole business; and that the expenses attending the arrangement and settlement of the accounts, shall be divided and charged in the same manner. In consideration of which promise, and that he the plaintiff then and there undertook and faithfully promised the defendant, to perform and keep the said agreement in all things in his part and behalf to be performed and kept, he the defendant then undertook and faithfully promised the plaintiff, to pay the plaintiff two-eighths of the whole of any sum or sums of money which he the defendant should receive upon the said contract, deducting the expenses attending the arrangement and settlement of the accounts as aforesaid. And the plaintiff in fact saith, that afterwards, to wit, on the 10th day of April, in the year aforesaid, in pursuance of the said agreement, the defendant did tender for the said government contract, and did include in the said tender the said steamboats of the plaintiff, and did afterwards, to wit, on the day and year last aforesaid, accordingly enter into contract with Her Majesty's Government for the conveyance and transport aforesaid; and although the said contract with Her Majesty's Government was afterwards duly performed by the said parties respectively, to wit, in and for the year aforesaid; and although the plaintiff hath in all things performed and kept the said agreement in all things on his part and behalf to be performed and kept; and although the defendant afterwards, to wit, on the 1st day of January, in the year of our Lord, 1839, did receive from Her Majesty Government, over and above all expenses attending the arrangement and settlement of the accounts, as aforesaid, a large sum of money, to wit, the sum of eight thousand pounds, of lawful money of Canada, for the business done on the said contract, and for the performance of the same; yet the defendant, although often requested so to do, did not, nor would, nor hath he paid to the said plaintiff two-eighths of the said sum of eight thousand pounds, to wit, the sum of two thousand pounds of the said sum of eight thousand pounds so by him, the defendant, received from Her Majesty's Government, for and in account of the said contract, over and above the said expenses or any part thereof, but wholly neglected and refused so to do, and still neglects and refuses so to do.

Plea: That the said contract, in the first count mentioned, with Her Majesty's Government, was not duly performed by the said parties (to wit, the plaintiff and the defendant respectively), in manner and form as the plaintiff hath above in his said first count in that behalf alleged; and concludes to the country, &c.

Demurrer to plea: For that there is nothing in the said plea stated, upon which the plaintiff can safely take issue; and also, that the same is no answer to the said first count of the declaration, for the said first count does not state that the contract was to be performed by the plaintiff in any way; and also, that the said plea is uncertain in this, that it does not state in what particular the plaintiff has not performed the contract, or what contract particularly; and also, that the same is uncertain in not stating by which of the said parties the contract was not performed; and for all that appears, it may be that the defendant is the party who has not performed his contract; and that the said plea ought to have concluded with a verification; and that the said plea is neither a plea in bar to said first count, neither is the same a plea in confession and avoidance of the said first count.

Phillpotts for the demurrer.
Alexander Campbell, contra.

ROBINSON, C. J., delivered the judgment of the court.

We think this plea bad. It assumes that the contracting parties mentioned in the declaration are the plaintiff and the defendant in this suit; whereas it is clear that the parties to the contract out of which the payment of eight thousand pounds arose (of which the plaintiff claims his share), was the government on the one side, and this defendant on the other. And I understand the plaintiff as alleging, that although the contract in the fruits of which he was to share was duly executed, and eight thousand pounds in consequence paid to the defendant; and although the plaintiff hath in all things fulfilled his agreement with the defendant, yet the defendant hath not kept his agreement with the plaintiff, but refuses to pay the one-eighth of the money received on their joint account. But if the defendant's reading of the declaration were correct, and we are to understand the plaintiff as asserting that he and the defendant both kept their contract with the government (though the plaintiff entered into no contract whatever with the government), yet the plea is bad, for it rests the defence on the assertion, that the contract with the government was not duly performed *by the plaintiff and defendant respectively,* thereby leaving it uncertain whether he means to charge the plaintiff with a failure, or to set up his own failure to perform his contract as a reason why he should keep all the money which he does not deny he has received; and this failure might, for all that is stated, have been in some trifling particular, which the government had waived, and if so, there could be no reason why the defendant should not divide the money according to the contract. If the fact really was, that after the contract was made, the plaintiff would not allow his boats to assist in performing it, that would be a good defence, but it is not the defence pleaded. Judgment for the plaintiff on demurrer.

BLEEKER V. COLMAN.

Where premises have been let, and the tenant is in possession, the landlord has no right of action against a defendant for breaking and entering the said premises and pulling down the fences, unless the defendant has at some other time removed the rails and converted them to his own use.

Trespass *quare clausum fregit,* for an alleged entering three closes of the plaintiff, being composed of the south half or front part of Lot No 3, in the

2nd concession of Thurlow, describing the tract by metes and bounds, for breaking gates, treading down grass, &c., cutting and carrying away hay and corn, destroying the trees, and breaking down, prostrating and destroying 100 perches of the fences of the plaintiff, of and belonging to the said closes respectively, and taking and carrying away divers, viz., 2,000 rails and 1,000 poles, composing the fences of the plaintiff of and belonging to the said closes, of great value, &c., and converting and disposing thereof to his own use.

The defendant pleaded, 1st, The general issue.

2ndly, As to breaking and entering the closes, and taking and carrying away the rails and poles, that they were his, and that the plaintiff wrongfully took them away and placed them in the said closes, wherefore the defendant entered and retook them.

3rdly, That the closes were not the plaintiff's.

4thly, As to the trespasses, except as to the gates, bars, fences, rails and poles, that the closes, grass, corn, &c., were not the plaintiff's.

Issue on all the pleas.

Verdict for the plaintiff, £2 10s. damages.

It appeared upon the trial, that the plaintiff had leased the premises for five years, to one Bath, who was to pay rent in kind, that is, a certain share of the produce; and that Bath was in actual possession as tenant, at the time of the alleged trespass. The defendant therefore maintained that he alone could bring trespass for entering upon the land and destroying or removing the rails; and leave was reserved to him to move in *banc* for a nonsuit on that point.

Wallbridge moved accordingly.

Benson shewed cause.

ROBINSON, C. J., delivered the judgment of the court.

We are of opinion that this plaintiff had not, at the time of the alleged trespass, such a possession of the *locus in quo* as entitled him to bring trespass for the wrongful entry. And as to the rails, they surrounded the field of which the tenant, and not the plaintiff, was in possession. The entry on the premises, and prostrating and removing the fence a few feet, was all one act, and was an injury to the tenant's enjoyment of the field, and his use of the rails. There was no conversion of them to the defendant's own use, nor any subsequent removal of them at another time; which would bring the Act within the principle of those cases where, if a stranger enters on land demised to a tenant, and cuts down trees, and afterwards cuts up the trees and removes the timber, it has been held that the tenant has an action for entering upon his possession and cutting down the trees, thereby depriving him of their use for shade and shelter; and the landlord may also sue, for the conversion of his chattels, which the trees became as soon as they were felled and made into timber.

Rule absolute for nonsuit.

McLeod v. Torrance.

A judge will not certify under the statute 4 Anne, ch. 16, sec 5, to protect a defendant against paying the costs of a plea which he knows is not true in itself, but which he pleads for a collateral purpose.

An application was made by the defendant, to the judge who tried this cause, to certify under the statute 4 Anne, ch. 16, sec. 5, in order to protect him against paying the costs of a plea on which he failed at the trial.

The plaintiff sued on a note. The defendant pleaded, besides other pleas, that he did not make the note declared on. It was proved at the trial that he did make it, and it was not pretended that he had any ground for denying that fact; but the defendant alleges as his reason for pleading the plea, that it was important to him to enforce the production of the note upon the trial, with a view to his defence on a special plea, that the note had been given upon an agreement with this plaintiff such as the law deems fraudulent, being intended to assure to him the full amount of his debt, in fraud of other creditors who had consented to a composition in which this plaintiff appeared also to them to be concurring. The defendant urged, that with a view to that defence it would be necessary to identify the note to which the evidence was to be applied; and he therefore put the plaintiff to prove the note in order that he might be compelled to produce it.

The learned judge to whom the application was made for a certificate, hesitated to receive this as a ground for certifying, and referred the party to the court.

Crooks now made a similar application to the court.

J. Hillyard Cameron shewed cause.

ROBINSON, C. J., delivered the judgment of the court.

We think the learned judge did right in refusing the application. The expression in the statute is, "unless the judge shall certify that the defendant " had *a probable cause to plead* such matter which upon the said issue shall be " found against him;" which can only be reasonably understood to mean, that he had *probable* cause for believing that to be true which he had pleaded; not that he had an excuse, in some ulterior object or motive, for pleading a plea which he knew to be contrary to the fact. Such a motive as the defendant alleges does not come fairly within the intention of the statute, and there need be no desire to strain this provision in his favour, for he did actually make the note for the fraudulent purpose intended, in which he was concurring, and he has no cause of complaint if he has relieved himself from the effect of his own voluntary undertaking at the expense of a few shillings, occasioned by his pleading a false plea, in order to help him in his defence.

Rule discharged.

Cramer v. Hodgson.

To an action upon a bond, the defendant cannot set up as a defence a *separate* agreement, not under seal, alleged to have been entered into *at the same time* with the making of the bond, varying the condition from that which the bond itself imports.

Debt on bond, conditioned to pay the plaintiff £75 with interest, after the expiration of one year from the date, in the following manner, viz., £18 15s.

on the 26th November, 1845, and the like sum in three annual instalments, with interest, on the 26th November in each of the three following years; assigning a breach, in not paying the first instalment.

The defendant pleaded a set-off for work and labour, and materials found, goods sold, &c. &c. &c.

2nd, Payment.

Verdict for the plaintiff, and damages assessed on the breach at £7 19s. 4½d.

At the trial the defendant offered evidence to prove that this bond was given for the price of a house, sold by the plaintiff to the defendant, and that at the time the bond was given, an agreement was made in writing between the parties, not under seal, that the plaintiff should, by a time specified, do certain work upon the house sold, and that if he failed in doing it, the defendant should be at liberty to get it done and deduct its estimated cost from the amount payable by the bond.

The learned judge rejected this evidence, on account of the alleged agreement not being under seal. It was not produced, the defendant alleging that it was lost.

A set-off was proved of the amount of goods sold by the defendant to the plaintiff, and the verdict is for the balance.

Wallbridge moved to set aside the verdict for misdirection and improper rejection of evidence.

Alex. Campbell shewed cause.

ROBINSON, C. J., delivered the judgment of the court.

We are of opinion that the evidence was rightly rejected. Any such agreement appearing on the same paper as the bond might be regarded as incorporated with it and forming part of it; but nothing of this kind being written on the same paper, we must take the bond and condition to be the only admissible evidence of what was then agreed. And if such an agreement as is spoken of, not being under seal, were advanced, it was an attempt to explain away the terms of a deed by an agreement not under seal, alleged to have been made at the same time.

The case of May v. King, cited from 12 Mod. 537, is the case of an agreement made subsequently to the bond to receive a horse of the obligee at £20, the money not being yet due on the bond. The court said that, the horse being accepted on that agreement, it had in law the operation of a payment, and ought to be so pleaded. But what the defendant set up here was, that whereas the defendant on a certain day made his bond to pay the plaintiff a certain sum of money, yet that it nevertheless was agreed between them *at the same time*, by another writing not under seal, that he was not to pay that full sum, unless the plaintiff should in the meantime do certain work for him.

This cannot be distinguished from any of those cases which have arisen, where the makers of promissory notes have attempted to set up as a defence that it was agreed at the time that payment should not be exacted at the day mentioned in the note, or some other alleged condition, varying from what the note itself imported, and such evidence has always been rejected.

The defendant's remedy in this case is upon his alleged agreement, as a separate undertaking; and if that has not been made in such a manner that it can be enforced, we cannot help it.

Rule discharged.

COMMERCIAL BANK v. CULROSS, HEWSON & LOVE.
COMMERCIAL BANK v. NEWMAN, HEWSON & LOVE.

Though a certificate of bankruptcy be no discharge to the bankrupt till it be confirmed, an interlocutory judgment entered up against him before the confirmation will be set aside, to allow him to plead his certificate by way of *puis d'arreine continuance;* and if he omits to make such application, the court will still relieve him, by staying the execution of the *fi. fa.* on a proper application being made, after judgment shall have been obtained and execution issued.

In these cases a rule was obtained by *Crooks*, to shew cause why the interlocutory judgment signed against all the defendants, or against Hewson & Love alone, and all subsequent proceedings against the defendants, or against Hewson & Love, should not be set aside, and why Hewson should not be allowed to plead, on payment of costs.

In the first case, in which Hewson is defendant with Culross & Love, a *ca. re.*, not bailable, was sued out on the 6th of February, 1846, and served on Hewson on the 10th of February. The plaintiff entered appearance for the defendant on the 26th of February. The declaration was filed on the 4th of March. The judgment was signed on the 28th of March; and damages assessed against Hewson at the assizes in May, 1846.

On the 21st of November, 1845, a commission of bankruptcy had issued against Hewson, on his own declaration of insolvency filed. On the 9th of March, 1846, he obtained his certificate, which, on the 21st of April following, was confirmed by the Court of Review.

Hewson swears that the note on which he is sued in this action, being provable under the commission, he supposed it would protect him against the verdict, and therefore he *refrained from pleading the commission as a defence.* A similar affidavit was made in the other cause.

J. Hillyard Cameron shewed cause.

ROBINSON, C. J., delivered the judgment of the court.

Our late statute, 9 Vic. chap. 30, contains no provision affecting this case, though it makes some changes in regard to the granting of certificates. Then, under the former Act (from the 59th to the 66th clauses), no doubt the certificate is no discharge till it be confirmed, which it was not here until after the interlocutory judgment had been signed. It could not, therefore, be pleaded before the interlocutory judgment had been signed. The defendant might have applied afterwards to set aside the judgment by default, which, while it stood, prevented him from pleading the bankruptcy and certificate by way of plea *puis d'arreine continuance.* But we think it would be too rigid to hold, that not having done so, he shall be precluded from availing himself of the matter of discharge. The plaintiffs do not in any manner controvert the fact of the certificate, nor shew any ground why the defendant should not have the benefit of it. There is therefore no reason why the defendant should be put to plead, or why the judgment should be set aside.

We think that, no discredit having been thrown upon the certificate which Hewson has obtained, he should have the benefit of it—not by our interposing between the assessment and the judgment, but by staying the execution of the *fi. fa.* as against this defendant, on a proper application being made after judgment shall have been obtained and execution issued.

This application must be discharged, but without costs.

[The plaintiffs hereupon consented to the rule moved being made absolute on payment of costs, wishing to put the defendant to plead his certificate; and it was ordered accordingly.]

PRACTICE COURT.

TRINITY TERM, 10 VICTORIA.

Before the HON. MR. JUSTICE MCLEAN.

MURPHY v. BOULTON.

Where the notice endorsed on the copy of a *ca re.* specifies no year for the appearance of the defendant, or where the service has been made by a person not duly authorized by the sheriff, the service of the *ca. re.* will be set aside.

A commissioner administering an affidavit need not state a designation of himself as a commissioner.

An application was made by *Crawford*, to set aside the service of *ca. re.* on the defendant, with costs, on the ground that no time was specified in the notice to appear, or year named for the appearance of the defendant; that the notice was not properly dated; and that the service had been made by a person not duly authorized by the sheriff.

A. Wilson shewed cause.

MCLEAN, J.—The notice to appear, endorsed on the copy served, is undoubtedly defective, the year being omitted, which, rendering uncertain the time of appearance, defeats the whole object of the notice; and on that account, as well as on the ground that the service was made by an unauthorized person, this rule must be made absolute, if the affidavits on which the application has been made are sufficient. It is objected to them, that the jurat is insufficient, because the commissioner who took the same has not added in words at length his designation as a commissioner of the Court of Queen's Bench for the Johnstown District, but has abbreviated the same thus: "a Comr. in B. R., "Johnstown District," in one of the affidavits; and in the other, "A Comr. of "B. R., and for J. D."

These objections have, in a variety of cases, been held valid; and in the case 10 M. & W. 673, where it was argued that the addition or designation was unnecessary, and that the court would recognize their own officers, Lord Abinger said, that he would not give effect to the objection if he could help it, but that the court could not judicially notice who were its officers. In the case, however, in our own court, of Henderson v. Harper, the objections, which were precisely the same as those now taken, were overruled, expressly on the ground that this court will take judicial notice of its officers, and that the designation of commissioner was not necessary after the signature of a person authorized to take affidavits. The latter decision, I confess, is more in accordance with my views, and appears to me to be altogether more reasonable than the opposite class of cases. The great object in all such cases is, to be certain that the individual by whom an affidavit is administered, has authority from the court to administer it; and that certainly cannot be effected by adding or withholding the designation of commissioner. If an indictment were preferred for perjury on any affidavit, the question would be, whether the individual before whom it was taken, had or had not authority to administer it; and I cannot conceive that any question whatever could arise from the mere fact of such individual having merely put his name to it, without his designation of office.

Entertaining this view of the case, and considering that the decision in our own court must be regarded as overruling the decisions in England, which have usually been taken as our guide, and that the profession in this province might be misled if I did not so regard it, my opinion is, that these affidavits must be received as having been duly sworn; and that this rule must be made absolute on the grounds to which I have referred.

Rule absolute.

BATES V. O'DONAHOE.

Where a witness attending the assizes on the part of the plaintiff is seen to converse with the defendant, and afterwards shews an unwillingness to remain, and leaves the assizes, this fact will entitle the plaintiff to enter into the peremptory undertaking upon a judgment being moved for by the defendant as in case of a nonsuit.

A rule *nisi* was obtained in this case by *A. Morrison*, for judgment as in case of nonsuit, the plaintiff not having proceeded to trial pursuant to notice.

Miller shewed cause, on an affidavit of the plaintiff's attorney, stating the absence of a witness, whose testimony was considered material, and who did not attend, though subpœnaed and paid on the part of the plaintiff; and that the witness being present on one occasion, and the plaintiff prepared to proceed, the cause was put off till the following day, at the request of the defendant's counsel; that subsequently the witness was seen in conversation with the defendant and his attorney, and from that period manifested an unwillingness to attend; and that the cause was put at the foot of the docket in consequence of his non-attendance, and the record ultimately withdrawn on the same account.

The defendant's attorney expressly denied, on affidavit, having been in any way instrumental in procuring or causing the absence of the witness.

McLEAN, J.—The defendant's attorney stands fully acquitted of any suspicion which the affidavit of plaintiff's attorney was calculated to raise against him. I think, however, there is abundant ground for refusing the judgment as in case of nonsuit, as the plaintiff seems to have used every exertion to proceed with the trial, and it was at one time deferred at the request of the defendant's counsel, when plaintiff was prepared to proceed. Under these circumstances, the rule *nisi* must be discharged, and I think without costs, on the plaintiff entering into the peremptory undertaking to go to trial at the next assizes; more especially as the unwillingness of the witness to attend seems to have commenced from the time of his conversation with the defendant, and there is no affidavit of the defendant, or of the witness (against whom an attachment has been applied for), disclaiming any interference on his part.

BURGER V. BEAMER ET AL.

During the *progress* of a cause, an affidavit to arrest a defendant cannot be taken before the plaintiff's attorney.

An application was made by *Eccles*, to set aside with costs the *alias* writ of *ca. re.*, the same being for a different cause of action from the original; or to set aside the arrest of the defendant thereon, on the ground that the affidavit to hold the bail was sworn before the attorney for plaintiff, and that the warrant of the sheriff is for a different cause of action from that mentioned in the *alias* writ.

McLEAN, J.—As to the first objection, that the *alias ca. re.* is for a different cause of action from the original, it is clear from the production of the former that it is not so, though from the circumstance of the sheriff's warrant being in a plea of trespass on the case upon promise, and the original writ being in debt, the defendants have had good ground for believing that it was so. On looking at the *alias ca. re.*, an alteration or correction in the statement of the cause of action appears, which might well strengthen the belief on that subject had it been seen by the defendant's attorney; but that alteration is explained satisfactorily in the affidavit of plaintiff's attorney, and shewn to have been made by the consent of the officer who issued the writ, and before the writ was actually issued. The second ground is, that the affidavit to hold to bail was sworn before the plaintiff's attorney, after the commencement and during the progress of the suit; and by the papers filed it appears, that the original writ, not bailable, was obtained on a *præcipe* signed by Mr. Foley, as attorney for plaintiff; that writ issued on the 3rd February, 1846, and was served on the defendant on the 12th February; that on the 11th March, an affidavit of debt was sworn before Mr. Foley, on which an *alias ca. re.*, bailable, was issued on the 14th March on a *præcipe* filed as in the first instance by Mr. Foley as attorney for plaintiff, which writ was endorsed to take bail from Jas. Beamer, one of the defendants, for the sum of £175.

It is objected by the plaintiff's counsel, that it is not stated in the affidavits, on the part of the defendant, that Mr. Foley was the attorney for the plaintiff at the time the affidavit of debt was sworn before him. It is however shewn, that Mr. Foley is the attorney who commenced the suit by non-bailable process; that the *alias* writ was obtained by him and returned to him by the sheriff, and this writ is now produced by him to shew that the causes of action are the same. These facts shew, as it appears to me, conclusively, without any express statement by affidavit, that Mr. Foley has been the attorney in all the proceedings since the commencement of the suit; being so, he was precluded by the practice of the court under the rule 15, Geo. II., from taking the affidavit to hold to bail. In England, by the rule 2 Wm. IV. (which has not been in force in this province till the new rules were adopted), an attorney could administer no affidavit in a cause except an affidavit to hold to bail; but there such affidavit was at the very commencement of a suit, no person being liable to be arrested in the progress of a cause commenced by non-bailable process; a suit commenced by process not bailable, had to be discontinued before bailable process could issue. In this province, our statute authorizes an arrest in the progress of a cause, but in such case the rule as to taking any affidavit, before the plaintiff's attorney while a cause is pending comes into operation, and no such affidavit can be received. The plaintiff also objects, that as the arrest was made in March, the defendant should have applied promptly, on account of the alleged iregularity. It does not rest, however, with the plaintiff, as it appears to me, to raise such an objection. He has not been delayed in any way in his proceedings, and if the defendant chose to remain in jail, and submit quietly to the arrest for so long a period, the plaintiff has no reason to complain. The defendant, at any time before the period has expired for entering bail or appearance, has a right to object to any irregularity in the proceedings, and he has done so in this case; and as the irregularity complained of is one which affects the affidavit, I am of opinion that the *alias ca. re.* and arrest, must be set aside, but on the conditions that the defendant do enter common bail, and that no action shall be brought.

Rule absolute on these terms.

Ross v. Calder.

An attorney will not be ordered by the court to pay the costs due by his client to the opposite party, unless he has, by himself, or by his agent expressly authorized in that behalf, positively engaged to do so.

Foster moved for a rule on John A. Macdonald, Esquire, attorney for the defendant in this cause, to pay over to Douglas Fraser, Esq., attorney for the plaintiff, the costs of the plaintiff in this cause, as also the costs of the rule; on grounds disclosed in affidavits filed.

By the affidavit and papers filed, it appeared that the plaintiff and defendant had cross actions; that each recovered against the other and had obtained judgments. That in Trinity Term, 7 Vic. (1844), an application was made to set off one judgment against the other, and on that application it was "ordered "on hearing both parties, that it be referred to the Master to ascertain the "amount of the verdict obtained by the plaintiff against the defendant, and to "set off the same against the judgment recovered by the defendant in this "court against the above named plaintiff, without prejudice to further pro- "ceedings for the recovery of the costs due to the plaintiff's attorney in this "cause."

After this rule was obtained on the part of the defendant, the plaintiff (4th September, 1845) issued an execution against the defendant for the whole amount of debt and costs in the plaintiff's suit, and placed the execution in the sheriff's hands of the Midland District, duly endorsed, to levy the whole sum claimed; that execution was returned no property by the sheriff, and the plaintiff's attorney now calls upon Macdonald for payment of the costs of the cause, on the ground that Burns, who acted as Macdonald's agent in moving to set off the verdict of the plaintiff against the judgment of the defendant, had undertaken, when that motion was made, that the costs in this suit should be paid to the plaintiff's attorney, Mr. Fraser.

In the affidavit filed by Mr. Fraser, he stated that application was made, and a rule *nisi* obtained sometime in the month of June, 1844, by Robert Easton Burns, Esq., the agent of John A. Macdonald, Esq., the attorney of the defendant in this cause, to allow the debt in the defendant's cause to be set off against the judgment and costs in the plaintiff's suit against the defendant; and that he had been informed, and believed it to be true, that part of the rule relating to the costs was disallowed, and the said rule was made absolute on the defendant's counsel undertaking that the costs would be paid. He also stated that Mr. Burns several times afterwards told him, that the costs would be paid when taxed, and that he understood that Mr. Burns had received instructions from Mr. Macdonald to that effect; that subsequently he informed Mr. Campbell, a partner of Mr. Macdonald, of his intention to move for an order of court upon Mr. Macdonald to pay the costs in question, and that Mr. Campbell then told him that the costs would be paid when ascertained.

Campbell shewed cause.

McLEAN, J.—This motion is grounded on the undertakings of Mr. Burns, as agent of Mr. Macdonald, and of Mr. Campbell his partner, for the payment of the amount of the costs; and unless there has been a distinct undertaking by Mr. Macdonald personally, or through some one authorized in his behalf for that purpose, this court cannot interfere to enforce payment.

First, then, with respect to the alleged undertaking of Mr. Burns, Mr. Fraser does not establish that there was any positive engagement to pay the costs, but he says that he was informed, and believes, that the rule was made absolute, on the *defendant's counsel* undertaking that the costs would be paid. Now, it does not appear who the defendant's counsel on that occasion was; Mr. Burns obtained the rule *nisi* as agent, as appears by the affidavit, but whether he was the counsel who procured it to be made absolute, and who gave the alleged undertaking, does not appear by the affidavit; and if he was, there is no positive undertaking sworn to have been made by him for the payment of the costs, nor does it appear that he had any authority for giving such an undertaking on the part of his principal, Mr. Macdonald. The statement of the counsel, in moving a rule, cannot be taken to amount to a positive engagement in behalf of an attorney to pay moneys, and unless expressly authorized could not be binding on the attorney. Then as to the alleged promise of Mr. Campbell, the partner of Mr. Macdonald, that is sufficiently explained by Mr. Campbell in his affidavit. Mr. Campbell denies having had any authority from Mr. Macdonald to make any promise or engagement on his behalf in reference to these costs, and he states moreover that his observations to Mr. Fraser extended no further than a statement, that if Mr. Macdonald was bound to pay these costs, they would be paid without any application to the court.

By the terms of the rule for setting off one judgment against the other, the plaintiff's right to proceed for the recovery of the costs due to his attorney is expressly reserved, and he has acted upon it in issuing execution. The right to set off his judgment, without interfering with the costs due to his attorney, was one which could not be denied to the defendant; there seems, therefore, to have been no reason why such an understanding as that alleged to have been entered into by Mr. Burns should have been made; it was wholly unnecessary for the purposes of his application, and if made must have been a gratuitous offer on his part.

As the plaintiff has acted on the remedy reserved for him for the recovery of his costs, and that remedy is still open to him, and the proof of any absolute undertaking on the part of Mr. Macdonald is not clearly established by the documents before me, the rule *nisi* in this case must be discharged.

Rule discharged.

GLENN v. BOX.

Where a defendant was committed to prison on a bailable writ, and afterwards and before the return day of the writ *was released* on bail, and on the return day of the writ, entered special bail, he is not entitled, under the third new rule of our court, to be served with a declaration before the end of the term then next after such arrest.

Miller moved to discharge the defendant from arrest in this cause, or from the custody of his bail, and that the bail-bond be cancelled on entering common appearance.

By the affidavit filed it appeared that the defendant was arrested and committed to prison, on a writ returnable on the first day of Easter Term last. He was released on bail, and on the first day of term (8th June) entered special bail. No declaration was filed or served upon the defendant or his attorney during Easter Term, or at any time up to the 29th July, the day of making this application.

Under these circumstances, *Mr. Miller* contended that under the third new rule of this court the defendant was entitled to be discharged from his arrest, on entering a common appearance.

Crooks shewed cause.

McLEAN, J.—The third new rule is, "That in all cases in which a defendant "shall have been, or shall be detained in prison, on any writ of *capias*, or, "being arrested thereon, shall go to prison for want of bail, and in all cases in "which he shall have been or shall be rendered to prison before declaration on "any such process, the plaintiff in such process shall declare against such "defendant before the end of the then next term after such arrest or detainer, "or render and notice thereof, otherwise such defendant shall be entitled to "be discharged from such arrest or detainer upon entering a common appear-"ance, unless further time to declare shall have been given to such plaintiff "by rule of court or order of a judge."

It is on the ground that defendant has been *detained* in prison on the writ of *capias* in this cause, that his counsel urged his right to be discharged; but, on a consideration of the terms of the rule, it will, I think, appear plain, that the first branch of it applies only to the cases of persons who, having been previously in custody, are *detained* in prison upon a suit subsequently instituted;

that part of the rule was intended to embrace all prior cases of detainer, or any which might occur thereafter, and the next clause of it applies to the cases of persons arrested on a writ of *capias*, and who go to prison for want of bail. The defendant's case comes within this branch of the rule. He was arrested, and went to gaol for want of bail at the time. He has, however, since been admitted to bail, and has entered special bail; so that he has not remained in the custody of the sheriff. The object of the rule was to hasten proceedings against prisoners in gaol; but, as the defendant was not in gaol, the plaintiff was not bound to serve his declaration before the end of the term next following the arrest, but was entitled to the usual time for that purpose. This rule must therefore be discharged.

Rule discharged.

GRAHAM V. QUINN.

Under the 8th section of the 8 Vic. chap. 36, the defendant, living in a district east of the Home District, is entitled to *twelve* days' notice to appear on a *testatum* writ issued from the Niagara District: the Niagara District, for the purposes of that Act, being held to be a district west of the Home District.

Phillpotts moved to set aside the service of the *testatum ca. re.*, issued from the office of the deputy clerk of the crown in the Niagara District, directed to the sheriff of the District of Bathurst, and served on the defendant in that district, on the ground of irregularity in the notice endorsed on the copy served.

Eccles shewed cause.

McLEAN, J.—The notice, said to be irregular, is in the usual form, but the period specified therein for the appearance of the defendant is at the return of the writ, or within *eight* days thereafter; and the defendant contends that, by the 8th section of the Act which authorizes the issuing of *testatum* writs from the outer districts (a), he is entitled in this case to *twelve* days, and that the notice should have been to that effect. By the clause referred to it is enacted "that in all cases where a writ shall have been sued out of the office "of any deputy clerk of the crown for any district east of the Home District "into any district westward thereof, or from such deputy in any district west "of the Home District into a district eastward thereof, the time for filing an "appearance, and for pleading, replying and rejoining therein shall be ex- "tended to twelve days, any existing provision to the contrary notwithstand- "ing." The object of this clause of the statute obviously is to give defendants additional time to appear and plead in certain cases, on account of the distance between the district offices from which *testatum* writs may be issued, and the districts in which the same may be served; and in this point of view I think the Niagara District must be regarded as a district west of the Home District. Its geographical position may not be altogether west of the Home District; but within the meaning of the statute, it must, so far as the issue of writs is concerned, and the time limited for pleadings, be regarded as either eastward or westward of the Home District. The ordinary communications between the Niagara and the Bathurst Districts are through the Home District; and in

---

(a) 8 Victoria, chap. 36.

fact a considerable portion of the Home District lies farther east than any part of the Niagara District. On this account, therefore, but more especially because the statute evidently contemplates that between those districts which cannot ordinarily be reached except through the Home District, a period of twelve days is to be given to enter appearance after the return of a *testatum ca. re*, I think the notice endorsed on the copy served in this is irregular, and that the service must be set aside; but as the question is a new one, on which doubts might reasonably be entertained, and as there is not much merit in the application, the service is set aside without costs.

Rule absolute without costs.

SLACK V. MCEATHRON.

Where either party to an arbitration objects to what he conceives to be an irregularity in the mode of conducting the arbitration, as for instance against a certain person administering the oath to the witnesses, but still goes on and examines the witnesses and takes his chance of the award, he cannot afterwards be permitted on the same ground to impeach the award.

Wherever a certain fact is relied upon to set aside an award, that fact must be distinctly sworn to, and if denied, the denial is conclusive.

Phillpotts moved to set aside the umpirage of Elisha Drew in favour of Alex. McEathron, on the following grounds:—1st, That the witnesses examined before the umpire were improperly sworn, or not sworn at all, and not sworn according to the bond of submission. 2ndly, that the umpirage was bad and uncertain, in not awarding specifically the amount allowed for damages and the amount allowed for costs, or what amount for either. 3rdly, Because the umpire made up his umpirage upon improper and illegal evidence, and upon mere statements of persons not under oath, and whom the said Charles Slack had no opportunity of examining or cross-examining. 4thly, Because no notice was given by Drew, the umpire, or McEathron, of the time of sitting of the umpire to hear evidence. 5thly, Because Slack has not been allowed the benefit of his set-off against McEathron. 6thly, On account of the improper conduct and corruption of the umpire, Elisha Drew. 7thly, Because the umpirage was exorbitant, and not in any way warranted by the evidence or circumstances of the case. 8thly, Because the award did not shew in any way what amount of costs was allowed in said umpirage, or what amount of damages. 9thly, And because the umpirage was beyond the submission between the parties.

The parties in this case submitted by bond, bearing date the 5th of March, 1846, certain matters of account then open and unsettled between them; and also all and all manner of action and actions, cause and causes of action, suits, costs of suits, bonds, specialties, judgments, executions, extents, quarrels, controversies, trespasses, damages and demands whatsoever, both at law and in equity, at any time before subsisting between them; and they selected John Ritchie, of the township of Bathurst, and Archibald Jackson, of Farmersville, millwrights, as their arbitrators, with power, either before entering upon the arbitration or at any time pending the reference, to appoint, choose and name an umpire. The award to be made in writing, ready to be delivered on or before the 14th March, 1846, and, in case of the arbitrators disagreeing, the umpirage to be made in writing, ready to be delivered on or before the 1st day of April, 1846. The submission and award to be made a rule of court; all costs, charges and outlays already incurred by Charles Slack, or for which he had rendered himself liable, as well as the costs of the reference, or in any manner relating thereto, to be in the discretion of the said arbitrators or umpire. There were also certain stipulations for further reference, in case of failure of award or umpirage, and that the witnesses should be examined on oath, to be sworn as the said arbitrators or umpire might lawfully direct.

Richards shewed cause against these objections.

McLEAN, J.—It must be admitted that, by the terms of the submission, the arbitrators or umpire were clothed with ample powers to decide upon all matters in difference between the parties, and to award as to the costs of the reference; and, on examining the award, I cannot discover that these powers have been exceeded. The last ground in the rule (that the award is beyond the submission) seems, therefore, to be wholly unfounded.

It is first objected that the witnesses were improperly sworn, or not sworn at all, and not sworn according to the bond of submission. By the affidavits it is shewn that the witnesses were sworn before a justice of the peace with the assent of both parties, and that the examinations were conducted on both sides under the impression that they had been legally sworn; no objection was at any time made, at least none is shewn to have been made till after the making of the award. The manner of swearing the witnesses, notwithstanding the assent of all parties, is now, however, urged as a sufficient ground for setting aside the award.

The case of Allan v. Francis (a) shews that, after a party has taken his chance of an award in his favour, he cannot be permitted to impeach an award made upon the evidence of witnesses examined and interrogated on both sides. That is a much stronger case than this; for in that case one of the parties (the same who afterwards moved against the award) protested against the manner of swearing the witnesses, and requested the arbitrator to take a note of his protest; yet, as he afterwards examined the witnesses so sworn, and took his chance of an award in his favour, he could not be allowed to succeed in his application to set aside the award which was made. On the authority of this case, therefore, as well as on the further ground that all parties expressly assented to the mode of swearing the witnesses, I think that this objection cannot now be sustained.

The second ground urged is, that the umpirage is bad and uncertain, in not awarding specifically the amount allowed for damages, and the amount for costs. The umpire had power to award as to damages and costs, and to fix the amount of both; both were payable to the same person, and there could be therefore no advantage or necessity for making a specific award as to each item. The sum awarded is certain, and stated to be including all and sundry the costs, charges and outlays laid out, incurred or expended by Alexander McEathron, or for which he has rendered himself liable, as well as the costs of reference and umpirage, or in any manner relating thereto; and the affidavits

---

(a) 9 Jurist, 691; 5 Law Times, 178.

shew clearly how the amount awarded has been arrived at, as the proper sum to be paid by Slack to McEathron.

The third, fourth, fifth and sixth grounds of objection are fully answered, by the affidavits of Elisha Drew, the umpire, and of John Ritchie, one of the arbitrators chosen by the parties. In the case of Bedington v. Southall (a), it is laid down that "the court requires strong facts, and to be distinctly stated, "in cases of setting aside an award, and that a denial of any such is conclusive." In this case the denial is so distinct and positive, that it is quite impossible to give effect to any of these objections.

The eighth objection is only a repetition in other words of the second, and must receive the same answer. All the grounds stated being thus considered insufficient to require or justify the setting aside the award, it follows that the rule *nisi* issued must be discharged, with costs. Rule discharged.

MASECAR V. CHAMBERS ET AL.

Where a cause was referred to arbitration at *nisi prius*, under a rule of reference containing these words, "that the costs of the said cause shall be disposed "of as follows: the costs on the demurrer to be subject to the judgment of "the court on the issues in law upon which the arbitrators are to assess the "damages sustained by the plaintiff, and the costs on the issue in fact, and "the costs of the said reference, shall be in the discretion of the said arbi- "trators, &c., &c.," and the award said nothing respecting the issues in law, and no damages were assessed thereupon: *Held*, that under this submission the award was good.

A. Wilson moved to set aside the award with costs, on the ground that the arbitrators had not determined or decided upon the issues in law between the parties, and had not assessed damages on the said issues in law.

This cause being brought down to trial at *nisi prius*, the record was withdrawn and referred to arbitration, and by the rule of reference it was ordered "that the said suit be left to the award, order, arbitrament, final end and "determination of Eliakim Malcolm and Thomas W. Walsh, Esquires, with "power to the said arbitrators to choose a third, so as the said arbitrators, or "any two of them, shall make their award in writing, ready to be delivered "on or before the first day of the then next term;" and it was also ordered, by the consent of the parties and their attorneys, "that the costs of the said "cause shall be disposed of as follows: the costs on the demurrers to be subject "to the judgment of the court on the issues in law upon which the arbitrators "are to assess the damages sustained by the plaintiff, and the costs on the "issue in fact, and the costs of the said reference, shall be in the discretion of "the said arbitrators, or any two of them, who shall direct and award by "whom and to whom, and in what manner, the same shall be paid."

The arbitrators named chose as the third person, Thomas W. Clark; and on the 15th June, two of them made their award in writing, finding £10 damages in favour of the plaintiff, together with costs on the issue in fact, and awarding that each party should pay a moiety of the costs of reference. No award was made, or damages assessed, respecting the issues in law; and *Wilson* moved on that account to set aside the award, contending, that as by the terms of the

---

(a) 4 Price, 235.

reference the suit was to be decided by the arbitrators, they were bound to dispose of all matters pending in the suit; and that the rule also shewed that the arbitrators were to assess the damages on the issues in law.

Foley shewed cause.

McLEAN, J.—With respect to the first objection, that the arbitrators have not by their award disposed of the issues in law as part of the suit, I think that from the rule of reference it is manifest that the parties, though they referred the suit, meant only thereby those matters for which the suit was brought, and not those which arose between them relative to pleadings in the progress of the suit. The rule expressly provides that "the costs on the "demurrers were to be subject to the judgment of the court on the issues in "law." From this it is plain, that the parties contemplated that a judgment of the court was to be given on the demurrers, as that judgment was to govern the costs; the arbitrators therefore could not be called upon *also* to decide issues in law, which were to await the judgment of a more fitting tribunal by the terms of the reference. Had they taken it upon themselves to decide on the issues in law, and had given a judgment different from that of the court, good ground would have been given to move against their award, as being contrary to law and beyond the scope of their authority; and had their judgment been the same as that of the court, no additional weight or authority could be attached to the decision. I think therefore they acted wisely, in omitting to award on matters of law which were to be adjudged on by the court, and in confining themselves to the issues in fact, which in all probability they were much more competent to deal with. Then with respect to the other objection, that the arbitrators have not assessed damages on the issues in law, it seems a rather singular objection against the award, coming from the defendants, that the arbitrators have not awarded all the damages against them which they might have done. This objection would however have some weight if upon the judgment of the court upon the demurrers, it were open to the plaintiff to go down again to a jury to assess damages on these issues. But it is, I think, quite clear, from the award, that this cannot be done, and that the suit is terminated, because the parties, on the payment by the defendants of the damages and costs awarded to the plaintiff, are directed to execute mutual releases; so that in fact everything connected with the suit is disposed of by the award, except the costs of the demurrers, which were clearly intended to abide the event of the judgment of the court.

The rule *nisi* in this case must therefore be discharged.

QUEEN'S BENCH.

TRINITY TERM, 10 VICTORIA.

Present—THE HON. CHIEF JUSTICE ROBINSON.
" MR. JUSTICE MACAULAY.
" MR. JUSTICE JONES.

THE HON. MR. JUSTICE MCLEAN sat in the Practice Court.
THE HON. MR. JUSTICE HAGERMAN was absent in England.

IN RE REGISTRAR OF THE COUNTY OF YORK.

Under the 7th clause of the new Registry Act, 9 Vic. ch. 34, the registrar of a county is bound to receive proof of deeds by affidavit sworn to before a commissioner *of this court*, as well where they are executed *within* the county as without.

A *mandamus* was moved for by *Hagarty*, to compel the registrar of the county of York to register a deed, upon proof of the due execution by an affidavit sworn to before a commissioner of this court.

Hon. *R. B. Sullivan* shewed cause.

ROBINSON, C. J., delivered the judgment of the court.

This court has been applied to in consequence of a question which has arisen upon the construction of the new Registry Act, 9 Vic. ch. 34. The registrar of the county of York, it appears, has declined to register a memorial of a deed executed within the county, and conveying lands situate within the county, upon an apprehension that he cannot properly receive proof of the execution by an affidavit sworn before a commissioner of this court, but that the deed must in such cases be proved before himself or his deputy.

It seems to us so plain, upon the language of the 7th clause, that we probably have not correctly understood the nature of the doubt which has occasioned this application. This is the language: "And be it enacted, that every memorial "shall be attested by two witnesses, one whereof to be one of the witnesses to "the execution of the deed or conveyance, which witness shall, upon oath "(except in cases otherwise provided for by this Act) before the said registrar, "or deputy, or before any judge of Her Majesty's Court of Queen's Bench, or "any judge of a district court, or any commissioner of the said Court of "Queen's Bench in Upper Canada, prove the signing and sealing of such "memorial, and the execution of the deed or conveyance mentioned in such "memorial."

If the registrar had, upon a proper affidavit of execution made before a commissioner of this court, registered a memorial of this deed of lands executed within his county, as we were told upon the argument he had done in many cases before any doubt was suggested, we do not see upon what possible pretence we could hold the registration void, in the face of the clear language of the 7th clause.

Then if proof of execution by affidavit made before a commissioner may be accepted by the registrar as sufficient, there is nothing in any part of the Act that gives him an option to reject it and require any other of the modes of proof allowed by that clause ; they all stand on the same authority. And it is not the general course or effect of any such provision, to give to the court or officer who is to receive the proof, any discretion of receiving one and rejecting another. On the contrary, in all such cases, as in certificates for barring dower, affidavits to be used before the heir and devisee commission, &c., the choice rests with the party to resort to that mode of proof which he may find the most convenient according to the circumstances.

We do not see that any difficulty is created by the words in the parenthesis "except in cases otherwise provided for by this Act ;" they refer to the 9th, 10th and 11th clauses, the first of which would seem to render proof of the execution of a deed insufficient if made by oath before the registrar or his deputy, where the deed has been executed in some other county of the province, but the 10th and 11th clauses are exceptions certainly to the modes of proof allowed or rather required by the 7th clause, and in regard to them the exception in the parenthesis in the 7th clause is consistent and proper.

We have no doubt that the legislature intended to afford the convenience of proving a deed before a commissioner as well when it was executed within the county as without. There is no good reason why they should not have done it. It may often save a witness a journey of 60 or 70 miles. The English Registry Act, 7 Anne, ch. 20, sec. 5, contains a similar provision allowing deeds to be proved before any of the Masters extraordinary of the Court of Chancery. Mandamus granted.

EBERTS ET AL. V. SMYTHE ET AL.

In order to enable the owners of a vessel that has been lost or injured by collision to recover damages for the injury, it must appear that the accident was not in any degree owing to the negligence, misconduct or want of skill in those navigating such vessel ; and that the provisions of our Provincial Statute 7th Will. IV. ch. 22, have been, where they are applicable, properly observed.

Action on the case for negligently and unskilfully managing and navigating a steamer of the defendants called the *London*, by means whereof she ran into and against a steamer of the plaintiffs called the *Kent*, which was in consequence wholly sunk and lost, together with goods, money, &c., then on board of her.

The defendants pleaded, first, The general issue.

Secondly, They denied the plaintiffs' property in the *Kent*.

Thirdly, They denied the plaintiffs' possession in the goods, &c.

The declaration charged, that while the said steamers of the plaintiffs and of the defendants respectively, were near to each other in the waters of Lake Erie, on the 12th of August, 1845, the defendants not regarding their duty in that behalf, by their servants, so incautiously, negligently, unskilfully and carelessly managed, conducted, navigated, steered and directed their said steamer, that through the mere default, and by and through the negligence, carelessness, unskilfulness, misdirection and mismanagement of the defendants and their servants, she ran foul of and struck against the steamer of the plaintiffs, whereby, &c.

The trial took place at Sandwich before Mr. Justice Macaulay, and much evidence being received on both sides, it went to the jury upon the question of fact submitted to them, whether the *London* was or was not solely to blame ; in other words, whether the unskilful or negligent manner in which she was managed before and at the time of the collision, was the sole occasion of the accident ; and such directions were given to the jury as the learned judge thought necessary for assisting them in coming to a correct conclusion ; it being intimated, though not in terms to interfere with the free exercise by the jury of their own judgment, that the impressions made on his mind by the evidence was, that it could not justly be said that the whole blame was with the *London*.

The jury retired, and found a verdict for the plaintiffs, £2500 damages.

A new trial was moved for on the law and evidence, and on the ground of misdirection.

Cameron, Sol.-Gen., and *Harrison*, Q.C., counsel for the plaintiffs.

Hon. *R. B. Sullivan*, and *Blake*, counsel for the defendants.

ROBINSON, C. J.—Cases of this kind, especially where the loss sustained is large, as it is in this instance, are often attended with rather a painful degree of responsibility on the part of those who are to determine them. According to the system of proceeding in common law courts, the loss must fall wholly on one or other of the parties ; there is no principle of adjustment acted upon, where both are partially in fault, and according to the influence which the misconduct of either party may have had in producing the misfortune. Where the party which has suffered mainly from the collision, seeks to relieve himself by fixing the whole blame upon the other, and the jury, after deliberately weighing, and as we must suppose without prejudice, a good deal of unsatisfactory and perhaps conflicting evidence, acquit the defendants, the court will be generally found disinclined to disturb their verdict ; because the effect of setting it aside is to put a man twice on his trial upon a charge of culpable misconduct, and this is opposed to the tendency of our laws. I have no hesitation in saying, after perusing the great mass of evidence given in the present case, that if, upon that evidence and the charge which they received, the jury had found for the defendant, I should have considered that we ought by no means to have granted a new trial. At the same time, it is just to consider, that where a vessel is struck by another and sinks in consequence, her owners (where they are not covered by insurance) have no alternative but to submit to a loss perhaps ruinous in its amount, or to seek their remedy by an action of this nature. The defence which the other party may be expected to set up, in almost every instance, and without much regard to the real merits of the case, is, that the plaintiffs were themselves in fault, and are therefore entitled to no indemnity. It may be said with some reason, that both are put upon their trial in such a contest, and that when the jury, upon doubtful or conflicting evidence, have given damages to the plaintiff which do no more than compensate him for his loss, they do in effect acquit the plaintiff of the charge of negligence or misconduct by which it was attempted to throw the loss upon him; and that the same consideration which should make the court reluctant to open the matter again, will apply as well on behalf of the plaintiff as of the defendant, though apparently not so directly, because it is the defendant who is attacked in the action.

The difficulty of arriving at a perfectly satisfactory conclusion in cases of this kind, is very much increased in general by the conflicting character of the testimony.

It is not merely that the persons on board the respective vessels have literally seen the occurrence from different points of view, but they too commonly have looked on what was passing with such opposite feelings and impressions, that it is hard to trust implicitly to their relation, even where we cannot imagine that there is any deliberate intention to deceive. In the case before us, it is impossible to rely implicitly on the accounts given by the witnesses, because they differ from each other in some essential particulars. A professional writer in a late publication, meaning to apologize for the apparently censurable eagerness with which opposing advocates at the bar enter into the cases of their respective clients, as if both had justice on their side, when one or the other must be in the wrong, remarks that "It is matter of curious observation, how any "event, which is shared or witnessed merely in a state of hurry or excitement, "presents different and even opposite aspects to the memory, and how a bias, "from some almost or wholly imperceptible cause, converts spectators who "are without interest and above suspicion, into partizan witnesses. Such is "almost every case of litigated collision, by land or water, in which it is "usual to find both passengers and bystanders differing, not only on the "looser points of sobriety and speed, but on such matters of direct opposition, "as on which side of the road or river each carriage or vessel was proceeding, "and even on which side of a carriage or vessel a blow was struck. If such "differences arise in the recollection of impartial persons, surely it cannot be "surprising that each party is confident that he is injured, and communicates " his case in that confidence to his counsel."

The notes of the evidence taken at the trial of this cause would well illustrate the truth of these remarks ; for while generally (yet not without exception) the officers, crew and passengers on board of each boat respectively, stated the occurrence in such a manner as to relieve their own vessel from blame, the relations in which they thus agree are not only directly opposed by those on the other side, but some statements are made by several witnesses, which, if they were uncontradicted, we could not bring ourselves to believe, because they are not consistent with other parts of the statement made by the same witnesses.

In applying the evidence upon the trial, it became very material to consider the effect of our Provincial Statute, 7 Will. IV. ch. 22, "For regulating the "navigation of the waters of this province," the intention and true construction of which I have no doubt is, that its provisions are to be acted upon throughout the lakes and rivers of this province, whenever two vessels are passing each other in opposite directions, and sufficiently near to make it necessary for each party to take any notice of the course and movements of the other, in order to avoid a possible collision ; and this without reference to the breadth of the water in which they are navigating.

The Act recites that "many serious accidents have of late occurred on the "lakes and inland waters of this province, by vessels navigating the same "running foul of each other during the night, by means whereof many lives "have been lost, and much property damaged and destroyed." It provides, among other things, that each vessel shall carry a light or lights on the bow or some conspicuous place "during every night that she shall be navigating "the lakes, rivers and channels, or either of them." And the fourth clause enacts "that all vessels navigating as aforesaid, shall be bound to take the "starboard or right hand side of every channel in proceeding up or down the "said lakes, rivers or channels, or any or either of them, so as to enable all "vessels meeting each other to pass in safety; and that where any two vessels "are trying to windward, and there may be a doubt which vessel should pass "to windward, the vessel being on the starboard tack shall keep her wind, "and the vessel on larboard tack shall bear up or go to leeward." I insert the last part of the clause which gives the rule in respect to vessels trying to windward, only to shew, what is hardly necessary, that the legislature had no intention of confining their provisions to rivers or narrow waters.

The last clause of the Act is in these words : "And be it enacted, &c., that "the owner and owners of all steamboats, schooners and other vessels, the "persons commanding or in charge of which shall neglect to comply with the "provisions of this Act, shall be liable for all damages to be sustained by any "person or persons from any accident arising from the non-compliance with, "or during such time as the provisions of this Act shall not be complied with ; "such damages to be recoverable by trial at law, before His Majesty's Court "of King's Bench in this province."

By the Statute 52 Geo. III. ch. 4, passed for preventing damage to travellers on the highways, the legislature provided that persons driving any carriage, &c., and meeting others driving on the highway, shall always pass each other by turning to the right. Then they add the rule, and merely give a penalty of ten shillings in case of its violation ; but they do not insert any provision that the party deviating from the rule shall be liable for all accidents.

They seem to have resolved to make obedience to their rule much more imperative in the case of the later statute, respecting vessels, than they had done in regard to travelling by land ; and we can easily understand why they should feel it proper to do so. The property lost or injured by a collision, would in general be much more valuable—more lives would be endangered— and above all, the avoiding the effect of the confusion and uncertainty which an unexpected deviation by the one party might occasion to the other would not be so simple and practicable a proceeding in the one case as in the other.

At any rate we must consider that the legislature intended that this express provision at the end of the statute, throwing all the loss arising from the collision of vessels on the water upon the party deviating from the rule, should have some effect. If the Act had stopped at that part of the sentence which says that the party deviating shall be liable for all damages to be sustained by any person from any accident "arising from the non-compliance with the "provision," it would not have gone beyond the common law principle in its effect; because, wherever the accident was clearly occasioned by the deviation, that would be such misconduct or neglect as would throw the loss upon the party disregarding the statute. But when the Act proceeds to direct further, that the party deviating from the rule shall be liable for all accidents arising "*during such time as the provisions of the Act shall not be complied with*," unless we set ourselves above the legislature, we can hardly conceive a case in which the party deviating from the rule, under circumstances where it is incumbent on him to comply with it, can be allowed in this court, in the face of this provision, to recover damages on account of the collision from the other party, who at the time was complying with the rule. That however would be precisely the effect of the verdict rendered in this case, if it be correct to say that the steamers met under circumstances which called for the application of the rule laid down by the statute. I think they did meet under such circumstances. I will purposely avoid, in this stage, any critical and minute examination of the evidence, as well as the use of nautical terms, with which I am not familiar. I have no doubt it will be readily admitted, as I think it was indeed on the argument of this rule, that neither party intended to injure the other, by seeking an encounter which must be perilous to both.

Then, this is the outline of the case. The *Kent*, a steamer owned by the plaintiffs, was proceeding down the lake, on her regular trip from Detroit to Buffalo; and the *London*, owned by the defendants, a steamer of superior size and speed, was proceeding on her regular trip up the lake between the same places. The *London* had touched at Port Stanley, and having left that port, was advancing in her proper course in the night, between 3 and 4 o'clock, A.M. on the 12th August. It was rather cloudy to the westward, as some of the witnesses state, which may have made it more difficult for those on board of her to discern any object advancing towards them, than if the horizon had been clear in that direction. She was not (as I think the evidence shews) out of her proper position, or in a wrong course, when the two steamers came in sight of each other's lights—for each carried a light, as directed by the statute. The *Kent* had passed Point Pelee on Lake Erie but a short distance, and intended to stop at Port Stanley, but having got beyond a shoal outside of the point, and the wind blowing off the shore, though moderately, she laid her course rather to the northward of Port Stanley, in order to gain smoother water. The *London*, on the other hand, for all that appears, was advancing on the course she would ordinarily take, without those on board of her being conscious that the *Kent* was off her course, or having any good reason for supposing that she would be. The master of each steamer had left the deck before the approach of either was perceived, and continued below till the moment of the collision. The evidence is contradictory, and therefore leaves it uncertain whether the people on board the *Kent* first saw the *London* on their starboard or larboard bow; but they continued advancing very nearly in opposite directions, with but one light displayed from each vessel, so that it could not be certainly made out by either which course the other was steering, the hulls not being visible till they had approached very near. They were about six miles from the shore along which they were coasting. If the *Kent* had continued on the course she was steering during their approach, she would have come upon the land some miles before she could have reached Port Stanley, to which she was going, and from which the *London* had last departed. If, therefore, those on board of the *London* could not see that she was upon that course, they were not likely to have made allowance for it. The people on board the *Kent* seem to have been first aware of the danger of a collision, probably because the *London* being a much larger vessel, they could sooner see the direction in which she was advancing. The speed of the *London* was about fourteen miles an hour—of the *Kent*, ten. When the danger of a collision became imminent, those on board of the *Kent* saw that their best chance of avoiding it was to bear still more away on the course on which they were steering, instead of attempting to take the starboard or right hand side of the channel, as the statute directs.

The *London*, which had throughout, as the defendant's witnesses swear, inclined to the shore in order to pass to the right of the *Kent*, as the statute directs, did what could be done, as it would seem, to avoid a collision at the instant, by putting her helm hard-a-port, but before the two could sheer sufficiently to pass free of each other, the *London* struck the *Kent* on the starboard bow, and with so much violence that she soon filled and sunk.

Now the first question is, whether the two meeting where they did were bound to observe the direction of the statute. I think they were. The lake to be sure is some thirty or forty miles wide in that part, but they were coasting in a frequented channel, upon the same line of navigation, and in opposite directions; and no matter how widely they *might* have passed from each other, it was reasonable to expect that each should expect to meet the other upon nearly the same line in passing to and from the same ports; and if under any circumstances, whether expected or unexpected, they did in fact find themselves so near each other that a prudent navigator would have thought any degree of caution necessary, then undoubtedly they were bound to remember that surest of all precautions, the keeping each to the right of the other, as the law directed they should do. That they *were* near enough to make it important to apply the rule is but too evident, because they came into fatal collision, which could not have been the case if the *Kent*, when they were approaching each other, had kept the *London* on her larboard side, as the *London* was vainly endeavouring to do by her.

In this, as in all other cases of the kind, we must consider that if there had been no positive law upon the subject, or if (which is hardly possible) usage had not in the absence of any statute established a well known rule to be observed when vessels meet, the consequence must be, that those navigating each of the respective vessels would be under the necessity of considering in each case what the other would be most likely to do under all the circumstances; a very painful degree of vigilance would have to be exerted on every occasion, especially in a dark night, to the last moment of the approach; and in case of any accident, it would be hard indeed to tell which ought to bear the loss, since it would be extremely difficult to measure the comparative degrees of skill and attention, and still more so to determine what influence any particular failure in either may actually have had in producing the accident.

To prevent any necessity for this extreme vigilance, to give confidence to all parties in pursuing a certain line of conduct, and to leave as little room as possible for doubt in determining which party may have been to blame, the legislature have laid down one certain uniform rule, proclaiming expressly to all who observe it that they shall be saved from all damage which may be occasioned by any who disregard it. They have thereby relieved masters of vessels from the necessity of that extraordinary care which would be called for if there were no rule; and they have entitled them to feel that they are safe so long as they adhere to the rule. Where a vessel meets another at night sailing in an opposite direction, and has no means of ascertaining that she is steering a point or two off her course, she may find, as in this instance, when it is too late, that while she is herself following in supposed security the plain direction of the law, she is by that means coming in contact with the other, instead of diverging, as infallibly must be the case if both had ported their helms when they perceived they were approaching each other. The collision which will thus be produced, by one observing the rule and the other venturing to disregard it, must be expected to occasion difficulty and confusion; in the hurry and alarm of the moment a wrong order may be given, or an order may not be understood, or punctually obeyed; various mistakes may occur from misapprehension of what the other is doing, or other causes; and in my opinion, from the moment such a crisis occurs the conduct of parties is not to be rigorously scanned, with a view of determining, after the confusion is over, whether by better judgment and greater coolness the sad effects of the deviation from the rule might not after all have been avoided. It is part of the accident, that in the surprise of the unexpected danger the course has not been taken which after all danger and alarm is over would seem the most likely to have avoided serious injury; and all is to be justly charged to the account of that neglect or mismanagement which first placed the parties in the wrong position (a). This would have been the fair and legal consequence, if the statute had merely given the rule, and had not declared that the person deviating should be made by this court to pay all damages; but with that express legislative provision to enforce a strict compliance with the rule, it is impossible to take any other view of the case.

The plaintiffs indeed endeavoured to make out by their evidence, that by reason of the *Kent* bearing rather to the northward of her true course, she first made the *London* on her starboard bow; that the course she persisted in kept them in that relative position, and so decidedly so, that when at length they had got opposite to each other and were actually passing, so that, as some of the witnesses expressed it, they lapped over, they were about 700 *yards apart;* that at that moment the *London* most suddenly swerved from her course, heading into the *Kent's* starboard quarter; that as the *Kent* went round, she rounded after her, as the mate of the *Kent* expressed himself, until she struck the *Kent* forward of the paddle box, which made her fill, and sunk her.

It is objected, as it was also at the trial, that it is absolutely impossible the collision could have occurred as it did, under such circumstances; for that if the *London* had turned so suddenly and shortly to the right when they were abreast and seven hundred yards apart, the distance, with the course and

---

(a) 3 Man. & Ry. 105.

rate of going of each, must to a demonstration have prevented their meeting as they did.

I fully believe this; and no one, I suppose, upon calmly considering the matter, can doubt it. But admitting it to be impossible, that would only prove that the accident could not have occurred precisely as the plaintiff's witnesses declare it did. It would not establish conclusively that it did not occur solely from the fault of the *London*, though it would no doubt tend to shew that it would be unsafe to throw the loss upon the defendants, by relying implicitly on the judgment or memory of the plaintiffs' witnesses.

Looking at the whole case, it can hardly be said that the *Kent*, although bound down the lake to Port Stanley, was not perfectly at liberty to deviate from the true course on one side or the other, for any reason, or for no reason; yet we must remember, that the natural expectation on board the other vessel would be, that she was pursuing her proper course to Port Stanley. The person in charge of the *Kent* was conscious, I dare say, that he was inclining and meant to incline so far to the northward that the *London* could pass free if she kept on her right course, without the person in charge giving himself the trouble to think of the *Kent* or of the statute; but he was bound to consider that the master of the *London* did not know, and most probably could not discern from any distance at night, that the *Kent* was not on her true course, and that he would naturally take the only warrantable and safe course of conforming to the law, by keeping to the right; which, however, (unless the *Kent* should do the same as they approached), would bring them nearer together instead of the reverse.

The evidence of McIntyre, one of the seamen on board of the *Kent*, is strongly in favour of the defendants; but it is possible he may have been inclined, by some dissatisfaction with the mate or his employer, to give an unfair statement, though nothing of the kind was imputed to him. The testimony of Captain Otway, of the Royal Navy, is clear of any such possible motive, and would seem entitled to great weight in such a controversy; he not only acquits the *London* of all blame, but declares the mismanagement of the *Kent* to have been the whole cause of the collision.

It is clear, as the jury were instructed upon the trial, that it is only in case of the damage having been occasioned altogether by the misconduct or negligence of the defendants, that they can be made liable for the loss. If neither was in fault, but the collision arose from mistake or error in judgment excusable under the particular circumstances, then neither would be liable to an action. Insurance is the proper precaution for security against such casualties. If both were in fault, so that the accident was in any degree owing to something improperly done or omitted by the plaintiff, or even unfortunately done or omitted by him, though not by design or from carelessness, but yet contrary to good seamanship, then he could clearly not recover for a loss which would be in part chargeable to himself.

When we take into consideration in this case the clear fact that the *London* did comply with the rule of law—that the *Kent* did not—that if the latter had done so, the collision could not have occurred; and then when we turn to the statute and see the very stringent provision which that contains, throwing as plainly as words can the whole peril of a deviation upon the party who disregards the rule, I confess I do not feel that we can do otherwise than submit this cause to the decision of another jury. We have been asked to do so without subjecting the losing party to the costs of the last trial, on the ground that the jury were not properly directed; but I cannot see the least ground for complaining of a misdirection. On the contrary, remarkable pains were taken at the conclusion of the long trial, to present clearly to the jury the points to which it was necessary they should apply themselves; and I think this was done by the learned judge with great precision and accuracy. The charge appears to me wholly unexceptionable.

It is rather intended on the part of the defendants, as it strikes me, to complain that the judge did not in terms sufficiently strong and peremptory instruct the jury in regard to ths conclusion of fact which the evidence established, than that anything was said which could mislead them. I infer from reading the notes of trial, that the evidence did make a strong impression on the learned judge that the case was not one in which the defendants could be properly made liable for the loss; and that he must have made it evident to the jury that he entertained that impression. But it must always be a matter of discretion with a judge, in what terms he shall convey to the jury his own impressions in regard to the preponderance of evidence on any doubtful or contested point. His province is to deal with the legal questions that present themselves; and how far he will go beyond that, with the view of assisting the jury in disposing of the questions of fact, must be left to his judgment under the circumstances of each case. When he does take upon himself to express clear and strong opinions upon the weight and effect of the evidence, and the jury act in concurrence with his opinions, there the party succeeding upon such a charge will always be well pleased that the judge, by taking that course, has diminished the chances of error; but the same person probably, if upon another occasion he should be the losing party when a verdict has been given upon a similar charge, will be ready to complain that the jury were not left to come to their conclusion upon the facts upon their own view of the evidence, without any such decided expression of the effect which it had produced on the mind of the judge.

My opinion is, that the defendants should have a new trial on payment of costs; because it appears to me that upon the evidence there was not such a case made out as entitled the plaintiffs to a verdict, even upon the general principles which govern such actions at common law, and still less in the face of such a positive provision as the statute contains.

MACAULAY, J.—The evidence was to the effect that the *Kent* was steering N.E., and by N., for Port Stanley, one point off her course, which was N.E.; that the *London* was steering from Port Stanley towards Point Pelee lighthouse, and supposed to be on a S.W. course, her true course. The *Kent* saw the *London's* light off the starboard bow; the *London* saw the *Kent's* light off the larboard bow. On approaching they were nearer on a line than was expected. The evidence for the *Kent* was, that the *London* was 600 or 700 yards to seaward, and suddenly ported her helm and sheered round on the *Kent*; on which the *Kent* put her helm to starboard, and the *London* struck her forward of the larboard paddle box and sunk her. The evidence for the *London* was, that on seeing the *Kent* nearly on a line, the *London* ported her helm, and that the

Kent should have done the same ; instead of which she starboarded her helm, and so caused the collision.

I told the jury that the question was, whether they were so nearly on a parallel course that each ought to have gone to starboard according to the statute ; for if so, the *Kent* was to blame ; but if not, was the *London* in error in porting her helm ? was *all* the *fault* on her part ? if it was, she was liable ; if not, otherwise. The *Kent* having starboarded her helm, was *prima facie* wrong ; had she ported it, it is probable no collision would have taken place. As to the distance between the vessels, either as respected the line of approach or the courses they were steering, or laterally, the witnesses differed much. This is clear, that they were near enough to come suddenly in contact ; and if I may hazard a conjecture, it would be, that if two vessels, differing in speed, were approaching nearly on the same line, and the slowest vessel first put her helm hard-a-starboard and began to sheer to the left, and the fastest vessel immediately afterwards put her helm hard-a-port and began sheering to the right ; and this being done when so near together that the arcs they were respectively forming would intersect, the one would strike the other much as these were represented to have done. The *Kent* having put her helm to starboard first would be more round, and the other rounding in the same direction would probably strike her in a line slanting forward. The angle at which the collision took place, rests a good deal on the evidence of the mate of the *Kent*, and on the appearance of the *London's* larboard bow afterwards. It shews the *Kent* was sheering from her at the moment of collision, but was not quite far enough round to avoid the contact. Had she been more round, the blow might have been more aft, if still within the range of intersection.

I concur in a new trial, because I think that on the evidence it is not the reasonable inference that *all* the fault was on the part of the *London*. The *Kent* would seem quite as much in error or fault as the *London*.

JONES, J., concurred.   Rule absolute, on payment of costs.

DOE ON THE SEVERAL DEMISES OF THE TRUSTEES OF THE PRESBYTERIAN CHURCH IN GALT IN CONNECTION WITH THE CHURCH OF SCOTLAND, AND OF THE HON. WILLIAM DICKSON V. BAIN.

Where by deed of bargain and sale land was conveyed to certain persons *named* as trustees, and "to others" *not named*, and their successors, to hold to the persons as named and " *to others* trustees as aforesaid, and their suc-
"cessors in office, in fee simple absolutely forever, to the only proper use
"and behoof of the said (the persons named) and others trustees as aforesaid
"and their successors in office, forever, for the use of the minister of the
"Presbyterian Church in Galt in connection with the Church of Scotland,
"and his successors in office, in all times coming, provided that such minister
"shall be a member of the Synod of Canada in connection with the Church
"of Scotland :" *Held*, That no action will lie on a demise in the name of the Trustees of the Presbyterian Church at Galt, as in a corporate capacity ; but that a demise might be laid by those named as grantees in the deed. though they were not in fact trustees, as the deed assumed them to be.

Ejectment for land in the township of Dumfries.

A verdict had been taken by consent for the defendant, subject to the opinion of the court, and with leave to move to enter a verdict for the plaintiff if he should be found entitled to recover on either demise.

It was admitted that Mr. Dickson was seised in fee of this land, and that on the 11th Nov., 1843, he executed an indenture of bargain and sale between himself, of the one part, "and Hugh Wallace, Walter Cowan, William Ranken, "and John Campbell *and others, the present trustees of the Presbyterian Church* "*in Galt in connection with the Church of Scotland,* all of the township of "Dumfries, &c., yeomen, of the other part." He conveyed by this deed the land in question, being seven acres more or less, to the four persons named, "*and others trustees as aforesaid, and their successors in office for ever;*" to hold the said land to the before mentioned four persons, naming them, "*and others* "trustees as aforesaid, and their successors in office, in fee simple absolute "forever, to the only proper use and behoof of the said Hugh Wallace, &c., "and others, trustees as aforesaid, and their successors for ever, for the use "of the minister of the church, and his successors in office in all time coming; "*provided that such minister shall be a member of the Synod in Canada in* "*connection with the Church of Scotland.*" The deed was executed by the grantor and the four trustees named, and was registered 13th Dec., 1843. No provision was contained in it for the succession to the trust.

The defendant was the minister of the Church of Scotland stationed at Galt, and as such had been admitted into the possession of the land in question, on which is the manse intended for such minister.

On the 10th of August, 1844, after a discussion had taken place which had terminated in a division between those members of the Presbyterian Synod in Canada, lay and clerical, who resolved to adhere to the Church of Scotland, and those who desired to separate from her, on account of the causes of difference which have of late years divided the Presbyterian body in Scotland, the defendant gave in a general protest, signed by himself and others, in which, after giving many reasons for dissolving all connection with the Established Church of Scotland, the defendant and the others declared, that "while at "the same time they continue to adhere to the Confession of Faith and other "standards of the church, they can yet no longer with a clear conscience hold "office in the Presbyterian Church of Canada in connection with the Church "of Scotland;" and they concluded thus : "And further, we protest that the "guilt of schism lies not on us, but on those who have acted in a way which "compels us to depart." And they further add: "We protest, on behalf of "ourselves, and those of the people of this church who may now or hereafter "adhere to us, that we hold ourselves entitled to all the property and emolu- "ments of whatsoever kind of which we are now in possession."

Hon. *R. B. Sullivan*, counsel for the plaintiff.

Cameron, Sol.-Gen., counsel for the defendant.

ROBINSON, C. J.—It is quite plain that the defendant in this case is in possession of the premises in question contrary to right. The point to be determined is, what party is entitled by law to dispossess him. Certainly not those persons, whoever they may be, who are made lessors of the plaintiff by the *quasi* corporate name of "trustees of the Presbyterian Church in Galt "in connection with the Church of Scotland;" for no foundation is shewn for their suing by that title. The deed itself, which Mr. Dickson made on the 11th November, 1843, is no evidence of the existence of such a body, for it does not create or profess to create any body of trustees for the purposes set forth in our Statute 9 Geo. IV. ch. 2, or 3 Vic. ch. 73, and who were to be capable of holding real estate under the provisions of those Acts ; and indeed if it did profess to appoint trustees by the mere act of the grantor, that would seem not to be sufficient under the statute 9 Geo. IV. ch. 2, for it is there required that the appointment shall be made by the congregation or society on whose behalf the conveyance is to be taken. The statute contemplates that the provision for succession to the trust shall be contained in the deed itself ; meaning, as I suppose, that it shall be stated on the face of the deed what arrangement the congregation has made respecting succession to the trust, rather than that the grantor of the land is himself to appoint the mode of succession. But however this may be (and the determination of the point is not necessary in this suit), it is plain that according to the statute the appointment of the first trustees is to be made by the congregation or society. We are not, therefore, to look at the deed as being the foundation of their appointment ; and it is evident that it was not intended or understood to be, because it describes the grantees as being the "present trustees" of the Presbyterian Church in Galt, &c., thereby clearly referring to them as a body already existing ; and besides, if the grantor had been assuming to create a body of trustees for the first time by the deed, he would never have left the number of such trustees undefined, and would not have omitted to name them all. He would have felt it to be absurd to grant land to certain persons *and others* (not naming them) as the "*present* trustees of the church," if that deed were to be itself the only evidence of who the "*others*" were. I think it clear, therefore, that if the grantor, Mr. Dickson, could by his deed have appointed a body of trustees who should be capable by his appointment of holding lands and commencing and maintaining actions in respect of them, under the power given by the statute 9 Geo. IV. ch. 2, yet he has not done so, but has left us to find out by other evidence of their existence who that body is ; and no such evidence was given upon the trial. Admitting then, that this conveyance of Mr. Dickson, for seven acres of land, to be held for the use of the ministers of the Presbyterian Church in Galt in connection with the Church of Scotland, is within the terms of the statute 3 Vic. ch. 73, as being "*for the support of* "*public worship and the propagation of Christian knowledge*," it is not shewn that any body of trustees has ever been appointed for such a purpose.

We thought it possible, when we looked at the deed of 11th Nov., 1843, that the words contained in it, "*Hugh Wallace, &c., and others the present* "*trustees of the Presbyterian Church in Galt,*" referred to trustees who might have been appointed to hold the legal estate in a certain church erected there, or rather in the ground on which such a church had been erected, and that proof of the existence of a body of trustees, capable of holding land in a corporate capacity, might be supplied by referring to such deed which had been made of the site of the church ; but nothing of that kind was shewn on the trial, and on referring to the counsel on both sides, we find it admitted that this was not a mere omission, for that no such deed is known to exist. If therefore we could properly by any such means have derived information of the existence of a body of trustees capable of making a demise for the purpose of this action, it seems that no proof of such a fact is within the power of the parties.

There is consequently no ground whatever on which we can hold, that there are any such trustees holding this estate in a corporate capacity; and this makes an end of the case so far as it depends on the demise made in the name of such trustees as an aggregate corporation.

Then upon the other demise stated to have been made by Mr. Dickson. As he is admitted to have been seized of the estate, we must look upon him as continuing seized at the time of the trial, unless it was proved that he had in the meantime parted with it. There is no evidence that he had parted with the estate, except by the deed of 11th November, 1843. For the reason given, I consider that we cannot hold, upon the evidence, that any body of persons have taken an estate under that deed in a corporate capacity as trustees for the Presbyterian Church in Galt; and therefore it only remains to be determined, whether the deed has had the effect of vesting the estate in the four persons named in it, as being some of the trustees. If it has, then of course the demise should have been by them, and not by Mr. Dickson.

It is objected that the deed given by Mr. Dickson cannot operate, on account of the uncertainty who were the grantees. He grants the land to certain persons by name, and to "others the present trustees, &c., and to their successors in office," not for their own benefit, but for a certain puplic purpose, which requires, as we know, that in order to effectuate the intention fully, such trustees should have been appointed in a certain manner, and a succession to the trust provided for; neither of which is shewn to have been done. It is evident upon the face of the deed, that the intention was not to grant to those four persons only, to hold in their *natural* capacity, but to certain trustees of whom these were a part, to hold in a corporate capacity for a religious use. Under such circumstances, it is true, as is contended, that the individuals named can hold the estate for their lives; and that the uncertainty as to who were to hold the estate with them, has not the effect of making the deed void? I have been stongly inclined to the opinion that the conveyance utterly fails of its effect, and has not vested an estate in the four persons named, for this is not the case of a person making a sale or grant upon a valuable consideration moving him to it; which would make it reasonable that it should be construed most strongly in favour of the purchaser, and against himself. It is the case of a grantor intending to vest an estate for benevolent purposes in certain persons, with others collectively, all of whom he designates as being at that time the trustees of the Presbyterian Church in Galt; and he conveys to none except as they are trustees of a particular church. The limitation to successors shews this. It will be a clear perversion of his intention, if we must hold that in case we can find any one or more persons of the same name, though they are not trustees, and though he could not make and has not made them trustees for any such purpose, the estate must pass to such one or more persons, to be held by them in their natural capacity.

It is not merely the identity of the person which the law in such a case regards. It is the character which the person is assumed to fill, (where that plainly moves to the grant,) which is necessary to enable him to take for the purpose declared. In such a case, the material test of identity is not the Christian and surname, but the name of office. It is not shewn to us, that there is any person now capable of taking as answering the description of trustee for the Presbyterian Church in Galt, &c. And it would not be sufficient that we can find a Hugh Wallace and others of the same names; but to enable them to hold under this grant, they must be capable of taking, according to the intention of the donor, in their capacity of trustees.

If it were a deed made under other circumstances, merely conveying an estate to A. B. C. D. "and others," the effect as I conceive would be, that the addition of the vague words "and others" would not wholly vitiate the grant; but those named would take all the estate; but in this case the evident intention is to convey to no one in his natural capacity, but to the whole of a certain body of supposed trustees; and there are no such persons.

If trustees had been regularly appointed under the Act, and by mistake this conveyance had misnamed any of them, the person whose name might thus have been erroneously inserted as one of them, would in my opinion take no interest.

In a deed made for such a purpose, the real *designatio personæ* is not the name of the party, but the post he occupies; the grant being plainly intended for him only in that capacity. "If a deed be made to one that is incapable, and "to others that are capable, it shall enure only to him that is capable" (a); but here none, for all that appears, were capable of taking according to the intention of the grant, for our statute 3 Vic. ch. 73, expressly declares that religious societies are not permitted to hold lands except according to the provisions of the previous statute, 9 Geo. IV. ch. 2; and that is, by trustees appointed as that statute directs. And it has been held, that if a deed be made to a class of persons (as here it is to certain supposed trustees), for example, to children living at a particular time (being a period too remote by the rules of law), it may be void as to all, though some of the persons were *in esse* capable of holding under the rules of law (b).

It is true that a deed intended and made to one purpose, may enure to another, provided it can have such effect *consistently with the intention of the parties;* but it certainly would be an entire deviation from the intention of this grant, that it should have the effect of conveying the estate to four individuals, all of them unconnected with the trust with which the donor imagined them to be clothed. Before we could give such an effect to it, we should have besides to consider, whether a mere conveyance of lands not made under our statute 9 Geo. IV. ch. 2, or 3 Vic. ch. 73 (which this is not shewn to be), would not be void under the English statute 9 Geo. II. ch. 36, which this court has determined to be in force here under the legislative recognition of it by several of our provincial statutes; or whether we could accept of registry in a county register as equivalent to its being enrolled in Chancery, provided it were registered within six months, as the 9th Geo. II. requires. Upon this point, it is my opinion that the registry under our statute 37 Geo. III. ch. 8, would supply the place of enrolment for this purpose; and we should be more inclined to hold this, from seeing that the legislature, in their statute 8 Vic. ch. 15, have considered it a fit substitute.

If we should have been compelled to hold this deed void under 9 Geo. II.

(a) Sheph. Touchstone, 82.   (b) 1 Cox. 324; 2 Merivale, 363.

ch. 36, then the difficulty, I think, would not have been overcome by any of our provincial enactments respecting these trusts; for in the first place, as to the 9 Geo. IV. ch. 2, no deed can be made valid by that Act which was not taken for some of the purposes specified in it, none of which apply to the particular trusts of this deed; and again, the deed is not shewn to have been made to trustees appointed according to the provisions of that Act. In the next place, admitting that the trusts in this deed do come within the more general purposes stated in the 3 Vic. ch. 73, yet this latter Act expressly requires all conveyances to be taken in the manner directed by the former, and it is not proved that this conveyance was so taken. For these reasons I incline to think the estate did not pass from Mr. Dickson to the four individuals named in it, and that he consequently remained seized, and could make the demise stated.

Perhaps, in forming this opinion, I have not given sufficient weight to the circumstance, that four individuals of the same name as those who are made grantees have executed the deed, whether in the presence or with the knowledge of the grantor does not appear; while, at the same time, it does plainly appear that they were not members of an aggregate corporation of Presbyterian trustees, as he took them to be. If this must be taken to be conclusive, that the grantor meant to vest the estate in those four persons, whether they were trustees or not, then clearly the opinion will be correct which I understand my brother judges have come to, that we must look upon the estate as becoming vested in the four grantees named. My brothers, I believe, do not think it necessary to rely on the fact of execution of the deed by the grantees, as serving to identify them incontestably, but are of the opinion that at any rate, and without that, they take the legal estate. I have not yet been able to bring myself satisfactorily to that conclusion, though it is very probably correct. But it being the opinion of my brothers that the estate was divested from Mr. Dickson by his deed, the grantees named must bring the ejectment; and the case, so far as it depends upon the demise by Mr. Dickson, is at an end.

Then with regard to the objection, that a demand of possession was necessary, it has become unnecessary to determine it; but I consider that the defendant, by his declared separation from the Church of Scotland, put an end to his interest in the possession, upon the terms on which he received it. He stood in the same situation as if he had divested himself of holy orders (if that had been in his power), and had entered into any other profession; or in the same situation as he would have done if he had entered as an intended purchaser, and had afterwards declared that he would not fulfil his bargain, but would keep the estate in defiance of the vendor. His separation from the church is his own act, and terminates his right to the possession. If the demise by Mr. Dickson had been found sustainable, I do not at present think there would have been difficulty on the point of notice.

These contests about the possession of churches, or lands granted to religious societies for religious purposes, are to be regretted; not merely from the expense to which the litigation gives rise, but from their tendency to disturb the harmony of those societies. We had some years ago to determine what effect had been produced in regard to estates held for the use of certain Methodist congregations in this province, by changes which had been made in the constitution of the Methodist Society. I observed that in the argument of the case now before us, no reference was made to the points which were determined on the occasions to which I allude, after discussions at the bar which took a very extensive range. I suppose they were not alluded to from an impression that the facts and circumstances which called for our opinions in those cases were so different from those now before us that the judgments were, on that account, not material to be referred to. I think that is the case; for with regard to the Methodist Society, there the body for whose benefit the deeds in question had been taken, had, by a proceeding intended to be in accordance with their constitution and discipline, made a change in their system, which those dissenting from it contended had so completely changed the character of the body or church that they could not continue to hold in their altered condition the estate which had been conveyed for their use. Whether that had or had not been the effect of the change was the point thrown upon this court to determine. It rendered necessary a laborious search into the origin and distinctive features of Methodism, in order to determine what could or could not be held as indispensable requisites to the continued existence of the church for whose benefit the lands had been conveyed. There was room for diversity of opinion, and we were not all able to view the matter in the same light; though the conclusion which the majority of the judges came to was submitted to without appeal, and so far settled the doubt.

But the case now before us is one of a much more simple character. The Church of Scotland has made, so far as has been shewn to us, no change in her constitution which could give rise to a question whether she any longer exists as the "Church of Scotland" in connection with which the minister must necessarily be, according to the plain terms of Mr. Dickson's deed, as a condition of his enjoying this estate under the trustees. While she remained in the same position which she had formerly occupied, the defendant in this case, Mr. Bain, who was one of her ordained ministers, has, for reasons into which we have no motive to inquire, determined no longer to adhere to the Church of Scotland, but to separate from her. And it was proved, upon the trial of this ejectment, that he had by a formal written protest declared his connection with the Presbyterian Synod of Canada, in connection with the Church of Scotland, to be dissolved. It is true, that in this protest he imputes to the church herself (as I understand his declaration) "*the guilt* "*of the schism*" which he alleges has compelled him *to depart*. The fact of departure, however, would be the only thing material for us to have considered, if the defendant had been in fact holding under such a trust as the deed appears to have contemplated. And we certainly should have been driven to say, that the departure alone, and *ipso facto*, put an end to all pretension which the defendant could have to hold possession under this deed, as being a member of the Synod of Canada in connection with the Church of Scotland.

The defendant himself, it appears, seems to have entertained the idea that notwithstanding he was withdrawing from the Church of Scotland in the most formal and unequivocal manner, he could still retain the property and emoluments of which he was in possession as a minister in connection with that church; for he asserts such a right at the conclusion of his protest. Upon what principle he could think that just and reasonable it is difficult to understand ; for certainly no one can read the deed by which the former proprietor of the land now in question granted it for the use of the ministers of the Church of Scotland, so long only *as they should continue to be members of the Synod of Canada in connection with the Church of Scotland*, without feeling that the donor evidently designed that the moment the minister should break his connection with the church, his enjoyment of the land should cease.

I have made these remarks only for the purpose of preventing fruitless litigation, so far as any expression of my own opinion upon this main question, in the present stage, can have that effect.

The result of the consideration which we have given to this case is, that for the reasons stated, the court is of opinion that the plaintiff cannot recover, either upon the demise of the trustees in a corporate capacity, or on the demise of Mr. Dickson ; and therefore, according to the terms of the case submitted to us, the verdict is to be entered for the defendant.

MACAULAY, J.—The only demise by the trustees is in a corporate capacity, by the name of the Trustees of the Presbyterian Church in Galt in connection with the Church of Scotland ; and the first consideration is, whether they are entitled to sue and recover in that name. If so, it can only be because they are constituted such a corporation under the statute 9 Geo. IV. ch. 2. Now this Act does not make the congregations or societies corporations, *but empowers them to appoint trustees ;* to which trustees, and their successors, to be appointed in such a manner as shall be specified in the deed, the land may be conveyed, and they shall, by the name expressed in such deed, be capable of taking, holding and possessing, and of maintaining actions, &c. ; but how the congregation or society are to *appoint* such trustees, or whether they or the donors are to provide for the succession ; or whether the *deed* mentioned in the statute means the deed of appointment, or the deed of conveyance is uncertain—the latter is probably intended.

In whatever manner trustees are to be appointed, it is I think clear, that to enable them to take and hold in a corporate capacity under the statute, they must be appointed in some form by the congregation ; and that when they claim to exercise corporate rights in ejectment, they must as part of their title prove that they are such corporation. Though appointed under a statute, they are not created by the statute so as to enable the court to take judicial notice of their existence, as it can of many other corporations ; and being only a private body, created through the congregation, their appointment must be shewn, in ejectment, like the appointment of assignees of bankrupts, and other parties having a right conferred upon them in relation to private matters, by the observance of certain proceedings authorized by law. It is not in the discretion of any individual, by merely conveying lands to trustees in trust for some of the purposes mentioned in the statute, to constitute such trustees a corporation, nor will they take and hold in a corporate capacity ; for individuals may of their own good will, and without consulting the congregation, convey lands to trustees of their own selection for such like purposes, without the intervention or even the knowledge of the congregation for whose benefit the land conveyed is intended. In such cases the trustees take as individuals, not as a corporate body ; and the donor may, in the conveyance, provide for the substitution of other trustees, as occasion may require, for continuing the trust.

Now in the present case, the conveyance is by deed of bargain and sale, indented between Wm. Dickson, of the one part, and the trustees of the other part, and therein described as Hugh Wallace, Walter Cowan, Wm. Rankin and John Campbell, and others, all of Dumfries aforesaid, yeomen, the present trustees of the Presbyterian Church in Galt, &c.; and the indenture is executed under seal by the grantor and the four above-named grantees; and the land is conveyed for a nominal consideration of five shillings to them and *their successors in office*, for ever. There is not, on the face of this deed, any allusion to the congregation as having appointed the parties of the second part trustees, under the statute, unless it be in the word "successors;" and consequently, (for the contrary cannot be intended,) it only appears on the face of the deed to have been a spontaneous act on the part of Mr. Dickson, with the assent of the four grantees who have sealed the deed. But those four and others, being therein described as Trustees of the Presbyterian Church in Galt, it further imports, that they and others were such trustees already appointed, and their *succession* provided for, on some other occasion, and in some other way; the uncertainty on this head might be supplied by reference, and that made clear which on the present deed is uncertain; and it might, on such reference, be seen whether they were trustees appointed according to the statute, with a corporate name, and capable of taking and holding in a corporate capacity in such name; or whether they were merely trustees under some previous deed from Mr. Dickson himself, or some other individual, apart from the statute, in which they were termed and made trustees of the Presbyterian Church in Galt, &c.; how this is, does not appear in the evidence, and on reference to the counsel of both parties, we are told that there are no such trustees as the deed supposes. Under such circumstances, it seems to me that the case must depend on the construction of the deed itself. It has not been contended that the deed, having attributed to the grantees a previously existing trusteeship (corporate or otherwise) the parties who have executed the indenture, and the defendant who entered into possession under them, are estopped from denying it; and perhaps, (were it material to be decided,) the doctrine of estoppel would not strictly apply; because, if it were urged in favour of the conclusion, that the grantees take as a corporation by the name used in the demise, the answer would be, that the deed is not executed by a corporation, but by four individuals, not lessors of the plaintiffs, who call themselves and others Trustees of the Presbyterian Church in Galt, and who might be individually estopped from denying it, but who could not therefore exercise corporate rights and assume a corporate name, although their names are used in the deed merely as members of a supposed corporate body. It is however material to shew the identity of the four grantees, and to designate with certainty who are meant by the grantor.

Then can it be intended, on the face of the deed, that there were trustees of the Presbyterian Church at Galt, &c. when the deed was executed, composed of the four named grantees and others? and if so, can it be further intended that they were a corporation under the statute? I think it is to be intended *prima facie*, that there were such trustees, but not that they enjoyed a corporate capacity, though the limitation to *successors* may imply it. There is nothing to indicate it with certainty, and if there was, there would still be nothing to shew beyond mere presumption, that the name used in the demise is the name given to them, either by the congregation, or the deed which created such corporate capacity.

The present case depends, I think, on this point: If it is to be intended that the land was meant to be conveyed to the grantees as a corporation, and not otherwise, and by the name used in the demise, there arises the question, whether it is (as between the parties to this ejectment) to be intended, till the contrary is shewn, that there is such a corporation, with the capacity to take upon the trusts declared; and if so, whether it is competent to the defendant to deny it, or shew the contrary? If it is conclusively to be intended, then the demise is sustained; if it may be denied, it is then admitted there is no such corporation; and I have said that I do not think it can be intended.

Then the further question arises, whether it can be gathered that the intention of the donor was not to grant to the four persons named, and others, as individual trustees, but to a corporate body, of which they were members, and in whom it was kept alive; in other words, whether, on the face of the deed, the grantees are the individuals named and referred to, or the trustees of the Presbyterian Church in Galt, as a *quasi* body corporate; whether the latter designation is used in the deed, not as mere addition to the names therein mentioned, but as itself a name, and the name of the grantees; like a grant to A., B., C. and D., the president, directors and company of the Bank of Upper Canada, the latter and not the former being the grantees; or if not to be viewed in this light, whether it is nevertheless to be intended that the grantor meant to convey to a body corporate, or to the persons named as the members composing such body corporate, and not otherwise; so that the operation of the deed is conditional, and depending upon their being such trustees as the deed supposes and asserts. If I could see, on the face of this deed, that the trusteeship therein mentioned is not used as matter of addition or description, but as a name of grant, and that the intention of the grantor was that the deed was only to operate as a conveyance to a supposed body corporate, or to a number of trustees having a corporate capacity, or at all events to the parties named and referred to, in the event only of their being such trustees in whatever sense the deed attributes to them, I admit it should be held not to operate otherwise than according to such intent. My difficulty is, that I do not see enough on the face of the deed to ascribe to it and to limit it to such an intent. The leading object and intent was to convey the land to trustees in trust for the purposes therein declared; and that main design and intent ought, I apprehend, to be fulfilled, if by law it may, rather than that the object of the grantor should be defeated, and the deed entirely fail. It fails as a grant to a corporation under the statute, because their corporate capacity is not shewn; it fails as a grant to the parties named alone, or with others, only as trustees of the Presbyterian Church in Galt, though not possessed of a corporate capacity, because it is not proved they were such trustees, and the contrary is admitted. Then shall the object and intent of the trust therefore fail *in toto* for want of parties to take. I think not. There are sufficient parties to take; and the intent being that they, or they and others, should take (perhaps in a different capacity, that is, as being a body corporate, or as being otherwise trustees of the Presbyterian Church in Galt) upon the trusts declared, if they cannot all take in the manner intended, I do not see why some, who are sufficiently described and identified, may not take in their individual capacity upon the same trusts, rather than that the whole intent and object of the deed should fail. It is clear the grantor intended that the four persons named should be trustees (apparently with others); and because the others are uncertain and cannot take jointly, or because they cannot take in a supposed corporate capacity, or because they did not fill another office of trust, as was supposed, I do not see that they may not take independently as trustees created for the first time under this deed to give it effect. Whether the trust would cease with their lives, or whether the Court of Chancery could supply trustees, or the legislature be induced to provide for the permanency of the trust, it is unnecessary to anticipate; if they can take, they may hold for life; and the present question is, where is the legal estate? in the grantor still, or has it passed from him, and if so, to whom? In my humble judgment it did pass from him to the four grantees named in the deed in trust for the purposes declared. There being no proof *aliunde* to designate "the others" alluded to as grantees, the grant fails as to them for uncertainty, and the trusteeship or corporate capacity attributed to them not being shewn to have existed under the statute, or to have been otherwise conferred; indeed, being admitted on both sides not to exist, the estate, if it has passed from the grantor, can only be in the said four grantees for life upon the trusts contained in the deed.

I think it did pass to them, and that the demise should have been in their own names, and not in the corporate name adopted.

Upon the point of identity, I cannot say I entertain any doubt. The question is, whether Wallace, Cowan, Rankin and Campbell are known individuals or not? Are there such persons? and if so, are they the persons to whom the grantor intended to convey the lands? If so, his having by mistake supposed they were, and called them trustees of the Presbyterian Church in Galt, will not invalidate the deed. It becomes surplusage, as if he had called them executors or administrators, or as filling any other office, erroneously. It is only matter of description. If resort must be had to the alleged trusteeship, in order to identify the grantees, then, of course, it would be void if there were no trustees; but if the individuals are otherwise identified, and sufficiently named and described, the addition of trustees, though incorrect, would not destroy the grant. I think the true distinction is where the office or situation attributed is designed to designate the grantee, or is necessary to establish the identity of the grantee, and where it is for that purpose immaterial. The conveyance, though for a nominal consideration, is to be construed most strongly against the grantor, and in favour of the grantees; at all events, with a desire to fulfil the intent desired; and here four individuals are designated and have signed the deed, to whom (with others) it was intended to convey the estate upon the trusts therein declared, which trusts those four, and those four only, have accepted by executing the deed; and I do not see why they may not take, although *the others* be not known, and the succession be unprovided for. The addition of trustees, &c., to the names of the grantees, may aid the grant in respect of the parties to take, but will not defeat it if otherwise sufficient.

The intention of the deed may have been that they should take in a corporate capacity under the statute; if it cannot so operate, I do not see why they may not take individually on the same trust.

If the deed is not made in conformity with the provincial statutes, the second question is, whether the four named grantees do not take the estate in trust independently of the statute.

Being a valid conveyance on the face of it, the only doubt that can arise must be touching the Mortmain Acts.

That the trust is for a charitable use, within the meaning of those statutes, is, I suppose, undoubted; but being a transaction *inter vivos*, it is not prohibited, but merely regulated by them. It is a deed indented, sealed and executed by the grantor, in presence of two credible witnesses, more than six months previous to his death, and it was duly registered within that period, but it wants enrolment in the High Court of Chancery, and its validity depends therefore upon the sufficiency of registration to supply enrolment.

It was held in the case of Doe ex dem. Anderson v. Todd et al., (a) that the Statute 9 Geo. II. ch. 36, is in force here; not having been specially adopted, it must have obtained force of law under the first Provincial Act of Upper Canada, by which the English law generally was introduced, and, among other things, the law of England respecting conveyances by bargain and sale, and the statute 27 Hen. VIII. ch. 16, for the enrolment thereof. This Act requires conveyances by bargain and sale to be in writing, indented and sealed, and enrolled in one of the King's Courts of Record at Westminster (or otherwise, as therein provided), within six months next after the date thereof. The statute 9 Geo. II. ch. 36, requires conveyance to charitable uses to be by deed, indented, sealed and delivered, in the presence of two or more credible witnesses, twelve calendar months at least before the death of the donor or grantor, and to be enrolled in his Majesty's High Court of Chancery, within six calendar months next after the execution thereof.

Now it is clear from the provincial statute, 37 Geo. III. ch. 8, that it was not intended that deeds of bargain and sale made in this country of lands in this province, should be enrolled in one of her Majesty's Courts of Record at Westminster, nor can it be supposed that conveyances of lands in Mortmain were to be enrolled in the High Court of Chancery, which is the literal reading of the 9th Geo. II. ch. 36. In the year 1797, the want of some local provision on the subject of enrolment was felt more immediately in relation to deeds of bargain and sale, the early and usual form of conveyance of real estate in Upper Canada; the like want, however, equally extended to all conveyances under the Statute of Mortmain, 9 Geo. II. ch. 36, as well by reason of its own terms as the want of any organized Court of Chancery in the province, with an office or department for the enrolment of deeds, &c., as it is said there is in England (b). And although the 27 Hen. VIII. ch. 17, mentions the King's Courts of Record at Westminster, I apprehend it includes the Court of Chancery (although not generally speaking a Court of Record), and that a deed of bargain and sale enrolled in that court would be a sufficient compliance with the statute. This, I think, will appear from 14 Viner, 443, Enrolment, A. 4, and 2 Roll. R. 119; Worsley v. Filisker, and 2 Merivale, 363; and if so, the

---

(a) 2 Cameron's Reports, 82.   (b) 2 Mer. 363.

two statutes, 27 Hen. VIII. and 9 Geo. II., are identical on this point as respects the Court of Chancery, though the former is not, like the latter, restricted to that court alone.

Such being the state of the law, and there being no Court of Chancery here in which deeds of lands to charitable uses could be enrolled, although there was a Court of Record, viz., this court, constituted by the 34 Geo. III. ch. 2, the statute 37 Geo. III. ch. 8, was passed to supply the want of enrolment of deeds of bargain and sale. It recited the particular evil felt, that lands had been intended to have been conveyed by deed of bargain and sale, but that such deeds not having been enrolled *in a Court of Record* (not saying at Westminster) were not valid in law, and then to prevent the injury that might thence arise, *and* for the *better regulating the conveyance of land in future*, it was enacted, that whenever any lands had been sold or should thereafter be sold under deed of bargain and sale, and such deed should be therefore duly registered, according to the 35 Geo. III. ch. 5, the *same* should be and was declared to be a good and valid conveyance in law.

As applied to ordinary deeds of bargain and sale, it has been considered that this Act so far modified the 27 Hen. VIII. ch. 16, that they need not be *indented* or registered within six months after the date; but that a bargain and sale by indenture, or a deed poll, registered at any time, was good and valid in law, like a deed of bargain and sale in England, indented and duly enrolled within six months; no question of *time*, or of the form of the conveyance, arises here; the only point is whether the 37 Geo. III. ch. 8, extends to the 9th Geo. II. ch. 36, when the deed is by bargain and sale.

It is a principle in the construction of statutes, that a remedial Act, as this is, is to be construed liberally (*a*), and to embrace all cases within the same mischief or emergency, and such principle clearly applies here, independent of the general language of the enacting part of the Act, beyond the recital or preamble (*b*).

It appears to me the statute was meant to substitute registration for enrolment of conveyances, in all cases where the conveyance was by deed of bargain and sale. Indeed this seems implied in the 3 & 4 Vic. ch. 78, the Church Temporalities Act, on which much reliance was placed in the case of Doe ex. dem. Anderson v. Todd et al., as recognizing the 9 Geo. II. ch. 36. It requires deeds under that statute to be executed six months before the death of the donor, and to be registered within six months after his decease (*c*).

I had written the above before seeing the late Act of 9 Vic. ch. 34, sec. 14, which seems to set this point at rest.

The Act incorporating the English Church Society of this diocese, I have not been able to find.

As to the defendant's right to continue in possession, he was clearly but a tenant at will; and if such tenancy was not determined by his own act in signing

---

(*a*) Dwarris, pp. 718, 719, & 720; 2 Inst. 111; 2 Jo. 62; 1 Coke, 131; and Ib. 88.
(*b*) Dwarris, 655; 3 East. 165; Lofft. 783; 4 T. R. 193.
(*c*) 9 Geo. IV. ch. 2, s. 3 & 4; also 8 Vic. ch. 15, last clause.

a disavowal of the connection with the Church of Scotland, and in connection with which he received possession, it was determined by the demand of possession, &c., made by the grantees, or some of them.

But there being no demise in the name of those in whom, according to the evidence, on my view of it, the legal estate is, there must, I think, be a nonsuit, or a verdict entered for the defendant.

Questions of this kind are novel and very important, liable as they are to affect the interests of various religious congregations and societies, and the want of unanimity which prevails in the court on this occasion naturally induces me to express the opinion I entertain with great diffidence and distrust of my own judgment (a).

JONES, J.—It was contended that the deed from Dickson to Wallace et al., trustees, &c., was void, because it did not specify the mode in which the successors of the trustees named should be appointed, in order to keep up the succession according to the Act 9 Geo. IV. ch. 2; and it must be so regarded as far as respects the trustees named in a corporate capacity. It does not appear from the deed, or in any other manner, that trustees under that Act have ever been appointed according to its provisions. The deed having been executed more than a year before the decease of the grantor, and having been duly registered, which registration by law is substituted for enrolment, I do not see that the deed is void under the Statute of Mortmain, or rather the Statute against Charitable Uses. If the grantees cannot hold as a corporation under our statute, the question is, whether the individuals named do not take an estate under the deed, to hold, according to the *habendum*, "to the only "proper use and behoof of the said Hugh Wallace, Walter Cowan, William "Rankin and John Campbell and others, trustees as aforesaid, and their suc- "cessors in office for ever, for the use of the minister of that church, and his "successors in office in all time coming, provided that such minister shall be "a minister of the Synod in connection with the Church of Scotland;" that is, an estate in fee upon the trusts mentioned. There is, it is admitted, a church in Galt in connection with the Church of Scotland; and if so, it appears to me that the grantees named take the estate, subject to the trust, which can be carried into effect by the Court of Chancery.

It is questioned, whether the grantees are so named that they can take the estate; the objection is, that the deed is to the grantees named, and others not named, trustees, &c. Now there are no trustees as contemplated by the grant, but the persons named were known as in being at the time of the grant, and capable of taking and holding, although they were not, as called, "Trus- "tees, &c." Therefore the deed cannot be void for want of a grantee distinguished by name or description capable of taking and holding. That the grant is to those named and others not named, does not create that uncertainty which should make void the deed; it is quite certain that the persons named are intended to be grantees; the others called trustees, if such there are, not named, cannot be ascertained, and as it regards them it fails; there is not that uncertainty which clearly exists when a grant is made to A. or B., and

---

(a) See Hobart, 277; 6 East. 105; Cow. 600; S. Touchstone, 300; 3 Atk. 136; Wills. 684; 2 Wil. 75; 2 Sal. 561; 2 T. R. 254; 1 East. 450; 2 B. & P. 45; 6 Taunt. 325.

not being to either, is therefore void. I consider the grant to those named as good, and void as to the "others" not named, for the same reason that a grant "To J. S. and to his first-born son," or to "J. S. and her that shall be his wife," and J. S. has at the time of the grant neither wife nor son, is void as to the wife and son, and good to J. S.—2 Wood's Conveyancing, 12 Co. 101 ; 2 Coke, 31; Prest. s. 52 & 54.

The grant was intended to convey the estate to the individuals named, and others, as trustees under the statute. If trustees had been appointed under the statute, by the congregation of Galt, &c., they would have held this estate, whether all had been named or none, or if the names of some had been mistaken; because it would have sufficiently appeared that the grant was to the corporation. The difficulty is, that there is in fact no corporation known by the name of the Trustees of the Presbyterian Congregation of the Church of Galt.

After a good deal of discussion, and upon the best consideration of the case which I can give, the opinion I have formed is, that the grant is good to Hugh Wallace, Walter Cowan, Wm. Rankin, and John Campbell, and void as to the other intended grantees not named. That those grantees named hold in trust, for the same purposes that they would have held as a corporation, if they had been legally appointed trustees under the statute 9 Geo. IV. ch. 2, and the deed had in all respects been in conformity with the provisions of that Act. That Mr. Dickson having divested himself of the estate, the plaintiff cannot recover upon his demise ; and there being no corporation by the name of "The Trustees of the Presbyterian Church at Galt," neither can he recover upon that demise. The action should have been upon the demise of the grantees named in the deed. Upon such a demise it appears to me at present that the plaintiff would succeed ; the defendant not being a minister of the church at Galt, nor a member of the Synod in connection with the Church of Scotland, he can have no pretence for retaining the possession of the premises, disclaiming, as he does, to hold under those by whom he was put into possession.

Verdict to be entered for the defendant.

GRANTHAM v. THE CITY OF TORONTO.

Where an inhabitant of a corporate town being overrated, pays the overrate to the collector, without at the time making any remonstrance, he cannot afterwards recover back such rate, in an action for money had and received.

Semble : If he *voluntarily* pay the overrate, even though protesting at the time of payment, he cannot recover it back.

This action was brought upon the common count, for money had and received.

Plea, *non-assumpsit.*

Upon these pleadings, the following statement of facts was agreed upon and submitted to the consideration of the court :

1st. That this is an action brought by the plaintiff, who is at present, and for many years has been, a livery-stable keeper in the city of Toronto, and during such occupation has, since the year 1840, owned the usual property and appendages to a livery establishment, including horses, waggons, carriages, cutters, gigs and various other property, and which were during that time used and let by the said plaintiff for hire and reward in the city of Toronto and liberties thereof, in the usual course of his business as a livery-stable keeper as aforesaid ; to determine the right of the city of Toronto to rate, assess, levy and collect the several rates, taxes and assessments on the above-mentioned property, as if the same were used for *pleasure* only. 2nd, Whether the city of Toronto can collect any taxes or rates on such property, in any other manner than by exacting a fee for a license ? 3rd, For the recovery of moneys paid at various times since the year 1840, by the plaintiff to the defendants, for city rates and assessments levied and collected on the above-mentioned property, under the circumstances hereinafter stated.

2nd. That there has been no statute or by-law passed by the Corporation of the city of Toronto, nor is there any by-law made or passed by the city of Toronto, licensing livery-stables, in accordance with the 68th clause of the Act of Incorporation.

3rd. That the assessors of the city of Toronto have from time to time, since the year of our Lord 1840, assessed the said livery-stable and establishment of the plaintiff, including horses, waggons, carriages, cutters, gigs and various other property, and which were during that time used and let by the said plaintiff for hire and reward in the city of Toronto and the liberties thereof, in the usual course of his business as such livery-stable keeper as aforesaid ; and that the said property was respectively assessed in the same manner as other articles of the same kind used for pleasure only, as mentioned in the eleventh section of the amended Act of Incorporation passed the 4th March, in the year of our Lord 1837.

4th. That the said assessments were respectively collected, demanded and received by the collectors under their usual authority, and were treated by them as any other of the city assessments ; that they had the general power of distress as referred to in the Act of Incorporation in case of non-payment of rates or assessments, and that they had the same power of distress in this as in other cases of city rates and assessments in case payment was refused ; and that the collectors acted under the usual authority of "The City of Toronto," and collected and paid over the moneys hereinafter mentioned to the proper officer appointed to receive them ; and that all such moneys were placed in the city funds, and were made use of for city purposes ; and that the plaintiff, at the time such moneys were paid, did not know but that these rates were legally and regularly imposed and collected.

5th. That the sums assessed and paid as aforesaid were regularly mentioned in the particulars of the plaintiff's demand attached thereto, and as mentioned in the collector's receipts.

6th. That in the year 1845, the rates amounted to £22 5s., which amount the plaintiff refused to pay, on the grounds above in the first statement mentioned ; that he was threatened with distress in case of his continued refusal, but that the amount was subsequently reduced to £3 3s. 9d., which was paid under protest, and this action was immediately afterwards commenced ; the said reduction was made by the Court of Appeal, under the 13th section of the amended Act of Incorporation, on an appeal made by the plaintiff in the usual form.

7th. That at the time such rates were demanded, the plaintiff paid them without refusal, except the last payment, and under the impression that the corporation had a right and the power to collect them; and they were paid without any distress warrant having been issued.

If the court shall be of opinion that the plaintiff was legally liable to such rates, and was legally obliged to pay them, and that they were legally and regularly imposed or collected, and that the plaintiff is not entitled to recover on the above statement of facts in this form of action, then a verdict to be entered for the defendants; and that execution in either case be issued as if a verdict had been taken; and that in case it shall become necessary to have this cause referred for revision or decision by a court of error, this statement may be turned into a special verdict or otherwise, by consent of counsel.

If the court shall be of opinion that, on the above statement of facts and the pleadings in this cause, and on the construction of several Acts of Incorporation, that the plaintiff was not legally liable to those rates, and was not legally obliged to pay, and that the payments were not voluntary in a legal sense, and that they were not legally and regularly imposed or collected, then a verdict to be entered for the plaintiff for the sum of £71 10s. H. c'y, provided also that the court is of opinion that interest, under the hereinbeforementioned circumstances of the case, and under the declaration herein contained, can be allowed; but if not, then for the sum of £59 5s. 6d.

D. G. Miller, counsel for the plaintiff.

Cameron, Sol.-Gen., and *J. Lukin Robinson*, for the defendants.

ROBINSON, C. J.—The first question presented is upon the liability of the different descriptions of property to taxation, under the facts stated. This part of the case seems to me free from doubt. We must take it wholly upon the statute 7 Will. IV. ch. 39, sections 8 & 11, and it is clear, that for whatever horses were kept by him, the plaintiff was liable to be assessed, as all other inhabitants of the city were, and without reference to the purposes for which he may have kept them.

It is equally clear, that for his carriages, gigs, sleighs, and every vehicle of that description, he was not liable to be assessed, except in regard to such of them as he was keeping "for pleasure only." The words of the statute are explicit.

The only points that admit of argument are:

1st. Whether the plaintiff can recover back any money which he has unnecessarily paid, or been improperly made to pay (as he contends), on account of rates assessed upon his carriages not kept for pleasure; or whether he is not precluded, 1st, by omitting to appeal, as the Act directs; or, secondly, upon the principles which govern the action for money had and received when brought under such circumstances.

2nd. With regard to the obligation upon the plaintiff to pursue his remedy by appeal against the rate; the appeal given by the 13th clause of 7 Will. IV. ch. 39, is confined obviously to the case of alleged overcharges made by assessors in the value put by them on real property under the 9th clause. And the same court which is to decide upon such appeals has also a jurisdiction conferred upon it under the 16th clause, in respect to the exempting from assessments unoccupied buildings, and granting relief to persons unable, from poverty, &c., to pay the rate, which jurisdiction is not properly applicable here.

If this plaintiff had at any time resolved to contend against the liability to rates, either in respect to his horses or carriages, I do not see clearly that his remedy was by appeal, and that he can be held to have waived any other remedy by not appealing.

The only ground that really seems to admit of discussion, is whether the plaintiff can be said to have paid voluntarily such taxes as he has paid with a full knowledge of the facts, and whether, in that case, he can recover the money back in this action.

As it is stated in the case that this action is brought to try the right, it would seem to be rather inconsistent with this intention to rely upon any objection against being liable to refund the money, if the question of right should be determined against the defendants; but it is, I see, expressly submitted by the case, as a point to be adjudged by us, whether the payments are or were not voluntary in a legal sense, and this must therefore be decided.

As nothing is said in the statute 7 Will. IV. ch. 37, to the contrary, I think we are to assume that the assessors for the city are to obtain an account of the ratable property possessed by each householder, in the same manner as is done under the general assessment laws, that is, by calling upon the owner to give in a list; and the inference, in the absence of any statement to the contrary, is that the plaintiff Grantham had himself stated in former years the number of horses kept by him, and for which he was accordingly assessed. It is not shewn that he did at any time, either when giving in the list, or before paying, or at the time of paying the rates now claimed to be recovered back, give any information to the collector or assessor, or to the corporation, that there was any certain number of his carriages which were not kept by him for pleasure, and on that ground not liable to be taxed; nor is it shewn that the corporation or their officers received the rates with the knowledge that any portion of them had been paid in respect to such carriages. The plaintiff himself must have well known how the fact was, and if the assessor did not obtain from him the list of the carriages, but took upon himself to set down the number, still it is clear that by law the plaintiff had full opportunity of knowing for how many carriages he had in fact been rated, and of objecting (as it was incumbent on him to do), if he found himself assessed for more than he ought to have been. Instead of this he paid the rates as assessed, without remonstrance or objection, and now after the lapse of some years, brings his action to recover back all that he unnecessarily submitted to pay. In the meantime we must suppose the corporation must in the ordinary course of things have applied the money received by them in each year to public purposes; and it would be most unreasonable to hold them liable to an action to recover back what has been thus expended, having been received under such circumstances. It is unreasonable to contend that the plaintiff paid the rate under compulsion, for the just presumption is, that if the plaintiff had made the defendants aware of the fact, nothing more would have been exacted than was right. If this action could lie, then it must follow that whenever an inhabitant of the city has been assessed for property which he did not own, or for more than he owned, and has paid the tax without objection, he can harass the corporation with an action to recover it back again. Both parties in this case were equally bound to know the law; the defendants were certainly not bound to know what use the plaintiff made of his carriages. The plaintiff of course knew which were liable to be taxed, as being kept for pleasure, and which were not; and what he, with this knowledge of the fact, consented to pay, the collector was warranted in receiving; the plaintiff might as well bring an action upon the ground, that four years ago he paid a tax upon four horses, when he owned only three. The defendants could not be expected to have it in their power to protect themselves against such action, by proving what the fact really was, especially after years had elapsed.

If, when the several payments were made, the plaintiff had stated the facts, and insisted that he was not liable to the extent claimed, but had nevertheless paid the money because it was demanded, then the question of voluntary payment, with the cases decided upon it, must have been carefully considered by us. It is my impression, that this not being a case of extortion or fraud, the money could not have been recovered back even under such circumstances. The language of the courts has varied, but I believe the cases of Bilbie v. Lumley et al. (a), and of Brisbane v. Dacres (b), are still regarded as having been correctly decided, and they are strongly in point against this action. The case of Baldwin v. Johnson, in our own court, (c), bears also upon this question.

I am of opinion that, upon the facts stated, the defendants are entitled to a verdict.

MACAULAY, J.—The plaintiff was clearly *overrated*. From overcharge the statute gives an appeal. It is silent as to overrating. Being thus overrated in respect of the number of his carriages kept "for pleasure only," the plaintiff, being called on, paid the rates without objection or remonstrance. He had full knowledge of the facts, and though mistaken in law, his conduct shews a tacit acquiescence in the correctness of the rate. He should have remonstrated at first; for if actions like this are tenable, any number of persons accidentally overrated may pay the rates without saying a word, and then bring actions for money had and received. It is too late.

JONES, J., concurred.   Verdict to be entered for the defendants.

O'HARA v. FOLEY.

A person passing a toll-gate more than once on the same day, could not, while the statute, 3 Vic. ch. 53, was in force, be legally charged more than one toll in the twenty-four hours.

NOTE.—No further difficulty need be apprehended from the construction the court have given to this Act, as a recent proclamation from the government, founded upon an Act passed the last session of Parliament, has made express provision on the subject.

The plaintiff declared on the common count, for money had and received.
The defendant pleaded the general issue.

It was agreed between the counsel for the above-named plaintiff and defendant, that a verdict be taken for the above-named defendant, subject to the opinion of the court on the following case. It is admitted:

1st, That the servant of the plaintiff, on the 18th day of November,

---

(a) 2 E. R. 469.   (b) 5 Taunt. 145.   (c) 2 Cam. 475.

1845, with a waggon, and a pair of horses drawing the same, passed though Toll-gate No. 1, on Dundas Street, at which gate the defendant was the gate-keeper, and paid the toll of nine pence, and returned on the same day, through the same gate, with the same waggon and horses.

2nd. That on the said 18th day of November, 1845, with the same waggon and horses, the plaintiff's servant a second time passed through the defendant's gate, when the defendant demanded the payment of nine pence as toll, which the plaintiff's servant was obliged to and did pay, under protest. That the same fact occurred between the same parties at the same place, on the 7th day of February following. That this action was commenced within the three months mentioned in the statute, after the said 18th day of November. That the table of rates upon which are painted the tolls payable at Toll-gate No. 1, on Dundas Street, amongst other tolls, authorizes the toll-gate keeper to take and exact for every waggon drawn by two horses the sum of of nine pence, and that such sum was authorized to be taken on the aforesaid 18th November, 1845, and 7th February, 1846.

That if the court should be of opinion that the exaction of the said second tolls on each or either of the said days was legal, the said verdict is to be entered for the defendant; if of a contrary opinion, a verdict to be entered for the plaintiff, and the court to draw all inferences, &c.

R. P. Crooks, counsel for plaintiff.
J. Lukin Robinson, for defendant.

ROBINSON, C. J.—I do not perceive in the statutes passed, respecting that particular road in question, any existing provision on the subject of tolls which can affect the point submitted to us. It must turn, then, upon the enactments of the general Act for regulating Turnpike Trusts, 3 Vic. c. 53, and on what has been done under it. The 25th, 28th, 29th, 30th and 40th clauses appear to be the only clauses of that statute which require to be considered. Our attention has not been called to any more recent statute that can affect the question, and we are not aware of any.

The 25th section authorizes the commissioners to continue to demand and receive the tolls which were at the time of that Act passing directed to be taken and collected by any Act passed for making and maintaining the macadamized roads.

With respect to what has been done under any prior Act towards imposing tolls, all that we are told in the case is, that "the table of rates on which are "painted the tolls payable at the toll-gate in question, amongst other tolls, "authorizes the toll-gate *to take and exact for every waggon drawn by two horses,* "*the sum of nine pence,*" and that such sum was authorized to be taken by statute 3 Will. IV. ch. 37, sec. 9, which clause has been repealed by 3 Vic. ch. 53.

Whether that statute provided that such toll should be taken upon every waggon, &c., as often as it passed through the gate, or imposed the toll precisely in the words here given, is not stated; but I find it was silent on the subject.

Under the same 25th clause, the commissioners have power given to them to reduce or increase the previous tolls, which power they have not exercised in regard to this gate No. 1, but have left the toll to stand, as stated in the case.

Now the 28th clause of this Act, 3 Vic. ch. 53, enacts that it shall be lawful for the collector of the tolls *to be taken by virtue of that Act,* (which I take clearly to include these tolls, because though previously established, they are now received by virtue of this Act, and not under the one repealed by it,) "*to demand and take every day* (such day for the purposes of this Act being computed from 12 o'clock at night to 12 o'clock at the next succeeding night,) "the several tolls directed to be taken at the several toll-gates, &c., and which "tolls or sums of money shall be demanded and taken as aforesaid, before any "horses, cattle, or carriage whatsoever shall be permitted to pass through any "toll-gate," &c.

And it is upon the effect of this clause that the question turns; for if the commissioners or the trustees, under the former Acts, could have made any express regulations that would not have been controlled by the operation of this clause, explaining whether the tolls should or should not be exacted more than once in the day from the same waggon and horses passing through the same gate, it is not shewn that they have made any regulation of that kind.

We are left then to declare our sense of the construction of this clause; and we do not see in the 29th, 30th or 40th clauses, or elsewhere in the Act, anything that can warrant us in giving to this 28th clause a different construction from that which it should receive, if it stood alone.

Our opinion is, that the 28th clause imposes the toll of nine pence upon every waggon drawn by two horses for using the gate, during each day, and not for every time that it goes through the gate in the course of such day.

The Act is faulty in not being more explicit in this respect, as the English Turnpike Acts usually are, some of which allow the party only to return free during the same day that he has paid, and others allowing him to pass free during the day for an unlimited number of times after having paid once.

The collectors are to take tolls every day; that is, every day that the team goes through they are to take nine pence,—the day is described as extending from midnight of one day to midnight of the next,—which provision, as well as all that is said in the clause respecting the day, would be insensible if the intention was to impose the toll as often as the waggon should go through.

The concluding part of the clause is not repugnant to this construction; it merely, in effect, enjoins that every day in which any waggon, &c., shall pass through the gate, the toll shall be paid before it shall be allowed to go through. This is complied with by exacting the toll on the first occasion of its passing; when it comes a second time it has no toll to pay.

There is, doubtless, force in the argument that the toll is fixed as a reasonable compensation for the use of the road, for the benefit received, and the injury done to the highway, and therefore that there is no injustice in exacting the toll as often as the waggon passes.

Perhaps in this case the legislature meant nothing less; though the person framing the Act may have inadvertently copied in this part the language of some English statute, which, in another part of such statute, provided that the toll should be levied but once in the day—upon which point this Act contains nothing express, while the clause (28th) which it does contain is reconcilable (so far as it goes) with no other construction than that which we feel ourselves compelled to give it.

We must take our Act altogether as it stands. We consider that the collector can only demand under it one toll in the twenty-four hours from the same waggon—any other construction would make those words which declare how the day shall be reckoned useless and inapplicable for any purpose whatever ; and we cannot reject the construction which seems to us the only natural and reasonable one, upon the idea that it would be a construction intolerably or unreasonably injurious to the public, because we find the fact to be, that in turnpikes in England (where they have long been familiar with them) the payment of tolls is often placed by law upon precisely that footing, and by language so clear as to leave no room for doubt.

The Act for Honiton Turnpike, in England, 47 Geo. III., upon which the case of Loaring v. Stone, 2 B. & C. 515, arose, was one of that kind, and even went further, for it makes a payment at one gate sufficient to pass the same waggon during the same day through all the other gates on the same road. And such provisions are very general in the English Acts.

If the legislature, in passing the 3 Vic. ch. 53, did really not mean what we think the clause imports, it will be easy to make the Act so explicit as to leave nothing to be taken by surmise or intendment ; and such precision is necessary, for as was observed by the court, in Waterhouse v. Keen, 4 B. & C. 200, "Acts of Parliament, such as those now in question, must be construed with "reference to the particular language in which they are expressed ; but when "there is any ambiguity in the language used, the construction must be in "favour of the public, because it is a general rule, that when the public are to "be charged with a burden, the intention of the legislature to impose that "burden must be explicitly and distinctly shewn."

My opinion is, that the plaintiff is entitled to a verdict upon the case stated.

MACAULAY, J.—It is a result not probably contemplated by the legislature, nor does it appear to me a very reasonable one, but the cases are emphatic that statutes such as these are to be construed strictly in favour of the public or payer, and that the person using the road is not to be charged with double toll, or twice on the same day, unless *clearly* made liable thereto. It is not clear in this case, and I do not therefore feel authorized to uphold the exaction, although if a double toll had been distinctly directed to be taken by the commissioners before the statute 3 Vic. c. 53, it might have been confirmed by that Act in ss. 25 and 27.

The toll is not for passing the gate, but as compensation for using the road ; and the Act only strictly authorizes one toll for one day's use.

JONES, J., concurred.

Verdict to be entered for the plaintiff.

IRELAND, CLERK TO THE COMMISSIONERS OF THE MIDLAND DISTRICT TURN-
PIKE TRUST V. GUESS ET AL.

Commissioners appointed under an Act of Parliament limiting their powers with respect to demises, and to the collection and appropriation of rent when due, make a demise beyond the scope of these powers; the tenant is put into possession and enjoys his term; the commissioners at the expiration of the term take a promissory note from the tenant for the amount of rent, giving time for payment: *Held, per Cur.*—That the commissioners, by their clerk, could not sustain an action upon such note, upon two grounds :—first, because the promise to pay the note arose upon an illegal consideration, viz., the illegal demise; and, secondly, because the commissioners had no power, though the demise were legal, to give time of payment for rent already due. (The Chief Justice dissenting from the judgment of the court on both grounds.)

The plaintiff declared in *assumpsit*, for that whereas before the making of the promissory note hereinafter mentioned, the commissioners of the Midland District Turnpike Trust demised to the defendants Toll-gate No. 1, in the township of Kingston, together with the house erected at the said toll-gate, on the macadamized road, between the town of Kingston and the village of Napanee, in the said district, and the tolls and rents, revenues, profits and incomes thereunto belonging and appertaining, according to the provisions of the statute in such case made and provided; to have and to hold the same to the defendants for a certain term, to wit, from the first day of January, in the year of our Lord one thousand eight hundred and forty-three, for and during, and unto the full end and term of one year from the first day of January, in the year of our Lord one thousand eight hundred and forty-three, for and during and unto the full end and term of one year from thence next ensuing and fully to be complete and ended; yielding and paying therefor to the commissioners of the Midland District Turnpike Trust the rent or sum of fourteen hundred and twenty-five pounds, by even and equal payments of fifty-four pounds sixteen shillings and two pence each, payable every fortnight in advance, by virtue of which demise the defendants entered into the said demised premises with the appurtenances, and were possessed thereof during the term so demised to them, and until the same was fully complete and ended.

And whereas the defendants, at the expiration of the said term, and before and at the time of the making of the promissory note hereinafter mentioned, were indebted to the commissioners of the Midland District Turnpike Trust in a certain sum of money, to wit, the sum of six hundred pounds, for so much rent due and owing to them from the defendants, and then in arrear and unpaid, for and upon the said premises with the appurtenances so demised to them as aforesaid, which said sum of six hundred pounds should have been paid to the said the commissioners of the Midland District Turnpike Trust, at certain days and times then past, and thereupon, in consideration of the premises, and in consideration that the said the commissioners of the Midland District Turnpike Trust, at the request of the defendants, would accept and receive a large part of the said last mentioned sum of money, to wit, the sum of one hundred pounds, at the end of the period in the promissory note hereinafter mentioned specified, and would in the meantime give time to the defendants for payment thereof, the defendants, on the tenth day of July, in the year of our Lord one thousand eight hundred and forty-four, made their promissory note in writing, and thereby jointly and severally promised for value received to pay the commissioners of the Midland District Turnpike Trust or order, the said sum of one hundred pounds, eighteen months after the date thereof, which period had elapsed before the commencement of this suit, and the plaintiff, as clerk as aforesaid, in fact saith, that the said the commissioners of the Midland District Turnpike Trust did forbear and give day of payment to the defendants for the said sum of one hundred pounds, for the period in the said promissory note mentioned, to wit, from the said tenth day of July in the year aforesaid, during and until the expiration of eighteen months therefrom, and the defendants thereupon became jointly and severally liable to pay to the said the commissioners of the Midland District Turnpike Trust the amount of the said note, according to the term and effect thereof, and being so liable, afterwards jointly and severally promised the said the commissioners of the Midland District Turnpike Trust to pay them the same. Yet they the said defendants have not, nor hath any or either of them, paid the said sum of money in the said promissory note specified or any part thereof, to the damage of the said the commissioners of the Midland District Turnpike Trust of two hundred pounds, and therefore the plaintiff, as said clerk according to the said statute, brings suit, &c.

To this declaration the defendant demurred on the following grounds : that the said the commissioners of the Midland District Turnpike Trust cannot by their clerk bring an action under the statute 3 Victoria, ch. 53, s. 17, upon the contract declared upon in the said declaration, the same being a contract not within their proper jurisdiction as commissioners of the Midland District Turnpike Trust, and therefore the present action is improperly brought in the name of their clerk. That the promissory note declared upon in the said declaration, is an instrument upon which the plaintiff, as clerk to the said the commissioners of the Midland District Turnpike Trust, could not bring an action, the same being, as set forth in the declaration, founded on a consideration and given for a subject-matter not accruing to the said the commissioners of the Midland District Turnpike Trust, as commissioners, nor within the objects of the Midland District Turnpike Trust, but as private individuals, and for which the plaintiff as clerk could not sue; that the consideration upon which the said promissory note in the declaration mentioned is founded, is in direct contravention of the said statutes and law from which the commissioners of the Midland District Turnpike Trust derive their authority as commissioners; that is to say, forbearance and giving a day of payment for money due from the same parties, is not a proceeding or subject-matter within the power of the said the commissioners of the Midland District Turnpike Trust as commissioners; and then the clerk cannot bring an action upon a contract or note founded on a matter not accruing to them as commissioners: that it is not alleged or set forth in any part of the said declaration, that the said Toll-gate No. 1, therein named and alleged to have been demised by the said the commissioners of the Midland District Turnpike Trust to the defendants, is a toll-gate erected under authority of the said statutes, or under the authority of any law whatsoever, on or across any road macadamized under the said authority of law, to collect tolls, but merely "Toll-gate No. 1," so that it does not appear whether the said toll-gate is a subject-matter of demise within the objects of the trust or otherwise, by the said commissioners as commissioners, and for which the plaintiff as clerk could sue; that it is not alleged in the said declaration as it ought to be, that the said plaintiff is clerk to the said the commissioners of the Midland District Turnpike Trust "for the time "being;" that the said alleged demise of Toll-gate No. 1, being made contrary to the form and direction of the said statute, any claim founded thereon cannot be a subject-matter of action for which the said commissioners of the Midland District Turnpike Trust could sue by their clerk; that it is not alleged that any matter set forth in the said declaration was due to or accrued to the said the commissioners of the Midland District Turnpike Trust as such commissioners, but merely commissioners; that the said declaration is doubtful and confused in this, that there are three distinct causes of action set forth in the said declaration, that is to say, use and occupation, forbearance and giving a day of payment and a promissory note, all include in one count, and by the general breach in the declaration it does not appear certain for which cause of action the plaintiff relies in his said declaration, and that it is uncertain whether the plaintiff alleges the joint and several liability to arise from the making of the said promissory note, or from the giving a day of payment and forbearance; that the forbearance for eighteen months for the payment of a sum of money already due to the said the commissioners of the Midland District Turnpike Trust, as commissioners for tolls collected at a toll-gate erected by authority of law, as appears on the face of the declaration, is not a consideration sufficient for a promissory note to bring an action upon by the said plaintiff as clerk, the same forbearance being contrary to law; that the commissioners as commissioners have no authority in law to take a promissory note, and that their clerk cannot bring an action for the same; that it is alleged in the said declaration, the said the commissioners of the Midland District Turnpike Trust "did forbear and give a day of payment to the defend- "ants for the said sum of one hundred pounds for the period in the said promis- "sory note mentioned," and "that the defendants thereupon became jointly "and severally liable to pay to the said the commissioners of the Midland Dis- "trict Turnpike Trust the amount of the said note according to the tenor and " effect thereof," from which it is uncertain whether the liability of the defendants arose from the said forbearance, or the making of the said note; that it is not averred in the declaration that the forbearance was given and made by the said the commissioners of the Midland District Turnpike Trust to the said defendants "at the request of the defendants;" that the consideration shewn on the face of the declaration for which the said promissory note was given is an illegal consideration, which makes the said promissory note void in law; that it is not alleged in the declaration, that the defendants were requested by the said the commissioners of the Midland District Turnpike Trust to pay the amount specified in the said promissory note, to the said the commissioners of the Midland District Turnpike Trust, at any time after the same became due, and before the commencement of this suit; that it is shewn on the face of the declaration, that the demand for which the plaintiff declares in the said declaration, did not accrue to the said the commissioners of the Midland District Turnpike Trust in the course of their business as commissioners, and is then invalid, and a contract for which the said plaintiff as clerk cannot bring an action; that the commissioners have no right to give further time or credit as commissioners for money due to them for tolls arising from any lease of a toll-gate, and the promissory note declared upon being founded upon such consideration, cannot be sued for by the plaintiff as clerk.

McKenzie, counsel for the demurrer.

Campbell, contra.

ROBINSON, C. J.—The substantial objection urged on this demurrer is, that the turnpike commissioners could not by law take a note from a person owing them rent for a toll-gate, especially if the note gives time for payment. Cases may be conceived in which it would be for the public advantage that they should take such notes. If a third party should join in it as surety, there might be manifest advantage; that, however, was not the fact here. Again, the commissioners, in reckoning with the lessee of a toll-gate, might accidentally, from error in reckoning or otherwise, have given a receipt for more than had been actually paid, and having no means of proving the mistake, might well be willing to give time, if the lessee would give on such terms only his note, for a sum which would otherwise be wholly lost. We cannot tell that some motive of this sort may not have led to the taking this note. It may be said that in such a case the commissioners would be liable themselves to make good the money which they ought to have received, and therefore ought to pay it promptly, and that the recovering it back of the lessee must necessarily be regarded as a matter between the lessee and them in their natural capacity, and not a transaction with them as commissioners. But I do not understand the law to be so rigid. Where there has been no connivance or wilful wrong (and we are never to assume fraud or illegality) it is not, in my opinion, a principle of law that a public officer may not in his public capacity accept an undertaking of this nature to protect himself, whether he might or might not be held in strictness to have made himself responsible, in consequence of indulgence granted by him. His being responsible to the government, when he had intended no wrong, would be no reason that the person whose conduct had made him responsible should not be liable to him. It would furnish a very just reason for holding him liable.

But supposing this to have been the mere case of a lessor of tolls obtaining indulgence from the commissioners as to time for part of the rent, it may have been just under the circumstances. Suppose, for instance, that the toll-house had been robbed, or that the lessee had taken the gate at so high a rate that he could not pay it out of the receipts; in such a case, if the commissioners were to wait some months and then sue for the rent, it would be no defence for the lessee to say that they had been guilty of a breach of duty in not suing him before, and that therefore they should never recover; but such a defence would be as reasonable as the present. Before we can allow a defendant to set up as a defence, that a forbearance shewn to himself was a culpable breach of duty, and by that means defeat the action, we ought to be referred by him to some express authority on which he can claim an advantage against justice and good conscience, as that would be. The defendant's counsel cited no such decision in any case like the present in principle, and I believe he could not produce any. The statute 23 Henry VI. ch. 9, which makes void all obligations taken by the sheriff, for ease and favour from persons in their custody, unless such as are taken in the form prescribed by that statute, affords a stronger argument against what is contended here; for if bonds taken by sheriffs to indemnify them for indulgences granted, were in all cases void at common law, that provision of the statute would not have been necessary. Beaufage's case (*a*), Lenthall's case (*b*), Rogers v. Reeves (*c*), contradict the principle, that no undertaking given by a party to a public officer in consequence of forbearance shewn to him, can be legal at common law. It is a strong circumstance, too, that even since the statute, a bond taken by the sheriff from a defendant in a *fi. fa.*, to pay the money at the return of the writ, upon receiving which bond the sheriff had forborne to execute the writ, may be enforced by the sheriff.

I have no doubt that every transaction or undertaking, the *object of which* is the violation of a public or private duty, is void (*d*); but here, are we to assume that in taking this note there was any such object in view? For all that appears on this record, the government of the country may, under some special circumstances, have authorized a delay in payment. The case of Cole et al. v. Gower and Piggott (*e*), was not relied upon as an authority against recovering in this action; it may seem at first sight to be so, but upon examination it will be found not to apply. It turned on the evident and certain impolicy of the contract under the circumstances of that case, and also upon the express provisions of a statute, which were contravened by the note being taken. On the other hand, Green v. Pilkington et al. (*f*), and Sugars v. Brinkworth (*g*), and especially the latter, strongly support the action. There a warrant had been directed to the plaintiff, to levy penalties on the defendant's goods, he having been convicted of smuggling salt; half of the penalty was to go to the informer, and half to the crown. Instead of levying, the plaintiff took the defendant's promissory note for the amount, payable in two months. Mr. Scarlett contended that the note could not be recovered; that it was the plaintiff's duty to have levied the penalties instead of taking a security, and that great abuses might follow such a practice. Lord Ellenborough observed: "If there were any reason to think the law had been abused by the plaintiff, "he could not be allowed to enforce payment, but he appears to have acted with "perfect good faith; and the defendant, instead of being the subject of extor- "tion or violence, had a benefit conferred upon him. He gave the note at "two months in redemption of his goods, which were liable to be instantly "sold for what they might fetch; this surely was sufficient consideration. I "do not think any previous consent by the commissioners of excise or the "magistrates was necessary to the arrangement; I will look to such a trans- "action with extreme jealousy; but the party to whom indulgence has been "laudably extended, is not to evade his engagements by attempting to crimi- "nate his benefactor."

(*a*) 10 Co. 100.   (*b*) 1 Saund. 161.   (*c*) 1 T. R. 418.
(*d*) Collins v. Blanton, 2 Wills. 347; Parsons v. Thompson, 2 H. B. 322, 327; Blachford v. Preston, 8 T. R. 89.
(*e*) 6 E. R. 110.   (*f*) 2 B. & P. 151.   (*g*) 4 Campb. 46.

This language of Lord Ellenborough is very applicable here; the mere delay in payment was a favour to this defendant who urges the objection, and it is the commissioners to whom he owed the money who grant him the indulgence, not a stranger, as the bailiff in the case last cited, who had no interest or discretion in the matter. At the trial on that case, the facts might all be brought out under the general issue, and we may suppose were; and that from the language used by Lord Ellenborough the consent of the plaintiff's superiors to the forbearance had not been proved. If they had prohibited the bailiff from taking the note, and that would have been a defence, then it was necessary for the defendant to shew it. At the present day it would be necessary also to plead it; and I take it to be no objection upon demurrer, that a note sued upon *may have been* illegal, under circumstances which are merely supposed or surmised, but not shewn. If the circumstances were such as made it illegal, these things must be pleaded and proved; if it might be free from illegality for all that appears, we are to suppose that it was. In the case of public officers, the maxim, "*omnia presumunter rité esse acta,*" has a very general application.

We were referred to several clauses of the 7 Will. IV. ch. 81, and 3 Vic. ch. 53, as tending to shew that it must be a violation of their duty for the commissioners in any case to grant forbearance to the lessee; I think we cannot reasonably construe any of the provisions so strictly. It is true that all the moneys paid into their hands they are to pay over regularly, and that the tolls are to be applied to meet the interest on debentures; but we cannot infer as a certain fact that enough had not been already paid to cover the interest.

So far as this objection then is concerned, I think we cannot give judgment for the demurrer; the defendant admits that he owes the rent, and owes it to the plaintiffs; his having been allowed some months' credit is no reason why he should never pay it; and if being liable for the rent, as he unquestionably is, and liable to the commissioners, he cannot be sued upon the note which he has voluntarily given for the amount, it must be because the commissioners have no legal capacity to take a promissory note for rent or other money due to them as commissioners. That was made another ground of objection in this case, and it is one of substance if it be well founded; but I know of no authority or principle on which it can be supported.

The foundation of this note is averred by the declaration to have been a transaction had with the commissioners, in the course of the business which they are by law authorized to manage. The objection on which some cases have turned, that corporations cannot give or take promissory notes, unless where they are expressly authorized by law to do so, does not apply in this case; and if it did, that is, if the commissioners were a corporate body, we should not hastily decide, I think, that it would not be within the scope of their power to take a promissory note for a debt legally due to them. In all such cases, respect must be had to the objects of the corporation, and to the common method at the present day of conducting the kind of business which it is allowed to manage.

It has not been contended that so far as regards the mere technical law of bills and notes, a promissory note may not be made payable as this is, to persons not named by their Christian and surname, but designated by the office which they fill, as "to the sheriff of such a district," or "to the executors of "A. B.," or "to A. B. and company," &c. The objection is to the legality, by reason of the nature of this particular transaction. It is urged that these turnpike commissioners cannot take a note at all for any debt due to them in their public capacity. I do not know any reason why they cannot; of course, there being several of them can make no difference. In Cole et al. v. Gower and Piggott (a), and Sugars v. Brinkworth (b), it was not objected that upon general principles a public officer may not take a promissory note or bond upon a contract made with him in his official capacity, where it is not prohibited by any statute, or would not be void as being against morality or public policy. By the 5th clause of the statute under which this action is brought, the commissioners may sell in some cases the former road allowance; and upon such a transaction why might they not sell on credit, and take a note for the purchase money? If they could in any case they could for a plain debt of this description, subject only to the doubt raised upon the legality of their giving credit, which doubt has been already considered. For all we see upon this record, the credit may have been given for good reasons, and with the assent, or even at the instance, of those to whom the commissioners are accountable, and under circumstances which made it manifestly proper and just. If it were not so, but were a mere act of indulgence granted without necessity, and in prejudice of the public, that might have the effect of exposing the commissioners to liability, but would be no reason why this defendant should not pay his rent due, and as well upon the note as in action for the rent itself.

So far then as all objections of this nature are concerned, I am of opinion that there is no reason why the plaintiff should not recover on this declaration. The note does appear by the record, as I think it should, to have been taken by the commissioners for a debt accruing to them in the discharge of their duty under the statute 3 Vic. ch. 53. They may take a note for such a debt; and as to giving time by the note for such a debt already due, there may under the circumstances have been nothing in that unjust towards the public, or in any manner censurable. Its having a tendency, if generally practised, to create abuse, would not authorize us to hold the note void, as the cases shew; and if there may have been circumstances in the particular transaction which would make this note void, it is for the defendant to shew them in his plea. As I do not feel justified in holding the note void upon the face of the declaration, and as the statement of facts shews it to be for a debt to the commissioners in their public capacity, their clerk may sue under the 17th section of 3 Vic. ch. 3.

There are some other objections taken by the special demurrer; with regard to these, I think it does sufficiently appear that the toll-gate leased was within the sphere of duty of these commissioners, being described to be on the macadamized road between Kingston and the village of Napanee, in the Midland District. Then as to the next objection, the plaintiff rightly sues as clerk to the commissioners, &c., without adding "for the time being;" the declaration imports that this plaintiff was the clerk at the time of his filing this declaration; in other words, clerk for the time being, as the Act expresses it,

---

(a) 6 E. R. 110.   (b) 4 Camp. 46.

which merely means that when the suit is to be brought or defended, he may sue or be sued as such; not that he must call himself in the declaration, clerk *"for the time being."*

I do not understand on what particular ground it is objected, that the tolls appear to have been leased contrary to the directions of the statute. It is not explained whether the lease was made upon a letting by bidding after due notice, &c., or by private contract, as the 27th section of the statute in certain cases allows.

It was not necessary that these preliminary matters should be stated. Enough appears, I think, when it is shewn, that the lessee engaged under a demise at a certain rent, and owing a debt to the commissioners on that account, gave this note for the sum due. As to the demise not conforming in its terms to the statute, that forms an objection against suing on the demise itself, but is not a reason why the defendant should pay no rent in any shape.

The other objections are evidently not tenable, and were not pressed in the argument.

The commissioners, from either paying no attention to the provisions of the statute, or choosing to act in disregard of them, have unnecessarily given rise to several perplexing questions, both in this case and in the case of Ireland v. Noble, in which we have given judgment this term. It may seem that upon the same principle upon which I have held the plaintiff unable to maintain an action on the alleged contract of demise made by the commissioners, I ought also to hold that the plaintiff cannot recover upon the promissory note sued on in this action; but to my own mind, the cases and the principles which must govern the decision of the objections raised in them are perfectly distinct. In the action against Noble, the plaintiff was assuming to sue under the statute as clerk to the commissioners, upon a demise made by them under its provisions, and the question was whether that demise, being made in a manner substantially different from what the statute directs, can be enforced by the clerk suing upon it under the statute. If it could be, then if the commissioners had chosen to demise the tolls for ten years instead of one, exacting the whole rent in advance, or postponing it all till the last year, I do not see how we could refuse to say that such a demise would also be legal, and could be enforced in the name of the clerk.

In demising the tolls at all, the commissioners are merely executing an authority, and they must pursue in substance at least the directions by which the authority is limited, or their contract will be invalid; they have no private legal interest in their tolls, they have only a power to demise them upon certain terms.

It is true the 27th clause of the Act in one part of it says, that after they shall have found a bidder for the tolls at auction, they are to enter into a proper agreement with him for the letting thereof, with sureties, &c., *" and " under such conditions and in such manner as the commissioners shall think fit,"* and these words may seem to give an almost unlimited discretion to the commissioners, but I think it is plain that they apply only to the form of binding the lessee and his sureties, and that they can give only a discretion in regard to any conditions respecting matters on which the Act is silent, or that may seem most advisable for carrying the positive directions of the statute into effect, not a discretion to substitute conditions quite repugnant to those expressly directed by the Act.

The cases of Fairtitle dem Myton v. Gilbert et al. (a), and Cole et al. v. Gower (b), are in point upon the objection taken in the action against Noble, which was by the clerk upon the demise itself.

In this case against Guess, Beamish and McKellar, the defendants are sued upon a promissory note given by them to the commissioners, not in their individual capacity, but as commissioners.

It was considered necessary by the plaintiff to shew that the note was taken by the commissioners in the course of the execution of their duty; in other words, that it was not on a private transaction of their own, but that the money was sued for on behalf of the public, and was a debt connected with the trust.

In Curling v. Johnson et al. (c), where a clerk of a turnpike trust was suing in *assumpsit* under a similar provision in an English Act of Parliament, Lord C. J. Tindal said, "The plaintiff stating himself to be suing on a contract as "clerk to commissioners, under an Act of Parliament, we must see therefore "whether he discloses such a contract as the commissioners can enter into." In order to shew this, the demise is stated in this action as the demise was in the other; the difference in the effect is this—in the other action the plaintiff sues wholly and expressly on such a contract as I think the commissioners could not by law enter into, and therefore that their clerk could not in their behalf recover *on that contract*, though as the lessee had enjoyed the tolls for the term, he might in another form of action by the clerk have been made to pay a compensation for them; I mean in an action for use and occupation. In this it is not the illegal demise that is sued upon; and the same objection does not apply in the same form. The lessee had entered and enjoyed for the whole term, and whatever he owed for such occupation was a debt due to the commissioners. Their clerk in their name could clearly have sued on an account stated, for any balance which the lessees might have admitted themselves to owe on account of their occupation; that debt became due to them like any other debt, and notwithstanding any difficulty which might prevent the clerk suing for it under the lease itself on account of its being made contrary to the statute, yet after the term was ended, and the defendant had had all the benefit contemplated, the difficulty of maintaining an action on the lease could surely not have the effect of absolving the lessees from all obligation to pay in any shape for what they had enjoyed. The statute directs in what terms the rent shall be made payable by the demise, and therefore a contract on a demise made in other terms, cannot, as I think, be sued upon. But the statute does not say that for rent or any other debt, after it had become due, the commissioners shall not under any circumstances grant any forbearance, nor does it provide that the clerk shall sue only upon the demise for toll itself, and on no other cause of action. The case of Peacock v. Harris (d), is an authority on that point, if any were wanting, and that case, as well as those I have already cited of Green v. Pilkington et al. (e), and Sugars v. Brinkworth (f), are also authorities to shew, that if no provision had been

---

(a) 2 T. R. 169.   (b) 6 E. R. 110.   (c) 10 Bing. 89.
(d) 10 E. R. 104.   (e) 2 B. & P. 115.   (f) 4 Camp. 46.

made in the Act for enabling the clerk to sue, and if the commissioners had been left to sue in their own names, the fact of their having granted indulgence to the defendants, which may have been done from the most just and fair motives, would have been no reason for the defendants to urge against paying them according to their promise. I see no reason either, why they might not take a note for that or any other debt accruing to them as commissioners; and my opinion is, that whenever an action could have been sustained by them for money which when received would be public money of the trust, their clerk may recover in an action under the statute, shewing, as I think he must do in any such action, that the cause of action was acquired by the commissioners in the course of their duties under the statutes. The averments which this declaration contains are not to be regarded as necessary for laying a consideration to support the note, because a consideration would be presumed till the contrary was shewn, but they are necessary for shewing the right of this plaintiff to sue upon a security which upon the face of it has no reference to them.

We know what the commissioners for the Midland District Turnpike Trust are; that they are not a corporate body, but are certain individuals discharging a public duty under a public Act of Parliament which we are bound to notice; that no question therefore can arise about their capacity as a corporation to take a promissory note, or to make any contract except under their seal, because we know they are not a corporation, and are not therefore required so to contract. A note therefore may, as I conceive, be legally made payable to them as commissioners, as a note might be made payable to the sheriff of the Home District, or to the executors of A. B. Such a note may, for all we can certainly infer from the note itself, have been publicly given to them upon a transaction had with them in their public capacity, or it may have been given to them upon a transaction of their own, unconnected with their public duty: when the former appears upon the record, then the right of their clerk to sue upon it is apparent on the record; when it does not appear, then we cannot see, and therefore cannot acknowledge the right; for I apprehend that the right of A. B. to sue upon a promise made by C. D. must be specifically shewn.

In holding that this action on the promissory note may be sustained, I consider that we are carrying into effect the obvious justice of the case, which it is incumbent on us to do, so far as the rules of law will allow. There is nothing in the statute, it is true, giving express permission to the commissioners to grant forbearance for a debt due to them, or to take or give promissory notes; but there is no prohibition in the statute against their doing either. Indeed the statute does not pretend to direct them in every step of their duty, or to lay down in terms everything that they may or may not do. It does direct that they are to demise the tolls upon certain conditions; and therefore I think it follows, in consequence of that direction, that a demise upon other conditions repugnant to the statute cannot be sued upon as a legal demise, not merely because it is unauthorized, but because it is made in violation of so explicit a law.

As to other points, on which the statute is silent, I consider that where the legislature have imposed upon these commissioners onerous duties, they have confided to them a liberal discretion; they have extensive works to carry on;

much money to be received and expended; and a great deal of business to transact, which it is reasonable to suppose may require, both for the public interest and the just convenience of those with whom they have to deal, the same kind of facilities, and the same occasional relaxation of what might be rigidly exacted, as is found necessary in other concerns of life; and where there is nothing in the statute restraining them, I am of opinion that, in the execution of their trust, they may buy and sell, lend and borrow, give credit and take securities, as other persons may who have the same description of business to manage. They are liable to be controlled by superior authority; but I do not see why that should be fraud, or abuse, or oppression in them, which would not be viewed in the same light in transactions between individuals; and when these defendants gave them their note for £100, which they admitted to be due to them for tolls which they had received, they gave a note upon a very sufficient consideration certainly, without any necessity of relying upon forbearance as a further consideration; and it does not lie in the mouth of these defendants, who have received the forbearance, to advance that as a reason why they should not pay their debt, which is certainly no less a debt because they have given a note for its payment.

I do not look upon the statement of facts which led to the giving of the note, as inserted for the purpose of shewing a consideration to support it; but for the purpose of explaining that it was given, not merely to the plaintiffs *being* commissioners, as a note might be given to the collector of a port or sheriff of a district, but was given to them for a debt accruing in the course of business done by them in that capacity, in order that this plaintiff might appear entitled to sue on it as their clerk. The plaintiffs, as I conceive, are as much entitled as other payees of notes to have a valuable consideration from the promise presumed from the mere giving of the note; and the defendants as much bound as other defendants, by that presumption, till they shew an illegal or insufficient consideration in fact.

The case disclosed in the declaration does indeed shew that the defendants had taken the tolls from the commissioners on such a demise as would not enable them to sue through their clerk on the instrument itself, as their deed, valid under the statute; but it shews also that the defendants entered into the enjoyment of the tolls, and received them for a year, and acknowledged themselves indebted to the plaintiffs in consequence of their occupation, in a sum for which they gave their note; a sum which might be legally as well as justly due by them, whether the demise made to them was a valid contract or not.

MACAULAY, J.—It was held, in the case of Cumming v. Guess et al., that an action would not lie in the name of the clerk, upon a promissory note made to the commissioners, unless it appeared on the face of the declaration that the *demand* accrued to them in the course of their business as commissioners.

It may be that a note, expressed on the face of it to be for value received in tolls or for rent in arrear, or any other description of debt due to them as such commissioners, would be sufficient; but when the note itself is silent on the subject, it is not very clear to me how the deficiency can be supplied by averment, without stating the consideration. Whatever averment may be necessary would, I suppose, be traversable, and I do not see that a count so framed could be properly called declaring on the note; it would rather be a special count setting forth a consideration executed, or executory, and a special promise in writing to pay for such consideration. It is the principle of a promissory note that if it contains that which makes up the constituent parts of such an instrument, it may be declared on *per se*, without any extraneous statement of the consideration on which it is founded; a good and sufficient consideration being *prima facie* presumed. When it cannot be declared upon as a promissory note, and the consideration must be stated, it becomes virtually a mere evidence of a special promise to pay. Whether essential or not, the consideration is, in the present case, fully stated.

Now the consideration set forth is twofold: first, rent in arrear upon the alleged demise, and a promise of forbearance for eighteen months; and if they fail, the note or promise will want any sufficient consideration to support it. As to the first, it was a past or executed consideration; and being (as alleged) for rent in arrear upon a parol demise, the law would (if valid) imply a joint promise to pay the same on request; and the subsequent joint and several special promise contained in the note (treating it as merely evidence of such special promise) would seem to fail for want of a new consideration, according to the case of Hopkins et Ux. v. Logan (a). But even treating the instrument as a promissory note, and declared on as such, that consideration fails on the same ground that the covenant fails in the case of Ireland v. Noble, viz., because the alleged demise was not authorized by the statute 3 Vic. ch. 53, and therefore void as a demise; to which the defendant might plead or demur, as not valid within the powers conferred upon the commissioners by the Act. If a covenant or promise in writing to pay such rent, made contemporaneously with the alleged demise, cannot be enforced on the ground that in law there was no such demise, even after enjoyment during the whole period, I do not see how it can be correctly said that rent was in arrear upon such a demise, for part of which a valid promissory note could be afterwards given. If a covenant or promise to pay, as upon an executory contract, fails because there was no such demise, I do not see how the same demise can be treated as an executed consideration, to support a subsequent promise to pay the rent said to have accrued under it. If there was no such demise, there could be no rent in arrear upon such a demise; and the foundation or consideration seems to me to fail, as well in relation to the subsequent as to the original promise. If there was no demise for a year, as stated, the defendants were indebted, not upon such a demise, but for use and occupation at the end of the year; but a liability for use and occupation is not laid as the consideration for the promissory note in question.

If there was not in law such a demise as laid, there would not of course be any implied promise to pay the rent on request; and if there was no consideration to support an implied, I do not see how it can support a special, promise as upon an executed consideration. There was enjoyment for a year, and an implied promise in law did result to pay therefor on request, not upon a demise at a fixed rent, to be paid by instalments every fortnight in advance, but for the use and occupation according to what it was reasonably worth. The demise

---

(a) 6 M. & W. 241. See also, 1 March, 567; 6 Taunt. 300; 6 M. & W. 458; 7 Dowl. 360; 8 M. & W. 790; 1 D. N. S. 96; 3 A. & E. N. S. 234; 2 Gale & D. 508; 8 Scott New Rep. 502.

itself as laid could not be declared upon; and if not, neither can it be declared upon as inducement or consideration to support an action on a promissory note given for rent that never was legally due under it. It may be said that the defendants, having enjoyed, there was a legal liability to pay whatever was reasonable: and that having enjoyed at a specified rent, though under a void demise, such liability constituted a sufficient consideration to support a subsequent promise to pay the amount. This might be so in ordinary private transactions; but if the original covenant or promise fails notwithstanding such enjoyment and liability, owing to the peculiar circumstances of the trust held by the commissioners, and it is on that ground that it does fail, I should think the subsequent promise or undertaking fails upon the same principle; at least I have not been able satisfactorily to distinguish between them.

As to the second consideration, viz., forbearance, which is not mere passive forbearance, but a contract and promise to forbear as the condition for the note, that fails also; so much so that I have not been able to satisfy myself that the note was not invalid by reason of such superadded consideration, even were the demise laid perfectly valid and unexceptional. The objection to it is, that the commissioners having no power to extend the time for payment of rent in arrear for eighteen months, such a contract on their part, even if under seal, would not bind the board or trust. An action might at any time within the eighteen months have been brought by the clerk for such rent, against which neither the promissory note nor the promises to forbear could be pleaded; nor could any action for breach of such promise or covenant be instituted by the defendants against the board of commissioners for the time being in the name of the clerk for the time being. The commissioners were acting in the execution of a public trust, and such a contract as this was an excess of authority, not binding on the trust; and, as a consideration moving from them as such commissioners, void. The case of Nerot v. Wallace (a) is not inapplicable. It was there held, that a promise made by the friend of a bankrupt, when upon his last examination, that in consideration that the assignees and commissioners would forbear to examine him touching moneys which he had received and not accounted for, he, the friend, would pay such sum as he the bankrupt had received and not accounted for, was void. One objection was, that no sum was specified; but there, as here, the forbearance promised was averred to have been granted. The principal grounds relied on were, that the agreement was illegal, and against the policy of the bankrupt laws; and among other things, Lord Kenyon said, that every person who in consideration of some advantage, either to himself or another, promises a benefit, must have the power of conferring that benefit up to the extent to which that benefit professes to go, and that not only in fact but in law; and, per Ashurst, J., in order to found a consideration for a promise, it is necessary that the party by whom the promise is made should have the power of carrying it into effect.

Tried by the test of policy, there is much to shew that a right of action on this note cannot be said to have accrued to the commissioners

---

(a) 3 T. R. 17.

in the course of their business as commissioners. A right of action for the rent in arrear did not accrue to them for want of a demise such as the statute empowered them to make ; and if this note be valid, this consequence follows, that although the demise was void, and no action could be maintained thereon for the rent, still it was competent to the board to take negotiable promissory notes every fortnight the day after the rent should have been paid in advance, and payable eighteen months afterwards, or at any other period they might please. Such notes being the property of the trust, might be negotiated or disposed of by endorsement, and if not retired by the makers at maturity, actions might be brought by their holders against the commissioners for the time being in the name of their clerk as endorsers. The clerk and commissioners are liable to constant change, but all the property, contracts, choses in action, &c., belonging to the trust, go to the successors, upon whom also attaches the liability for all demands against the trust ; and if on a demise of toll the rent is required to be reserved payable monthly, and secured by a proper agreement and sufficient sureties, I do not see how it can be competent to the commissioners for the time being, instead of exacting the rent when in arrear, to take promissory notes for the same, payable at distant periods, at the risk of discharging the sureties they ought and must be supposed to have responsible to them, and this without the new security beyond the tenant's own note, founded upon nude promises of a forbearance not in their power to grant. It looks so much like a breach of authority (however laudable the object), that I cannot believe it consistent with the object and policy of the Turnpike Acts, or that the courts can assume as valid such contracts of such public boards, founded on such transactions and considerations.

It is true that promissory notes, taken under the circumstances of the present, may not discharge the rent, or suspend any remedy that existed therefor : and that such note may not have in the case of the commissioners the same binding effect upon the board that it would have in the case of private individuals ; still forbearance is promised on their part and delay granted, without authority, and if the consideration of forbearance be invalid, and all previous remedies remained unaffected, it follows that the note could only have operated as a *collateral security*, and in this light only could it I think be correctly regarded and upheld. But if the demise was void, and there was therefore no principal debt, it would not seem capable of operating as a collateral security, nor was it given or received with such intent ; the contrary appears in the declaration ; it was not payment or satisfaction, and could not operate as collateral security. In whatever light viewed, therefore, the action brought by the clerk on behalf of the commissioners in their public capacity, upon a note treated as the property of the trust and a valid security in law, seems to me to fail.

Although this seems to me to be the construction to be placed upon the transaction as set forth in the declaration, judging from the provisions of the statute, and what I find upon the subject in the English books, I cannot say I am by any means confident in the opinion I have expressed. I find no case of the kind in relation to the tolls in England, which are managed under statutes from which ours are very closely though not literally copied. The commissioners of turnpikes seem to be there regarded as executing public trusts under powers conferred and limited by the statutes under which they act, and in the cases I have seen, it appears to be considered that they are confined strictly to the duties and authorities therein prescribed.

I should rather have adopted the opposite view, if I felt it to be safe, as being more consistent with the justice of the case and the faith of contracts; but regarding the board of commissioners as acting within circumscribed powers, I do not find authority or discretion vested in them to farm out the tolls in any other mode than the statute provides, or to deal with the rents accruing for toll so demised otherwise than according to the terms of the original contract or agreement of lease; nor do I perceive anything in the Act, nor can I find any adjudged cases, sanctioning their extending the time of payment for rents already due, at their discretion, or making rent in arrear the foundation of new contracts in relation thereto; it does not appear to fall within the scope of their business as such commissioners in execution of specified trusts; in other words, the declaration does not shew this demand to have accrued to them in the regular course of their business as commissioners, being based upon an alleged demise, and an extension of credit for rent claimed to be due, and a promise of forbearance, not authorized by the statute or binding on the trust, proving it to be beyond the scope of the powers thereby conferred. I come therefore (but with much hesitation) to the conclusion that this action is not sustainable on the present declaration. I am by no means prepared to say the commissioners may not take promissory notes, either in original transactions, or as further or collateral security for debts to accrue or due to them, or that such notes would not become the property of the board, and be capable of collection in the name of the clerk for the time being. I restrict myself to the present case as it appears on the face of the declaration.

JONES, J.—I have reluctantly come to the conclusion that this action cannot be sustained.

The commissioners are not by any provision in the statute authorized to make a contract like the present, that is, to take a promissory note the consideration for which is for tolls due upon a lease.

The law points out the mode to be pursued in farming the tolls, and it is the duty of the commissioners to proceed according to its directions, and it is doubtful whether a lease taken upon terms not prescribed, or different from those prescribed, can be sued upon. Here, however, the defendants had enjoyed under the lease, and a debt had accrued to the commisioners for rent of tolls for which they could sue for use and occupation, if not under the lease, and in such action upon a contract implied by law could sue in the name of their clerk. This contract is not authorized by the Act, and I think is one upon which no action accrued to them as commissioners, and therefore not capable of being enforced in the name of the clerk.

It is not a void note, but such a one as I think could be enforced in the names of the commissioners, it being a debt due to them personally, they having paid, or being liable to pay to the government the rent, for the payment of which the extended credit was given by the note.

The case of Sugars v. Brinkworth (a), is an authority to shew that the note

---

(a) 4 Camp. 46, and 2 Bos. & P. 151.

is not altogether void, although a transaction of this nature should be strictly scrutinized where parties profess to contract in the character of commissioners acting in the discharge of a public duty.

There is no reason here to doubt that the commissioners acted in good faith, and that the defendants have reaped the benefit of their indulgence, and now attempt to get rid of their own contract growing out of an Act in all probability regarded by them at the time as highly favourable.

The case in 10 East. is also very satisfactory to shew the right of the commissioners to collect the amount due, notwithstanding the extended credit; but the note being a contract made upon consideration of forbearance, as well as in consideration of a debt due, which is an executed consideration, I do not think it a contract which can be sued upon in the name of the clerk; as in the case of this plaintiff against Noble, I think it would be better to require the commissioners to pursue the directions of the statute, and make only such contracts as are authorized, or such as are necessary to discharge their duty as commissioners under the Act.

I see no action brought upon a note in all the cases which have grown out of the proceedings of commissioners under Acts like that under consideration, and it is scarcely possible, if such an action could be maintained, that one should not have arisen in the multiplicity of litigation and the cases reported arising out of the proceedings of commissioners and trustees for public works. *Per Cur.*—Judgment for defendants on demurrer.

ROBINSON, C. J., *dissentiente*.

IRELAND, CLERK TO THE COMMISSIONERS OF THE MIDLAND DISTRICT TURNPIKE TRUST, V. NOBLE.

A. sues as clerk to the commissioners exercising a public trust under an Act of Parliament (3 Vic. ch. 53) upon an alleged demise of tolls for a year, at a rent payable *every fortnight in advance;* the 27th section of that Act requiring the rent to be made payable *monthly;* the lease stated in the declaration is said to be subject to the provisions of the Act.

Held, on demurrer to the declaration, that the plaintiff, as clerk to the commissioners, could not be permitted to recover on such a contract, because it is a contract substantially different from the one which the commissioners are expressly directed by the statute to make.

The plaintiff declared in debt for rent, as clerk to the commissioners, upon a contract of demise made by the commissioners, to the defendant, for that whereas heretofore, to wit, on the 6th day of December, in the year of our Lord 1844, by a certain indenture then made between the said the commissioners of the Midland District Turnpike Trust, of the one part, and the defendant, and one William Breden and one John Wiley of the other part, (and which said indenture, sealed with the seal of the defendant, the plaintiff as clerk as aforesaid now brings here into court,) the said the commissioners of the Midland District Turnpike Trust did demise, lease, and to farm, let unto the defendant and the said William Breden and the said John Wiley, their executors, administrators and assigns, Toll-gate No. 1, in the township of Kingston, in the said district, together with the toll-house erected at the said toll-gate, on the macadamized road, between the town of Kingston and the village of Napanee, in the said district, and all the tolls, rents, revenues, profits and incomes thereunto belonging and appertaining, according to the provisions of the statutes in such case made and provided, and except as in the indenture is excepted: to have and to hold the said toll-gate, toll-house, with all and singular the appurtenances thereto belonging, to the defendant, and the said William Breden and the said John Wiley, their executors, administrators and assigns, from the first day of January, in the year of our Lord 1845, for and during and unto the full end and term of one year from thence next ensuing and fully to be completed and ended, subject nevertheless to the provisions of an Act of the Provincial Parliament of Upper Canada, passed in the seventh year of the reign of his late Majesty, King William the Fourth of that name, entitled, "An Act to raise a "sum of money to macadamize the road between the town of Kingston and "the village of Napanee, in the Midland District, and for other purposes "therein mentioned," and of an Act of the Provincial Parliament of Upper Canada, passed in the third year of her present Majesty's reign, entitled, "An Act to repeal, alter and amend the laws now in force for the regulation "of the several macadamized roads within this province," and (excepting as aforesaid) yielding and paying therefor to the said the commissioners of the Midland District Turnpike Trust the rent or sum of £990 12s. 11d. of lawful money of Canada, by even and equal payments of £38 2s. 0½d. each, payable every fortnight in advance, and the defendant and the said William Breden and the said John Wiley did thereby for themselves and each of them, and each for the other jointly and severally, covenant, promise and agree, to and with the said the commissioners of the Midland District Turnpike Trust, that they, the defendant and the said William Breden and the said John Wiley, their executors, administrators and assigns, should and would well and truly pay, or cause to be paid, to the said the commissioners of the Midland District Turnpike Trust, the said two-weekly rent thereby reserved, at the times and in the manner hereinbefore limited and appointed for the payment thereof, as by the said indenture, reference being thereunto had, will more fully and at large appear, by virtue of which said demise the defendant and the said William Breden and the said John Wiley afterwards entered into and upon the said demised premises with the appurtenances, and became and were thereof possessed, and received and enjoyed the said tolls, rents, revenues, profits and incomes thereto belonging as aforesaid, from thenceforth until and upon the 1st day of September then next following, when a large sum of money, to wit, the sum of £667 14s. 8½d. of the rent aforesaid for the space of seventeen fortnights of the said term, ending on the day and year last aforesaid, and then last elapsed, became and was due and payable from the defendant and the said William Breden and the said John Wiley to the said the commissioners of the Midland District Turnpike Trust, and still in arrear to the said the commissioners of the Midland District Turnpike Trust, and unpaid, whereby an action hath accrued to the said the commissioners of the Midland District Turnpike Trust, to demand and have of and from the defendant the sum of £667 14s. 8d., being the sum above demanded. Yet the defendant, although often requested so to do, hath not paid the said sum above demanded, or any part thereof, to the damage of the said the commissioners of the Midland District Turnpike Trust of £60, and therefore the said plaintiff, as clerk as aforesaid, brings suit, &c.

The defendant demanded oyer of the lease, which was set out, demising the premises as in the declaration mentioned, and with a covenant to pay rent, &c., and at the conclusion of the lease the following words were used: "In witness whereof, the *seal* of the commissioners aforesaid hath been hereunto affixed by *Charles Cumming*, their clerk, who hath also hereto set his hand," &c.

To this declaration the defendant demurred, on the following grounds:

1st. That the indenture being executed by Cumming, as clerk, he should have sued.

2nd. That it did not appear that Cumming was not still clerk, or when he ceased to be so.

3rd. That it did not appear in the declaration *by whom* the lease was executed on behalf of the commissioners.

4th. That Cumming, as a fact, had no authority to execute it.

5th. That the commissioners never did lease the tolls, or execute the lease.

6th. That the cause of action should have been stated to have accrued to the plaintiff, and not to the commissioners.

7th. That the commissioners had no authority to reserve rent payable, except monthly.

8th. That the declaration should have averred that the plaintiff was clerk "for the time being," the indenture having shewn another clerk.

Henderson, counsel for the demurrer.

Alex. Campbell, contra.

ROBINSON, C. J.—Ireland, as clerk to the Midland District Turnpike Commissioners, *declares* in this action upon a contract of demise made by them to the defendant; oyer is demanded, and he shews a deed which on the face of it indeed is a demise by the commissioners, but which, if we are at liberty on the pleadings to look at the conclusion, "*In witness whereof,*" &c., or at the manner of its execution, we must see is not really a demise by them, but a contract of demise, which their clerk has assumed to make in their name. He had no right, by the Act of Parliament or otherwise, to bind them by deed or by a contract in any form; and the first question that arises is, whether that defence is or is not one which the defendant is bound to avail himself of upon the trial, upon a denial of the demise pleaded; or, whether we can look at what is stated in the attestation part of the deed, and at the manner in which it professes to have been signed and sealed; or whether the *contents* of the alleged deed are not all that is before us upon the oyer, and for the purpose of deciding on the demurrer. In the case of Cooch et al. v. Goodman (a), that point came up in a case very like the present in some respects, but it does not seem to have been satisfactorily cleared up by the court. They were not driven there to decide it, nor are we here; for there is at least no doubt that the deed which is set out on oyer, becomes in effect part of the declaration, so far as its contents are concerned, and that it does open to us all the objections which the defendant has taken to the legality of the contract. I must first remark, however, that if we could treat this deed as not being executed by the

(a) 2 A. & E. N. S. 580.

commissioners, then there would be no demise such as is stated in the declaration; and that would present the question, whether the defendant would not be bound nevertheless to pay the rent, upon his covenant. The case of Berkeley v. Hardy (a), is a very clear decision that the landlord could not in such a case sue for rent upon the covenant, although the covenantee had well executed the deed; the principle, I suppose, being, that as the landlord did not execute, he cannot prove his averment that he demised for the term mentioned; and as he would not be estopped by a deed which he had never executed, so the tenant would not be estopped from denying that he had demised.

In the latter case, however, referred to, the Court of King's Bench held otherwise, and that an action upon the covenant might, under such circumstances, be supported. I do not at present see how these decisions are to be reconciled; but this case before us presents a substantial ground on which I think we must hold that the action cannot be supported. It is an action brought, not by the lessors, but by this plaintiff as their clerk. He has no authority to sue as such generally, but only under the power expressly given by 3 Vic. ch. 53, sec. 17; and we have held, and I think rightly, and in accordance with English decisions, that it must appear on the record, in any action brought by him, that the cause of action accrued to the commissioners in the course of their duty under the Act (b); otherwise he might be suing, or might undertake to answer, in their name, upon matters wholly foreign to the trust, relating to their private transactions (c). But it is objected, that the alleged contract on which this action is brought, is on the face of it one which could not be made consistently with the statute, and that the clerk of the commissioners can therefore not sue on such a contract; I feel there is great force in that objection. The 27th section of the Act directs that commissioners shall let the tolls by public auction, and that the lessee shall give surety that he will pay the rent monthly. If after repeated attempts they can find no bidder who will enter into the proper conditions, they may then let the tolls by private contract; in which case, I consider, that as in the other, though the provision is not repeated in the clause, the commissioners must make the rent payable monthly, and take sureties for the payment. But this contract (if we must look at it as the deed of the commissioners), instead of reserving a rent payable monthly, which means at the end of each month, the rent growing with the enjoyment, reserves a rent payable every fortnight *in advance.*

In the case of Cummings v. Glassup et al. (d), it appeared that the same commissioners had, in another lease of tolls made by them, reserved the rent payable in the same way; but that case did not come before the court till after the trial, and then upon objections which appeared to be fatal to the plaintiff's recovery, and the verdict which the jury had given for the defendants was confirmed. Here the objection is taken and insisted on upon demurrer. I do not say that I am perfectly clear in my opinion and free from all doubt, in holding that the clerk to the commissioners cannot legally recover under the Act upon such a contract, but upon the best judgment I can form, he cannot.

(a) 8 D. & R. 102. (b) 10 Bing. 89; 2 G. & D. 621.
(c) Cummings v. Guess, 2 Cam. Rep. 125. (d) 1 Cam. Rep. 340.

In the case of Cole et al. v. Gower et al. (a), the question was discussed, how far a public officer contracting under the provisions of a statute is bound to make his contract in conformity with the statute. Parish officers had there taken a note to themselves in their public capacity, from the father of a bastard child, for a certain sum of money intended to indemnify the parish for the charge of the child, instead of taking, as the statute required, a bond, with security, *to indemnify the parish.*

The court held that the note could not be recovered upon, being taken in violation of public policy and of the directions of the Act. Lord Ellenborough remarked, "The parish officers are to take the security as a matter of public "duty, in the form prescribed by the Act; and taking it in the form they "have done, is contrary both to the direct letter and to the general policy of "the law." The other judges were not less decided in their opinion of the necessity of following the directions of the Act. Mr. Justice Lawrence conceived that the practice which had prevailed, of taking notes of that kind, was probably rather expedient than otherwise, so far as regarded the public interest; but he agreed, nevertheless, that it was better to abide by the strict, letter of the statute (b).

Now as to public policy in the present case, certainly the exacting rent to be paid once a fortnight and in advance, gives terms less favourable to the tenant than making it payable monthly, and may therefore have the effect of prejudicing the leasing at the auction; it is at all events a substantial variance, and if we were to sanction such a departure from what the Act directs, where and how could we on any principle draw the line within which the commissioners must keep themselves?

They might lease the tolls for five years instead of one, and might make a year's rent, or the whole rent, payable in advance; or they might rent for a term of years, and postpone the payment altogether till the end of the term. Public policy is clearly concerned in their observing, as they ought to do, the directions of the legislature. And this case is stronger against the action than the case to which I have referred, because there the payees of the note were themselves suing in their own names, upon a security which had certainly not been given without consideration. Here a third party, not named in the contract, sues upon it. He can only derive his right to sue under the statute, and it would be inconsistent with the principles which govern the execution of powers and authorities, if we were to allow him to derive, under the Act, a right to sue upon a contract taken in violation of the substantial provisions of the Act.

There may, to be sure, be some of the provisions in the law which we could treat as merely directory, and we will not prejudge any future case by laying it down as an inflexible rule that all must be done in exact conformity with the statute, or must be void; but for the reasons given, I am of opinion that the plaintiff, as clerk to the commissioners, cannot be permitted to recover on the contract which is set out in this case; not because it is a contract which the Act gives the commissioners no express authority to make, (for that, I think, may not be necessary,) but because it is a contract substantially

---

(a) 6 E. R. 110.   (b) 2 Smith, 246.

different from the one which they are expressly directed by the statute to make.

MACAULAY, J.—According to what is said in the case of Cooch et al. v. Goodman (a), the demise as stated in the declaration, and as appears on the face of the deed set out in oyer, is by a corporation; but it does not appear to me that the statute 3 Vic. ch. 53, constitutes the commissioners of turnpike trusts corporations (b): the execution of the lease, therefore, by the clerk, affixing a common or corporate seal, was not valid; nor does it appear to have been done by the direction of the board; the deed was not signed or sealed by any of the commissioners personally; nor does the Act empower the clerk to sign his name in this place and stead. The provincial statute does not on this head contain provisions that may be found in some English statutes. The lease was not therefore a demise by a corporate body by deed; and as a demise of tolls, it could only be well made by deed, unless let at public auction or otherwise, under the 27th section, which may perhaps authorize a demise in writing without seal, although the Act does not (like the Imperial Statute 3 °Geo. IV. ch. 126, ss. 55-57) expressly render a lease in writing, signed by two of the trustees, or their clerk, &c., good and valid, though not by deed or under seal. It was not therefore a demise such as the declaration, apart from the deed itself when set out on oyer, imports. It is however alleged and admitted that the defendant covenanted to pay the rent, and that he entered and enjoyed during the period for which such rent is claimed in this action; and the case of Cooch et al. v. Goodman is much in point to shew that he is liable on his covenant, although the lessors did not duly execute the lease. The difficulty arises from the terms of the alleged demise, in respect of which the defendant did so covenant; and the question occurs, supposing the trustees had all signed and sealed the lease, whether an action thereon could be brought in the name of the clerk. The plaintiff is suing as clerk to the commissioners, exercising a public trust under an Act of Parliament upon an alleged demise of tolls for a year, at rent payable every *fortnight* in advance; whereas the 3 Vic. ch. 53, s. 27, required it to be reserved, payable *monthly;* and section 33 authorizes the expulsion of the tenant, in case the tolls shall be in arrear for seven days. The lease stated is declared to be subject to the provisions of this Act; so that (if within it) the tenant might be expelled at the end of the week, because they had not been paid in *advance*, though they might be ready with the rent the next day; and if the commissioners could require the rent to be paid every fortnight in advance, so they might every *month*, or for the whole year, were they not restricted to a monthly letting. I do not find that it is such a contract as the commissioners can enter into, and if not, the clerk cannot sue thereon on their behalf (c). If this action lies, it follows that actions might have been brought, as upon a demise under the statute, for the rent reserved every fortnight, if not paid in *advance;* and further, if not paid within a week after it became due, the commissioners might have expelled the tenants, although the statute only intended to subject them to a monthly

---

(a) 2 A. & E. N. S. 580.
(b) Sections 7, 14, 45.
(c) Section 17; 10 Bing. 89.

rent, payable at the end of such period. The proper remedy under the circumstances seems to be, for use and occupation (a).

JONES, J., concurred.

Judgment for the defendant, on the demurrer.

CAMPBELL V. ELLIOTT, BLACK, MOORE AND SOUTHWICK.

A county superintendent of common schools, signing together with the trustees a contract with a teacher, will be considered to have signed the same only as approving the appointment, and in pursuance of the direction of the statute, and not as a party contracting with the teacher.

The plaintiff sued in *assumpsit* on a special agreement by the defendants, to employ the plaintiff "as teacher and master of a school, for a year from "the 1st of July, 1845, at a certain salary, to wit, £166 5s. for the year."

The declaration averred that the plaintiff did enter into the employment of the defendants as such teacher, on the terms aforesaid, and continued to serve the defendants therein, as such teacher, &c., till the 19th of September, 1844, when the defendants wrongfully discharged him, without any reasonable or probable cause whatsoever, and refused to employ him for the remainder of the term, or to pay him his wages for such period.

The declaration also contained a count for work and labour as a schoolmaster, in teaching a school for the defendants, and counts for money had and received, and an account stated.

The defendant Elliott, pleaded, 1st, *non-assumpsit*.

2ndly, To the first count, that the school mentioned therein was a county model school for the District of London, according to the statute, of which the other three defendants were trustees; that they appointed the plaintiff teacher for one year, subject to the provisions of the statute, with the special approval of him, the defendant Elliott, who then was, and still is, the County Superintendent of Common Schools for the said District of London; and that the said defendant Elliott, as such superintendent, afterwards, viz., on the 18th September, 1845, "*considered it was necessary to dismiss, and did "then actually dismiss*, the plaintiff, as such teacher of the said model school, "as it was lawful to him to do under and by virtue of the said statute," of which the plaintiff had notice, which is the said non-performance complained of. This plea was demurred to.

The other defendants, Black, Moore and Southwick, pleaded to the first count the general issue.

2ndly, To the second and third counts, except as to £27 6s., parcel, &c., they pleaded *non-assumpsit;* and as to the £27 6s., a tender before action brought, and payment into court; and a set-off to the whole action.

The plaintiff replied to the tender, damage beyond the £27 6s., which he took out of court.

The case was tried at the last moment of the assizes for the District of

---

(a) 6 T. R. 62; 6 C. & P. 608.

London, upon a record made up by consent, and entered a few hours before the trial, and the jury gave a verdict for the plaintiff, £132 15s.

The plaintiff had, on the third day of the assizes, served the defendant's attorney with a notice to produce the written agreement or memorandum on which the plaintiff was engaged to teach for a year; no paper was produced by the defendants on the trial, and their counsel objected that the notice was served too late. The plaintiff was allowed to give secondary evidence of the agreement, which was in substance, that the plaintiff was to keep the county model school (for the County of Middlesex,) at a salary of £166 6s., per annum, and that his engagement should be for the term of one year, beginning on the 1st of July then next (1845).

There was a paper put in, which the plaintiff's attorney swore he was satisfied was a copy of the agreement or memorandum intended for heads of an agreement which was drawn up between the parties when the contract was made. The plaintiff entered upon his duty as teacher, under the contract, and taught from the first of July to the 18th of September following, when he was dismissed.

The salary due to him to that day, according to the contract, was tendered and refused, and this action was brought to recover damages for not retaining him in service, but wrongfully dismissing him.

The paper which was produced at the trial as a copy of the agreement, but not admitted to be such, and the production of which was objected to after stating the terms, concludes thus: "It is understood that Mr. Campbell's "engagement shall be for the term of one year, beginning on the 1st of July "next;" and it professes to give the signatures, thus:

"Signed,   DUNCAN CAMPBELL, H. Mr.
"MR. NOTT, Assistant.
"DR. SOUTHWICK.
"MR. BLACK.
"MR. MOORE.
"MR. ELLIOTT."

Elliott was in fact the school superintendent for the county, and he contended that he had signed the paper in no other capacity but merely to signify his approval, as the School Act required.—7 Vic. ch. 29, sec. 61.

The learned judge, when the case was gone through, left it to the jury to find for the plaintiff, if they were satisfied that all the defendants signed the agreement as contracting parties, but not otherwise; and on that direction, they found for the plaintiff, giving him damages, as it appears, to the amount of the wages which would have been payable to him, under the agreement, if he had been allowed to serve out the whole of his year.

J. H. Hagarty, counsel for the defendants, now moved to set aside the verdict without costs, as being contrary to law and evidence and for misdirection, and for admission of improper evidence, and for excessive damages; and in support of his motion, produced Elliott's affidavit, in which he swore positively that the contract was made by all the parties under the School Act, having that before them at the time, and that he signed, and was known by the plaintiff to sign, as superintendent only, and with no other intention than to signify his approval of the engagement made by the trustees which the Act required him to do; and also annexed to this affidavit a paper which Elliott swore was a copy of the memorandum, in pencil, made at the time, and subscribed by the parties in the same form as that was subscribed.

This paper agreed with the paper which was produced, except as to the manner in which the signatures were given, thus:

"DUNCAN CAMPBELL, Hd. Master.
" ELIAS C. NOTT, Assistant.
" WM. ELLIOTT, Dist. Superintendent.
" HENRY BLACK,
" MARTIAL T. MOORE, } Trustees."
" G. SOUTHWICK,

Blake and *Becher* shewed cause, contending that the defendants had waived all objections as to time of serving notice, by having delayed pleading till the evening of the day before the assizes terminated.

ROBINSON, C. J.—The case certainly, in my opinion, calls for a new trial. Taking only the evidence which the jury had before them, it was not reasonable to suppose that Elliott signed otherwise than as superintendent. This plaintiff had been some time before teaching a school under the Act, and must be supposed to be cognizant of all its provisions, and to have intended to make the contract under it. There is no ground for supposing that the plaintiff expected to be remunerated otherwise than out of the public funds, and through the operation of that system which the legislature had established. The paper which was given in at the trial as secondary evidence of the agreement, could not be relied upon by any one as an accurate transcript of the signature, for it was manifestly not a copy of them, but merely a memorandum, shewing by what persons it was subscribed. It does not give the Christian names of the parties signing, but merely "signed, Mr. Southwick, Mr. Elliott," &c., giving no additions, either to the trustees or to the superintendent. According to the paper which is now put in, annexed to Mr. Elliott's affidavit, the parties did in fact sign very differently, both as to the order in which they set their names, and the additions which they appended to them. This plaintiff, in making the engagement, doubtless looked to the public funds for his salary, and not to the private responsibilities of the parties; and I cannot for a moment imagine that he considered the trustees to be acting in any other manner than as trustees, or that Elliott was or would have been a party to the transaction in any other manner than in virtue of his office as superintendent. If Elliott had produced at the trial the paper which he has annexed to his affidavit, the jury would hardly have come to any other conclusion than that the contract was made under the statute, and by the trustees alone on the one side, and Campbell on the other side; though the district school was inconveniently mixed up with the model school in the arrangement.

If, having that paper before them, the jury had found the verdict which they did, I must have considered the defendants entitled to a new trial, without costs; and as it is, I have difficulty in determining that they should not have it on those terms, because the plaintiff must have known that the paper which he placed before the jury, as a copy of the agreement, did not represent truly the manner in which the parties had signed. But, on the other hand, the defendant Elliott, who was present at the trial, had it in his power to shew all that he shews now. It is not asserted by him that he had not the paper with him in court; but it seems he declined to bring it forward, relying, as I suppose, that the plaintiff, for want of notice to produce the agreement being served in time, would be found not entitled to give secondary evidence; and being unwilling to help him through the difficulty by producing this copy, which he now advances in aid of the application for a new trial.

I am of opinion, under all the circumstances, that the verdict should be set aside, and a new trial granted on payment of costs.

The question of Elliott being or not being a contracting party, affects the whole verdict; for if the contract was in reality made by the trustees only, the misjoinder of Elliott, as a contractor, is a fatal variance.

MACAULAY, J.—The verdict is warranted by the evidence given at the trial of this cause, but the copy of the agreement now produced imports that Mr. Elliott signed only as superintendent, and not as a contracting party. The statute authorizes the trustees to engage teachers with his approbation; and as the damages are large, I have no objection to a new trial on payment of costs. The issue is, whether the defendants jointly contracted or not; and the question does not arise whether the superintendent could dismiss the plaintiff of his own discretion, without assigning any cause; if it did, it is not clear to me that he could do so, after signing the engagement by which the parties agreed to abide by the arrangement therein contained, the last item of which was, that the plaintiff was engaged for a year.

The 7 Vic. ch. 29, sec. 61, empowers the trustees to appoint the teacher, with the approval of the superintendent in writing; and it gives him *power* at any time to *suspend* or dismiss such teacher, if he shall consider it necessary to do so; but it does not follow that he can exercise such power without *any cause*. Without such authority he could not have dismissed at all. The trustees had power to dismiss for adequate and justifiable cause; and as to them the statute is silent, but seems to confer a like *power* on the superintendent. Nor has he such power, except in relation to the model school, by sec. 44, No. 2; and the trustees are to contract with and employ all teachers within the same. But in this case he specially agrees to abide by the agreement to hire the plaintiff for a year.

JONES, J., concurred.

Rule absolute, on payment of costs.

DOE ON THE DEMISE OF PETER VANCOTT V. ROBERT READ.

Where lands are devised to A. and B. and C., as trustees, and C. is incapable of taking, the estate may nevertheless vest in A. and B.

The devise of an estate is not wholly void because the estate has been charged *to some extent* with an illegal trust.

Where trustees are directed by a will to dispose of an estate, "as the ministers " of a certain church may see fit," the devise is good, not being *necessarily* a devise to charitable uses.

This was an action of ejectment to recover the north half of Lot No. 25, on the east side of Pinnacle Street, in the town of Belleville.

The defendant pleaded the general issue.

The cause came on to be tried before the Hon. Mr. Justice McLean, at the assizes holden for the District of Victoria, when a verdict was found for the plaintiff for one shilling damages and costs of suit, subject to the opinion of the court on the following case:

The lessor of the plaintiff proved that Anne Sparrow, before the day of the demise laid in the declaration, in the year 1839, died, seized of the *locus in quo;* that she had been married, and that her husband had died without issue; that she was the daughter of John Vancott, deceased; that John Vancott and wife were both dead, and that Peter Vancott, the lessor of the plaintiff, was her eldest brother and heir-at-law; and it was admitted that his heirship was sufficiently established; this closed the plaintiff's case.

The defendant, in his defence, claimed a purchase from two of the trustees, devisees in trust, mentioned in the will of Anne Sparrow, a copy of which, and the evidence to establish it, is subjoined:

"In the name of God, amen.—Know all men, by these presents, that I, "Anne Sparrow, of the town of Belleville, in the Midland District, and Pro- "vince of Upper Canada, widow of the said John Sparrow, deceased, being of "sound mind, do make and ordain this my last will and testament, hereby "revoking all former and other wills by me made.

"I do give and bequeath and devise all my real estate in the town of Belle- "ville, which I hold by a deed signed by James Bickford, and dated Belleville, "May the fifth, one thousand eight hundred and thirty-five, that is to say, my "town lot number twenty-five on the east side of Pinnacle Street, in the town "of Belleville, to the board of the Upper Canada Academy, and Benjamin "Ketcheson, joiner, and James Jameson, millwright, of the town of Belleville, "as my trustees in trust, to hold, to use and to dispose of the same as they, "the annual meeting of the ministers of the Wesleyan Methodist Church "in Canada, see proper, only however in accordance with the following "directions:

"1st. I direct and hereby give and bequeath to my brother, Cornelius Van- "cott, the sum of twelve pounds ten shillings, lawful money.

"2nd. I give and devise to my brother, David Vancott, the sum of twelve "pounds ten shillings, lawful money.

"3rd. I give and devise to my sister, Sarah Badgley, the sum of twelve "pounds twelve shillings, lawful money.

"4th. I give and devise to my nephew, Benjamin Vancott, the sum of five "pounds, lawful money.

"5th. I direct, also, that the sum of one pound five shillings shall be "applied annually to the regular support of the Wesleyan Methodist minister "in the Belleville circuit or station; and that the amount be paid by my "trustees into the hands of the stewards of the Wesleyan Methodist Society, "for the same purpose, year by year.

"6th. I direct, further, that each of my nephews and nieces be furnished "with a copy of the Holy Scriptures.

"7th. And lastly, I require that all my personal and movable property be "sold, and the proceeds applied in the same manner and to the purposes above "mentioned, after the expenses of my funeral, and all the lawful demands "against me are paid. I hereby do appoint the above named trustees, namely, "the board of the Upper Canada Academy, Benjamin Ketcheson and James "Jameson, to be my executors of this my last will and testament; and in view "of either of the above named persons ceasing to be members of the Wesleyan "Methodist Church in Canada, that the board of the Upper Canada Academy "shall select some other suitable persons to act in that capacity; and any "such person or persons, from time to time, shall, and are hereby declared to "be, to all intents and purposes, my trustee or trustees, executor or "executors.

"Done in Belleville, this tenth day of September, in the year of our Lord "one thousand eight hundred and thirty-nine."

The parties agreed that a verdict should be taken for the plaintiff, subject to the opinion of the court as to the validity of the devise of the premises in question, and the right of the devisees to hold under that will; a verdict to be entered for the defendant if the devise should be held valid, and the evidence sufficient to entitle him to a verdict.

Verdict for plaintiff, one shilling, subject to these points.

D. B. Read, counsel for the plaintiff.

A. Wilson, counsel for the defendant.

ROBINSON, C. J., delivered the judgment of the court.

We are of opinion that the devise of the land in question in this action vested the estate in the two devisees named, Ketcheson and Jameson, admitting that no estate could pass under it to the "board of the Upper Canada Academy," which board the testator intended to make a trustee, jointly with the persons named.

The objects of the trust are of course unexceptionable as regards the legacies to the testator's relatives, which she directs to be paid from the lands, and we do not hold the devise to be void as regards any other object of the trust than the £1 5s. annually to be paid to a Methodist minister, which certainly was within the Act 9 Geo. II. ch. 36, against charitable uses. That statute, this court, for the reasons stated in Doe dem. Anderson v. Todd et al. (*a*), have held to be in force in this province, but it has not been so rigidly construed in England that it has been taken to make void the devise of an estate, because it has been charged to some extent with a charitable trust; that might occasion a most ruinous consequence in some cases to a testator's family.

The case of Doe dem. Toone & West v. Copestake (*b*) is quite in point to shew that the direction to the trustees to dispose of the estate as the annual meeting of the ministers of the Wesleyan church may see proper, is not void under the statute, inasmuch as it is not necessarily a devise to a charitable use, since they have it in their power to apply the estate to any use not prohibited. There are many later decisions to the same effect.

We are of opinion, therefore, that as the estate vested in Jameson and Ketcheson for some purposes clearly legal, the plaintiff suing as heir cannot recover, and that a verdict is to be entered for the defendant (*c*).

Per Cur.—Verdict to be entered for the defendant.

(*a*) 2 Cameron's Reports. (*b*) 6 E. R. 328.
(*c*) See 1 Ves. Sen. 80; 9 Ves. 400; 10 Ves. 532; 18 Law Mag. 294; Ambler, 636; 10 Ves. 265; 1 Ves. 320; 14 Ves. 537; 1 Cox. 316; Shelford Mort. 71; Drake, 109-82; 1 Ves. Jun. 390.

THE QUEEN V. KERR, IN THE SUIT OF BATES V. O'DONOHUE.

The court in *banc* has no power to punish, by attachment, a witness disobeying a subpœna, issued at *nisi prius* by the clerk of assize.

Quære: Can the court at *nisi prius* punish a witness for contempt of its authority, in disobeying a subpœna.

In this cause, D. G. *Miller* obtained a rule *nisi* to shew cause why an attachment should not issue against one Kerr, who was subpœnaed to attend as a witness on the part of the plaintiff, at the last assizes for the Home District. It was stated that he was duly served with the subpœna, and money tendered to him, and that he did attend during part of the assizes, but afterwards stayed away, and, as the plaintiff swore, wilfully, and for the purpose of defeating his action, and that the record was withdrawn in consequence.

W. Hume Blake shewed cause, filing an affidavit of Kerr.

ROBINSON, C. J.—The witness has answered the application, and filed an affidavit, by which he attempts to shew that his conduct was not improper. How far the answer given by him is satisfactory, we need not determine ; for it is first to be considered whether we have any power to attach a witness for contempt in disobeying a subpœna not issued from this court, but by the clerk of assize, as this was.

I apprehend we have not the power. The cases of Rex v. Ring (*a*), and Rex v. Brownell (*b*), are against it, as well as the reason of the thing ; for it is not a contempt of this court to disobey the command of another court.

If it could have been so treated, the statute 45 Geo. III. ch. 9, s. 3, need not have been passed in England.

The party injured in such cases, has of course a remedy by action, which often, perhaps, would be no remedy ; and he might, as I suppose, upon a proper application to the court at *nisi prius* which issued the subpœna, have the witness punished by that court, for the contempt of its authority. The case of The King v. Clement (*c*), seems to assume this.

I hope we might find some authority for holding, that as issues out of this court are tried before a judge of this court, the command of such judge might be regarded, by reason of his connection with the court, as the command of this court, because necessary for enabling him to try the cause; but he sits under a distinct commission, and holds a court apart from this court. We cannot punish a party summarily, upon any doubtful authority.

MACAULAY, J.—I can find no instance in which disobedience to a subpœna issued by the court at *nisi prius*, through the clerk of assize, as in this case, has been held to be a contempt of the Court of Queen's Bench ; although the witness may have been supœnaed to give evidence in a cause pending and to be tried under a *nisi prius* record of this court; on the contrary, it would seem, that to bring the witness into contempt of this court, the subpœna should issue from the crown office, be personally served, and the original be shewn at the time of such service.

(*a*) 8 T. R. 585.   (*b*) 1 A. & E. 598.   (*c*) 4 B. & Ald. 218.

The constant practice of making rules of *nisi prius*, and judges' orders, rules of this court, in order to enforce them by attachment, also shew it (a).

JONES, J., concurred.

Rule discharged, but not with costs.

EWING ET AL. V. LOCKHART.

An affidavit on which a *ca. sa.* is to be sued out, stating that the plaintiff had good reason to believe that the defendant had made some secret *and* fraudulent conveyance of his property, &c., and not some secret *or* fraudulent conveyance, is good under the statute.

Semble: Under our rule 2 Will. IV., it is not necessary in any case to state, in an affidavit of either the plaintiff or the defendant, the deponent's degree: certainly not where the affidavit is sworn in a foreign country.

Quære: Whether the fact of a defendant having given bail to the limits, would not preclude him from taking a formal objection of this kind.

In this case *R. P. Crooks* moved to set aside the *ca. sa.*, and to discharge the defendant, and to cancel the bailbond given for the limits.

1st. Because the affidavit on which the *ca. sa.* was sued out stated that the plaintiffs had reason to believe that the defendant had parted with his property, or made some secret *and* fraudulent conveyance thereof, in order to prevent its being taken in execution; instead of stating, as the statute requires, that he had made some secret *or* fraudulent conveyance, &c.

2ndly, Because there was no addition or description of degree added to the name of the deponent in that affidavit. (The affidavit ran thus: "Henry "Fowler, of the city of Montreal, in the province of Canada, assignee and "agent of the above plaintiffs, maketh oath and *saith*," &c., and was sworn in Montreal, before a judge of the Queen's Bench there.) The *ca. sa.* issued upon a judge's order, on account of the affidavit being sworn abroad.

ROBINSON, C. J.—With regard to the first objection, it would be unreasonable to hold that when the statute requires the plaintiff to swear that the defendant has made some secret *or* fraudulent conveyance of his property, it would be sufficient if he should swear that the defendant has made some secret *and* fraudulent conveyance; for that includes both, when either is all that is required. If there were any repugnancy in the two, so that they could not co-exist, then it would be different; but a defendant may make a conveyance of his property both secret and fraudulent, and when the plaintiff swears that he has done so, he swears to all that the statute requires, and more.

The second objection ought not, in my opinion, to prevail; the deponent's place of abode is stated; all that is given by way of addition is "*assignee and agent of the above plaintiffs.*" Our rule of court, Trinity Term, 3 & 4 Will. IV., is the same in effect, though not exactly in words, as that of Michaelmas Term, 15 Car. II., in the King's Bench in England. Within a short time of its being made, this court thought proper to modify it, by a rule, Easter Term, 4 Will. IV., declaring that it was not

---

(a) See 8 T. R. 585; 1 A. & E. 598; 3 N. & M. 725; 9 Jurist, 1003; 7 Dowl. 178.

to apply to the case of a defendant in a cause making an affidavit; and one cannot imagine any good reason why a similar exception should not there be made in favour of the plaintiff in a cause. The making that exception shewed that the only objection in contemplation by the court was to identify the deponent; and a reference to the cases cited in the argument shews, that though we might be warranted by some decisions, yet we should not be warranted, as I think, by the general course of the practice in England, either before or since the rule 2 Will. IV. (Hilary Term), in holding the addition here to be insufficient.—2 Dowl. 473; 3 Dowl. 487; 4 Dowl, 26; 3 Scott, N. R. 235; 2 Tyr. 495; 2 Dowl. N. S. 332.

But especially I think we ought not so to hold in respect to an affidavit sworn in a foreign country, where we are not to suppose persons to be cognizant of our rules of practice, which regard, not the substance of the contents of the affidavit, but a mere requisite of a formal kind, certainly not essential for subjecting the deponent to a prosecution for perjury in case of the affidavit being false. In this case, too, the defendant has acted as if he were legally in custody, by giving bail for the limits; and I am not prepared to say that this should not preclude him from taking a mere formal exception of this kind.

MACAULAY, J., and JONES, J., concurred.

Rule discharged.

DOE ON THE DEMISE OF GRAHAM V. NEWTON.

Where a tenant in tail makes a lease for lives, and dies without issue, the lease is absolutely determined by his death, so that no acceptance of rent by him in remainder or reversion can make it good.

The acceptance by the remainderman of a yearly *nominal* rent, is not a confirmation of the lease, especially where the party disclaims to hold as his tenant.

Special case. Ejectment for north half of No. 19, in the third concession of Whitchurch. A verdict was taken in this case for the lessor of the plaintiff, subject to the judgment of the court upon the following facts as they appeared in evidence at the trial.

William Graham, by his will, made the 26th February, 1813, "*bequeathed* "to his son William the half lot in question, with other lands, to have and to "hold, to him and to the heirs of his body lawfully begotten, and then for "want or in default of such issue, unto the testator's heirs at law, males in "the same degree always to take before females."

The testator died in 1813. On the 3rd of November, 1823, the devisee, William Graham, made a lease by indenture to Abijah Newton (husband of this defendant) of the 100 acres in question, to hold to him during the lives of him, the said Newton, stated therein to be 37 years old, and of two of his sons, stated to be respectively 16 and 17 years of age, or of the survivor of them, at the annual rent of two shillings and sixpence, payable on the 1st of January in each year.

William Graham afterwards died without issue, and Adam Graham, another son of the testator, being his right heir, accepted the annual rent from the lessee, and afterwards from the defendant, his widow.

The question for the opinion of the court under these facts was, did the lease executed by William Graham absolutely determine with the wife of the tenant in tail? or did the acceptance of rent by the remainderman confirm the lease and render it effectual? Should the court be of opinion that the defendant became a mere tenant from year to year to the lessor of the plaintiff, by reason of the receipt of rent, it was then admitted the verdict must stand.

Wm. Hume Blake, counsel for the plaintiff.

J. Duggan, counsel for the defendant.

ROBINSON, C. J.—Where tenant in tail makes a lease for years, and dies without issue, the lease is absolutely determined by his death, so that no acceptance of rent by him, in remainder or reversion, can make it good; for the estate out of which it was derived being determined, it must fall with it; and the intent of the statute 32 Hen. VIII. ch. 28, was only to enable the tenant in tail by such leases to bind his issue, which in no case before he could do; and not to bind, or in any way affect those in remainder or reversion, after the estate had determined.—Bac. Abr. Leases, D. page 27-28; Doe Martin v. Wallis, 7 T. R. 82; 1 New Rep. 158.

This is precisely the case before us: The lease in such case being void, and not merely voidable as those leases are which are made conformably to the statute 32 Hen. VIII., it follows that no acceptance of rent could confirm the lease, so as to make it binding on the remainderman for the three lives mentioned in it. The utmost effect which could be thus given to the acceptance of rent would be, to create thereby a tenancy from year to year upon the terms of the lease.

But I am of opinion that the tenant in this case, upon the facts stated, cannot maintain her possession as a tenant from year to year, who has not received a legal notice to quit; because in the first place, the acceptance of a mere nominal rent of two shillings and sixpence for 100 acres of land would not have that effect. In the case of Right v. Bawden, 3 T. R. 267, the receipt of a year's rent of six shillings was relied upon under similar circumstances. Mr. Dampier, who was counsel for the plaintiff, resisted the defence on that ground. "It "may be argued," he said, "that the receipt of six shillings rent from the "husband of the defendant made him at least tenant from year to year, and "entitled him and those claiming under him to six months' notice to quit, "was holden in the case of one who became originally tenant under a void "lease. But that lease was at a rack rent; and the doctrine has never been "extended to the case of a mere conventionary rent; for the receipt of such a "rent as six shillings cannot furnish any evidence of a tacit agreement between "the lord and tenant, that the latter shall hold premises worth fifty pounds a "year as tenant from year to year. The principle on which courts have inferred "such a tenancy is, that the rent is a compensation for the land, and that both "parties have acted upon that understanding. But here the circumstances of "the case furnish decisive evidence against such a conclusion. It is clear that "neither the lord nor tenant conceived the holding to be on a tenancy from "year to year. The tenant did not hold it upon the footing of receiving notice "to quit, but upon a claim which such notice could not defeat."

This was but the argument of counsel, but I consider it to have been affirmed by the decision of the case, and to have received the sanction of the court also in a later case, of Doe dem. Brune v. Prideaux, 10 E. R. 188. We are to put ourselves in the place of a jury as to all inferences to be drawn from the evidence; and in the case to which I have last referred, Lord Ellenborough held, that a jury would probably in such a case receive a very strong direction to decide against a tenancy where the rent accepted bore no proportion to the annual value of the estate. But it is not really necessary that we should determine whether this acceptance of the nominal rent of two shillings and sixpence for several years, can have the effect of creating a tenancy from year to year; because if it could, the only effect would be to render a six months' notice necessary, unless there has been something which dispenses with it. In this case a sufficient notice seems not to have been given. But it is not necessary that any should have been; for the tenant held the estate, or attempted to hold it, "upon a claim which such a notice could not defeat," as the point was stated in Right v. Bawden. When possession was demanded of the defendant, she constantly refused to give up possession, claiming a right to hold under the lease for the three lives, and denying the plaintiff's right to turn her out as a tenant from year to year. She claimed to hold an estate not created by him or determinable by him, or over which he could have any control. In other words, she set up her right against his; not till she should receive notice merely as a yearly tenant, but upon a footing that denied his right to give such notice, and which would have made the giving of it a nugatory act. She disclaimed being a yearly tenant. This evidence was given in the cause before me at *nisi prius*, and is to be taken in connection with the written admissions made at the same time.

It is clear, on the whole case, that William Graham being a tenant in tail, in effect assumed to sell the estate for three lives; he reserved no real rent to himself or those in remainder as a continuing compensation for the enjoyment of the property; and the effect, while it was submitted to, was to deprive the remainderman of all benefit from the estate. When therefore this remainderman accepted the two shillings and sixpence a year, he can only be looked upon as submitting, in ignorance of his right, to a disposition of the estate which he imagined was beyond his control; he could not have conceived that he was *creating* a tenancy; and it would be a perversion of reason to hold that he was accepting two shillings and sixpence a year as a rent taken by himself in compensation for a year's enjoyment of 100 acres of land, acknowledged by him to be held solely by his permission.

I am of opinion that the lessor of the plaintiff is entitled to a verdict.

MACAULAY, J.—Although it seems to be understood that a lease for lives by a tenant in tail is not void, but voidable only, by the issue in tail, and therefore susceptible of confirmation by such tenant in tail; and that acceptance of rent after the death of the lessor by such issue, will constitute or be evidence of an implied confirmation thereof; yet it seems to be assumed that, as against the remainderman or reversioner, such a lease is *void* at the death of the lessor, and not confirmed by the subsequent receipt of rent (a). Here the person to whom the estate was by the will limited, in default of issue of the tenant in tail, being the testator's right heir, I apprehend the lessor of the

---

(a) Stat. 32 Hen. VIII. ch. 21, s. 1; Willes, 176, (n); 5 Bing. 469; 3 M. & P. 59; 1 N. R. 158; 1 B. & P. 531; Cow. 482.

plaintiff takes as reversioner, and not as remainderman, which (if anything) strengthens his right to treat the lease as void.—Dyer 156, a, place 4.

Then as to a yearly tenancy, and notice to quit; payment of rent is *prima facie* evidence of a subsisting term corresponding with the periods of such payments; but where it is paid by a tenant who has entered under a lease which had ended or had become void by matter *ex post facto*, as in this case, it has relation to the old contract (a). Consequently the notice to quit in this case would be insufficient, as not ending in the *year*, and the demise being laid within six months.

But it would not seem that acceptance of a nominal rent of 2s. 6d. a year, though evidence, is sufficient evidence of a demise from year to year; the rent being a compensation for the land, and the presumption only arising where the compensation is proportional to the value. It cannot, therefore, be considered that the plaintiff received the rent otherwise than as under the lease of the tenant in tail, and which, being void at his death, was not confirmed by such acceptance; nor was a yearly tenancy created. As a mere tenant at will, the notice was sufficient.—See the case in 1 Dougl. 53, where Lord Mansfield said that it did not appear to have been any intention either to confirm the old lease, or to grant a new one. That both the lessor of the plaintiff, and the defendant, had proceeded under a mistake, and had supposed the original lease good. See also 3 East. 267-8, Right v. Bawden, where it said that the rent of six shillings was not received as between landlord and tenant, but was attributable to another consideration. Also 10 East. 158, 187-8; Roe ex dem. of Brune v. Prideaux et al.

The defendant claiming to hold as tenant for lives, independent of the plaintiff, except as entitled to the rent, as following the reversion, supports this construction.

JONES, J., concurred.

Per Cur.—Verdict to be entered for the lessor of the plaintiff.

HENDERSON V. PERRY ET AL.

A *ca. sa.* commanding a sheriff to detain the defendant in custody until he should satisfy the plaintiff, without stating the amount of the debt recovered, is void.

D. B. Read moved to rescind an order of Mr. Justice Macaulay in chambers, directing that Simeon W. Perry, one of the defendants, should be discharged from custody on the writ of *ca. re.* in this cause with costs, on the ground of the said writ being irregular and void; and that the said defendant should be remanded to custody on the *ca. re.*

1. Because the affidavit on which the judge's order was obtained should not have been received, being an affidavit of Simeon W. Perry, sworn before his attorney employed in making the application, and at the same time agent for the plaintiff's attorney.

2. Because the order was made on insufficient grounds.

3. Because the judge should have allowed the writ to be amended, instead of discharging the defendant.

(a) 7 T. R. 83; *Ib.* 178; 1 H. B. 97; 1 T. R. 161; Dougl. 51; 2 Taunt. 109.

4. That the order should be amended, inserting a condition that the plaintiff should bring no action.

5. That the writ should now be amended, and made conformable to the judgment.

In this case judgment had been recovered in assumpsit; and a *fi. fa.* issued for £52 10s. 8d.; and afterwards a *ca. sa.* issued, which, by mistake, stated no sum to be made, but directed the sheriff to take the defendants "to satisfy "Lawrence H. Henderson, which in our court before us, at Toronto, were "awarded to the said plaintiff for damages, &c.," referring as usual to the judgment. The writ was endorsed to levy £32 8s. 3d., with interest; and Simeon W. Perry was arrested upon it.

The plaintiff's attorney resides at Belleville, and sent the *ca. sa.* to A., living at Kingston, requesting him to deliver it to the sheriff, which A. did on the 23rd June, 1846. Simeon W. Perry was arrested upon it, and employed A. to procure his discharge, and the affidavit for that purpose was drawn by A.'s clerk and sworn before A.

On shewing cause against the summons, the plaintiff's attorney prayed to be allowed to amend the *ca. sa.*, but the learned judge considered that it was a void writ, and not amendable so as to admit of the party being legally detained under it; he also considered that in such a case he could not properly restrain the bringing an action; and he made an order discharging the defendant, with costs. This order was made on the 21st of July, 1846, and was now appealed from (a).

(a) In making this order in chambers, the learned judge (Macaulay) delivered the following judgment:

If it appears that A., the commissioner, was acting as the defendant's attorney in this matter when he took the affidavit (*e. g.*, if he drew up the affidavit as such), it cannot be read. If it does not so appear, then I find no authority for making such an amendment as this, which would be to make a writ, void on the face of it, good and valid. In all the cases in the books, it will be found that the writs of execution amended were *prima facie* good on the face of them. It is not so here. The writ is void, and the defendant entitled to his discharge, on *habeas corpus*.

On looking at the above cases, it does not appear to be stated with sufficient precision that A., the commissioner, who took the defendant's (S. W. P.'s) affidavit, is A., the attorney, who makes this application, and is one and the same person; nor does the fact of the latter being the defendant's attorney in making such application otherwise appear, than by his own admission after it was made. As to the district officer issuing a *ca. sa.* after a *fi. fa.*, the 2 Geo. IV. ch. 1, enacts that a *ca. sa.*, after final judgment, may issue from a district office, in the same manner as may be done in the principal office; and 8 Vic. ch. 36, sec. 1, repeats this in effect as to all writs of execution, except against lands; section 3 is very general as to the issue of an *original* or *testatum ca. sa.*, although section 6 requires all *alias* or *subsequent* writs, and writs against lands, to be from the home office; a good reason is, that the *original writs* are always made *returnable* at *Toronto*. The reason does not apply to several *original writs*, or to an original *testatum ca. sa.* If it depended on this objection, I should refer the defendant to the court in term; because, taking 2 Geo. IV. ch. 1, secs. 32 and 33, and 8 Vic. ch. 36, together, there is much in favour of the regularity of the proceeding, the 7 Will. IV. ch. 3, having dispensed with any *testatum clause*, and authorizing an original writ of execution ostensibly to be issued into any district other than that in which the venue is laid. But on the main ground, I think the order to discharge the defendant must be made absolute, with costs. As to the writ itself, I look upon it as *void*, and say nothing about it, unless parties wish it set aside. It is said I cannot set it aside; if not, it may remain as it is, and the plaintiff can, if so advised, move

J. H. Hagarty shewed cause.

ROBINSON, C. J.—I am of opinion that we ought not to rescind the order made in chambers.

The objection to the writ is entirely such as was determined in the case of Billings v. Harvey, in this court, to make the writ not voidable merely, but void. If the *ca. sa.* had been for a sum varying from the judgment, the writ would nevertheless have been good upon the face of it, and would have supported the arrest made under it, unless it had been set aside for the irregularity, which would not appear until it had been compared with the judgment; but this was a writ manifestly illegal, for it commanded the sheriff to detain the defendant in custody until he should satisfy the plaintiff, without stating any sum. In Kenworthy v. Peppiott (*a*), the court, being applied to for amendment of a writ which had been made returnable on a *dies non*, refused the amendment, saying that the writ was altogether void, and was distinguishable from the cases of amendment of the party's name; as a writ it was good, though not applicable to the particular case.

It is not, however, easy to satisfy oneself that the distinction between void and voidable process has been always consistently maintained in granting or refusing amendments. For my own part, I look upon the allowing an amendment, with a view to cure mistakes which have been committed, as a matter of discretion with the court or judge, even where there may be no doubt of the power to grant the indulgence, and where an error of so glaring a nature as this had been committed, it can never be pronounced wrong to leave the party to the consequences of it. I see no instance of a judge's order being reviewed on the ground that he should have allowed the irregularity to be cured by ordering an amendment. I think I should probably not have allowed an amendment in such a case, even if the power were unquestionable; certainly I should not if the defendant had agreed to bring no action, for the party complaining of so gross an irregularity may well be allowed to prevail.

As to the preliminary objection that the affidavit on which the defendant moved should not have been received, because it was sworn before the defendant's attorney, I think, under the circumstances appearing in the affidavits, the plaintiff's attorney had reason to complain of A.'s assisting the defendant to take advantage of the error. It would have been much better that he had not done so, but referred the defendant to some other attorney; for he subjected himself to the suspicion, which the plaintiff's attorney may naturally entertain, of having himself detected and exposed the error, and suggested its being taken advantage of, when he had acquired the knowledge of the fact in consequence of being employed for the plaintiff to forward the execution of the process. As to the objection founded on the rule of practice (15 Geo. II.), that the attorney of

---

to amend it next term; but in the meantime, the defendant, S. W. Perry, must, I think, be discharged.

I have no objection to grant leave to move, so far as I may without prejudice to such application, by reason of the defendant's bringing an action for false imprisonment in the meantime; for if *amended*, it would, by relation, be good *ab initio*, and afford a good justification for the arrest.—See 1 A. & E. N. S. 914, 319; 3 Dowl. P. C. 464.

(*a*) 4 B. & Ald. 298.

the party could not as a commissioner take the affidavit, it would seem, according to several decisions, to have been considered as coming within the spirit of the rule when the commissioner is the attorney of the party for the mere purpose of the application, though he is not his attorney of record; but the courts are strict in requiring that it shall appear in support of such an objection that he was his attorney at the time of swearing the affidavit, and not only at the time of making the application. That was not distinctly sworn in this case; on which account the objection was not entitled to prevail. It was to little purpose, indeed, to make such an objection, because in favour of a defendant in custody on a void writ; the court would have allowed the party to move again on an affidavit free from such exception.

As to the learned judge not having exacted an undertaking to bring no action, he might, as it seems to me, even in such a case, have granted the order, with costs, on that condition only (a); but that was quite a matter of discretion.

JONES, J., concurred. *Per Cur.*—Rule discharged.

THE QUEEN V. JAGGER AND GARRISON.

Where goods subject to a duty ad valorem, have been entered at a port in this province upon the importer's own declaration of value, which the collector has accepted and acted upon, the same goods cannot be afterwards seized by the collector of another port on the ground of their having been undervalued upon their entry with the first collector.

In this case the *Attorney-General*, on the part of the crown, and the defendants, went to trial upon certain admitted facts.

The information charged the defendants with importing cotton "from the "United States of America into this province, and landing the same by virtue "of an entry and warrant not corresponding with the characters and circum- "stances according to which such cottons were charged and could be imported, "contrary to the form of the statute."

The defendant pleaded not guilty; and the point raised was, whether when an importer of goods subject to a duty ad valorem, has entered them at a port in this province upon his own declaration of value, which the collector has accepted and acted upon, the same goods can be afterwards seized by the collector of another port, on the ground of their having been undervalued upon their entry with the first collector.

The defendants, by their counsel *P. Vankoughnet*, contended at the trial, that whether the goods had or had not been declared to be of less value than they really were when they were entered with the collector of Cobourg, and the duties paid to him, yet that they could not for that cause be seized as liable to forfeiture, by the collector of another port to which they were removed, after they had been once entered and duties paid to the satisfaction of the other collector.

They contended also, that in point of fact the goods had not been undervalued.

(a) 4 B. & Ald. 298.

The object of the trial was, to take the verdict of a jury upon that fact; in order that if they found it against the defendants, the case might be afterwards argued in *banc*, upon the other point.

The jury found a verdict for the defendants.

F. Carruthers, on the part of the crown, now moved to set aside the verdict, as being contrary to evidence.

P. Vankoughnet shewed cause.

ROBINSON, C. J.—The evidence was strong to shew, that the cotton which the defendants had entered with the collector at Cobourg, as being worth six cents per yard, was in fact worth eight; and there was evidence also to shew, that the defendants, intending to dispose of their cotton at Toronto, had artfully entered them first with the collector at Cobourg, because they found or supposed that he was less vigilant, or less informed upon the subject, than the collector of Toronto, and would therefore be more easily satisfied with their declaration of value.

When I gave the case to the jury, I remarked upon the objection which the defendants had raised to the seizure in point of law, even admitting that the collector at Cobourg had allowed them to be entered and the duties paid at an undervalue; and I stated my impression to be, that the seizure would be found not to have been properly made, for that the owner of the goods having used no false invoices (they had not bought the goods, as it appeared, but were themselves the manufacturers of them in a foreign country,) and having openly entered them and submitted them to the inspection and judgment of the proper officer, who had contented himself with their declaration of value, had received the duties and allowed them to pass, it did not seem reasonable, that any or every collector might in like manner exercise his judgment upon them, after the entry and payment of duties, and at any distance of time. But I intimated to the jury that this was the point intended to be discussed hereafter, and that all that they were to determine was, whether the goods had been in fact undervalued or not, and I repeated the evidence to them on that point.

The jury retired, and after some time, brought in a verdict for the defendants; not giving any particular opinion upon the value of the goods. It was evidently their intention to find them not guilty of the charge—perhaps upon their view of the law as well as of the fact.

Under these circumstances, I am of opinion that we could not at any rate set aside their verdict, consistently with the general practice of the court, when a verdict has been given upon the merits for the defendant, in an action for a penalty, and where there has been no misdirection. The jury seem, contrary to the recommendation given to them, to have determined upon their view of the whole case, as undoubtedly they had a right to do, and would not conform themselves to a mere expression of opinion on one part of it—that is on the value of the cotton.

If I erred in the opinion which I formed and expressed as to the legality of the seizure, upon the general facts of the case, yet I was particular in giving the jury to understand that it was desired, and would be more advisable, that this should be left for decision hereafter, and that they should consider only the one question, whether the defendants had knowingly entered the goods falsely at less than their true value. I do not think that they could have believed that the defendants had declared the true value of the goods, or that they could have had much doubt that they were acting unfairly; but we are not authorized to assume, in face of their verdict, that they were satisfied with their guilt.

Upon the ground that, independently of the legal question, the verdict of the jury should now be set aside under such circumstances, my brothers are of opinion that we ought not to grant a new trial, and I concur in that opinion. The case of Gregory v. Tuffs (a) is perhaps as strong a case as could be cited in favour of granting a new trial, if we could say that the circumstances were similar. There the jury took the Act of Parliament into their own hands, and construed it for themselves, misapplying its provisions, or rather, refusing to apply them in what the court thought a perfectly clear case. In this case the court submitted a certain fact, and that only, to the jury, and they found for the defendants a general verdict; not, as I think, against law or fact, and not under any misdirection; for they were requested to assume the point of law for the time to be against the defendants, and to confine themselves to the facts alone. Whether they did so or not, we cannot certainly say; though whether we should set aside their verdict, if we saw clearly that they had taken upon themselves to decide the law, and had decided it wrong, would be another question.

For my own part I will add, that I see nothing in any of the statutory provisions to which we were referred, which subjects the party to have his goods seized in any part of the province, by any collector, upon a suspicion of their having been undervalued, where they have been openly entered at the first port to which they were brought from a foreign country, and submitted to the judgment and claim of the proper officer there, without imposing upon him by any false invoice.

The collector at Cobourg must be supposed competent to the discharge of his duty; if he was satisfied with the value which the importer named, and inquired no further, he waived any of those methods of proceeding which the law allowed, and accepted the entry on behalf of the crown. And when the crown has once exercised its judgment through its proper officer, and allowed the goods to be landed, the law is satisfied. If false documents had been used to deceive the collector, the case might be otherwise. The goods were, in truth, not imported into Toronto from the United States, as the information states; they had been imported into Cobourg from the United States, and were afterwards, in the same condition, to be removed from place to place in the province, as other goods are.

Of course, if it be true, as was suspected, and I think upon good ground, that these defendants were profiting by the want of knowledge or want of vigilance of the collector at Cobourg, and that circumstance become known to the collector of Toronto, he would be doing quite right in putting the other collector on his guard, and if he found him still remiss, it might be necessary to report the fact to their superiors, otherwise the business of the fair trader might be destroyed; and there could be no doubt that the collector of this port acted to the best of his judgment, and from a correct motive, in making the seizure as he did; but I think it was not the proper course; for upon the same principle an importer of goods might be questioned by every collector of

---

(a) 2 Dowl. 713.

every district through which he passed, and the judgment of each upon the value of his goods exercised in succession, and sometimes under circumstances which might make it extremely difficult for him to prove the real value. That would not be reasonable as a general rule, whatever might be proper in a particular case, where some palpable fraud has been practised.

MACAULAY, J.—I have not been able to find the statute referred to; but it seems to me it was for the jury to decide as to the price per yard, and they decided in favour of the claimant; and new trials, under such circumstances, are not granted. But, independently of this consideration, the other allegations contained in the information do not seem to have been proved.

JONES, J., concurred.

Per Cur.—Rule discharged.

HURLBURT V. THOMAS.

While an agreement is open between the parties, and the time for performance has not arrived, a new agreement may be substituted for it, postponing the period for performance ; and the original consideration will be regarded as being imported into such new agreement, and will be sufficient to support it.

The plaintiff declared specially in assumpsit, stating : That whereas heretofore, to wit, on the 16th day of May, in the year of our Lord 1843, in consideration that the plaintiff, at the special instance and request of the defendant, had then agreed with the defendant to take and receive two daughters of the defendant to board, and to give them tuition for eight or nine terms of eleven weeks each, the tuition to be in music, needle-work, and common English branches, the said board and tuition to commence on the 25th day of May, in the year of our Lord 1843; he the defendant then undertook, and faithfully promised the plaintiff, that he the defendant would furnish the plaintiff with a pianoforte worth £85 or £100, and as good as any piano of his the defendant's make at the above mentioned prices, and did then also agree to deliver the said pianoforte to the plaintiff within fifteen months from the time of the making of the said agreement, as aforesaid; and the defendant and the plaintiff did then further agree, that the wife of the plaintiff should decide which priced pianoforte the said plaintiff was to have and receive, as aforesaid. And the plaintiff further saith, that he, confiding in the promise of the said defendant, as aforesaid, did afterwards, to wit, on the said 25th day of May, in the year of our Lord 1843, take and receive the said two daughters of the said defendant, to board and to give them tuition, as aforesaid; and the plaintiff further saith, that they remained with him the plaintiff for a long time, to wit, from the said 25th day of May, in the year aforesaid, until the 1st day of September, in the year of our Lord 1844; and the plaintiff further saith, that the said two daughters of the defendant did, during all that time, receive good and sufficient board and lodging, and also tuition in music, needle-work, and common English, and the said plaintiff was then, and continuously from thence, until the commencement of this suit, willing to keep the said two daughters of the said defendant, and to give them the board and tuition, as aforesaid, for the full term of nine terms of eleven weeks each ; of all which the defendant afterwards, to wit, on the 1st day of September, in the year of our Lord 1844, had notice ; but the defendant, before the expiration of the said nine terms, to wit, on the 1st day of September, in the year last aforesaid, without any cause, and without the consent of the plaintiff, and against the will of the plaintiff, took and withdrew his said two daughters from the school of him the said plaintiff, and hath ever since refused to allow them to return ; and the said plaintiff further saith, that the wife of the said plaintiff decided that she would have the piano priced at £100, of which the defendant afterwards, and before the expiration of the said fifteen months, within which the same was to be delivered as aforesaid, to wit, on the 1st day of September, in the year of our Lord 1844, had notice ; and he the plaintiff has always been willing to receive from the defendant a piano priced at £100, for the board and tuition of the said two daughters of the defendant for nine terms of eleven weeks each, of which the defendant afterwards, to wit, on the day and year last aforesaid, had notice ; and the plaintiff afterwards, and after the expiration of the said fifteen months, to wit, on the 1st day of August, requested the defendant to deliver to the plaintiff the said piano priced at £100, so agreed to have been delivered as aforesaid ; yet the defendant, not regarding his said promise and undertaking, but contriving and intending to defraud and injure the plaintiff in this behalf, did not nor would furnish and deliver to and for the plaintiff the said pianoforte priced at £100, and as good as any piano of his the said defendant's make at that price, at any time within the fifteen months from the making the said agreement in this count mentioned (which time had elapsed before the commencement of this suit), nor hath he since furnished and delivered to and for the plaintiff a pianoforte valued at £100, and as good as any pianoforte of his make at that price, but hath hitherto wholly neglected and refused so to do.

To this special count the defendant pleaded fourthly, That after the making of the undertaking and promise of the defendant in the said first count mentioned, and after the plaintiff had received the daughters of the defendant to board and to give them tuition as in the said first count mentioned, and had given them board and lodging, and tuition in music and needle-work, for a part, to wit, five terms of the said eight or nine terms of eleven weeks each, in the said first count mentioned, and before any breach in the said undertaking or promise of the defendant in the said first count mentioned, to wit, on the said 21st day of June, in the year of our Lord 1844, it was, at the request of the plaintiff, agreed by and between the plaintiff and the defendant, that the plaintiff should take and receive the two daughters of the defendant to board and to give them tuition for the said eight or nine terms of eleven weeks each, as in the said first count mentioned, and for part, to wit, five terms of the said eight or nine terms, the said daughters of the said defendant had received board and lodging and tuition as hereinbefore in this plea stated, the said tuition to be in music, needlework and common English branches, as in the said first count mentioned ; and that the defendant should furnish the plaintiff with a pianoforte worth £85 or £100, and as good as any piano of his the defendant's make at the last above mentioned prices, and that the defendant should deliver the said pianoforte to the plaintiff in the spring of the year of our Lord 1845 (which period was distant more than fifteen months from the time of the making of the said undertaking and promise of the defendant in the said first count mentioned), and that the wife of the said plaintiff should decide which priced pianoforte the said plaintiff was to have; which said agreement of the defendant in this plea mentioned, he the plaintiff, before any breach of the undertaking or promise of the defendant in the said first count mentioned, accepted in full discharge of that undertaking and promise, and thereby then wholly released and discharged the defendant from the further performance of that undertaking and promise; and this the defendant is ready to verify, &c.

To this fourth plea the plaintiff demurred, on the following grounds:

1st. That the plea only argumentatively, and without sufficient certainty, alleged the new agreement to have been before breach; also that the plea was too large, in saying before *any* breach, without saying before *the* breach complained of.

2nd. That the plea did not confess and avoid or traverse the plaintiff's breach in direct terms.

3rd. That the plea was inconsistent, &c., in saying it was agreed the plaintiff should receive and board the defendant's daughters for eight or nine terms, of which five had elapsed and been performed; that it did not deny the board and tuition as alleged, but implied that the defendant, having taken them away wrongfully, the plaintiff was willing to receive them back again.

4th. That there was no averment of performance, or offer, or readiness to perform the second agreement, though the time had elapsed; nor any excuse therefor.

5th. That the plea did not go to the whole consideration stated in the declararation; nor stated any new consideration.

6th. That an agreement to deliver goods exceeding £10 in value was not shewn to be in writing.

7th. That the alleged discharge from further performance, imported a part performance, and yet not shewn or explained.

8th. That the plea was double.

9th. That the defendant did not confess or avoid or traverse the plaintiff's allegation, that the defendant wrongfully withdrew his two daughters.

10th. That the plea set up an agreement in answer to an agreement required to be in *writing*, and admitted to be a valid one, without shewing the last agreement to be in writing also.

The defendant then objected to the *declaration* as bad on general demurrer, on the following grounds:

1st. That the averment that the plaintiff's wife decided that *she* would have the pianoforte at £100, was not a proper election according to the agreement which required the plaintiff's wife to decide which priced piano *the plaintiff* was to have.

2nd. That the award by the plaintiff's wife was absolutely void, she being incompetent on account of her marriage.

3rd. That her decision, if of any avail, was not, and is not according to the agreement, for she has decided she would have *the* pianoforte priced at £100, while the agreement was not to deliver *a* particular piano of any price, but *any pianoforte* at the price she decided the plaintiff should have.

4th. That her award ought to have shewn that she decided the plaintiff should have a piano priced at £100, and as good as any of the defendant's make at that price.

5th. That the averment of plaintiff's willingness to receive a pianoforte priced at £100, was defectively set out, without the addition of the other material part of the agreement, "and as good as any of the defendant's make "at that price."

6th. That in such averment it was not shewn the defendant had notice of plaintiff's willingness to receive a piano before the expiration of fifteen months, or even before the commencement of this suit.

7th. That it was not in such averment shewn the plaintiff elected to have a piano priced at £100, or that he adopted his wife's award in that respect, but only that he was willing to have received a piano at that price, while it may have been he had elected and ought to have taken a piano priced at £85.

8th. That in such averment the plaintiff stated that he was willing to have received a piano priced at £100, for *nine terms* of eleven weeks each, while he had before alleged that the defendant had taken his daughters from the plaintiff's school *before* the expiration of the nine terms, and that the defendant had, since his so taking them away, refused to let them return to the plaintiff's school; and as the defendant's two daughters were to receive from the plaintiff board and tuition for eight *or* nine terms, and not for nine terms absolutely, it may have been that the defendant, rightly before the expiration of the nine terms, *but after* the expiration of the *eight terms*, took his daughters away.

And if the defendant had submitted to the plaintiff's claim, of being willing to have received a piano priced at £100, for *nine* terms, while his daughters had only received the benefit of the eight terms, and all they were entitled to, the defendant might have prejudiced his right by acquiescing in the plaintiff's claim so advanced.

9th. That the plaintiff's averment of request on the defendant, to deliver the said piano priced at £100, &c., was defectively stated; because the request was, to deliver the *said* piano priced at £100, while the defendant was only to have delivered *a* piano, and not any one in particular; because the request is not shewn to have been before the commencement of this suit; and because the request ought to have been to deliver only such a piano priced at £100, "as good as any of the defendant's make at that price."

10th. That the breach was inconsistent with the award of the plaintiff's wife stated in the declaration; and with the subsequent averments in the same declaration; because the breach states that the defendant would not deliver the said piano priced at £100, " and as good as any of the defendant's make at "that price," while the award of the plaintiff's wife, and the following averments, were silent as to *such a piano* having been awarded upon to be received by the plaintiff, or that the plaintiff was willing to have received such a piano, or that he requested such a piano.

D. B. Read, counsel for the demurrer.

A. Wilson, contra.

ROBINSON, C. J.—The pleadings on both sides are such as to give rise to several perplexing questions; but I do not see that any of the exceptions raised to the declaration are such as ought to prevail on general demurrer.

The breach complained of, I take to be solely the non-delivery of a pianoforte at the end of fifteen months from the making of the agreement. The taking away the defendant's daughters is only alleged as an excuse for the plaintiff not averring that they had been taught for the whole period agreed upon.

The agreement, as set out in the declaration, is such as by the Statute of Frauds should be in writing, not being to be performed within a year; but it is not contended that it was necessary on that account that the declaration should have stated the contract to have been in writing.

The plea is very inartificially framed, and inaccurate in its language, but I see no ground on which we can hold it to be bad.

It is objected that it amounts to a defence of a mere gratuitous promise by the plaintiff to forbear or give further time, which is *nudum pactum*, and not binding. No doubt, when a debt has become due, a mere promise by the creditor to give further time is not binding. In De Symons v. Minchwick, 1 Esp. 430, where such a defence was set up in evidence, Eyre, C. J., said, "If the "credit given was voluntary, subsequent to and not making any part of the "original contract, it certainly might at any time be retracted."

But this is said in regard to the forbearance of a debt or duty already due or incurred, and is not to be applied to the case of an agreement being substituted for another before the time for forbearance of the original contract has arrived. Mr. Starkie, in his Treatise on Evidence, states (a), "that the defendant may "show that the promise has been discharged by the plaintiff before breach, or "by a subsequent contract inconsistent with the former; as if A. promise to "marry B. within three weeks, and it is afterwards agreed that he shall marry "her in half a year, this will discharge the former promise; for, by taking the "latter promise of a longer time, the parties must be supposed to intend to "discharge the former; for otherwise the latter could have no intent at all;" and for this he cites the authority of Chief Baron Gilbert, and of Trials per Pais, 402 (b).

The effect of the defence set up here is, that although the defendant did at first agree to deliver such a piano as the plaintiff's wife might prefer, in fifteen months from the 16th of May, 1843, yet that afterwards and before that time arrived, viz., in June, 1844, it was agreed between them that the piano should not be delivered till *the spring of* 1845; this may not have been a mere act of forbearance on the plaintiff's part, the time may have been altered to suit his convenience, as well as that of the other party; he may for various reasons have preferred not receiving the piano till the time last agreed upon.

No new consideration seems necessary to support the second agreement in such a case. The courts say the original consideration continues and is imported into the new agreement, which is merely substituted for the other (c), and certainly it is good sense so to regard it.

Then as to the Statute of Frauds, it is contended by the plaintiff, that where an agreement would only be valid if in writing, such agreement when averred

---

(a) Vol. 2, page 103.
(b) See also Buller N. P. 152; 2 Sco. 144, 1 Mod. 262.
(c) 10 A. & E. 57.

in a plea must be stated to be in writing, and that is certainly the rule. This new agreement is not averred to have been in writing. Then was it necessary to be in writing under the statue? If it stood alone and considered only in itself, it need not be in writing on account of the time it covers, for it is alleged to have been made in June, 1844, to be performed in the spring of 1845, and so not to extend beyond a year; but it is an alleged alteration of an original agreement, which, as stated in the declaration and admitted by the plea, was not to have been performed within the year, but might cover eighty-eight or ninety-nine weeks. It is stated in some books, that any alteration of an agreement which requires to be in writing, must also be in writing; and applying the principle to this case, are we to assume that the first agreement was in writing (*a*), though it is not stated by the plaintiff to have been so? But it seems to me not material to consider that point, because the first agreement was abandoned, and a second substituted for it, which was all to be performed within a year, and the case seems in this respect to come within the decision in Taylor v. Rilay (*b*). The principle that a written agreement cannot be varied by a parol contract, seems not to create difficulty here, because the first agreement is not stated to have been in writing; it may not have been, though both parties have agreed to treat it as valid.

As to that part of the statute which requires agreements for goods of more than £10 value to be in writing, I think we cannot hold this contract to come within that section; the piano was not *in esse*, as it appears; the defendant was to furnish one of his best make, which might be made up at any time within the period, so that it resembles those cases which have been treated rather as contracts for work and labour and materials to be found. The statute 9 Geo. IV. which has been passed in England regarding contracts of this nature, subjecting them to the statute, is a strong argument that the conviction before was that the statute did not apply in such cases. We are left to the effect of the Statute of Frauds without the aid of the latter statute.

MACAULAY, J.—The case of Cuff v. Penn (*c*), and what is said founded thereon; Whitcher v. Hall (*d*), and also Warren v. Stagg, cited in Littler v. Holland (*e*), and Thresh v. Rake (*f*), so far as they hold that an undertaking to extend the *time* for performance of an executory contract in writing, though by oral promise, is an extension merely, a continuance of the original bargain, or the same contract; the mere substitution of another day, and not a new agreement, must be considered as overruled by Goss v. Lord Nugent (*g*), Stowell v. Robinson (*h*), Stead v. Dawber (*i*), Marshall v. Lynn (*j*); which seem to decide that whether for one day, or a month, or more, it is in legal effect a new agreement. When the contract remains executory partly or in toto on both sides, although there be no *new* consideration, the old consideration is imported, as it is expressed by Lord Denman in Stead v. Dawber, into the new agreement; I am obliged to relinquish, therefore, the impression I

(*a*) Goss v. Lord Nugent, 5 B. & Ad. 58; 1 T. Rayd. 450; Stephens' Pl. 5th Ed., 412, 40.
(*b*) 3 Dougl. 462.   (*e*) 3 T. R. 591.   (*h*) 3 Bing. N. S. 928.
(*c*) 1 M. & S. 21.   (*f*) 1 Esp. 53.   (*i*) 10 A. & E. 63; 2 P. & D. 447.
(*d*) 5 B. & C. 275.   (*g*) 5 B. & Ad. 67.   (*j*) 6 M. & W. 109.

previously entertained, that the substituted agreement, as pleaded in this case, shews but a continuation of the original agreement, with a postponement of the time for its execution on the defendant's part.

The original agreement is not in the declaration alleged to be in writing, and if oral it might be abandoned or varied while executory in like manner (a). And I look upon the agreement pleaded as oral, superseding the old one, and substituting a new agreement varying only in the time of performance on the defendant's part. If, therefore, that plea is good in substance and form, the matter of it seems sufficient in law. But it is objected, that it should be shewn to be in writing; 1st, as varying an agreement that must be presumed to be in writing; 2nd, because in itself required to be in writing, &c., being set out in a *plea*, it should be so stated.

The first ground I do not think a good one, because the *declaration* does not aver the first agreement to be in writing (b). As to the second, the plea does not import a contract for the sale of goods exceeding the value of £10, and it appears to me to fall within that class of cases where the thing contracted for is not *in esse* but to be made. The agreement, as pleaded, is not that the defendant should *make* a piano for the plaintiff or deliver him one of his make, but that he should *furnish* the plaintiff with one worth £85 or £100, and as good as any of his make at such prices, and should *deliver* the same to the plaintiff in the spring of 1845; now if the defendant had pianos of his own make ready made, or afterwards made one, or had or afterwards procured one made by another, as good as any of his own make, at the prices specified, and delivered any such instrument to the plaintiff, it could not be said not to be a performance of his agreement. It is probable that one of his own make was intended, but still he may have had dozens on hand, out of which he might have selected one for the plaintiff, upon being apprized of his election as to price.

It appears to me to be a contract for a piano to be delivered at a future day, but whether made or to be made is uncertain; neither is it clear that the new contract on the plaintiff's part was to be performed within a year. The terms of tuition were to be eleven weeks each, but vacations or holidays might intervene. However, it does not appear that *the* agreement was *not* to be performed within a year, and therefore it is not clearly within that section of the Statute of Frauds.

It appears therefore to me, that the plea must be upheld as good. The case of Stead v. Dawber (c) and others, serve to establish that where an oral agreement continues partly executory on both sides, a postponement of the time of performance, as in this case, is in effect departing from or altering the old one, and making a new agreement; clearly so on the defendant's part, for a more remote day is substituted, and also on the plaintiff's part, for the original consideration, part of which remaining executory, was imported into the new contract.

I still think there is great force in Cuff v. Penn, &c., as shewing that at least where both are oral, an extension of the time only is merely a continu-

---

(a) 2 Bing. N. S. 359.
(b) Whittaker et. al. v. Mason, 2 Bing. N. S. 359.
(c) 10 A. & E. 63.

ance of the former agreement, there being no other new consideration on either side. Where there is a reciprocity of advantage in the delay, payment or performance being deferred on both sides, or where there is a mutual agreement to cancel or rescind an executory contract, I can perceive a consideration operating mutually. The difficulty here is, that no perceptible consideration exists for the plaintiff's consenting to the new arrangement; but it is alleged to have been at his request, and that he accepted it in discharge of the defendant's former promise. This is admitted by the demurrer, and according to the recent cases it seems a valid cancellation of the first agreement by the substitution of another, though differing only in the *time* for performance on the defendant's part.

JONES, J., concurred.

Per Cur.—Judgment for the defendant, and against the demurrer.

WHEELER V. SIME & BAIN.

The plea of "*non tenuit*" to an action of replevin does not necessarily oust the District Court of its jurisdiction.

The mere fact of the plaintiff in his declaration in replevin stating the value of the goods distrained at a higher sum than £15, does not shew that the action could not have been brought in the District Court. The plaintiff, to entitle himself to Queen's Bench costs, must prove at the trial that the goods are really of greater value.

Macaulay, J., *dissentiente* upon this last point.

Replevin.—To avowry for rent *non tenuit* was pleaded, and no rent in arrear.

Verdict, £4 damages.

The Master taxed Queen's Bench costs.

Mr. Justice Jones was moved in chambers to revise taxation, on the ground that "*non tenuit*" did not bring in question the title to lands, and that there was no reason why more than District Court costs should be taxed.

An order for revision was granted by the learned judge (*a*).

(*a*) In making the order the learned judge (Jones) delivered the following judgment:

This was an action of replevin, in which the defendant avowed for rent; and to this avowry the plaintiff pleaded, amongst other pleas, "*non tenuit*," no rent in arrear, and payment under special circumstances. The jury found for the plaintiff that the rent had been paid, and for the defendant upon the other pleas; but the issue of no rent in arrear should have been found for the plaintiff. The damages were nominal. No certificate was moved for or granted to enable the plaintiff to tax more than District Court costs. Queen's Bench costs having been taxed by the Master, this application was made for a revision of the costs. It is contended on the part of the plaintiff, that the Master was justified in taxing Queen's Bench costs on the pleadings; that upon the plea of "*non tenuit*," the title to land might be brought in question; and also, because it appears that the defendant's claim was for an annual rent.

It is true that upon *non tenuit* the title to lands might be brought in question, but the jurisdiction of the District Court is not ousted, unless the title *shall* be brought in question. If it could be regarded otherwise, the plea of *non tenuit* would in all cases prevent a party from suing

D. B. Read, counsel for the plaintiff, now moved to rescind this order,

1st. Because "*non tenuit*" brought in question the title.

2nd. Because the goods distrained were of more than £15 value (they were described in the declaration as being of more than £60 value).

J. H. Hagarty shewed cause, and cited 6 E. R. 283; Willes, 66; 2 Saund. 320, note 1.

ROBINSON, C. J.—I have some difficulty in this case; but the opinion I have formed is, that we ought not to rescind the judge's order, which is intended to have the effect of limiting the plaintiff's costs in this action to District Court costs. There is no doubt that the district courts can take cognizance of actions of replevin : our Act gives them jurisdiction, "when the value of the "goods distrained does not exceed £15" (*a*).

The damages given by the verdict being merely nominal, as is usual in replevin, does not on the one side shew the case to be one in which the action could not properly have been brought in the District Court; nor does it shew the contrary, because the damages for the taking the goods are not the principal object of the action. The one party is contending for his rent, and the other for his goods replevied; and if the contest about either involves a question of amount beyond the jurisdiction of the District Court, then, when that appears, it becomes evident that the action was properly brought in the Queen's Bench; but not before that does appear, so far at least as the question of amount affects the jurisdiction. It is contended that, as the declaration states the goods to have been of greater value than £15, it makes an end of the question without the aid of any judge's certificate, such as the District

---

in replevin in the District Court, which would be inconsistent with the law, which expressly authorizes such actions to be brought in that court, when the matter in dispute does not exceed £15.

To oust the jurisdiction of the District Court in any case, it is not sufficient that the title to lands *may* be brought in question—the title *must* be brought in question; and in such case, according to the 13th section of 8 Vic. ch. 13, the plea must be accompanied with an affidavit stating, amongst other things, that it is not filed "for the mere purpose of excluding such "court from having jurisdiction."

The objection that the action being for an annual rent, it could not be brought in the District Court, appears to me not tenable.

The same section says, when "the *title* to any annual rent" shall be brought in question, and if this objection were good, the Act authorizing the action of replevin to be brought in the District Court would be a dead letter; for these actions almost invariably grow out of a distress for annual rent.

I am therefore of opinion that in a case like the present, where the damages are less than £15, the Master can only tax District Court costs, unless the usual certificate entitling the plaintiff to Queen's Bench costs has been given by the judge at the trial. The cause was tried before me; and, if the certificate had been moved for, I should have granted it.

The issue upon the plea of no rent in arrear should have been found for the plaintiff, and I make the order upon condition that the defendant waives any right to costs on that issue.

The case is now rested upon the fact that the claim for rent exceeded the amount which authorized the bringing of the action in the District Court. If this would justify the withdrawal of the cause from the District Court, and authorize the taxation of Queen's Bench costs in all actions of trespass or assumpsit for any amount, the plaintiff would only be required to state his cause of action to be beyond the jurisdiction of the District Court; but this court has invariably held that that is not sufficient.

(*a*) 7 Will. IV. ch. 7, sec. 7.

Court Act requires (a). If that be so, and a certificate is not required to be moved for by the plaintiff, then, as the statute makes no provision for the defendant obtaining a certificate in order to restrain the costs, it will follow that in all actions of replevin, in which the plaintiff may choose to declare for the taking of goods which were not taken, in order to swell the amount, or to assign to a sheep or a bushel of wheat distrained the value of £20 in his declaration, he must thereby be taken to shew that the action was not of the proper competence of the District Court, and no certificate will be necessary, but the plaintiff will have Queen's Bench costs without it. It may be said that the defendant may, by entering a suggestion, deprive the plaintiff of costs, as in cases in England which are within the jurisdiction of the courts of conscience. Upon that point I do not desire to add anything to what was said by me in the case of Gardner v. Stoddart, which was determined in this court in Easter Term, 2 Geo. IV. I still think as I then did, that the reasons and purposes for which suggestions are resorted to in those cases in England, do not apply in questions of costs as between the Queen's Bench and the district courts; which latter are |not limited in their jurisdiction by the evidence of the parties, or the place where the cause of the action arose.

The legislature have enabled the judge at the trial, by a method of proceeding, summary, convenient and inexpensive, to determine whether a cause which the District Court might or might not have tried, according to circumstances, was in truth such as could and ought to have been brought there; and I do not see why we should drive the party to the necessity of entering a suggestion.

The argument for the plaintiff here is, that we must first see that the cause is of the "proper competence of the District Court," before we can hold that a certificate was necessary in order to give him Queen's Bench costs; that he complains of goods being taken of a value much beyond £15; and that his statement must be taken as conclusive, because the verdict does not, from the nature of the action, ascertain the value of the goods, and therefore imports nothing to the contrary—so that the statement in the declaration is unrepelled. I think it is a reasonable answer to this argument, and a reasonable mode of acting upon this remedial statute, to hold that the plaintiff's own statement of value in his own favour is not sufficient to shew whether the action could or could not have been brought in the District Court; that, unless he was in fact suing for the taking of goods of greater value than £15, he could and ought (so far as value merely is concerned) to have sued in the District Court; that the actual value of goods was what ought to govern; that the trial afforded means and opportunity of shewing what the truth in that respect was; that the judge could and should have received evidence for that purpose, and would have been in a situation, if it had been given, to have certified according to the fact—while the mere fact that there was a trial precludes the plaintiff from resorting to any proceeding, under our rule of court, for obtaining full costs, such as is prescribed when judgment has been confessed, or has gone by default, or been obtained in any manner without trial.

My opinion is, that we should hold the party to the necessity of shewing the judge at the trial that the cause was really such as could not properly have

---

(a) 8 Vic. ch. 13, sec. 39.

been tried in the District Court, which he can do conveniently when the facts are in his favour, and therefore ought to do. Nokes v. Fraser (a) shows how liberally the courts act in applying provisions of this nature.

Where there is an issue of *non cepit*, the particulars must necessarily appear. That was not the case in this instance; but, although the value of the goods distrained need not be shewn for the mere purpose of the verdict, because the plaintiff had his goods already, yet it is not irrelevant to the cause to shew what goods and of what value were actually taken out of the possession of the plaintiff, since, by the record, damages for the taking are to be assessed, though these are in practice nominal; and more especially the evidence would not be irrelevant, when it would have the effect of governing the judge in an essential part of his duty at the trial; namely, the giving or withholding a certificate.

We have been in the frequent habit at *nisi prius* of hearing evidence of parties, or their witnesses, with a view to govern the judge in his discretion, in regard to the certificate required for giving Queen's Bench costs; and by requiring a certificate in this case, and declining to take the plaintiff's own statement of the cause of action as conclusive in his favour, we shall be acting consistently, I think, with the spirit and intention of the Act, as well as in accordance with many English decisions, which maintain that the plaintiff's statement of his action in the record is not what is to govern for the purpose of entitling him to costs.

This case, I conceive, turns wholly upon the question I have stated. The title to the land was not necessarily brought in question by the plea of *non tenuit*, and was not in question upon the trial; and the amount of rent in question was not such as to take the matter out of the jurisdiction of the District Court.

MACAULAY, J.—I think the order restricting the plaintiff to District Court costs should be rescinded on this short ground, that it does not appear upon the face of the record, either expressly or impliedly, that the suit is within the competence of the District Court, and it cannot be presumed or intended.

The jurisdiction depends upon the value of the goods distrained, &c.; and here the value laid in the declaration far exceeds £15, and there is nothing to shew or indicate the contrary. In this respect the case differs from Gardner v. Stoddart, where the verdict or sum assessed as damages was within the jurisdiction, which jurisdiction depended thereon. If the goods did not exceed £15 value, the defendant should have moved to enter a suggestion of that fact on the roll. Where new extraneous facts (as the value of the goods distrained) are to be brought in question, and the right to liability for costs is to depend upon it, the parties should be at liberty to contest such value, if disputed, before a jury; and for such purpose, if the value assigned in the declaration is disputed, the defendant should suggest the same.

Per Cur.—Rule discharged.—MACAULAY, J., *dissentiente.*

(a) 3 Dowl. P. C. 339.

WOOD ET. AL. V. CAMPBELL.

Alien friends residing in their proper country cannot, upon a summary application to this court, be deprived, under the words of the statute 5 Geo. II. ch. 7, of their right to an execution against the lands of their debtor.

Semble, The alienage should be pleaded in bar of execution.

Quære, If alien friends residing in this Province would be differently situated? A writ of *fi. fa.* directed to no one is void, and cannot be amended.

P. Vankoughnet moved to set aside, with costs, the *fi. fa.* issued in this cause against the defendant's lands, to the sheriff of the Midland District, on the ground that the plaintiffs were aliens, and therefore not entitled, under 5 Geo. II. ch. 7, to execution against the lands of their debtor, and also for irregularity, on the ground that the writ was not directed to the sheriff of any district, while the same was in the hands of the sheriff of the Midland District, who had acted thereon; and cited 2 B. & P. 363; 4 M. & S. 329; 3 Dowl. 353.

It was shewn that the præcipe was for a writ to be directed to the sheriff of the Midland district.

The *fi. fa.* was one of the usual printed writs, and ran—

"To the Sheriff of the ———— District."

The sheriff, in consequence of this defect being pointed out to him, declined to sell certain lands which he had seized and advertised for sale.

It was sworn, and not denied, that the plaintiffs were aliens, being citizens of the United States of America, residing in New York, and carrying on business there as merchants.

S. B. Harrison, Q. C., moved for the plaintiffs to amend their *fi fa.* by the præcipe, directing it to the sheriff of the Midland District; against the first objection he cited 1 Burge's Col. Law, 710; 9 East. 321.

ROBINSON, C. J., delivered the judgment of the court.

As regards the first objection, it assumes that the plaintiffs, though alien friends, cannot have execution for the debt against the lands of their debtor, as a subject may. That turns on the construction proper to be given to the words "or any of his subjects," used in the statute 5 Geo. II. ch. 7; and on this a doubt might be raised, if the plaintiffs were alien friends residing in this province, and owing, on account of such residence, a temporary allegiance. But the plaintiffs here do not stand in that situation it seems, but are alien friends residing in their proper country, and in no sense entitled to be regarded as subjects of Her Majesty. Still they are suing in her courts; and I take it this court should not interfere, upon a summary application, to deprive them of the privilege common to all suitors, to be regarded as subjects, till the contrary is found of record.

In the case cited on the argument, of Doe dem. Richardson v. Dickson, decided in this court in Hilary Term, 2 Will. IV., the point was noticed but not decided; and it is not necessary to be determined here. I think it must be held that the objection is one which must be taken, if at all, by pleading it in bar of execution against the lands (*a*).

(*a*) Str. 732.

But upon the other objection, there can be no doubt. The writ not being directed to any one, conveys no authority, and is on the face of it void. By giving it a direction now, we should be making a new writ, and not merely waiving an irregularity. The writ is not only erroneous, it is defective and imperfect (a).

Rule absolute.

PRENTISS V. BEEMER.

In an action upon a foreign judgment, rendered in an inferior court, it is not necessary to aver that the cause of action arose within the jurisdiction of that court.

The plaintiff sued in *assumpsit*, on a foreign judgment.

The declaration stated that the plaintiff, on the 7th January, 1845, viz., at Niagara, in the said District of Niagara, by the judgment of a certain court called a Justices' Court, in Niagara County, in the State of New York, one of the United States of America, before Alonzo T. Prentice, Esquire, a justice of the peace in the said county and state, and within the jurisdiction of the said Alonzo T. Prentice, recovered against the defendant the sum of 100 dollars, &c., equal in value to £25, for damages, and 1 dollar and 88 cents, or 9s. 5d., for costs, &c., whereof the defendant was convicted, and concludes in the usual manner as to that judgment being unsatisfied, &c.

The defendant suffered judgment by default, and damages were assessed at £27 9s. 5d.

H. Eccles moved to arrest the judgment, and objected that the declaration shewed a judgment of a court holden in the District of Niagara, in this province, and out of the jurisdiction of the court as described.

Boomer shewed cause.

ROBINSON, C. J., delivered the judgment of the court.

We must look upon the record now as we would upon a general demurrer, and it certainly is substantially alleged, that the judgment was rendered by a justice in the State of New York, within his jurisdiction, and holding a court called a Justices' Court.

We think it sufficiently certain, and that it was not necessary to aver that the cause of action arose within the jurisdiction of the court. The forms of declaring in actions of debt or assumpsit on foreign judgments, to be met with in the books, do not contain any allegation of the kind; and admitting that we are to assume that the court described is one of local jurisdiction, yet we ought not to take it for granted that it cannot take cognizance of any cause of action arising out of its locality, since the inferior courts in our own country are not so limited in their jurisdiction.

Rule discharged.

GOULD V. FREEMAN.

The court will not allow judgment to be entered on a verdict taken subject to a reference, on account of the attempt to arbitrate having failed.

At the assizes held in London on the 14th May, 1846, this cause was referred and a verdict taken by consent for plaintiff for £700, subject to the award of

---

(a) 4 B. & Ald. 288.

two arbitrators; or, in case of their disagreeing, of an umpire to be appointed by them. The cause only was referred, with power to confirm, reduce or annul the verdict, or enter a verdict for defendants—the award to be made on the 1st of June then next, or umpirage by the 4th June; with power to the arbitrators or umpire to enlarge the time. Costs of the cause to abide the event.

The usual clause was inserted in the rule, that if either party should wilfully prevent the arbitrators or umpire from making an award, he shall pay such costs to the other as the Court of Queen's Bench should think just.

No award had been made.

J. H. Hagarty, for the plaintiff, moved to be allowed to enter judgment and issue execution on the verdict rendered, or for the sum of £554 5s. 3d., being the sum sworn to by the plaintiff in his affidavit filed as being due to him from the defendant: or that he should be allowed to enter judgment and sue out execution as aforesaid, unlesss defendant should, *on or before 18th June instant*, effectually carry out the reference to arbitration by enlarging the time, or entering into a new submission: and he moved also for costs to be paid by defendant under the rule of reference, for wilfully preventing the arbitrators from making an award.

The affidavits shewed that the arbitrators chose an umpire, intending that the three should sit together and hear the case; that a day and place were appointed by the arbitrators; and, upon notice thereof, both plaintiff and defendant attended with their evidence, &c., and that the arbitrator chosen by defendant did not attend; and in consequence they could not then proceed.

The defendant swore that his arbitrator's absence was occasioned by illness; that he was exceedingly anxious to have the meeting postponed to the next day, or some other day within the time limited, but that the other arbitrator declined.

The plaintiff swore to his belief that the defendant's arbitrator was absent at his request, or by his contrivance. The defendant, on oath, denied this.

The arbitrator (Jones) who stayed away, had declined or omitted to give any account of the cause of his absence.

ROBINSON, C. J., delivered the judgment of the court.

Looking at the affidavit on which the rule was moved, we do not consider that we can properly go farther in this case, the verdict which was taken by consent being for a large amount, than to remove the impediment to the plaintiff's further proceeding by setting that verdict aside and granting him a new trial, unless the plaintiff should prefer availing himself of an order which we shall make in the alternative, under our statute 7 Will. IV. ch. 3, sec. 29, enlarging the time for the arbitrators making an award to Tuesday, 8th September next, and for the umpirage to the 10th September. If the plaintiff chooses to proceed to arbitration within the enlarged time, the verdict will of course stand; but in case the arbitrators or umpire should make an award, or in case the plaintiff should desire rather to take his cause to trial and waive any further attempt at arbitration, then he may have a new trial—the costs of the former trial to abide the event.

The plaintiff does not seem to have requested the arbitrators to enlarge the time, which they might have done by the terms of the rule; nor has he taken the other course which was open to him under our statute, of applying to the court to enlarge the time, according to the statute 7 Will. IV. ch. 1, sec. 20, which, upon the authority of Parberry v. Newnham (a), we might have done under the circumstances of this case. Whatever it might have been proper to have done under other circumstances, we should certainly not allow the plaintiff to enter up his judgment for so large a sum when there had been no investigation of the merits, and when the plaintiff had not resorted to the remedy which the statute gives him.

As to granting costs to the plaintiff under the rule at *nisi prius*, on the ground that the defendant had wilfully hindered the award being made, we do not find that we can properly do so, upon considering the statements contained in his affidavit on which he moved the rule, and the manner in which these are denied on the defendant's part.

Conditional order granted as above.

IRVING V. MERYGOLD.

Before a defendant can be charged with deceit in a contract for the sale of land, he must be shewn to have entered into a contract such as is required by the Statute of Frauds, and to have clearly practised or intended the deceit alleged against him.

The plaintiff sued in case for deceit, and declared that the defendant had publicly advertised himself to be the purchaser, from the government, of a lot of land mentioned, and that he was then entitled to sell the lot to any person who might wish to purchase the said land, being a clergy reserve, and who would make immediate application to him for it; and that the defendant, wrongfully contriving and intending to deceive, defraud and injure the plaintiff, falsely, fraudulently and deceitfully represented to the plaintiff that he had become the purchaser of the lot, and was entitled to sell the same to him; whereupon the plaintiff, confiding in the representation, bargained with the defendant for the land at a certain price, and paid him £10 on account of it; that the defendant afterwards entered upon the land and made improvements; and that in fact the defendant had not at the time when, &c., become the purchaser from the government of the land, and was not entitled to dispose of the same to the plaintiff, as the defendant then well knew, and that after the plaintiff had gone into possession, he was compelled to yield up the same to the rightful purchaser.

The defendant pleaded: 1st, Not guilty.

2nd, Payment of £10 in full discharge and satisfaction of the grievances in the declaration, and of all damages sustained thereby.

The plaintiff took issue on this second plea.

The only evidence given by the plaintiff in support of his case was, an advertisement produced, which was proved to be in the defendant's writing, and which was headed " List of Clergy Lots in East and West Oxford, pur-"chased by Edward Merygold," among which was the lot in question; and under the numbers of lots was written—" Persons wishing to become pur-"chasers of any of the above mentioned lots of land, had better make imme-

---

(a) 7 M. & W. 378.

"diate application to the subscriber, as there are continual applications made "for them, and he intends selling them without reserve." It was not shewn that this advertisement had been ever in any way made public, or that it had come to the knowledge of the plaintiff.

It was proved that the defendant had in conversation admitted to a third party that he had sold the land in question to the plaintiff, and had received £10 on account; that the plaintiff finding, not long after, that another person had purchased the lot from the government agent, went to the defendant and acquainted him with it; upon which the defendant returned him the £10, but declined making him any recompense for the disappointment.

On the defendant's part, it was proved that he had gone to the government agent, and agreed to purchase the lot at the upset price, and not having paid the first instalment within a few days, as he had engaged to do, the agent had sold it to another.

The agent swore that the defendant had stated to him that he considered that the regulations of the government extended the time for paying the first instalment to the 1st of January, and that many other persons had so construed the regulations.

The land in question, being a clergy reserve, was sold at ten shillings an acre, being the upset price; though it was proved that land not so good, in the same neighbourhood, had been sold for thirty shillings.

The learned judge at the trial held that there was not such evidence as entitled the plaintiff to recover; that there was no evidence of such a representation as the declaration averred; no written evidence of the contract, such as required by the Statute of Frauds; and no proof of any deceit practised or intended.

When the defendant received the £10 he gave him a written receipt, in these words: "This is to certify that I have received from Robert Irving the "sum of £10, and have applied it to the sale of Lot No. 9, in the 5th conces- "sion of West Oxford, and so soon as I get a bond I will give him one for the "lot."

The case went to the jury, with a direction to find for the defendant, but they returned with a verdict for the plaintiff, and £25 damages.

S. B. *Harrison*, Q. C., moved for a new trial, on the law and evidence.

J. W. *Gwynne* shewed cause, and relied upon 3 T. R. 51; Cro. J. 196; 5 B. 66.

ROBINSON, C. J., delivered the judgment of the court.

We consider that the defendant should have a new trial, without costs, It was not a mere question of fact for the jury to decide; in which case, if they had taken a different view of the evidence from that which it might appear to us reasonable to take, we should not probably have relieved against the verdict on other terms than the defendant paying the costs of the last trial. There were in this case several legal objections to the plaintiff's recovery, and so the learned judge informed the jury; but they found, nevertheless, for the defendant, and it is our duty to see that the defendant has the benefit of the protection which the law extends to such cases. The defendant is charged in this action with deceit in a contract for the sale of lands. The foundation of the action is the alleged contract; and though it is not an action to enforce the contract, yet it is an action charging him upon the contract, for until that is established, there is no ground for the complaint. Then there was not that certain evidence of the contract which the Statute of Frauds requires, for the receipt relied upon does not specify the terms of the bargain, but merely that £10 had been paid on account of a certain lot. We agree with the learned judge who tried the cause, that the representation which is alleged as the ground of the action was not proved; for though the defendant's signature was proved to the handbill produced on the trial, yet it was not shewn either that that had been in any way made public, so that the defendant must be assumed to have had knowledge of it, or that particular communication of it had been made to him.

There was indeed no proof of any deceit practised or intended. According to the evidence of the crown agent, Mr. Carrol, the defendant had agreed with him for the lot, and only lost it by not having paid his first instalment in time; but he seemed to think that the defendant might have been under the impression, as he says many were, that by the public regulations of the government, the purchasers had till the 1st of January to pay their first instalment. It would seem, then, that this defendant had only lost by a mistake, or possibly by neglect, or inability to pay the means of making good his purchase, and so could not convey to the plaintiff what he says (but did not legally prove) he had undertaken to convey; but there is a great difference between failing in a promise, and being guilty of fraud and deceit; and independently of the legal objections, there seems no pretence for an action of this kind. The defendant undoubtedly was bound to return the £10 which he had received on account, and this he did without difficulty.

Rule absolute, new trial without costs.

HORNBY v. HORNBY.

Though an order to change the venue had been granted and served, unless the venue is in fact changed, by taking out the rule and making the alteration in the record, the plaintiff is at liberty to proceed to trial according to the original venue.

Assumpsit on the common counts.

Plea, general issue and set-off.

Verdict for the plaintiff.

Richards moved to set aside the verdict for irregularity, on the ground that the cause was tried at Kingston, after a judge's order had been granted, and a copy thereof served on the agent of the plaintiff's attorney, for changing the *venue* to the Home District.

The legal point for decision was, whether the judge's order for changing the *venue* merely, served as it was, not on the plaintiff's attorney but on his agent in Toronto, had the effect of disabling the plaintiff's attorney from proceeding in the trial, the change of *venue* not having been in fact made in the declaration, and the plaintiff's attorney having no knowledge of the order.

Alex. Campbell shewed cause against the rule.

ROBINSON, C. J., delivered the judgment of the court.

There is an early decision of this court precisely in point—I refer to McNair v. Sheldon (a); and we think it right to conform to it, and to hold that until

---

(a) Taylor's Reports.

the *venue* was in fact changed by taking out the rule and making the alteration in the record, the plaintiff was at liberty to proceed to trial according to the original *venue*. It would be unfair indeed in a case like this, if the effect should be otherwise ; for the service of the rule upon the agent resident here of the plaintiff's attorney could be of no service in arresting the trial—the time did not admit of it.

Per Cur.—Rule discharged.

AINSLIE V. RAPELJE, SHERIFF, &C.

It is no objection on the part of a sheriff, in an action against him, that the jury have been summoned by himself, and not by the coroner.

In an action against a sheriff, by an execution debtor, for the surplus of money remaining in his hands after satisfying a *fi. fa.*—no demand before action brought is necessary.

The plaintiff sued the defendant in a common action of *assumpsit* for goods sold and delivered, &c., &c., the causes of action as laid in the declaration having no relation to his office of sheriff, but the declaration described the defendant as sheriff of the District of Talbot.

The defendant pleaded the general issue.

The *venue* was laid in the District of Gore, but a suggestion had been entered that the trial could be more conveniently had in the District of Talbot.

The plaintiff recovered a verdict.

C. Foster moved to set it aside upon the grounds—

1st. Because the *venire juratores* ought to have been awarded to the coroner.

2nd. Because the plaintiff recovered for a sum of money, being a surplus in the defendant's hands of the proceeds of the plaintiff's goods sold on a *fi. fa.* by the defendant, as sheriff, and he did not shew that he demanded his money before he brought his action.

Notman shewed cause.

ROBINSON, C. J., delivered the judgment of the court.

Upon the first point it has been several times held in this court, that it is no objection in the mouth of the sheriff that the jury has been summoned by himself, and not by the coroner. If the opposite party were to raise such an objection, of course it would be fatal ; but every one may waive the benefit of a rule made for its protection ; and if the plaintiff is content that the sheriff may summon the jury, it surely is not for the sheriff to complain.

No authority has been cited which goes the length of supporting the second objection. The case of Dale v. Birch (*a*), before Lord Ellenborough, so far as it applies, is against it ; and it seems to have been hitherto treated as a correct decision. There it was the plaintiff in the *fi. fa.* who sued the sheriff for money which he had acknowledged to have levied by his return ; and the court held that, in strictness of law, no demand was necessary before action. Longdill v. Jones (*b*) is a similar case ; and Jeffries v. Sheppard (*c*) is consistent with what Lord Ellenborough held ; for the court there relieved the sheriff by

---

(*a*) 3 Camp. 347.   (*b*) 1 Starkie, N. P. C. 345.   (*c*) 3 B. & Al. 696.

staying proceedings on paying the debt without costs, because the action had been brought without first demanding the money—this appearing to be the only proper way of relieving him from the effect of a course of proceeding which certainly seems unreasonable, where the sheriff can be supposed not to have known where to find the party entitled to the money, or where he is not easily accessible.

We can give no good reason why the sheriff is not as much under the necessity of finding the defendant entitled to the surplus as the plaintiff, to whom he is to pay the money levied. The probability is in favour of his knowing more precisely the situation and circumstances of the defendant than of the plaintiff; and we cannot state any legal principle upon which a sheriff, having in hands money due to another person, is not as much bound to pay it over without any other demand than the action itself, where that is resorted to, as any other person. There is a case in Noy's Reports in which it is held that the surplus must be demanded from the sheriff before an action will lie for it, but later decisions are inconsistent with this. The case of Ruggles v. Beikie, decided in this court, was under very different circumstances. The action was not brought there by the person whose goods the sheriff had sold; and, admitting that decision to have been correct, we cannot carry the principle further. In that case the lands of a deceased debtor had been sold under the statute 5 Geo. II., upon an execution against the administrator, and the surplus money was claimed by the heir of the debtor who sued for it. Whether he or the administrator was entitled to it, was a difficult question, not for the sheriff merely but for the court. *Prima facie* the sheriff might naturally have considered himself accountable for the surplus to the person against whom the *fi. fa.* had been issued; and, if the heir was the person legally entitled to it, under the circumstances he had no means of knowing who the heir was. The decision turned wholly on the particular facts of the case. This is the common case of the sheriff selling the defendant's goods under an execution against him, and having a surplus in his hands which he must have been well aware belonged to the defendant.

We cannot accede to the defendant's argument that it was for the defendant to shew that the second execution (for there were two), was not for such an amount as would have absorbed the whole sum levied. He naturally stated what the sheriff had alleged as his reason for not paying over the surplus, but it was for the sheriff to shew that the reason was well founded. If he had executions to cover the whole sum levied, he should have shewn them. It was for him to discharge himself of the residue above the first writ.

Per Cur.—Rule discharged.

Downs v. McNamara et al.

An agreement to do certain work cannot be declared upon as a promissory note. The consideration for such agreement and breach must be properly averred.

Demurrer. The plaintiff declared in *assumpsit*, for that the defendants in, &c., made their agreement or promissory note in writing, and thereby jointly and severally, for value received by the defendants from the plaintiff, promised to pay the plaintiff £14, to be paid in carpenters' or joiners' work, such as might be required; the declaration then stated the defendants liability to pay.

There were other common counts in the declaration, and the usual breach, wherever a note is declared upon together with the common counts.

Demurrer to the declaration: Because it did not state what the consideration for making the said agreement was, or that the defendants did not perform the said work, and because no breach was shewn.

H. Eccles, counsel for the demurrer.

R. P. Crooks, contra, relied on Teal v. Clarkson, Hilary Term, 6 Will. IV.

ROBINSON, C. J., delivered the judgment of the court.

The defendants are entitled to judgment on the demurrer.

There is nothing in the case cited of Teal v. Clarkson, decided in this court, to support such a declaration. An agreement to do work is sued upon as a promissory note, which it certainly is not.

No consideration is laid to support the promise, no request to do the work, though the undertaking is only to do such work *as might be required;* and no breach is laid, for the plaintiff only sets out the promise, and does not charge that it is unperformed.

Per Cur.—Judgment for the defendants, on the demurrer.

THE QUEEN V. ROBERT LAND.

A. and B. enter, as co-sureties, into separate bonds to the crown, for C.: C. becomes a defaulter. The crown proceeds by *sci. fa.* on each bond, and obtains a separate judgment against each surety. A. satisfies to the crown the judgment against himself. B. moves the court to be allowed, on paying the judgment against himself in full, to stand in the place of the crown, and to have the benefit of the crown process against his co-surety for a moiety of the judgment.

Held, That the court could not thus relieve B. from the effect of the judgment against himself; all that they could have done would be to allow him to proceed in the name of the crown to enforce the judgment which had been obtained on *sci. fa.* against A., and this they could not now do, as it appeared the crown had already enforced that judgment.

S. B. Harrison, Q. C., on the part of this defendant, obtained a rule upon Abel Land, a co-surety with the defendant in a bond to the Queen for Wm. Scott Burn, late Paymaster of the 3rd Regiment of Gore Militia, to shew cause why, upon payment of what is due to the crown upon the judgment recovered against the above defendant in the above suit, he the said Robert Land should not stand in the place of the crown, and have the benefit of the crown process against the said Abel Land, for his re-imbursement, as well of a moiety of the amount of the said judgment, as of so much thereof as he the said Robert Land has or shall have paid as for his costs and expenses already incurred, or which he may incur in prosecuting the prerogative process in his aid, and why he should not have the aid of this court to recover the same from the said Abel Land; and why the Attorney-General should not thereupon acknowledge satisfaction upon the record of the judgment in this suit, and the said bonds be delivered up to this defendant.

On the 6th of April, 1838, this defendant gave his bond to Her Majesty in

£1000 penalty, with a condition, to be void if one W. S. Burn should faithfully pay over all sums of money which he should receive as Paymaster of the 3rd Regiment of Gore Militia. Abel Land at the same time entered into a like bond as another surety for Mr. Burn.

In January, 1840, a board of officers assembled for the purpose, reported that Mr. Burn was a defaulter in £406 5s. 6d. Proceedings were in consequence taken by *sci. fa*, on each of these bonds, and in December, 1840, judgment was entered in each case, and execution was issued against the goods of Robert Land for the amount thus found due, and he paid thereupon £362 14s. 0d., and Abel Land paid £52 14s. 0d. on the judgment against him.

This is the manner in which the case was stated by Robert Land in his affidavit.

Abel Land, in opposition to this application, made affidavit that a verdict in the action on the *sci. fa*, was rendered against him for £104 or thereabouts, being the whole sum claimed from him by the Attorney-General on account of his bond; that he paid that sum to the sheriff upon an execution issued upon the judgment; and that he called upon Robert Land to repay him half of the sum thus paid by him, which the said Robert Land did accordingly pay.

H. Eccles shewed cause against this application, filing Abel Land's affidavit.

ROBINSON, C. J., delivered the judgment of the court.

We have carefully considered the affidavits and papers filed in support of this application. The books supply us with very few cases to guide us in the course to be pursued in such cases; and the text books are short and unsatisfactory upon the subject. More is to be found in the case to which Mr. Harrison referred us in Wightwick's Reports, page 1, and in the short notes of cases appended to it, than can be found elsewhere in any quarter to which we have access.

The courts in England are compelled in general, where questions arise upon such proceedings, to gain information by searching into the records of what has been done on similar occasions. This is a source of information to which we cannot have access, but upon the reason of the thing, it appears plain to us, that the application which has been made to us on behalf of the surety, Robt. Land, is one to which we cannot accede.

Mr. Manning, in his Exchequer Practice, lays it down, upon the authority of the short note given in Wightwick's Reports of the case of the Queen v. Doughty, that where one of two sureties to the crown pays the debt, "it may "be ordered that he shall stand in the place of the crown, and have the aid of "the court to recover either the whole against the principal, or moiety against "a co-surety." Assuming this then to be so, what we are asked to do here is to allow to the surety, Robert Land, the aid of the prerogative process in enforcing for his benefit, against Abel Land, the payment of so much of the debt due by him on his bond to the crown, as will make good a moiety of what Robert Land has been compelled to pay on account of Burn, for whom they were each bound to the crown in separate bonds.

Now, admitting that this course may be pursued as well where such surety binds himself in a separate bond as where they both unite in one undertaking, it is still certain that all the assistance the court can give to Robt. Land, is to allow him to proceed in Her Majesty's name to enforce the judgment which has been obtained on *sci. fa.* against Abel Land. But upon the paper before us it appears that the crown has already taken its proceedings against Abel Land, upon the bond, to the full extent of the demand which it has been thought just to urge under it.

All the proceedings are not laid before us; but it is sworn by Abel Land, and nothing to the contrary is asserted on the other side, that £104 was proved and returned by the jury as the debt against him on the extent, and that he paid it, and afterwards required his co-surety to repay him the half of it, which he did.

The debt demanded and found against Robert Land in the proceeding against him was £300; whether he had paid that before he submitted to the demand of Abel Land, and paid him £52 as a contribution which he ought to make in respect to the £104, or not till afterwards, does not appear. If it was after he had paid his own £300, that he yielded to that demand, it would seem a strong acknowledgment on his part that in paying the £300 he had paid no more than was incumbent on him to pay, while his co-surety had a claim upon him for half of the £104 paid on his bond. However that may be, the crown certainly would not think it right to pursue any further proceedings against Abel Land after the judgment against him, after he had fully satisfied the whole amount which had been claimed as being due under it, for there is no new demand as between the crown and Abel Land by reason of anything discovered accruing since the crown consented to limit its claim to £104.

And the papers indeed furnish a very just reason, as it appears to us, why the crown should have proceeded against these two sureties in the manner they have done, claiming of Robert Land £300, and of Abel Land only £104. The latter sum is evidently the amount of sundry claims made by three or four militia officers upon Mr. Burn, the paymaster, for sums which he had not paid to them, although he had received funds for that purpose. This was a plain defalcation, coming within the express condition of the several bonds, for which both the sureties were equally liable, and as Abel Land had paid it all, he might justly look to his co-surety for contribution.

But the £300 which the crown has exacted from Robert Land stood on a very different footing, as the documents placed before us explain.

That was money which had found its way from the government into the hands of Robert Land himself. It had never been issued by the government to Mr. Burn, as paymaster, to be applied in paying the officers and men, according to the regulations of the service, as the conditions of the bond require; and Mr. Robert Land allowed Mr. Burn to apply it on a particular occasion in paying the men of his regiment, in anticipation of the regular payment to be made when the money and pay-lists should arrive. He directed Mr. Burn to stop from the men afterwards such sum as he had thus advanced, and to return it to the bank, in which it had stood in his (Robert Land's) account before he had irregularly made this use of it, instead of returning it to the government, as ought properly to have been done. Mr. Burn, it seems, did not return the money to Robert Land's account in the bank, as he was desired, and it was not discovered that he had failed to do so till a considerable time had elapsed. This was a collateral transaction, out of the course of those duties for which the sureties had become responsible. The £300 was, in fact, a sum for which Robert Land was himself responsible to the paymaster. If lost by Mr. Burn's misapplication of it, it would be lost to him, and not to the government; and lost, not in consequence of any trust as between the crown and the paymaster, but in consequence of an irregular transaction between Robert Land and him. There is no doubt that nothing wrong was intended on the part of Mr. R. Land; he acted for the best, to meet some passing exigency of the service ; but he was unfortunate in the steps which he took with regard to this £300, and we think it would be unreasonable that under such circumstances he should look to the co-surety, who had nothing to do in the matter, to make good half the loss. What he became responsible for was, that the paymaster should faithfully disburse the sums which should come to him as paymaster, to be paid out to the regiment; not that he would punctually return to A. B. or C. D. any sum irregularly advanced to him, in anticipation of his receipts from the government.

We do not go so far as to hold that the £300, thus misapplied, might not be in strictness treated, if the crown chose so to regard it, as money belonging to the crown ; nor that in strictness of law, Mr. Robert Land may not be able to compel contribution in an action on that sum from his co-surety.

It is not necessary that we should now determine these points; but we think that the Attorney-General acted reasonably in looking to Robert Land exclusively for the £300, and that we should do wrong if we were to lend any particular facility to him in his efforts to throw part of the loss on Abel Land.

Per Cur.—Rule discharged.

BEEKMAN, ASSIGNEE OF MCKAY, A BANKRUPT, V. JARVIS, SHERIFF OF THE HOME DISTRICT.

A *fi. fa.*, at the suit of an execution creditor, placed in the sheriff's hands before a commission of bankruptcy against the debtor was sealed, but on *the same day* on which it was completed and delivered to the sheriff, has priority over the commission.

Where goods are already in the custody of the law, a writ of *fi. fa.* at once attaches upon them without an actual seizure.

In determining the priority of writs, the court will look to the fraction of a day.

Assumpsit for money had and received.

General issue.

The action was brought to recover the sum of £218 and interest, being money made by the defendant, as sheriff, from the goods of the bankrupt, and which his assignee claims under the commission, the defendant having paid it over to Hooker and Henderson, as entitled to preference under a *fi. fa.* at their suit, which was placed in the defendant's hands on the same day on which the commission was delivered to him, and some hours before the commission was completed.

The jury, by consent of parties, found for the plaintiff, subject to the opinion of the court above, whether, upon the facts proved and admitted, the verdict ought to stand, or a verdict be entered for the defendant.

W. H. Blake moved to enter verdict for the defendant, on leave reserved.

R. P. Crooks shewed cause, and relied on there being no fraction of a day, and that the goods had been seized under a prior *fi. fa.*, at the suit of The Bank of Upper Canada and Maitland & Co., and that there was no occasion for a further seizure, and could in fact be none. He also cited 7 M. & G. 251; 2 B. & Ald. 586.

Blake admitted the *fi. fa.* was in fact in the sheriff's hands before the commission of bankruptcy, but then there was no evidence of anything done under it; there was no seizure. He referred to the 37th section of our Bankrupt Act, 7 Vic. ch. 10.

ROBINSON, C. J., delivered the judgment of the court.

We are of opinion, upon the facts proved and the admissions made, the defendant is entitled to the verdict. It is not disputed that under the circumstances the *fi. fa.* which had been placed in the sheriff's hands at the suit of Maitland & Co. was entitled to be satisfied before Hooker and Henderson could come in with their writ, because it was first in the sheriff's hands. It is admitted, also, that that writ would have more than absorbed all the assets, so that nothing would have remained to be applied on Hooker and Henderson's writ, if things had been left to take their course, without the intervention of any commission of bankruptcy.

But all this became immaterial when Maitland & Co. gave up their claim as execution-creditors, and were content to come in as creditors of the bankrupt estate. Then the impediment of Maitland & Co.'s writ was removed; and if the *fi. fa.* of Hooker and Henderson was entitled to priority over the bankrupt commission, it would from that moment assume its true position, the pressure of the former superincumbent writ having been withdrawn.

The question of priority as between Hooker and Henderson's writ and the commission, depends upon whether we can divide the day on which the commission issued, or rather on which it was dated; and can hold that the execution was entitled to priority, because it was actually in the sheriff's hands before the commission was delivered, and before it was even signed, though it was proved that both took place on the same day.

We have already determined that under our bankrupt law the act of seizing under a *fi. fa.* is sufficient to make the creditor's claim to priority good as against the assignees, under the 37th clause of the statute. The point came up first in Hales v. Tracey (*a*), and Moulson v. Kissock (*b*). It has been urged that there was no actual seizure of the goods under this *fi. fa.;* but the answer to that is, that under the circumstances none was necessary. The goods were already in the custody of the law, being in the sheriff's hands under the prior writs. He could not seize them again, but the writ attached upon them as if he had seized under it.

Then the remaining question is upon the effect of the commission coming out on the same day, and after the seizure must be considered to have taken place. The plaintiff contends that since the 37th clause requires that the seizure should be made *before the date of the commission*, and as this was made *on* the same day that the commission bears date, and not before, the *fi. fa.*, cannot have priority under that seizure. We are not of that opinion. We have no doubt that generally speaking the "*date*," and the "*day of the date*," mean

---

(*a*) 1 Cam. Rep. 541.   (*b*) 2 Cam. 338.

the same thing, as was determined in the well known case of Pugh v. The Duke of Leeds (a). In most cases it would be inconvenient, and would tend to confusion, to take the words in any other sense; but we must always look to the whole of a statute to determine its meaning, and we must also have regard to the purposes to which the construction in any such case is to be applied.

We think that we are bound, from the reason of the thing, to hold that the "date of the commission," as the words are used in the clause, cannot be understood to include or extend to any time anterior to the actual completion of the commission. If, for instance, by any accident, or from design, the commission was to be dated some days back, it would be a plain contravention of the will of the legislature, that it should have by that means the effect of overreaching an execution levied before the commission had been engrossed. The British statute, 6 Geo. IV. ch. 16, and 2 & 3 Vic. ch. 29, in their corresponding provisions, are careful to use the words "*date and issuing,*" which they apply to the fiat for the commission, and not to the commission itself; and in construing those words it has been determined, in the case of Pewtress et al. v. Annan (b), that the courts may regard the fraction of a day, and give effect to a seizure under a *fi. fa.* which has been made on the same day the fiat issued, and on which it was dated. I fully admit that that case is not expressly in point upon our statute, because the *issuing* of the writ or commission points to the moment of an act being done; and there can therefore be less difficulty of dividing the day according to the hour when the act was performed. But when we look at the 16th, 18th, 19th, 22nd, 23rd, 25th, 31st, 35th, 37th, 38th, 48th, 51st, 60th, and 74th clauses of our statute 7 Vic. ch. 10, and consider the nature and effect of the several provisions contained in them, it is quite obvious that the legislature never could have meant to give to the commission the effect which the plaintiff claims for it here, before the time of its being actually made out. That might lead to most inconvenient and unjust consequences; and it is evident that the legislature, by the term "*date,*" mean nothing distinct from the issuing of the commission; for in the 16th, 18th, and 19th clauses they use the term "*issuing,*" and not the term "*date;*" and when the objects of the several enactments are considered, it will appear very incongruous to suppose that, on those clauses in which "the date" is the term used, the legislature intended to give a binding authority to the commission, not merely from the time of its issuing, or even from the time of its being *sealed,* but from any day that may happen, whether truly or otherwise, to be inserted as its "date."

The date of a deed or instrument, when it is not referred to as matter of description, means the time when the deed was really made or delivered, not always the day that may have been inserted in the date, which may sometimes be an impossible day.

The 23rd clause of this Act provides that the first meeting of creditors shall be appointed on some day not less than fourteen, nor more than thirty days, after the date of the commission.

If we suppose a commission not sealed till the 20th of January, though improperly dated on the 1st of January, there could be no legal meeting of creditors take place under it, if by the term "date" we could only intend

---

(a) 2 Cowp. 720.   (b) 9 Dowl. 828.

the day inserted as the date, and not the true *date* or *giving*, that is, the issuing of the commission.

We are of opinion that the *fi. fa.* at the suit of Hooker and Henderson being in the sheriff's hands, and a levy made upon it, as we must consider, before the commission was sealed, though on the same day, the execution-creditors are entitled, as against the assignee, to the benefit of the levy; and that the sheriff has done right in retaining for their use, or paying over to them, as much of the proceeds of the sale as was necessary for satisfying their debt; and that he is consequently entitled to a verdict.

Per Cur.—Postea to the defendant.

VINCENT V. SPRAGUE.

Where a witness, being called to prove the plaintiff's case, persists in making a positive though very improbable statement disproving it, the court, in the absence of any other witness, will not allow the case to go to a jury. (MACAULAY, J., *dubitante.*)

Action for seduction of the plaintiff's daughter.

Plea: General issue.

Verdict for the defendant.

The daughter was the only witness called, and she swore that the defendant had had criminal intercourse with her on more than one occasion, but always by force, and against her will; and that she forbore to tell of it only because he promised her marriage. She persisted in this account; and refusing to declare that she had at any time consented, but repeating that the defendant succeeded only by force, the learned judge directed a verdict for the defendant.

Cameron, Sol.-Gen., moved to set aside the verdict, for misdirection, on the ground that it should have been left to the jury to weigh the probability of the witness's story, and to find for the plaintiff against her evidence, if they were satisfied that it was not in fact a case of rape.

J. W. Gwynne shewed cause, contending that as the attention of the witness was directed to the effect of her statement, and she persisted in adhering to it, she thereby put an end to the action.

ROBINSON, C. J.—I do not see that we can properly hold this verdict to be wrong on the ground of misdirection. A plaintiff must recover according to his allegations and proofs. This plaintiff sues for the seduction of his daughter; and, like other plaintiffs, was bound to prove his case. He called only his daughter, and relied on her testimony, and she was a perfectly good witness for him, if she proved what was indispensable to the support of his case.

At first she did apparently prove the case, for she began by saying that the defendant had seduced her; but when pressed to relate the particulars, she gave such evidence as must lead us to conclude that what she meant by being seduced by the defendant, was that he had had criminal intercourse with her. When desired to swear whether it was with or against her will, she stated positively that it was by force, and against her will, and would not admit by any means that she was consenting. The case then, as she stated it, was not one of seduction, but a felonious charge. It is true, that when we consider that there was a child born, and at such a time that the connection must have taken place a longer period than usual before the birth; that the girl was willing to have married him, and made no complaint of violence, so far as appeared at any time, there is great reason to doubt whether the fact was as she represented it to be in this respect; and the inconsistency between her own conduct and her evidence upon the trial is such, that it might well shake the confidence of the jury in her testimony, so that if there had been other witnesses whose evidence conflicted with hers on any particular point, they might be disposed to discredit her and believe them; but here the plaintiff brought no other evidence. He was bound to prove the civil trespass charged, by some witness, but he proved it by none; and what he now contends is, that the jury might and ought to have inferred in his favour a fact which nobody proved, and might upon her evidence alone have given damages for her seduction, while she swore that she was not seduced, and there was no other evidence to prove that she had been.

It is no doubt correct to say, that although a jury must have the whole of a witness's statement, they are not bound to believe it all, but may accept part of it as true and discredit the rest; but then, if what the witness before them has sworn not to have taken place be essential to the action, it must be proved by some one else. The jury cannot found their verdict affirming a certain fact upon the mere disbelief of the witness who denies it. It is true, that if this defendant should be indicted for a rape, on the same evidence only, the jury might probably acquit him, as they should do, if they doubted the truth of the girl's evidence.

When it is necessary to prove a fact affirmatively, in order to found a verdict upon it, some proof must be given of it; the proof cannot consist merely in calling on the jury to disbelieve all that is sworn to respecting it. If this evidence was demurred to, I cannot conceive that it could be held to support a verdict for the plaintiff.

MACAULAY, J.—I cannot say I am satisfied that the case ought not to have been left to the jury on this evidence. The plaintiff's object was to prove the seduction of his daughter. Had he, instead of an action for seduction, prosecuted the defendant for a rape, he would doubtless have been acquitted, and the plaintiff would have exposed himself to an action for a malicious prosecution; if therefore it was not a question of doubt on the evidence whether a felony had been committed or not, there could be no duty resting on the plaintiff to satisfy the end of criminal justice before seeking private satisfaction by a civil suit. If on the evidence it was doubtful, then of course the criminal charge should be first disposed of. The facts in evidence to shew seduction were, that the defendant was an inmate in the plaintiff's family, where the daughter lived, whence an intimacy was likely to arise; that such intimacy did take place, and that he paid his addresses to her as a suitor; that he had carnal knowledge of her so early as in harvest of the year 1843, which was repeated, how often not appearing, and that a child was born in December, 1844, of which he was the father; the dates shewing that this intercourse must have at all events been renewed in March, 1844, or about that period. Connected with all this is his promise to marry, the delay of the ceremony, and his subsequent marriage to another person. On such a statement, can anyone doubt the fact of seduction? It is true that in the course of her evidence the daughter said that every time he had connection with her it was done by force, and against her will; but her whole evidence must be taken together, and if so, it follows that she must misrepresent the conduct of the defendant, if she meant to assert a forcible and felonious violation of her person against her will; or she must have used the terms "force and against her will" in a milder sense, which I think she did, if stating the truth. No doubt, if she positively and distinctly charged the defendant with having ravished her, it put an end to the case; but if not, though she used language calculated to imply such a charge, it might, I should think, have been left to the jury to acquit the defendant, by reason of the felonious charge, if they saw any reason for doubt on that head, or to convict him of the seduction, if satisfied that such was the fact, and that there existed no ground for a criminal prosecution. The learned judge understood her expressly to charge a felonious violation of her person, and he of course had the best opportunity of knowing in what sense she was to be understood; still, judging from the whole of her evidence, as it appears in the notes, I should have been better satisfied had her evidence been left to the jury, but I find no case like it in the books of evidence.

JONES, J.—At the trial, the daughter of the plaintiff, the only witness in the cause, after swearing to the seduction, upon the cross-examination stated most positively that she had not assented to the criminal intercourse with the defendant, but on the contrary, that it took place against her will, and by force. In this she persisted, although the ingenuity of the counsel was exerted to make her state otherwise. She either proved seduction or a rape; persisting in a statement which proved the crime, there was no evidence to prove seduction, and I so directed the jury, and I cannot understand how I could with propriety give any other direction.

MACAULAY, J., *dubitante.*

Per Cur.—Rule discharged.

LEMESURIER V. WILLARD.

In an action on a covenant for title, where defendant pleads that he was seised, in the terms of the covenant, the onus of proof lies upon him; and plaintiff need not first give evidence of a breach, in order to entitle himself to a verdict.

The plaintiff sued upon a covenant in an indenture of bargain and sale, whereby the defendant and his wife sold and conveyed to the plaintiff certain lands in the township of Burgess, and the defendant thereby covenanted, "that he then was the true, lawful and rightful owner of the said land, and "was lawfully and rightfully seised, in his own right, of a good, sound, perfect, "absolute and indefeasible estate of inheritance, in fee simple, of and in the "premises, and without any condition, encumbrance, &c., to change or defeat "the same;" and the plaintiff assigned as a breach of the covenant, that defendant, at the time of making the indenture, was not the true, lawful and rightful owner of the said land, nor was lawfully and rightfully seised in his own right of a good, sure, perfect, absolute and indefeasible right of inheritance, in fee simple, of and in the said premises, according to the form and effect of the said indenture; and so that the defendant, although often requested, had not kept the said covenant, &c., &c.

The defendant pleaded that " he was, at the time of making the said inden-
" ture, the true, lawful and rightful owner of the said tract of land, &c., and
" was then seised lawfully and rightfully, in his own right, of a good, sure
" and perfect estate of inheritance, in fee simple, of and in the premises," and
concluded to the country.

Upon this record the parties went to trial. The plaintiff gave no evidence,
contending that it lay on the defendant, upon the issue joined, to shew himself
seised, in the terms of his plea.

The defendant, on the other hand, maintained that the plaintiff must first
give evidence of a breach, and he declined to offer any evidence himself till a
prima facie case should be established against him.

The plaintiff was allowed by the learned judge to recover, as the defendant
had failed to support the affirmative of the issue, and he recovered a verdict
for £120.

Alexander Campbell, of Kingston, moved for a new trial on the law and evidence, and for misdirection.

Benson, of Belleville, shewed cause against the rule, contending that the
onus probandi under the pleadings lay on the defendant, and cited in support
of this position, 9 Co. 60; Sheph. N. P. 1282; Raym. 14; Cro. Jac. 369;
3 T. R. 307; and McKinnon v. Burrows, decided in our own court, Easter
Term, 3 Will. IV.

Campbell supported his rule, and relied upon 7 C. & P. 289, 307, and 613;
6 C. & P. 64, 772.

ROBINSON, C. J., delivered the judgment of the court.

It was contended in the argument (and the fact is so), that this is the
identical point determined by this court in a case of McKinnon v. Burrows,
Easter Term, 3 Will. IV., and that this verdict cannot be set aside on the
ground moved, without overruling that decision. I have looked at the note
of the judgment in that case, and find that I came to the opinion which I then
expressed with hesitation and reluctance.

My inclination, I confess, is against that decision, and I should have been
glad, if upon this occasion, with the advantage of reference to later English
cases and test books, it could be clearly shewn that it was wrong; but I have
not succeeded in finding any authority that would warrant us in departing
from it.

The *onus probandi* is governed in its application by two principles:

1st. That the party who alleges the affirmative of any proposition must
prove it.

2ndly. That a party who seeks to support his case (or defence) by a particular
fact of which he is supposed to be cognizant, must prove it.

It would seem reasonable to hold that the vendee, in charging a breach, takes
upon himself the burthen of proving it; that he should be the person regarded
as advancing the affirmative, of the vendor having broken his contract; and
that the defendant, in advancing, on his side, the affirmative, that he was seised
in fee, should be looked upon as doing it only as an introduction to the
negative, or denial of the breach charged upon him; upon which principle,
the affirmative would be with the plaintiff, and the negative with the defendant, and the plaintiff must begin by shewing a breach. There could be no
hardship in this; because the plaintiff must be supposed to have a knowledge

of some defect in defendant's title, or some encumbrance, otherwise why should he harrass him with an action. Nevertheless, this argument seems not to hold; for when the plaintiff declares in covenant, for non-payment of a sum of money, which the defendant pleads he has paid, the issue is taken to be made up of the affirmation of payment on the one side, and the denial on the other; and the plaintiff's allegation that the defendant has broken his covenant, is not treated as forming the affirmative of the issue. In such a case, indeed, the proof could hardly be thrown upon him, because he could not prove the non-payment; whereas, in a case like the present, the vendee could prove the title in some one else, or shew an encumbrance.

I find no recorded authority expressly upon the point; nothing but the repetition in modern books of the old dicta and decisions upon which we held it necessary to decide as we did in McKinnon v. Burrows. These are very clear to shew that the plaintiff's declaration in this case is not more general than it may be; that he need not state an eviction, nor point to any particular defect in the title, but may assign a breach in the terms of the covenant, merely asserting that the vendor was not seised. If the defendant, in answer, should choose to set out his title, the plaintiff might reply by pointing out what was defective, or shewing title in another; but we cannot deny the defendant's right to plead as he has done; and as his plea is a simple affirmation of what the plaintiff has denied, he rightly concludes to the country, which closes the pleading; and it seems that in such a case the plaintiff is held entitled to recover, unless the defendant proves that of which the affirmative is advanced by him, and which is a fact especially within his knowledge; but I conceive it would rest with the jury not to give him damages beyond any injury which he may shew himself to have sustained.

Referring, therefore, to the authorities cited in the judgment in McKinnon v. Burrows, and which will be found collected in a note to Browning v. Wright, 2 B. & P. 14, I will add to them Lancashire v. Glover, 2 Shaw, 460; 2 Saunders, 181 (c) note; and 2 Ch. Pl., 7 East. 389, note.

Per Cur.—Rule discharged.

BALDWIN QUI TAM V. HENDERSON.

A vendor, in order to have the benefit of the exception under the statute 32 Hen. VIII. ch. 9, must *really and in truth* claim under some person in possession a year before the bargain made: a mere pretended, fraudulent claim, under a person of whom *in fact* the vendor knew nothing, and with whom he had *in truth* no privity, will not satisfy the statute.

In an action for the sale of land under this Act, the court will refuse a new trial merely on the ground that no direct evidence was given as to the value of the property; the situation and condition of the land having been proved, and the sum acknowledged to have been paid for the land in the deed by the defendant being considered as evidence of the value to go to the jury.

This action was brought on the statute 32 Henry VIII. ch. 9, to recover a penalty for purchasing the pretended right of one Abel Conat to 400 acres of land in the township of York. It was averred, as the statute required, that "neither the said Abel Conat, nor any of his ancestors, nor any other person or "persons by whom he then claimed the said premises with the appurtenances, "had been in possession of the same, nor of the reversion or remainder thereof, "nor taken the rents or profits thereof, by the space of one whole year next "before the aforesaid bargain made;" and that the defendant well knew the same, and that he also well knew that the said Abel Conat had only a pretended right to the said lands.

The case was tried at Toronto; and it was objected that there was not sufficient evidence that the defendant, at the time of his purchasing the pretended right, knew that neither the vendor nor "any person by whom *he* then claimed "the premises had been in possession of the same, nor taken the rents or profits "thereof, by the space of one whole year next before the bargain made," &c.

It was further objected, after the plaintiff's case was closed, that he had given no evidence of the value of the estate, and so the jury had nothing before them to shew what ought to be the amount of the penalty.

Alexander Phillpotts moved for a new trial, on the law and evidence and for misdirection, and in arrest of judgment.

A. Wilson shewed cause against the rule, and relied upon 5 T. R. 19; 3 Taunt. 232; Peake's U. P. C. 163; 1 Stark. Rep. 117.

Phillpotts, in support of the rule, cited Cro. Car. 233; 1 Hawkins, P. C. 472; Co. Litt. 369.

ROBINSON, C. J.—With respect to the first objection, it appeared to me that the evidence was strong and perfectly sufficient, if the jury gave credit to it, to shew that the defendant when he made the purchase knew that the vendor (A. Conat) was not at the time, and had not been for the year next before that time, in possession of the estate, by himself, or his tenants or servants, or in any manner, actually or constructively; but that, on the contrary, he was himself residing in another part of the country, and not receiving the rents and profits,—while there were other persons in actual possession, living upon and cultivating the lands, which they held under no privity with Conat, or with any person under whom Conat claimed. It was indeed ingeniously argued at the trial, and has been here again insisted upon, that, as Conat professed to hold under a deed made to him by the heir of one Smeethman, the original grantee of the crown, and as the persons in possession were shewn to have been holding as tenants, with the permission of Mr. Baldwin, the agent of Smeethman, he came in that way within the exception in the statute, because those under whom he claimed (namely, Smeethman and his ancestor) had been for the year next before the making of the deed in possession thereof by their tenants; but it was too clear on the evidence to admit of any reasonable doubt, that Conat the vendor was setting up a mere sham conveyance from some unknown person whom he had procured to sign it as the heir of Smeethman; and I told the jury that if they entertained the same conviction, it would be an absurd and shameful evasion of the law to look upon him as in fact claiming under Smeethman's heir, and so entitled to the exception in the statute by reason of the possession held under the agent of Smeethman's heir. I consider the statute undoubtedly to mean that the vendor must really and in truth claim under some person who has been in possession, in order to have the benefit of the exception. His fraudulently pretending to claim under a person of whom in fact he knew nothing, and with whom he had in truth no privity, could be of no consequence. The jury could have no doubt about the fact, and found a verdict for the plaintiff for a penalty of £500, taking that to be the value of the land.

My brothers take the same view of this point. It is in fact as flagitious a case of buying up a pretended right as can well be imagined; and if the old statute 32 Henry VIII. ch. 9, must be admitted to be still in force, though almost fallen into disuse in England, I do not know that a plainer case for applying its provisions can ever present itself. It is certainly much to be desired that the legislature would apply some more convenient and suitable remedy to the case; but we have only to determine upon the law as it stands; and we have had occasion in the case of Beasly v. Cahill, determined not long ago in this court, to express the opinion that we cannot refuse to act upon the 32 Henry VIII. as binding, being adopted with the rest of the law of England by our legislature.

The objection that no evidence was given upon the trial of the actual value of the estate purchased, was urged in time to entitle the defendant to the benefit of it, if it ought to succeed. When it was made, the plaintiff desired to be allowed to repair the omission by calling witnesses then to prove the value. I have no doubt but I could have granted the indulgence, and that the testimony then given would have been legally admitted, if in my discretion I had thought it right to admit it at that stage. Perhaps I should have received it, as it was a mere inadvertent omission; but I thought it better not to do so in a prosecution of this nature, by an informer for a penalty. Sometimes persons render themselves liable to penalties without corrupt intentions, and there may be hard cases of this kind under this statute, or under others. We should on such occasions feel it right to leave the plaintiff to make out his title to a penalty without any special indulgence of the court, and hold him to proceed strictly. To allow a plaintiff to call new evidence after he has formally closed his case and the defendant has moved the exception, is certainly an indulgence; and it would not, as I think, be a very clear course for a judge to be more or less indulgent in any such case, according to the view which he may happen to take of the merits of each particular case while it is still before the jury.

I considered that I might be creating a precedent that would embarrass myself at least on some future occasion, and therefore would not let the plaintiff go again into his case by calling new evidence. I was the less disposed to allow it because it did not seem to me that the case was fatally defective as it stood. The jury heard the premises described; the estate consisted of 400 acres of land in the same township that the court was sitting in; it was proved that it was in part improved; and there could be no one of the jury who did not know that the land must be worth more than £500, which they adopted as its value. They were led, I dare say, to adopt that sum by my reminding them that in the conveyance put in by the defendant that sum was stated as the amount paid by him for the land, which supplied some evidence of its value, as it would not be reasonable to infer that he gave more for it than he considered it to be worth. There was no evidence of any bargain being concluded for the land before the day on which the deed was given; and it was shewn that just before the 10th July, when it was executed, the defendant was hesitating about concluding the purchase, as he well might under the circumstances. The sum, therefore, which he was stated in the deed to have paid, might be, in fairness to the defendant, taken as the value, at the time when the estate was "by "him bought or taken," which is the language of the statute.

It is not attempted to shew that the estate is worth less than £500; and, if we were to grant a new trial, it is impossible that there could be any difficulty in proving it to be worth considerably more. Still the defendant would be entitled perhaps to have a new trial, as he pressed it, if we could say that under the circumstances the jury were not warranted in giving any value to the land; but I am of opinion that we cannot hold that, and that therefore the rule should be discharged.

MACAULAY, J.—There seems to be evidence sufficient to go to the jury to shew that the defendant knew his vendor (Conat) had not been in possession for the year preceding, and at the time of the sale of his pretended right, and that he also knew it was but a pretended right.

As to value, in addition to the local situation and quantity of the lands, and the general state of the improvements thereon, there was the admitted consideration as between defendant and his vendor, as stated in the deed of sale, which (for all that appears) shews the time of the bargain and the price agreed on, and as against defendant is evidence of value. The case of The King and Barnes v. Hill and Windsor (a) is not in point so much as was supposed at the argument. There it was a motion in arrest of judgment for a defect in the declaration, not in the proof, and it arose in this way: it was alleged that Hill, not being seised, &c., on the 31st October, 4 Car., *conveyed* the *tenements*, &c., to Windsor; and for *confirmation* of the said conveyance, the said Hill and his wife, by *fine*, Hilary, 4 Car., granted the said tenements, &c., to Windsor. And the third objection made was because the value of the land at the *time* of the *fine* was £800; and plaintiff did not shew what was its value at the time of the *bargain*; and it might be they were of greater value at the time of the fine than at the *grant*; and that the *grant* of them was the offence. It is said, that for the several defaults urged, the court conceived the information to be ill and the verdict ill, *but they would advise thereupon*.

Here it is a point of evidence, and the only question is whether the consideration stated in the deed of sale, *grant* or *bargain*, imports the value sufficiently for the jury to consider, as upon the admission of the parties thereto in connection with the other evidence; and I think it does. Had the jury placed a higher value upon the premises than the defendant has done, it would be perhaps a fair case for relief. But that is not so; nor is the value placed upon them by the jury objected to as excessive.

JONES, J., concurred.   *Per Cur.*—Rule discharged.

WEST v. BOWN (ROBERT R.)

A party endorsing his name on the back of a note not negotiable, or if negotiable, *not endorsed* by the payee, cannot be sued as endorsee by the payee.

The plaintiff declared in *assumpsit* on a note as made by one J. Y. Bown, payable to the plaintiff, and that the defendant endorsed the same to the plaintiff, &c.

(a) Cro. Car. 233.

Demurrer : that the plaintiff did not shew in his declaration any right of action against the defendant, the note being payable to plaintiff and not to his order, and consequently not a negotiable instrument.

W. H. Blake for demurrer.—The declaration is bad—a payee cannot sue a defendant as endorser of a note not negotiable.—Thew v. Adams (*a*). There is no authority to shew that a note not made payable to bearer or order can be endorsed.

The Hon. *R. B. Sullivan* contra, relied upon Scott v. Douglass (*b*), and that the defendant could not set up his want of authority to endorse.—2 B. N. C. 249 ; 1 C. M. & R. 439 ; Byles on Bills, 108.

ROBINSON, C. J.—It is impossible to hold that any right of action is stated in this declaration, unless we can hold that any one, by endorsing a note not negotiable made payable to another, renders himself liable to that other, and may be sued as an endorser.

This action is not against Robert R. Bown as a new maker of the note, independent of any right to be derived through the payee. It is an action by the payee against the defendant as endorser upon a note not negotiable, and yet treating the defendant as endorser. We have never decided anything in this court that would seem to support such an action, nor can anything be found in English cases to warrant it. Thew v. Adams in this court, decided in 1838, was the case of the payee of a negotiable note, suing the endorser who had put his name on the back of it, though the payee himself had not endorsed; and suing him as endorser, we held that he could not recover.

If Hill v. Lewis (*c*), which is recognized by Mr. Justice Bayley in his Treatise on Bills, page 98, would sanction, under such circumstances, an action by this plaintiff against this defendant, it could only be as by charging him in another form, not as the endorser of a note not negotiable.

The cases of Gwinnell v. Herbert (*d*), Penney v. Innes (*e*); and Plymly v. Wesley (*f*), do certainly not warrant this action. but the contrary, and especially the observations of Patterson, J., in Gwinnell v. Herbert.

MACAULAY, J.—This case is similar to Thew v. Adams, in which, after the best consideration, I could not find that a party endorsing his name on the back of a promissory note not negotiable, or if so, not endorsed by the payee, could be made responsible to the payee as a maker, or endorser, or guarantor. Here it is sought to charge him as an endorser to the payee—a thing inconsistent in itself.—JONES, J., concurred.

Per Cur.—Judgment for defendant on demurrer.

WEST v. BOWN (J. Y.)

To an action by the payee against the maker of a note, the defendant pleaded that the note was obtained by fraud, *and* without consideration. *Held*, on special demurrer, plea bad for duplicity.

Assumpsit, by the plaintiff as payee, against the defendant as maker of a promissory note.

(*a*) Hilary Term, 3 Vic. ; 5 A. & E. 436.
(*b*) Mich. Term, 6 & 7 Will. IV , and 1 Salk. 132.
(*c*) Salk. 132.   (*d*) 5 A. & E. 436.
(*e*) 1 C. M. & R. 439.   (*f*) 2 Scott, N. C. 249.

Plea.—That the note was obtained by fraud, covin and misrepresentation, *and* without any value or consideration from the plaintiff to the defendant for making the same, or for his paying the same or any part thereof.

Demurrer.—That the said plea is double.

The Hon. *R. B. Sullivan*, for the demurrer, cited 13 M. & W. 651; 4 Bing. N. C. 658; 2 M. & G. 347; 8 Dowl. 87; 1 Dowl. N. S. 458; 2 G. & D. 386.

W. H. Blake, contra, relied upon the forms in 3 Ch. Pleading, 6th Ed., p. 832, as being exactly similar. He also cited 13 M. & W. 34; 1 Tyr. & Gr. 181.

ROBINSON, C. J.—It is objected that the first plea is bad for duplicity. The defendant being sued as maker of a promissory note, made payable to the plaintiff, pleads that the note was obtained from him by the plaintiff by fraud, covin and misrepresentation, practised upon him by the plaintiff, and without any value or consideration given by the plaintiff to him for the making of the note. It is objected upon special demurrer that this plea is bad for duplicity; and I think it is. The cases decided in England of Stephens v. Underwood (*d*), and Leaf v. Robson (*b*), are not distinguishable from this.

That part of this plea which states that there was no consideration would not be a good defence if it stood alone and were specially demurred to, because it ought to state how it came to be given in order to shew that it is invalid for want of consideration (*c*). But upon a general demurrer the plea would be good, as I apprehend; at any rate, it is not only in cases where two defences are well pleaded that the objection of duplicity applies. I am of opinion that the plaintiff must have judgment on the demurrer.

MACAULAY, J.—I find forms in the books similar to the present plea, and cases in which similar pleas have been pleaded without exception; but the objection is here made on special demurrer, and the case of Stephens v. Underwood (*d*), seems expressly in point. There duress of imprisonment and want of consideration were pleaded together, and the plea was held double. The use of this form has, I suppose, arisen from its being required that in pleas for want of consideration it should appear on what ground there was such want; as that the instrument was given for the accommodation of the party, or that the consideration had entirely failed, or the like: the two allegations, of want of consideration, and the ground thereof, together constituting one defence. But here the allegations include two defences: first, fraud; and, secondly, want of consideration. Either would establish a full defence, viz., fraud, though there was consideration, or want of consideration, though there was no fraud; whereas, when the plea merely denies consideration on a ground alleged, the defendant is held to prove the absence of consideration on the ground stated. Under a plea of accommodation, and no consideration, he could not prove failure of the absence of consideration on a different ground. This I take to be the distinction; and, though sanctioned by the forms and

---

(*a*) 4 Bing. N. C. 653.   (*b*) 13 M. & W. 651.
(*c*) 1 Dowl. N. C. 458; 1 B. N. C. 267; 5 M. & S. 97; 3 Dowl. 453.
(*d*) 4 Bing. N. C. 655.

cases in which like pleas have passed without exception, and been traversed, I cannot but think it bad for duplicity on special demurrer.

JONES. J., concurred.   *Per Cur.*—Judgment for plaintiff on demurrer.

DOE DEM. SULLIVAN V. READ.

In an action of ejectment against a defendant pretending no title in himself, *prima facie* evidence is sufficient to prove that a party through whom the lessor of the plaintiff claims is heir-at-law to the title: no express evidence of the fact is necessary, till the presumption in favour of the title has been repelled.

A party cannot obtain a new trial on the ground that an incompetent witness has been examined against him, unless he took the objection to his incompetency at the trial.

Ejectment for land in the township of Toronto.

The lessor of the plaintiff claimed under a deed made by one John Kenney, as heir of his uncle, John Kenney, the grantor of the crown.

The uncle, John Kenney, died in this province, intestate, leaving his widow, Julia Kenney, who has since intermarried with Daniel Sullivan. They had no issue, and John Kenney, nephew of the said John Kenney, being a poor and illiterate man, resident in Ireland, had made a deed as his heir-at-law to the widow of his late uncle. The action was brought upon that title. The proof of heirship consisted in evidence taken in Ireland under a commission from several members of the family.

They all agree in swearing that John Kenney, the grantee of the crown, was the son of John Kenney, now dead; that he had several brothers, of whom Thomas Kenney, now dead, was the eldest; that this Thomas Kenney left several children, who are yet surviving, and they named them thus: John, Mary, Thomas, Michael and Peg; not saying expressly that John was the eldest, but naming him first in order. It was this John who, as heir-at-law, had made the deed in question. He was examined himself as a witness, and swore expressly that he was the eldest of the family.

Read, the defendant, for all that appeared, was a stranger to the title, as he was to the family.

The jury, under this evidence, found John Kenney to be the heir-at-law.

J. Duggan moved to set aside the verdict upon the law and evidence and for misdirection. He objected that John Kenney, having given a covenant for title, was an incompetent witness; and that without his evidence there was no positive testimony to shew the title in John Kenney as heir-at-law.

A. Wilson shewed cause, contending that the verdict could not be disturbed. There was no attempt at the trial, or since by affidavit, to throw doubt upon the fact of John Kenney being the heir-at-law, and no objection was made at the trial to Kenney as an incompetent witness. Besides, the defendant set up no claim to the land himself—he was not a person disputing the inheritance; and being a stranger to the title, the proof of heirship was not required to be given with the same degree of certainty as in the case of a contested title.

ROBINSON, C. J.—I am of opinion that the verdict should stand. If the evidence of John Kenney were to be wholly set aside, it is still proved by others that he is the son of the eldest brother of the deceased, and as such must be the heir, unless another son of the same brother is entitled to be preferred to him as being older; no other son is described as the elder brother by any witness who was examined, nor is it pretended that he is, though that could easily be shewn if the fact were so. We are asked to set aside this verdict, because he perhaps may be. The circumstance that the witnesses who enumerate the children of Thomas Kenney, place John the first on the list, is some evidence to the contrary. If there is a nearer heir in fact, he has only to bring an ejectment and shew his title. The present defendant sets up no title by inheritance or otherwise. It is obvious, that any seeming defect in the evidence of pedigree merely arose from the circumstance that neither party asked these witnesses to name the children in the order of their birth; they were requested to do so with respect to the children of the grandfather, but the request was not repeated in the interrogatory respecting the children of Thomas. No one, however, who reads the whole of the questions and answers, can have any doubt that the witnesses mean in fact to represent John as the oldest son of Thomas Kenney. He himself swears expressly that he is, and that is not contradicted; and his evidence was read without exception at the trial.

MACAULAY, J.—It appears to me, on reading the commission, that there was sufficient evidence to go to the jury, exclusive of that of John Kenney, the immediate grantor of the lessor of the plaintiff, and nephew of the grantee of the crown. The sixth interrogatory inquires whether John Kenney, the grantee, had brothers and sisters; and if so, their names, and the order of their birth, and times of death, &c. The seventh inquires whether any of the said brothers or sisters were married; and if so, their issues, &c. The fifth inquires as to the father and mother of John Kenney, the grantee. James Sugue says, the said John Kenney had brothers and sisters, but he only knew four, viz., Thomas and three others; that he did not know the order of their birth, *save* that *Thomas* was the eldest, and died nine or ten years ago; that the said Thomas was married, and left *a son* named *John*, whom he knew, and other children, whom he did not know, but who are living; that the said John Kenney is the nephew of John Kenney, the grantor.

Marian Sugue says, that John Kenney was the father of John Kenney, deceased, and Margaret Neil, his mother, both dead, when he died.

To the sixth interrogatory, that the said John Kenney, meaning the grantee, had brothers and sisters, viz., Thomas and others; that Thomas died ten or eleven years ago, and was married to Mary Crowly, and that Thomas had children, of whom *John*, Peg and Michael are the survivors.

I think this evidence is sufficient to shew *prima facie* that John, the nephew, is the oldest son and heir of Thomas, the brother of John, the grantee (a). Besides, the evidence of John Kenney, the nephew, or that he had covenanted for title to the lessor of the plaintiff, was not objected to at the trial, and his evidence is express on the subject of his own right as heir of Thomas, heir of John, deceased, grantee of the crown.

(a) See 7 Bing. 346; Str. 445; 2 Roll. Ab. 685.

JONES, J.—The testimony of John Kenney, junior, the grantor in the deed under which the lessor of the plaintiff claims, proves the right of the plaintiff to recover, and there is other evidence to establish his right. It is now objected that Kenney's testimony was inadmissible, his evidence going to support his own deed containing covenants for title: this objection to his interest is too late; it should have been taken at the trial. But if his testimony were rejected, I cannot say that the verdict is wrong. The lessor of the plaintiff is clearly entitled, unless there is a person more nearly related to the intestate; and under such circumstances, I think that as against a wrongdoer he is entitled to recover. Having shewn his relationship, he was entitled to succeed unless the defendant could shew that another had a better right: when that better right is shewn, the person so entitled can recover from the lessor of the plaintiff. But I have no reason to doubt the right of the lessor of the plaintiff in this action. *Per Cur.*—Rule discharged.

GATES V. TINNING.

The proprietor of a race-course is not responsible for the purse run for, unless upon clear proof of an express undertaking to that effect.

A winner at a horse-race has no right to recover back his entrance-money, because the purse has not been paid over to him.

The plaintiff sued in *assumpsit*, to recover from the defendant, the proprietor of a race-course, a turf-club purse of £75, run for and won by the plaintiff's horse; and which the plaintiff averred that the defendant, as proprietor of the course, had, before the race was run, engaged to pay to the winner.

There were several special counts in the declaration, all claiming the payment of the club purse of £75, laying the undertaking in different ways and upon different considerations, and averring the payment of £5 entrance money by the plaintiff upon entering his horse for the race, as one of the candidates, on which he was to be allowed to run for the purse, and as part of the consideration for defendant's undertaking to pay the £75 if plaintiff's horse should win the race.

There was no special count claiming a return of the entrance-money; but there were common counts for money had and received and for money paid.

The defendant pleaded the general issue.

At the trial, evidence was given of the facts on which the plaintiff grounded his claim, and by consent a verdict for the plaintiff was recorded for £75, subject to the opinion of the court whether he had shewn a case which entitled him to recover.

A printed advertisement was put in at the trial, as that upon which the race was run (in June, 1845), in which there was this notice: "The turf-club "purse of £75, entrance £5 each, for all horses; turf-club weights; three-mile "heats."

This advertisement was signed by the defendant as proprietor.

W. H. *Blake* obtained a rule *nisi* for a nonsuit, or a verdict to be entered for the defendant, on the leave reserved at the trial.

D. G. Miller shewed cause. He contended that there was ample proof to shew an express contract by the defendant, as proprietor of the race-course, to pay the purse; that the £5 entrance-money was a good consideration for such promise; and that, at all events, whether the plaintiff was entitled to the £75 or not, he could recover back the £5 on the common money counts.

Blake, in support of his rule, denied that any contract upon a sufficient consideration was made with any one; that at the utmost, a mere promise to the stewards was shewn, which was afterwards retracted; that the advertisement contained the only terms the public were to look to; and that though there might be a contradiction in the evidence as to the fact of a promise by the defendant to pay the purse, there was nothing to prove a legal valid contract. He also contended that the £5 entrance-money could not be recovered back; it was not money run for, but a sum contributed by each party for permission to run the race, which privilege had been made use of. Having received value for the £5, there could be no claim for its return. He cited 3 M. & G.; 5 Jurist, 508; 4 M. & G. 5; 2 M. & W. 369; 1 Jurist, 242; 7 Price, 540. He also objected that nothing had been said about the entrance-money at the trial.

ROBINSON, C. J., delivered the judgment of the court.—The questions are, 1st. Does the evidence supply proof of an *assumpsit* by the defendant to the plaintiff to pay him £75 if he should win the race? 2nd. If so, was the promise made in a manner and upon a consideration that gives this plaintiff a right to sue upon it? and 3rd. If the plaintiff cannot recover for the amount of the stakes, can he maintain his action for a return of the £5 entrance-money paid by himself?

We are of opinion that the plaintiff cannot recover for either of the alleged causes of action. The race must be taken to have been run upon the conditions and understanding expressed in the printed advertisement, which was the final declaration made to the public of the terms, after the discussions which were said to have taken place at a previous meeting. There is certainly nothing in the printed hand-bill which can make the defendant liable for the amount of the purse. He was not stake-holder: his merely being proprietor of the course would not make him responsible for any of the stakes, though an express undertaking to see them paid might have done so. But no such undertaking was proved, at least not satisfactorily.

There was some evidence that the defendant had said, at a public meeting called for settling preliminaries, that he would see all stakes paid; but this was contradicted by other evidence. The plaintiff was not shewn to have been at that meeting, nor to have had any knowledge of defendant having made such a promise; and the printed advertisement which came out afterwards is the only safe evidence of what the final understanding was.

With respect to the claim to recover back the plaintiff's entrance-money, under the count for money had and received, there is, in our opinion, no principle on which it can be supported.

It was not claimed upon the trial; it was not a sum contributed, which was to go to the winner; but was the consideration paid by each person whose horse was entered, for permission to run the race. The plaintiff used the privilege for which he paid, and has therefore received value for his entrance-money. He acquired by it the right, as winner, to receive the purse, or to sue for it, in case of non-payment, whatever person he may find to be responsible. We cannot hold that he has a right to sue for his entrance-money back, because, being the winner, he has, from some cause, been disappointed in receiving the stake. *Per Cur.*—Rule absolute.

DOE DEM. DISSETT V. McLEOD.

It is not necessary, under the statute 43 George III. ch. 1, that there should be a year between the date and return of a writ of *venditioni exponas* against lands.

The deed given by the sheriff after a sale of lands under a *fi. fa.*, whereby he conveys all the estate and interest of the debtor, is not to be considered as a mere deed of "release," in the strict sense of the term.

Any want of regularity in giving public notice of an adjourned sale under a *fi. fa.* will not invalidate the sale, where the debtor attended the sale, by his agent, and afterwards ratified what had been done.

Ejectment for Lot 37, in the village of Portsmouth, part of the broken front of the west half of Lot 19, in the 1st concession of Kingston.

Plaintiff made title as assignee of a purchaser at sheriff's sale under a *fi. fa.*, in the suit of McGlashan v. F. Logan and John McLeod.

At the trial, an exemplification of the judgment was produced, and of the record of award and return of *fi. fa.* against goods, and of award of *fi. fa,* against lands, returnable on first day of Michaelmas Term, 1844; to which the sheriff returned, lands seized and remaining unsold for want of buyers; whereupon a *venditioni exponas* was awarded, and the lands were sold to Alexander Campbell, Esq., who sold soon after to the lessor of the plaintiff.

In one respect the sale was alleged to have taken place under circumstances which made it unfair towards the execution debtor, as they did not afford proper notice of the intended sale. It was proved that the sale had been several times postponed at the request of one of the defendants in the *fi. fa.*, and at length it was agreed, that on a Saturday, at a certain hour, if the plaintiff in the cause was not in the meantime satisfied, the land should be sold.

The plaintiff in the cause remained unpaid on that day, but for some reason not explained, the sale did not take place then, but on the following Monday, either upon a verbal notice, or a notice put up in the sheriff's office. The lot, said to be worth £30 or £40, was then sold for £9; a gentleman of the profession attending on the part of the defendant, at whose request the sheriff, after selling this and several other small parcels of land, stopped the sale, on his undertaking to pay the balance the next day, which he did.

The defendant was on the lot at time of the sale, and had been for a year before, as tenant to F. Logan and J. McLeod, according to his own declaration after the sale by the sheriff.

1st. The defendant objected at the trial, that the *ven. exp.* was tested the first day, and returnable on the last of the same term, whereas there should have been a year between *teste* and return, according to the statute 43 Geo. III. ch. 1.

2ndly. That the deed from the purchaser at sheriff's sale to the lessor of the plaintiff being a mere quit claim, a release of all his interest could convey nothing to the lessor of the plaintiff, who had no estate for the release to operate upon, nor even possession, the defendant being at that time in possession.

3rdly. That the sale was void, for want of a regular postponement, or notice of the sale.

The learned judge allowed the plaintiff to recover, reserving leave to the defendant to move on these objections in *banc*.

Thomas Kirkpatrick, of Kingston, moved for a nonsuit or a new trial, on the law and evidence, for misdirection, and for the admission of improper evidence. He urged the several objections which had been previously taken at the trial, and contended that Mr. Campbell, the purchaser under the sheriff's deed, was an incompetent witness, upon the ground that he had covenanted for a good title, the words "bargain and sell" in his deed to the lessor of the plaintiff implying a covenant, though none was expressed in the deed. He cited 15 E. R. 530; Com. Dig. Cov. A. 4.

Alex. Campbell, of Kingston, shewed cause, and relied upon Doe Spafford v. Brown et al. in our court, E. Term, 3 Will. IV. ; 4 M. & W. 468. As to a year not having elapsed between the *teste* and return of the writ of *venditioni exponas*, he contended that this writ was clearly but a continuation of the *fi. fa.*, and that there could be no necessity therefore for a year between its *teste* and return.

ROBINSON, C. J., delivered the judgment of the court.

We are of opinion that there is no necessity that a year should intervene between the *teste* and return of a writ of *venditioni exponas* to sell lands. The defendant in this case had the advantage of the delay which our statute directs, by the time which elapsed between the *teste* and return of the *fi. fa.*, which conformed to the statute, and of which the writ of *venditioni exponas* is to be regarded as a mere continuation, the two together making but one execution. The same point has been already determined in this court. With regard to the sheriff's deed being a mere release, and on that account incapable of operating, for the want of some previous estate in the grantee, the deed is more than a mere release; it is a conveyance of all the debtor's right and interest in the land, in the usual form of sheriff's deeds. Its containing the words "release," and "quit claim," coupled with words of grant, does not necessarily confine the instrument to the operation of a release; the other words will also have their effect. As to the objection that the land was sold on a day of which a formal notice had not been regularly given, it is not clearly shewn that there was not a public advertisement of the postponed sale. But the purchaser's title could not be affected by an inquiry now into the point of notice, when it is shewn that the sale was in fact attended by a gentleman employed by the debtor for that purpose, at whose request the sale of this and other property was made, and the proceedings so far acquiesced in and confirmed, that on the following day the balance of the execution, remaining unpaid above the proceeds of these sales, was finally settled.

Per Cur.—Rule discharged.

McLaren v. Cook et al.

A proprietor of land on a stream has a right to the use of the water flowing past him in its natural course, undiminished in quantity and quality; and nothing short of a grant or a twenty years' user (which presumes a grant) of the water in a particular way and for a special purpose, can entitle some one proprietor on a stream, in violation of this common right of all, *injuriously to divert or pen back* the water from or upon proprietors living above or below him on the stream.

Where at the time of making a dam the plaintiff sustains no injury, but afterwards, having built a mill, he suffers real damage by the dam penning back the water upon the mill, he has no right of action against those who built the dam—he can only sue those who are *continuing* the dam at the time of the injury.

The plaintiff declared in case for obstructing his mill, by backing water upon it.

The declaration stated that before and at the time of the injury the plaintiff was possessed of a grist mill on the river Castor, in the township of Osgoode, and of right ought to have enjoyed the benefit of the river or water-course for the supplying his mill with water, and that the water-course ought of right to have run and flowed from the mill of the plaintiff through divers lands in the said district, without being penned back upon and obstructing the plaintiff's mill, and free from obstruction by any person whatever; yet that the defendants, well knowing, &c., on the 1st of August, 1845, wrongfully erected a dam in and across the said river, below the plaintiff's mill, and wrongfully continued, &c., and thereby injuriously *obstructed* and *diverted* the usual and proper course of the water of the said river, whereby it ran and flowed out of its usual course, and became and was penned back upon the mill of the plaintiff, and prevented it from working, &c.

The 2nd count was for overflowing the plaintiff's land, and it charged that the defendants erected and continued a dam, whereby they injuriously obstructed and diverted the usual and proper course of the water, so that it *ran and overflowed* out of its usual course and channel, *upon the plaintiff's land*, &c.

The defendants pleaded, 1st, the general issue; 2ndly, to the 1st count, the plaintiff not possessed of the mill; 3rdly, to the 1st count, denied the right of the plaintiff to have the water flow past his mill in its usual course, without being penned back or obstructed; 4thly, to 2nd count, that the plaintiff was not possessed of the close in manner and form, &c.

The case was tried by a special jury, and a verdict given for plaintiff, £100 damages.

Philip Vankoughnet moved for a new trial on the law and evidence, for misdirection, and for excessive damages. He contended that the plaintiff could not recover upon the first count, because it was not proved that he had the enjoyment and possession of the mill. The injury, as stated in the first count, was clearly such as could only be an injury to the *plaintiff's* possession (*a*); and the son, and not the plaintiff, being proved to be the beneficial owner, he was the party who ought to have brought the action. It was also shewn in evidence that the gates, and not the dam, as alleged in the declaration, occasioned the injury: this, he submitted, was a fatal variance (*b*). He also contended that four of the defendants were merely workmen employed in erecting

---

(*a*) 2 B. & C. 910.   (*b*) 6 Price, 1; 5 Taunt. 534.

the dam, and not answerable for the use of it. At all events, they would not be liable if the plaintiff, *at the time of the building of the dam,* had not erected the mill alleged to have been injured in the declaration; and it was shewn that the mill was not *then* in existence. Upon the last ground he submitted with confidence that the verdict must be set aside.

J. H. Hagarty shewed cause.—He contended that, though it might be said upon the evidence that the son had apparently the enjoyment of the mill, yet it was clearly proved that the father had the title to the property, and no evidence was adduced to shew that the son had any estate in the land for a term of years or otherwise, or that he was occupying the mill for his own use or benefit; he might, for all that appeared, be the mere agent or servant of his father. In the absence, therefore, of any proof of title in the son, the title of the plaintiff, he submitted, ought to prevail, to establish a right of action under the first count. He contended that the workmen were all liable, being the servants of the principal, Cook. He also submitted that the damages, considering the wilful conduct of Cook, the owner of the mill below, in obstructing the use of a grist mill for months, were not excessive; the injury occasioned may have been no more than compensated by the verdict the jury had given.

ROBINSON, C. J.—With respect to the grounds on which damages are claimed in this action, I am of opinion that the mere fact of the defendant having put his mill in operation lower down the stream, and thereby appropriated the water, as it flowed past him, to the special purpose of his mill, did not give him a right to pen back the water upon the plaintiff living higher up the stream; and that although the plaintiff, at the time when the obstruction began, had not erected his mill, and had not then occasion for the use of the water for the turning of his mill, yet when he did, not long afterwards, erect a mill higher up the stream, and found the wheels obstructed by the defendant's dam penning back the water, he could then bring an action for the damage which he received by the act of the defendant in obstructing the flow of the water in its natural course, although such damage arose by the plaintiff's applying the water to a special purpose, inconsistent with the defendant's enjoyment of it for a similar purpose, to which the defendant had applied it. In other words, I conceive the principle to be settled, that nothing short of a grant, or use for such length of time as will support the presumption of a grant, will entitle the proprietor of land on a stream to divert or *pen* back the water in such a manner as to occasion damage to those living above or below in the same stream, by disabling them from making any special use or appropriation of the water which would have been in their power, if the stream had been allowed to flow in its natural course. I do not say that they can bring their action for the loss of a possible privilege merely which they have not proceeded to use, but that when they have erected their mills or other works, and suffer damage by the water being diverted or obstructed, then their right of action accrues. The cases of Bealey v. Shaw, 6 E. 213; Howard v. Wright, 1 S. & T. 190; and Mason v. Hill, 3 B. & Ad. 304; 5 B. & Ad. 1, sustain this doctrine. It applies only to the injury to the plaintiff's mills, which is the principal cause of action. Some injury was proved at the trial from the plaintiff's land being overflowed, and of the right to recover for that injury there could be no question, but it was trifling in its extent.

An objection is taken which would apply to both causes of action—namely, that Peter McLaren, and not this plaintiff (his father), appeared by the evidence to be the person entitled to damages for the injury. It certainly was proved that Peter McLaren was the person using and apparently enjoying the mill, as well as the person asserting his right to the water, and taking the active part in forbidding the defendant to erect the dam ; but, on the other hand, the title to the property was shewn to be in this plaintiff, and it was not shewn that Peter McLaren had any estate in the land for a term of years or otherwise, or that he was occupying the mill for his own use or benefit. He certainly acted as the beneficial occupant, but he was not proved to have been so ; in fact, for all that appeared, he may have been merely acting as the agent or servant of his father, the plaintiff. It is not now shewn by affidavit that he was not; and therefore I think we should not interfere with the verdict on that ground.

That the damages are excessive has been another ground of moving. There does not appear in the evidence any sufficient materials for a computation leading to any sum; but considering that Cook, the principal defendant, proceeded wilfully in deliberate defiance of the plaintiff's rights, and that the obstructing the use of a grist mill for some months may very probably have occasioned an injury to that amount, the case does not call upon us to interfere as regards the amount of damages ; for we cannot say that they are manifestly excessive.

But we cannot properly, in my opinion, allow the verdict to stand, for this reason, that four of the defendants certainly, against whom this verdict is rendered for backing water on the plaintiff's mill, are not legally chargeable with that damage. They were merely employed as workmen in building the dam across the river, and at a time when this damage of which the plaintiff complains could not have accrued, because he had no mill there then receiving injury from the back-water. When he had placed his mill there, and made the appropriation of the water and found his free use of it obstructed or impeded, then it was that his injury commenced; but none except Cook, the owner of the mill below, who had the control of the gates in the dam, and by the use he made of it actually backed the water, can be said to have occasioned the injury to the plaintiff. The mere building a dam in or across the river gave no right of action to the plaintiff, till he received from it the damage of which he complains. Those who penned back the water after that, by making or continuing the dam, and thereby injuring the plaintiff's mill, are liable under the first count, but none others. This does not seem, however, to have been objected to at the trial.

MACAULAY, J., and JONES, J., concurred.

Per Cur.—New trial, on payment of costs.

NUGENT V. CAMPBELL AND HIS WIFE, ADMINISTRATRIX OF
JOHN TAYLOR, DECEASED.

Under the statute 5 Geo. II. ch. 7, real estate in the colonies is liable to satisfy a judgment *for damages in an action of covenant.*

Plaintiff sued in covenant on an indenture dated 18th January, 1833, whereby Taylor bargained and sold to plaintiff certain lands, and covenanted that at the time of making the deed he was lawfully seised in fee simple, and had good right to convey; that the lands were free from encumbrances; that plaintiff should quietly enjoy, &c.; and that he Taylor would warrant and assure the same to plaintiff, his heirs and assigns, for ever.

Plaintiff then averred that at the time of making the indenture there were 200 apple trees growing on the said lands, bearing fruit; and which said premises, with the appurtenances, at the time of the sale, were not free and clear of all encumbrances; but on the contrary thereof, one Jane Taylor, who before and at the time of making the indenture, &c., had and still hath lawful right and title to one half of the fruit which from year to year, since the making of the said indenture, had grown on the said land, during her life, and who is still living, on, &c., impleaded the plaintiff in an action of trespass on the case for converting and disposing of the fruit which, since the making of the said indenture and before the suing out the said writ, &c., had grown upon the premises, viz., 2400 bushels of apples.

Plaintiff then averred a recovery against him in that action for £50 damages for disposing of the share of the fruit which was thus claimed by Jane Taylor, and £23 for the costs of the action, contrary to the force and effect of the covenant so entered into by the said John Taylor; and that plaintiff has been forced to pay and had paid the said damages and costs.

Defendants pleaded *plene administravit.*

Plaintiff replied, lands of the intestate sufficient to satisfy the judgment, which defendants confessed.

Plaintiff recovered a verdict at the trial, and £250 damages.

Alexander Campbell, of Kingston, moved in arrest of judgment, contending—

1st. That the declaration did not shew, as it ought to have done, that the encumbrance was created before the deed made.

2ndly. That it was not clear on which covenant the action was brought; and, so far as regarded the quiet enjoyment, it must appear on the record that the interruption or disturbance did not arise in consequence of any title created by the covenantee himself after he took the conveyance.

3rdly. That the plaintiff could not have judgment by reason of the issue raised on the plea of *plene administravit;* for that plaintiff relied on there being lands liable to satisfy his judgment, and did not aver that the intestate died seised of an estate not determinable by his death; further, that the lands would not be liable to satisfy damages in an action of this nature, but only a debt on contract; and that plaintiff having acknowledged that defendant had fully administered her goods, his recovery was thereby barred, and defendant was entitled to the costs of the cause. He cited Buller's N. P. 139; 4 M. & S. 53.

Adam Wilson shewed cause.—He contended that the declaration did sufficiently aver that the encumbrance upon which the plaintiff had been disturbed existed before the covenant sued upon (*a*); and that, as to the issue raised by the replication, that testator had lands, and that they were not liable except for debts in contract, and that this was an action for damages, he submitted

---

(*a*) 2 Saund. 181, a, note 10.

that, if this were the case, that would only shew that an immaterial issue had been raised. It was no ground for arresting the judgment. Could not the plaintiff, if he chose, take judgment of assets *quando* of the personal estate of the debtor? and if he could, and there could be no question upon that point, what ground could there possibly be for arresting the judgment on such an objection?—3 T. R. 688 ; 12 E. R. 232 ; Will. Ex. 1221.

ROBINSON, C. J., delivered the judgment of the court.

We consider it perfectly clear, upon this record, that the plaintiff has stated a good cause of action, upon the alleged breach of the covenant that the estate was free from encumbrance ; for the declaration contains a direct statement that, before the covenant was made, one Jane Taylor had a legal right to one half of the fruit to be annually grown there ; and, in pursuance of such right, brought an action against this plaintiff and recovered damages against him for converting the fruit, which would have been his own if the intestate, John Taylor, had had a right to convey the premises free from all encumbrances, as he professed to have. No doubt the statement must be such as to shew that the encumbrance under which the plaintiff had been disturbed existed before the covenant sued upon, otherwise the injury might have arisen from some deed given by the covenantee himself after he had taken the conveyance ; but certainly it sufficiently appears upon this declaration that such could not have been the case in this instance.

As to the objection that the issue upon the plea of *plene administravit* must prevent the plaintiff from recovering, I do not see that it presents any such difficulty, because the plaintiff, as was urged on the argument, would be entitled at any rate to judgment of assets *quando* as regards the personal estate of the debtor. I think there is no room for doubt that, under the statute 5 Geo. II. ch. 7, real estate in the colonies is liable to satisfy a judgment for damages in an action of covenant. They certainly come within the very comprehensive words, "all just debts, duties and demands of what "nature or kind whatsoever ;" and it would be strange indeed if the legislature did not intend to make them liable to satisfy such damages when they would be liable to it by the law of England in the hands of the heir, where the heir is named in the covenant, as he usually is. The covenant here was broken the moment it was executed ; and the land of deceased covenantor is liable to the demand for damages occasioned by the injury, which is strictly pecuniary in its nature, as much so as a covenant to pay an amount in money.

Per Cur.—Rule discharged.

SEATON v. TAYLOR, EXECUTOR OF TAYLOR.

Plaintiff declared in *indebitatus assumpsit*. The defendant pleaded *plene administravit*, except as to £20. The plaintiff replied, admitting that the defendant had not any goods and chattels except, &c., yet that the defendant died seised *of lands*, and that said lands, &c., were at the testator's death and when suit brought assets in the hands of the defendant, as executor, and *liable to satisfy the plaintiff's damages*. Demurrer to replication, on the ground that executor had no control over the lands, or could not as such executor dispose thereof : *Held*, replication good.

The plaintiff declared in *indebitatus assumpsit* for work and labour, goods sold and delivered, and on an account stated with the testator—there were also counts on promises by the executor.

2nd plea—*Plene administravit* except as to £20.

Replication to 2nd plea, admitted that the defendant had not any goods and chattels of the testator except as excepted in the 2nd plea, yet that the testator died *seised* of divers houses, lands, hereditaments and real estate in Upper Canada; that plaintiff is a natural born subject resident in the Home District; and, being such, that the said houses, lands, &c., were at the testator's death and when suit brought, and still are, assets in the hands of the defendant as executor as aforesaid, and liable to satisfy the damages sustained by reason of the non-performance of the premises in the declaration mentioned, concluding with a verification.

Special demurrer, on the ground that the plaintiff had averred that the houses, lands, &c., mentioned in the declaration, are assets in the hands of the defendant as executor, whereas the defendant, as executor, had no control over the same, or could not as such executor dispose thereof, &c.

The Hon. *J. E. Small*, for the demurrer, contended that the replication was bad in stating that the lands were assets in the hands of the executor liable to satisfy the testator's debt. The executor could not dispose of the land, by any voluntary act of his own, to satisfy this defendant.

Chas. Durand contra.—There is nothing in this objection. The plaintiff does not aver that he can dispose of the lands; he merely alleges that the lands are assets in his hands, liable to satisfy this judgment; and the recent decisions in our court, upon the effect of the British statute 5 Geo. II. ch. 7, clearly establish that these lands would be so liable. He submitted, therefore, that the replication must be held good, and that the demurrer could not prevail.

ROBINSON, C. J., delivered the judgment of the court.

The replication is good in our opinion; whether the executor could, under the operation and effect of the British statute 5 Geo. II. ch. 7, dispose of the lands by his voluntary act, in order to satisfy this or other debts, is immaterial. The plaintiff does not aver that he could, but that the lands of H. Taylor, of which he died seised, are assets in the hands of his executor, the defendant, and liable to satisfy the testator's debt. The statute 5 Geo. II. expressly makes them assets for that purpose, though it does not say *assets in his hands;* but they may be regarded as assets *in his hands* in contemplation of law to satisfy a judgment; and, if not, then these words are mere surplusage, and cannot vitiate what is besides stated in the replication, viz., that the lands were liable to satisfy the plaintiff's damages, which certainly is a sufficient reason why he should be permitted to retain his judgment in order that he may, through that, reach the lands thus liable. The defendant, when he demurs upon the ground that he has no control over the lands and cannot dispose of them, cannot mean that plaintiff's replication is bad in asserting that he could dispose of the lands, for the plaintiff has said nothing of the kind; and, if he means that the lands are not assets liable to the plaintiff's execution, because the executor cannot sell them, he advances a *non sequitur*. The question raised by this demurrer has been at various times before us, and has been both directly and incidentally decided. I refer to Gardner v. Gardner in this court, in which the effect of the statute 5 Geo. II. ch. 7, was considered very much at large; and there have been many cases since that, in which the point raised here has been decided or assumed. The plaintiff is, in our opinion, entitled to judgment on the demurrer.

Per Cur.—Judgment for the plaintiff and against the demurrer.

BACON V. MCBEAN ET AL.

Plaintiff declared in *assumpsit* on a foreign judgment against *two defendants*. *Defendants* pleaded *that one of them* had never been served with process, and had no notice whatever of the proceedings in the foreign court: *Held*, plea bad, as setting up a matter of defence for both of the defendants which applied only to one of them.

The plaintiff declared in *assumpsit* on a judgment rendered in the State of New York against the two defendants, Alexander McBean and John McBean.

The defendants pleaded "that, though the said recovery in the declaration "mentioned was in fact obtained by the plaintiffs against the defendants, the "said defendant John McBean was not at any time arrested or served with "any process issuing out of the said supreme court of judicature of the people "of the State of New York, at the town of Utica, at the suit of the plaintiff, "for the cause of action upon which the said recovery was obtained as afore-"said; nor had the said defendant John McBean at any time notice of any such "process; nor did he the said defendant John McBean at any time appear in "the said court to answer the plaintiff in the said action in which the recovery "was so obtained, as in the declaration mentioned; and this the defendants "are ready to verify," &c.

Replication set out a law of the State of New York, supporting the proceedings of the plaintiff.

Demurrer to replication, that it was a departure from the declaration.

Cameron, Sol.-Gen., for the demurrer, admitted that the plea might be bad, but contended that it was cured by the replication supplying the defect in the plea.—11 A. & E.; McPherson v. McMillan in our own court; also the June No. of the Law Times, 1846. The replication was bad as not shewing a conformity to the laws of the State of New York; it was not averred that either of the defendants had been served (as the Act required).

Philip Vankoughnet contra, submitted that the defects in the plea were not, in this case, cured by the replication. With respect to the replication itself he contended that, as the plaintiff had judgment, it must be intended by the court rather that *one* of the defendants was served, which under the Act would be sufficient, than that a foreign judgment was void, which the Act shews might have been good; that the court could hardly intend otherwise, when Alexander McBean, who joins with John McBean in the plea, does not say that he was not served himself, or did not appear; that the judgment obtained against Alexander was not charged by either to be bad, and therefore must be assumed to be good; and if so, under the Act, it would support the recovery against John.

Cameron, in reply, contended that there could be no such assumption in the face of the pleadings; besides, the replication was bad in not shewing that either of the defendants resided within the jurisdiction of the State of New York.

Robinson, C. J., delivered the judgment of the court.

We are of opinion that the plaintiff should have judgment on this demurrer. The plea sets up as a defence for both the defendants a matter which only concerns one of them; and if there were circumstances which might have shewn that in this case what discharges the one must necessarily discharge the other, yet no such facts are stated, and it does not appear to us that the replication cures this defect.

Per Cur.—Judgment for the plaintiff on the demurrer.

Taylor v. Carr.

A defendant will not be allowed, in an action of slander, to single out some of the words of a count and demur to them as not being actionable, while the same count contains other words, uttered in the same conversation, which are clearly actionable.

Where a defendant charges the plaintiff with being "a public robber," and the plaintiff shews that the defendant used the expression in a mitigated sense by an innuendo that "he the plaintiff had defrauded the public in his dealings "with them," it is not necessary for the plaintiff to aver that he is in any office, trade or employment, in which he could have defrauded the public.

Macaulay, J., *dissentiente* on both points.

Action on the case for slander.

The declaration charged that the defendant falsely and maliciously spoke and published of and concerning the plaintiff these false, scandalous, malicious and defamatory words, that is to say: "You (meaning thereby the plaintiff) "need not say much, for every one knows your character" (meaning thereby that the plaintiff was a person of bad and doubtful character). "You (again "meaning the plaintiff) are a public robber, and all you have got you have got "it by robbing the public" (meaning that the plaintiff was guilty of dishonesty, and that he had defrauded the public in his dealings with them, and that whatever he the plaintiff was worth was obtained by dishonest and fraudulent practices, as aforesaid). "You (again meaning the plaintiff) are a damned thief, "and every one knows it" (meaning thereby that the plaintiff was guilty of the crime of feloniously stealing, and that the same was well known to the public). "You (meaning again the plaintiff) are a thief" (meaning thereby that the plaintiff was guilty of theft).

Demurrer, "for that as to so much and such parts of the said declaration of "the said plaintiff, and to so much and such part of the grievances in the said "declaration mentioned as relates to the speaking and publishing of and con- "cerning the plaintiff, the false, scandalous, malicious and defamatory words "following, that is to say: 'You (meaning thereby the plaintiff) need not say "'much, for every one knows your character' (meaning thereby that the "plaintiff was a person of bad and doubtful character); 'You (again meaning "the plaintiff) are a public robber, and all you have got you have got it by "'robbing the public' (meaning that the plaintiff was guilty of dishonesty, "and that he had defrauded the public in his dealings with them, and that "whatever he the plaintiff was worth was obtained by dishonest and fraudu- "lent means and practices as aforesaid); defendant says that the same and "the matters therein contained and above referred to, are not sufficient in "law;" and he shews the following causes of demurrer thereto, that is to say: "because as an innuendo or explanation to the said words, '(You (meaning " 'thereby the plaintiff) need not say much, for every one knows your character,' "the plaintiff alleges as such innuendo the following, that is to say : meaning "thereby that the plaintiff was a person of bad and doubtful character: "whereas the words alleged to have been spoken cannot bear the construction "or meaning as alleged, or that the plaintiff's character was doubtful, unless "they were spoken ironically, which is not alleged and does not appear. Also, " as relates to the words charging the plaintiff with being a public robber and "of robbing the public, there is no inducement or allegation of any trade, "profession or employment in which the plaintiff is said to have been engaged "in, or in reference to which such words were spoken." And as to the other and the residue of the said supposed grievances, the defendant pleaded not guilty.

D. G. Miller for demurrer.—The first words, as to character, could of course maintain no action ; and as to the words "public robber," the plaintiff himself by his innuendo, admits the defendant used the term in a mitigated sense, viz., as meaning to charge him the plaintiff with having defrauded the public. He ought, therefore, to have averred that he was in some office or trade in which he could have defrauded the public (a). As to the right to demur to part of the words in the declaration, he cited Str. 696.

J. Duggan contra, contended that nothing could shew more forcibly the absurdity of allowing a defendant to select certain words from a count in slander and demur to them as not being actionable, than the fact that a verdict might be rendered against the defendant on other words in the same count clearly actionable ; and in this very case a verdict has been given for the plaintiff upon other words in the same count passed by in the demurrer. The principle seems to be clearly established that, where some words in a declaration for slander are not in themselves actionable. yet, if they be coupled with words which clearly are so, the insufficient words are only aggravation ; and if so, as they cannot be traversed, neither can they be demurred to (b). He submitted that, notwithstanding the innuendo explaining the words "public "robber," the plaintiff need not aver that he was following some trade or occupation in which he could defraud the public.

ROBINSON, C. J.—This demurrer seems at least unecessary ; because, if words are charged in a count which are not actionable but joined with those that are, the defendant would always be safe in assuming that the latter were alone relied upon for sustaining the action. He could always request at the trial that the jury should be directed to give no damages in respect to those words, which the judge would take care they did not, except indeed as they might serve to shew a more deeply malicious feeling and intent to injure, when they might properly be allowed to enhance the damages, and it is for that purpose they are usually inserted. If they have been treated as giving a substantial ground of action, and the plaintiff allowed to recover upon them,

---

(a) 1 Nev. & M. 455 ; 3 Campb. 461 ; 1 Campb. 48.
(b) 10 Coke, 131 ; 3 Wils. 185 ; 1 Chit. Rep. 641.

when the actionable words were not proved, the defendant would not be without a proper remedy. This is the first attempt I have seen to single out some of the words of a count and demur to them as not actionable, while the same count contained, as this undoubtedly does, words which are clearly actionable. It is all one conversation which is laid in this count. The defendant is charged with prefacing his slander by saying, "You need not say much, for every one "knows your character;" if he had stopped there, then clearly he would have spoken no actionable words ; but he does not stop there, but proceeds to charge him plainly with a felony. It seems to me that it would be very absurd if the defendant could apply himself to these prefatory words alone, and demur to them upon the ground that they will not bear an action, when the plaintiff has not rested his action upon them, but has proceeded without interruption to complain of the actionable words which the defendant uttered in the same conversation. In Osborne's case (a) the court say, "An action "for slander is an action on *the case*, and therefore the plaintiff may well "declare his *case* as it really was. All together is but one scandal; and "although no action lies for the words 'thou art an arrant knave,' a 'cozener,' "by themselves, yet being spoken at one and the same time, and coupled with "the other words actionable, they aggravate them;" and they proceed to state the difference where the words are charged as being spoken several times, and are declared upon as several causes of action. In Onslow v. Horne (b) the court allow this to be good law; and they say, "Words insufficient may be "rejected where they are laid to be spoken at the same time with other words "that are actionable; for the insufficient words, coupled with the actionable "words, are only aggravation." I find cases in the old books in which, after verdict in such cases in which damages have been assessed in respect to certain words in a count, and other damages for other words laid in the same count, the court have arrested judgment where they said that some of the words in respect of which damages had been expressly given were not actionable, because they held the judgment must be entire, and they could not strike out a part. But there is no doubt at this day, if on one count general damages were given, the court would not arrest the judgment because some of the words are not actionable. Indeed, if it should appear that, from inadvertence, judgment had really been given for the words not actionable, no doubt there would be a new trial. If it be a good general rule, as I believe it to be, that where the words are charged in the same count as being all spoken in one conversation, any which are not actionable are to be considered as spoken merely in aggravation, then, I conclude, they cannot be demurrable, for matter laid merely in aggravation is not traversable (c), and for the same reason not demurrable. I do not know, indeed, where demurrers in actions of slander would stop, if there was not this limit. If the defendant had begun here by saying, "You are a pretty "fellow," and the plaintiff had inserted it as part of the conversation, gravely adding an innuendo, "meaning that he was not a pretty fellow," a demurrer might as well have been filed to those introductory words as the present. The plaintiff does not mean or undertake to shew that all the words are actionable; as Lord Coke says, he is bringing an action on the case, and he relates his case

---

(a) 10 Co. 131.   (b) 3 Wils. 185.   (c) 1 Chit. Rep. 641.

as it was, and it is sufficient for him if the whole conversation as he gives it will bear an action.

As to the other words charging the plaintiff with being "a public robber "and robbing the public," I think they are actionable without the aid of a colloquium, or the averment of any particular trade. The cases of Surman v. Shelleto (a) and Smith v. Cary (b), I think shew that to be so, on the ground that they import a felony, robbing being a proper term of legal signification describing an offence which is felony, and it may receive that meaning when applied as it is here. But here the plaintiff cannot contend that the words are actionable in that construction of them, for he has himself assigned to them a mitigated sense, which they will also bear. He says the defendant meant that "he had defrauded the public in his dealings with them." The objection is that he has not averred himself to be in any office, trade or employment in which he could have defrauded the public; but surely a man may defraud the public in any individual transaction he may have without filling any particular trade or office, or having any common course of dealing which brings him in contact with the government; if, in fact, the plaintiff never had such an office, or trade or course of dealings, he could not have averred it, because he could not have proved it; and yet the words would have been no less a slander if they were false. I have more doubt in regard to this objection upon the demurrer than the other; but I think the answer which the objection should receive is, that defrauding the public is generally an indictable offence, though, doubtless, there may be frauds on the public which are not indictable. But the plaintiff, so far as these words are material to be proved (which they need not be to support the action on the count), undertakes to prove that the defendant did mean, not that he had actually robbed the public by violence and feloniously, but by defrauding them, which is often called robbing; and we cannot say that he cannot prove that the words were spoken with intent to convey that meaning—he undertakes to prove that he meant that by the words, as certainly he might. I think, though I have some doubt on the second ground, that the plaintiff is entitled to judgment on the demurrer.

MACAULAY, J.—It appears to me it is competent to the defendant to demur to that part of the declaration which is demurred to, and to plead to the residue. The test, I think, is, whether that part demurred to contains a substantive charge or complaint against the defendant, or whether it is merely introductory to what follows, not of itself laid as a ground of action, but merely to explain or aggravate what follows, or as being the first part of a continued conversation and in itself immaterial and surplusage. The words that follow are, "You "are a damned thief and every one knows it (meaning that plaintiff was guilty "of stealing). You are a thief (meaning that plaintiff was guilty of theft)." Now, these words, distinctly charging criminal offence, did not require any innuendo to explain that they meant to charge defendant with being a thief or guilty of theft; nor did it require any inducement, much less could they require the aid of what goes before, to assist in giving to them the meaning alleged ; nor do they at all affect the meaning unless to shew that larceny was *not* intended

---

(a) 3 Burr, 1688. (b) 3 Camp. 461.

to be imputed; and, although laid as one continued discourse, much other matter may have intervened, and the expressions alleged to have been used made at intervals; they have no necessary connection. Thus, looking back to the inducement, and then to the words demurred to, and the innuendoes attached thereto, it is clear to me that the plaintiff intended to make those words a ground of action, and that the defendant ought to plead to them, denying the speaking, or justifying them, without regard to what follows. If the words respecting theft were struck out, and the others constituted a good ground of action either as laid or if prefaced by a proper inducement, it is clear the plaintiff might recover. The innuendoes separate them from the words alleging theft, and shew they are treated as of themselves actionable; and if actionable, as laid, it is clear the demurrer must fail; but why should it if they are only introduced in order to illustrate the *quo animo* with which the following words were used, and not as of themselves a ground of action. If actionable, they are well laid as a ground of action, and all about theft may be struck out, and the plaintiff must recover; and if the words of themselves or in connection with the inducement and innuendo, import a criminal indictable conduct to the plaintiff as a robber or guilty of fraud, the demurrer should be overruled on that ground. But the plaintiff does not treat them as *per se* actionable; nor does he treat the words "robber" and "robbing the public" in the criminal sense of the word, as a highway robber or the like, but as guilty of fraud in his dealings with others—Day v. Robinson (a); and his own interpretations of them (being equivocal) may be adopted by the defendant, who admits having used them in the sense imputed. Nor is the imputed fraud explained to have charged plaintiff with a criminal fraud; and so, there being no inducement of any trade or profession, or any allegation that the words were spoken in relation to any trade or profession, or any special damage alleged, that part of the count is bad in law.—2 A. & E. 645. Prudhomme v. Fraser (b) was a long single count for libel containing one hundred and eighty innuendoes. And the present argument, if good, amounts to this, that if defendant had demurred to all that declaration except one passage, and that passage would sustain the action, the demurrer should be overruled, though all the rest were not actionable or well laid. Besides, in this demurrer the rest of the declaration is not before us, to determine whether what follows be actionable *per se* or not, or even whether only so in connection with what is demurred to. It is only looked to with the latter view, however, that is, to see whether what is demurred to is mere introductory matter, immaterial in itself and surplusage, or only used as inducement to explain or aggravate what follows. If it is to be regarded in such a light, then the demurrer is bad as going to that which is not substance or laid as a ground of action. But in such a light I cannot regard it—the inducement and innuendoes, and words that follow, prove the contrary.

JONES, J., concurred in opinion with the Chief Justice.

Per Cur.—Judgment against the demurrer.

MACAULAY, J., *dissentiente.*

(a) 1 A. & E. 554.   (b) 2 Tyr. 411; 2 C. & J. 362.

THE BOARD OF POLICE OF LONDON V. TALBOT.

A., upon being appointed clerk to the market of the Board of Police of London, enters into a bond for the payment of a certain sum of money in compensation for the market tolls, which the board allowed him to receive. Being sued on his bond for non-payment of the money, he pleads, "that he discovered, "after the execution of the bond, that the plaintiffs had no legal authority "to erect a market, or make by-laws respecting fees to be taken thereat;" he then avers that they had no such authority, and that on this account the bond is void.

Held, plea bad in not shewing that no market was erected, or existed, and in not averring that fees were not in fact received by him.

Quære ? Does the Act 3 Vic. ch. 31, give the Board of Police of London power to establish and regulate a market, and appoint fees to be taken thereat ?

Declaration. Debt on bond, which appeared on oyer to be conditioned that the defendant should pay to the plaintiff certain sums of money, provided the plaintiff should at all times uphold and enforce the several by-laws of the said president and Board of Police, made or thereafter to be made, relating to the collection of market fees, and all other things appertaining to the office of clerk of the market, by trial, conviction, distress or otherwise, so that the said John Talbot shall not be injured or damnified by reason of the refusal or neglect of any person or persons required by the said by-laws to pay, or otherwise, the said sum of £173 3s. 3¾d., being in lieu of all fees payable to the said president and Board of Police, and also if the said John Talbot, during the said period, that is to say, between the day of the date of the above-written obligation and the fourth day of March next, shall and do well and truly perform and keep and execute the several duties appertaining to the office of the clerk of the market, and shall do, observe, perform and keep, and enforce the several by-laws, rules, orders and regulations, which are now or may be passed for the regulation of such public market.

The defendant pleaded as his defence, "that prior to the execution of the "said supposed bond, the president and Board of Police of London pretending "a right to erect a market in the said town of London, and to enact by-laws "regulating the same, and establish certain tolls, fees and dues appurtenant "to the said market, and claiming right further to appoint a certain officer, "to wit, the clerk of the said market, with power to collect such tolls, fees "and dues, did propose to the said defendant to become the clerk of the said "market, upon the terms in the condition of the supposed writing obligatory "mentioned, and thereupon the defendant, believing that the plaintiffs had "power to erect such market, and to establish tolls, dues and fees to be paid "to the clerk of the same, did agree to accept such office, upon the terms "aforesaid, and did, at the request of the plaintiffs, execute the said supposed "bond ; but the defendant discovered that the plaintiffs had not any legal "authority, or any charter from the crown, to erect a market or to make by-"laws, rules, orders or regulations respecting the fees to be taken thereat, and "the defendant averred that the president and Board of Police of London had "not, at the time of the execution of the aforesaid bond, nor have they at any "time since acquired any legal authority, or any charter from the crown "authorizing them to erect a market or to make by-laws, rules, orders or "regulations respecting the fees to be taken thereat, whereupon the said bond "was and is wholly void, and this the defendant is ready to verify," &c.

Demurrer to first plea, not sufficient in law.

W. H. Blake, against the demurrer (a).—The question to be decided upon this demurrer is, whether the defendant is estopped by his bond from denying the recital it contains, viz. : that the Board of Police of London has authority to establish a market in the town of London, and to impose fees to be taken thereat? It is submitted that the defendant cannot be held estopped from urging such a defence. Has the Board of Police legally the power, under the Act 3 Vic. ch. 31, to erect a market in the town of London, and to exact tolls? He would contend they had not. The principle is well established, that before a corporate body can impose tolls which are a burden upon the public, they must be able to point to clear and precise language in the Act of Parliament authorizing the very toll sought to be exacted. O'Hara v. Foley, in our court, was decided upon this principle. Now does the Act 3 Vic. ch. 31, incorporating the town of London, contain specific language upon the right to erect a market and demand toll such as is here contended for? No such construction can fairly be put upon any of its clauses: on the contrary, it will be found materially to differ in its terms from other Acts incorporating other towns, where the right has been unequivocally conferred. Why then, was not a similar clause, as express in its terms, inserted in this Act? The legislature must for some reason have designedly omitted such clauses in the London Act? Assuming, therefore, that the Act 3 Vic. ch. 31, conferred no right upon the Board of Police in London to erect a market and appoint tolls to be taken thereat, was not the bond executed by the defendant upon the assertion that such a right existed, an illegal bond? and if an illegal bond, a plea denying the condition to be legal would, it is submitted, be a good plea. The law will not allow an estoppel to work in favour of an illegal act.—6 Vesey, 776 ; 6 Bing. N. C. 34 ; 10 B. & C. 826.

Cameron, Sol.-Gen., for the demurrer.—There may not be language in the Act incorporating the town of London (b) as expressly conferring upon the Board of Police there the right to build a market and take tolls, as in other Acts incorporating other towns ; but it is submitted that the Act does contain clauses evidently relating to the establishment of a market in London, and does in general words, which is all that can be required, authorize the passing of a by-law by the Board of Police with respect to the imposition of market toll. The 9th clause says expressly "that they may raise funds for building "a market house, and may make such by-laws as they may think reasonable "for the improvement, good order and government of the town, not repugnant "to the laws of the province." This demurrer however, must, it is submitted, be determined upon grounds wholly independent of the view the court may take upon the general question of the right of the board to impose market toll. It is perfectly consistent with all that is stated in the plea, that the board may have in fact, whether legally or not, erected a market and imposed fees to be there taken ; the plea does not aver that no market was erected, or that fees were not in fact received by the defendant ; and how can the defend-

---

(a) This demurrer was argued in the order as above, it having been intimated by mistake that Mr. Blake had abandoned the plea.   (b) 3 Vic. ch. 31.

ant, after admitting the plaintiff's title in his plea, and deriving, as it must be assumed he has done, all the benefits of his appointment, under the plaintiff's authority, question the legal right of the board to do what they have done. If the defendant had found, when entering upon his office, that he was obstructed in collecting his fees, he had his proper remedy ; but while admitting that he has received the fees—as his plea must be held to do—it would be contrary to all law to allow him to dispute the right under which the board had been acting ; the defendant, reaping all the benefit stipulated for in this bond, cannot resist payment of the consideration money upon which such benefit was conferred.

ROBINSON, C. J.—The defendant, having obtained from the plaintiffs the office of clerk of the market of the town of London, for a year from the 4th of March, 1845, has given a bond with surety to the plaintiffs for the due performance of the duties, and also for payment of a certain sum in compensation for the market tolls which he was to be allowed to receive. Being sued upon this bond, for the non-payment of the money due under it, he pleads that he discovered, after the execution of the bond, that the plaintiffs had no legal authority, or charter from the crown, to erect a market, or make by-laws respecting fees to be taken thereat, and denying that they had any such authority, he pleads that the bond is on this account void. As regards the assertion that the plaintiffs had no charter from the crown for erecting a *market*, the plaintiffs, by demurring, must be taken to admit that to be true ; but if the plaintiffs had otherwise by law, that is by any statute which we must judicially notice, a right to erect a market, then the defendant must fail upon the demurrer. Upon that point, I think, there is much room for doubt. There is certainly nothing so express in the statute incorporating the Board of Police of London, respecting the establishment of a market, as there is in the other statutes of that nature regarding other towns ; but I have not made up my mind that the Corporation of London have not the power, under the Act, to establish and regulate a market, and appoint fees to be taken. The Act 3 Vic. ch. 31, gives the board power (sec. 9) to make such laws for the internal government of the town as to them shall seem meet, to appoint such officers as shall be required for the due execution of them, and take security from them. They may *raise funds for building a market-house ;* may make such by-laws as they may think reasonable for the improvement, good order, and government of the town, not repugnant to the laws of the province. They may "fix upon and appoint such days and hours for the purpose of selling "butchers' meat, butter, eggs, poultry, fish and vegetables, and make such "other orders and regulations relative thereto, as they shall think expedient."

These are very extensive powers given to them, and evidently having relation to the establishment of a market, at least for the sale of the articles enumerated. I should have difficulty in saying that the board had no authority under them to establish a market in some particular part of the town, and to impose tolls and fees. It is true that tolls or other impositions upon the subject must rest upon some clear and precise authority, and consequently if any tolls are to be collected at a market in London, there must at least be shewn some express by-law of the board authorizing the toll in precise terms ; but I cannot go so far as to say that the power to make such a by-law cannot be conferred by the legislature in general terms, but that the words market fees or market tolls must be used, and authority given to impose them.

The statute 31 Geo. III. ch. 31, which constituted the legislature of Upper Canada, gave it power to make laws for the peace, welfare and good government of the province; and under that general authority it has always been understood and admitted that they might impose taxes and duties, and authorize fees, though no specific words are used in the statute giving power to pass such laws more than others. Still the law of England is so scrupulous in regard to the authority upon which Acts of this nature must rest, that unquestionably it was an omission not to provide, in the Act establishing the Board of Police of London, in express words for the establishment and regulation of a market, and the imposing of tolls, and it will be prudent to have that omission supplied without delay. What I have said upon it was not necessary for determining this demurrer, because I think the plea bad upon grounds independent of the general question. The defendant sets up as his defence that the plaintiffs, pretending a right to erect a market and to appoint a clerk to collect fees, &c., proposed to him to become the clerk. We cannot tell from this whether he means us to understand that they acted upon their pretensions or not; it is consistent with all that is said in the plea that the board may never have proceeded to establish a market or to appoint fees, but may have left the defendant to pay his money without doing anything towards enabling him to receive the fees which were to form the emolument of his office, and on the other hand it is equally consistent with what is stated in the plea, to infer that the plaintiffs may have set up a market and established fees, and that the defendant may have collected and received them under their authority; and now, after having availed himself of their regulations and of his appointment, and received all the benefit of it, he may be endeavouring to evade payment of his bond, by questioning their legal right to do what they have done. This would be contrary to all legal principles. If the fact were that the defendant, after entering on his office, found his claim to fees contested, and was obstructed in the receipt of them, then his plain remedy was under the condition of the bond. He should have called on the board to enforce them by law, and if they failed to do so, then by the very terms of the condition, he would be exempt from paying. But as the plea does not exclude the supposition that he may in fact have received all the benefits he stipulated for, I am of opinion that it is bad, and that judgment must be for the plaintiffs on demurrer.

MACAULAY, J.—The plea does not distinctly aver that the plaintiffs did erect a market, only that prior to the execution of the bond, not saying how long prior, the plaintiffs, pretending right to erect a market and to establish tolls and fees and to appoint officers, proposed to defendant, not saying when, to become clerk of the said market: that he accepted the office and gave the bond, and then avers that after the execution of the bond (not saying how soon after, and it may have been after the year had expired, and he had received all the fees and emoluments as clerk of a market then existing, during the whole period), he discovered that they had no legal authority or charter to erect a market, &c., at the time the bond was executed, nor since had they any such authority or charter, &c. He does not say no market was erected, or existed, or any fees received. It is consistent with all that is stated, that in point of fact there was a market, and fees imposed, as mentioned in the bond, and the plaintiffs long in possession thereof as ostensibly entitled. It is not competent to the defendant, after admitting their title under the statute, and reaping the fruits of the appointment, to dispute their title. If the plaintiffs have usurped powers that do not belong to them, in claiming a franchise such as a market is, with tolls and fees, &c., the mode of proceeding is by information *quo warranto*, or some other course that shall deny and resist their pretensions, and not one that acknowledges the right and shews not that it was impeached by any regular proceeding. Whether the plaintiffs can, by virtue of the Act 3 Vic. ch. 31, erect a market, or have done so, or whether they may do so if a site has been reserved or dedicated by the crown for that purpose by force of the 9th, 11th and 21st sections; or whether they can legally impose tolls or fees by their own by-laws, is not by any means clear to me, though it was no doubt contemplated by the legislature in passing the Act. I do not think the plea shews the absence of any market, or the usurpation of powers not belonging to the plaintiffs in relation to the market mentioned in the bond, so as to render it void on the ground of illegality. The right and title is admitted by the defendant, and he seems estopped from disputing it, after having received the benefit; it would be a different thing if he shewed disturbance, or a total failure in the condition, owing to the plaintiffs having made an appointment, and guaranteed tolls and fees they had no legal right to dispose of. If there be a market, in fact, of which they have the possession and control (as I think must be intended), I do not see that a bond securing a sum upon farming the office of clerk to such markets is illegal and void, so long as the market subsists, and the benefit of the office is enjoyed without disturbance or obstruction. I do not look upon it as illegal (however unauthorized) so as to invalidate the bond. The defendant is estopped from denying the right.

JONES, J., concurred.

Per Cur.—Judgment for the plaintiffs on demurrer.

SMITH ET AL. V. HALL.

It is not necessary to state in the notice of non-payment to an endorser of a bill, that the holder looks to him for payment.

The certificate of a notary in Lower Canada at the foot of the protest, that he had put a notice into the post addressed to the endorser, is evidence of that fact under the statute 7 Vic. ch. 4, sec. 2.

The law of Lower Canada with respect to time of giving notice, is to govern when the note was made payable and was presented there, though the endorser resides in Upper Canada.

Endorsee against endorser. *Assumpsit* on a promissory note made by one Ritter, on the 1st of May, 1845, payable to her own order, at the office of the plaintiff, in Montreal, for £124 10s., four months after date, endorsed to defendant, and by him to the plaintiff.

Pleas. 1st. That the note was not duly presented at the office of the plaintiffs, in Montreal, in manner and form, &c.

2ndly. Denied notice of non-payment.

The plaintiff recovered at the trial.

There was another count on another note, in which the plaintiff also recovered.

In the learned judge's report of the case, it appeared that the first note falling due on the 4th of September, was presented on the 6th, at the office of the plaintiffs, in Montreal, and protested on the same day, by a notary there; and in the protest it was stated, that the notary "had duly signified "these presents by post to the endorser;" and to the copy of the protest a note was added, "I certify that I put true and correct copies of this protest "into the post-office, in the city of Montreal, this 6th day of September, 1845, "for J. L. Ritter, addressed to Moy, near Windsor, Sandwich, C. W." Signed, "W. Ross, N. P." On the same sheet of paper with this copy of the protest, was a certificate signed by W. Ross, N.P., 6th September, 1845: "At the "request of Joseph Wenham, Esq., on the other side named, holder of the "original promissory note and protest, of which true copies precede, I beg "leave to notify you in your quality of endorser of the said note, the protest "thereof, and to which and the foregoing will serve."

This notice was addressed to the endorser, at Moy.

J. Duggan moved for a nonsuit, or to reduce the verdict. He stated three grounds for nonsuit. 1st, the delay in giving notice; 2nd, the want of proper evidence to prove the sending of the notice; and 3rd, that the notice sent to the endorser did not state that the holder looked to him for payment, but simply the presentment and non-payment. He strongly relied upon this last objection.

Cameron, Sol.-Gen., shewed cause.—There are express authorities in this court against the two first grounds for nonsuit. Bank B. N. A. v. Ross; Bank U. C. v. Grover; also Matthewson v. Cameron. The notice is in the usual form; there is no necessity to state that the endorser is looked to for payment; he must take that for granted after receiving the notice; for what other purpose could the notice be sent?

ROBINSON, C. J., delivered the judgment of the court.

The points raised in this case have been already determined in this court. In Matthewson v. Cameron (*a*), it was decided in respect to the time of giving notice to an endorser resident in this province of a note made payable in Lower Canada, and protested there, that the law of Lower Canada was to govern, and the endorsement in that as well as in this, was made in Upper Canada. The facts were the same. The notice was clearly in time, according to the statute in force in Lower Canada.

Upon the other point, it has also been decided in this court that the certificate of the notary, at the foot of his protest, of his having sent notice to the endorser, shall be evidence of the fact stated in the certificate, as indeed the statute 7 Vic. ch. 6, sec. 2, expressly provides.

The objection which seemed to be chiefly relied upon in this case was, that the plaintiff could not recover upon the first note because the notarial certificate did not state that in the notice sent to the endorser an intimation was given that the holder looked to him for payment.

We are of opinion that that is not necessary. It is sufficient if the endorser has notice in due time that the note has been duly presented and is unpaid.

(*a*) 1 Cam. Rep., 259.

There have been opinions to the contrary; but we take it to be now well settled that it is not necessary that the notice should inform the endorser that he is required to pay the note.

Per Cur.—Rule discharged.

BALLARD V. POPE.

A party suspected of stealing a horse is brought up on a warrant before a magistrate; he investigates the alleged larceny and dismisses the charge; the suspected individual pretends no right to the horse, and the magistrate, after dismissing the charge, restores the horse to its supposed owner (the party prosecuting), but before doing so takes a bond of indemnity from the owner. In an action brought upon this bond, the defendant pleads that the bond is void, relying upon its being contrary to the general policy of the law that a magistrate should take such a bond; the plaintiff demurs to the plea.

Held, plea bad, as it does not shew any statute expressly prohibiting bonds of this description being taken, and does not aver any corrupt purpose or undue motive on the part of the magistrate to whom it was given.

Declaration debt on bond.

The condition of the said bond, as set out in oyer, was, "that the defendant "should indemnify the plaintiff from all damages which might be incurred "by reason of the plaintiff releasing a certain horse to the defendant, then in "the custody of one Wycott, a constable, and which was said to belong to the "said defendant."

The defendant pleaded secondly the following special plea, containing a full statement of all the facts of the case: "That before the making of the said "bond or writing obligatory in the said declaration mentioned, to wit, on the "twentieth day of June, in the year of our Lord one thousand eight hundred "and forty-four, the plaintiff was one of Her Majesty's justices of the peace in "and for the district of Prince Edward, and continued and was such justice until "and at and after the making of the said bond or writing obligatory as herein-"after mentioned; and thereupon afterwards, to wit, on the day and year first "in this plea mentioned, at Picton, within the said district, information and "charge upon oath was made by one Benjamin R. Davis, the servant of the said "defendant, before the said plaintiff as such justice as aforesaid, that one George "Haight did on the nineteenth day of June then instant, at the barn of James "Cotter, Esquire, in Sophiasburgh, in the said district of Prince Edward, felo-"niously steal and lead away a certain horse or stallion of the said now defendant, "commonly called 'Sir Archy,' being then in the lawful care and possession "of the aforesaid Davis as the servant and keeper thereof for the said defendant; "and thereupon afterwards, to wit, on the said twentieth day of June, in the "year last aforesaid, the plaintiff, as such justice as aforesaid, at Picton aforesaid, "within the said district, did upon such information so made upon oath as afore-"said, issue his warrant under his hand and seal, directed to one Thomas Wycott, "constable, and to all other persons, peace officers within the said district, com-"manding him and them in Her Majesty's name forthwith to apprehend the said "George Haight and bring before him, the said plaintiff, or some other of Her

"Majesty's justices of the peace in and for the said district of Prince Edward, the
"body of the said George Haight, as well as the said horse if found in the pos-
"session of the said Haight, that the said Haight might answer to the charge so
"as aforesaid made against him, and be further dealt with according to law ;
"which said warrant was then, to wit, on the day and year last aforesaid, de-
"livered by the plaintiff as such justice as aforesaid to the said Thomas Wycott,
"to be executed according to the tenor and effect of the said warrant. And
"thereupon the said Thomas Wycott, after the delivery to him as aforesaid of
"the said warrant, to wit, on the day and year last aforesaid, to wit, at Picton, in
"the said district, under and by virtue of the said warrant, did apprehend and
"arrest the said George Haight by his body, and did then take into his possession
"and custody the said horse 'Sir Archy,' in the said warrant named, the said
"horse then and at the time of the apprehension and arrest of the said George
"Haight as aforesaid, being found in and being in the possession of him the said
"George Haight; and did afterwards, to wit, on the twenty-fourth day of June,
"in the year last aforesaid, bring before him the said plaintiff as such justice as
"aforesaid within the said district of Prince Edward, to wit, at Picton, in the
"said district, the body of the said George Haight, as well as the said horse, as
"by the said warrant he was commanded, of all which premises the defendant
"afterwards, to wit, on the day and year last aforesaid had notice. And the
"defendant further saith, that the plaintiff, when the said George Haight and
"the said horse were so brought before him as aforesaid, to wit, on the day and
"year last aforesaid, within the said district of Prince Edward, to wit, at Picton,
"in the said district, did examine into the circumstances of and attending the
"said alleged felonious taking and stealing of the said horse, and after hearing
"the testimony adduced before him, did consider and decide that there was no
"evidence of a felonious taking, stealing, or leading away of the said horse, and
"that the said horse had not been feloniously taken, stolen, or led away as
"charged against the said George Haight; and as such justice did then decide to
"discharge, and did there, to wit, on the day and year last aforesaid, release and
"discharge the said George Haight from custody under the said warrant, and of
"and from the said charge, and did then permit him the said George Haight to
"go at large ; and the defendant further saith, that thereupon it became and was
"the duty of the said plaintiff, as such justice as aforesaid, to have restored or
"caused to be restored the said horse to the said George Haight, who was the
"possessor of the said horse at the time of the apprehension and arrest of the
"said George Haight, and also at the time the said horse was taken into posses-
"sion and custody by the said Thomas Wycott as aforesaid, or to have permitted
"the said George Haight to have had and taken possession of the said horse; yet
"the defendant saith that the plaintiff, not regarding his duty as such justice,
"did not restore or cause to be restored the said horse to the said George Haight,
"nor permit him to take or possess the said horse; but on the contrary thereof
"it was there, to wit, on the day and year last aforesaid, while the said horse
"remained in the custody and keeping of the said Thomas Wycott as such con-
"stable within the said district, to wit, at Picton, in the said district, under
"and by virtue of the said warrant, and under and by virtue of the order and
"authority of the said plaintiff as such justice, and subject to the direction and
"order of the said plantiff as such justice as aforesaid, unlawfully agreed by and
"between the plaintiff as such justice as aforesaid and the said defendant, and

"against the will of the said George Haight and without his consent, that he
"the said plaintiff, as such justice as aforesaid, should give possession of and
"release the said horse to the said defendant, who then claimed the said horse
"adversely to the said George Haight, of which the defendant then had notice;
"and that he the said defendant, in consideration thereof, should sign, seal,
"execute, make and deliver to the said plaintiff a bond in the penal sum of two
"hundred pounds, conditioned to indemnify the said plaintiff, his heirs, exe-
"cutors and administrators, from all damages, suits, costs, penalties, loss or
"charges whatever, which the said plaintiff might incur or make himself liable
"to in consequence of his releasing to the said defendant the said horse pursuant
"to the said agreement; and the defendant further saith, that in pursuance of the
"said unlawful agreement and in part performance thereof, he the said plaintiff
"as such justice as aforesaid, afterwards, to wit, on the day and year last
"aforesaid, and while the said horse remained in the charge, custody or
"keeping of the said Thomas Wycott as such constable, under and by virtue
"of the said warrant, and under and by the authority and order of the said
"plaintiff as such justice as aforesaid, ordered and directed the said Thomas
"Wycott to release and give possession of the said horse to the said defendant,
"and the said Thomas Wycott did then give possession of and release to the
"defendant the said horse, under and by virtue of the said order and direction
"so given as aforesaid, and the defendant did then accept and receive the
"said horse of and from the said Thomas Wycott, under and by virtue of the
"said order and direction, so given as aforesaid by the said plaintiff as such
"justice as aforesaid; and in further pursuance of the said unlawful agreement
"and in performance thereof, did then, to wit, on the day and year last afore-
"said, sign, seal, execute, make and deliver to the plaintiff the bond or writing
"obligatory in the said declaration mentioned; and this the defendant is
"ready to verify."

There was a third plea differing a little in point of form from the second.

To these second and third pleas the plaintiff demurred, as well upon some points of form which were not noticed in the judgment of the court, as upon the following substantial grounds of demurrer:

1st. That it did not appear that the said bond was given to induce the said plaintiff to adjudicate in any way, but to do an act after his authority had ceased, and which his duty as a magistrate would neither compel him to do, nor make him liable for not doing.

2nd. Also, that it did not appear that the said plaintiff acted knowingly and maliciously in the matter, or that he did not act *bona fide* and without collusion.

D. G. Miller, for the demurrer, contended that the bond was perfectly legal; the judicial character of the magistrate was at an end when he dismissed the charge; the bond could not therefore have been given with any intention of influencing a just adjudication upon the complaint. There was no averment of a corrupt purpose or *mala fides* on the part of the magistrate; the act of the magistrate upon which the bond was requested and assented to by the defendant was for the benefit of the defendant, and upon an express agreement made with himself; he could not therefore set up its illegality as a defence; the defendant shews no statute prohibiting such a bond, and there is nothing, it is submitted, in the common law, which would make a bond given under the circumstances of this case invalid. He cited the 30 Eliz. ch. 11, sec. 3, and 2 Hawkins 25, 2 Hawkins P. C. 243 ; he relied also strongly upon the plea admitting the horse to be the defendant's.

S. Richards, contra, contended that the magistrate was acting judicially, and could not take a bond to indemnify himself ; he denied that the plea admitted the horse to be the defendant's. Haight claimed the horse and had him in possession, which was *prima facie* evidence of property ; what right had the magistrate to give the horse to the defendant upon dismissing the charge against Haight? Burns' Justice, Search Warrant, 2 Hale, 151 ; he admitted he could find no authority which went the length of deciding that a judicial officer could take no indemnity for any act done, but submitted that a bond like the present would clearly be contrary to the general policy of the law, and, if upheld, very likely to prove a most pernicious precedent.

ROBINSON, C. J.—In this plea the defendant is setting up as his defence the illegality of an act done for his own benefit, upon an express agreement made with himself. He does not shew any statute which makes such a bond as is here sued upon illegal, but he relies upon its being manifestly illegal, as being contrary to the general policies of the law. We have lately had occasion to consider defences of this kind in the two cases of Ireland v. Guess et al., and the same plaintiff v. Noble. Upon the principles which were then stated, I consider that there is a distinction between cases where anything is done contrary to an express direction or prohibition contained in a statute, and where a party, not having such a ground to rest upon, is seeking to evade his own contract by averring the illegality of an act done by his own procurement and for his own benefit. As we have had these cases before us so recently, I will only refer to the cases of Sugars v. Brinkworth (a), and the others cited on that occasion. The defendant does not aver that the bond which he is sued upon was taken for any corrupt purpose, or under circumstances which would necessarily imply a bad motive ; and in support of it we are at liberty to assume that any facts did exist which (if they existed) would have made the transaction just in intention and *bona fide*. It is argued that it was the duty of the justice to do what the law required, without exacting any such security. The same may be said of bonds of indemnity, taken by sheriffs, and which are constantly sustained without any statute to aid them. The effect of that argument is only to shew that the bond was given without consideration ; but that is no defence to a contract by speciality.

Then the objection is pressed further. The act, it is said, was judicial, and therefore that a bond of indemnity taken on the occasion was illegal. No doubt it would be illegal, as being manifestly contrary to duty as well as public policy in a judge to take from the party in whose favour he purposes to decide, an undertaking to indemnify him against all the consequences of his decision. If that were allowed, the parties litigating would not be before him on equal terms, for one might be poor and not able to offer satisfactory indemnity. But is it right to look upon this alleged giving up of the horse by

(a) 4 Campb. 46.

the justice in the strict light of a judicial decision? If it could only be so regarded, no action would lie for his directing the constable to give the horse to Pope. But we know judicially that the justice in this case has not been held to be protected against an action on that principle. As the facts are stated in the plea, the charge was disposed of, and the case decided, by the justice determining that Haight had not taken the horse feloniously, and on that ground discharging him. I think the judicial duty was then ended, and that the alleged subsequent direction of the justice to the constable, to give the horse to the defendant, was no more a judicial act than any other commands and directions of justices, which are regarded as mere ministerial acts, and held to be trespasses or otherwise according as they are legal or illegal. Now, consistently with all that is stated in these pleas, the facts may have been such as would have made it manifestly proper and reasonable that the horse should be placed in the possession of Pope. Suppose, for instance, that Haight had owned a horse that had been long astray, and finding a horse of Pope's on the common, and supposing it to be his own, he had taken it up and kept it, and that he had in consequence been brought up before the justice on a charge of stealing Pope's horse. He might have been so clearly convinced of his error, that he had nothing to urge in his favour but that he had acted under a mistake. His own horse might have been produced; he might have acknowledged his error and been properly dismissed from the charge of felony. Surely in such a case the horse might without hesitation be delivered over to the person acknowledged to be his true owner; but yet Haight might not be willing, as the plea says, and might not assent to this being done. It is not said in these pleas that he forbade the justice to do it, or said anything on the subject, or manifested openly any dissent. It is the general rule, undoubtedly, that when goods are brought before a justice on a search warrant, with the person upon whom they have been found, if the justice discharges him upon the examination, he is to return the goods into his possession. But surely this rule, like other rules, is not to be applied indiscriminately. I will suppose another case. A gentleman, walking in the street, loses his purse, and in the course of his search after it, hears of a man having it in his possession and shewing it to a third party; upon which he has him arrested by a warrant, and charged with felony. When he is brought before the justice, with the purse found upon him, he proves clearly that he found it lying in the street, and picked it up, not being able to tell to whom it belonged, but shewed it openly to several for the purpose of finding an owner, and had even advertised it. He would of course be discharged. Surely, if he admitted the property to belong to the other, it would be absurd that the purse should be restored to his possession. The justice would, without hesitation, place it in the hands of the true owner. It might be possible that in such a case the finder, repenting of his honesty, might be *unwilling*, as the plea says, to part with the purse, and might not assent to it; and the magistrate might, in consequence, feel some doubt whether he would be quite safe from being harrassed with an action, if he was to give any express order upon the subject, and the constable might not choose to act without an order. To quiet all apprehensions, the owner of the purse might offer an indemnity against any action, and give such a bond as has been given here. How can we tell upon this record that there was not in the case in question, as complete an absence of any wrong done or intended, in delivering up the horse to Pope, as in the case I have supposed; we ought to intend that this was the case, rather than intend the contrary, for the purpose of relieving the defendant from an undertaking of which he has reaped the benefit. It is palpably unjust for the defendant first to obtain his horse by offering this indemnity, and then to endeavour to evade payment upon the pretence that the magistrate should not have done for him what he did, and that he must therefore suffer the consequences. He does not pretend that the horse was Haight's, or deny that he himself was the true owner; but rather than pay his bond, he pleads that the magistrate should have let the other man take him away and not complied with his request. There are many cases no doubt in which a party who has had his own ends served, may thus turn round upon the person who has confided in his promise. Contracts made in violation or disregard of the statute law, may be thus resisted; and there are other cases which rest on other grounds at common law; but there is in my opinion not enough on this record to authorize us to hold that this is one of them. I look with no favour on this kind of defence, but would undoubtedly give the defendant the benefit of it, if he could shew us any decided case of good authority that will support the plea; he admits he cannot. The cases cited in the judgments which I have already referred to—Humphrey's Case, 10, Co. 100; Southwick's Case, 1 Saund. 161; Rogers v. Reeves, 1 T. R. 418; Green v. Pilkington, 2 B. & P. 101, and Sugars v. Brinkworth, 4 Camp. 46—are in principle, I think, against it, when it is not shewn, as it is not here, that there was any intention to pervert justice, or any abuse in fact practised.

MACAULAY, J.—I am by no means free from doubt in this case, there being much force in the argument that it is against public policy to uphold bonds given under the circumstances of the present; the case arises, however, upon demurrer, and if under any supposable circumstances consistently with the facts pleaded, the defendant could have legally taken the bond of indemnity, he is entitled to judgment. There is no imputation of collusion or *mala fides;* and the case in effect is no more than this, that a man's servant having laid an information on oath before a justice, of the larceny of his master's horse by a suspected individual, the justice issued a warrant against the accused party, with directions to bring him and the horse, if found in his possession, before the magistrate, which being done, the case was investigated and the complaint dismissed, and the party discharged; after which the horse was delivered by order of the justice to the master or alleged owner. If this (though wrong, strictly speaking), being done *bona fide*, would not subject the justice to an information or any criminal prosecution, it follows that the act not being criminal, it was no more than a civil wrong or injury to the party from whom the horse had been taken, or any other person better entitled thereto; and I cannot find that for protection in such an act, which may be a civil wrong and expose the magistrate to a civil action, he may not take a valid bond of indemnity. If any collusion or contrivance, or other sinister or corrupt motive could be shewn, it would certainly alter the case and frustrate his remedy; so it would expose him to a criminal information. But such is not the case here; the plaintiff's judicial duty had ended (a), and had he given

---

(a) 3 Burr. 1262.

no directions respecting the horse, the constable might, I suppose, have required a bond for his indemnity upon delivering the horse to defendant; strictly it was the duty of the plaintiff to have returned the horse to the possession from which it was taken, if the result was not merely to exonerate the party charged with the larceny, but to repel the charge of any larceny at all by any one; but if the larceny was not repelled, though the imputation upon the party might be removed, it was perhaps the plaintiff's duty to have retained the horse till criminal measures were taken against the real offender (a).

The plea alleges that the complaint of a larceny was dismissed, and the *prima facie* duty of the plaintiff was to restore the horse to Haight; but there may have been peculiar circumstances, and certainly nothing corrupt, however irregular, is shewn. I should not think the precedent likely to prove pernicious. If he undertook to investigate a dispute about the property, and to decide between the parties, it would be another question.

JONES, J., concurred.

Per Cur.—Judgment in favour of the demurrer and against the defendant.

CURTIS V. FLINDALL.

A defendant casually observing to a third party, in the presence of the plaintiff, that he had paid the whole price for his land, except a certain sum, without any further explanation of the circumstances, is not satisfactory evidence of an account stated.

Semble, that if there had been satisfactory evidence of an account stated, the Statute of Frauds would not have applied, though the sum was due in respect of the sale of lands.

Plaintiff sued in *assumpsit*.

The first count was special, on an agreement to pay £600 for a certain lot of land to be conveyed to the plaintiff by the defendant, averring the conveyance of the land and a refusal to pay the money.

A count was added upon an account stated.

The defendant pleaded to the first count,

1st, That the plaintiff did not convey the land to him.

2ndly, *Non-assumpsit* to the first count.

3rdly, Payment.

Non-assumpsit to the second count.

Upon the trial, evidence was given of an acknowledgment by the defendant that he had owed the plaintiff a certain sum for land that he had bought of him; they were conversing together in presence of a third party, and the defendant said he had paid for the land except £75.

The learned judge, considering the nature of the demand, held it to be necessary that the plaintiff should give evidence in writing of the contract for the sale of the land, signed by the defendant, according to the Statute of Frauds; and was proceeding to direct the jury that, in the absence of such writing, they must find a verdict for the defendant.

The plaintiff thereupon accepted a nonsuit.

(a) 1 Chitty's Cri. Law, 67; 2 Hale, 151; 19 Howell, 1066; 15 Vin. Ab. 18 Justice of the Peace, L. 8.

W. H. Blake moved to set aside the nonsuit. He contended that the plaintiff was improperly nonsuited. There was sufficient evidence of an account stated between the parties, and it is clear upon the authority of several cases, that upon a contract like the present for the sale of land, evidence of an account stated between the plaintiff and defendant would enable the plaintiff to recover the sum admitted to be due, without proving a contract in writing to satisfy the Statute of Frauds. He cited 4 B. 459; 1 M. & P. 227; 3 Car. & P. 170; also Dalton v. Botts, in Taylor's Reports.

D. B. Read shewed cause. He admitted the principle contended for by the opposite counsel, that upon clear and satisfactory evidence of an account stated between parties who had contracted for the sale of land, the plaintiff might recover upon an account stated without producing a written contract under the Statute of Frauds; but he denied that any such evidence had been offered in the present case. The parties had not met together with any view towards a settlement of accounts, but the plaintiff happening to be present some four years ago when the defendant and a third party were arranging a transaction of their own, the defendant casually observed that he had paid the plaintiff for his land all but £75; there was nothing further said upon the subject; could any evidence be more slight or unsatisfactory than this to support an account stated? What specific conversation is here proved to shew that this sum of £75 was the balance due to the plaintiff upon the sale of his land? He also contended that the plaintiff, having a special count in his declaration, could not be allowed to resort to the count on the account stated to prove the same transaction. He cited 1 C. & M. 89; 3 Tyr. 26.

ROBINSON, C. J.—I am of opinion that in a case like the present, the plaintiff might be allowed to recover upon satisfactory evidence of an account stated, without producing any written evidence of the alleged contract for the sale of the land, if it was clear that the contract had been executed and a balance plainly admitted to be still due. In Knowles v. Mitchell (*a*) a similar question arose; but the court held, that if there were a verbal acknowledgment by the defendant of a debt due *upon any account*, it was sufficient to enable the plaintiff to recover upon the count for an account stated; and Lord Ellenborough said he was in the frequent habit of receiving such evidence at the sittings. The case of Dynes v. O'Neill, 1 Crawford & Dix (an Irish report), 329, is expressly in point; and 4 Bing. 459, 1 M. & P. 227, and 3 Car. & P. 170, are authorities to the same effect. But, though the law seems to be clearly so settled, I do not think that the plaintiff was improperly nonsuited, for I do not think the plaintiff gave such evidence of an account stated as was sufficient to enable him to recover; he is endeavouring to sustain an action as upon an account stated of a debt still subsisting, and of money actually payable to the plaintiff as being due upon the land, and his only evidence was a casual conversation with a stranger in the plaintiff's presence some four or five years ago. The parties were not settling accounts, nor conversing with any view to it; but while the defendant was paying some money to a third party on account of land, he remarked he had paid the plaintiff for the land he had bought of him all except £75. Now, there was no evidence that that sum was due in this

---

(*a*) 13 E. R. 250.

sense, that the plaintiff had a right to exact it from him. It may have been that the defendant merely bargained for the land on condition that if he made certain payments he was to have the land, otherwise not. It was not shewn that the defendant had agreed absolutely to pay any sum of money, or that he had means of compelling plaintiff to convey to him. It would be dangerous indeed to allow a party to recover upon no other evidence than this casual conversation with a stranger, though in the plaintiff's presence, and after a lapse of four years, without any explanation of circumstances. A jury could have no confidence that they would be doing justice by such a verdict.

MACAULAY, J.—Strictly speaking, I think there was evidence sufficient to go to the jury of an account stated, but it was slight and unsatisfactory; and the plaintiff having accepted a nonsuit rather than risk the case with the jury on this evidence, it ought not to be set aside unless it *prima facie* entitled the plaintiff to a verdict. Had the jury found for the defendant on such evidence, the verdict could not have been disturbed as against evidence; nor do I look upon it as a case that ought to be restored in order to its being submitted to a jury hereafter. I am not dissatisfied with the nonsuit on the merits as in evidence (a).

JONES, J., concurred. *Per Cur.*—Rule discharged.

BANK OF UPPER CANADA V. LEWIS.

Endorsees v. Endorser of a promissory note. The defendant pleads that *before* and *at* the time when the note became due, and at the time of the commencement of the suit, the plaintiffs, as bankers and agents, had in their hands divers sums of money of the maker of the note, amounting to £500, and were *then* indebted to the maker in that amount, and that the maker *then* directed the plaintiffs to retain to their own use the amount of the said note out of the said moneys, which exceeded the amount of the said note, &c.
Demurrer to plea.
Held, plea bad, in not averring the particular time when the direction was given.

The defendant was sued as the third endorser of a note, made by one Blasdell, for £200, payable to the order of A. Christie, at the agency of the Bank of Upper Canada, in Bytown.

He pleaded that *before* and *at* the time when the note became due, and at the time of the commencement of this suit, the plaintiffs (at whose office in Bytown the note was made payable), as the bankers and agents of Blasdell, had in their hands divers sums of money of Blasdell, amounting to £500, and were *then* indebted to Blasdell in that amount; and that Blasdell *then* directed the plaintiffs to retain to their own use the amount of the said note out of the said moneys, which exceeded the amount of the said note, and all damages sustained on occasion of the non-payment thereof.

Demurrer to plea for uncertainty and upon other grounds appearing in the judgment.

S. Richards, for the demurrer, contended that the plea was bad, in not stating

---

(a) See 1 C. & M. 89; 3 Tyr. 26; 13 East. 250; 1 A. & E. 488; 1 C. & D. 329 (Irish Rep.); 12 Law Jour. 15; 1 Arch. N. P. 193; Dalton v. Botts, Taylor's Reports (in this court).

when the direction was given by Blasdell to the plaintiffs to retain his moneys in their hands to pay the note; it did not even shew that it had been given before the commencement of the action. He cited 10 M. & W. 371; 2 M. & G. 329; 2 U. C. Jurist, 226; and submitted that the plea was clearly bad for uncertainty in a very material and traversable fact.

Eccles, contra, contended that the plea was sufficiently certain; that the words "*then directed,*" as used in the plea, meant that the direction was given when the note became due.—3 Chitty Pl. 168; 7 M. & W. 512; 5 B. & Al. 815.

ROBINSON, C. J.—I am of opinion the plea is bad on several accounts. The defendant merely states certain facts, without shewing what defence he relies upon as arising out of them, and leaving it doubtful on the facts stated what defence, if any, they could constitute. Nothing but Blasdell's express direction to the plaintiffs to appropriate his money in their hands to the payment of this note, could possibly make the other facts stated of any consequence. The alleged direction, therefore, was a material traversable fact, and ought to have been stated with an allegation of a particular time when the direction was given; instead of that, it is merely averred that Blasdell *then* directed, and it is uncertain whether we are to apply the word "then" to the time "*before* "*the note became due,*" or "*when it became due,*" or "*at the time of the com- "mencement of the suit,*" for all these are mentioned just before in the same sentence.

If we should properly refer them to the last preceding time named, then the direction would appear not to have been given till this suit had been commenced.

If the direction being given was binding upon the plaintiffs, and was before the action brought, then it was a payment, and should have been pleaded as such; but to make the plea good in that case the plaintiffs should have been holders of the note on their own account, which is not averred.

If not given till after the suit was commenced, then the plea could only operate as a defence by shewing money paid and *accepted* in satisfaction and discharge, which the plea does not shew.

MACAULAY, J.—The plea appears to me insufficient, for the causes assigned. It is not certain whether the direction to the plaintiffs to appropriate funds in hand to the payment of the note, was before, at, or after maturity, or indeed whether before or after suit. If before maturity, and if the funds remained in hand until and at maturity, it is probable the maker had a right to direct the application of a sum sufficient to satisfy the note, and the maker was not indebted to the plaintiffs on any other account, even without the plaintiffs assenting thereto; but if afterwards, in that event it must be pleaded not as a plea of *solvit ad diem*, but of accord and satisfaction, in which assent would be essential. If before due, it would be in effect a plea of payment; but if the funds continued in hand till the time of suit unappropriated, it would follow that the note had not been previously paid.

JONES, J., concurred.

Per Cur.—Judgment for plaintiffs on the demurrer.

KEESER v. McMARTIN, SHERIFF, &c. ET AL.

Semble, that when the sheriff, on a *fi. fa.*, seizes goods in the possession of the debtor, and a third party claims them as his, under a bill of sale, which is impeached as being merely pretended and colourable, the sheriff, when sued in trespass for taking the goods, may, upon a plea that the goods are not the plaintiff's, contest his right on the ground of fraud, without proving the judgment; and the learned judge reporting that the non-production of the judgment was not objected to at the trial, the court would not afterwards entertain the objection.

Declaration. 1st count. Trespass *quare clausum fregit* and for taking goods.

2nd count, for taking goods.

Pleas. 1st. General issue.

2nd. Property of the plaintiff denied in the house and goods.

The defendant, as sheriff, had sold certain goods on a *fi. fa.*, as being the goods of one McCosh, the defendant in a suit at suit of Hutchinson and Birss.

The plaintiff claimed the goods under a bill of sale from McCosh, which was impeached at the trial on the ground of fraud.

The *fi. fa.* was produced in evidence at the trial, but not the judgment. No objection was taken to the non-production of the judgment.

Verdict for the defendant.

P. M. Vankoughnet moved for a new trial on the law and evidence and for misdirection; he relied upon 1 Taunt. 381; 2 B. & Ald. 134; 8 A. & E. 111; 1 Ld. Rayd. 724; 1 M. & S. 251, submitting that the defendant ought to have produced at the trial, before being allowed to question the assignment on the ground of fraud, the *fi. fa.* and judgment upon which the seizure had been made.

S. B. Harrison, Q.C., shewed cause. The *fi. fa.* was produced at the trial; there was no objection urged at the trial to the non-production of the judgment; it was now too late; under all the circumstances of the case, however, he submitted that fraud in the alleged assignment could be shewn without proving either the *fi. fa.* or judgment; he cited 8 A. & E. 121.

ROBINSON, C. J.—The learned judge reports that no objection on account of the non-production of the judgment was made at the trial, though there were other points raised by the defendant's counsel which are noted.

The bill of sale was palpably a mere colourable and fraudulent assignment on the evidence, and was so found by the jury, on the case being left to them on that point. The transaction was not open and public, and there was no adequate consideration to support it. The debtor, McCosh, remained in possession after the sale the same as before, disposing of the goods and keeping no account of them, and he actually made payments to the plaintiff, out of the proceeds after the alleged sale, on account of the very debts which it was pretended formed the consideration for the transfer.

A clearer case of fraudulent assignment could not be shewn. The plaintiff's counsel rested his objection on the ground that the debtor being placed in possession after the bill of sale by the plaintiff, must be regarded as being his servant or agent, holding possession for him, and that the possession, under such circumstances, was not fraudulent; but upon the evidence the fraudulent nature of the transaction was apparent. In such a case, where the goods were not taken out of the plaintiff's possession, but out of the possession of the defendant on the *fi. fa.*, and where consequently the plaintiff shews no right to damages till he has shewn his interest in the goods, I do not take it to be necessary that a judgment or execution must be shewn on the part of the defendant in order to let in the defence that the alleged transfer was a mere deceitful pretence; and in fact there was enough evidence here to lead to the conclusion, that if there was a transfer of the goods, it was afterwards repudiated and abandoned.

But if it was necessary to prove a judgment, that point was not urged at the trial; and it would be wrong to entertain the objection now as a ground for granting a new trial. If the objection had been taken at the trial, it is possible the evidence might have been supplied; and it would be only harassing the parties with useless expense to set aside this verdict, when it is clear the result must be the same on a second trial, for the judgment and *fi. fa.* would then be proved; and it is clear that the transfer of the goods was a mere colourable contrivance not intended to pass the property.

MACAULAY, J., and JONES, J., concurred.

Per Cur.—Rule discharged.

JONES v. GEORGE ROSS, JOHN ROSS AND JOHN BARNES.

The plaintiff declares against the defendants in trespass for an assault, beating, bruising and ill-treating. A., one of the defendants, justifies, alleging that upon suspicion that plaintiff had stolen his goods, he laid his information before a justice of the peace of the Niagara District, who granted a warrant directed *to the constable of Thorold*, in the Niagara District, authorizing him to search the plaintiff's house at the *township of Louth*, in the said district, for the said goods; that B., another defendant, being *the constable of Thorold, in the said district*, at the request of A., searched the house, found the goods, and arrested the plaintiff at Louth, and, *at the request* of A., carried her before a magistrate. Demurrer to plea.

Held, plea bad, in assuming to answer the whole injury complained of, and yet not denying, nor confessing and avoiding the arrest.

Held also, that the direction of the magistrate *to the constable of Thorold*, not naming him, to execute the warrant in *the township of Louth,* was good.

Quære, whether, when a defendant is charged with arresting, bruising, beating and ill-treating the plaintiff, a justification of the *mere arrest* will be sufficient?

Declaration.—1st count, trespass for assault, beating, bruising and ill-treating the plaintiff, and for false imprisonment for one hour.

2nd count, common assault. *Venue,* Niagara District.

Pleas.—1st, not guilty, per statute.

2nd plea, by *George Ross,* to the 1st count, a justification, alleging that divers goods and chattels of his had been stolen (not saying when); that he had cause to suspect the plaintiff, whereupon he made oath before Hobson, a justice of the peace in and for the district aforesaid, of the arceny, and his suspicion that the goods were concealed in the plaintiff's house in the said district; upon which information the said justice granted a warrant under his hand ånd seal, directed to *the constable of Thorold*, authorizing him, with necessary assistance, to enter the plaintiff's house, at the township *of Louth* in the said district, and to search for the said goods, &c.; that the defendant Barnes, being constable of Thorold *in the said district*, at the request of *the defendant* (not saying which), and under the authority of the said warrant, entered and searched the plaintiff's house, &c., in Louth, and there found the said goods, &c., and took the same into his possession, &c., and the said Barnes *gently laid* his hand on the plaintiff and took and arrested her at *Louth* aforesaid, on suspicion of the said felony, and to take her before a justice, and did accordingly, *at the request of the said George Ross*, carry and convey her before — Lovell, Esq., a J.P., &c., who discharged her, &c., which were the said supposed trespasses in the first count mentioned.

Demurrer to the 2nd plea.—That it neither confessed nor denied that the said George Ross was guilty of the trespasses complained of in the declaration, but merely justified the trespasses of Barnes; and that if the act of one defendant could be justified as the act of another, it was not stated with sufficient certainty at the request of which defendant the said Barnes committed the said trespasses, &c.; that it was not stated that Barnes acted within his jurisdiction, or that he was a constable of the Niagara District, or that Louth was within that district.

Eccles, for the demurrer, contended that the plea was bad upon two grounds: first, that it professed to answer the whole of the injury complained of in the first count, yet that it certainly did not deny or confess and avoid the first act of trespass, viz., the arrest by Barnes the constable, which was the very gist of the action: this was clearly a fatal defect in the plea. Secondly, a search warrant is averred to have been issued by the magistrate to *the constable of Thorold*, and it is then shewn that the constable went to the *township of Louth*, and there executed his warrant. It did not appear that the constable had any authority in the township of Louth.—Cro. Eliz. 94.

Cameron, Sol.-Gen., contra, contended that the township of Louth being averred to be in the Niagara District, was all that was necessary; for by our Township Act, constables appointed to a township had authority to execute warrants throughout the district in which the township was situate; that at all events, supposing the plea formally defective in this respect, it would sufficiently appear from the statement of facts which the plea disclosed, that the defendant Ross could have arrested the plaintiff without reference to the warrant at all, and that therefore the averment that related to the direction the magistrate had given in his warrant might be rejected as surplusage; the defendant Ross might rely on the constable's right to act without a warrant. He cited 1 B. & C. 288; 1 Hale, P. C. 459; 5 Tyr. 186. It was averred that the plaintiff was carried to the justice at *the request of Ross;* this, he submitted, was a sufficient admission of the trespass by the defendant Ross.

ROBINSON, C. J.—The first point which this demurrer presents is, whether the defendant John Barnes, being constable for Thorold, could legally execute the warrant, the township of Louth not being named in the warrant, and Barnes being specially directed by the magistrate, *as the constable of Thorold*, to execute the warrant upon the plaintiff in the township of Louth. My brothers are clear in the opinion that he could, taking the view of the case which Mr. Justice Holroyd seems to sanction by his judgment in Rex v. Wier (a). At present I should not feel clear in so ruling; but, however this may be, I agree in the opinion that the plea is bad, for it professes to answer the whole injury complained of in the first count, and yet neither denies nor confesses, and avoids the taking part in making the arrest complained of. For all that is stated in this plea he may have been absent at the time, and may have had no knowledge whatever of the arrest when it was made; he does indeed state that after Barnes had made the arrest, he (George Ross) requested him to take the plaintiff before a magistrate, but that does not connect him with the arrest.

It is consistent with all the statements in this plea that George Ross may in the first instance have merely gone before a magistrate and made his complaint, which he had a right to do; but upon that the justice may, as his own act, and without any request of Ross, have made his warrant to the constable of Thorold. If the execution of that warrant in Louth would, under the circumstances, have made Barnes a trespasser, it clearly could not have made G. Ross liable, because he had done nothing more than made his complaint on oath, and it was the duty of the magistrate to make a good warrant upon it, if he made any, and the duty of the constable to execute the warrant in a legal manner—Ross would not be responsible for the error or excess of authority of the one or the other. If the plaintiff was illegally arrested by Barnes, the defendant George Ross would not be liable for it unless he was present and acting in aid of the constable, or had given him some express direction apart from the warrant, and nothing of this kind is stated in the plea; though it is stated that after he had been arrested Ross requested the constable to take him before a justice. If that was a trespass, he would be liable for it; but the previous arrest he neither confesses nor denies, and therefore does not answer the whole count, though he undertakes to do so. The plea is bad.

MACAULAY, J.—The plea does not shew that the defendant George Ross was present aiding or assisting in the *arrest*, or that it was made at his request. He alleges that he *requested* Barnes to search the plaintiff's house for the stolen goods, and requested him to take her before Mr. Lovell; both of which, especially the former, the warrant commanded him to do.

It is not alleged that the defendant George Ross procured the warrant to issue. It was not *his act*, but *the act* of the justice upon his information and oath, and for its execution he would not be liable in trespass, though responsible in case. Then, is it shewn sufficiently that he was *prima facie* a co-trespasser with Barnes in making the arrest, which is the gist of the action, for the tort to the plaintiff's person? Upon not guilty pleaded, the defendant would be entitled to a verdict, if the plaintiff merely proved that upon his information (as stated in the plea) the justice issued the warrant under which Barnes arrested her. It would not shew it to be *his act*. It is not like a civil action, in which the plaintiff in the writ sues it out and delivers it to the sheriff to execute. Its issue, &c., is his act, and he is *prima facie* a trespasser for an

---

(a) 1 B. & C. 294.

arrest under it as made at his request and for his benefit; not so in criminal cases, where the warrant is the act of the justice, judging and exercising his discretion upon the complainant's statements.

On the ground that the plea professing to answer the whole count does not sufficiently confess and avoid the *arrest*, which (if any) is the assault and battery which the plea professes to answer, and the gist of the action as respects the tort to the person, I think the plea bad (*a*). It is not objected that a mere arrest does not sufficiently justify a battery, bruising and ill-treating, though it is perhaps open to such objection.

As to the warrant, I am of opinion that it is good. The provincial statute 33 Geo. III. ch. 2, empowers the justices in quarter sessions to appoint a sufficient number of persons as in their discretion shall be necessary to serve the office of constable in each and every township, &c. It is alleged that Barnes was constable of Thorold, and that the warrant was directed to the constable of Thorold. If it appeared there were several persons appointed to the office of constable of Thorold, it might be more questionable, But it is alleged that Barnes was such constable, and, if so, the writ commanded him to enter the plaintiff's house in Louth and search for goods, &c. Now, although a warrant to a peace officer by the name of his office gives him no authority out of the precincts of his jurisdiction, still it does not follow that such authority may not be expressly given on the face of the warrant, as in this case.

The case of The King v. Weir et al. (*b*) and of Davies v. Jenkins (*c*), are instances of warrants worded in general terms, and not like the present; and in the former, Holroyd, J., seems to have anticipated a case like the present, and approved of a warrant like the one now in question (*d*).

If a certain individual (A. B.), for example, is constable of Thorold, and if a warrant, directed him by the name of A. B. to search a house and arrest a party in Louth, would be valid, I do not see why a similar warrant addressed to him by the name of office [the constable of Thorold] should not be equally good. It seems to me correct in substance; and I can find no case that warrants me in holding the constable who executes such a warrant, and all who aid and assist him, trespassers.

JONES, J., concurred.   *Per Cur.*—Judgment for plaintiff on demurrer.

IN RE McLACHLAN, AN OVERHOLDING TENANT.

The court will not grant an attachment against an overholding tenant, under the 4 Will. IV. ch. 7, sec. 55, for the non-payment of costs, until an order to pay the costs has been first served upon the tenant and a demand made.

This was the case of a tenant overholding, and proceeded against by his landlord, under the provisions of the Real Property Act, 4 Will. IV. ch. 7, sec. 53.

Upon an inquisition taken and returned under the Act, a precept issued to

---

(*a*) 3 M. & W. 418, West v. Smallwood.   (*b*) 1 B. & C. 288, and 2 D. & R. S. C.
(*c*) 11 M. & W. 745.   (*d*) 1 Hale, P. C. 459; Comb. 446.

put the landlord into possession, and a writ to levy the costs, to which the sheriff had returned *nulla bona*.

The landlord applied to the court for an attachment to be issued at once, under the 55th clause.

ROBINSON, C. J., delivered the judgment of the court.

We think before an attachment can properly go, there must be an order to pay the costs, which being served upon the party and a demand made, an attachment can then go, as in other cases for non-payment of costs.

Per Cur.—Rule refused.

QUEEN'S BENCH.

MICHAELMAS TERM, 10 VICTORIA.

Present,—THE HON. CHIEF JUSTICE ROBINSON.
" MR. JUSTICE MACAULAY.
" MR. JUSTICE JONES.
" MR. JUSTICE MCLEAN.

MR. JUSTICE HAGERMAN sitting in the Practice Court.

McGRATH v. COX.

A plaintiff charging a defendant with *publishing* a libellous pamphlet against him, is not entitled to have the alleged libellous matter read upon the production of evidence merely leading to the presumption that one or two pamphlets, seen in the defendant's hands, and delivered by him to others at their request, *but not produced at the trial*, and which, for all that appeared, had never been read, were in all respects identical in their contents with a pamphlet which somebody else, unconnected with the defendant, had been proved to publish.

JONES, J., *dissentiente.*

Before secondary evidence of the publication of a libellous pamphlet can be received, it must be shewn that notice to produce the identical pamphlet has been served; or that it has been either lost or destroyed.

Quære: When a declaration complaining of the *publication* of a libel contains but *one count*, can a plaintiff, having already given evidence of the publication of a certain pamphlet as the cause of action, be allowed to introduce evidence of *another and distinct publication*, the defendant being neither the author nor printer of the libel charged?

A plaintiff *requesting* a nonsuit, rather than risk his case with a jury, cannot afterwards be allowed in *banc* to move against the nonsuit.

This was an action for libel.

The defendant pleaded the general issue; and as to several of the passages charged as libellous, pleaded their truth in justification.

The case was tried at the Home Assizes, before the Chief Justice.

The plaintiff's counsel, Mr. *Cameron*, after opening his case to the jury, went into evidence to prove the publication of the libel, which was stated to have been contained in a printed pamphlet; and after examining several witnesses, he represented to the court that his evidence to prove the publication fell much short of what he had been led to suppose it would have been in his power to produce. He stated that he was not aware that he could carry his proof further, except by shewing one or two additional circumstances which might not be thought material, and he submitted that it might be more convenient to the parties to ascertain in that stage of the cause whether, in the opinion of the court, the publication was sufficiently proved. The Chief Justice observed, that it might lead to embarrassing discussions hereafter, if anything was to be taken on the plaintiff's statement of what he could have proved in addition to what he had proved; and he suggested therefore that he should go on, and produce whatever evidence he was able to give of the fact of publication, and when it should all be heard he would give an opinion on the sufficiency of the proof. Some further evidence was then given, and the plaintiff having closed his case, the Chief Justice said, that as the parties were both there with many witnesses, to prove or disprove the special pleas, some of whom they might be unable to procure upon another trial, he was willing to go into the whole case, however tedious it might be, there being no less than ten pleas of justification on the record, applying to as many distinct passages in the libel, on all of which the plaintiff had joined issue; and he proposed, that although he did not consider there then was such evidence as would be found to warrant the jury to find the publication of the alleged libel by the defendant proved, yet with the consent of the parties he would reserve that point for consideration in *banc*, and give the defendant leave to move to enter a nonsuit, if it should be determined that there was not sufficient evidence of publication to be left to the jury. One, if not both of the parties, preferred that the question of the sufficiency of evidence to prove publication should be first disposed of by the court; and the Chief Justice then proceeded to state his opinion that the evidence of publication was not such as ought to satisfy the jury, and that their verdict should on that ground be given for the defendant; and the plaintiff's counsel thereupon accepted a nonsuit.

Cameron, Sol.-Gen., moved to set aside the nonsuit. He relied upon Gathercole v. Miall, 10 Jurist, 23rd April, 1846; 7 A. & E. 223, 233; 3 Camp. 228, as authorities to shew that the evidence adduced at the trial in this case (which appears at length in the judgments of the court), was sufficient to prove publication, so as to entitle the pamphlet in the possession of the witness James McGrath, which he produced at the trial, to be read against the defendant.

W. H. Blake shewed cause.—He contended that the evidence given was far too loose and unsatisfactory to shew a publication, by defendant, of the alleged libellous matter contained in the pamphlet produced in court by the witness McGrath. He referred to the cases cited by the opposite counsel, and submitted that in all of them the contents of the publication were certainly shewn, and that the only doubt was whether the defendant had published; but in this case the contents of the pamphlets traced to the defendant were not proved.

He also strongly contended that, upon the principle of law as applicable to secondary evidence, the plaintiff had entirely failed to place himself in a position to resort to this mode of proof; he had given no notice to the defendant to produce any one of the three identical pamphlets proved to have been delivered by the defendant to three different individuals, and had given no evidence of their being lost or destroyed. He cited 4 M. & Gr. 598; 2 A. & E. 49; Jurist, 1846, page 347.

ROBINSON, C. J.—The defendant objects that, under the circumstances which occurred at the trial, the nonsuit is conclusive upon the plaintiff. That objection depends upon a principle which, where it does apply, is in itself very reasonable and just. When a plaintiff, finding that the case is going to the jury upon a charge so unfavourable to him upon the merits, that rather than take the risk of a verdict against him, he interposes with a request to be nonsuited, then he is held to be precluded from moving afterwards against the nonsuit. But I think it would not be fair, under the circumstances of this case, to hold the plaintiff to be within the rule. It was raised as a preliminary question, whether the publication had been sufficiently proved; and although I was willing to have let the case proceed, and to have left to the jury the evidence of publication, such as it was, yet I certainly gave the plaintiff's counsel to understand, that unless I should change my opinion on that point during the trial (which I thought not probable), I should tell the jury that in my judgment there had not been such proof of publication as the law required, and that it would not be proper for them to convict upon such evidence. It appeared to me that both parties were unwilling to press the cause on, from a reluctance to enter upon a very tedious and disagreeable mass of evidence under the special pleas, while the preliminary objection was open and unsettled. Mr. Cameron, the counsel for the plaintiff, had reason to suppose that the jury would be finally instructed that the libel had not been proved; and when he acquiesced for the time in the view which he understood the court to take of it, I have no doubt he considered, and I think he was warranted by what passed in considering, that if my impression at the trial was erroneous, he would be relieved from the nonsuit. Then the effect of the evidence was this: the alleged libel, it appeared, was contained in a printed pamphlet, of which it was not pretended that this defendant was either the author or printer; but he was charged, upon the following testimony, with having published it. Sometime in the autumn of 1844, there was a large public meeting in the township of Chinguacousy, on an occasion connected with an election; a person named Dean was on the ground and had a number of pamphlets in a waggon, which he was disposing of to the bystanders. This professed to be a history of the plaintiff and his family, and it contained the passages charged in the declaration to be libellous. The defendant was not shewn to have been acting in privity with Dean, or to have had any part in publishing the identical pamphlet produced, which was the only copy intended to be submitted by the plaintiff to the jury. But it was proved that a gentleman, seeing the defendant have two copies of a pamphlet in his bosom, asked him for one of them, and got it from him; that, before reading any part of it, he put it in his pocket, and afterwards gave it to a third person, by the name of Bell, never having perused any part of it; that Bell took it home, but did not himself read it;

that it was out of his possession for a time, and that he understood a pamphlet was brought back to his house, which he supposed might be the same; and being examined on the trial, he swore that he did not know where that pamphlet then was. He did not say that he believed it to be lost or destroyed, or that he had ever searched for it, or been requested to search for it; and not having read any part of it, he could give no account whatever of its contents. It was further proved, that upon the same day that the defendant had parted with this pamphlet, whatever it was, he had given a pamphlet also to another person upon the ground, by the name of Silverthorn: that Silverthorn, being asked by the plaintiff's son to let him have this pamphlet, declined, and returned it to the defendant, without reading any part of it. It was proved by the plaintiff's son, that while he held in his hand the pamphlet which afterwards got into Bell's hands, he had observed its general appearance; had looked at the title page and read the dedication; and from this comparison alone, he came to the conclusion that the pamphlet was the same in its contents as the one which he produced in court. He had not read in it any of the passages charged in the declaration as libellous, and did not describe the number of pages, or give any other proof of similarity than I have mentioned. In addition to this, it was proved, that some time after the day of this meeting, the defendant had asked a person who proved this upon the trial, whether he had read the history of the McGrath family? and being told he had not, the defendant produced a printed pamphlet, and read from it various passages, which the witness swore related to some of the matters set forth in the declaration, which he particularized; he could not repeat any of the language, but merely recollected the general subject-matter. The plaintiff had served the defendant's attorney with a notice to produce a certain pamphlet, called "History of the McGrath "family," not making any particular reference to the copy which Silverthorn had returned to the defendant; that is, not calling on him to produce the identical book. When the plaintiff's counsel referred to the court for its opinion, whether he was entitled to read the alleged libel, he had not given any evidence of the comparison, such as it was, which had been made by the plaintiff's son between the pamphlet which he produced in court, and the one which Mr. Morrison, the first witness, had shewn to him. The plaintiff had no pamphlet to lay before the jury, which the defendant had in any manner published, and there was therefore no such pamphlet which I could direct to be read; what was requested was, that the copy which Dean, or some other person, and not the defendant, had published to the plaintiff's son, and containing, I believe, fifty or sixty pages, should be read against the defendant; and that he should be held to have published a libel precisely identical with that, upon the grounds of presumption afforded by the evidence, that one or other of the pamphlets which had been seen in the defendant's hands, and had been handed by him to others at their request, but which, for all that appeared, no one had ever read, was in all respects the same in its contents. I consider that the plaintiff, when he brought his action, must necessarily be understood to have had some particular act of publication in view, which he complained of as the injury. If what he complained of was the publication of the pamphlet which had got into the hands of Bell, then the difficulty was, that he neither produced that pamphlet to the jury, nor entitled himself to give secondary evidence of it, by shewing it destroyed or lost: I mean no such evidence of loss after diligent search as the law requires, and if I could have received secondary evidence of that publication, yet none was offered that could have been received, for no examined copy was in the possession of the plaintiff; no one had read it, or could describe its contents, or had in any degree compared it with any other pamphlet produced to the jury. The declaration contained but one count, and charged but one publication; and if the plaintiff, having given such evidence as he could of a publication to the first witness, was at liberty to go into proof of another cause of action, and recover for a distinct publication of another pamphlet, and to another person, then it became necessary to consider how the case stood, in regard to the copy delivered by the defendant to Silverthorn, and returned by him unread. As to that pamphlet, it was no more before the jury than the other which had been attempted to be proved; and when it is considered how much in anything written or spoken may depend upon the difference of a few words, or a single word, and how strictly a party is held to the necessity of proving publication, in all essential particulars, exactly such as he declares upon, I thought it too much to assume, if secondary evidence could be admitted, that the book handed by the defendant to Silverthorn contained all the libellous passages which might be found in another pamphlet which Dean had given to the plaintiff's son; and there was no more proof that it contained any one of these passages than that it contained all of them: no one had read it, and the evidence which was afterwards given by Mr. James McGrath of his having looked at the title, and read the dedication, did not appear to me to be sufficient to lay a safe foundation for the inference that it contained the same number of pages as the pamphlet which he had got from Dean, and that the contents of each page were the same. It was some evidence certainly to give to the jury, and which would have been given to them, if the case had proceeded but with a direction that in my opinion it was insufficient to establish the fact of publishing the libel charged. Before, however, I could have submitted this evidence of a publication to Silverthorn, I must have considered in the first place whether the plaintiff, having before given evidence of the publication of a pamphlet to the first witness as a cause of action, was at liberty to introduce evidence of a distinct publication also as a cause of action, upon a declaration containing but one count, complaining of the publication of a libel (a); and next, whether he had entitled himself to give secondary evidence of that libel alleged to have been published to Silverthorn. The only notice proved, made no mention of the particular pamphlet re-delivered by Silverthorn, but of a pamphlet so described, that any other copy which the defendant may have had in his possession, answering to such a description, would have been a compliance with the notice; whereas, what the jury required to have proved to them was the contents of a certain pamphlet which had once been in the possession of Silverthorn; and until the defendant had been duly called on to produce that same pamphlet (not one like it), or until it could be shewn to have been lost or destroyed, no secondary evidence of its contents could properly be received. The plaintiff, as I conceive, must be

---

(a) See 1 Lewin, 83—Rowbattle's case.

looked upon always as prosecuting for the injury arising from publishing some
one certain libel, to which particular act of publication his cause of action is
confined; and if he relied upon the giving a certain book to Silverthorn, as
constituting that act of publication, he must produce that book, or prove it to
be lost or destroyed, or call upon the defendant to produce that individual
book, not any book having merely a similar title-page, which book the defendant may never have published; and then if he could have given evidence of
its contents satisfactory to a jury, he could recover. It was proved on the
part of the plaintiff, that when the defendant was asked by the first witness
to let him have one of the two pamphlets which he had in his possession, he
referred him to Dean (from whom therefore we may suppose he got his copies);
this afforded, no doubt, strong ground for inferring that the copy which he
gave to that witness was a pamphlet of the same sort as those Dean was
selling; but if that had been proof strong enough to convict the defendant of
the offence, which I did not think it was, still there were the difficulties, that
in regard to that copy, no one had examined or read a word of it; and in
respect to it, as well as the other copy, the plaintiff was not in a position, as
it appeared to me, to give secondary evidence, if sufficient secondary evidence
had been in his power. I do not suppose that the plaintiff intended to rely
upon the evidence of the defendant having, on a subsequent occasion, read
passages from a pamphlet to a third witness, as proof of a distinct substantive
cause of action under the single count. If he did it would be subject to the
same observations as the others, for no notice had been served on the defendant
to produce the pamphlet which had been read to that witness; and as it was not
imputed to the defendant that he was either the author or printer or publisher
of the book, or in any manner connected with the press from which it emanated, a case could only be established against him by shewing that some one
book, containing the passages complained of, had come from his hand. For
the reasons I have mentioned, I did not think that sufficiently proved. And
it is my opinion at present, that if I had allowed the evidence to go to the
jury, as I was willing to have done, if it had been pressed, though with a
charge unfavourable to the plaintiff upon the mere fact of publication, I should
have taken a wrong course. If my brothers think otherwise, and if they are
also of opinion that in case the jury had been satisfied with the proof of publication, their verdict in the plaintiff's favour could have been sustained, then
the plaintiff should be relieved from the nonsuit. The cases of Johnson v.
Hudson & Morgan, cited in a note to Watts v. Fraser (a), and of Gathercole
v. Miall, in the Court of Exchequer, cited in the Jurist (b), were referred to
by the plaintiff's counsel, as being the most strongly in point upon the question of evidence, and they do, I believe, go as far in support of the plaintiff
in this case as any that could be cited. In the first of those cases, the plaintiff
complained of the publication of a libellous song : Morgan was sued as the
printer, and Hudson as the vendor; and the question was not as to the contents of the song, but rather as to the sufficiency of the evidence to connect
the two defendants with it. The plaintiff rested his case upon a publication,
by singing the ballad in the street from a printed paper; and it was for him

---

(a) 7 Ad. & El. 233.   (b) 23rd April, 1846.

to satisfy the jury that that identical printed paper had been printed by Morgan and sold by Hudson. It was proved to have been actually bought at Hudson's shop, out of a parcel of 300, and that Morgan had printed 1,000 copies of it, of which he had sent 300 to Hudson. If that sufficiently identified the paper that had been in the hands of the ballad singer, then a publication was shewn for which the printer and vendor were responsible. With regard to the contents of the paper, there was no legal question of difficulty, for the proof was positive and clear that the paper itself was destroyed. That let in secondary evidence, and the person who sang the song, and the journeymen of Morgan who printed it, swore that the contents were the same as those of another copy produced, which Morgan had printed. In the case before us, the defendant was neither printer, nor proprietor, nor editor, and had no connection with the alleged libel further than as he could be shewn to have made himself liable by publishing some particular book which contained it. Then again, the particular copy which the plaintiff did open his case upon, he did not prove to have been either lost or destroyed, and he gave no such evidence of its contents as was given in Johnson v. Hudson & Morgan, for there the evidence was clear and positive, as it well might be, of the language of a song which had been committed to memory. In the other case of Gathercole v. Miall, the principal point, and that to which the arguments of counsel and the attention of the court were chiefly given, was, whether a sermon preached to a congregation was a fair subject of criticism, in the same spirit as the public acts of public men are? The question respecting proof of publication arose only incidentally, and did not affect the publication of the identical copy of the newspaper which was made the foundation of the action; that was proved precisely and beyond doubt, so that the plaintiff, without any question, was entitled to a verdict, if the action was libellous. But the plaintiff, in order to shew an unusual degree of malice in the defendant, desired to prove that he had been busy in circulating copies of this paper among persons who were not subscribers to it. That evidence did not go to the ground of action, but applied to the question of damages only; and it is obvious that evidence introduced for this subsidiary and secondary purpose, would not in general be so scrupulously sifted, after the foundation had been properly laid. And there again, as in the other case, the defendant was not a stranger to the libel before it was composed and printed, and therefore one that could only be made liable upon some one copy specifically traced to his hands: he was admitted to be the responsible editor. Then the proof which the plaintiff wished to give of further publication of the same libel, which he had already proved, was that it had been sent to a public reading-room. He proved that the same number of the same newspaper had been lying on the public table; that it had been taken away by some one and *never returned*, and had been searched for, and could not be found. Now, not to lay stress upon the reasonableness of the presumption, that one number of a well known daily newspaper is the same in its contents as another number of the same newspaper purporting to be issued on the same day, especially where the evidence was given only for the secondary purpose of shewing a more extensive circulation of that which had been already clearly proved against the defendant, the difference between that case and the present is, that the copy spoken of there was sworn to have been taken away and never returned; the copy of the pamphlet given to Bell, although it had been taken away, had been returned. It had not been searched for, and it had not been sworn that it could not be found. In giving judgment in the case of Gathercole v. Miall, Ch. B. Pollock says: "Several witnesses "appear to have been called, who were examined up to the point of saying "that they were not able to produce the newspapers sent them, and were then "not allowed to proceed in their evidence. I own it would have occurred to "me that unless the case were carried further, that evidence would go for "nothing. This appears to have occurred with several of the witnesses; and "no stress at all was laid on this kind of evidence, except where the copy "spoken of was either produced or proved to be lost, and evidence given of "its contents." And his lordship is careful to explain what he means by a paper being lost: "A paper of importance (he says), and which was not likely "to be permitted to perish, may call for a more minute investigation; but "that which may be viewed almost as waste-paper, and which no person is "likely to take care of, might be considered as lost, so as not to be produce- "able before a court and jury, after a search has been made in the place where "it is likely to be found, and it is not found there; and no person can suggest "any one place in which it is more likely to be than another."

Now, admitting that a pamphlet may, like a newspaper, be regarded almost as waste-paper, and as little likely to be preserved, still the evidence to prove loss in this case came altogether short of what his lordship ruled to be necessary. Then as to the contents: supposing it to be a case clearly open for the admission of secondary evidence, the learned Chief Baron, in the case referred to, remarks of the witness who had been examined,—"He appears to have "seen a newspaper which he took upon himself to say was one of the copies "of the number complained of. He must have been understood as meaning "to say that on grounds more or less clear and positive, but on some grounds, "he saw a paper, the contents of which he was ready to state." Now, Mr. James McGrath did not speak in any such terms of either copy of the book which he saw, and which had come from the defendant. He could only speak as to the general appearance, and the title-page and dedication. And when both the cases referred to are compared with the present, and it is considered that the proof wanted here was not for the purpose of proving additional circulation in order to shew malice or enhance damages, but was the proof necessary for shewing any cause of action whatever against the defendant, and any connection whatever with the libel, it is my opinion, that if we were to hold the publication of the libel set out in this declaration to have been proved upon the evidence that was given, we should carry such kind of proof further than can be shewn to have been ever done before, and further than it appears to me safe and right to do.

The language of the publication complained of is so extremely offensive, and the evidence of a deliberate intent to defame and injure the plaintiff and his family is so plain upon the face of it, that no judge could feel a reluctance in giving to a plaintiff who had been so assailed the full benefit of every legal and proper facility for making out his case; but I considered that by allowing the proof that had been given to be accepted as satisfactory, or rather as legal evidence of publication, I should be straining the law in a particular instance, which it is not permitted us to do. I think this rule should be discharged.

MACAULAY, J.—This is an application to set aside a nonsuit voluntarily taken by the plaintiff's counsel, without requesting the case to go to the jury. It is noted by the learned Chief Justice, in relation to the nonsuit, that the plaintiff could of course move against it, but no leave was expressly asked or given, and the Chief Justice did not rule that there was no evidence of publication, nor would he have refused to permit the pamphlet produced by the witness McGrath to be read, had it been desired ; in short, he would not have peremptorily stopped the case; but being strongly of opinion against the plaintiff as to the sufficiency of his proof, and intimating that he should advise the jury not to find a publication on evidence so slight and general, the plaintiff's counsel yielded to a nonsuit ; and considering the way in which it occurred, as has been fully explained by the learned Chief Justice, I do not see that it can be set aside, and the costs of the day on the defence be thrown upon the defendant, unless we see that he was wrong. The evidence, in the opinion of the Chief Justice, fell short of proof of publication ; but he would (if pressed to do so) have left it to the jury for their consideration, advising them at the same time that, in his estimation, it did not warrant the inference they were desired to draw from it, namely, that the defendant had published the libel set forth in the record ; and I am not sure that such advice would have been wrong, for if there was sufficient evidence to go to the jury, it was loose and slight, and it was quite open to the learned Chief Justice to give his advice to the jury as to the weight he thought it ought to have with them. In its circumstances, the case very much resembles that of a counsel electing to be nonsuited, upon hearing the judge, in leaving the case to the jury, strongly incline against the plaintiff, as to the results to which the evidence ought to lead. In Butler v. Dorant (a)—*assumpsit* on a special agreement—at the trial by special jury, Mansfield, C. J., in summing up, told the jury, the plaintiff not having distinctly proved any special damage, was entitled to nominal damages only, whereupon Best, for plaintiff, elected to be nonsuited ; and upon a rule *nisi* to set such nonsuit aside, Lawrence J., said : "His lordship did not say you should be "nonsuited ; he directed the jury that you should have nominal damages only, "*but you did not choose to trust your case with the jury.* If there was a mis. "direction, you should have abided the verdict, and then moved for a new "trial. I believe this has never been done, that a counsel shall lie by until he "hears the opinion of the judge at *nisi prius;* and that if he thereupon "chooses to be nonsuited, he shall come to the court to set aside his own act." Now, in the case before us, the views of the learned Chief Justice were not communicated to the jury in summing up, but a discussion arose upon the plaintiff's counsel moving that the pamphlet should be read, which was objected to by the defendant's counsel, and a nonsuit moved for ; but certainly, as I understand it, the nonsuit was the voluntary act of the plaintiff's counsel; of course he could not be nonsuited without his own consent ; and it appears to have been taken not so much in deference to the opinion of the learned Chief Justice, in opposition to his own, as in submission to or acquiescence in that opinion. See Robinson v. Cook (b), that if the plaintiff's counsel acquiesces in the judge's ruling at the trial, whereby the defendant takes a

---

(a) 3 Taunt. 229.   (b) 6 Taunt. 336.

verdict without going into his case, he will not be permitted to move for a new trial on the ground of misdirection. In that case the court inclined to think both the objections good, but peremptorily refused, after the points had been abandoned by the plaintiff's counsel at the trial, and the defendant thereby precluded from going into his defence, to permit them to be even mooted. Had the present case gone to the jury without any defence, and a verdict been rendered for the defendant, it would very much have resembled the above case. McL. 69; McL. & Y. 286; Attorney-General v. Good, 2 Bing. 528; Elsworthy v. Bird, 13 Price, 222; per Garrow (Baron), "whatever objection plaintiff's "counsel might have had to be nonsuited, it should have been expressed in "some manner to the learned judge, and not having done so, I am of opinion "they must be taken to have acquiesced. In all cases where counsel does not "*expressly* object to be nonsuited, I should consider it to be the nonsuit, not "of the judge but of the plaintiff's own counsel, who are entitled if they please "to elect to be nonsuited, and they are certainly the judges of what is most "for the benefit of their client." In Ward v. Mason (*a*), Garrow (Baron) expressed the same opinion, but the Lord Chief Baron and other Barons set aside a nonsuit. This case favours the application in some points of view, but the dictum of Wood (Baron) is against it under any circumstances. Meredith v. Gilpin (*b*); Alexander v. Baker (*c*). That submission to the opinion of the judge will not preclude the party if his opinion be incorrect. McCullough v. Green (*d*). When there is evidence which by possibility might, if believed by the jury, lead to a verdict for the party relying on its effect, the judge is bound to submit such evidence to the jury, *if required so to do by the counsel for that party;* and if he do not, and a verdict is found against that party, the court according to its best judgment may set it aside, and grant a new trial.

Vacher v. Cox et al. (*e*); Simpson v. Clayton (*f*).—When plaintiff's counsel, after a judge has begun to sum up, proposes to be nonsuited, he cannot move to set it aside, although the judge may have expressed a strong opinion as to the *effect* of the plaintiff's evidence. Kindrid v. Bog (*g*).—The court will not set aside a nonsuit on the ground that the case ought to have been left to the jury, unless this was desired on the part of the plaintiff at the trial.

Wilkinson v. Whalley (*h*); per Erskine, J.—The distinction seems now to be, that upon a misdirection in point of law the plaintiff may elect to be nonsuited, and afterwards move to set it aside; but not if the misdirection be upon the facts, such as the expression of a strong opinion on the part of the judge. Creswell, J., was unwilling to go so far as this when the plaintiff elects to be nonsuited for misdirection in point of law. 4 Bing. N. S. 83; 9 Dowl. 181.— That a bill of exceptions will lie on a nonsuit. The explicit terms of the form in this case shew that an express request to leave the evidence to the jury was deemed necessary. Gibson et al. v. Johnson (*i*).—On a demurrer to circumstantial evidence, the party offering the evidence is not obliged to join in

---

(*a*) 9 Price, 291.   (*b*) 6 Price, 146.   (*c*) 2 Tyr. 150; 2 C. & J. 130, S. C.
(*d*) 1 All. & Nap. 5 (Irish Report).   (*e*) 1 B. & Adol. 145.
(*f*) 2 Bing. N. S. 467; 1 Hodg. 483.   (*g*) 1 Taunt. 10.
(*h*) 5 Man. & Gr. 590, 592.   (*i*) 2 H. B. 187, 206.

demurrer, unless the party demurring will distinctly admit upon the record every fact and every conclusion which the evidence offered conduces to prove. It therefore appears that the defendant could not have demurred to this evidence, and that the plaintiff's most formal mode of objection would have been by bill of exceptions, which would of course have raised the question whether the facts in evidence, if true, proved a publication by the defendant of a pamphlet identical with that produced by the witness McGrath, and whether the non-production of such published pamphlet was sufficiently excused to admit secondary evidence of its contents.

I have also considered the case as at *nisi prius*, at the close of the plaintiff's evidence, when the question was whether the facts in evidence, if true, were sufficient in law to entitle the plaintiff to have the libel read, and to warrant the jury in finding publication, in which event the court ought to have left it to them for their consideration.—5 Burr. 2689, Rex v. Ammon. To sustain the action the publication must be proved upon the defendant, and the libel cannot be read against him until it is proved upon him. If the evidence be sufficient in point of law, and the jury believe it, they should find accordingly. So the question for the court was, whether the evidence was sufficiently conducive to prove the publication on the defendant.

The plaintiff's object was to prove the publication of the libel as set forth in the declaration, and to do this through the medium of secondary proof by aid of the pamphlet produced by the witness McGrath; three efforts were made to establish the publication: first, by proof that it was rumoured that a pamphlet existed against the plaintiff's family, and that one Dean was on the ground at an election meeting with a waggon load of them; that the defendant was there, and seen in possession of several pamphlets, one of which he delivered to Mr. Morrison, who on request shewed it to the witness McGrath, who looked at the dedication or title page, and finding the outside appearance and dedication to correspond with the one he then had in his pocket, returned it to Mr. Morrison, after which Mr. Morrison delivered it (unread) to Mr. Bell; Mr. Bell did not read it, nor was it produced or proved to be lost, nor was any one called who had read it. Secondly, by proof of a pamphlet delivered by defendant to Silverthorn, who returned it to defendant. Thirdly, by proof that defendant asked Mr. Andrews if he had seen *the* pamphlet against the McGraths, and being told "no," sent his man for one and read about half of it; the portions read being about the McGraths leaving Ireland, the bear, Ann Simpson, and the defendant saying of some passages, "This we know to be true." As to No. 1, the pamphlet being traced to Mr. Bell was not produced, or proved to have been lost or destroyed; it was, apparently, last seen in the hands of his boy. No. 2 was not produced or read by any one who was examined; although it might be considered sufficient to supply the absence of the pamphlet in Bell's hands, on the ground that it was identical in its contents, and was in the defendant's hands, who had notice to produce not *it*, but *the* pamphlet against the McGrath family; this if admissible would be a circuitous way of proving the contents of that pamphlet, through the medium of secondary evidence. No. 3. Mr. Andrews did not read the pamphlet, nor did he examine the record with the pamphlet produced by Mr. McGrath, to say whether they correspond with what he heard the defendant read, if the purport of it could be suggested to him in that way; and the substance of what he heard so read, as related by him from memory, was not specific enough to establish the contents of the pamphlet he heard read as identical with the passages set forth in the declaration.

It did not appear when or where the witness McGrath obtained the pamphlet he produced; it was not connected with those said to be in Dean's possession, nor was any one called who, from having examined any of them, could speak of the contents of those which Dean had. Without recourse, therefore, to the pamphlet produced by Mr. McGrath, a publication of the libel laid in the declaration was not proved by any one, and the question was, whether that pamphlet was admissible as secondary evidence of the contents of some one or other of the pamphlets which the defendant was shewn to have published; it was not admissible in relation to the one delivered to Mr. Morrison, the original not being sufficiently accounted for; clearly not as respected the one received by Silverthorn, unless it could be connected with the one traced to Bell, as above suggested; even if the general notice to produce *the* pamphlet entitled, &c., was sufficient to admit proof of its contents; no one could speak to them; the same remark applies to the one partly read to Andrews. It may then be asked whether, taking all the evidence together, there was sufficient proof of the publication of one or more pamphlets not produced, to admit the reading of Mr. McGrath's as identical in point of contents. I have looked into several works upon evidence, and various cases, and however confidently it may be conjectured that all the pamphlets spoken of were identical in point of contents, I do not find any case in which an indictment, a criminal information, or a civil action (all requiring a like degree of proof on this head) has been sustained upon evidence so loose and unconnected as this. There seems to me a deficiency of legal proof to shew the *contents* of any pamphlet proved to have been published by the defendant identical with that produced by Mr. McGrath; his pamphlet was not connected with those Dean had; nor were those circulated by the defendant connected with them or with McGrath's, any further than that the one delivered to Mr. Morrison corresponded in general appearance, and the dedication and title page. It would be a violent presumption to infer in a prosecution for libel, that therefore all the libellous passages set out in the record, and which it may be assumed were contained in Mr. McGrath's pamphlet, were also contained in the one he so casually inspected, without comparing them. It appears to me there was a want of sufficient connection to constitute legal proof of publication upon the defendants. I do not see that the nonsuit was wrong, and without being so satisfied, it cannot be expected that, taken as it was, it can be set aside. I have read the cases of Watts v. Fraser, 7 A. & E. 223, and Johnson v. Henderson and Morgan, ib. 233, and consider the proof of publication far stronger in those cases than in the present; in the last a clear connection was shewn, and the proof was cogent and satisfactory to prove the publication upon both the defendants, even if restricted to the single printed copy sung from in the street. It was proved that Morgan had printed and published one thousand copies, of which Henderson received three hundred, one of which three hundred was evidently the one used by the singers, and that was proved to have been *destroyed*, and its *contents* were fully established. In the case of Gathercole v.

Miall, 10 Jurist (1846), page 337, and Law Times (17 April, 1846), the publication was clearly proved upon the defendant. The absent copy of the same number of the newspaper was only offered in aggravation of damages ; not even with a view to shew malice in the defendant, but only to prove that the paper had been circulated widely by some one or other. The remarks of the judges, especially of Mr. Baron Alderson, are however in favour of the admissibility of Mr. McGrath's evidence as sufficient for the jury in proof that the pamphlet produced and the one delivered by the defendant to Morrison were from the same types, or identical in point of contents. But the evidence there was obviously much stronger, and the object of the proof did not, as here, involve the very gist of the action, the fact of publication being clearly shewn previously. Upon the whole, therefore, I am of opinion that no sufficient ground is shewn for setting aside the nonsuit.

JONES, J.—The first question is, whether the plaintiff has a right to set aside the nonsuit, having submitted to be nonsuited at the trial. I think he has. The plaintiff's counsel having given such evidence as he had to offer, to prove the publication of the libel charged in the declaration, appealed to his lordship the Chief Justice (before whom the cause was tried) to express his opinion whether he considered the evidence sufficient to go to the jury to prove publication, and the Chief Justice "ruled the evidence insufficient to prove " publication, and directed a nonsuit," observing, "*Of course, Mr. Cameron* " *can move against it.*"

The plaintiff, a clergyman of the Church of England, sued the defendant for the publication of a libel, parts of which were set out upon the record as mentioned in the libel published ; and, amongst many other things, the improper conduct of the plaintiff and his son Charles, the clerk of the church at Springfield, of which the plaintiff was rector, "in proceeding to the church on a "Sunday with a bear, and his son Charles, on the termination of Divine "service, for the amusement of the children, and the plaintiff's pious family, "swimming the bear in the River Credit ;" also the advice of the plaintiff to his sons, "as to how they should act towards the girl Simpson." The defendant pleaded to the action not guilty, and several special pleas of justification. The identical libel charged to have been published by the defendant was not produced, but, being contained in printed pamphlets, the plaintiff attempted to prove the publication by the production of a printed pamphlet entitled, "The "sayings and doings of the self-styled royal family of the McGrath's, of " McKenzie Castle, Springfield," dated "Credit, Nov. 1, 184– ;" in which was contained all that was set forth as libellous in the declaration ; and by proving that a copy handed to Mr. Morrison, another sold to Silverthorn, and a third from which the defendant read certain passages to Andrews, were all of the same impression with that produced by the witness James McGrath. A notice to the following effect was proved or admitted to have been served upon the defendant's attorney : "Take notice, that you are hereby required to produce to the "court and to the jury, on the trial of this cause, a certain book or pamphlet "entitled, 'The sayings and doings of the self-styled royal family of the Mc- " 'Grath's, of McKenzie Castle, Springfield,' dated 'Credit, 1st Nov., 184–.'" It was proved by James McGrath, that in a public meeting in Chinguacousy, for the nomination of candidates for a member to be returned to Parliament, the defendant Cox had several pamphlets in his possession, and a large number was at the same time in a waggon upon the ground in possession of one Dean, said to be against the McGrath family. The defendant handed one of the pamphlets in his possession to Mr. Morrison, and referred him to Dean for others. McGrath requested Mr. Morrison to let him see the pamphlet which he said Cox handed to him; he had at the time in his pocket the copy produced at the trial, entitled "The sayings and doings of the self-styled royal "family of the McGraths, of McKenzie Castle, Springfield," and he desired to see this to ascertain whether it corresponded with the one in his possession. He examined the title-page and read the dedication, which, with the general appearance, corresponded with his copy, and he made the examination for the purpose of satisfying himself that it was one of the pamphlets which had been published against the McGrath family. Mr. Morrison afterwards gave the copy received from the defendant to one Bell. After Mr. Morrison had shewn the pamphlet to James McGrath, he told the defendant that the McGraths would prosecute him; to which the defendant replied, "that he did not think "that he did wrong in distributing them while McGrath was on the ground."

It was proved by Silverthorn, another witness, that being at the nomination before mentioned, he understood there was something in circulation about the McGrath family; that, seeing some pamphlets in the defendant's possession there, he asked him for one of them, and the defendant handed him one, for which he paid him 1s. 3d.; that James McGrath requested to see it, but he declined shewing it to him, and afterwards returned it to the defendant without opening or reading it. One Andrews proved, that last autumn a year the defendant was at his house and asked him if he had received any of the pamphlets against the McGraths; upon his replying in the negative, the defendant sent for one and read parts to him: he read passages about Jane Simpson, and about the bear, and about the gagging major, and about the McGraths leaving Ireland—he read about half the book, which the witness could not more particularly describe. He did not give the copy to witness. It does not appear that the witness knew what the contents were of the pamphlet produced by McGrath, or what the libel was as charged in the declaration, and was not therefore asked whether in his opinion they were the same. Upon this evidence the question is, was there sufficient to go to the jury upon which they were at liberty to find that the defendant published the libel. And first, with respect to the pamphlet handed by the defendant to Mr. Morrison and by him to Bell, it is not proved to have been lost or destroyed, or traced back again into the hands of the defendant; so that, with regard to it, the notice to produce is of no consequence; but if upon the evidence it appeared that it was of the same impression as that produced by McGrath on the trial, both were originals, and the latter could be proved without a notice to produce, the object of such a notice being to let in secondary evidence. The one sold to Silverthorn was returned, and the one read to Andrews was retained by the defendant; so that, with regard to those copies, the notice to produce would let in secondary evidence, if all were not to be regarded as originals. The defendant had several pamphlets in his possession —he gave one to Mr. Morrison, and sold another to Silverthorn, and read parts of a third to Andrews; neither of which being produced, the contents may be proved by the production of another of the same impression, by a copy, or by *viva voce* testimony, to correspond with the libel set out in the declaration, there being no degrees of secondary evidence. The contents are only proved, if proved at all, by the testimony of McGrath, which goes to establish that those delivered to Morrison and to Silverthorn are of the same impression, and that the one read to the witness Andrews was also of the same impression; or, with respect to the last, that the *viva voce* statement of the contents was sufficiently proved, the original being in the possession of the defendant, which he does not produce upon the notice served. I am of opinion that there was pregnant evidence to go to the jury that the copy produced by James McGrath and all the other copies spoken of by the witnesses were of the same impression. McGrath satisfied himself that the one handed to Mr. Morrison was the same as that which he had at the time and which he produced at the trial; and his reasons for believing so were from the correspondence in general appearance in the title page and in the dedication, and the defendant had several copies in his possession. It is not alleged that any other libel has been printed or published regarding the McGrath family; and the defendant fails to produce the two copies issued by him, and which were traced back into his possession, by which he could, if such were the case, shew that they did not correspond with the one produced, or that charged in the declaration. Under such circumstances, it appears to me the testimony is sufficient to establish to the satisfaction of any reasonable mind, that all of which we have had any evidence or have heard, are of the same impression. The cases cited in the argument, and which I shall notice, fully justify me in the conclusion to which I have arrived. Now, setting aside the evidence with regard to the identity, what are the facts with regard to the libel read to Andrews? All the witnesses speak of a pamphlet in circulation against the McGrath family. The defendant himself went to Andrews and asked him if " he had *received* any " of the pamphlets against the McGraths;" upon being informed that he had not, he sent for a pamphlet, from which he read passages upon the subjects as those contained in the libel sued upon, and to prove the identity, the plaintiff gave the defendant notice to produce the pamphlet itself; when he declines to do so, is not the evidence sufficient to satisfy a jury that he read from a pamphlet the same passages described in the declaration? I think the jury would be at liberty so to conclude, and that such finding would be upheld; in the case of Johnson v. Hudson and Morgan, in a note, 7 Ad. & Ell. 223, Littledale, J., says, "The paper from which the actual publication " was made being lost, the plaintiff was to give secondary evidence, another " paper is produced, and the journeyman swears that Morgan printed papers " similar to it, and then evidence is given of the correspondence of the paper " produced with that which is lost. I think that is sufficient; the journey-" man does not pretend to speak of the contents, but that papers similar to " that produced were printed, and the other testimony proves the correspon-" dence of the paper produced with that which was lost." In the case under consideration, McGrath proves correspondence in general appearances. In the title page and dedication, they must be the same, unless a different impression of a libel was published corresponding in general appearance with the title page, and the dedication were the *same*. The object of the testimony in the case referred to was to shew that the copy produced was the same as that which was lost. The object in the case under consideration is to prove that the copies circulated by the defendant were the same as the one produced, and the evidence was that they corresponded in general appearance, and had the same title and dedication. This is much stronger than proof of their similarity, and the correspondence of the paper, not of the contents. Coleridge, J., says, " Can it be that on all the facts there was not evidence for a jury ? There is " no rule with respect to the proof of identity peculiar to the case of a printed " paper; the evidence may depend upon correspondence in size, appearance, " and other circumstances." Lord Denman, C. J.—" The question then was, " whether it was one of the parcel taken to Hudson's shop from Morgan; " that was shewn from the correspondence of the paper produced with those " printed by Morgan, in *name, appearance,* and contents, by the evidence of " the journeyman. If we drop the recollection that this was a printed paper, " and examine the question of its identity as we should a question of the iden- " tity of a bale of goods, it is clearly impossible to say there is not some evi- " dence." In Gathercole v. Miall, Jurist, April 23rd, 1846, one of the questions before the court was, whether a newspaper called the *Nonconformist,* sent to a literary institution and proved to have been lost, was the same as a copy put in, which was an authenticated copy of the *Nonconformist* in which the libel was contained, and of which the defendant was admitted to be the responsible editor. A witness at the trial said it was entitled the *Nonconformist* newspaper, that it was like the authenticated copy before the court, and so far as he could judge from a *glance* at the time it came in, contained the libellous article. It was objected that there was no proof that the copy spoken of by the witness was issued by the defendant. Pollock, Chief Baron, in giving judgment on a motion for a new trial, one of the grounds upon which it was moved being the reception of this evidence, stated, "I think there was evidence " to justify the jury in the conclusion that it was issued by the defendant, and " that it was one of the copies struck off at the time when the newspaper was " published." Alderson, Baron, observes, " Was there reasonable evidence " that the newspaper spoken of by the witness was a copy of that proved to " have been published by the defendant? In order to determine this, we must " consider what was the nature of the document. It appears that it was the " impression of some newspaper ; in dealing with these questions we must use " our common sense, and we know that when a newspaper is published, a great " many copies are struck off for circulation among the public at large. This " then appears, from the evidence of the witness, to be one of the copies of " the number of the *Nonconformist* which contained the libel, for if you com- " pare two prints in two different parts, and find they agree, you conclude " they are from the same types." Here a copy of a newspaper which had been sent (how does not appear) to a literary institution, and being supposed to be lost, was admitted as proof of the circulation of a libel in an authenticated copy of a newspaper having the same title, and proved to be of the same number, or rather containing the same libellous article, so far as the witness could "judge at a *glance* at the time it came in," for the purpose of enhancing the damages. In the case of Rex v. Watson (a), it was decided that all the impressions of a placard were to be regarded as originals; so that the question then is, whether there was sufficient evidence to go to the jury to warrant

---

(a) 2 Starkie, 129.

them in the conclusion that all the pamphlets spoken of at the trial were of one impression. In using what common sense I possess in dealing with this question, as Baron Alderson says should be done, I was of opinion that the evidence was sufficient to warrant the jury in finding a publication in the delivery of the one copy of the pamphlet to Morrison, and also in selling the second copy to Silverthorn, and in reading parts of the third to Andrews; but when I read the cases referred to, I felt that I had clear and undoubted authority to justify me in differing from both my learned brothers.

McLEAN, J., having sat in the Practice Court during the argument, gave no judgment.

JONES, J., *dissentiente*.   *Per Cur.*—Rule discharged.

HENDERSON V. MOODIE, SHERIFF.

A. has a reversionary interest in goods leased to B.; the sheriff *seizes* the goods under a *fi. fa.* against B., but does not sell or remove them. A. sues the sheriff for an alleged injury to his reversionary interest. *Held*, that if any trespass was committed by the seizure, B. should sue, and not A.

The plaintiff sued in case for an injury to his reversionary interest in certain household furniture, which was in the possession of one O'Reilly upon a lease made of it for three years by the plaintiff, and which the defendant, as sheriff, sold under a *fi. fa.* against O'Reilly, or rather he sold the interest which O'Reilly had in the furniture.

The jury, in accordance with the charge of the Chief Justice, found a verdict for the plaintiff, and £62 10s. damages, being the estimated value of the goods; leave being reserved to the defendant to move the court in *banc* to decide whether the plaintiff was to enter his verdict for that sum or for only nominal damages.

John Duggan moved to be allowed to enter a verdict for the damages assessed by the jury.

Cameron, Sol.-Gen., and *D. B. Read*, shewed cause. The goods were merely seized by the defendant; they were not shewn to have been removed or injured. The simple act of seizure could occasion no injury to the reversioner's interest in the goods. What possible right then had this plaintiff, the reversioner, to recover damages? The verdict must clearly be entered for nominal damages only (a).

ROBINSON, C. J., delivered the judgment of the court.

The goods, as it appeared in evidence before me at the trial, had never been taken from the possession of O'Rielly, and as the sheriff could not in fact transfer this plaintiff's interest in them, I could not see what injury the plaintiff had sustained. The mere seizure of the goods, if wrongful, was an injury to the person having the temporary use of them, and not to the plaintiff; they had not been injured or removed. The defendant and the alleged purchaser may, for all that appeared, have discovered that nothing could legally pass by the sale, and they may never have intended to remove them. In the mean-

---

(a) 3 Campb. 187; 2 B. & B. 452; 6 D. & R. 551.

time the plaintiff's reversionary interest in the goods has not been prejudiced, and cannot be, if the sale could not in law affect it.

I nevertheless allowed the jury to assess the value of the goods, or rather what they might be worth when O'Reilly's interest in them would expire; they estimated it at £62 10s., and I reserved it for the court to say whether the plaintiff should be allowed to enter his verdict for that sum, or only for nominal damages. The difficulty, in our opinion, is in seeing that this plaintiff has really a ground for recovering any damages whatever. If it were not for the demurrer, upon which contingent damages were directed to be assessed, I should, I think, have directed a verdict for the defendant. If the sheriff had had no authority whatever to seize the goods, still the mere act of seizure would have given no cause of action to this plaintiff, but to O'Reilly, who was in actual possession of the goods, and entitled at the time to the beneficial use of them. And if the sheriff had assumed wrongfully to set up to sale the absolute property in these goods which did not belong to the debtor, still that occasioned no damage to the reversioner so long as the goods had not in fact been taken from the possession of his lessee. Mr. Chitty, in his notes to the form of declaration in a similar case, suggests the question, whether the averment that the defendant "absolutely sold the goods," shews a sufficient cause of action, in as much as the sale could only pass the tenant's temporary interest in the goods, and could not affect the reversionary interest (a).

Per Cur.—Verdict to be entered for one shilling damages.

BROCK ET AL. V. BOND.

The attorney is entitled to recover, against his client, fees paid to counsel conducting the case at the trial.

A client, not having obtained a regular order for the taxation of his attorney's costs before the trial, will not be allowed, by producing the Master's allocatur at the trial, to dispute the item of his attorney's bill.

The plaintiffs sued in *assumpsit* for services rendered as attorneys, adding the common counts.

The defendant pleaded the general issue and a special plea, which is demurred to.

At the trial the plaintiffs proved the retainer and services rendered in defending an action brought against Bond, and it was shewn that the amount of costs, exclusive of a fee of £5 paid by plaintiff to the counsel who conducted the defence at the trial, was £12 16s. 3d.

The defendant's counsel offered to give in evidence the Master's allocatur, certifying the costs taxed in the suit referred to at £7 0s. 7d., but the learned judge rejected it on account of there having been no order for taxation.

A verdict was rendered for £12 16s. 3d.

Eccles moved for a new trial, on the law and evidence. He contended that the Master's allocatur, certifying the costs taxed in the suit referred to, to amount to £7 0s. 7d., should have been received in evidence.

(a) Chitty's Pleadings, Vol. I., p. 580.

Cameron, Sol.-Gen., shewed cause. There was no judge's order for the taxation of costs, and therefore the Master's allocatur could have no effect upon the verdict. If the defendant wished to dispute the items in the bill, he should have obtained an order for taxation before the trial. No injustice has been done, as a counsel fee of £5, to which the plaintiffs were clearly entitled, was not included in the allocatur; if it had been, the verdict rendered would have been for the precise sum mentioned in the allocatur.

ROBINSON, C. J., delivered the judgment of the court.

It is sworn on the part of the plaintiffs, that the £5 paid to the counsel was not included in the allocatur, though undoubtedly it is a disbursement for which the plaintiffs were entitled to recover, and this would account for the difference, and shew that the defendant had no injustice done him by the verdict. But, besides this, I do not consider that the learned judge did wrong in not allowing the allocatur to affect the case. It was the defendant's business, if he questioned the correctness of the bill, to take the proper steps before the trial to have it taxed under the statute, and not having done so, and having obtained no order for taxation, subject to the condition imposed upon the client in such cases by the statute, he can no more dispute the items in consequence of that irregular proceeding, than he could enter into a discussion upon the charges at the trial, without any such taxation, and this the court constantly refuses to permit (a).

Per Cur.—Rule discharged.

GALLAGHER V. BROWN ET AL.

Plaintiff and defendant own adjoining lots of land; they had a fence between them, supposed to be on the true division line; a correct line is however run, and the defendant is found to be encroaching some acres on the plaintiff's land; the plaintiff takes possession of the disputed piece of ground, though under a protest from the defendant, and cultivates it. When the crop is fit to cut, the defendant enters and takes it away. The plaintiff sues the defendant in trespass.

Held, that the plaintiff had such a possession as would enable him to maintain an action of trespass.

Trespass *quare clausum fregit* against Thomas Brown and William Brown.

The defendants pleaded first, general issue; secondly, that the close was not the plaintiff's in manner and form, &c.

The plaintiff and defendants owned adjoining lots of land; they had a fence made between them, supposed by them to be on the true division line, and the defendants had been allowed to clear up to the fence on their side, and had taken crops off the land for six or seven years. In March, 1846, the plaintiff, having had the line correctly run by a surveyor, found that the fence encroached upon his land, and deprived him of seven or eight acres, and, though forbidden by the defendants, he moved the fence and placed it on the true line.

The defendants openly declared their dissent, and protested that they would retain possession till they had been paid for clearing the land; still the plaintiff

---

(a) Douglas, 188; 5 B. & Ad. 400.

occupied without disturbance up to the fence as he had lately placed it, till the month of July following, when the hay being fit to cut, the defendants entered and cut and took away the hay, about four or five tons, being forbidden to do so.

A verdict was given for the plaintiff, subject to the opinion of the court, as to whether the plaintiff had such a possession as would justify him in bringing an action of *trespass*.

George Sherwood, of Brockville, for the plaintiff, contended that the plaintiff could clearly maintain trespass under the evidence against the defendants; he was shewn to have the legal title to the whole lot, and the actual possession of the very piece of ground in dispute. The plaintiff having the title, his mere entry, without proof of a continued possession such as was given, would have been sufficient.—He cited 7 B. & C., 399; 7 T. R. 431; 4 Taunt. 507; 1 T. R. 292.

J. Duggan, for the defendants. The plaintiff could not recover in this action. The defendants must be considered as being legally in possession of the piece of ground on which they entered to cut and remove the hay; they may not have been in the actual visible occupation of the ground a few months before their entry, but that fact did not divest them of the legal possession. They had never abandoned the possession. Whatever the plaintiff may have done, he acted under the protest of the defendants; and the defendants never having acquiesced in the encroachment of the plaintiff beyond his original boundary, they cannot be proceeded against as trespassers.

ROBINSON, C. J., delivered the judgment of the court.

The evidence shewed the plaintiff to have the legal title to the *locus in quo*, and he would therefore be in possession by construction of law, even if he had not been actually occupying the lot of land of which this field formed a part, unless some one else had been in actual possession, holding adversely to him, but so far from the defendants or any other person being in actual possession of this field, keeping him out, he was himself in the actual visible possession of this field, having openly and with defendant's knowledge inclosed it; and he was, besides, in possession of the other part of the lot of which this formed a part, having title to the whole. It is impossible, therefore, to maintain that he was not in a situation to bring trespass for entering into the field which he had so inclosed, and held exclusive possession of for some months. The defendants seem to have imagined that they could be looked upon as being actually in possession by virtue of the possession which they had once held, though they had allowed themselves to be deprived of it. There was a time when they might have attempted to stand upon their possession, namely, when the plaintiff entered upon them, and removed the fence; but if they had complained of that removal as an injury, the plaintiff could have put his defence upon the right; and now having acquiesced for a considerable time in the change, they have neither the right nor possession to justify them in what they did.

Per Cur.—*Postea* to the plaintiff.

DOE DEM. STEPHEN & WIFE V. FORD.

The declaration of a deceased testator respecting his age at the time of the execution of his will, are not admissible as evidence.

Ejectment of the west half of Lot 7, in the 2nd concession of Etobicoke.

The lessor of the plaintiff claimed as heir at law of one Matthew Henderson.

The defendant claimed under a devise of the land made to her by the same Matthew Henderson, on the 3rd of December, 1843.

The pedigree on the one side, and the execution of the will on the other, were admitted, and the only question to be tried was, whether Matthew Henderson was or was not of full age when he made the will; evidence was given upon that point on both sides, and the jury found their verdict in favour of the defendant.

J. Lukin Robinson moved for a new trial, on the ground that the verdict was contrary to the weight of evidence and the judge's charge; he contended that the evidence strongly preponderated in favour of the lessors of the plaintiff; that Mrs. Gouldthorp, the most, if not the only satisfactory witness at the trial, was clear and positive in her conviction that Matthew was under age (about 19), when he made his will; and that having been an intimate friend of Matthew's parents at the time of his birth, living near them for years as next neighbours, and well acquainted with the ages of the whole family of the Hendersons, from having had children of her own at corresponding periods, her testimony should have prevailed with the jury over the very loose and general evidence given by the defendant. Mrs. Lafferty, a witness for the lessors for the plaintiff, though equally positive as to the fact of Matthew being about nineteen when he executed his will, had evidently fallen into some mistake as to the age of Matthew's next elder sister, making her older than she really was, and confounding her with one of her older sisters; and it was upon this error that the jury, with an inclination perhaps in favour of the defendant, found their verdict. The declarations of the testator himself as to his being of full age, may also have had much weight with the jury; now there was great doubt whether such evidence should have been received; the objection however was not taken at the trial, as the testator had made admissions to others, witnesses at the trial, of his being under age when executing his will. He submitted upon the whole evidence a new trial should be granted.

Adam Wilson shewed cause. He contended that the evidence was at least doubtful; that Mrs. Lafferty had given evidence more favourable to the defendant than appeared on the judge's notes, and that there was other evidence, besides the declarations of the testator himself, strongly confirming the fact of Matthew's being of full age when he executed his will. This was one of those cases in which he admitted the jury had to deal with very conflicting testimony; but having decided in favour of the defendant, the court ought not to disturb their verdict. It was natural enough that the testator should wish to devise the land to the defendant, his grandmother, who had provided for him since the death of his parents. It was clearly a voluntary act on the part of the testator, and nothing more than a proper compensation for the great kindness he had for many years been receiving from his grandmother; and he thought the court would have every disposition, under the doubtful evidence and circumstances of the case, to establish the will by refusing to set aside the verdict.

ROBINSON, C. J., delivered the judgment of the court.

We have some reluctance in interfering with this verdict; Matthew Henderson was the owner of the land, and could have devised it as he pleased, if he was clearly of legal capacity to make a will. The defendant, to whom he did in fact devise, is his grandmother; she had taken care of him in his last illness, and he might naturally desire to give to her what he had to leave, as the person best entitled to it at his hands. We have no doubt that the disposition which he endeavoured to make was voluntary. On the other hand, the original owner of the land was the father of Mrs. Stephens, one of the lessors of the plaintiff, and she being his only surviving child (upon the death of her brother), she has a just as well as a legal claim to the property, unless it can be proved to have been legally devised away from her. Now that wholly depends upon what the fact was with regard to the age of Matthew Henderson at the time of making his will; he died a few days afterwards. The evidence is certainly strong to shew that he was only about nineteen years of age, and though there is some evidence to the contrary, yet it is much less circumstantial and satisfactory. Still we should not have disturbed the verdict, if it had not seemed to us most probable that the jury were much influenced by the evidence given of the declarations of the deceased Matthew Henderson in regard to his own age, which declarations we consider were not admissible as evidence, for they regarded a fact of which he could not have any personal knowledge, namely, the exact time of his own birth, and they were declarations tending to confer a disposing power upon himself, and not therefore receivable, on the ground of being against his interest. Declarations of the infant might be made in such a case for the express purpose of setting up a will made or intended to be made by him. No objection seems to have been made on the trial, to the reception of this evidence, and therefore we grant the new trial, only on the condition of paying costs.

Per Cur.—Rule absolute on payment of costs.

CUVILLIER ET AL. V. BROWN.

To an action of trover, the defendant pleads that the plaintiffs "were not law-"fully possessed of the goods and chattels, &c., as of their own property, "as in the 2nd count alleged." *Demurrer* to plea.

Held, plea bad in not shewing *at what time* the defendant means to allege the plaintiffs were not possessed—the words "*at the said time when, &c.,*" should have been added.

The plaintiff sued in trover for two hundred barrels of pork.

Plea: That plaintiffs were not lawfully possessed of the said goods and chattels, or any or either of them, or any part thereof, as of their own property, *as in the second count alleged.*

Demurrer to this plea, on the ground that it did not shew at what time the defendant alleged plaintiffs were not possessed.

Cameron, Sol.-Gen., for the demurrer. He contended that the plea was bad; there was no sufficient averment of time; that it might be true that at the time intended by the defendant the plaintiffs were not possessed, though they might have been possessed at the time of the alleged conversion.—2 M. & W. 9; 2 Chitty's Pleadings; Com. Dig. Pleader, E. 5, ch. 19.

Alexander Phillpotts contra. The words "as in the second count alleged" are a sufficient allegation of time; they include a reference to the time of being possessed.—6 C. & P. 620; 2 Chitty, Jun. 437.

ROBINSON, C. J.—The defendant has, by the omission of the words "at the "said time when, &c.," failed to apply the denial of the plaintiff's property to the time of the injury committed, which of course is indispensable. The precedent cited from Mr. Chitty's Pleadings, of a form of such a plea in trover brought by the assignees of a bankrupt, is not applicable, because the time there is not meant to have relation to the injury committed. The general current of precedents is the other way. "As in the second count alleged," cannot fairly be strained to mean more than the preceding words cited from the count, which do not include any statement of time. On general demurrer we might hold the plea to be sufficiently certain, but not on special demurrer. The defendant should have amended at once when the departure from the common form was pointed out. In Williams v. Jarman, 13 M. & W. 133, the learned Chief Baron justly remarks, "the object of having certain recognized "forms of pleading is to prevent the time of the court from being occupied "with vain and useless speculations as to the meaning of ambiguous terms."

McLEAN, J.—The defendant contends that the words "as in the said second "count alleged," put in issue the time as well as the possession of the goods, and these words are probably equivalent to saying that plaintiffs were not possessed *in manner and form* as in the second count alleged, but neither of these forms of expression appears to me, in a case like this, to apply to the particular time at which the possession of plaintiffs is disputed or denied. The words, that *"plaintiffs were not possessed as in the second count alleged,"* appear to me to refer solely to the possession, leaving (as stated by the plaintiff) the time uncertain, and not shewing clearly that the defendant intends to dispute the possession at *the time* of the conversion.—Cro. Eliz. 97; Com. Dig. Pleader, E. 5, ch. 19; 6 C. & P. 620; 2 M. & W. 9.

MACAULAY, J., and JONES, J., concurred.

Per Cur.—Judgment for plaintiff on demurrer.

RATTRAY V. McDONALD ET AL.

The plaintiff sues defendant on two counts: 1st, on a promissory note; 2ndly, on an account stated. The defendant pleads that he did not make the note in the *said declaration mentioned.* Demurrer to plea.

Held, plea bad, as professing to answer the whole declaration, while it in fact answers the first count only.

The defendants plead, 2ndly, that the note was endorsed to the plaintiff by the payee in fraud of the defendants, and without consideration, to deprive the defendant of a right of set-off, which he had at the time of the endorsement against the payee. The plaintiff replies "*de injuria.*" Demurrer, that the replication is inapplicable, the plea being in *discharge of the note.*

Held, replication good, the plea containing matter *of excuse*, and not matter of discharge.

Quære.—Is not the plea double?

Assumpsit: First court on promissory note.

Second count on an account stated.

First plea by J. S. McDonald, that the defendant did not make the promissory note in *the said declaration* mentioned.

Secondly, that the plaintiff received the note from G. Washington Campbell, endorsed by him and Lane to the plaintiff in fraud of defendant, and without consideration, to deprive the defendant of the right which he had, at the time of such endorsement, to set off a certain demand alleged to be due to the defendant at that time by George W. Campbell, for work and services as attorney, &c., concluding to the country.

Third plea to the last count, that defendant, J. S. McDonald, did not promise.

Demurrer to first plea, on the ground that it professed to answer the whole declaration, and only answered the first count.

To the second plea plaintiff replied *de injuria.*

Defendant demurred to the replication of *de injuria*, on the ground that it did not traverse or confess and avoid the defendant's second plea; that it was double, and attempted to put in issue several facts stated in plaintiff's plea; that it was inapplicable and insufficient, as the plea did not consist of matters of *excuse*, so as to enable the plaintiff to adopt that general form of replication; that the second plea was pleaded by way of *discharge* of the amount of the promissory note; that therefore the replication was inapplicable.

P. M. Vankoughnet for the demurrer. He contended that the first plea by the defendant, J. S. McDonald, was clearly bad. It professed to answer the whole declaration, whereas it was, in fact, but an answer to the first count.— Wood v. Rogers, 2 Cam. Rep. p. 399; 1 Dowl. N. S. 874. As to the replication of *de injuria* to the defendant's second plea, the defendant by his plea admitted a *prima facie* right in the plaintiff to recover, but *excused* himself from the payment of the note by averring certain facts, which, if true, would repel the *prima facie* right of the plaintiff to sue, and give a good defence to the action. The defence was not in *discharge* of the defendant's liability in the first instance, it merely contained matter excusing the defendant from performing his promise; the replication, therefore, of *de injuria* he submitted was good. He cited 4 M. & G. 351; 13 M. & W. 33; 5 A. & E. 237; 6 M. & W. 559; 10 M. & W. 367; 2 D. & L. 49; 7 Jurist, 812.

S. Richards, contra. He admitted that the decisions were against him on the demurrer to the first plea. As to the replication of *de injuria* to the second plea, he contended that that replication, upon the principles laid down for its use, was inapplicable to this case; the facts stated in the plea were matters in *discharge* and not in *excuse*. A plea was in effect a plea of set-off. Now the plea of set-off, he would urge, was a plea *in discharge of the action;* it admitted a cause of action to the time of plea pleaded, but from that time it operated as a discharge of the action, just as a plea of payment.—7 M. & W. 214.

Vankoughnet, in reply. This was not a plea of set-off; it wanted an averment, which was necessary to make it substantially a good plea of set-off; it claimed a right of set-off, *but did not offer to set-off anything*. Besides, it was clear that the set-off was mentioned in the plea, not as a substantive defence to the action, but as one of the ingredients establishing the charge of fraud. —6 M. & G. 692; 9 M. & W. 50; 2 C. M. & R. 364.

ROBINSON, C. J.—I am of opinion that the exception to the first plea must prevail; it is not expressly confined to the first count, and must therefore be taken to have been pleaded in bar of the whole action, whereas it is only a defence to the note (41st rule of Easter Term, 1842) 1 Dowl. N. S. 874.

The replication to the second plea is, in my opinion, not open to exception as being too general. I take this to be clearly a case in which the defence specially pleaded may be met by the replication of *de injuria*. The defendant is not pleading any matter that goes to deny his liability in the first instance, and *prima facie*, as maker of the note, nor anything that goes to discharge the action. He gives as an excuse or reason why he should not be made to perform his promise to the present holder of the note, that the payee, when he endorsed it away, owed him a debt of large amount, and that the plaintiff took the note with a knowledge of that fact, and in order to deprive him of the benefit of a set-off, paying no consideration for it; all this amounts only to an excuse for not paying the note. The set-off, if the note were still held by the payee, would not *ipso facto* discharge the debt, though it might be made to bar the action if the payee, being sued, chose to avail himself of the statute. The endorsement conveys to the plaintiff a *prima facie* right of action, which the plea does not deny, while it states something collateral which is relied upon for excusing the defendant from performing his promise. This case comes within the principle of the decision in this court of Davidson v. Bartlett and Murney, 1 Cameron's Reports, 50.

The plaintiff is, I think, entitled to judgment on both demurrers, and it is not necessary to consider whether the special plea is liable to the exceptions which have been taken.

MACAULAY, J.—The first plea is pleaded to the whole declaration, though it answers only the first count, and is therefore bad. The second plea appears to me to be double, but it is not demurred to on that account.—9 M. & W. 196. The subject matter of it is in excuse of performance of the *prima facie* promises of the defendant to pay the plaintiff as endorsee and holder of the note. It is not a plea of set-off, for the defendant does not offer to set off the debt alleged to be due to him by the payee of the note, he merely excuses payment to the plaintiff by reason of his having such a right of set-off against the demand in the hands of the payee, and the other facts and circumstances alleged. If the replication seems to traverse too much, it is the fault of the duplicity of the plea.

JONES, J.—The plaintiff demurs to the first plea because it professes to answer the whole declaration, and is in fact an answer to the first count only; the plea is bad for that reason; 1 Dowl. N. S. 874, is express upon that point. The plaintiff is therefore entitled to judgment upon the demurrer to the first plea.—2 M. & W. 72. The facts stated in the second plea are a good defence to the action upon the note, and are so stated that it cannot be held bad on general demurrer. Then the question is whether the replication to this plea, being *de injuria*, and specially demurred to, is a good replication? I think it is ; the defendant by it admits a *prima facie* right to the plaintiff to sue, but excuses himself from the payment of the note by shewing that under the circumstances he is not bound to pay it to the plaintiff. The plea is not in denial of the plaintiff's right to sue, or any fact in discharge, but an excuse as before stated for not paying. This replication therefore is in my opinion good, and the plaintiff is entitled to judgment ; see Cam. R. 32, 50 ; 6 Dowl. 498 ; 2 Dowl. N S. 78. The language of Lord Denman in Herbert v. Sayer, 2 D. & L. 53, is applicable to this case, and conclusive. His lordship says : "If Rogers "had been the plaintiff, the direct transaction with him *might perhaps* have "been matter of discharge, but as the plaintiff is a stranger to the defendant, "and *prima facie* there is a promise in law by the defendant to pay the plain- "tiff, arising out of the endorsement of the bill, the plea, which discloses "transactions with the former holder Rogers, and the circumstances under "which the plaintiff took the bill from him, amounts only to an excuse for not "performing to the plaintiff that *prima facie* promise, and the replication *de* "*injuria* is therefore good."

McLEAN, J.—If the plea is in fact a plea in discharge of the ground of action, as the defendant contends, then it seems to be settled that the plea of *de injuria* would be inapplicable ; but the defendant, as it appears to me, is in error in considering his plea as in discharge. He alleges various reasons why he should not pay *the plaintiff* the amount of the note, admitting in his plea the making of the note and the endorsement to the plaintiff, but stating as an excuse for not paying it to the plaintiff, that the original payee was in his debt at the time of the endorsement, and that in fact the endorsement was made to defeat his right to set off his demand against the note, no value being paid by the plaintiff for the note. If these facts were all established on the trial, they would shew that the plaintiff was not entitled to recover, but they could not prevent another action being brought by the payee of the note, in which the amount of set-off could be contested, so that the plea could not affect the validity or value of the note, but could only operate "as a reason why in "equity and good conscience this plaintiff should not have the benefit of the "undertaking which the note on the face of it imports."

I think the replication *de injuria* is a full answer to the second plea, and puts in issue those facts on which the defendant rests his excuse for not paying his note to the plaintiff ; judgment must therefore be for the plaintiff on his demurrer to the first plea, and also on the defendant's demurrer to the replication.

Per Cur.—Judgment for plaintiff on demurrer to plea, and also on demurrer to the replication.

The Bank of Upper Canada v. Smith.

In order to charge the endorser of a promissory note, it is not necessary that the holder should prove the notice to have been absolutely received: if he shews that due diligence has been used in putting a letter into the post, though the post miscarry, that is sufficient.

The fact that there is a post office in the township in which the endorser resides, does not make it incumbent on the holder to direct his notice to that office, if there be a nearer office in an adjoining township, to which the endorser's letters are generally sent.

The defendant was sued by the plaintiffs as last endorser of a promissory note, dated at Mosa, in the District of London; it fell due on the 5th of August, 1846, on which day the bank clerk put the proper notice of non-payment into the post office at London, directed to the defendant in the township of Mosa. Ekfrid and Mosa are adjoining townships. The defendant in fact lived in Ekfrid, and had lived there for some years continually, but within a mile of the division line which divides the two townships. There is a post office in each township; according to the testimony of one witness, the Mosa post office is a mile and a half nearer to the defendant than that in Ekfrid. Another witness described the Ekfrid post office as being nearer by half a mile. The office in Mosa was first established, and it was proved that newspapers for the defendant came to that office, and that business letters were frequently addressed to him there. The clerk of the payee and first endorser swore that he informed the bank agent, when he took the note there, that the defendant lived in Ekfrid, but that he had better direct the notice to him in Mosa. One witness swore, that having corresponded with the defendant, he usually addressed to him at Mosa, and that on one occasion, having directed a letter to him at Ekfrid, and not receiving an answer, he wrote again to him, directing to Mosa, and got an answer by return of post. The note was made payable to Anderson and Beebe. Anderson, one of the payees, was postmaster at Mosa, and it was sworn by his clerk that he believed Anderson destroyed the notice, and that the defendant had never received it, though he was told a week afterwards that it had come to the Mosa post office. The learned judge who tried the cause had some doubt whether the notice could properly be said to have been misdirected under the circumstances; but it was objected by the defendant, that as the evidence shewed that he did not in fact receive the notice in time, and as it was not addressed to him at his place of residence, the plaintiff could not recover, but must fail upon the issue on the plea that the defendant had not due notice.

The jury found for the defendant.

James Givens, of London, moved for a new trial on the law and evidence, and for misdirection. He contended that under the circumstances of the case, due notice had been sufficiently proved. It was not necessary that the plaintiffs should shew the notice to have been absolutely received by the endorser; there is abundant authority upon this point. All that the law requires is to give the notice punctually, by putting a letter into the post office, directed to the endorser's usual address. If this be done, though the letter miscarry, the plaintiffs having legally taken every step in their power to charge the endorser, he will be held liable. In this case the evidence clearly proved that a letter was sent to the usual address of the defendant at Mosa within the period limited by law for giving notice. The fact that the letter was not sent to the Ekfrid post office is immaterial; the defendant may have been living in the township of Ekfrid, but that did not make it imperative on the plaintiffs to send the notice there, if another post office was nearer, and was shewn to be the usual channel through which the defendant received his papers. The witnesses proved this to have been the case with respect to the post office at Mosa: it was nearer than the one at Ekfrid to the defendant's residence, and his letters were almost always delivered there. The plaintiffs are clearly entitled to a new trial upon the weight of evidence; and the direction of the learned judge at the trial not having been, it is submitted, as strong as the law would warrant, as to the proof of notice being legally sufficient, though not traced into the defendant's possession, a new trial should be granted without costs.

John Wilson, of London, shewed cause. He contended that the only fact for the jury to try was, whether the notice was more likely to reach the defendant addressed to him at the post office at Ekfrid, than to the one at Mosa—this was a fact exclusively for the jury to decide; and they have found that the letter should have been sent to the post office at Ekfrid, and not to the one at Mosa; and determining this fact in favour of the defendant, they gave him a verdict. There was clearly evidence sufficient, though contradicted, to warrant the jury in arriving at such a conclusion; and the jury having given a verdict for the defendant upon conflicting testimony as to a particular fact entirely within their province to determine, he submitted the court ought not to set it aside. He cited Chitty on Bills, page 472; 3 M. & W. 166; 1 R. & M. 249.

ROBINSON, C. J., delivered the judgment of the court.

We think there should in this case be a new trial without costs. It is of much importance that the law should be duly administered on settled principles in regard to commercial transactions of this nature, occurring so constantly, and in which so many persons are interested. We take it to be well settled that it is not by any means a rule that because there is a post office in the same township in which the endorser lives, therefore the letter must be sent to *that* office, although there may be an office nearer to him in an adjoining township. We take it also to be a principle of law, that when the holder of a note in such a case acts with proper diligence, and does what the law requires for giving notice, he is not to lose his remedy because it is shewn that the endorser did not in fact receive the notice, or as in this case, did not receive it in due time. If the holder of a note puts a proper notice into the post office in due time, and so addressed as that it might be reasonably supposed it would be more likely to reach the party than if it had been sent or directed in any other manner, he does what is sufficient to entitle him to recover, so far as giving notice is in question. It was a strong fact in this case in favour of the plaintiff that the Mosa post office was that which had been longest established, and as near if not nearer than the other. The defendant usually received the newspapers which he subscribed for through that office, and others addressed to him through that channel, and with better success than when they adopted the other. I apprehend the jury must have taken upon themselves to judge that since the defendant did not get the notice in due time, he should as a necessary consequence escape from his liability; but the law is not so unreasonable; it is no part of an endorser's contract that he must receive notice of non-payment by the maker in one day or two, or at any time. It is a mere condition superinduced upon his contract by the effect of a rule of law established upon certain considerations of the protection which it is just to afford to him, but the same rule of law has certain qualifications as well established as the rule, and one qualification is, that if the holder does what the law considers sufficient for giving notice he can recover, though the notice should in fact miscarry. How it happened not to reach the defendant in this case as soon as it should have done, was not certainly shewn, but it did appear that the maker of the note for whom he endorsed was the postmaster at the office to which the notice was sent, and strong ground was laid, by the evidence of his clerk, for supposing that he knew well enough when the notice came, and what it was, and that he took care that his endorser should not receive the notice as soon as he should have done. A case of this kind tends strongly to shew the reasonableness of determining as the courts in England have done, that the holder should not as a matter of course lose his remedy whenever the notice is not punctually received, provided it has been punctually sent.

Per Cur.—Rule absolute for a new trial without costs.

COMMERCIAL BANK v. REYNOLDS ET AL.

Endorsees against the endorsers of a note. The plaintiffs declare on two counts: 1st, on the note: 2ndly, on an account stated. The defendants plead that "*they did not endorse the said promissory note in the said first count of the said declaration mentioned*" in manner and form, &c. Demurrer to plea.

Held, Plea bad on two grounds: 1st, because, not being limited in the introductory part of it to the first count, it must be taken as pleaded to the whole declaration, and thus, while professing to answer the whole, it in fact only answers the 1st count. 2ndly, because in its mode of traversing the endorsement it contains a negative pregnant with the admission, that one or two of the three defendants did endorse.

Declaration : 1st count, endorsees against the endorsers of a promissory note.

2nd count, account stated.

Plea : That *the defendants did not endorse the said promissory note in the said first count of the said declaration mentioned*, in manner and form, &c.

Demurrer: 1st. That the plea contained nothing, in the introductory part of it, to shew that it was meant to be pleaded to a part and not to the whole of the declaration, and that professing therefore to be an answer to the whole declaration, it was in fact only an answer to the first count of the declaration.

2ndly. That the plea was uncertain, and contained a negative pregnant with the admission, that one or two of the three did endorse.

Alexander Campbell, of Kingston, for the demurrer, contended that the plea was unquestionably bad upon both the grounds stated in the demurrer.— Wood v. Rogers (a) ; also the case of Worley v. Harrison (b), were authorities precisely in point.

(a) 2 Cam. Rep. 399. (b) 5 N. & M. 173.

D. B. Read, contra, submitted that the authorities, though apparently against him, did not go the length of shewing that this plea must necessarily be considered by the court as an answer to part only.

ROBINSON, C. J., delivered the judgment of the court.

Both the objections taken to this plea, we think, are entitled to prevail; the case of Wood v. Rogers, 2 Cam. 399, decided in this court, cannot upon any clear ground be distinguished from this case. It is true that the plea here refers to the first count as being that part of the declaration in which the note is mentioned; but that does not remedy the defect, that the plea is not in terms and expressly pleaded only to that count. For want of being so confined by proper introductory words, we must look upon it as intended to bar the whole action, and yet it clearly would be no answer to the second count. The exception is a strict one, but our 41st rule is positive, that all pleas, unless otherwise expressed, shall be taken as pleaded in bar of the whole action, and it was meant to preclude captious and doubtful objections as to the necessity in particular cases of the *actionem non*. In Worley v. Harrison, 5 Nev. & M. 173, there was precisely such a plea as the present, and the same objection was taken to it on special demurrer. The plea was also excepted to on another ground, and it became unnecessary to determine the first point; but the court evidently looked upon the plea as bad on special demurrer for the same cause that is assigned here. The plea was, "*as to the "promissory note in the first count mentioned.*" The Chief Justice said it professed to be the whole action. Littledale and Williams gave no opinion on that point. Paterson, J., begged to be understood as *not* saying that it was not a good objection on special demurrer.

The other objection is more one of substance. The effect of the plea would be, that in order to entitle the plaintiff to recover against any of the defendants, as he would by our statute be able to do in this joint action, he must prove the endorsement by all; whereas it could be no defence by the last endorser, that the one before him had not endorsed. The plea does not rest the defence in regard to each upon the assertion that *he* did not endorse; but for all that is stated in it, the defendants may be taken to admit that one or two of the three did endorse, but to rest their defence on the plea that the other did not, leaving it uncertain which, and thus calling for more proof than would by law be necessary to establish a cause of action against them separately. *Per Cur.*—Judgment for the plaintiff on demurrer.

THE COMMERCIAL BANK v. J. L. HUGHES, COTTINGHAM, G. HUGHES, & BURTON;

AND

THE COMMERCIAL BANK v. J. L. HUGHES, LEE, & COTTINGHAM.

Plaintiffs charge defendants upon a *joint contract;* one of the defendants allows judgment to go by default: the plaintiffs at the trial have a verdict against him, and elect to be nonsuited as to the other.

Held, that the plaintiffs, suing the defendants on a joint contract, could not have a verdict against one, and be nonsuited as to the other; and that the verdict must be set aside, and a new trial granted without costs.

In the first of these cases, the plaintiffs sued on a note stated to be made by Charles Hughes on the 4th of February, 1846, promising to pay in three months, to the order of J. L. Hughes, £200, and endorsed by the other three defendants successively. There was also a count on an account stated.

J. L. Hughes pleaded to the 1st count, that he did not endorse the note; 2ndly, that the other three defendants did not, nor did either of them, endorse the note.

The other defendants all pleaded severally like pleas, and all pleaded jointly the general issue to the 2nd count.

In the other action the plaintiffs declared on a note made by Charles Hughes, dated 31st January, 1846, payable in three months, to the order of J. L. Hughes, for £200, and endorsed by each of the other defendants in succession; with a count on an account stated.

Lee pleaded, 1st to the first count, denying that he endorsed the note; 2ndly, general issue to second count.

J. L. Hughes pleaded to the first count, 1st, that he did not endorse the note; 2ndly, that the defendant, Lee, did not endorse; 3rd, that Cottingham did not endorse.

Defendant Cottingham pleaded, 1st, that J. L. Hughes did not endorse the note; 2ndly, that Lee did not endorse; 3rd, that he did not himself endorse.

And Hughes and Cottingham pleaded the general issue to the second count.

In the first case, the plaintiffs proved the endorsement by the defendant, Burton, and desired to be nonsuited in regard to the other defendants. A verdict was taken against Burton on the count upon an account stated, £206 2s.

In the second case, the endorsement by the defendant, Hughes, was admitted, and the plaintiffs elected to be nonsuited as to the other defendants, and a verdict was taken for the plaintiffs against the defendant, J. L. Hughes, for £206 4s. 8d., and on the fourth and fifth pleas for the defendant.

The Hon. *R. B. Sullivan* moved to set aside the verdict rendered in each case against one of the defendants, or to arrest the judgment.

Cameron, Sol.-Gen., shewed cause. The verdict, he submitted, was correct. The case of Hannay v. Smith et al. (*a*) was in point to shew that the plaintiffs could not be nonsuited at the trial in regard to one or more of the defendants, when others have allowed judgment to go by default; and if there could be no nonsuit upon the record as to one of the defendants, the joint contract declared upon does not appear to be disproved, and the verdict may stand.

Sullivan, in reply. The practice, he admitted, was formerly such as stated by the learned counsel, but the case establishing that practice has been expressly overruled. Murphy v. Dolan et al. (*b*) has now determined that the plaintiff, not succeeding at the trial against one of the defendants who has pleaded, may be nonsuited as to him, though others have suffered judgment to go by default, and of course the effect of such a decision must necessarily be that the joint contract will appear upon the record not to have been proved; the plaintiff must therefore fail as to all the defendants. He submitted a new trial ought to be granted, without costs.

(*a*) 3 T. R. 662.   (*b*) 5 B. & C. 178; 7 D. & R. 618, S. C.

ROBINSON, C. J., delivered the judgment of the court.

In both of these cases the plaintiffs seem by a strange inadvertency to have sued the maker and several endorsers of the notes in one action, as if it were a case which would come under our statute 5 Wm. IV. ch. 1, which it is clear that it does not, being for a larger sum than £100. The consequence is, that he has improperly charged the defendants with having entered into a joint contract, when the evidence shewed the contrary. Under such circumstances it was formerly held, that the plaintiffs could not be nonsuited at the trial in regard to one or more of the defendants, when others had allowed judgment to go by default. In Hannay v. Smith & Williams, 3 T. R. 662, it was so decided; but in Murphy v. Dolan et al. 5 B. & C. 178; 7 D. & R. 618, S. C., the court overcame the supposed difficulty, and determined that the plaintiff, failing on the trial to make out his case as against the defendants who had pleaded, might as to him be nonsuited. Then the consequence of this we take to be, that being thus nonsuited as to one defendant, he appears on the record to have failed in establishing the joint contract as declared upon, and cannot therefore have judgment against any. The case of Porter v. Harris, 1 Levinz, 63, determines that in such a case the judgment must be arrested, even if one of the defendants had confessed the action; and in such a case the court said, the defendant for whom a verdict had been given on the trial should have his costs against the plaintiff, and that the plaintiff should have neither costs nor damages against the other. In the cases before us, I conceive that as it was undoubtedly necessary for the plaintiffs to establish a joint contract, no verdict should have been taken against one of the defendants when the plaintiffs elected to be nonsuited in regard to the other defendants, but unless the plaintiffs chose to be nonsuited in the action, a verdict for all the defendants should have been returned. There should we think be a new trial without costs; the plaintiffs will then find the expediency of discontinuing, which they can only properly be allowed to do on paying the costs of the last trial. If this nonsuit as to some of the defendants, and a verdict against one of them in this joint action, were not set aside, judgment must necessarily be arrested.

Per Cur.—Rule absolute.

COMMERCIAL BANK v. CAMERON.
COMMERCIAL BANK v. CULVER.

Endorsees sue the defendants separately, as payees and endorsers of a promissory note. The declaration avers a joint endorsement by the defendants—*a due presentment* and *notice*, and the liability of the *defendants*. Demurrer to declaration : 1st, Because presentment at a particular place is not averred ; 2ndly, Because a joint liability is shewn on the face of the declaration, and no excuse for omitting the party jointly liable alleged ; 3rdly, Because *due* notice is not alleged, or a special averment of notice, with time, &c.

Held,—Declaration good upon the 1st and 2nd grounds, but bad on the 3rd.

Two suits. Endorsees sue defendants separately, as payees and endorsers of a promissory note. The declaration averred a joint endorsement by the defendants—*a due presentment* and *notice*, and then averred the liability of the defendants.

Demurrer—1st, Because presentment at a particular place was not alleged; 2ndly, Because a joint liability was shewn on the face of the declaration, and no excuse for omitting the party jointly liable was averred; 3rdly, Because due notice was not alleged, or a special averment of notice, with time, &c.

Miller, of Niagara, for the demurrer. He contended, upon the first point, that where the maker of a note payable at a particular place was sought to be charged, no averment of a presentment *at the place* need be stated—that he admitted; but it was different with respect to an endorser—to charge him, presentment *at the place* must be shewn. The cases of 8 Bing. 214, 2 B. & B. 165, clearly establish this distinction. Upon the second point he admitted the general principle to be, that the non-joinder of a joint contractor should be pleaded in abatement; but he contended that it appeared upon the *face of the declaration* in this case, that there was a joint endorser, who ought to have been sued; and the omission of the joint contractor, he would submit, when thus apparent, was a good ground of demurrer.—1 Saund. 134, note 1—291, note 6; 6 T. R. 770; Cro. Car. 494; 1 B. & P. 73; 8 T. R. 507; 2 Taunt. 254. Upon the last objection, he submitted that the averment of notice, without the words *due notice*, as prescribed by our forms, was clearly bad on special demurrer. The case of Grant v. Eyre in our own court was expressly in point.

J. Lukin Robinson contra. He contended that the case in 8 Bing. relied on by the opposite counsel as establishing his first point in favour of the demurrer, was inapplicable: the averment in the declaration of *due presentment* was all that the forms required, either in the case of a maker, or drawer, or endorser of a bill or note. Under the allegation of *due presentment*, the fact of presentment at the place specified in the body of the note is matter of evidence. In the case in 8 Bing. the bill was averred to have been presented at a different place from that mentioned in the bill—the evidence, therefore, could not possibly shew presentment at the place mentioned *in the bill*—it was, in fact, presented at a totally different place. Here, however, no particular place was designated in the averment as the place of presentment; and evidence could have been given to shew a presentment, under the averment of *due presentment*, such as the note specified.—1 C. & M. 429, 3 Tyr. 364, 2 Cam. Rep. 116. Upon the second objection, the cases cited by the learned counsel have been expressly overruled. The law now is, that the non-joinder simply of a co-contractor appearing on the face of the declaration is not ground of demurrer; other facts must appear on the face of the declaration before the defendant can demur—the co-contractor not joined must be shewn to be alive and *within* the jurisdiction of the court. Now it does not appear in this declaration that the party omitted was within the jurisdiction of the court. The defendant therefore was precluded from demurring; he should have pleaded in abatement; at least that plea was open to him, if accompanied by an affidavit that the co-contractor was alive, and within the jurisdiction of the court.—2 Saund. Rep. (last edition), page 110; 6 T. R. 766; 3 Scott, N. R. 149. Upon the last point, he submitted that the English forms fully warranted the averment of notice simply without the allegation of *due* notice.—2 M. & R. 359; D. & L. Rep. 151; 8 B. & C. 387. When it is alleged the endorser had notice of the non-payment by the maker, it must be assumed that due notice is meant; and the defendant could easily by his plea compel the plaintiffs to prove such a notice as the law requires. The case of Grant v. Eyre, decided in this court, might seem opposed to this averment; the court, however, were not unanimous in that decision, and evidently came to it with reluctance; and the English authorities not being found to support the judgment, the court, it is submitted, might see fit, upon a re-examination of the point, to determine it otherwise. With respect to the new rules having prescribed forms which the plaintiffs were bound to follow, the new rules clearly do not make it compulsory upon the pleader to adhere to those forms; he may adopt others, if he thinks it advisable, subject of course to the risk of a demurrer.

ROBINSON, C. J.—Upon the first objection my judgment is against the demurrer, for the reasons stated in the case of the Bank of Upper Canada v. Parsons et al., determined in this term, and upon the authority of former decisions there referred to. The second objection I do not take to be ground of demurrer, as the defendant can no longer plead the non-joinder of a joint contractor in abatement, without shewing that the person not joined is resident within the jurisdiction, and verifying his plea by affidavit. It would be incongruous to hold that a declaration is demurrable for not stating that, of which a denial by a plea in bar would be no defence. There is no doubt of the general principle, that non-joinder of a defendant who ought to be sued as a joint contractor must be taken advantage of by pleading in abatement. The distinction relied upon in this case is, that here it appears on the declaration that there was a joint endorser, who ought to have been sued. But that distinction does not, in the opinion of the learned editor of Saunders, make the declaration demurrable, or dispense with the necessity of pleading in abatement.—Saunders, 134, note 1; 291, note 6; Addison v. Overend, 6 T. R. 770; Cro. Car. 494, 544; 1 B. & P. 73; Churchhill v. Gardiner, 7 T. R. 567, very nearly resemble the present, and there the court intimated that the non-joinder might perhaps be made the ground of a special demurrer. And in South v. Tanner and Jones, 2 Taunt. 254, the court threw out in the course of the argument, that non-joinder of a joint contractor, when the objection appeared upon the record, might be taken advantage of in arrest of judgment, and this without its appearing upon the record that the person not joined was still living. But this does not seem in accordance with decisions upon that point in cases both preceding and following it. Mr. Chitty, in his Treatise on Pleading, I. 53, considers that in order to make the non-joinder an objection on the face of the record, it must appear that the party omitted is still living, notwithstanding the general principle of law that a party is presumed to be living if he has been heard of within seven years. And it fortifies this conclusion, that our statute makes it necessary that another fact should appear, namely, that the person omitted is within the province. When those two facts must not only be stated, but sworn to, in order to make a plea in abatement good, it can surely not be consistently held that a declaration is on the face of it bad, because a party is not sued, of whom it does not appear that he is living within the province, or living anywhere.—4 M. & S. 478; Archbold on Pleading, 68, 280; Cro. El. 544; Cowper, 832.

The last objection turns upon the averment of notice of non-payment. It is in these words: "Of all which the defendant (an endorser) had notice." It is contended, that either a certain day of giving notice should have been stated, or the form followed which is given by the new rules; "of all which "the defendant had '*due*' notice." The answer to which is, that the courts have frequently decided that notice, and due notice, mean precisely the same thing; so that when the defendant simply denies that he had notice, he puts the plaintiff by that plea to the necessity of proving due notice (a). In the case of Grant v. Eyre et al., decided in this court, it was held that the allegation, that the defendant *endorsed* the note, without laying a certain day when he endorsed, would not suffice, because it neither followed the general principle of pleading, which requires each traversable fact to be laid within a certain time, nor with the form given in the rule, which does dispense with any statement of a day, and allows the plaintiff to aver instead, that the defendant duly endorsed. I confess I concurred in that decision with a reluctance which I expressed, because I thought it more reasonable as well as more convenient to hold, that when the rule permitted the mention of any certain day to be omitted, it made it no longer material that the declaration did not contain it, and "*duly*" could hardly be regarded as a substitute for that statement; and I do not think that the form was given as one that must be used at the peril of a demurrer, but as one that *may* be used. What is pressed upon us here, it seems to me, would carry the principle of a strict adherence further. Endorsing, and duly endorsing, may not mean precisely the same thing; but notice, and due notice, have been adjudged to be perfectly the same; and if so, it would seem a strange ground of demurrer, that a word admitted to be insignificant when so applied, has been omitted. On the same principle we ought to decide, that any verbal deviation from the form, though in a part however immaterial, would be fatal on special demurrer, for between things wholly immaterial there can be no degrees of importance. That was not the intention of the form; it was to sanction a short and convenient form of declaration, not to compel a literal adherence to every word of it, so as to afford no choice between that and the old form of declaring. My brothers, however, I understand, think it will be more convenient to insist upon the word "duly" as it is prescribed by the form; therefore the defendant will on that objection have judgment.

MACAULAY, J.—The declaration, as respects the joinder of defendants under the statute, follows in the frame of it the new rules—as I think it may do. It should conform strictly to one or the other. In the form prescribed by the court, an averment of *due* notice is sufficient, and supplies the place of a more special averment. Here *due* notice is not alleged, but merely notice; and in this respect I think the declaration imperfect.

As to the non-joinder—if it appeared on the face of the declaration that there was a joint contractor alive and within the province—in other words, if those facts appeared which the defendant would have to shew in a plea in abatement for non-joinder, the objection would be good on demurrer; but it does not so appear in the present case. The mere circumstance of there being a joint contractor alive, does not compel the plaintiff to join him in the action; he may be out of the jurisdiction of the court, and it does not appear that he

---

(a) M. & Ry. 359.

is within it. The Act authorizes the omission where the party is without the province, and requires the defendant to shew him *within* it, if he pleads the non-joinder in abatement; *prima facie*, therefore the omission seems sanctioned by the statute. Presentment at the particular place, if material, is matter of evidence. A due presentment is alleged, and the form of the court requires no more ; whether such special presentment must be shewn in proof upon a plea denying *due* presentment, is a question not necessary to be now decided.

JONES, J.—The note being made payable at the Commercial Bank, at Hamilton, but the words "and not elsewhere" not being added, was payable generally. The declaration alleges the default of the maker, although the note was duly presented on the day when it became due ; a due presentment is a presentment according to law, which would be a presentment at the office of the Commercial Bank at Hamilton, to an officer of the bank, at the time it fell due. The allegation is according to the form prescribed by the rule of court, and is therefore sufficient The word *due* being omitted in the averment of the notice of non-payment, the declaration is in this respect insufficient, as it does not follow the form. The liability of the defendant and Culver was joint, and not separate ; but such joint liability is only matter required to be pleaded in abatement.

MCLEAN, J.—The case of the Commercial Bank v. Johnson (*a*) is very like the present case, so far as the allegation of presentment goes. It was there objected that the note was payable at the Com. Bank at Bytown, but there was no averment of presentment there for payment; here the objection is, that it was not shewn to whom or where the note was presented for payment, or that it ever was presented. In that case it was decided that the note, being payable at a particular place, and not stating that it was not payable elsewhere, must be regarded as payable generally, and that presentment at the place mentioned or to the maker, was a sufficient presentment, and that the allegation that the note was duly presented was sufficient. In the statement of presentment in that case the word "*duly*" was omitted, but in this case (which does not come within the statute 3 Vic. ch. 8) the non-payment and presentment are averred in the very words of the form given in the New Rules (*b*), and we must hold the form there given to be sufficient. There is an omission in the statement of notice ; in the form it is, that the defendant had *due* notice ; but in this case it is averred that the defendant *had notice*, the word *due* being omitted. When it is alleged that the defendant had notice of the non-payment by the maker, it must be assumed that he had *due notice*, and if he had not, he may put that fact in issue by his plea, and make the plaintiff prove the particular notice given. In law the notice cannot be regarded as any notice, unless it was in fact *due* notice, and what constitutes due notice is now pretty well settled by authorities in such cases. In the case of Grant v. Eyre, in this court, it was stated that the defendant *duly* endorsed the note declared on, but the omission of the word "*afterwards*," as given in the form prescribed by the statute 3 Vic. ch. 8, was not considered as supplied by the word *duly*, and the declaration was held bad on special demurrer on that account. I could not

(*a*) 2 Cam. Rep. 127.   (*b*) Cameron's Rules, page 46.

then concur in so considering it, and I cannot now see that the objection as to the omission of the word *due* in reference to the notice, ought to be sustained as a good objection.

As to the other objection, that the defendant only became jointly liable with Chester Culver, I cannot see that it is entitled to prevail, as the law authorizes actions to be brought in particular cases against one of joint contractors; and this, for aught that appears, may be one of these cases; if not, the defendant might have pleaded in abatement, and given the plaintiff a better writ; he cannot, however, on special demurrer, object to a proceeding which the law sanctions, where owing to the absence from the province or death of a joint contractor, only one of such contractors can be served with process. On these grounds, I think the demurrer must be overruled, and that the plaintiffs are entitled to judgment.

Per Cur.—Judgment for the plaintiff on the first and second grounds of demurrer. Upon the third ground of demurrer, the court being equally divided, the Chief Justice, in order to afford a rule for the future, agreed to confirm the decision in Grant v. Eyre, now sanctioned by the judgments in this case of Macaulay, J., and Jones, J., and subsequently concurred in their opinion.

Per Cur.—Judgment for the defendant on the third ground of demurrer.

McLean, J., *dissentiente*, on the third ground of demurrer.

The Kingston Marine Railway Company v. Gunn.

Under the Acts 1 Vic. ch. 30, and 7 Vic. ch. 16, the Kingston Marine Railway Company may give and receive promissory notes in the course of transacting their legitimate business.

In declaring upon such notes, the plaintiffs need not aver the consideration upon which they are received.

The omission of the words "value received" in a note, or the fact that a note is made payable at a certain time after date, afford no inferences that such notes were taken in violation of that clause of the Act of Incorporation prohibiting the company from banking operations.

Payees against maker of a promissory note. The declaration contained the usual averments, without alleging any particular consideration.

Demurrer to declaration on six grounds:

1st. Because the Kingston Marine Railway Company, the plaintiffs in this cause, could not bring an action on a promissory note, payable with interest, the Act incorporating them as a corporate body not authorizing them to deal in negotiable paper.

2nd. Because the promissory note, as declared upon in this cause, was void, it being given to a corporate body who had no authority in law to receive the same.

3rd. Because it was not shewn on the face of the declaration, that the consideration for which the said note was given to the plaintiffs, accrued to them in their corporate capacity, or within the objects of their corporation.

4th. Because, as it did not appear on the face of the declaration that the note declared upon was given for any value whatever, the plaintiffs could not sue the defendants for the amount thereof.

5th. Because it appeared on the face of the declaration that the note declared upon in this cause was an accommodation note.

6th. Because the defendant was not liable to pay the said note to the plaintiffs, then being a corporate body prohibited banking powers.

Kenneth McKenzie, of Kingston, for the demurrer. He contended, that as the Act incorporating the Kingston Marine Railway Company, 1 Vic. ch. 30, contained no clauses empowering the company to sue, they could not sustain the present action. The statute says that they may be sued, not that they may sue. This was clearly an omission; but the effect must be, that the company are not legally in a position to sue until the legislature has supplied this defect in the existing Act. He also contended that this corporation, under the Act, had no power to take negotiable paper; also that the consideration upon which the note was given should have appeared in the body of the note. The statute 7 Vic. ch. 16, prohibits the plaintiffs from acting as bankers, and what is there apparent upon the face of this note to shew that it did not originate in a banking transaction between the parties, and was not therefore illegal as an infringement of the statute? Had the consideration been expressed, it might then have been seen whether the consideration was connected with the objects for which the plaintiffs were incorporated or not.—Cumming v. Guess, 2 Cam. Rep. 125; 4 Bing. 283; 12 Moore, 533; 5 B. & Ald. 204; 3 B. & Ald. 1. The words "value received" were omitted in the note. This, he contended, was a very material omission, leading to the presumption that the note was an accommodation note, and therefore prohibited by the Act. It was also payable one month after date. This fact was another strong ground for supposing the note to have been discounted in the way of a banking transaction between the parties, and not to have been received on account of a previously existing debt. Upon all these grounds, he submitted, the demurrer ought to prevail.

Thomas Kirkpatrick, of Kingston, *contra*. There is no weight whatever in the first objection: if there was, the result must be that this corporation could bring no action whatever. The right to sue is clearly incident to a corporation, unless express provision to the contrary be contained in the Act. There is no such provision in this Act, 1 Vic. ch. 30. Besides, our provincial Act, 7 Will. IV. ch. 14, sec. 14, gives express authority to corporations generally, such as this, to sue and be sued, unless the special Act of incorporation shall otherwise provide. The company are certainly prohibited from banking by their Act of incorporation; but there was no clause in the Act restraining them from making or taking promissory notes for debts due to them upon any contract within the scope of their legitimate business. It need not appear on the face of the note that it was given for a consideration valid under the Act of Incorporation. If the note was to be impeached on the ground of its illegality, that was matter of defence. The averment of such illegality in the first instance was unnecessary. The case of Cummings v. Guess, and the other cases referred to by the learned counsel, were clearly distinguishable from the present. In these the company was not suing, as in this case, but a clerk, who was in no way connected with the note; he was expressly authorized by the statute to sue for debts contracted by certain trustees under certain provisions of the Act; and in order to make his title to sue apparent, the court held that there should be an averment that the note was given to the trustees in the course of their duty as trustees under the Act. This is a totally different case; the parties suing are not strangers to the note, but the very payees themselves —5 Taunt. 792. He also contended that there was nothing to shew that the note was an accommodation note. The omission of the words "value received" in the note, relied upon for that purpose, could lead to no such presumption. These words were not essential to a note, and need not be inserted; they were wholly unimportant, and no inference could be drawn one way or the other from their omission or adoption. The inference that because the note was made payable one month after date, it must therefore necessarily have originated in a banking transaction, and could not have been given for a subsisting debt, was absurd; many a creditor, having a *bona fide* existing debt, would be very willing to give time to his debtor, upon having an easy and tangible mode of proving his debt placed in his hands. He felt convinced that the defendant must fail upon all his grounds of demurrer.

ROBINSON, C. J.—I am of opinion that the plaintiffs are entitled to judgment on the demurrer. The objection insisted on in argument, in addition to those specially assigned as causes of demurrer, is the most material in its nature, because it would deny to the plaintiffs not only the right to bring this action, but the right to bring any action whatever; and that is grounded on the circumstance that the Act constituting the Kingston Marine Railway Company, 1 Vic. ch. 30, does not contain the ordinary clause that the corporation may sue and be sued. We take it however to be clearly incident to a corporation, that it may sue and be sued where nothing is mentioned to the contrary, and besides our statute 7 Wm. IV. ch. 14, sec. 14, leaves no room for any such objection, for that expressly provides that all such corporations as this in question, created by the legislature, shall be capable of contracting and being contracted with, and of suing and being sued, unless it shall be otherwise provided in the Act. As to the causes of demurrer assigned, I am of opinion that they are none of them tenable. The statute, 7 Vic. ch. 16, does not support the objection that this company cannot give or take a promissory note in the course of transacting their proper business; it affords rather an argument to the contrary, for the 4th section, while it gives them express authority to enter into contracts and agreements relating to their business (not excepting contracts through the medium of notes or bills), prohibits them from acting as bankers, or from issuing or keeping in circulation notes in the nature of bank notes. Now, if they could not by law either make or take a promissory note of any description or for any purpose, such a prohibition would have been useless. But on general principles I hold that a corporation established, as this was, for trading purposes, and not composing a mere municipal body for purposes of government only, may take a promissory note for a debt due to them, or upon any contract in the transaction of their business. We have never held otherwise in this country, and there is no decision in modern times in England which can be relied on as supporting the contrary opinion. Whenever we have had occasion to express any conclusion on the point, we have assumed that a corporation such as this may take a note for a debt due to them; for we consider that where they have the power to transact business of a commercial character (and nothing is said to the contrary), they may transact their business and take securities according to the usual course of such matters. I hold it also to be unnecessary that it should appear on the face of the note that it was given for some consideration connected with the objects of their incorporation. It would be matter of defence if it were given for any purpose illegal, as being prohibited by their charter or unauthorized. But it need not be shewn in the first instance that it is free from such exception. The defendant argued, that on the principle which we stated in Cumming v. Guess, 2 Cam. 125, it ought to appear on this note for what purpose it was taken; but there is an evident distinction which it is only necessary to state, and which was noticed by us in a latter case of Ireland v. Guess et al. In these cases, the clerk was suing in his name upon a note to which he was in no shape a party, but which he was authorized by statute to sue upon, if it were a note given to the trustees of a turnpike under a certain statute. To make this derivative authority to sue appear, we thought it should be averred that the note was given to the trustees in the course of their public duty. Here the parties who sue are the payees of the note. I refer on this point to what is said in Chitty's Treatise on Bills, &c., and to Slack v. Highgate Archway Company, 5 Taunt. 792. It is quite clear that the consideration of a note need not appear upon the face of it for the mere purpose of making it a valid note. The words "value received," are unimportant; a note good with them would be good without them. There is nothing to shew this to be an accommodation note; it is not to be inferred from the absence of the words "value received," and it is equally clear that the taking of a promissory note for £100, payable a month after date, does not carry on the face of the transaction any appearance of being an infringement of the prohibition against carrying on banking, to which I have referred.

JONES, J.—The principal objection to the action is, that the plaintiffs being a corporate body created for specific purposes, cannot take and sue upon a promissory note, no express authority having been given in the charter to take such notes The plaintiffs were incorporated for the purpose of repairing steamboats and other vessels, and their powers were extended by the 7 Vic. ch. 61, so as to enable them to purchase, to have and to hold any estate, real, personal, or mixed, to and for the use of the company, and to let, convey, and otherwise depart with the same for the benefit of the company. It was evidently contemplated, that the business of the company by the latter Act should be most extended in the objects for which it was created, but it was expressly prohibited from acting as bankers, or issuing notes in the nature of bank notes. No prohibition is contained against the issuing of notes as evidence of debt, or of receiving such notes given for the same object. Indeed, it may be said to be almost necessary for the convenient carrying on the business contemplated, that such power should exist, and there appears to me to be nothing in the charter, or by common law, to prevent a corporation, established for such purposes, exercising the right of giving and taking promissory notes in the natural course of their business; and when such power is given or incident to a corporation, notes given or taken by them are *prima facie* to be regarded as so given or taken, and need not express the consideration upon which they are given, nor need it appear upon the declaration in any action upon such note.

The strict rules with regard to corporations have been relaxed in consequence of the necessity produced by the changes in the circumstances of the times, and the great increase of trading and other institutions like that under consideration.

MACAULAY, J., and McLEAN, J,, concurred.

Per Cur.—Judgment for the plaintiffs on the demurrer.

BOULTON ET AL. V. WELLER.

Where a plaintiff declaring upon a deed sets it out untruly, but in a particular *not material* to the action which has been brought upon the deed, the defendant wishing to take advantage of the variance, should plead *non est factum;* he cannot crave oyer and demur.

The plaintiffs declared against the defendant in an action of covenant, "for "that by certain articles of agreement, &c., it was agreed by and between the "parties, that the defendant, in consideration of the sum of twelve pounds ten "shillings, to him in hand paid by the said plaintiffs, should shut up a certain "hotel known by the name of the Albion Hotel, in the town of Cobourg, in "the said district, then kept by one James Lambert, as soon as a certain hotel "then building near the dwelling house of the said defendant should be opened; "and that the said defendant should keep the said Albion Hotel closed and "shut up as an hotel for the space of two years then next ensuing the date of "the said agreement ; and for the due performance and satisfaction of the said "agreement, the said defendant did thereby agree and bind himself unto the "said plaintiffs well and truly to observe and perform all and every the said "agreement therein mentioned, as by the said articles of agreement, reference "being thereunto had, will more fully and at large appear ; and the said "plaintiffs in fact say, that the said new hotel so to be finished and opened "as aforesaid, was on the first day of August, in the year of our Lord one "thousand eight hundred and forty-five, finished and opened for business as "an hotel as aforesaid.

"Yet the said plaintiffs say, that although the defendant did for a short "space of time, to wit, the space of nine months from the day and year last "aforesaid close and shut up and keep closed and shut up the said Albion Hotel "pursuant to the said agreement, yet he hath not since the expiration of the "said nine months, nor at any other time between that day and the commence- "ment of this suit, nor did any in his behalf close or shut up the said Albion "Hotel, or cause the business of hotel-keeping to be discontinued, according "to the form and effect, true intent and meaning of the said articles of agree- "ment, but on the contrary thereof, to wit, on the first day of May, in the "year of our Lord one thousand eight hundred and forty-six, before the "expiration of the said two years, and before the commencement of this suit, "opened and allowed the said hotel to be kept open, and did keep the same "open as such hotel as aforesaid, contrary to the force, form and effect, true "intent and meaning of the said articles of agreement, to the damage of the "said plaintiffs of three hundred pounds."

The defendant craved oyer of the said articles of agreement, and they were set out in these words :—

"I hereby agree and bind myself unto D'Arcy E. Boulton and John Vance
"Boswell, Esquires, managers of the new brick hotel now about being finished
"next my dwelling-house, in the sum of three hundred pounds currency, to
"shut up the present Albion Hotel now kept by Mr. James Lambert, as soon
"as the new hotel is opened, and keep it shut up as an hotel for the space of
"two years, under the above penalty of three hundred pounds, in consideration
"of twelve pounds ten shillings to me in hand paid.

"Signed, sealed and delivered in the presence of
      (Signed)   "WM. WELLER. [L.S.]
"The word 'three' being interlined twice before execution.
      (Signed)   "R. ROBINS.
      (Signed)   "H. H. JACKSON."

And then demurred to the declaration upon the ground that "the said articles "of agreement were not correctly stated or set forth in the said declaration "in this particular, that is to say, that by the said articles it was agreed that "the defendant should shut up the said Albion Hotel as soon as the other new "hotel in the said agreement mentioned should be opened, and keep the said "Albion Hotel so shut up and closed for the space of two years thereafter, "whereas it was stated in the declaration that the said Albion Hotel was to "be so kept closed and shut up for the space of two years next ensuing the "date of the said agreement."

Several other grounds of demurrer were stated in the pleadings, but were abandoned on the argument.

The Hon. *R. B. Sullivan*, for the demurrer, contended that the agreement was not truly stated—that the two years were to be reckoned from the opening of the new hotel, and *not* from the date of the agreement, as alleged in the declaration; this variance was fatal on demurrer.

J. Lukin Robinson, contra, admitted that the agreement had been incorrectly set out in the declaration; he contended, however, that the variance was in a particular perfectly immaterial to the action which had been brought upon the agreement. The breach complained of was equally within the agreement as set out in the declaration, or as set out on oyer. This being the case, the defendant could not demur; he might perhaps have taken advantage of the variance under the plea of *non est factum* (a).

ROBINSON, C. J.—The only point which we have been called upon by the argument of this demurrer to consider is, the variance between the deeds as declared on, and as set out in oyer, in regard to the time from which the defendant was to close his hotel. It is laid down certainly in many places in our books, that when a plaintiff in declaring upon a deed sets it out untruly, the defendant may either plead *non est factum*, or may pray oyer, and having set out the deed as it is, may demur for the variance, and this is sometimes stated in such terms as not to call attention to a distinction which certainly is

---

(a) 1 B. & C. 758; 4 B. & C. 750; 2 C. M. & R. 304; 2 Saund. 366, note 1 (last edition).

very reasonable, and is by no means a distinction first taken in modern times, namely, that in order to afford ground for demurrer, the variance must be in some particular, not merely of substance as regards the effect of the deed, but some particular material to the action which has been brought on the deed. In Com. Dig. Pleader, Q. 3, it is said, if the declaration is founded on a bond or other speciality, the defendant may demand oyer, and if it shews no cause of action he may demur. In Ross v. Parker, 1 B. & C. 358, the court, upon demurrer for a variance between the deed set out in oyer, and that which had been declared on, observe, "The part of the deed upon which this objection is "founded, is quite immaterial to the present action, and therefore supposing "that there was a variance between the deed as described in the declaration "and as set out on oyer, still it would be no ground of demurrer. In Snell v. "Snell, 4 B. & C. 750, Bayley, J., says if the meaning of a deed when set out, "varies from that attributed to it in the declaration, in order to take advantage "of that variance he should plead *non est factum*, without setting out the "deed; if it does not support the breach, he should set it out and demur." It is the deed which is set out on oyer that is to be regarded as the deed on which the action is founded, so that if the defendant, after setting it out on oyer, should demur for a variance merely, he would fail, and it is therefore that Mr. Justice Bayley says, the way to take advantage of the mere variance as a variance (where it is not in a matter affecting the right of action), is to plead *non est factum* without craving oyer, because then the plaintiff is confined to the deed which he has declared upon, and upon its existence being denied he must shew it. In Paine v. Emery, 2 Cr. M. & R. 304, this matter is clearly treated by Lord Abinger; he says the deed set out in oyer is the plaintiff's statement of it, and unless the variance is such as to shew that the plaintiff has no cause of action for such a breach as he sues on, it is no cause for demurring. The judgment of Mr. Justice Patterson, who is of great eminence as an authority on special pleading, in the case of Smith v. Jennings, 9 Dowl. 161, renders questionable some part of what Mr. Justice Bayley has laid down in the case cited of Snell v. Snell, but the editor of the last edition of Mr. Chitty's Treatise on Pleading, adopts the conclusion, that a defendant cannot demur on account of a variance in an immaterial part between the deed as set out in the declaration, and as set out on oyer (a). Now the variance pointed out in this case is certainly not one that is material in this action. The defendant by his deed covenanted to shut up the Albion House for two years, commencing after the plaintiff's new hotel should be opened, which was not completed when the deed was executed; he is charged with having shut it up for a time after the new hotel was opened, thereby submitting to his covenant. but with not keeping it shut between a certain day and the commencement of the action. That period, when the injury complained of accrued, must clearly therefore be comprehended within the breach as the deed is set out, and equally so if the deed had run as it was first stated in the declaration. The reckoning the two years from the opening of the new hotel, might support a breach better than reckoning it from the date of the deed, that is, it would continue longer to give a right of action. It is a variance which in its effect makes the

---

(a) 1 Vol. 449. (2 Saunders, 366, note 1.)

covenant less extensive as against the defendant. The breach complained of is equally within the covenant as set out at first on an oyer, and therefore the variance is immaterial to the action. No other objection was relied on in the argument, and the declaration does not appear to be open to any other.

JONES, J.—The action is covenant, and although the deed as set out in the declaration is not correctly described, and upon a plea of *non est factum* the defendant would succeed, still there is not that variance from the deed set out on oyer that would entitle the defendant to judgment. It is immaterial in this action whether the Albion Hotel was to be shut for two years from the date of the deed, or from the opening of the new hotel. The deed is dated the 11th of July, 1845, and the hotel is stated to have been finished and opened on the first day of August following, and that the defendant did not close the Albion Hotel, but on the contrary, on the first day of May, 1846, opened and continued it open, which was within two years from the date of the deed and the time of opening the said hotel.

MACAULAY, J., and McLEAN, J., concurred.

Per Cur.—Judgment for the plaintiffs on demurrer.

Leave was given to the defendant to amend on payment of costs, and to the plaintiffs to amend their declaration as they desired.

THE BANK OF MONTREAL V. BURRITT.

Under the 51st and following clauses of 8 Vic. ch. 13, a writ of trial may go from the Queen's Bench to the judge of the District Court in a case in which *an attorney* is the defendant.

This was an action brought against an attorney on a promissory note, and the question raised was, whether, under the 51st and following clauses of 8 Vic. ch 13, a writ of trial could go from the Queen's Bench to the judge of the District Court in a case in which an attorney was the defendant.

ROBINSON, C. J., delivered the judgment of the court.

We are of opinion that we cannot properly withhold the writ on the ground that it is an interference with the defendant's privilege as an attorney. It is true that there are no words in these provisions of the statute expressly taking away the privilege referred to, under which an attorney claims the right of suing and being sued in his own court; and it is true that his claim of privilege is generally recognized here, as it is in England. But, on the other hand, it is to be considered that the giving effect to these provisions of the statute does not take the suit out of the Queen's Bench; it merely authorizes, for greater convenience, cheapness and expedition, the verdict of a jury to be taken by a judge of the District Court, at a sitting of that court, upon a writ emanating from this court, and which is afterwards to be returned into this court, where all subsequent proceedings are to take place. We do not see that this differs in principle from the common case, both in England and this country, of trying causes at *nisi prius*, in which attorneys are defendants, upon a record emanating from our court, but tried before a judge of another court; or assessments of damages before the under sheriff. The attorney is in fact sued in his proper court, and that is the extent of his privilege. If he desires to be present at the trial, he must leave the place where the court having cognizance of the cause sits, and go down into the country, when it is tried there, as it may be, before a judge of another court; and we can make no difference in principle, because the judge to whom the legislature has thought fit to assign the duty happens to belong to the District Court. The effect of the claim of privilege advanced in this case is to set up a right of attorneys to have every case against them tried at bar, unless they should choose to waive it. That, however, is not a right recognized at the present day. We are of opinion that the writ of trial should go in this case.

Per Cur.—Rule absolute.

DOWLING v. EASTWOOD ET AL.

A note signed A. and Co., by A., jun., *prima facie* imports that A. signs the note for the firm, and not as one of the firm.

The plaintiff sued upon a promissory note made by one Ketchum, payable in ninety days to Messrs. Eastwood & Co., or order, for £125.

The note was endorsed "*Eastwood & Co., per J. Eastwood, Jun.*"

The plaintiff sued John Eastwood and John Eastwood the younger, as payees and endorsers, averring that the defendants, under the name and firm of Eastwood & Co., by the said John Eastwood the younger, endorsed the note.

The defendants pleaded, among other pleas, that they did not endorse the note in manner and form, &c.

Upon the trial it was proved, that John Eastwood, junior, had never been a partner with his father; that John Eastwood, the father, was formerly in partnership with one Skinner, who died; and that he had always since continued to use the name of Eastwood & Co., though alone in business.

The learned judge left it to the jury to say, whether it was the intention of Eastwood, jun., to hold himself out to the plaintiff as a partner, or whether he intended to endorse the note as jointly liable, or led the plaintiff to think so. Under that direction the jury found for the plaintiff.

Alex. Grant moved for a new trial, on the ground of misdirection, and on affidavits.

Blake and *Gwynne* shewed cause. There was no misdirection: it was left to the jury to say whether the defendants were partners or not; they found that they were, and gave a verdict to the plaintiff. The evidence warranted the finding of the jury, and the verdict therefore ought not to be disturbed.

Grant, in support of his rule. The learned judge appeared to consider at the trial that the signature was *prima facie* binding on both the defendants as partners; in this there was a misdirection: the signature, he would submit, *prima facie* imported that Eastwood, jun., signed for the firm and not as a partner. There was no evidence whatever to shew that the plaintiff could have any fair reason to believe that Eastwood, jun., was a partner, or that he had in fact taken the note supposing him to be such; the verdict as to him ought to be set aside without costs.

ROBINSON, C. J., delivered the judgment of the court.

There does not appear in the evidence any ground that could warrant the jury in holding John Eastwood, junior, liable, either as a partner or as a joint endorser. The signature *prima facie* imports merely that he was signing for the firm, not that he was one of the firm. The affidavits filed raise no inference to the contrary, and they repel any pretence that the plaintiff was induced to take the note by being led to suppose that John Eastwood, junior, was a partner. There does not appear upon the evidence anything to warrant a recovery against that defendant, and we are therefore of opinion that there must be a new trial without costs.

Per Cur.—New trial without costs.

DOE DEM. YEIGH V. ROE.

The rule for judgment *nisi* against the casual ejector must be taken out within two days after the end of the term.

Judgment under the rule cannot be entered upon *the same day* on which the rule is issued.

The objection taken to the regularity of the judgment in this case against the casual ejector, was that the rule *nisi* for judgment was not taken out till the 28th of September, in vacation, and long after two days after the end of the term.

ROBINSON, C. J., delivered the judgment of the court.

We think it clear that the practice does not allow this, and that there was a decided irregularity in not having taken out the rule for judgment *nisi*, within two days after the end of the term, and as clear an irregularity in entering up judgment under the rule on the day on which it issued. It is not stated in the affidavit at what time the notice required the tenant to appear; but it is impossible that the proceedings taken can have been regular under any circumstances.

Per Cur.—Rule absolute.

REYNOLDS V. SHUTER ET AL.

Defendants are taken by plaintiff to a quantity of timber already made upon the ground. Having seen the timber, they contract with the plaintiff to draw it out, and well and truly to deliver it to the plaintiff on the bank of a river.

Held, that the timber cut in two by the defendants, to suit their convenience, and without the permission of the plaintiff, and drawn out to the river in that *altered state*, was not a delivery within the meaning of the contract.

The plaintiff had agreed with the proprietor of a tract of land to purchase from him all the standing trees that would make merchantable timber of a certain description; and in order to get the same to market, he entered into an agreement with the defendants, under seal, by which they covenanted, "that they would well and truly deliver, or cause to be delivered to the

"plaintiff, on or before the 15th of March then instant, all the timber that is
"now squared or hewn, and all other the timber that may be squared or hewn
"on or before the first day of March next, and lying and being on Lot, &c.,
"all of which said timber the defendants covenanted to deliver unto the plain-
"tiff or his assigns, on the banks of the River Trent, at White's Landing, at
"the time mentioned."

The plaintiff, in his declaration, after charging a breach in not delivering the timber, assigned as a further breach that the defendants "cut in two and cut "in pieces, and thereby made unsaleable, forty pieces of the said timber, which "were squared and lying on the lot, and rendered themselves incapable of "delivering the same to the plaintiff in the manner agreed upon, &c., and did "not deliver the same to the plaintiff in manner agreed upon, &c.;" and he averred that he received great damage from "the timber not being delivered "in the state in which it ought to have been."

The defendants pleaded performance in the terms of the covenant, not noticing that part of the declaration which charged them with having cut many of the sticks of timber, and not delivering them in the state in which they ought to have delivered them.

It was proved at the trial, that the timber was a particularly good lot of pine timber; and that as it lay in the woods, after being squared and dressed for market, it averaged about 120 feet a stick, forty or fifty of the sticks averaging more than 150 feet, and twelve of them exceeding 200 feet; but the defendants went with plaintiff and examined the timber before they entered into the agreement, and that in consequence of the size of the sticks, they demanded a higher price for drawing them than was usual, to which plaintiff assented. He agreed to pay them £6 5s. per thousand feet for drawing them out to the river—five pounds per thousand being the price paid to others by another lumberer, for drawing timber from the adjoining lot. It was proved, that although it might all have been drawn out without cutting, by employing more cattle with the larger sticks, yet that the defendants, to save themselves trouble and expense, cut about thirty of the finest sticks in two. The plaintiff remonstrated with them, as it would occasion a great damage to him; and declared he would make them pay whatever loss in price he might sustain. He offered to leave the matter to arbitration, and to take half of what should be awarded as the amount of damage. One of the defendants admitted that they had done wrong, and wished to make compensation, but the others declined.

It was proved by persons experienced in the trade that the alteration made in the timber by the defendant, which had the effect of reducing the average length of sticks in the whole lot from about one hundred feet to sixty, would throw upon the plaintiff a loss in the market of $1\frac{1}{2}$d. per foot, or about £65 in the lot.

The defendants objected that the plaintiff's proper remedy for such an injury would be either trespass or an action on the case; but he could not maintain his breach for not delivering the timber since it was all delivered.

The jury, in accordance with the direction of the learned judge, gave the plaintiff a verdict for £65, and leave was reserved to the defendants to move to set it aside.

L. Wallbridge, of Belleville, moved to set aside the verdict, as contrary to law and evidence. The defendants had contracted to deliver the timber on the bank of the river; this the evidence shews has been done; the timber was delivered at the place contracted for. It might not have been in the state in which the plaintiff may have expected to receive it; but the defendants were not bound at any sacrifice to deliver it on the river in precisely the same state as they found it before they proceeded to draw it off.—4 Price, 36.

D. B. Read shewed cause. The verdict is right. The court are to look at the *intention* of the covenant, and not at the bare words. The intention manifestly was that the plaintiff was to receive the timber on the river in the same state in which it lay upon the ground at the time the defendants contracted to remove it; the usage of the trade requires this. If the defendants can cut the wood into two pieces to suit their convenience in drawing it off, what is there to prevent them cutting it up into a dozen pieces? He cited 4 B. & C. 750; 13 E. R. 86; 11 E. R. 639; 2 B. & Ald. 746; 12 E. R. 179; 7 E. R. 116; 13 E. R. 63; Plowden, 87-89; 2 Stephens, N. P. 1368.

ROBINSON, C. J., delivered the judgment of the court.

I directed the jury to find for the plaintiff such damage as they should think he had sustained, leaving it to the defendants to move against the verdict. It was found on the trial, that according to the well known usage of the trade, persons contracting to draw timber to the water are never allowed to cut it into pieces, and it appears to me to be at least doubtful whether these defendants, who had engaged *well* and truly to deliver the timber, and who must be taken to have made their contract with a knowledge of what the usage of the trade required, could be said to have fulfilled their undertaking when they delivered it in a different state from that in which they ought to have delivered it, in consequence of an alteration wilfully made by themselves, not from any accident arising from negligence or otherwise.

We are of opinion that the verdict may be supported on legal principles, and upon authority; the plain intent of a covenant is to be regarded, and not barely its words. The cases cited for the plaintiff on the argument were strong authorities on that point. It is true that the timber was delivered, that is, the wood was taken to the bank of the river, and so it would have been if the defendants had mutilated the sticks in a greater degree, by cutting them twice instead of once, they would still have been timber fit for some purposes. When the defendants were taken by the plaintiff to this lot of timber already made on the ground, and contracted to draw it out, we must look upon them as having undertaken to deliver it in the state in which it then was. It was proved that the usage of the trade required this, and they must be supposed to have contracted upon that understanding. Then they did not *well* and *truly* deliver according to their contract if they did not deliver it as they received it, but in an altered state, not altered by accident or from negligence merely, but by their own wilful act. In Com. Dig. Condition M. 1, 3, it is laid down, that "it shall be a breach of the condition if the obligor acts contrary to "the very intent of the condition, or if he be disabled to perform it in the same "plight as it was when the condition was created."

Per Cur.—Rule discharged.

MANLY V. CORRY.

Where in an action for slander the declaration charged the defendant with saying of the plaintiff, "*he burnt Knox's barn,*" and the evidence was not that the defendant said simply, "*he burnt Knox's barn,*" but that he added the words, "because one of the girls would not marry him;" and no notice was taken of these latter words in the declaration. *Quære:* Would not there be a fatal variance between the words as laid and proved?

Where, by way of introduction, the declaration averred that the defendant, &c., "in a certain discourse which he then and there had, of and concerning "the plaintiff, and of and concerning a certain barn upon the premises of "the late Mrs. Knox, now deceased, which had been burnt," spoke and published of and concerning the plaintiff, *and of and concerning the said barn*, the false and scandalous words following, &c., "*he burnt Knox's barn.*"

Held, that mere proof of the defendant's saying of the plaintiff, "*he burnt* "*Knox's barn*," without *proof of the colloquium respecting the burning of Mrs. Knox's barn*, was insufficient.

The plaintiff sued for slander.

The declaration contained four counts, charging the words differently in each; and by way of introduction to the whole, it averred that the defendant, &c., "in a certain discourse which he then and there had of and concerning "the plaintiff, and of and concerning a certain barn upon the premises of the "late Mrs. Knox, now deceased, which had been burnt," falsely and maliciously spoke and published of and concerning the plaintiff, "*and of and* "*concerning the said barn*," the false and scandalous words following, &c.

In the first count the words charged were, "he burnt Mrs. Knox's barn;" in the second count, "he burnt the barn;" in the third, "he burnt it;" in the fourth count, "*he burnt Knox's barn.*"

The defendant pleaded the general issue.

The only proof of the words upon the trial was by one witness, who swore that the defendant came to him and endeavoured to persuade him to surrender the plaintiff (for whom the witness had given bail) to close custody; that he used several arguments to induce him to do so; and among other things said, that the plaintiff was the "worst man in Stamford; that he had shot Danton's "hogs; that he had killed Thomson's bull, because Thomson had impounded "his mare; *and that he had burnt Knox's barn, because one of the girls would* "*not marry him.*"

The plaintiff gave no evidence whatever upon the trial respecting the subject-matter of these last words. It was not proved that the defendant, in speaking of Knox's barn, meant to refer to Mrs. Knox, or was so understood; nor that there was any such person as Mrs. Knox, or that any barn was burnt belonging to a person of that name; or that there was any conversation about the burning of a barn of Knox or of Mrs. Knox.

The defendant moved for a nonsuit on that ground. The learned judge thought that there was a fatal variance between the words proved and those laid, and that the plaintiff ought to have given evidence that the words spoken were meant to convey the sense ascribed to them.

The jury found a verdict for the plaintiff for £100 damages.

The Hon. *R. B. Sullivan* moved for a new trial on the ground that the verdict was against law and evidence, and also in arrest of judgment. The words proved did not support the words laid in the declaration; there was no proof whatever that when the defendant said "he burnt Knox's barn," he made any allusion to Mrs. Knox's barn. The *colloquium* should have been proved. He relied upon 5 B. & Ad. 27.

Eccles shewed cause. The general issue under the new rules did not put in issue the declaration.—3 Dowl. 619 ; 3 M. & S. 548. The words were proved as laid in the fourth count. There was no necessity of proving more to support that count. He submitted the verdict ought to stand.

ROBINSON, C. J., delivered the judgment of the court.

The plaintiff contends that the words proved are sufficient to establish a cause of action under the fourth count. It is evident that they did not support any of the other counts, and I have great doubts whether the fourth count can properly be considered as having been proved, for the evidence was not that the defendant said simply "he burnt Knox's barn," but that he added the words "because one of the girls would not marry him," no notice of which latter words is taken in the count. It is true that the tendency of those words would be to aggravate the slander, because they imputed a deliberate design and a vindictive motive, and therefore it may be said that the plaintiff's case is not made stronger than the whole matter could warrant by omitting them. But my present impression is, that whenever the words proved are so closely connected as they were in this case with other words spoken at the time, which tend to give them force and application, the whole ought to be set out. The conversation shewed that the defendant intended to make the charge in connection with a certain supposed motive, and the motive is material in estimating the graveness of the charge. It might in the opinion of the jury be such in some cases as to shew plainly that a charge of felony or other crime was not intended, or, although so far as the mere words are concerned, the effect might not be such, yet they might seem to suggest a motive so utterly inadequate to form an inducement to the crime imputed, that the jury might be led to infer from that very circumstance, in connection with the tone and temper in which the words were described to have been spoken, that the bystanders could not have supposed that the defendant was uttering the words gravely, and as if he desired and expected them to be believed. The plaintiff is not, in my opinion, at liberty to divide an assertion as is done in this case, and give barely the words imputing the act, omitting those which relate to the motive or purpose. Where in conversation the defendant has made charges of several substantive offences, the plaintiff may complain of some one of those slanderous charges only, and may confine his proof to that ; but when the words constitute, as in this case, but one entire charge, they are not divisible ; the whole, if charged, ought to be proved, and the converse of the rule I think holds ; so that if the plaintiff having laid only part of the charge, proves other words uttered not relating to any distinct charge, but closely connected with the only charge made, whether serving to qualify or aggravate the charge, then I am inclined to think that the variance would be fatal.

But, independently of this doubt, the defendant is in our opinion entitled to succeed on the ground on which he has rested his objection. The words, "he burnt Knox's barn," have no reference to the barn of a Mrs. Knox deceased ; and there was no evidence, as it was indispensable there should have been, on this declaration, that the defendant was speaking of a barn that had belonged to a Mrs. Knox, and which had been burnt. If it had been shewn that the tenor of the conversation was such that the bystanders must have understood him to be alluding to a felonious burning of a barn belonging to a Mrs. Knox deceased, then it would have been immaterial whether there had or had not been a Mrs. Knox now deceased, or whether any barn of hers had been feloniously burnt or not. But, for all that was proved on the trial of this cause, the conversation might as well have related to a barn of Mrs. Knox which had been accidentally burnt. In such a case as this the colloquium was necessary to be proved, because the words proved do not obviously bear the meaning ascribed to them ; and when that is the case, there must be proof given that they were in fact spoken with that meaning. We are of opinion that there should be a new trial without costs.

Per Cur.—Rule absolute with costs.

O'REILLY v. MOODIE, SHERIFF.

The plaintiff sues the defendant, as sheriff, for an escape. The declaration contains the following averment : " That the defendant after and before the "return of the writ, took and arrested the said Rabure, and *then* had and "detained him in his custody."

Held, declaration bad on special demurrer in not alleging the arrest to have been made on any *certain* day.

The plaintiff sued the defendant as sheriff, for an escape.

The declaration, in setting out the arrest, contained the following averment: "That the defendants, after and before the return of the writ, took and arrested "the said Rabure, and *then* had and detained him in his custody."

To this averment the defendant demurred, " because it did not appear on "what day or at what time the defendant executed the said writ, and took "and arrested the said Rabure, and detained him in his custody."

Other grounds of demurrer were taken to the declaration, but not insisted upon in argument.

The Hon. *R. B. Sullivan*, for the demurrer. The declaration is clearly bad, in not laying the arrest on a certain day; the arrest is a material traversable fact, and the day on which it took place should have been alleged with certainty.

D. B. Read, contra. He submitted that the averment was sufficient, at least under the form in which the demurrer is taken. The demurrer is that no "time or day is stated ;" and the objection really is, that time is not stated with *sufficient certainty*. Now it is submitted that *time* is stated, the time being "from the delivering of the writ to the return ;" and it is alleged that the sheriff *afterwards* and before the *return*, arrested ; and if this is a traversable fact, the plaintiff could prove any time, from the delivery of the return. In Chitty's Pleadings, Vol. II, page 322, in note, it is said, " The allegation of the "arrest is not *necessary*, and is not traversable."—2 Saund. 596. The form in escape directs the pleader to follow the form above given precisely.

The words "*and took and arrested*," it is submitted, will also aid in giving a certain time to the arrest.—See Chitty's Pl. Vol. I. p. 273; Cro. Jac. 443. The words "and then had and detained," refer to the next antecedent day named.—14 E. 291.

ROBINSON, C. J., delivered the judgment of the court.

The demurrer to the second count is given up, and we are only called upon to consider the sufficiency of the first count. The question raised upon that is, whether upon special demurrer it is a good objection that the arrest is not alleged to have been made on any certain day. The statement is (after averring the delivery of the writ to the defendant on the 5th day of May, 1846) that the defendant *afterwards*, and before the return thereof, took and arrested the said Rabure, and *then* had and detained him in his custody. The word "then," I think, as here used, cannot reasonably be referred to the 5th day of May, though it might possibly be " afterwards," and yet on the same day that the writ was delivered ; that is, the sheriff might have executed the writ on the same day that he received it. The language, however, does not import that ; and as the general principle of the law is that there is no fraction of a day, we must, I think, *prima facie*, suppose that "afterward" means on a subsequent day. Then, as the reference is not plainly to the 5th day of May, some day should have been alleged ; for certainly the arrest is a material traversable fact, since there could have been no escape without it ; and the strict rule of pleading is, that a certain day and year must be alleged for every material traversable fact. The case in 2 Saund, 59 (a), to which we were referred, and where the arrest was held not to be traversable, was an action against the sheriff for taking insufficient sureties, which is altogether different, for there the sheriff had admitted the arrest by the act of taking sureties. No doubt the declaration would have been good on general demurrer, because it does sufficiently appear that the arrest was made under the writ while it was current, but the special demurrer particularly points to the defect in form —that the day is not alleged when the arrest was made ; and we cannot take the case, therefore, out of the rule recognized in Ring v. Roxburgh, 2 Tyr. 468, which we have acted upon in other cases.

Per Cur.—Judgment for plaintiff on demurrer.

THE BANK OF UPPER CANADA V. PARSONS ET AL.

An averment that the note was "*duly presented*" for payment to the maker, without specially stating either time or place, is sufficient to charge an endorser.

Semble: That even for the purpose of evidence, it is not necessary, in order to charge the endorser, since our statute 7 Wm. IV. ch. 55, to shew presentment of the note at the particular place.

Endorsees against the maker and endorser of a promissory note, under the provincial statute, 3 Vic. ch. 8 ; the note was made payable at the Bank of Upper Canada, and *due presentment* was averred in order to charge the endorser.

Special demurrer : Because it was not averred that the note was presented for payment *at the Bank of Upper Canada*.

H. Eccles for the demurrer.
J. Lukin Robinson, contra (a).

ROBINSON, C. J.—This declaration is in an action charging the maker and endorsers of a promissory note, as jointly and severally liable under our statute 3 Vic. ch. 8. The defendant Wetenhall, one of the endorsers, demurs. The ground of his objection is, that although the note set out is made payable at the Bank of Upper Canada, yet it is not averred that it was presented there, which he contends is necessary in order to charge the endorser. But the statute, in the form which it gives to be used in this joint action, does not lay the plaintiff under any peculiar necessity with regard to the averment which he is to make of presentment; and then our rule of court (34th rule) comes afterwards, and makes it sufficient to state in an action by endorsee against endorser, that the note was "*duly presented*," without specially stating either day or place. We must hold this form to be sufficient, as it complies with the rule which makes no exception with regard to notes payable at a particular place. If it were held to be necessary that the note should be presented at the particular place, in order to charge the endorser, that would be a question upon the sufficiency of evidence at the trial, as shewing what the averment of due presentment would bind the plaintiff to prove. But we have always held, that even for the purpose of evidence, it would not be necessary, since our statute 7 Will. IV. ch. 55, to shew presentment of the note at the particular place, in order to charge the endorser. This point was expressly so adjudged in this court in Commercial Bank v. Johnston, 2 Cam. Rep. 126; and the court recognized the principle of that decision in Grant v. Eyer et al., 2 Cam. 427. The course of evidence at *nisi prius*, in actions against endorsers, has been always in accordance with those decisions; and if it were clear that in England, under a statute nearly similar as regards bills of exchange, a presentment at the particular place has been held necessary, not merely to be proved, but to be averred specially, in order to make the endorser liable, yet we should not feel ourselves at liberty to decide in opposition to our own uniform construction of our own statute, in order to conform to the English cases. The mercantile community ought to feel themselves safe in adhering to the practice upon such a point, after it has been sustained by repeated decisions, safe (that is) till these cases have been overruled, or the law changed by a higher authority. We do not know what losses we might be inflicting upon the holders of bills, by varying from what has been hitherto held; and we cannot feel it difficult to adhere to the view we have always taken of the effect of our statute, when we rely upon the express words of the statute itself, which make the acceptance and promise "*to all intents and purposes* a *general acceptance* or "*promise*," unless the words "*and not otherwise or elsewhere*" are added. It certainly is no stretch of construction to hold that "*all intents and purposes*" includes the intent and purpose of making the endorser liable as well as the maker, and especially when the endorser's undertaking is to answer for the maker's default. It certainly seems good sense to hold, that when all has

---

(a) The point taken in this demurrer was argued and determined in The Commercial Bank v. Culver and Cameron, reported in the last number of the *Jurist* (February); the argument is therefore omitted in this case. The judgment is given, because it goes more fully into the reason of the decision than in the prior case.

been done which is requisite to charge the maker, and he has not paid, the endorser, upon due notice of his default, must come in his place. It would seem difficult to reconcile oneself to a contrary decision, but at all events we consider ourselves bound to adhere to the construction which our statute certainly has always received here. The other objection we think clearly not tenable; the mode of averring notice precisely follows the form given by the rule of court, which is not at variance with that given by the statute when a plaintiff declares in a joint action, for that form contains no specific direction on that point.

MACAULAY, J.—The form corresponds with the new rules, and the time and place, if material, become matter of evidence. If the case of the Commercial Bank v. Johnston has decided that presentment to the maker anywhere of a note made payable at a specified place is a sufficient presentment as against an endorser, such decision, till reversed, ought to be adhered to; but it seems to conflict with Gibb v. Mather in relation to endorsers of bills of exchange.

JONES, J.—Our statute 3 Vic. ch. 8, is a transcript of the British statute 1 & 2 Geo. IV. ch. 78, so far as respects bills of exchange; but it extends the provisions, with regard to presentment at the place at which payment is to be made, to promissory notes as well as bills of exchange. In Commercial Bank v. Johnston, 2 Cam. 126, this court has expressly decided, that under our statute the making a note payable at a particular place, without adding the words "and not elsewhere," is the same in effect as making it payable generally; and that there is no necessity to present it at the particular place to charge the endorser, thereby holding the provision with regard to presentment to extend to all the parties to a note, and I do not see with what propriety it can be otherwise determined. The words of the statute are, that where a bill is accepted, payable at a particular place, and not elsewhere, such acceptance shall be deemed and taken to be to all intents and purposes a general acceptance. The decision referred to is in opposition to Gibb v. Mather, 8 Bing. 214; but this court having so held, and as appears to me in accordance with the letter and spirit of the statute, and the intention of the legislature, I think the question should be considered a settled one till otherwise determined by a superior jurisdiction. In Grant v. Eyre, 2 Cam. Rep. 426, it was also held by the court that a presentment of a note need not be shewn at the place where it is made payable, the words "and not elsewhere" not being added in order to charge the endorser.

McLEAN, J., concurred.

Per Cur.—Judgment for plaintiffs on demurrer.

HARVEY FOWLER, SEN., APPELLANT, V. MCDONALD, RESPONDENT.

The court in *banc* will not overrule the opinion of the judge and jury in the District Court on the question of weight of evidence on a trifling matter, especially when a new trial could not be granted without paying costs.

This was a case of appeal from the District Court of the Victoria District.

Action—Trover for a cow.

Pleas.—"Not guilty," and "plaintiff not possessed," &c.

A verdict was given in favour of the plaintiff below for £4, and a new trial was moved for before the Judge of the District Court and refused. The case was left to the jury on contradictory evidence. The plaintiff proved by his father that the latter had lent him the cow, while he was working a farm on shares with the defendant. The plaintiff had left the farm, and sometime afterwards went and demanded the cow and other things he had left on the farm. The defendant gave up the other things, but as to the cow, he said he had sold her. On this evidence the plaintiff recovered.

The defendant called witnesses, who swore that plaintiff's father had given the cow to his daughter, who had sold her to one Lingham, and that it was not Fowler who sold her

D. B. Read for the appellant. The appellant cannot sue, as the cow was only lent to him and not his property; the defendant besides had her not when she was demanded, and could not give her up, and therefore refused, which was no evidence of conversion.

Campbell, of Kingston, for the respondent, The respondent is answerable over, and therefore may bring the action. The defendant on these pleas cannot shew title in a third party—the sale is a conversion, and so demand and refusal unnecessary to be proved.

ROBINSON, C. J., delivered the judgment of the court.

The evidence seems to preponderate for the defendant, as to the daughter being the person who sold the cow and not the defendant. But there was evidence to support the verdict as it stands, and it was left to the jury. They and the judge could best determine whether one witness on the one side, or several on the other, should be believed. It was not the intention of the statute that we should overrule the opinion of judge and jury below on the question of weight of evidence in a trifling matter, and when a new trial could not properly be granted without paying costs.

Per Cur.—Judgment below confirmed.

QUEEN'S BENCH.

HILARY TERM, 10 VICTORIA.

Present,—THE HON. CHIEF JUSTICE ROBINSON.
" MR. JUSTICE JONES.
" MR. JUSTICE MCLEAN.
MR. JUSTICE MACAULAY sitting in the Practice Court.
MR. JUSTICE HAGERMAN absent, from illness.

DOE DEM. MALLOCH V. THE PRINCIPAL OFFICERS OF HER MAJESTY'S ORDNANCE.

Quære: Whether any grant, improvidently made by the crown, of lands set apart for the Rideau Canal before the passing of the late Act 7 Vic. ch. 11, would not be void at common law, if injurious to the canal, without the necessity of a proceeding by *scire facias* to repeal it?

Held, that lands which had been so granted before the passing of the Vesting Act, 7 Vic. ch. 11, but afterwards marked out and reserved by the Ordnance Department, as necessary for the canal, became again re-vested in the crown.

This was an action of ejectment for broken Lots Nos. 7 & 8 in the first concession, from the River Rideau, in the township of Nepean. Verdict for the plaintiff.

W. H. Blake moved for a new trial on the law and evidence.

The Hon. *R. B. Sullivan* and *J. H. Hagarty* shewed cause.

The arguments of counsel, and the facts of the case, fully appear in the following judgment of the court, delivered by the Chief Justice.

ROBINSON, C. J.—The lessor of the plaintiff produced a patent dated 18th December, 1839, granted to him in fee, broken Lot No. 8, containing twenty-six acres; and also a patent dated 19th December, 1839, granting to him in fee, broken Lot No. 7, containing eighteen acres. With respect to the Lot No. 7, it was shewn upon the trial that so long ago as in 1806, the crown had made a grant of it by letters patent to a Mrs. Christiana Mount, so that independently of the grounds upon which the defendants claim a right to the possession of the property as having been necessarily reserved for purposes connected with the Rideau Canal, it was evident that the lessor of the plaintiff could not make title to that lot under his patent of 19th December, 1839, on account of the crown having divested itself of its interest in the land by the prior grant to Mrs. Mount. The question of title has been, therefore, confined to the Lot No. 8, described in the consent rule as being in the first concession from the River Rideau, in the township of Nepean; that lot is a clergy reserve. The township of Nepean, in that part of it, is bounded by the Rideau River, which prevents its eastern limit from being an even base line, there being a greater breadth of land towards the northern end of the township line on that side, than towards the southern end, on account of the course of the waters. The lots in the several concessions are numbered from south to north; the concessions are numbered back from the Rideau. Towards the northern end of the township line, it appears, a concession is laid out which fronts on the River Rideau, but where the second concession line which bounds that range in the rear is protracted southerly, it strikes the Rideau River upon Lot No. 6, and from that point, therefore, the second concession from the Rideau becomes in effect the first. In the early patent to Mrs. Mount for Lot No. 7, in the first concession, the land intended to be granted is so described as clearly to carry the boundaries down to the Rideau River, and there is no doubt, therefore, as I have already stated, that the plaintiff can hold nothing under the recent patent, which has from some inadvertence been made to him for what is called the broken Lot No. 7. That a grant should have been made to the lessor of the plaintiff of this broken lot, shews an unaccountable overlooking by the Surveyor-General's Department of what had been done before in regard to that land, independently of whatever had taken place under the Rideau Canal Act. With respect to the Lot No. 8, which lies between what in the plan of the township are designated as the second and third concession lines, the evidence is not clear to shew whether it should properly be called 8 in the first concession, or in the second. It seems most reconcilable with the evidence to call it Lot No. 8 in the second concession; and the small tract of land intervening between its eastern end and the river, might be properly described either as a broken Lot No. 8 in front of the second concession, or as the broken front of Lot No. 8 in the second concession. Although evidence was given on this point, it seems not to be material how it is settled, because it is clear that the whole space known as Lot No. 8, from the rear of the first range of full lots from the Rideau down to the river, including what the plaintiff claims in this action as broken Lot No. 8, was a clergy reserve lot, of which no grant had ever been made by the crown before the patent which issued to the lessor of the plaintiff in 1839; and the question is, whether under that patent, which undoubtedly does embrace the land in dispute, (*i. e.* the broken Lot No. 8, as I have described it,) the lessor of the plaintiff is entitled to be put in possession of the land, or whether it has not become vested in the Officers of the Ordnance, as part of the land appertaining to, and to be held with the Rideau Canal. That depends upon the provincial statutes referred to, and upon what has been done under them. The legislature passed in 1827 the Act (8 Geo. IV. ch. 1) for granting certain facilities to the government for the construction of the Rideau Canal. They recite in it that "the work would tend most essentially to the security of the Province "by facilitating measures for its defence, as well as promote greatly its agricul- "tural and commercial interests;" and when this double public advantage is considered, we cannot doubt that the legislature intended, that the discretionary powers which they were about conferring upon the military officers, to be intrusted by His Majesty with the superintendence and charge of the canal, should be such as would enable them to carry out the design on what they might consider an efficient and proper scale, with reference to the protection and security of the work in every point of view, and the uses that might be made of it, in war as well as peace. I have so held on several occasions, when it was made a question before me at *nisi prius*, whether the lands which the military engineers had taken were in fact necessary. Although there might possibly be such an evident abuse of the powers given by the statute, as would make it right to hold, that what was pretended to be done under its provisions, was not in fact done with a view to execute its powers, but only under colour and pretence of its authority, yet it has always appeared to me, that wherever there could be said to be any room for question as to the necessity, it ought to be assumed that the public officers had used their discretion fairly and in good faith, in which case, the question of the land being necessary or not necessary must be governed by their judgment and not by the judgment of any court, or the opinion of any other person, public or private ; and this appears to me to be not only legal but highly reasonable, when we consider the great public interests involved on the one hand, and on the other, the care taken to secure to every individual whose property may be taken possession of, a just compensation for its value. In the case of Phillips v. Redpath, Hilary Term, 10th Geo. IV., we had occasion to consider the intention and effect of the statute. The case before us, however, will not turn upon the extent to which the principle spoken of should be carried; and I should perhaps not have adverted to that, if it had not appeared to me that some of the evidence given at the trial must have been brought with the view of attempting to show that some part of the land for which the ordnance officers are defending, cannot in fact be required for any purpose connected with the canal.

The statute 8th Geo. IV. chap. 1, gives authority (sec. 1) to the officers employed to superintend the work, "to explore the country lying between "Lake Ontario and the River Ottawa, and to enter into and upon the lands "or grounds belonging to any person or persons, bodies politic and corporate, "and to survey and take levels of the same; and to set out and ascertain such "parts thereof as he shall think necessary and proper for making the said "canal, and all such other improvements, works and conveniences, as he shall "think proper and necessary for making, effecting, improving, completing and "using in the said navigation." Extensive powers are then given to take materials for constructing or repairing the canal, &c., "and also, to make, build, "erect and set up, in and upon the said canal, or upon the lands adjoining or "near the same, such and so many bridges, tunnels, aqueducts, sluices, locks, "wears, piers for water, reservoirs, wharves, quays, landing places, and other "works, roads and conveniences, as the officers aforesaid shall think requisite "and convenient for the purposes of the said navigation; and also, from *time* "*to time to alter the route of the said canal*, and to amend, repair, widen or "enlarge the same, or any other of the conveniences above mentioned, as well "for the conveying goods, timber and other things to and from the said canal, "as for the carrying and conveying of all manner of materials necessary for "making, erecting, finishing, altering, repairing, amending and widening the "works of and belonging to the said navigation," and after specifying other acts that may be done, such as getting materials, laying them on the lands of individuals, making drains, &c., the clause concludes in these very comprehensive words, which would appear to be intended to embrace everything that the officers employed should think it *necessary* or *convenient* to do for carrying the Act into effect according to its spirit. "And also, to construct, "make and *do all other matters and things* which he shall think necessary or "convenient for its making, effecting, preserving, improving, completing and "using the said canal, in pursuance and within the true meaning of this Act, "doing as little damage as may be in the execution of the several powers to "him hereby granted." The statute next provides in the second clause, that after any lands or grounds shall be *set out* and *ascertained* to be necessary for any of the purposes therein mentioned, the officer in charge is to contract and agree with the proprietor *for the absolute surrender* thereof to His Majesty; and when the officer in charge cannot succeed in making an arrangement with the party, then the compensation to be paid for the land is to be determined by arbitration, in the manner set forth in the Act. And it is declared in the third clause, "that such parts and portions of land as may be so ascertained "and set out by the officers employed by His Majesty, as necessary to be "occupied for the purposes of the canal; and also, such parts and portions as "may upon any alteration or deviation from the line originally laid out on the "said canal, be ascertained and set out as necessary for the purposes thereof, "shall be for ever thereafter vested in His Majesty, his heirs and successors." The twenty-third clause enacts, "that all the powers and authorities given by "the Act to His Majesty, or to the officers to be employed in superintending "the construction of the canal, or to the officer *at any time thereafter* in charge "thereof—shall extend, so far as may be required for the purposes of the Act, "to all and every, the persons employed *or to be employed in the execution of* "*any matter authorized to be done by the Act.*" It was proved upon the trial of the cause, that Col. By, the officer of engineers employed by his late Majesty to superintend the construction of the Rideau Canal, had under the authority given by the legislature, "*set out and ascertained*" lands along the route of the canal, which he considered necessary to be procured or reserved for the purposes of the Act; and in 1828 he marked these lands upon a plan in the Surveyor-General's Office, at the desire of the government—which plan, or copy of it, was produced from the Surveyor-General's Office on the trial of this cause. It was proved that Col. By had, before or about that time, had that part of Lot No. 7, which he desired to take possession of, marked out by stakes upon the ground; and that the government had made compensation to the proprietor of that lot, claiming under the patent which had been long ago issued to Mrs. Mount. As this land was the private property of an individual, the same measures had been taken as in other similar cases for vesting the land in the crown. But the broken Lot No. 8, with the 200 acres lot immediately in rear of it, having been marked, it seems, as a clergy reserve in the original survey of the township, had not been granted to any one; and being still vacant, and the title remaining in the crown, Col. By does not seem to have thought it necessary to mark it out by stakes on the ground, or to take any more formal possession of it than by designating the whole of the Lot No. 8, and the broken lot in front, upon the plan left by him in the Surveyor-General's Office, as land taken by him for the canal; most, if not all of the crown and clergy reserved lands were marked in the same manner upon the plan as having been thus reserved; probably more with the view in many cases of guarding against future claims for compensation, for lands flooded or other injuries occasioned by the canal, which might be set up, if the lands should be granted by the crown to individuals, than because they were at the time necessary to be occupied for any purpose immediately connected with the canal. But with respect to the broken Lot No. 8, I by no means intend to say that it was not essentially necessary to be occupied for the purposes of the canal, or that the reserving it was not strictly within the letter and spirit of the Act. Indeed, when one looks at the plans produced, and sees how the whole front line of that broken lot lies along the margin of the river, used as the navigable channel, and not far from a succession of locks; and how the whole of this small lot is traversed diagonally by the stream which has been made available as a by-wash for the canal, it can readily be believed, that if the land had not remained vested in the crown, but had become the property of any private person, the engineer officer would have thought it very expedient to take possession of it under the authority of the statute, making compensation of course as the law directs. That he could have done so can hardly be doubted, when it is considered that the adjoining Lot No. 7 was in fact so taken, and a large portion of the land in the rear of it—for which the proprietor was compensated—and when we find from the evidence and the plans produced, that an essential part of the work of the canal is actually upon this broken Lot No. 7, —and that the government nevertheless, after they had acquired it under the Act, made a grant of it to the lessor of the plaintiff, about the same time that they issued the patent to him for Lot No. 8, which has occasioned this litigation; it is but too evident, that neither of these grants was made to the lessor of the plaintiff upon any conviction entertained by the government that the land thus taken or reserved was really not necessary for any of the purposes embraced in the Rideau Canal Act, but that both grants were unfortunately made under some unaccountable error, or strange forgetfulness of what had been done with the knowledge and concurrence of the government, in respect to these lots. It seems impossible to doubt, that their situation in reference to the Rideau Canal must for the moment have escaped attention.

Whether the patent made in 1839 can have the effect of enabling the grantee to dispossess the crown, or in other words the officers of the Ordnance, of the broken Lot No. 8, about which alone it is admitted there can now be any dispute, is a question of much interest in a public point of view. If this had been left to be determined by the Rideau Canal Act alone, and by what was proved to have been done under its provisions, several considerations must have presented themselves; which it will be sufficient to state shortly. The first doubt might have been, whether the power given by the 8th Geo. IV. chap. 1, to take lands for the purpose of the canal, could be exercised in respect to land not belonging to any "private person or company of persons," but of which the title was yet in the crown. The first, second and third clauses of the statute are certainly confined in their language, as it seems to me, to lands belonging to any person or persons, bodies corporate or politic: and the provisions made for compensation also, shew that these enactments had only in view the securing such portions of land which had been granted to others, as the crown might desire to occupy. It may naturally be supposed to have occurred to the legislature while they were passing the Act, that no authority from them could be required for enabling the crown to retain in its possession, for the use of the canal, any portion of its ungranted lands which might be found necessary; and this consideration might be urged as a reason for not giving to the language of the first and second clauses of the Act an effect more extensive in this respect than the common rules of construction would warrant. But then supposing these two clauses not to be applicable to lands of which the title was still in the crown, the next question would be whether the third clause would be held to affect any lands which would not be affected by the operation of the first and second clauses; in other words, whether after the proper officers had set out and ascertained this broken Lot No. 8, being a clergy reserve, as being necessary to be occupied for the purposes of the canal, such lot would in consequence of having been so set out and ascertained, become, in virtue of the enactment in the third clause, for ever thereafter vested in His Majesty, his heirs and successors. If that would have been the effect under the statute 8th Geo. IV. chap. 1, then there would have been no room for further question, and we need have looked no further. But the statute might not have been considered to have that effect, on account of the apparently inseparable connection between the first, second and third clauses; and it might have been thought proper to hold, that such lands only as had been required under the first and second clauses, namely, lands which had belonged to "*any person, or to any body politic or corporate,*" could be vested for ever (or unalienably) in His Majesty, under the third clause. That would apply to the mere positive effect of the statute ; but it would have remained still to be considered, whether it might not be reasonably and upon sound legal principles maintained, that when the government, requiring no legislative authority, had through its officers voluntarily set out and ascertained certain portions of its waste lands as necessary for the purposes of the canal, and had consented to their being formerly marked out accordingly, in the same manner as the lands which they had been obliged to take from individuals, it did not by such proceeding disable itself from afterwards alienating such lands, to the prejudice of all the interests involved in this great public work. There can be no doubt that the government ought to have regarded the land reserved by them, and the land acquired for them, as standing in that respect on the same footing; and as little doubt that they intended to act on that principle. The legislature must have taken it for granted that they would do so, or we must suppose they would have taken care, by their Act 8 Geo. IV. ch. 1, to have made the lands appropriated to the canal unalienable in the one case as well as the other; in assuming any such caution to be unnecessary, as they might naturally do, they overlooked the possibility of the civil government not keeping always steadily in view the connection of adjacent lands with a work under the care of a distinct military department; and they overlooked also the possibility of the government being at some future time improperly asked to do what, if their attention were fixed upon the true facts of the case, they would see to be unwise and wrong. And they seem to have forgotten also, that there was no absolute security against accidents that might happen from the want of care in some public department, except by putting the matter wholly beyond their reach. Supposing that the omission of any express provisions in the Act, that any crown lands set apart by the government for the canal should be thenceforward unalienable, prevented the statute itself from applying directly to such grants; and that the government forgetting, or not acknowledging their obligation to retain such lands for ever in the crown for the use of the canal, had, as in the case before us, afterwards alienated some portion of land which they had thus appropriated, then I think there is no doubt in the mind of any of us, that so far at least as regards any of such land that had been actually occupied by the canal, or any works connected with it, or that was in the opinion of the proper officer necessary for the "*using, preserving, or improving the canal,*" the grant would be held to be illegal, on the ground that the crown must have been deceived when it made a grant so manifestly repugnant to the public good, and so inconsistent with what had before been done under its authority. There is a great deal which applies strongly to the case, in the language used by the court in the case of Lee v. The Manchester and Ashton Canal Company, cited by Mr. Blake from 11 E. R. 645, though the question then did not turn upon the validity of any act done by the crown. "Under every canal," Lord Ellenborough says, "the proprietors have rights, and the public have rights;" and again his Lordship says, "to allow the company to sell an indefinite right "of carriage, without the consent of the proprietors, would be doing what "was never intended, and what might ruin the concern. This argument "seems equally to apply when the rights of the public are concerned; the "public have an interest that the canal shall be kept up, and whatever has a "tendency to bring it into hazard is an encroachment upon their right in it." This language has a plain and very strong and reasonable application to the case before us, for the legislature had by their Act 8 Geo. IV. ch. 1, in which the king concurred, held out to the public the prospect of great benefits from the intended canal. They had made these expected benefits the ground of a measure directly interfering with private rights of property to a great extent; and by the sacrifices which they had exacted, as well as by the public nature of the objects in view, they had given the public an interest in the work; and it would be contrary to reason and justice, if the crown having deliberately set out and given up portions of its lands, through which the canal was to be constructed, or which were required to be occupied for any purpose connected with it, could afterwards at its pleasure resume those lands, indispensable, perhaps, to the preservation or beneficial use of the land, and by granting them to individuals, ruin or greatly prejudice a public work in which the whole country has an interest. In the language of Lord Ellenborough, that would be "an encroachment upon the right of the public;" as the effect of such an act would be against justice and right, so it would be against the honour of the crown, to suppose that the king could with knowledge have done it; and therefore it is, that in all such cases the law implies that the king must have been deceived when he made the grant, that those circumstances must have been withheld from him which it was the duty of the applicant to have laid before him, and therefore that the patent cannot be allowed to have effect. Whether these letters patent could be held to be absolutely void upon the circumstances appearing, so that the grantee could not be suffered to make title under it upon the trial of an ejectment ; or whether the facts would not rather afford ground only for repealing the patent upon a proper proceeding by *scire facias*, is another question. The learning upon that point is much gone into in the case of Alton Woods, 1 Co. 51, and is chiefly to be sought for in early cases, for reasons that are very obvious ; but at the same time we must remember that much of what may have been adjudged in these early cases may be found unsafe to rely upon without cautious examination, for in those periods of English history, the sovereign very frequently, under various influences which are now not felt, was prevailed upon to make improvident grants ; and as a natural consequence, we may apprehend, that when such grants were either distasteful to the nation, or were afterwards repented of by the sovereign or regretted by his successor, there might be too much facility allowed in getting rid of them by holding them absolutely void, upon maxims which, while the sovereign making the grant was admitted to have a power of alienation, it might seem difficult to uphold upon satisfactory principles of reasoning. Considering that the patent in this case does not bear upon the face of it any untrue recital from which we could say, without more being shewn, that it was evidently granted upon a false suggestion ; and considering also that if the interest of the crown had not been divested by what had already taken place, there was nothing doubtful or uncertain, or repugnant to law, or manifestly injurious to the crown or the public, on the face of the grant, I am disposed to think, that if this question rested solely upon the 8 Geo. IV. ch. 1, and the effect of what Col. By had done with reference to this land, the case would have been one in which the patent should be held to be voidable upon a proper proceeding by *scire facias* to repeal it *quia improvide emanavit*, rather than one in which we could have held it to be absolutely void. There is much, however, in the Alton Woods case, and in other cases which apparently support the opinion, that the patent might be held not merely voidable but absolutely void ; though the instances put are chiefly of cases where the objection went to the legal capacity to grant, as where the crown had before granted the land to another, in which case it would seem self-evident that no *scire facias* to repeal the second patent could be necessary, since the king can no more grant what he no longer owns, than a subject can. It is not necessary to go further into this point, because we think, as both parties indeed seemed to concede upon the argument, that this case cannot be taken up merely on the statute 8 Geo. IV. ch. 1, and the acts of the Engineer officer and of the government done under that Act ; but that it may be found to depend mainly or entirely on the effect of the later Act 7 Vic. ch. 11, to which I shall presently refer. This seems indeed so clear, that I should probably have applied myself at once to that statute and confined myself to it, as being necessarily decisive of the question, but for this consideration, that I do not desire it to be supposed, that if that statute had not been passed, the lessor of the plaintiff must, in our opinion, have been incontestably allowed to hold the estate under his patent, whatever might have been the inconvenience or injury occasioned to the canal. If no injury or inconvenience could arise from the government losing the possession of this piece of land, then it is not likely that any attempt would have been made to resist his claim to hold under his patent; but if from an unfortunate oversight in any public department, the government has been led to make a grant manifestly inconsistent with the rights and interests of the public, and if, being satisfied of this, they have availed themselves of the easiest means of rectifying the error, by exercising a power assumed to be continuing in the public officer in charge of the work, of acquiring from time to time any land which it may be found necessary to occupy for the purposes of the canal; then it may deserve consideration, whether a claim can, under such circumstances, be fairly urged by the person obtaining such a patent, for any compensation beyond a restitution of the price which he may have paid for the land, supposing him to have bought it from the government as crown land believed to be vacant and grantable. I consider that as the civil government of this Province, on the one hand, certainly ought not and could not advisedly and knowingly have granted any land which the Ordnance Department had specially marked out and described as being necessary to be retained for the canal, and which is in fact so necessary, that having inadvertently granted it, it has been found right to resume it; so I consider on the other hand, that no person having a knowledge of the actual circumstances ought to have moved the government to make such a grant. I think also, that in contemplation of law, the person who receives a grant made upon his own application, is presumed in such cases to have known what the circumstances really were; though the king, in the multiplicity of affairs in which he is engaged for the good of the public, may well be excused if he has not always present to his mind the particular facts of each. It is the duty of subjects, as the court declares in the Alton Woods case, to which I have referred, "to see "that the king be truly informed, for the king hath the charge of the common- "wealth, and therefore cannot, like a private individual, attend to his affairs; " the grants which he makes he makes as king, and therefore as king he ought to "be so instructed that his purpose and intent shall take effect." It may indeed be made to appear in any such case, that the person obtaining the grant did in fact not know those circumstances which the king or (which is the same thing) his officers were either ignorant of, or had at the moment forgotten, and that he had therefore no design to procure an advantage to himself to the prejudice and damage of the public. But the law holds that it was his business to inform himself, and that the public shall not suffer injury without redress because the grantee did not know what he was asking for. If that were really the fact in this case, as it perhaps may have been, there would be no hardship in the application of a principle so just in itself, because there can be no hesitation, I conceive, in admitting that as soon as it is discovered in any such case, that what had been inadvertently done would be unreasonable in its operation, and would work an injury to the public, the grantee should at once, and without compulsion, surrender his patent; and if not being so disposed, he should resolve to insist upon his grant, and it should be held void, there would be little ground to complain of hardship under such circumstances. In answer to any argument of that kind, it might well be said in the language used by the court on a similar occasion, "as to the mischief which hath been " supposed, if this grant should be adjudged void, no case can be adjudged but "it is mischievous to some, but a mischief (that is, a private damage,) is rather "to be suffered than an inconvenience, and great inconvenience would ensue "on the other side if this grant (forasmuch as the king is deceived in his grant) "should be adjudged good" (a). It may not rest with this court to determine any question that may be raised about compensation, but if any claim should be imagined to arise merely from the circumstance of the ordnance officers maintaining their possession under a new appropriation of the land, made after the lessor of the plaintiff had obtained his patent, then it might be material that it should not be erroneously supposed that we had come to the conclusion, that without such new appropriation, and without the aid of the late statute to which I have alluded, the patent must inevitably have been allowed to have effect, so that the crown could not even have avoided it by a proper proceeding upon *scire facias*. That is not my impression, nor, I believe, the impression of any of my brothers, ; on the contrary, I have for my own part no doubt that the lessor of the plaintiff could not have finally made good his title under it, if the effect would have been to impair the safety or usefulness of the canal. Besides the well established principles of the common law in respect to patents which have improvidently issued, there are express provisions in our Court of Chancery Act, and in the statute regulating the disposal of crown lands, to meet such cases. If the fact had been, that the military engineer, having taken this lot in 1828 as necessary for the purposes of the canal, had afterwards apprized the civil government, that upon further consideration and experience after the completion of the canal, it did not appear to be required, and that the ordnance were therefore willing to relinquish it; and if the civil government acting advisedly and not under a mistake, had made this grant in consequence, then the case, as regards justice and right, would have been different, and might also have been different as regards the legal effect. But it seems to be well understood by both parties, so far as we can gather from the argument, that the land had not been alienated upon any such change of views or intention, but that it was really an oversight.

I come now to the consideration of the recent statute to which I have referred, 7th Vic. ch. 11, which was passed for vesting in the principal officers of Her Majesty's Ordnance the estates therein described, and in which the legislature has been careful to provide for the cases of clergy reserves and crown reserves, or other crown lands which had been set apart for certain public purposes, and placed under the control of the Ordnance Department, as well as for lands which had been purchased for individuals for like purposes. The statute enacts among other things, "that all "lands in Canada then vested in Her Majesty, or in any person in trust for "Her Majesty, and set apart, used or occupied for purposes connected with "the military defence of the Province, or placed under the charge of the "Ordnance Department, or any military officers, whether the same have "been set apart or transferred from the lands of the crown or the clergy "reserves, or have been intended to be so set apart or transferred, or have "been purchased for such purposes, and conveyed to Her Majesty, &c., shall "be and remain vested in the principal officers of Her Majesty's Ordnance

---

(a) Alton Woods Case, 1 Co. 52.

"in Great Britain and their successors, in trust for Her Majesty and her suc-
"cessors, for the service of the said department, or for such other services as
"Her Majesty, her heirs and successors, or the said principal officers, shall
"from time to time direct. *Provided that nothing in this Act shall extend or be
"construed to extend, to vest in the said principal officers, any lands which may
"before the passing of this Act have been granted by Her Majesty or her royal
"predecessors to any other person or party, unless the same shall have been sub-
"sequently to such grant lawfully purchased, acquired or taken for the purposes
"of the said Ordnance Department, nor to impair, diminish, or affect any right,
"title, or claim vested in, or possessed by any person at the passing of the Act, to
"or in any lands:* nor to give to the said principal officers any greater or better
"title to any lands, &c., than is now vested in the crown, or in some person
"in trust for the crown." The Act contains various provisions respecting the
right to make future purchases or appropriations, which cannot affect this
case; and there is appended to it a schedule of the lands vested in the principal officers of the ordnance under the Act, in which is set down "the canal
"called the Rideau Canal, and the lands and other real property lawfully pur-
"chased and taken, or set out and ascertained as necessary for the purposes of
"the canal from the crown lands, or reserves or clergy reserves, under the
"authority of the Statute 8th Geo. IV. ch. 1, and *more especially those* marked
"and described as necessary for the said purposes, on a certain plan lodged by
"the late Lieutenant-Colonel By, the officer then employed in superintending
"the construction of the said canal, in the office of the Surveyor-General of
"Upper Canada, and signed by the said Lieutenant-Colonel By, and now filed
"in the office of Her Majesty's Surveyor-General of this Province." The effect
of the first clause of the Act, taken in connection with this schedule, and with
what was proved on trial to have been done by Col. By, would have been to
vest the Lot No. 8, now in question, in the defendants as principal officers of
the ordnance, if it had not been for the grant which in 1839 was made to the
lessor of the plaintiff, and which brings this case within that proviso at the
end of the clause which I have recited, and renders it necessary, as I think, to
shew that *since the making of the grant* the land has been acquired or taken for
the purposes of the Ordnance Department. That must clearly be necessary,
unless the specification in the schedule, embracing, in connection with Col.
By's map, this particular lot, can be considered as overruling the proviso, so
far as regards that canal—which I think it cannot. It may not be rightly
understood by us with what view the proviso in question was inserted; but
on looking at the map from the Surveyor-General's office, and observing how
remote from the canal some of the vacant crown lands are, which were marked
in 1828 by Col. By as reserved, it seems not unreasonable to suppose that it
may have appeared possible to the legislature that the government, upon an
understanding with the military department, might have subsequently made
grants to individuals of some portions of these vacant crown lands, which had
at first been reserved, but which they had afterwards perhaps found and
admitted to have been unnecessarily set apart for the purposes of the canal;
and it might seem just to guard, as the Act does by this proviso, against the
grantee losing his land by re-establishing all the reservations in the late Col.
By's map, and paying no regard to the intermediate acts of the government.

Then with regard to this Lot No. 8, it was proved upon the trial that after the 18th December, 1839, when the grant to the lessor of the plaintiff was made, viz., on the 22nd of February, 1840, upon an application which had been made by one Heliner, to purchase any part of the clergy reserve Lot No. 8, which might not be wanted for the use of the canal, Major Bolton, the officer of the Royal Engineers, then in charge of the Rideau Canal, did survey and mark out on the ground the part of the said lot which he considered necessary for canal purposes, embracing clearly the whole of this broken Lot No. 8, and a considerable portion of the two hundred acres (all numbered 8) beyond the concession line. A certificate, it appears, was granted in conformity with Major Bolton's recommendation, which enabled Mr. Heliner to purchase the rear portion of the reserve ; the other part, which includes this broken lot in question, remaining marked on the ground from that time as necessary, in the opinion of the officer in charge, for the purposes of the Rideau Canal. It seems that when Major Bolton marked out this ground, he was not aware that the civil government of Upper Canada had made any such grant to the lessor of the plaintiff, as had been made in December preceding ; at least on the 5th of May, 1840, he first communicated the fact to the chief officer of his department by an official letter, which was given in evidence on the trial, accompanied by a plan in which the land which he had marked out in February preceding was precisely delineated. In this letter he states, "that the broken "Lots 7 and 8, which he had been informed had been deeded to a Mr. Malloch, "were absolutely necessary to be retained for the preservation of the works "at Long Island ; and were taken and set apart by Col. By for canal pur-"poses, as well as other lands in their rear, which had been paid for by arbi-"tration," (alluding as I suppose to the lot in rear of Lot 7, which had been acquired and paid for to the person claiming under Mrs. Mount's patent). Major Bolton adds in this letter, that he had not given certificates that the broken fronts were no longer required, nor had any application been made to him on that subject ; and he states further (what very clearly shews the good grounds on which this land had been reserved in the first instance, and the want of care which must have led to its being alienated), that the broken fronts in question are situated between the waste channel, Mud Creek and the river, and include the abutment of the stone dam, and the whole of the new dam and waste weir. This statement shews that whether Major Bolton knew of the grant to Mr. Malloch or not, when he made his survey in February, 1840, and marked out the lands as I have described, he must have felt it to be his bounden duty to have marked them out immediately on acquiring the information, if it had not been sufficiently done before, to secure the public interests. Having in fact done it, however, though apparently for another purpose, and in order to enable him to report formally on Heliner's application, and having marked out the ground and made and reported the reservation subsequently to the grant to the lessor of the plaintiff, the land so marked out is in my opinion no longer prevented by the proviso referred to from vesting in the ordnance, by reason of the grant which had by inadvertence been made of it. The case is now brought, by the subsequent appropriation of the land, within the provision in the latter part of the clause which I have cited. The learned judge who tried the cause was of opinion, and so instructed the jury, that if the fact was that all the land covered by the patent for broken Lot 8 had been so set out by Col. By under the statute as to vest it in the crown under the third clause of the Act, no part of it could be afterwards granted away by the government; but that if there is any part of that lot which Col. By had not set out before the canal was completed, in such a manner as to bring it within the third clause of the Act, then that no more land could be taken up in addition after the canal was completed, and in that case their verdict should be for the plaintiff. The jury found for the plaintiff; from which we must infer that they did not consider that Col. By had set out the whole of the broken Lot 8, by such a proceeding as was sufficient under the statute, and that although his successor in charge of the work had undoubtedly marked out upon the ground in February, 1840, the whole of broken Lot 8 as being necessary for the canal, and had formally reported that he had done so, yet that this was an act not binding, for the reason suggested by the learned judge, that the authority to take land for the purposes of the canal had ceased upon the completion of the work, which I believe was in 1830 or 1831. The second clause of the 7th Vic. ch. 11, does not seem to have engaged attention at the trial. I consider that the parts of the statute 8th Geo. IV. ch. 1, which I have cited, and the whole tenor of the Act, shew that the authority given to take land for the purposes of the Rideau Canal was intended to be a continuing power, and that it did not cease when the canal was completed. If it were not so, indeed, the objects of the statute could not be fully carried into effect. I think the very language of the proviso in the first clause of 7th Vic. ch. 11, as well as other parts of that Act, shew that the legislature contemplated the authority to take lands as one still capable of being exercised. The whole of broken Lot 8 was in my opinion sufficiently set apart by Col. By to make the reservation binding under the 8th Geo. IV. ch. 1, if that Act could be considered as extending to vacant lands still belonging to the crown; and whether it did extend to such lands or not became an immaterial question, when the 7th Vic. ch. 11, in express terms vested in the Ordnance all the portions of crown or clergy reserves which had been in fact set apart, and especially those marked in Col. By's map, which this broken Lot 8 certainly was. The only remaining consideration then is, that the lot has been granted to the lessor of the plaintiff, and if we take the effect of that grant most favourably for the grantee, and determine (which may to some seem doubtful) that the proviso in the first clause of 7th Vic. ch. 11, extends to the case of grants improperly made by the civil government, in disregard of the reservation under the former statute, still the land in question was in my opinion "*lawfully acquired or taken for the purposes of the Ordnance "Department subsequently to such grant, and before the passing of the 7th Vic. "ch. 11,*" and has therefore become vested in the defendants by virtue of that statute.

The verdict was in our opinion against law and evidence; and as there appears to have been an error at the trial, in supposing that there could be no new setting out and appropriating after the canal was completed, there ought to be a new trial without costs.

Per Cur.—Rule absolute. New trial without costs.

GILLESPIE ET AL. V. GRANT.

The plaintiff declares in debt on a recognizance of bail, and sets out in his declaration that the bail came before *a Commissioner in the Newcastle District*, duly appointed to take recognizances of bail, according to the form of the statute in such case made and provided (2 Geo. IV. ch. 1, s. 40); and then, after stating the condition of the recognizance, makes this averment: "*As " by the record of the said recognizance, still remaining in the said court, fully "appears.*"

Held, per Cur. (MACAULAY, J., *dissentiente*): Declaration bad on special demurrer, in not averring that the recognizance *was filed in the office of the Deputy Clerk of the Crown in the district in which it was taken*, as directed by the 40th section of the Act (2 Geo. IV. ch. 1).

Debt on recognizance of bail.

The plaintiffs in their declaration alleged, "that the defendant on the 10th "June, 1846, as of Easter Term, in the ninth year of the reign of our Lady the "now Queen, at Port Hope, in the District of Newcastle, to wit, at Toronto in "the Home District, came in his own proper person before George C. Ward, "a commissioner for taking bail duly appointed and commissioned to take "and receive such recognizance or recognizances of bail or bails in the New- "castle District, as any person or persons should be willing to acknowledge or "make before him in any suit depending in the Court of Queen's Bench, "according to the form of the statute in such case made and provided, and "then and there, before the said George C. Ward as such commissioner, "became pledge and bail for one Charles Hughes, that if he should be con- "demned at the suit of the plaintiff in an action of trespass on the case upon "promises then depending in the said court, at the suit of the plaintiff, against "the said Charles Hughes, then the said Charles Hughes should satisfy the "costs and condemnation money, or render himself to the custody of the "sheriff of the Home District, or in default thereof, he the defendant would "do it for him, *as by the record of the said recognizance still remaining in the "said court fully appears;* and although plaintiffs afterwards, on the 15th July, "1848, by the judgment of the court recovered against the said Charles "Hughes, in the said action, the sum of £508 13s. 5d. for their damages and "costs in that suit, as by the record and proceedings thereof still remaining "in the said court more fully appears, yet the said Charles Hughes hath not "paid the said plaintiffs their said costs and condemnation money or any part "thereof, nor hath he rendered himself to the custody of the sheriff of the "Home District, nor hath the defendant paid the same or any part thereof to "the plaintiff, nor rendered the said Charles Hughes to the custody of the "sheriff of the Home District, according to the said recognizance, and the said "recognizance as well as the said judgment *still remain in full force,*" &c.

The defendant demurred specially to the declaration.

1st. Because the declaration commenced "for that," as in trespass, instead of "for that whereas," as in debt, by way of recital.

2nd. That it was not alleged by the declaration for what amount the defendant became bail, or the extent of liability in the original action.

3rd. That it did not appear by the declaration that the recognizance in the declaration mentioned was ever filed with the Deputy Clerk of the Crown in the Newcastle District, where it was alleged to have been taken, according to the statute; nor was it alleged or stated that the same was ever brought into court here or enrolled in the said court, notwithstanding which it was alleged, that the *record* of the *same recognizance still remained* in *the same court*, and it was not alleged that any affidavit, by any credible person present at the taking of the recognizance of the due taking thereof, was made and filed therewith.

P. M. Vankoughnet for the demurrer.

It is not shewn that the recognizance is a record in court. Had it been taken in open court, and so averred, then the allegation in the declaration might have been sufficient; but having been taken before a commissioner in the country, the 40th section of the 2 Geo. IV. ch. 1, requires that *before* "it "shall have the like effect as if it were taken in open court, it shall be filed in "the office of the Clerk of the Crown in the district where the same shall have "been taken, together with an affidavit of the due taking." Now the allegation that the recognizance was so filed is wholly omitted, and the demurrer being special, it must prevail. In England, the statute 4 W. & M. ch. 4, contains an analogous provision. It is necessary by that Act that a recognizance, when taken before a commissioner in the country, before it can bind the bail, should be transmitted to one of the justices of the court where the action may be pending. The forms of declaring upon such a recognizance invariably state "the transmitting," &c. It has never been considered safe by pleaders in England to omit this averment. They have inserted it, no doubt, as essential to the statement of a legal recognizance.—1 Marsh, 441; 6 Taunt. 45; 2 Cam. 329; 1 Cam. 241; 13 M. & W. 132; 7 Went. Pleadings, 59, 60, 61; 2 Ch. Pleading, 479. Now if the averment of a due transmission of the recognizance to a justice, under the English Act, cannot be dispensed with, because such transmission is required by the Act to make the recognizance legal, and to give authority for its enrolment, what good reason can be argued to shew that the filing in the office of the Clerk of the Crown, in the district in which the recognizance is taken, which our statute makes as essential to render a recognizance legal as the British statute does the due transmission, can be altogether omitted in the declaration? The declaration contains no averment to shew a valid recognizance, and is therefore bad.

R. P. Crooks, contra.

This declaration is clearly good on general demurrer.—Cro. Car. 209, 363; 4 Co. 65. It is also sufficient on special demurrer. It contains a direct statement of the recognizance being *enrolled of record* in the court; and this record while it exists must be taken to prove that it was duly entered into—that it was a legal recognizance binding upon the bail. The filing gives the recognizance no new force: it may be necessary to a regular entry of the bail, and if not regularly made, it might be set aside for irregularity. This was the course which the plaintiff should have pursued. He cannot treat the recognizance itself as null and void on the exception taken, and demur. The omission, if it in fact existed, was matter of practice, and no ground of demurrer.—10 B. & C. 539; 16 E. 39; 1 Bur. 447.

Vankoughnet, in reply.

As to the argument that the filing is mere matter of practice, that may be well enough to the objection that the declaration does not shew that an affidavit of due taking was filed, accompanying the bail-piece; but it is no answer to the non-averment of the due filing of the recognizance itself: the recognizance is the very ground of action, and must be shewn to have been perfected.

ROBINSON, C. J.—The question on special demurrer is, whether the declaration on a recognizance of a bail taken by a commissioner in the country, must not state that the recognizance was filed in the office of the Clerk of the Crown in the district where it was taken, as the 40th sec. of 2nd Geo. IV. chap. 1, requires it to be? Or whether it is not sufficient to state, that the bail came before the commissioner duly appointed to take bail and entered into the recognizance, "*as by the record of the said recognizance still remaining in the "said court fully appears.*" It is said on the other side, that this is sufficient even on special demurrer, for that it is a direct statement of the recognizance being enrolled of record in the court; that such record while it exists, incontrovertibly proves that the recognizance was duly entered into; that filing with affidavits of due taking, &c., are mere matters of practice which need not be pleaded in any case; and that if the recognizance has in fact been unduly enrolled without those necessary steps being taken, the only advantage the bail could take of the irregularity would be by moving to set the proceedings aside.

The statute says, "*which recognizance of bail or bail piece so taken and filed, "shall be of the like effect as if the same were taken in open court.*" In England the analogous provision is under 4 W. & M. chap. 4, which authorizes bail to be put in before a commissioner in the country in like manner, and then provides, "which said recognizance of bail or bail piece so taken as aforesaid, "shall be transmitted to some one of the justices of the court where the action "shall be pending, who upon affidavit made of the due taking thereof, by some "credible person, shall receive the same; which recognizance of bail or bail "piece so taken and *transmitted, shall be of the like effect as if the same were "taken de bene esse before any of the said justices.*" The form of declaring on a recognizance of bail taken in England under this statute, seems to have been uniform in this respect, that the declaration always contains a statement that the recognizance has been transmitted to a judge and by him produced in court, which, like the filing in the crown office under our statute, is what makes it a recognizance, and is the authority for enrolling it. In Lutwich, 1282, is a record of the pleadings in an action on such a recognizance transcribed verbatim. This was only two years after the statute was passed, when the proper averments to be inserted in the declaration were likely to have engaged particular attention. The form given in Wentworth's Pleadings, Vol. VII. 59, 60, of declarations on such a recognizance, signed by Mr. Vitruvius Lawes, contains the same averments. It is usual to speak of Wentworth's collection of precedents with very little respect, and it certainly is a confused ill arranged compilation; but it has not been imputed to him that he has appended forged names to his pleadings, and Mr. Lawes was a pleader of much experience in his day. Mr. Chitty, in all the editions of his work on pleading, inserts in his declaration the same averment, that the bail piece was transmitted, &c., without any intimation that it can be dispensed with. I can find no precedent of a declaration in England without it. The same form of declaring has been adopted generally here, and as I supposed universally; but the contrary was asserted in the argument. This court at least has never, to my knowledge, sustained a declaration without this averment, when it had been excepted against on special demurrer, and I have no knowledge that a declaration wanting the averment was ever before us in judgment. It is of little consequence to remark upon the want of authority in one book of precedents, unless when it is found to differ from others; nor is it reasonable to suppose, that from the passing of the statute in England to the present time, pleaders would have gone on inserting an averment for which there was no necessity whatever, and which might embarrass them by calling for unnecessary proof; unless we can see clearly that the averment is idle and unnecessary, we should not sanction a departure from precedent on such a point. There is a convenience in adhering to established forms of pleading, because their adoption prevents the raising of doubtful questions upon points of form, to be discussed at the expense of the parties. Experiments in pleading are on that account usually discouraged in the courts. But I have reason to apprehend from other proceedings which have taken place in this cause, and which have been brought before me in chambers, that this may not have been a mere experiment in pleading, but that, by some inadvertence, the bail piece was really not filed in the proper office as the statute requires. We cannot allow a knowledge of extraneous facts to influence our opinion upon a mere point of pleading arising on a special demurrer; but what I have mentioned shews the propriety of considering, that in this or any other case, the plaintiff may have omitted the averment, not from any slovenly disregard of form, or from any willingness to try what usual averments he might be safe in omitting, but because he could not venture to insert it on account of it happening not to be consistent with the fact, in which case he could not cure the defect by amendment. We must therefore consider the reasoning and principles involved in the question. If these should shew quite clearly that the averment of the bail piece being filed in the crown office is useless, then the declaration should not be held defective for the want of it even upon special demurrer. If they should not lead quite clearly to that conclusion, then the fact alone that the form of pleading in use contains the averment, would be decisive with me for exacting it—the demurrer being special. A recognizance is defined to be "an obligation of record," an "acknowledgment of a debt upon record." If the bail in this case had gone into the court of Queen's Bench while sitting, and entered into this recognizance, then it would have been matter of record from its caption. But the commissioner in the country cannot by his mere act make it a record; it must first *be filed*, and then, and not before, the statute gives to it the "*like* "*effect as if taken in open court.*" It is not properly a recognizance before that has been done, and therefore, both the English statute and ours, in speaking of it in this stage, call it a recognizance of bail *or* bail piece. It is in fact a paper which may become a recognizance in its proper sense by being filed, but never without that. In Botholeny v. Lord Fairfax, 1 P. W. 357, Sergt. Williams, in arguing in support of a recognizance of another kind than that before us, but to which the principle must equally apply, admits it to be plain " that when an Act of Parliament gives a particular power of taking a "recognizance, or statute, the Act of Parliament must be observed, and the "circumstances thereby required complied with; and if omitted, the recog-

"nizance intended to be given is not a recognizance." If the bail piece in this case was never in fact filed in the proper office, as directed by the statute, it cannot "*have the like effect as if taken in court,*" in other words, it can be no recognizance, and the court, by enrolling it, would not be enrolling a recognizance. If the bail piece being duly taken had been also duly filed, so that it became entitled "to have the *like effect as if taken in court,*" then the plaintiff might have felt himself at liberty to declare upon it, as if it had been in fact taken in open court, which is the usual course in the Queen's Bench in England, with respect to recognizances taken by a judge in vacation. His declaration then would have been consistent and complete, and would have shewed no defect; but here he avers bail put in before a commissioner in the country, which is no record, and shews nothing more done, but yet concludes, "as by the record of the said recognizance still remaining in the "said court fully appears." But before he could properly refer to a bail piece taken as this was, as being a recognizance still remaining in court, he should first have shewn it to be a recognizance, which he has not, and he should have shewn it to be a record, before he was in a condition to refer to it as "*remaining*" of record. If the plaintiff had declared on a recognizance taken in the country before any officer having nothing to do with taking bail, or before A. B. without averring that he was a commissioner, he could not declare upon it as a recognizance, and rely upon an averment, that it still "remained of *record in this court,*" for shewing it to be a recognizance of record, when there would be nothing to shew that the court could make a binding record of such a proceeding. Then a bail piece taken before a commissioner, till it is filed, is no more a recognizance than if it had been taken by any body not authorized. If the plaintiff had been suing on a recognizance that had really been taken in open court, he must have averred that the bail came into court on such a day before the Queen herself, and then acknowledged, &c.; all the forms are so; and I take it that such an averment would be indispensable, because he thereby shews in the first place that which is *matter of record,* and then, according to the judgment of the court in Glynn v. Thorpe, 1 B. & Ald. 153, he must go farther and shew it to be enrolled of record. It would not do for him to omit all mention of that which is necessary to constitute a binding recognizance. To say, for instance, that the said A. B. acknowledged himself to our, &c., and then conclude, as he has done here, with a common *prout patet per recordum,* saying nothing about his having appeared in court, and made the undertaking there. Then if a declaration in that form would be bad, as I think it would, it must be equally bad to omit the statement of the filing in the crown office, which our statute makes equivalent to the acknowledgment in open court. This reference to an alleged record of a recognizance as still existing, without directly averring a legal recognizance to be recorded, is relied on as sufficient even upon special demurrer; but I do not consider it to be so. What might be its effect upon general demurrer, or in arrest of judgment, or on a writ of error, it is not necessary to consider. The cases of Courtenay v. Grenville, Cro. Car. 209; Goldsmith v. Sydnor, Cro. Car. 363; and Fulwood's case, 4 Co. 65, bear upon this point and shew the distinction. As to the argument that the filing is matter of practice merely, and that we are to intend that all was rightly done or the court would not have recorded it, it is true that in general matters of mere practice need not be pleaded, such as the affidavit of due taking which is to accompany the bail piece, and without which it ought not to be filed. The forms of declaration used do not aver the making of such an affidavit, and we may therefore hold the omission of it in this case immaterial. When the recognizance is shewn to have been filed, we must intend that it was regularly done; at least till the contrary appears. But that is a different thing from assuming the very act of filing itself, which is necessary to make it a record. The maxim, that all things will be presumed to have been regularly done by the court or its officers till the contrary appears, cannot be pushed so far as the plaintiff contends for, or it would never be necessary to aver a judgment in order to support an execution; and when the maxim does apply, its general effect is rather to relieve parties in regard to the onus of proof, than from the necessity of making the averment. In this case, besides, the recognizance is not set forth as inducement merely, it is the very ground of action, and must be shewn to have been perfected. The *prout patet per recordum*, which this declaration contains, is relied upon, as being a direct averment sufficiently formal on special demurrer, though it is never so applied, but is merely used as a reference to a record of something that had been before shewn to be done as of record. It is only referred to as an existing proof by record of what is already affirmed, and which can only be regularly proved by the record. But it is not affirmed in this declaration that the recognizance was filed, and therefore it is not in effect affirmed that there is any record of such a fact, which there ought to be, because the recognizance roll sets out the bail piece as taken before a commissioner. And besides, when the plaintiff refers to it as a record *still* remaining, that is no averment that there existed any recognizance of record when he commenced his action; it refers only to the time the declaration is filed, which would not be sufficient. The *prout patet per recordum* is very well for the purpose for which it was inserted, and is in general necessary when it follows a direct averment of something being done which forms a matter of record; just as a *profert in curia* of a specialty is used after the plaintiff has set forth the making of that specialty; but they are never relied on in pleading as a sufficiently positive or formal setting out of themselves of the judgment sued upon being rendered, or of the bond or other deed being made. These are first distinctly set forth, and then the record or deed is referred to as *evidence of* that which, according to the previous description of it, is shewn to be a record or a deed. How far defects of this nature may be rendered immaterial by the defendant's plea, or may be cured by verdicts, is a separate question, upon which the cases turned which I have cited. There is no such circumstance to aid the plaintiff in this case. The case cited of Stevenson v. Grant, 2 N. R. 103, is not in the least in point; that was an objection raised for want of the *prout patet per recordum*. The averments in that declaration did set out a perfect recognizance entered into in open court. This case is just the reverse; there is here a *prout patet per recordum*, but the defect is, that there is not sufficient shewn, if it were all recorded, to make the recognizance legal. There is neither shewn the entering into the recognizance in open court, nor the filing in the district office, which is made by law equivalent to it. The defendant, I think, could have pleaded that the recognizance was not filed in the district office. It would not be traversing any matter alleged to be of record, for this plaintiff has done nothing more than aver that the debtor went before a commissioner in the country and acknowledged to owe, and that a record of this is recorded. We cannot infer from this declaration that the record would shew its being filed. The defendant is in my opinion entitled to judgment on demurrer.

MACAULAY, J.—When this case was before me at chambers, upon an application to set aside the demurrer as frivolous, I intimated my opinion, that while the entry of the recognizance of record remained, an action was maintainable, without its being averred or appearing of record, that the bail piece was filed in the office of the Deputy Clerk of the Crown in the district in which such recognizance was taken, and I have not been since able to satisfy myself that such impressions were erroneous. On the contrary, I am obliged to say, that I think the declaration good and sufficient in law.

A reference to the authorities will shew, that in England, where bail is entered into before commissioners in the country, under the statute 4 W. & M. chap. 4, sec. 1, from which our Act of 2 Geo. IV. chap. 1, sec. 40, is mainly copied, the entry in the Queen's Bench is always made as taken in open court, but in the Common Pleas it is made according to the fact as taken before such commissioner, and the consequence of such practice seems to be, that in the latter court the recognizance binds from the caption by relation, while in the former it binds only from the entry, which in the Queen's Bench is said to be always made as present in court.

I look upon this as mere matter of practice, and can see no reason why an entry in the Queen's Bench. similar to that in the Common Pleas, would not be of equal force and validity. The entry in the present case follows the practice in the Common Pleas, with the exception, that in all the precedents, the transmission of the bail piece to a judge according to the statute is there averred, whereas here its filing in the district office is omitted. There, when transmitted to a judge, it was declared to be good bail *de bene esse*. Here, when filed in the district office, it is declared to be of the like effect as if taken in open court.

When a recognizance of bail is taken before a judge in chambers, it is usually entered as brought into court by such judge to be enrolled, and enrolled accordingly, but not uniformly so; see 2 Chitty's Pleadings, 4th ed. 475; 4 B. & C. 403; Bevan v. Jones, 6 D. & R. 483, S. C.

Many cases may be cited in which the definition of a recognizance is given in terms more or less different, according to the nature of such recognizance and the authority under which it may be taken. See the following references and cases: 18 Viner's Ab. 163-171; 1 Vent. 360-1; 1 Saund. 7; 2 Saund. 8, 68, (a) 71, 291; 11 Mod. 53, 223; Bacon Ab. Exon. B; Hob. 195-222; Barnes, 97, 207; 2 L'd Ray. 1140; 2 Salk. 564, 654; Pl. 4, 659; Shettle v. Wood, 6 Mod. 42; 2 Lord Raym. 966, 756, 1140; 5 East. 461, 324; 1 H. B. 174-5, 181, &c. Brymer v. Atkins; 2 Keb. 750; Freeman, 355, Pl. 446; Vaughan, 103; Edgecomb v. Dee, Bro. Recog. 20; 8 Mod. 290; 10 Mod. 153; Aleyn, 12; Dyer, 306; 1 Co. Litt. 260, (a); 1 B. & A. 153, Glynn v. Sharpe; 1 Rolls Ab. 892, Pl. 11; 2 Rolls Ab. 393; 2 Smith, 14; 5 E. R. 461; Holt's R. 612; 2 W.

B. 768, Kenney v. Thornton; 2 Dow. P. C. 282; 1 E. R. 603; 2 Verners, 750; 1 P. W. 334, S. C.; Cro. Jac. 449; 8 A. & E. 932; Com. Dig. Bail R. 2; 2 M. & S. 565; Lut. 1283; 1 Browne's Entries, 164.

But I do not find that a recognizance is necessarily a record upon its caption, or of record whenever it becomes valid as a recognizance, although to support a *sci. fa.* or an action thereon, it must appear to be recorded; 1 B. & A. 153, and cases *supra*.

Here I think it is sufficiently averred to be enrolled or of record, and *nul tiel* record would be a good plea, which proves that the entry of record is sufficiently averred and might be traversed by the defendant. 4 B. & C. 407; 6 D. & R. 487; 15 E. 382; 2 D. & W. 434, Irish; 1 C. & L. 473; 2 L. Ray. 1139; 1 N. R. 108; 3 B. & P. 464; 5 E. 443.

It does appear therefore to be a judicial recognizance, duly acknowledged before an officer of this court within his jurisdiction, acting under a commission of this court authorized by law, in a suit pending in this court, and afterwards adopted by and recorded or enrolled herein, when not appearing, and it may have been the very day after the caption and before notice of bail. It is therefore a record of this court. I look upon its filing in the district office as directed by the statute, in order to a regular entry of the *bail*, but not as a condition precedent to its being valid and binding upon the bail as a recognizance. See Hale's Pleas of the Crown, 696; 2 Sid. 90; Timberley's Case; 4 & 5 W. & M. ch. 4, sec. 4; Tidd, 8 ed. 253, note h; Manning's Exch. App. 243; 2 E. P. C. 1009; 1 Vent. 301; T. Jo. 64; 1 Hawk. P. C. ch. 27, p. 421; Rule Mich. 654, No. 8. The filing gives it no new force: while it remains of record, such filing, if essential in point of practice only, and not conditional, may be presumed to have been done; or if such entry be irregular or unauthorized, the proper course appears to me to be to move to set it aside, not to treat all as null and void. See 10 B. & C. 207-216; 5 B. & C. 539; 16 E. 39; 1 D. & R. 50; 7 B. & C. 700; 1 Bur. 447; 19 Vin. A. 511-12. If invalid without filing, the enrolment is of course improvident, but the court will not, while the entry stands, treat its record as irregular or void. If unwarranted it should be set aside.

My opinion, therefore, rests on this short ground, that the recognizance, as respects its binding effect upon the bail, was a perfect recognizance upon its caption, which was a judicial act, and the principal, and was in effect the act of the court under its commission duly empowered; and being afterwards enrolled (as it is alleged and admitted to be), it is a record of this court, and contains all the essentials as such to bind the defendants. I cannot persuade myself that the omission to file it in the district office, entirely vacates it as a recognizance of bail there recorded. I cannot distinguish it in principle from a like recognizance taken before a judge in chambers at common law; both are judicial acts, the one authorized at common law, the other by statute; both alike under the sanction and on behalf of the court, both recognized and adopted by the court, both enrolled by the court, both equally records of the court; and why both should not be equally binding upon the bail while such records subsist, I cannot perceive (a).

(a) 3 B. & P. 460; 1 H. B. 81, 174; 2 Roll. Ab. 393 pl.; Noy's R. 25; 1 Keb. 552; 4 Inst. 125.

The Act says that the recognizance should be filed in the district office, and which recognizance so filed should be of the like effect as if taken in open court. Had the Act been silent on this subject, it would have the same effect upon being enrolled in the court, and surely its entry of record in the principal office is, as respects its binding effect, however irregular in point of practice, equivalent to the mere filing of it in the district office.

If a recognizance taken before a commissioner be equivalent to one taken before a judge in chambers, then although all the precedents I have found in the English books of forms of such recognizances, state the transmission to a judge, and that it was by him brought into court to be enrolled and was enrolled accordingly, I cannot satisfy myself that it is necessary, and in truth it is never done. And I think it certainly not necessary for the validity of the entry of record, that a recognizance taken before a judge of the court should be stated to have been brought into court by him to be enrolled. It is always in fact brought in by one of the parties. In Stevenson v. Grant, 2 N. R. 103, the *sci. fa.* against bail stated the recognizance to have been taken before Chambers, J., Common Pleas, in £2100 with the usual condition, and then proceeded to allege a subsequent recovery against the debtor, whereof he was convicted, *as by the record and process thereof now remaining in the same court manifestly appeared.* Demurrer, because it did not appear by the *sci. fa.* that the *recognizance* therein mentioned was ever enrolled in Her Majesty's Court of C. P. nor did the plaintiff verify or offer to prove the same by the record of the said recognizance; the plaintiff amended; the court intimated a strong opinion that the writ of *sci. fa.* was bad for *want of an averment*, that the recognizance was of record, and thought the words "as by the record and "process," &c., applied to the judgment, and not to the recognizance; see also Tidd P. 8th ed. 280; 6 D. & R. 483; 4 B. & C. 403; 2 Chitt. Pl. 476; P. S. 8 Vic. 13, secs. 20, 23, 50; 8 Taunt. 512; 2 Morris, 561, S. C.; 5 B. & A. 69.

The material questions, therefore, are, first, whether this recognizance being enrolled, is a record; and if so, secondly, whether a recognizance taken before a commissioner is *per se* a judicial recognizance as if taken before a judge, and as such binding upon the bail upon being enrolled, though not averred to have been proved by affidavit of the caption, or filed in the office of the district where taken.

An affidavit taken before a commissioner of this court in a cause pending in this court, is an affidavit made in a judicial proceeding, and in which wilful false swearing would incur the penalties of perjury; so a recognizance of bail duly acknowledged before a commissioner (3 Burr. 1261, Medherst v. Waite) of this court for taking bail in a suit pending herein, is a judicial recognizance deriving its effect from the caption, and though requiring ulterior steps *to perfect* it as bail, is still in itself a recognizance taken by competent authority, and when enrolled binding as a record equally with a like recognizance taken before a judge in chambers. If the entry of record is irregular or unauthorized by the real state of the proceedings, the defendant should move to set it aside, but while it remains it is conclusive upon him.

The defendant might plead *nul tiel record* to this declaration, and that would be clearly a good plea. This proves that the entry of record is sufficiently averred and might be traversed by the defendant. By demurring, its being so of record is admitted, and the defence is, that a valid contract or obligation of record is not shewn to sustain an action of debt founded thereon, to which my view of the subject does not warrant me in assenting.

JONES, J.—The defendant is in my opinion entitled to judgment upon the demurrer. The declaration of the plaintiff cannot be supported. The 40th section of the Provincial Act, 2 Geo. IV. chap. 1, is almost a transcript of the British statute, 4 W. & M. chap. 34, sec. 1. By the latter the recognizances of bail taken before a commissioner, are required to be transmitted to a judge of the court, who is directed to receive the same upon an affidavit of the due taking, and the recognizance is declared to be of the like effect as if it were taken *de bene esse*, before a judge.

Our statute enacts, that recognizances of bail taken before a commissioner, shall be filed in the office of the clerk of the crown in the district where the same shall be taken, together with an affidavit of the due taking, which recognizances *so taken and filed* shall be of the like effect as if taken in open court.

This, it appears to me, is positive and peremptory, and that no recognizance taken by a commissioner can be effectual, unless filed as directed, while there is room to argue, that in the British statute that which is required is merely directory.

Nevertheless the forms of declarations referred to in argument, in actions upon recognizances thus taken, contains the averment, that such recognizance was duly transmitted to a judge, and by him recorded in court. This declaration, however, contains no averment, that it, with the affidavit of due taking, was filed in the office of the deputy clerk of the crown for the District of Newcastle, where it was taken, or that it was ever recorded. It cannot therefore be regarded as a valid recognizance under the statute.

It is nowhere expressly averred in the declaration, that the recognizance was made a record, nor are the facts stated which in law would make it one, and therefore the objection taken upon special demurrer is fatal. The declaration would be sufficient upon general demurrer.—6 Taunt. 45; 2 Cam. 329; 1 Cam. 241; 1 P. W. 336; 1 B. & Ald. 153.

McLEAN, J.—The commencement of the declaration which is objected to, varies from the usual form, but that is not as it appears to me a sufficient ground of demurrer; in the mode adopted, the facts stated in reference to the appearance of defendant before a commissioner and having become bound as bail, are more positively stated than the ordinary form requires, but I cannot see that, on that account, it is bad on special demurrer.

The second ground of demurrer seems also to fail, inasmuch as the plaintiffs could not state any specific sum for which defendant had become bail, or the extent of liability in the original action; that must depend upon the amount of verdict and the costs incurred in the cause, and the latter could not be ascertained. The defendant it is alleged became bound, that the debtor in the original action (Hughes) should pay the costs and condemnation money, or render himself to the custody of the sheriff of the Home District, or that he would do it for him. The costs and condemnation money being together uncertain, the plaintiffs could not be required to allege any specific amount as the extent of defendant's obligation.

The objections, that the declaration contains no allegation that the recognizance was filed in the office of the deputy clerk of the crown in Newcastle District, in which it was taken, as required by the statute in order to give it the same effect as if the same were taken in open court; and that it is not alleged or stated that the same was brought into court here or enrolled, appear to me to be well founded. The recognizance, so long as it remained in the custody of the commissioner who took it, or of the party who gave it, could not become a matter of record in this court, and the statute provides the mode of proceeding to be pursued in order to make it a record, which is by filing it, with an affidavit of the due taking, in the office of the clerk of the crown in the district where the same has been taken, in which case it declares it *shall be of the like effect as if the same were taken in open court.* It was necessary for the plaintiffs to shew how the recognizance was taken: if they had alleged it to have been, and the fact was that it had been, taken in open court, that would have been sufficient, but if taken before a commissioner in the country it was necessary, in setting it out, to shew that all those measures had been taken which the statute requires in order to give to a recognizance the like effect as if the same were taken in open court. It is not shewn to have become matter of record, either by its being taken in court or being taken by a commissioner, that it was filed in the office in which alone by the statute the filing could give it the effect of a record. The forms of declaration in cases like the present, drawn with great care by eminent special pleaders, all contain the allegation of the taking of the recognizance either in open court or before a judge in chambers, or other person out of court, and in the latter cases it is always stated that they have been brought into court by the judge, or have been transmitted to a judge and brought into court *to be recorded,* and that the same *has been recorded as by the record of the same remaining in court will more fully appear.* When suing on a record, it is necessary to shew what the record is, and it is not sufficient to say that certain matters appear by record remaining in court. It is, I think, but reasonable to assume, that the allegations which shew how a recognizance has become a record, which appear in all the forms of declarations on such recognizances, are inserted because they are necessary; if they were mere surplusage they certainly would not have been preserved in such forms, after the revision to which they have been subjected from time to time by men of great learning and ability.

My opinion is, that in the present case the want of an allegation, shewing how the recognizance declared on has become a record of this court, is not supplied by the statement, that the taking of the recognizance before the commissioner, and the condition of it, *appear by record* of the said recognizance remaining in court.

Judgment must therefore be for the defendant on this demurrer.

Per Cur.—Judgment for defendant on demurrer.

MACAULAY, J., *dissentiente.*

DOE DEM. SMYTH V. LEAVENS.

Where the landlord places a tenant in possession of Lot No. 1, and the tenant knowingly encroaches on part of Lot No. 2, to which the agreement as between himself and the landlord gives him no right whatever:

Held, that the tenant's occupation does not enure to create for the landlord a title to Lot 2, by means of a twenty years' possession of the lot.

Quære: As to the effect of the Statute of Limitations. Where the twenty years' possession has not been an adverse one—where the party has gone into possession with the consent of the plaintiff, as an act of kindness on his part, and has remained there under the same assent, paying no rent and acknowledging no title.

This was an ejectment for land in Sidney. The declaration gave no name or particular description of the tract claimed.

The defendant entered into a consent rule, calling the land of which she admitted herself to be in possession, the west half of Lot 13, in third concession of Sidney.

It was proved on the trial, that about twenty years ago, Richard Riley had agreed with one Taylor, to purchase the south half of Lot 12, in the third concession of Sidney, of which he and Mr. Patrick Smyth, father of the lessor of the plaintiff, were joint owners; that he went upon the land under his contract to purchase in the spring of 1818, and began to improve and cultivate it, no one being in possession of the adjoining lot at that time. After he had been three years in possession, he took a bond (16th November, 1821,) from Patrick Smyth, to convey this south half of Lot 12 to him, on condition of his making certain payments. In the same year one Wood went into possession of Lot 13, as tenant of Bleeker, who owned the lot; and from that time to the present, there has always been some one in possession of a part of Lot 13, and claiming the whole lot under a chain of title derived from Bleeker. The lots number from west to east. Lot 11, the adjoining lot on the other side, was owned and occupied by one Bonnisted, when Riley went upon the south half of 12, and he was then making improvements on what he supposed to be be his lot, but Riley having the line run by a surveyor, found that Bonnisted had encroached upon the south half of 12, and he forbade him to continue clearing on what he found to be his side of the line. Bonnisted, however, persisted, and rather than have difficulty with him, Riley for the time acquiesced; and while he continued on the 100 acres which he had purchased, he made his improvements very considerably to the east of his own line, thereby encroaching upon Lot 13, in proportion as the owner of 11 had encroached upon him. He built his house near the line between him and 13, but upon 12 as he intended and supposed, and as it would have been if the line which he had had run by the surveyor had been correct, but the side lines of all the lots in this concession have been lately established by the boundary line commissioners, and it turns out that the house, as well as the greater part of the clearing made by Riley and those who followed him in the possession, are in fact upon the west half of 13. Whether the person then occupying 13 was aware of the true line, and that Riley was encroaching upon him, did not appear. He was perhaps ignorant of it; there seems to have been an error prevailing as to the division line of the lot in that part of the concession, for the occupant of 13 had in like manner encroached upon 14, and they seem to have continued these encroachments till the lines were established by the boundary line commissioners, only three or four years ago. Riley continued to occupy as described, from the spring of 1818 till March, 1822, when he gave up possession to one Irving, to whom he had sold out his right, having made an assignment to him in 1821, of the bond which he had received from Patrick Smyth. The nature of Riley's possession was this: he had made a contract with the owner of the south half of Lot 12, for the purchase of it, and had taken possession, not claiming or pretending to derive from them any part of Lot 13, upon which nevertheless he had, as he swears, knowingly encroached, making a large improvement upon Lot 13, as he well knew at the time, and living in fact upon Lot 13, though he supposed that his house was on the south half of 12. Taylor, from whom he had purchased in the first instance, died before the bond was given to him by Patrick Smyth, but not till after Riley had taken possession. It was not shewn that either Taylor or Patrick Smyth had any knowledge of his having taken possession of more land than they had sold to him. Irving, who followed him in the possession, having purchased his right to the south half of 12, lived five or six years on the lot, maintaining, as it appears, the same possession that Riley had done. He has been long dead, and whether he was conscious that he was occupying any part of Lot 13 or not, was not proved. At the end of five or six years he moved off with his family, and surrendered up his possession, as the witnesses stated, to the lessor of the plaintiff, as the owner of the south half of 12, his father Patrick Smyth having died not long before. From the whole evidence, one cannot gather anything more from the witnesses' statement of his having "*given up possession*" to the lessor of the plaintiff, than simply that he relinquished the purchase and moved away. It was not shewn that the lessor of the plaintiff, or his father, received from him any delivery of actual possession upon or in view of the land, or that he ever saw the land, or was aware that the possession of Riley or Irving had extended beyond the hundred acres they had bargained for. Before Irving went away, one Peter Smyth it seems, had, to the knowledge of Irving, made some arrangement with the lessor of the plaintiff to lease the place, and he succeeded Irving in the possession as tenant to the lessor of the plaintiff. Whether he went in immediately or not, was not stated; he certainly did without any considerable interval, living in the same house that Riley had built, and occupying the same land that he and Irving had done. He stated that while he was clearing land on what now appears to be 13, the owner of that lot came and forbade him, in consequence of which he desisted, but still retained possession, as the others had done. He continued there about four years, leaving the place in 1831, when the lessor of the plaintiff leased the hundred acres (south half of 12) to one Bonnisted, who possessed it for three years, and left it; and then one Phillips leased it from the lessor of the plaintiff for three years. Both of these tenants, for all that appears, held possession of the same land that the others had done. Riley had in the meantime gone to live in the United States, and before Phillips' term was out he returned, and, contrary to the will of the lessor of the plaintiff, made some arrangement with Phillips by which he got into possession, with the idea it seems of attempting to hold under his original purchase; for he had got a copy of his bond, and instituted a suit in chancery to compel a conveyance. While this suit was pending, and while he was in possession, holding the place as those before him had held it, Peter Leavens (now deceased) the husband of this defendant, who had purchased in the meantime from Bleeker Lot 13, brought an ejectment against him to recover possession of that part which had been so long encroached upon, the boundary line commissioners having lately established the true division lines, and Riley (as he stated) not choosing to contest the matter, accepted payment from Leavens for his improvements, and gave up possession to him in April, 1843, of all the land which by the survey was found to be part of Lot 13. It appeared that much the greater part of the land cleared by Riley, and those who succeeded him, was in fact upon Lot 13, and that according to the true line, about forty acres only of that which had been so occupied as part of Lot 12 really belongs to it. It was stated in the affidavits and not denied, that upon Leavens getting possession of the part of Lot 13 which Riley had occupied wrongfully (paying him for his improvements upon a valuation), he gave up to the proprietor of Lot 14, on the other side of him, all the land which according to the commissioners' survey he had improperly occupied as part of 13. Whether the lessor of the plaintiff could or could not right himself (in the event of failing in this ejectment), by recovering from the owner of Lot 11 any part of 12 which he has occupied, did not appear. It was not shewn whether he would or would not be precluded by the Statute of Limitations. The facts in regard to any continued possession of that land were not proved. Riley was examined upon the trial, and he swore distinctly that he always thought, while he lived on the place, that he was improving on 13; that he expected at some future day he and the proprietors of Lots 11 and 13 would have the boundary properly adjusted, and that he would get on the one side as much land as he might have to give upon the other, and was therefore not careful about it; and that he never considered himself to be holding under Patrick Smyth the part of Lot 13 of which he knew himself to be in illegal possession.

The learned judge instructed the jury, that if the plaintiff and those under whom he claimed had been twenty years in possession of the land now in dispute, not acknowledging the title of the defendant or of any other person, he would be entitled to recover whether the land formed part of 12 or not. It appeared in evidence at the trial, that the lessor of the plaintiff had leased the south half of 12 to one Haight for two years, not yet expired, and it was objected by the defendant, that as the lessor of the plaintiff only claimed a right to one hundred acres, and as Haight was in possession under a lease of the one hundred acres, it was not Smyth but his tenant Haight who could maintain this action. The objection was overruled. The jury found for the plaintiff.

A. Wilson moved for a new trial without costs, on the law and evidence, and upon affidavits.

Cameron, Sol.-Gen., shewed cause (a).

ROBINSON, C. J.—I think the objection as to Haight was properly overruled. The question at the trial was expressly about the right of possession in the *west half* of 13. Haight's lease did not cover that, and therefore could not obstruct the plaintiff's right to possess that land. Haight under his lease could

(a) The present reporter had not been appointed till after the argument in this case.

enjoy for two years whatever right Smyth had in the west half of 12, and that only ; and if by the encroachments of his tenants or otherwise, Smyth had besides acquired a right to a part of Lot 13, that would be an additional property, which he was not bound to include in his lease of the south half of 12, and which it was not shewn that he had included in it. Then upon the question of title, it was correctly stated to the jury, that if the plaintiff by himself, or through those holding under him, had been in possession of the premises for twenty years, not acknowledging the right of the defendant or those under whom she claimed, such possession would give him a right to recover. It would in fact constitute a title, and as I understand the learned judge to have been satisfied with the verdict, I infer that the jury were led to believe that the evidence was in his opinion sufficient to enable the plaintiff to recover on that ground. I cannot say that I take that view of it, and it is due to the defendant in this case to examine scrupulously the grounds on which the plaintiff rests his claim, because what the plaintiff is seeking does not seem to be in accordance with justice. The award of the boundary line commissioners, as we must suppose, gives a fair and equal quantity of land to each of the Lots 11, 12, 13 and 14, according to the intention of government in making the grants. By some common error not explained, they had each made their improvements too far to the east, that is, beyond the proper boundary of their respective lots. The error has been discovered and corrected by public authority ; and what each lot does embrace is now ascertained and fixed. Public convenience, and the claims of private justice in such cases, would be best consulted by each party at once adjusting his possession according to the true line. Particular circumstances, such as improvements of a substantial kind, and of great value, made before the error was discovered, may in some cases furnish reasonable grounds for desiring to make such instances exceptions ; especially when, from any peculiarity in the case, pecuniary compensation would not afford a satisfactory indemnity ; but generally speaking, wherever the Statute of Limitation interferes to prevent a correction of the boundary being made throughout a concession into which an error has crept, it will operate unjustly. Either all ought to be made to conform to the true line or none, for positive injustice must be done by shifting the lines unless the change can be carried through ; and I confess I think it calls for serious consideration by the legislature, whether the supposed effect of the Statute of Limitations should not in this respect be controlled. Why should mere lapse of time be allowed in general to prevent the correction of a manifest error, and the rendering equal justice to all ? While the statute 21 Jac. I. continued to be our rule, and the question of the nature and effect of a possession which had been held inconsistently with the title was a matter to be left open to the jury upon all the facts of the case, I always inclined to the opinion, that under ordinary circumstances, a possession held for twenty years of another man's land, not in defiance of his right nor upon any intention to claim what his title covered, but upon a mere mistake as to boundary, was not to be looked upon as a possession held adversely by one claiming title, and would consequently not bar the remedy of the true owner. In the case of Denison v. Chew, determined in this court (Trinity Term, 6th and 7th Wm. IV.), that point was discussed. It appears in the case before us, that Mr. Leavens allowed his neighbour on the east side of him to take the land properly belonging to *his* lot, as soon as he had by his agreement with Riley gained possession on the other side of the land properly belonging to his own lot. If this plaintiff can in like manner move his line upon his neighbour to the west (the proprietor of 11), so as to embrace in his Lot No. 12 all that properly belongs to it, then the plaintiff's possession would be according to his title; he would be as well off as his neighbours, and could have all that he can have any just pretence to claim. And if by the effect of the Statute of Limitations or otherwise, he should be found to be disabled from righting himself on that side, still he should not on that account be allowed to save himself from loss by grasping the property of his neighbour, unless he can make good his title upon perfectly clear grounds. Now, what is shewn here? Riley, in the spring of 1818, is the first person to take actual possession of the land in dispute, part of 13, not as tenant or agent, or servant of the plaintiff, or of Patrick Smyth, but on his own account as a contracting purchaser entitled to the rents and profits. He soon finds, according to his own evidence, which is not contradicted, that he had encroached on lands which he had not agreed to buy from Patrick Smyth, or from any one, but nevertheless he resolved to retain wrongful possession of them. In doing this he was a mere trespasser upon the right owner. The person who had sold to him part of Lot 12, and had given no authority, express or implied, to take possession of any other land, would not be responsible for his trespass upon Lot 13, and should therefore derive no advantage from it, any more than if Riley had gone into possession of Lot 20, instead of 13. If Riley had continued on the land twenty years, he and not Smyth would have gained by such possession what the true owner would have lost, and he would not the less have held his right to the hundred acres under his purchase from Smyth. Irving having taken an assignment of Smyth's bond succeeded Riley in his wrongful possession, and when he gave up to Smyth the right which he had bought from Riley and left the place, the effect of what had happened up to that time was, that he and Riley between them had dispossessed the true owner for about ten years, which would count as so much of twenty years towards making a title under the Statute of Limitations in favour of Irving, if he had continued to occupy, or in favour of those who might follow him in the possession, that is, I mean, who might have followed him in the possession, deriving down from him a right or supposed right to occupy; for whatever effect an uninterrupted possession for twenty years by successive trespasses, not holding or claiming under or by any privity with each other, might have in barring the remedy and even extinguishing the right of the true owner, I do not consider that the last of such occupants could be allowed to add the possession of the others to his own in order to strengthen his title. Then from the end of these ten years, Peter Smyth, Bonnisted and Phillips occupied in succession for six or seven years, bringing the time down to 1833 or 1834, and making in all about fifteen or sixteen years of occupation, for the dates are not precisely given. The leases are not produced; they were probably verbal. There was no proof that the lessor of the plaintiff, who gave them as heir to his father, Patrick Smyth, had ever been on the land or seen it, or knew what Riley or Irving had occupied, or that he did anything more than simply lease to these parties in succession the hundred acres of Lot 12 which he owned. Under such circumstances, I am not of opinion that their occupation, any more than the possession of Riley and Irving, could do more than count as so many years of occupation in their own favour. It was no continuation of the ten years' possession of the others, for it was not derived from Irving, and there is nothing to shew that when he went away and abandoned his purchase, he pretended to give up to Smyth anything more than Riley had got from his father, which was an undertaking to convey a part of 12, but no part of 13; and moreover Riley expressly swore, on the trial, that he never considered himself so holding under Smyth any part of 13, but that he occupied it advisedly, knowing that Smyth had no right to it, and had not pretended to sell it to him. And considering that Irving followed him in the possession, and that Peter Smyth followed Irving, not wholly independently of each other, but with privity and knowledge of the other's interest, I think it may fairly be presumed, that they knew as well as Riley did that Smyth's title did not cover the land now in dispute. Fifteen or sixteen years' possession having been thus held adversely to the true owner, Riley came in again, not by any means upon agreement with the lessor of the plaintiff, but against his will, and then endeavoured to set himself up as owner of the fee adversely to Smyth, so far as regarded anything that he had ever held under Smyth, relying on his old bond obtained in 1821, which he had assigned to Irving, and the right under which bond Irving had abandoned. The three or four years' possession necessary to make up the twenty years were held by Riley under these circumstances, and can surely not go to make up part of a twenty years' possession, to be relied on by the lessor of the plaintiff as a title which he has acquired. Then having remained on the place and holding possession with that view, and by no privity with the lessor of the plaintiff as regards any part of Lot 13, till after the twenty years had run out, he abandons that land, and surrenders whatever right or interest he had as occupant into the hands of the husband of this defendant, the very person against whom it is the object of this action to establish a right as having vested in the lessor of the plaintiff under the twenty years' possession. Surely if it ever was in the power of any one to make out a title under the twenty years' possession of this property, it is the defendant, who now represents that right, Peter Leavens her husband having received possession from him in whose hands it was first perfect, and not the lessor of the plaintiff.

There is one view of the case, however, which, though not insisted upon in argument, must receive attention. The effect of the new Statute of Limitations (4 Wm. IV. chap. 1, admitting it to extend to the case of a possession held while the true owner is labouring under a mistake as to his boundary), is to extinguish the title of a person who has suffered himself to be "dispossessed" for twenty years. There is much in this statute to be considered—much, in regard to its intention and effect, on which text writers have expressed doubts, and which has not yet been elucidated by the cases (not numerous) which have occurred in England since the statute from which it was framed was passed there. Among other things, I doubt at present whether the statute will apply in its strict sense, excluding I mean all distinction and discussion about adverse and non-adverse possession, and extinguishing the right, except in those cases where the twenty years' occupation has followed an *actual dispossession*, not an intrusion upon the mere constructive possession which follows the right of property, where the soil is vacant, or a *discontinuance* of an *actual possession* (by which I mean a visible occupation, not a mere legal seisin), or a discontinuance of the actual receipt of rents or profits. I suggest this, however, only as a doubt which, if there is any ground for it, would extend equally to the case of an alienee not taking possession for twenty years after his purchase, only that there the doubt would be whether the statute would apply except to the alienee of a vendor, who had not been in actual visible possession, or receipt of rents and profits. The statute has evidently been carried farther in its application than the commissioners upon whose report it was framed intended, as appears to me upon considering their published reports, and Mr. Sugden has expressed that opinion (a). In this country, from obvious causes, rights are likely to be acquired under its provisions by surprise upon the true owner, in so much greater a proportion of cases, that we must be very careful not to carry the effect of its provisions further than we can find clear authority for doing, either in its express language, or in cases which have been adjudged, and which have settled its construction. Now in the case before us, we have to consider on the one hand, that although this plaintiff, having, as it is admitted, no title in the common sense of the term, that is no paper title, may be also unable, as I think he is, to rest his claim to a verdict upon having acquired a title by twenty years' possession of himself, or those under whom he claims; yet the defendant, if there had been a clear twenty years' dispossession proved against her, within the meaning of the statute, has not only lost her right of entry, but her title. Being in possession, she has no occasion to bring ejectment, but taking the case for the present to be clearly against her as to the dispossession, she then would stand in this light; that she is shewn to be in possession of land to which she has no title, and the consequence of that would be, that if we may look upon her as a mere wrongdoer, then any one might recover the possession from her in ejectment, who could shew possession previous to her's of such a nature that the presumption of title would arise from it. What I mean is, that it might not be necessary for the lessor of the plaintiff to shew as against her a perfect title by documents, or by what is equivalent, twenty years' possession; because it is true that the doctrine, that a plaintiff in ejectment must recover on the strength of his own title, and must shew a good title, is admitted to have this qualification, that as against a wrongdoer a former occupant may stand upon a previous peaceable possession, though short of twenty years, and without shewing the foundation of that possession. But in the first place I do not consider this defendant, even if her first legal title has been extinguished by long acquiescence in an adverse possession, as a mere wrongdoer within the reason of the few cases on this point which are reported in the books, beginning with Allen v. Rivington, 2 Saunders, 111. Supposing her to stand in the place of her late husband as devisee, or otherwise, (though her connection with his title seems not to have been inquired into on the trial), then her possession is derived from Riley, in whose hands the twenty years' possession must, in the view which I take of the case, have

---

(a) 1 Hayes' Conveyancing, 171; 2 Sugden on Vendors, 349.

conferred a title if upon any one, and it is not he who is questioning her right in this action, but the plaintiff, whose title is no longer capable of being supported by the presumption arising from possession (if he ever had possession of this land), because the evidence given disproves his title, shewing that the right was in Leavens till he lost it (if he had lost it) by the title vesting in Riley from twenty years' possession. And it is clearly admitted, that on the trial of an ejectment, a defendant may prevent a plaintiff recovering, if he can shew that the title is in any third party. Whether Riley, after receiving payment from Leavens in 1843, for improvements which he had wrongfully made upon land known by him to belong to Leavens, and after formally giving up a possession which he admitted to have been wrongful, could or could not afterwards turn round upon him and eject him, by standing upon the twenty years' possession which he had surrendered, I will not undertake to say; but I feel very certain that the Statute of Limitations never could have been intended to have an effect so repugnant to justice, and I think it ought never to have received a construction which would admit of that, though I do apprehend that the view which has been taken in some cases of the English statute may lead to results as difficult to be reconciled with one's ideas of right. But whatever Riley could have done (supposing him to have made no deed to Leavens when he went out of possession), it is clear I think that the lessor of the plaintiff has no footing whatever to stand upon. He had no actual possession at any time, and if the title of Mrs. Leavens has been extinguished, it has only been so by a twenty years' possession, which under no principle can be held to have accrued to the plaintiff's benefit.

Before the late statute, the case of Doe dem. Burrough v. Reade, 8 E. R. 353, would have been decisive against this plaintiff, where the court held clearly "that a defendant, being lawfully in possession, might defend himself "upon his title, though twenty years had run against him before he took pos- "session, *such twenty years not being the possession of the lessor of the plaintiff.*" In Archbold's N. P. 318, this case seems to be considered equally applicable now, as before the new statute; and although it is provided by the late statute, that after twenty years' adverse possession, the title of the true owner shall be extinguished (which it was not before), yet that has not created such a difference of circumstances as to render the person who had by dispossession lost his title, but who is again in possession by the assent of the only person who could have acquired a title by the adverse possession, liable to be turned out by anybody and everybody who can shew, which this plaintiff indeed does not, that he has ever been in possession, and though such person has neither a documentary title, nor twenty years' possession to stand on. If Riley, after the twenty years' possession had run out, admitting the unreasonableness of retaining possession of land which he was conscious he had never any legal or just claim to, had surrendered up the possession (as in fact he did) to the person who had been wrongfully dispossessed; and if, repenting of his honesty, he had afterwards turned round upon the person to whom he had so restored possession, and had brought this ejectment instead of Smyth, then it would, I dare say, have been contended, and it might have been found, that the effect of the new Statute of Limitations would have enabled him to recover, on the ground that by his former possession he had acquired a perfect title; that his having allowed the defendant to go into possession did not extinguish his right; that it was not that written acknowledgment of title which the statute requires; and that if it would be accepted as equivalent, still it would have no effect, not coming till after the twenty years had run out, when all question about interrupting the twenty years was at an end. I have not met with any decision in England upon such a state of facts, and can only say, that if it must be determined in any such case that the former owner, to whom possession has been restored, is by the effect of the late statute liable to be turned out again by the very person who had relinquished possession or any one claiming under him, it will shew a state of the law which no just person can have desired or intended to introduce; but that is not the case before us. The case of Doe dem. Thompson v. Thompson, 6 Ad. & Ell. 721, bears upon this point; and whether the court only took up that case upon the ground of the twenty years having all run out before the statute came into force, or not, is a question, in my mind, of much interest. The injustice which Lord Denman there spoke of as too monstrous to be supposed, would be as strong in such a case, where the twenty years had not run out till after the statute came into force, as where they had run out before the statute.

We have kept this case under consideration, in the hope that we might be able to concur in opinion upon the several points it involves; and if there is now any difference of opinion on the part of either of my brothers, I believe it arises chiefly from the view taken of the effect of Riley's encroachment. In Colclough v. Mullener, 1 Esp. C. 460, Lord Kenyon held, that a landlord could not recover in ejectment against his tenant a piece of land which the tenant had inclosed from the waste by encroachment; revolting, as the reporter says, at the idea that the tenant could make the landlord a trespasser, which he said must unavoidably follow if the landlord could recover in the ejectment. "If (his lordship said) the tenant had acknowledged that he held such inclosed "part of his landlord, it would make a difference." In the next case reported in the same volume, under similar circumstances (a), his lordship was inclined to rule in like manner against the plaintiff, but allowed the plaintiff to take a verdict, as being told that several other judges had held, that in such cases encroachments by tenants "were for the benefit of their landlords." The question, even when thus confined to encroachments upon the waste, is treated by Sergeant Adams in his Treatise on Ejectment as a very unsettled point, that is, whether it gives to the lessee or to the landlord a possessory right after the end of the term; and he states that Kenyon and Lee, Chief Justices, and Thompson, Baron, have held that it belongs to the lessee, and that Heath, Buller and Perrin, Justices, and Graham, Baron, have held that the landlord becomes entitled. I find nothing very recent on the subject. But admitting that the weight of authority is in favour of holding that the lessee does not acquire the right in regard to encroachments upon the waste or common, and especially where the fee of the land inclosed was in the landlord, yet the case before us is not the case of a tenant, but of a purchaser, taking possession of land for himself as owner of the equitable freehold, so far as he acted under his contract at all. Then again, the land was not a waste or common, belonging

---

(a) Doe Dem. Challnor v. Davies.

in any shape or degree to the vendor, and instead of Riley acknowledging that he held the part inclosed as Lot 12 under his purchase, or leaving us to infer that he did so, he swears positively to the contrary, and no proof was given that he did. I will not venture to extend a principle which has been so much doubted, even in regard to landlord and tenant, to the case of vendor and vendee, and under circumstances so much stronger against the application of the principle. My conviction is, that we should be unwarranted in doing so by any authority that can be produced. If it had been shewn that Irving did anything more than abandon his purchase of the south half of Lot 12, that he had done some act manifesting that Smyth received from him actual possession of all the land which he and Riley had occupied; if it had been shewn that what Smyth leased to Peter Smyth, Bonnisted and Phillips, was not merely the hundred acres to which alone he had title, but the land which his intended vendee had wrongfully inclosed, then there would have been ground for holding that the last of his tenants, Phillips, was in possession under him of that part of 13 which is now in question. But nothing of this was proved, and I think the jury were not at liberty to infer it without proof, in order to give an enlarged effect to a statute so extremely stringent in its provisions, that when it is applied it ought to be on clear grounds established by evidence, and not upon surmises of things not appearing. If all this had been shewn, then it might have followed that Riley, by putting himself in Phillips' place, with whatever intention, could not have held against the landlord anything that Phillips could not have held against him; and if so, then neither I suppose could the defendant be in a better situation than Phillips, in consequence of any treaty made with Riley after he had bought Phillips out; but as I view the case, it stands on a very different ground. Smyth could never, I think, upon anything that has been shewn, have been sued by Bleeker or Leavens for the trespass on 13, which Riley or any of the subsequent occupants of 12 had committed, nor could he have sued Riley or any one for use and occupation of that land. I see therefore no right vested in Smyth under a twenty years' possession demised from one person to another, and terminating in him, but a mere dispossession of the rightful owner by a succession of trespassers, and the right of the lessor of the plaintiff, if it be grounded on the possession of two of these tenants only, (which I think is the utmost that can be contended for,) would be grounded only on a possession of eight or ten years; and though the defendant's title might under the effect of statute be extinguished, yet I do not consider that it follows as a consequence that she is liable to be dispossessed by any person who can shew that he has once been in possession, either for ten years or for ten days, when it is shewn that his possession was nothing more than a constructive possession for a time derived from his own wrongful act, in pretending to lease what he had no right to.

The rule for a new trial should, in my opinion, be made absolute; costs to abide the event.

MACAULAY, J.—I have no objection to a new trial, in order to ascertain more distinctly some material points in the case, especially whether the lessor of the plaintiff was at any time, and particularly at the expiration of twenty years after Riley first entered thereon, in possession by himself or through his tenants of the tract of land claimed in this case, or of any part thereof. For assuming it to constitute a part of Lot 13, it forms a question how far the encroachments of those entering upon No. 12, under the plaintiff or his ancestor, or their wrongful entering upon part of No. 13, should enure to the benefit of the plaintiff, or whether he was at any time possessed thereof, through, or in succession to them. As a mere encroachment, it would form a question of law rather than of fact, whether the possession of his vendee or tenants should enure to his benefit; if, in fact, they did encroach for his benefit; in other words, if he was in fact possessed through them, or upon their surrender of the usurped possession to him, it would of course and as a fact then enure to his benefit.

The difficulty arises from the inferences on this head to be drawn from the evidence. The jury have found that in point of fact the lessor of the plaintiff was possessed, and the evidence appears to me to warrant such finding, but their opinion was not asked as to how far the witness Riley's account of his original occupation of No. 13 was correct; or whether, when Irving relinquished possession, the plaintiff or his ancestor succeeded to the whole of the improvements made, whether on 13 or 12, or whether he afterwards leased or became possessed of the same through subsequent tenants. They were not required to distinguish between 12 and 13, and so far as material I have no objection to the case going back for this purpose.

At present it certainly seems to me, that in 1818 or 1819 Riley entered upon the land in dispute, claiming it to be part of Lot 12, or else knowingly intending to encroach upon No. 13, and ousted the owner of 13 therefrom, so far as any actual or constructive possession is at that time to be attributed to him. Riley entered on No. 12, under a contract or purchase with the then owner of the whole or half of this Lot 12 (on this point there is a want of clearness), and while so possessed he extended his improvements over the tract in question. Irving succeeded him, and at the end of ten years he relinquished possession, or surrendered the premises to the vendor, the plaintiff's ancestor. Stopping here, a question may be asked, whether all that Riley and Irving occupied was so occupied in the *bona fide* belief that it was all on No. 12, or whether as to part it was a known encroachment upon the owner of 13; and if the former, whether it enured to the vendor's benefit when the purchase was afterwards abandoned; if the latter, whether when Irving went out of possession, possession was in fact given or immediately taken by the vendor of the parcel in dispute. If the possession was not thus continued, then another question would arise, viz.: whether the owner and possessor of No. 13 would constructively be remitted, as it were, to his former possession, as being part of 13, upon Irving's ceasing to be possessed.

Beyond this period, the vendor appears to have leased the premises to different tenants for a period covering about 18 years, when Phillips became tenant. But whether the lessor of the plaintiff demised, or through his tenants occupied the tract in question, is uncertain; no leases are produced, and if the demises were of 12 merely, a question of fact would thereon arise, viz.: what tract of land was actually thereby embraced, or demised under that designation. While Phillips was possessed Riley regained possession from him, but against the plaintiff's will; whether twenty years had expired when Riley had thus re-entered is not clear. If they had, and if the plaintiff at that time was, through his tenant Phillips or Riley, in possession, it would follow, I suppose, that the title of the owner of 13 became extinguished, and that the plaintiff, as being in possession and thereby having a *prima facie* possessory right, became entitled against all who could not shew a better right. But if the twenty years only expired after Riley had regained possession, a different question would arise, involving the point how far the plaintiff was at that time possessed of the *locus in quo*, through Phillips, and if he was, how far Riley's entry and possession (though against the will of the plaintiff's lessor), continued to enure to his benefit; and how far, entering as he did under the plaintiff's tenant, Riley could himself set the plaintiff (Phillip's landlord) at defiance, or by any act of his towards the defendant's husband pending an ejectment against him, compromise the right of the plaintiff without notice to the plaintiff, if such ejectment and no such notice is shewn. In other words, whether Riley himself or the defendant through him, can acquire any better position than Phillips could have maintained, as against the plaintiff his landlord. Riley and Irwin were originally possessed of 12 under a contract to purchase, and stood in the relation of tenants at will to their vendor, the plaintiff's ancestor. But notwithstanding this, I should think, that so far as they or the subsequent tenants encroached upon 13, it would enure to the plaintiff's benefit if he adopted the encroachment, though of course he might have repudiated it to avoid responsibility, as far as a trespass committed for his benefit. How far the encroachment was inadvertent, or supposed to be within the limits of 12, or a known excess beyond them, is, on the evidence, a question; but the case presents other questions, namely, the effect of the compromise with Riley, and the restoration of possession by him to the owner of 13, after twenty years' dispossession of the latter—the death of such owner since acquiring possession (*a*)—and the right of the plaintiff to recover though less than twenty years in possession, if he was possessed at the time when the owner of 13 had been twenty years out of possession.

These questions, in connection with the statute above mentioned of limitations, need not be now considered. When the facts or rather the inferences to be drawn from the facts are more distinctly settled by a jury, I do not apprehend any serious difficulty in determining the legal rights of the parties.

I will merely observe further, that in any view of the case the plaintiff would seem entitled to recover up to what is called Smith's line, being eighteen or twenty feet to the east of the house erected by Riley on No. 12. as he supposed, at the time of erection. The possession previous to, and since the commissioners of boundaries established the new line, seems to have been the same. The questions are, how far such possession, as the possession of the plaintiff, extended, and had been by him enjoyed, either personally or constructively through others holding under him, or for him, or on his behalf.— Tapley v. Wainwright, 5 B. & Ad. 895; Doe ex dem. Lewis v. Rees, 6 C. & P. 610; 2 Bing. N. S. 98; 2 Saund. 111; 3 M. & R. 111; 8 E. 356; 1 Esp. 460; 1 Taunt. 208.

(*a*) See 4th Wm. IV. chap. 1, sec. 42, and 1 D. & W. 289 (Irish).

JONES, J.—I think the plaintiff cannot recover.

In ejectment the plaintiff must recover upon the strength of his own title, and not upon the want of title in the defendant.

On the trial the plaintiff attempted to recover the south half of Lot No. 12, in the 8th concession of Sidney, together with a portion of the adjoining Lot No. 13. His claim upon No. 12 was supported by a paper title; that to a part of 13 was rested upon a twenty years' possession by his ancestor and by himself and his tenants. He had from time to time leased the south half of Lot No. 12, and at the time of the trial of this cause it was under lease, so that he could not properly recover for any part of it, the tenants being entitled to the possession. As to that portion of No. 13 sought to be recovered, it was first occupied by one Riley, who purchased the south half of No. 12 from the ancestor of the lessor of the plaintiff, and in clearing upon it he encroached upon 13, of which he was perfectly aware, as stated by himself in his evidence; he did not, he swears, occupy it as a part of No. 12 under the plaintiff's ancestor, for he knew that it was a part of 13. After an occupation of about four years, he abandoned it or gave up possession to Irving. If this occupation of 13 can enure to the benefit of the lessor of the plaintiff, he with his ancestor and his tenants, may be regarded as having had a twenty years' possession, otherwise not. I cannot say that the possession of 13, so taken by Riley, can be regarded as the possession of the plaintiff. It was a trespass by Riley, and his occupation for ought that appears was not with the assent or knowledge of the plaintiff, and according to the testimony was the act alone of Riley. If the plaintiff had been asked what land he had sold to Riley, his reply would undoubtedly have been, part of Lot No. 12; and if Riley, entitled to take possession of 12, trespassed or encroached upon 13 during his occupation of 12, it can no more be regarded as the possession of the plaintiff, than if he had gone upon Lot No. 1, instead of 13; and surely it would be absurd to hold that his taking possession of No. 1, instead of 12, and either ignorantly or knowingly trespassing upon the owner of that lot, could entitle the plaintiff to regard Riley's possession of No. 1 as his possession. . Whether the possession of Riley and others after him for twenty years, can be regarded as an extinguishment of the defendant's title, is another question. I think there was not proved to have been in the lessor of the plaintiff and his ancestor and those claiming under him, such a possession of the *locus in quo* as entitles the plaintiff to succeed in this action.

MCLEAN, J., having sat in the Practice Court during the argument, gave no judgment.   *Per Cur.*—New trial without costs.

DOE ON THE SEVERAL DEMISES OF HENRY AUSMAN AND JOHN MONTGOMERY V. MINTHORNE.

A., the owner of land, agrees to sell to B.—B. goes into possession—B. fails in making his payments.—A. then conveys the land to C. in B.'s presence, and apparently with the consent of B., who says that he will *at once* leave the place—B. nevertheless continues uninterruptedly in possession for more than twenty years, paying C. no rent, and making no written or other acknowledgment of C.'s title.

Held, that B.'s twenty years' possession under these circumstances, gives him the legal title.

Held also, that a notice to quit given by C. to B., within the twenty years, does not save C. from being barred by the statute.

Held also, that a judgment in ejectment recovered by C. against B., within twenty years, but upon which B. had never been dispossessed, is no bar to the statute.

Quære: If B. in undisturbed possession for twenty years, voluntarily restores the possession to C., can B. turn C. out again, by reverting to his title under the Act?

The sheriff, under a *fi. fa.* against lands, can only sell the *debtor's interest in possession*, whatever that interest may be; he cannot sell the debtor's mere right of action, while a third party is in adverse possession of the land.

This was an action of ejectment for the east three-fourths of Lot No. 10, in the third concession of Markham, on the several demises of Henry Ausman and John Montgomery.

On the 20th of February, 1816, the crown granted Lot 10, in the third concession of Markham, to John Walden Myers, upon certain trusts for the benefit of the estate of one Machofsky, deceased.

Henry Ausman, one of the lessors of the plaintiff, had gone upon the lot in 1800, or soon after, and had continued upon the land and improved it from that time; but upon what pretence or expectation of title he had entered did not appear, further than that a witness who saw them together in 1819, after Myers obtained the patent, understood from their conversation that he had been in possession for some years by permission of Myers, intending to purchase, and upon his undertaking to make certain payments, in which he had failed; and upon that occasion it was agreed by Myers to wait upon him for another year, when if he did not make a payment, Myers was to look out for another purchaser.

In January, 1820, the parties again met, and Ausman not being prepared to make any payment, Myers sold to one David Lick, and on 18th January, 1820, made him a deed of the premises, Ausman being present and agreeing to leave the place as soon as he could remove his family; nevertheless he still continued to reside on the lot and cultivate it, though it was not shewn that he had any permission from Lick, or any understanding with him, after the day on which the deed was given, when he promised to leave the place without delay; on the contrary, it was proved, that while he was so in possession he stated openly to a neighbour that he had once bargained for the lot, and had a bond for a deed but had not paid for it; that Lick had since bought it from Myers, and would probably try to turn him off, but that he would have hard work to do so.

In 1823 or 1824, Lick served Ausman with notice to quit, and soon afterwards brought an ejectment against him and obtained a verdict; but for some reason not appearing in evidence at the trial, judgment was not entered for the plaintiff till the 27th December, 1842. The demise in that action was laid in 1824, to hold for seven years, and the time thereof having expired long before the entry of the judgment, there was no term to be recorded. No *habere facias*, consequently, was issued; but a *fi. fa.* was taken out for costs, £65 11s. 2d., under which the interest of Ausman in the premises in question was put up to sale, and was bid off by John Montgomery, the other lessor of the plaintiff, who received a deed from the sheriff. Ausman had many years before given or sold to his son one-fourth of the lot (fifty acres), and the other three-fourths of the lot (one hundred and fifty acres) are claimed in this action. It was further proved at the trial that Ausman had continued to live upon the place and cultivate it till April, 1841, when his house being burnt down, he went to live with his son upon another part of the same lot, for a short time, and afterwards with a neighbour, exercising occasionally acts of ownership on this land now in question; but not long after the fire (how long was not precisely made out) he left the farm altogether, and went to live in another township; and the defendant Minthorne, who is married to the daughter and only child of Machofsky, went upon the place in July, 1841, and still remains there, that is, on the one hundred and fifty acres for which the action is brought, one Monro being in possession of the other fifty acres as assignee of Ausman's son, to whom Ausman had given that portion.

The case was tried before his lordship the Chief Justice, at Toronto, and he directed the jury to find for the plaintiffs, if they were satisfied that Ausman had been in actual possession without interruption for twenty years after the 18th day of January, 1820, otherwise to find for the defendant.

The jury found for the plaintiffs, expressly declaring that they were satisfied by the evidence that Ausman had enjoyed possession without interruption for more than twenty years after the 18th day of January, 1820, without paying rent or giving any written acknowledgment of title; and that he was not within that time in possession by Lick's permission.

The plaintiff's counsel at the trial desired it to be understood that he went upon the demise by Montgomery alone.

W. H. Blake moved for a new trial on the law and evidence, and for misdirection. He relied upon 11 E. R. 488; 8 E. R. 353; 7 Bing. 345; 6 A. & E. Thompson v. Thompson.

The Hon. *R. B. Sullivan* shewed cause, and cited 8 M. & W. 533; 6 M. & W. 395; 2 M. & W. 894; 5 A. & E. 532; 6 M. & G. 816; 5 A. & E., s. c. 291; 7 M. & W. 226; 9 M. & W. 643; 4 Q. B. R. 767; 5 M. & G. 30; 2 Q. B. R. 601; 5 Beavan, 67; 8 M. & W. 119.

Thomas Ewart, same side, cited 2 Smith's Leading Cases, 416; 11 A. & E. 44; 2 Sugden, 351; 6 A. & E. 721; 2 Hayes, 268; 2 N. & P. 656; 7 M. & W. 226; 2 Saund. 111 (*a*).

ROBINSON, C. J.—If the case had gone to the jury upon the demise of Ausman. I do not see on what ground the propriety of the plaintiffs' recovery could have been questioned. The defendant Minthorne stands in no other light upon the evidence than a mere stranger to the estate, and whatever should enable Ausman to recover against anyone, should enable him to recover against this defendant. The land had been granted to Myers, it is true, upon some trust to pay the

---

(*a*) The present reporter had not been appointed till after the argument in this case.

debts due by one Machofsky, deceased, who was as I suppose the locatee of the land ; and Minthorne, it appeared, had married his only child, but that shews no connection either on his part or his wife's with the legal estate, which on the 18th day of January, 1820, was vested in Lick. How it happened that Lick had allowed himself to be so long dispossessed of the estate did not appear. Lick was himself examined as a witness, but did not account for it. It seemed to me that neither party was disposed to question him upon the point. All the evidence that was given went to shew that on the 18th day of January, 1820, when Lick's title accrued, Ausman with knowledge of his title engaged to go immediately out of possession, but did not ; that he afterwards declared to others that he would not leave the place, and that Lick might get him out if he could ; that he lived upon the place and used it in all respects as his own, paying no rent to Lick, nor giving any acknowledgment in writing or otherwise of his title. The jury found that this possession against the true owner had been held continuously for twenty years from the 18th January, 1820. I did not see, and do not now see, why upon the facts proved the statute should not begin to run from that time, whatever were the previous relations between Ausman and Myers. Nothing had passed between him and Lick that I could take to have created a tenancy at will ; he left Myers and Lick with the knowledge and understanding, that all claim on his part to continue possession, and all expectation of being a purchaser, were at an end, and that he was *at once* to leave the farm ; nevertheless, he continued after this for more than twenty years to occupy it, without paying rent, or acknowledging in writing the title of the true owner ; and more than five years of the twenty were running after the new Statute of Limitations came into force. If a tenancy at will could be created between Lick and Ausman, when Ausman promised to go out immediately as soon as he could remove his family, by ascribing to Lick an implied assent that he might retain possession till he could remove his family, still that could have no greater effect, at the utmost, than to postpone the time for the statute commencing to run for one year, or to the 18th of January, 1821, under the 19th clause of the statute, which provides for the cases of tenants at will ; and two witnesses swore expressly that Ausman constantly resided on the farm till April, 1841, when his house was burnt, which would still give the full period of twenty years ; nor do I think that his possession could, according to the evidence, have been considered as clearly terminating even then. The defendant endeavoured to avoid the effect of the statute by setting up the notice to quit which Lick had given, before bringing his action of ejectment in 1823 or 1824, as conclusive evidence of a tenancy existing then ; but to give this any effect against the statute, we must hold it to have created a new tenancy from year to year. It certainly is not an acknowledgment in writing by Ausman ; it is at most the mere admission of the other party that a tenancy then existed. Such a notice we know is often given by a plaintiff, where the facts do not really call for it, and as a measure of precaution when he apprehends that the other party may endeavour to set up a tenancy. It was not proved that Lick recovered at the trial upon proof of a tenancy. If within the twenty years Ausman had given a notice to Lick as his landlord, in order to put an end to an alleged tenancy, the case would have been very different ; but if we were to treat this notice given by

Lick as landlord, as having the effect of interrupting the twenty years, then we must hold, that in any case of a tenant holding over and paying no rent, a mere notice to quit given from time to time by his landlord and followed up by no effectual proceeding would save him from being barred by the statute; such a notice, I conceive, would be of no avail for that purpose, even in cases in which a previous tenancy had been clearly shewn; still less can it avail when there is no proof that a tenancy ever existed.

The defendant next relied upon the effect of the judgment in ejectment rendered in 1842 in favour of Lick, as establishing that the title was in him. But, in the first place, a judgment in ejectment is not conclusive as to the right, because it does not affect the inheritance (*a*). Then the record that was given in evidence contained nothing on the face of it to connect the recovery with these premises. It might as well have been a judgment to recover any other land in Markham; and it proved nothing more than that Lick had a right to demise the premises in question in that action (whatever they were) for the term of seven years from the 20th October, 1824, which is no proof that he owned the fee either then or at any time. The fact might be, consistently with that record (even if it clearly related to the land now in dispute), that Lick might have derived his right to make the lease for a term which the owner of the fee had granted to him; and, after all, if the judgment could be taken to establish certainly that Lick was the owner of the land in 1824, it would only shew that he had then lost the possession which he has never since regained. But admitting that to be so, still the fact which constitutes the bar under the statute would nevertheless exist; for if the true owner of an estate allows another to possess it for twenty years, without paying him rent or acknowledging his title in writing, he loses the estate. The case of Doe dem. Jukes v. Smith, decided in the Exchequer in Easter Term, 1845, is a strong decision on that point, on which indeed the statute is explicit.

On the whole, considering that the title of Lick undoubtedly commenced in January, 1820—that Ausman was at the time in actual possession, with the assent of the person from whom Lick received his conveyance—that he continued uninterruptedly in possession for more than twenty years, as the jury found, paying no rent, acknowledging no one's title, and not even with the permission of Lick during any part of the twenty years (I mean of the last twenty years)—we can see no ground on which we can hold otherwise than that Lick lost his title, and that Ausman acquired the estate. The ejectment brought within the period, since it had not the effect of changing the possession, it must be evident upon reflection can have no influence in the case. It is rather a circumstance against the then alleged owner of the fee (Lick), so far as it shews that the possession was at that time at least against his will. If judgment had been entered in his favour in 1824, and he had made no use of it for regaining possession, but merely held the judgment and had the power of turning Ausman out, it could only prove, what in most cases of the kind can be clearly shewn, that he had the title to the estate and the right to possession, and therefore came clearly within the statute; it could not prevent the Act running. Lick's only security would have been in making use of his

---

(*a*) 7 Bro. P. C. 145.

title for gaining possession. If Ausman had after the twenty years voluntarily restored the possession to Lick, and was now seeking to turn him out again, by reverting to his title acquired under the statute, I do not say that the result must be different. Such a state of facts, however, would introduce considerations which do not apply here, and which therefore we need not now dwell upon. The fact here is, that Ausman, having acquired the right under the statute, has gone out of possession, for what reason we know not, and a stranger to the title has entered. So far as making title under the demise from Ausman is considered, we see no other difficulty than the difficulty of reconciling to one's sense of right the apparent injustice of a person acquiring a title to an estate said to be worth £1,500 or more, merely because he has been from good nature or negligence allowed to live on it so long rent free, that he now can turn round on the true owner and call it his own. But that is the operation of the Statute of Limitations, in every perfectly clear case, of which we take this to be one. The effect of the statute in such cases, (to use the language of the court in Doe dem. Jukes v. Smith), "is to make a present of "the estate to the person in possession. It is a parliamentary conveyance."

I have one difficulty, however, in sustaining the verdict. I have reported to my brothers, that upon the trial the plaintiff's counsel expressly desired to limit his case to the demise laid by Montgomery. It is so stated in my note of the trial, and my recollection confirms it: but on the argument of this rule, it did not seem to be intended to take up the case solely on that demise. If, however, we are to understand that the plaintiff's case must depend on the title of Montgomery, then we have to consider whether there is anything substantial in the objections raised in the argument to his title. I see only the one objection which was urged on the argument, that the sheriff could not sell, upon an execution against Ausman, an estate of which Ausman was not at the time in possession, or rather of which he had been dispossessed. It was proved that in July, 1841, this defendant Minthorne entered into possession of these 150 acres as soon as Ausman had left the place; not upon any privity with Ausman, but holding the estate in opposition to him, and that he was holding possession in this manner at the time of the judgment, execution and sale. Ausman had at the time as it appears the title, but not the possession. He was dispossessed, and could not under such circumstances have conveyed the property by deed.

The question then is, whether upon a *fi. fa.* land could be sold as his, or his interest in it sold, when he could not by any voluntary act of his have disposed of the land, or of his interest in it; in other words, whether the sheriff under a *fi. fa.* can sell, not the debtor's interest in possession, whatever that may be, but his mere right of action. This question was but lightly discussed on the argument, for the plaintiff's counsel seemed not to apprehend that there was anything formidable in the objection. It is not a technical objection unconnected with the merits of the case, but is one altogether too substantial to be overlooked or waived; for of course if the land was not under the circumstances in such a condition that it could be legally sold under a *fi. fa.* against Ausman, then the title under the demise of the purchaser at sheriff's sale wholly fails, and it would be but just, that if the sale of a mere right of action cannot take place under an execution against lands, the title of the purchaser under an attempted sale of that kind should not be upheld; because it is very evident that no purchaser would bid the same substantial price for a lawsuit that he would for the land; and it is not fit that an estate, of which A. B. is at the time in actual occupation, claiming it as his own, should be sold under legal process to satisfy the debt of C. D., unless the law sanctions such a course, which I consider it does not. Chief Baron Gilbert, in his Treatise on Executions, page 42, lays it down "if a man be disseised against whom judg-"ment is recovered, the lands in the hands of the disseisee shall not be liable, "for though the disseisor has the right of possession, yet they are not his till "he recovers." Taking this view of the case, I am of opinion that there ought to be a new trial, letting the costs of the last abide the event; for if the defendant's counsel had at the trial opposed the recovery on the demise of Montgomery, upon the ground that the estate could not be sold and conveyed by the sheriff in consequence of Minthorne being in possession, it might possibly have been shewn that the possession of Minthorne was not adverse, or that he was concurring in the sale.

MACAULAY, J.—It appears to me that Lick's right of entry accrued on the 18th January, 1820, as a person claiming the land in respect of an estate in possession granted or otherwise assured to him by an instrument, other than a will, by a person (Myers) being in respect of the same estate in possession, under the 4th Wm. IV. chap. 1, sec. 17, and that he never afterwards made such entry. That previous to that time Ausman had been in possession in the relation of tenant at will to Meyers, which was at the time he conveyed to Lick expressly determined, and if not, was impliedly determined by force and virtue of the conveyance in fee to Lick. It does not appear that Ausman ever became a tenant at will to Lick, or otherwise held under him; on the contrary, he promised to go out of possession forthwith, as soon as he could move his personal property, and nothing then or afterwards occurred between them to deprive Lick of the right to enter or to bring an ejectment against Ausman, which accrued to him upon the execution of the deed of conveyance from Myers. Then it appears that Ausman continued in undisturbed possession of the premises for upwards of twenty years afterwards, and by reason thereof the title of Lick became extinguished under the Provincial statute, 4th Wm. IV. ch. 1, sec. 37.—See 14 M. & W. 392; 9 Jur. 413; 10 Jur. 705; 5 Q. B. 767; 10 Jur. 815. The defendant afterwards entered in July, 1841, ousting Ausman, who acquired a title by being in possession under the statute previously, or treating it as a vacant possession, and whatever equitable claims he on behalf of his wife might have had, he shews no legal right; as against him therefore Ausman is entitled to recover.—1 Lord Ray. 741; M. & M. 346; 7 Bing. 346; 3 N. & M. 331; 3 T. R. 13; 1 Bur. 119.

I do not see that Lick's recovering in ejectment can affect Ausman's right. The fictitious demise laid in the declaration had expired long before such recovery, and the utmost effect of the judgment, as evidence, would be to shew that on the day of the demise the lessor of the plaintiff had a right to enter—Co. Lit. 285 (a); 3 Camp. 447; and Bul. N. P. 105;—and that he was not lawfully in possession; that is, was liable to be treated as a trespasser when the action was brought—1 B. & C. 455-6; 11 E. 56;—but it only strengthens the claim of Ausman, now that twenty years have expired, when it is shewn that no possession under such ejectment was ever obtained by the therein lessor of the plaintiff. I do not find that the undertaking in the consent rule, to confess *entry*, as well as ouster, estops the tenant in possession. It is in the first place a known fiction, exacted of him by the court, as a condition of his being let in to try the title; and as respects the defendant was *res inter alios acta*. The effect of even a recovery of possession under an ejectment, was much considered in a case in this court Doe ex dem. Young v. Marsh, and is well laid down in Taylor v. Hide, 1 Bur. 78, and in 89, 90, 111, 114; 3 T. R. 13-17. Per Lord Mansfield—"He who enters under it, can only be "possessed according to right. If he has a freehold, he is as a freeholder; if "he has a chattel interest he is in as a termor, and in respect of the freehold " his possession enures *according* to the *right*. If he has no title, he is in as a "trespasser, and without any re-entry by the true owner, is liable to account "for the profits."—13 M. & W. 13; Tew v. Jones.

The demise in Ausman's name is therefore sustained. But the plaintiff seeks to recover exclusively on the demise by Montgomery, in order to raise the question of *title* in him as against Ausman. He seems to have brought this action, and to have used Ausman's name as a lessor to fortify the case, and if the plaintiff is entitled to recover on either demise it is not usual to go further in order to settle the rights of different lessors, except as between the defendant and them, with reference to costs. It would be unreasonable to expect the court to determine Ausman's right as conflicting with Montgomery's claim, without hearing the parties as antagonists. Here they are ostensibly in the same interest appearing and heard by the same counsel, and that counsel contending for a valid title in Ausman, as against the defendant, and then in Montgomery as against Ausman, by virtue of the Sheriff's sale.—5 A. & E. 520; 4 N. & M. 381.

I find no cases in which the court has been called upon to interpose between the conflicting claims of the lessors, to possession, under an ejectment where the recovery has been on several demises; but of course as both lessors cannot be entitled to the possession, it may be proper to decide which of them is.

I see no reason why lands and tenements may not be sold under a *fi. fa.* for costs in ejectment, if saleable for costs at all; nor do I perceive any objection owing to the judgment being for costs in relation to this land. Ausman may have owned it when sold, though not when the ejectment was brought, and indeed it is so now held. The only difficulty arises out of the defendant's adverse possession before and at the time of the sale.

Gilb. Exon. 42, *Tit. Elejit*, says, "if a man be disseised against whom judg-"ment is recovered, the lands in the hands of the disseisor shall not be liable, "for though the disseisee has the right of possession, yet they are not his till "they be recovered.

Co. Lit. 222 (a); S. 358 (n). "If feoffee be disseised, and after bind himself "on a statute staple or merchant, or in a recognizance during the disseisin, "the land is not chargeable therewith, neither is the land in the hands of the "disseisor liable thereunto."—2 Co. 59; 8 Co. 62; 1 Roll Ab. 888; Com. Dig. Exon. B. 5.

Ausman himself could not have conveyed the land without a previous entry, and if not it could not be extended, and if not extendible, it is not saleable.—Doe ex dem. Dunn v. McLean, 1 Cameron, 150; Doe dem. West v. Howard, 2 Cameron, 270; Doe dem. Williams v. Evans, 1 M. Gr. & Scott, 717; 9 Jur. 712; 14 L. J. 237, C. P.; 2 Dowl. N. S. 694; 7 Jur. 375.

JONES, J., and McLEAN, J., concurred in granting a new trial.

Per Cur.—New trial: costs to abide the event.

DOE DEM. TALBOT V. PATERSON.

In regard to a survey made before the 50 Geo. III. ch. 14, the provisions of that Act will not have the effect of *necessarily* confining the grantee to the land designated by the posts planted in the original survey, if the plan of survey had been altered by the government before the issuing of the patent, and before the passing of that statute; therefore, when the government had added to the ends of the several concessions a strip of land which the surveyor had left unsurveyed between his concessions and the adjoining townships, and in consequence of such addition had changed the numbering of the lots throughout the concession—*Held*, that the patents issued in accordance with such reformed survey would cover the land which the government intended to be included within the boundaries expressed in the patent, though the number of lots would not correspond with the posts set by the surveyor.

Ejectment for Lot A, in the first concession, and Lot A, in the broken front on the River Thames, in the township of Aldborough.

Verdict for the defendant.

Becher, of London, moved for a new trial on the law and evidence, and for misdirection.

John Wilson, of London, shewed cause.

The facts of the case, and the arguments of counsel, fully appear in the judgment of the court, delivered by the Chief Justice.

ROBINSON, C. J., delivered the judgment of the court.

The defendant claimed the land under a title to him for the north half of Lot 1, in the first concession, and the broken front on the River Thames, in the township of Aldborough.

On the 17th of May, 1802, letters patent issued to Peter Green, for the north half of Lot 1, in the first concession, and broken front in the township of Aldborough—300 acres. The land was thus described: "Commencing where a "post has been planted in front of the first concession on the River Thames, "at the N.E. angle of the said lot; then south, forty-five degrees east, to the "centre of the first concession; then south, forty-five degrees west, twenty-"seven chains, seventy-five links, more or less to *the line of Orford;* then "north, forty-five degrees west, to the River Thames; and then easterly "along the shore to the place of beginning."

On the 26th of July, 1821, the crown granted to the lessor of the plaintiff Lot A, and the S.W. part of Lot B, according to Hambly's survey, in the broken front on the River Thames, in the township of Aldborough, containing 250 acres more or less, and Lot A in the first concession of the said township; which broken Lot A, and south-west part of B in the broken front, are bounded as follows: "Commencing on the River Thames at the westerly angle of the

"said Lot A ; then south, forty-five degrees east, seventy chains more or less
"to the allowance for road in front of the first concession ; then north, forty-
"five degrees east, fifty-five chains fifty links to Lawes' line ; then north,
"forty-five degrees west, twenty-two chains fifty links more or less to the River
"Thames ; then westerly along the water's edge with the stream to the place
"of beginning." And Lot A in the first concession is thus described : "Com-
"mencing in front of the said concession at the northerly angle of the said lot ;
"then south, forty-five degrees east, sixty-seven chains fifty links more or less
"to the allowance for road in the rear of the said concession; then south,
"forty-five degrees west, twenty-nine chains eighty links more or less to the
"southern limit of said lot; then north, forty-five degrees west, sixty-seven
"chains fifty links more or less to allowance for road in front of said con-
"cession ; then north, forty-five degrees east, twenty-nine chains eighty links
"more or less to the place of beginning."

The sole question is, whether the patent to Peter Green covers the land which the lessor of plaintiff claims, or not. If it does, it must of course prevail, being the elder grant ; and the patent issued in 1821 to the lessor of the plaintiff, would convey nothing. There has been evidently a confusion in the Surveyor General's office, which has led to the government issuing inconsistent patents. It appears that the government has, without including this patent to the lessor of the plaintiff, actually granted seventeen lots of 200 acres each, in the first concession of Aldborough, as lying between the township of Orford, and what is called the big bend of the River Thames ; whereas if the land granted to the lessor of the plaintiff in 1821, as Lot A, in the first concession, and broken front, is to be considered as not covered by any of the series of numbers, from one to seventeen inclusive, which have been described to other patentees, there would be but fifteen lots on the ground. In order to make out the seventeen lots, before reaching what is called the big bend of the River Thames, which is higher up the river, No. 1 must occupy the ground which has been called Lot A, in the patent to the lessor of the plaintiff. It was proved that in 1797, the Surveyor General gave his written instructions to Lawe, a surveyor, to lay out four concessions in the township of Aldborough, running from west to east ; the first being next to the River Thames. These written instructions are produced, but not the sketch referred to in them, and sent to Lawe for his guidance, and for the better explanation of the instructions. This sketch it is stated cannot be found, and for want of it some points in the instructions are obscure. It is plain, however, from the instructions, that beginning at a certain oil spring on the River Thames, Lawe was to scale the river upwards, till he should be at least two miles above a point referred to, as marked B on the sketch. Then he was to *ascertain, with as much precision as possible the station* C, and open a line from thence to Lake Erie, on a course south, forty-five degrees east, affixing a stone boundary at C. Where, or how he was to find the point C, is not intelligible for want of the sketch. Lawe was then directed to run concession lines, from this line between C and the lake, on a course north, forty-five degrees east ; making the lots in the concessions twenty nine chains eighty links wide, with a chain between every two concessions for a road. The instructions shew that a line to be run from a point A on the river to the lake, on a course south, forty-five degrees east,

DOE DEM. TALBOT V. PATERSON.   433

was intended to be the line from whence concession lines were to run easterly. Mr. Lawe made the survey, and reported that he had ascertained the oil spring to which the instructions referred, and had scaled up the river; but finding the station B higher up than he expected, he had "*removed to the distance of "about fifty-five chains fifty links higher up the river,*" and marked the post with the letter A, and with other marks as described. He then reports his course to Lake Erie, and describes the point on the shore at which he arrived in such a manner as that it can be always clearly ascertained where the southern termination of his line was, and about that I presume there is no doubt. He stated further, that he had laid out the concessions as directed, and represents the first concession as containing fifteen lots between the line which he had run from the point A to Lake Erie, and the big bend of the River Thames. He numbered these lots, it appears, by his field notes, from the western side line easterly, making Lot No. 1 the lot commencing at the point A, and No. 15 the lot lying next to the big bend of the river. The line thus laid down in the original survey of the township between the point A and the lake, seems to be well known to the witnesses examined on the trial as "Lawes line;" and there can be no doubt that he laid it down and reported it, according to his plan of operations, as the western boundary of his survey. It is evident also, that the government intended that the line which he was directed to run to the lake should be the western line of the survey, which he was instructed to make in Aldborough. The instructions directed him to run a line to Lake Erie, from a point marked B on the plan sent to him, which he was to ascertain; and also another line from a point C to the lake. But where these points A, B and C, referred to in the instructions for the survey, would stand on the ground, it is impossible to make out without the aid of the sketch. It seems clear, however, that the lines from the points A, B and C, were all intended by the Surveyor-General to constitute township lines; for he says expressly in his instructions, that the points A, B and C, are "to form *angles "of townships.*" If the Surveyor-General's instructions had been closely followed, it is plain that the point A would have formed the north-west angle of the township of Aldborough, and would have been at, or immediately near the oil spring described in the instructions as being at the corner of the Indian lands. In other words, the same point A would have formed on the west side of the line the N.E. angle of the township of Orford, for it is well understood and was assumed in the argument, that the Indian lands spoken of in the instructions composed the township of Orford. In the Act for the division of the Province passed in 1798, the Legislature speaks of the "*Moravian tract of "land called Orford.*" The name "Moravian tract" took its rise from the circumstance, that the Indians living on the tract were superintended by Moravian missionaries.

But Mr. Lawe departed from his instructions, not inadvertently, but for a reason which he assigns; and it is this deviation which seems not always to have been borne in mind by the government, or at least not to have been constantly allowed for, that has afforded ground for the dispute between the parties in this cause. He reports in his field notes, which have been always since in the possession of the government, and are now produced from the Surveyor-General's office, that he had adopted as his point A, not the oil spring referred to, but a point fifty-five chains, fifty links higher up on the bank of the river, that is, further to the east, in order to make his survey accord better, as he conceived, with the general tenor of his instructions. He had been induced to do this, as he says, from not finding the point B on the ground to correspond with its supposed position as marked on the sketch; though by what natural or other marks he was to find the point B on the ground does not appear. However this may be, the government was fully apprised of what Lawe had in fact done by his field notes, and as we must suppose by the plan of survey which accompanied them; though none such it seems has been discovered in the late search in the office; and in May, 1802, having, as it would seem reasonable to presume, these documents before them, the government made the patent to Green, under which the defendant claims, granting to him the north half of *one* in the first concession, and broken front of the township of Aldborough; in which patent they make the tract commence "*where a post* "*has been planted* in front of the first concession on the River Thames, at the "N.E. angle of the lot," (*i. e.* the Lot No. 1.) Now as the instructions to Lawe merely directed him to lay out lots from the point A easterly, of an equal width, one must infer, if there is nothing on the face of the patent inconsistent with it, that the government intended No. 1 to be the tract immediately adjacent to the line running down from A to Lake Erie, as Lawe had laid it out. He reports in his field notes, that he had laid out fifteen lots from that line to the big bend of the river, numbering from west to east. According to his survey, therefore, No. 1 was the first lot in that range, and lay in the N.W. angle of the tract surveyed by him. He had laid out no Lot A, and was not directed to lay out any, and he had left no vacant space between his western side line and the commencement of his range of numbered lots. If therefore it *must* be assumed, as the plaintiff's counsel has strenuously contended, that the government meant to grant to Green, in 1802, the lot and broken front forming the N.W. angle of Lawe's actual survey, or if the words of the patent must have effect according to what Lawe did actually lay down as his intended Lot No. 1, without regard to what the government, having their own instructions in view, rather than his survey, chose to regard as No. 1, and without conceding to the government any discretion to depart from his plan of survey in making their grants, then the case would be plainly with the plaintiff; for there is no room for doubt, after reading Lawe's field notes, that his Lot No. 1 did not cover the ground which the plaintiff claims, so that the patent to Green could not interfere with the right of the lessor of the plaintiff to what the government afterwards granted to him by the name of Lot A. Whether that is the conclusion to which the jury ought to have come, is the question for us to decide. The case is by no means a satisfactory one, upon the facts appearing before us. One would think that the Surveyor-General's office must contain documents which would throw more light upon it; but it is said that diligent search has been made, that no trace of any plan of Lawe's has been found, nor of the sketch referred to in the instructions sent to him, nor any plan on which the patents which the government had issued for lands in the first concession of Aldborough can be certainly shewn to have been founded. It is evident that there has been a confusion and inconsistency in the acts of the government, as they regard the land in dispute, by which of course we mean only the acts of the Surveyor-General. Mr. Lawe's survey differed from his instructions, and the descriptions of the Surveyor-General issued in 1802 and 1821, are not reconcilable with either of them, or with each other. What is to be the legal result of such errors, it is not always easy to determine. In contests about other matters turning upon mere pecuniary claims, whatever is just will in general be found to be legal; for the law in such actions has often the power of adjusting itself so as to meet the good conscience and real merits of the case; but where the claim is specific, as it is here, to certain property, and especially real property, there is seldom any discretion to be exercised by the jury or the court, according to their views of what may seem just between the parties. For the sake of certainty in questions of real property, there are rules established by which all parties must abide, whenever they clearly apply, though in some cases the effect of the rule may seem unreasonable under the particular circumstances. Where any palpable injustice may appear to be thrown on a party, in consequence either of the errors or misconduct of any public department, it may be proper to look for redress to the government or the legislature, or to seek it in some cases according to the facts, through a proper proceeding before a legal or equitable tribunal: but while the single question is pending, whether a particular piece of land is the property of A. or of B., that question must receive its decision upon legal evidence, and according to legal principles. In this case, with the patents and other documents which the jury had before them, it was impossible for them to doubt that the government intended to grant to Peter Green in 1802, and supposed they were granting to him, 300 acres of land, subtended by the eastern limit of Orford on the one side, by the River Thames on another side, and by a line drawn north, forty-five degrees east, from the eastern limit of Orford, through the centre of the first concession of Aldborough, on a third side; being the very land in dispute in this action, and which the defendant now claims to retain possession of, under that patent. It is not disputed in this case, that when the government made that grant, they had power to grant the land which I have so described, for it was still vacant, not having been before granted to the lessor of the plaintiff, or to any one. If then it is plain that the government did intend to grant to Green, in 1802, the land of which the defendant is now in possession, and if they had also the power at the time to grant it, it must follow that that land did pass by the patent, unless there be something on the face of the patent itself, which prevents its operating according to his apparent intention, or unless there be some other legal obstacle, apart from the patent, which must prevent the intention of the government from taking effect. When I say, that it is plain on the face of the patent and other documents, that the land described as granted to Green, was intended to be the tract which is in dispute in this action, I refer to the language of the description, which in express words carries the boundaries to the line of Orford. No doubt that line, supposing it to extend from the oil spring to Lake Erie, was not the line that Lawe had run; but it is equally clear, that the line which he did run, though he may have intended it for the west line of Aldborough, and may have supposed that the government would adopt it as such, was never intended by him to be laid down as the limit of Orford on the other side. On the contrary, he very clearly explained to the government in his field notes, that he was leaving a space of unsurveyed land of about fifty-five chains, fifty links in width, between the plot which he had laid out into lots, and the Orford line. Whether therefore the government had before them Lawe's actual survey or their own instructions, they could not have supposed that they were granting to Green a tract of land beginning at a point fifty-five chains and fifty links higher up the river than the oil spring, and yet joining the Orford line. On the contrary, the very mention in Green's patent of twenty-seven chains seventy-five links, as being the distance from the east, or upper side of the Lot No. 1, to the Orford line, is a strong circumstance to shew that the Surveyor-General must have had before him, or at least in his mind, the exact extent of the departure from his instructions which Lawe had reported he had made, for that is just half of the width of the space, (fifty-five chains, fifty links) which Lawe had left between the Orford line and his No. 1. The Surveyor-General therefore seems to have resolved to divide this space just equally into two lots of twenty-seven chains, seventy-five links wide, the first of which was granted to Green, leaving all the other lots, fifteen in number, which Lawe had run out between the point A and the big bend, to remain twenty-nine chains eighty links wide, as he had been instructed to run them, and as he had actually laid them out. It is true that the Surveyor-General, meaning, as I think, to describe just half of that unsurveyed space between Lawe's line and Orford, does not call it twenty-seven chains and seventy-five links absolutely and precisely, but adds the words "more or less." This, however, is no argument against what I am stating, because Lawe in his field notes reported that he had "removed to the distance of '*about*' fifty-five chains, "fifty links higher up the river," not binding himself to an exact distance, and therefore as I take it, the Surveyor-General, meaning in the description for Green's patent to embrace just half of that width, whatever it might be, thought it right to use the same latitude of expression. It would be strange indeed if the Surveyor-General, in 1802, had described land of which the survey had been reported to him in 1797, without referring to that survey. The description, I think, shews that he did refer to it; that he quite well understood that he was describing half of the space which Lawe had left between Orford and his western line, and that he therefore made that the breadth of the lot which he was describing, and not twenty-nine chains eighty links, which Lawe had made the width of his Lot No. 1, as well as of his other fourteen lots. When it is besides considered, that the government has actually granted patents for fifteen lots besides these two, or seventeen in all, as lying in the first concession between Orford and the big bend of the river, the conclusion seems clear that the Surveyor-General, knowing the true state of the case, resolved after receiving Lawe's survey, to take the fifty-five chains fifty links into the concession run out by Lawe, making two lots of it, and changing the numbers throughout the range, in order to designate the whole as one series of lots, from Orford upwards; and to describe them as if they had been in fact so surveyed. It was an arrangement that could as well be made in the office as on the ground, after the ground had been chained and with Lawe's notes before him; and I think the reasonable inference to be drawn from the whole evidence is, that the description inserted in Green's patent was framed with that intention. That the Surveyor-General's department has not acted throughout in a manner that can be reconciled with such intention is too clear, but no subsequent act of that department, or of the executive government, could destroy or diminish whatever right Green had acquired in 1802, under his patent. Nothing short of a legislative Act could have that effect. I do not conceive that the Surveyor-General, in his description, spoke of No. 1 as the lot which Lawe had marked with that number on his plan, but rather as the lot which, having Lawe's survey before him, he had determined should be No. 1, adding the fifty-five chains fifty links to the end of the concession, and dividing it, as it is plain he did, into lots.

The objections to our so construing Green's patent are, that it speaks of a post as "*having been planted at the N.E. angle* of the lot" which the crown was then granting as No. 1; and there is no evidence of any survey on the ground between Lawe's point A and Orford, nor any proof of any post having been planted to mark the N.E. angle of any Lot No. 1 in the broken front, except such as Lawe may be supposed to have planted at that angle of his No. 1. That is very true, and it would appear to create a difficulty even, as to what might have been the intention of the government with respect to the No. 1, if we did not know, as every one at all conversant with such matters must know, for it has often been in proof before us judicially, that the descriptions in patents do in a number of instances refer to posts as planted and profess to start from them as points of departure, when in fact no such posts had been planted, nor any actual survey made in detail, though the exterior lines had been run, so as to ascertain how many lots there would be room for. If in this case the Surveyor-General must be supposed to be really and actually referring to the post planted by Lawe on the N. E. side of his No. 1, then there would be this gross inconsistency in his description, that he would be giving twenty-seven chains fifty-five links as the distance from that side of No. 1 to the Orford line, when it would be in fact eighty-five chains and thirty links, being the whole breadth of the fifty-five chains and fifty links added to twenty-nine chains and eighty links, the width of Lawe's No. 1. But it is contended that whatever the crown may have intended, still as the patent refers to the post at the N. E. angle of No. 1 in the broken front, that necessarily binds the grantee to the only post that was in fact planted to mark that angle of No. 1; and this objection is founded on the statute 58th Geo. III. ch. 14. But in the first place, that statute only makes the posts decisive as governing the breadth of the lot, when there is no dispute about the identity of the lot itself; it does not in its effect declare, that whatever had in any survey before that Act been marked as No. 1, should be No. 1, whatever changes the government may have made in the plan of survey after the posts had been planted, and before that Act was passed; and we have indeed already decided in several cases, that the legislature, by the Act 58th Geo. III. ch. 14, only intended to establish all original monuments of survey as they had been allowed by the government to stand, as they were then recognized; otherwise the statute would have had the effect of restoring many erroneous surveys that had been corrected, and would have produced great confusion and injury by reviving and giving permanence to surveys which the government had abandoned, substituting more convenient arrangements for them. There was nothing before that Act to prevent the government from remodelling a plan of survey after it had been reported to them, by changing the numbers of lots, and the divisions of ascertained spaces, and in regard to any case in which they had done so, it cannot be supposed that the legislature meant by the Act 58th Geo. III. chap. 14, to reverse such arrangements after the government had acted on them. There could be no motive for intending to do so. It must have inevitably created great confusion and injury to patentees ; and the language of the Act does not compel such a construction.

Another difficulty that has been raised is, that Green's patent grants land "in the first concession, and broken front *of Aldborough;*" that we cannot by law go out of the concession, and still less out of the township, to find the land; and that the concession and the township must be taken to be such as they were laid out in the original survey. But this again rests upon a more strict construction of the statute 58th Geo. III. chap. 14, than this court has hitherto given to it. As to the township line of Aldborough, it had not been made an unalterable boundary by setting up monuments, under any proceeding taken under the statute 38th Geo. III. chap. 1. The government clearly intended by their instructions to Lawe, that it should join Orford, and when they found that he left a vacant space between the western end of his concession and Orford, they could still, if they pleased, make that vacant space part of Aldborough, even if they could not have made it part of the concession. Then again, as to the concession, the government could, if they pleased, add this strip of land to the concession, and could divide it and designate it as they chose. Indeed, as the plaintiff's patent, no less than the defendant's, grants the land as being "*in the first concession, and broken front of Aldborough,*" he could not recover in this action, if both the township and concession must be held to be bounded by Lawe's survey, and if all the land beyond that must be excluded as not being in Aldborough, On the whole, we are of opinion, that the verdict of the jury was consistent with the evidence, without resorting to any proofs about the reception of which there can be any question. It would have been satisfactory if more particulars had been shewn respecting the patents which have issued for the other lots in the first concession, particularly for Fleming's lot, which Lawe notices in his field notes, making it correspond with his No. 4, and which I apprehend the government has nevertheless granted as No. 6, thereby making 1 and 2 different from what Lawe had called them in this instance also, and shewing that Lawe's numbers had been changed by taking in two additional lots between Orford and his point A. This seems, however, clearly enough proved, by the government having actually granted by an old patent the lot next to the big bend as Lot 17, when according to Lawe's numbering it would be 15. How the possession of the land in dispute had been actually held, from what period the land has been cultivated, and by whom, does not appear ; but this defendant claiming under Green's patent is in actual possession, or this action would have been unnecessary. If the plaintiff under his later patent were to dispossess him, the defendant could find no land that Green's patent would cover. The lot called No. 1 by Lawe has been granted, it appears, to one Scram, whether by a patent earlier or later than Green's was not proved, but it seems to have been granted to Scram as No. 3. This is the land which, according to what the plaintiff contends for, must have been intended to be covered by Green's patent, or at least must be held to be so. The broken front between Lot No. 1, in the first concession (calling that No. 1 which lies next to the Orford line), is very nearly as large as a full lot, or 200 acres; and added to the half lot in the first concession, which is granted along with it (as the defendant contends) in Green's patent, it makes up the 300 acres which was the quantity expressed to be granted to him. On the other hand, the broken front between the lot which Lawe laid out as No. 1 and the river is but a trifling piece of land of a few acres, and if the defendant could dispossess Scram, and hold these two pieces of land under Green's patent, he would still have not more than half as much, I believe, as his patent professes to grant, and would have a tract which, instead of coming up to the line of Orford, as Green's patent expresses, would not be within half a mile of it in the nearest part. These are strong circumstances to shew, that to give such an effect to Green's patent would be quite inconsistent with what the government intended when they made the grant. Then it is to be besides considered, that by the same rule by which we should hold the No. 1, mentioned in Green's patent, to be the identical lot which Lawe had called No. 1 in his field notes, we must also hold that the patentees of the other lands between Lawe's No. 1 and the bend of the river, must hold according to his numbers, and this would leave no land at all to the grantees of Lots 16 and 17, and would probably change the possessions throughout, so far as possession may have been taken, and this although many, if not the whole of these lots, may, for all we know, have been granted under the present understood numbers, before the patent was made to the lessor of the plaintiff, in 1821. Unless we could see that the case was so clearly in favour of the plaintiff, as to be absolutely free from all doubt, and unless we could say that the jury has been misdirected, which we do not think they were in any respect, we should certainly do wrong, if we were to grant a new trial for the purpose of giving such an effect to the latter patent as must produce so much injury and confusion; at the same time, it does seem unaccountable that the Surveyor-General, after giving the evidence, which he seems to have done by the description in Green's patent, that he was aware of the space between Lawe's line and Orford, and intended to embrace part of it in that description, should have described the same land for grant to the lessor of the plaintiff in 1821, though under a different name, as if it were still vacant and grantable. And the perplexity is still greater, when it is proved, as it was on this trial, that in 1803, the next year after the patent had issued to Green, the government instructed Hamblin, another surveyor, to survey the remaining part of Aldborough; and in their written instructions to Hamblin, they speak of Lawe's line as the western line of Aldborough, and they directed him to lay out the space west of that (fifty-five chains and fifty links), and take it into the township of Aldborough, marking the post on the south side of the Thames at the north-west angle of this small tract, A. O.; on the one side for Aldborough, and on the other for Orford. This intermediate act, however, of the government, taken by itself, seems to strengthen the conviction that the government did intend their patent to Green to cover the land which the defendant contends for, as they surely could not have forgotten that only the year before they had actually granted the land up to the Orford line as being in Aldborough; and they would hardly have directed this survey with the view of granting the same land to another person: they merely intended by it, as I should infer, to complete the survey of the ground, as they had by anticipation completed it on paper. They already knew the outlines; they had resolved to take this small strip in at the end of the concession; they had already granted it as if it formed a part of the concession, numbering the lots accordingly; and it was reasonable that they should give directions to have the land staked out on the ground in a manner to correspond with their official arrangements, and to remove the corner post of the township, from where Lawe had planted it of his own accord, to the point where they had originally designed it to be, and where they had assumed it to be by their patent to Green, issued only the year before. Taken by itself, therefore, as I have said, the directing Hamblin to make such a survey, in 1803, would confirm the opinion, that they intended, by their patent to Green, to grant him the land which the defendant claims, and wished to have in the office an actual survey corresponding with what they had done in anticipation of it, shewing the township line on the ground to be where they had in Green's patent assumed it to be. But there is this great apparent inconsistency with this supposed intention, that in 1821 they make this grant to the lessor of the plaintiff, which most clearly does embrace the very land now in dispute, and in which they call the same tract lot A, and treat it as if it had remained to that time vacant and ungranted. How to reconcile this contradiction is a question which the Surveyor-General's office may have some means of shewing, but we do not yet see it accounted for; and the difficulty is increased by the circumstance, that the survey made by Hamblin, in 1803, is said, in the written instructions from the Surveyor-General, to have been made at the request of Colonel Talbot, the lessor of the plaintiff, to whom, eighteen years afterwards, the land in question was granted. This would look as if the survey had been made rather with a view to the future grant (though it followed at so long an interval) than in order to confirm the past. But still these facts remain, that in 1802 the crown had really granted to Green the 300 acres next to the Orford line, in express words; that Lawe's line was never treated by the government as the boundary of Orford, nor ever so considered or understood by any one, as the evidence proved; and that the area of the grant, and the length of the lines, as expressed in the patent, shew clearly that it was the line run, or supposed to be run, from the oil spring to the lake, that the government then considered as the Orford line, and not the line east of it, which Lawe had actually run.

The facts proved, in our opinion, entitle Green's patent to prevail, as being the elder grant, and covering the land in question. If there are other public documents, or proofs of any kind, which can place the matter on a different footing, this verdict in ejectment will not be conclusive; but as the case stands, we think the verdict right, and that the rule for a new trial must be discharged.

Per Cur.—Rule for new trial discharged.

MACDONALD V. WEEKS ET AL.

Since the repeal of the Act 7 Vic. ch. 31, *Held* that recognizances taken under its authority are not binding upon the bail, except in regard to cases in which the debtor has been notified, and has made default, while the Act was still in force.

MACAULAY, J., *dissentiente.*

Debt on recognizance of bail. The declaration averred a recognizance of bail to have been duly acknowledged before a commissioner of this court, after the passing of the statute 7 Vic. ch 31, and before its repeal, to wit, on the 7th February, 1845, conditioned that if the defendant in the original action should be condemned, &c., *and* should neglect and refuse to pay the costs and condemnation, *or* to appear personally in open court of this court, or before any judge or commissioner of the said court when thereunto required by notice, &c., at least twenty days previously, and there to answer such questions or interrogatories as should be propounded to him touching his lands, tenements, moneys, rights and credits, then the defendants (the bail) should pay the same, which said recognizance was filed in the office of the Deputy Clerk of the Crown in the district where taken, according to the statute, *as by the record thereof* in said court, &c., doth fully appear. The declaration then averred, that the Deputy Clerk of the Crown of the district in which the recognizance was filed, before final judgment, to wit, on the first day of May, 1845, transmitted the said recognizance to the Home Office, when it was *filed of record* in the said court, as by the record thereof still remaining, &c., fully appears. The plaintiffs then averred recovery of judgment afterwards, to wit, on the 19th day of November, 1845, and notice to appear, &c., served, to wit, on 29th November, on Monday, the 22nd of December, 1845, before Christopher Alexander Hagerman, a judge of this court, &c., then and there to answer such interrogatories as should be propounded to the said debtor touching his lands, tenements, *goods, chattels,* moneys, rights and credits, &c., upwards of twenty days, &c. Breach, non-appearance to answer in the terms last aforesaid.

Demurrer, that the recognizance declared upon was not legal.

Campbell, of Kingston, for the demurrer. He relied upon 2 Cam. Rep. 276; 9 B. & C. 752; 6 Bing. 582; 8 A. & E. 405.

Kenneth McKenzie, of Kingston, *contra,* cited 6 A. & E. 943; 8 M. & W. 234; 9 Dowl. 200; 2 Mod. 210; Dwarris on Statutes, page 670.

ROBINSON, C. J.—Upon the best consideration that I can give this case, I consider that this declaration cannot be sustained. The recognizance is not only founded upon a statute which is repealed, but the action is brought for a non-compliance with a condition which, though good at law when it was entered into, could not be legally enforced at the time when the performance was exacted, because the statute was repealed which authorized such a proceeding as was contemplated in the condition. By the law as it stood before the 9th December, 1843, when 7th Vic. ch. 31 was passed, the condition of a recognizance of bail was, "that if the defendant in the action shall be condemned, "he will satisfy the costs and condemnation money or render himself to the "custody of the sheriff, or that the bail shall do so for him." While that form of recognizance was used the defendant could be taken in execution for the debt; and the bail knew and understood that they were in effect undertaking that his person should be forthcoming after judgment, or he or they must pay the debt; and they could only be liable in case they could not be ound. By 7 Vic. ch. 31, it was provided that thenceforward no person should be taken or charged in execution, *whether he shall have been held to bail or otherwise;* and it is further provided (by the 6th section) that if the defendant in any action shall upon examination on oath in open court, or before a commissioner, appear to have acted fraudulently in contracting the debt or evading satisfaction, or shall refuse to make a full discovery of his lands, goods, chattels, credits, &c., the court may commit him to the common gaol until he complies with their order, or for such period as the court may think reasonable, not exceeding a year; such commitment not to operate as a discharge of the judgment. And to suit this new condition of the law as regarded the debtor, it was enacted that the condition of the recognizance should thenceforward be, " that if the defendant shall be condemned in the action, and shall neglect and " refuse to pay the costs and condemnation money, *or to appear personally in* " *open court, or before any judge or commissioner of the court wherein the bail* " *shall be taken,* when thereunto required by notice to be left with either of " such bail and with the defendant, or at his last place of abode, twenty days " before the day on which he shall be required to appear, there to answer such "interrogatories as shall be propounded to him touching his lands, goods, " chattels, moneys, rights, or credits, then and in such case the bail will pay " the costs and condemnation for him." And the statute further provides, "that it shall be lawful for the court wherein any such recognizance shall " have been entered, or for a judge thereof in vacation, after any defendant " shall have submitted to any such examination, or in case no examination " shall be had within two terms after judgment shall have been signed " in any such cause, then upon hearing the parties, to order in their discre- " tion an *exoneretur* to be entered upon such bail-piece." Then on the 29th March, 1845, the legislature, by statute 8 Vic. ch. 48, reciting that it was expedient to repeal the above Act 7 Vic. ch. 31, and at the same time to afford protection to honest debtors, by establishing a system of proceeding for the relief of such as were insolvent without fraud or culpable negligence, enact that the 7th Vic. ch. 31, "*shall be and the same is thereby repealed.*" This statute creates in effect an insolvent debtor's court, to be held in each district by the judge or the commissioners in bankruptcy, who may examine into each case, and give orders of protection from arrest, and may discharge debtors from execution, according to circumstances. The effect of this statute, in repealing the Act 7 Vic. ch. 31, was to restore the law to its former footing in regard to the suing out execution against the body upon any judgment for debt, except as to the affidavit required to be made for that purpose, in which an alteration is required by the 44th clause of this Act, making it correspond with that prescribed by the same Act for suing out mesne process. The recognizance in this case is stated to have been entered into while the 7th Vic. ch. 31 was in force, and before its repeal, viz., 7th Feb., 1845. It is further averred that it was transmitted to the crown office 1st May, 1845, to be filed of record; that plaintiff recovered judgment on 19th Nov., 1845; that on 29th Nov., 1845, notice was given by plaintiff to appear on the 22nd Dec., 1845, before one of the judges, to answer interrogatories touching his lands, goods, chattels, &c., by service on one of the bail, and by leaving it at the last place of abode of Whelan, the debtor : and the breach of the recognizance charged is, "that Whelan did not appear before the judge on the 22nd December, "1845, there to answer such interrogatories which plaintiff was then and there "ready to propound to Whelan before the said judge, touching his lands, &c., "according to the form and effect of the recognizance and notice, but therein "made default ; nor hath Whelan paid the costs and condemnation money, or "any part thereof, according to the recognizance ; nor have the bail paid the "same according to the recognizance, and that the said judgment and recog- "nizance remain in full force, not satisfied or discharged ; whereby an action "has accrued to the plaintiff, to have from the defendants the costs and con- "demnation money—(£28 14s. 0d.)."

The defendants demur, assigning several causes ; the most substantial being, that since the repeal of the statute under which the recognizance was taken, it no longer remains in the power of the plaintiff to sue upon the recognizance, and to claim the debt and costs by reason that the debtor did not appear and answer interrogatories, there being, after the repeal of the statute, no law under which the plaintiff in the case could call upon the defendants to appear and answer interrogatories. Some perplexity has been occasioned by the legislature having merely repealed the statute, without making any provision for carrying on to a conclusion, as before, any proceedings in cases in which recognizances had been taken under the Act, or making any other provision for obviating difficulties. This is not like the case in 3 Taunton, 46, of Clark v. Hoppe et al., because there the bail were in difficulty, from the neglect of the defendant to plead (as he might have done) his bankruptcy and certificate in discharge. It was contended that the bail could not be in a better condition than their principal, and could not therefore have the benefit of a matter of discharge of which he had neglected to avail himself. The court admitted "that bail in every case put themselves in hazard of suffering by the *folly and* "*negligence* of the defendant ;" but nevertheless they did on that occasion afford equitable relief to the bail upon motion, after some hesitation. In this case the question does not arise upon the effect of any act or omission of the debtor, but upon its having been rendered impossible by law for the plaintiff in the original action to have the advantage of the condition of the recog- nizance ; that proceeding being now placed by law out of the power of the plaintiff, which it was the very object of the recognizance to secure. I con- ceive the effect of the recognizance, when it was entered into, to be wholly different from that of a condition on a bond to do either of two things ; that is, whichever of the two the obligor or the obligee may choose. There, if the performance of one of them has become impossible, we may assume that he must perform the other. This is not a condition in the alternative that the cognizor shall do one of two things ; it is a condition that, if a third party does not pay a certain debt, or appear before a judge to answer interrogatories, then the cognizor *will pay the debt, &c., for him*. The cognizor has only one thing to do ; but that is to be done or not according as the third party shall do one or other of the two things which at the time were incumbent upon him by law ; and the question arises, not upon a contract made by one individual with another, which the parties may shape as they like to suit their own purposes— it is an obligation in the terms of an Act of Parliament—a step in a cause, with a view to certain legal proceedings and results, always under the control of the legislature. While the recognizance and the Act under which it was taken were in full force, the plaintiff could not have sued the bail merely because the defendant had not paid the debt, for they were only to be liable in case he neither paid the debt nor appeared upon notice to answer interrogatories. The plaintiff could not at his option have forborne to examine the defendant, and yet have called on the bail to pay the debt because the defendant had not paid it. He might of course omit as long as he pleased or wholly to examine the defendant, and might take his chance of enforcing payment from him as he could; but while he took this course he would have no right to look to the bail, because they had not undertaken absolutely to pay the debt if the defendant did not, but to pay it if he did not either pay it or attend upon notice to answer interrogatories. The attending to answer interrogatories was, by 7th Vic. ch. 31, put in the place of the liability to be taken on a *ca. sa.* and imprisoned—a liability which the legislature had by that Act put an end to; and the plaintiff, under this new form of recognizance, could no more call on the bail to pay the debt, without first notifying the defendant to attend and be examined on interrogatories, than a plaintiff could formerly have called on the bail to pay the debt without first suing out a *ca. sa.* against the defendant. If, after the old law of imprisonment for debt had been abolished, a plaintiff had called upon bail who had entered into a recognizance in the old form to pay the debt, claiming that to be the necessary consequence of his being no longer able to imprison his debtor, he must have failed in my opinion, because the bail had entered into no undertaking that could bind them absolutely to pay the money, but only in case the defendant did not render himself or pay the money, and then in case they should not render him. They might say truly, "neither the defendant nor we can comply with the condition of render-"ing, because the defendant cannot legally be imprisoned; our undertaking "was intended only to secure your having his person, which has now become "impossible by the law of the land, and by no fault of ours." So I think the bail here may with some reason say, that the recognizance was given only to secure the defendants' attending to answer interrogatories; and though that proceeding has been abolished, so that the condition in that respect cannot legally be exacted, yet that has not legally or reasonably thrown upon the bail a liability which they never contemplated; namely, a liability to pay the debt at all events. The legislature could never have intended to place the bail in that situation; for that would be transforming their undertaking into one which it could never be thought reasonable to exact in such cases, and which would seldom or never be given. Persons may be found willing enough to undertake that a debtor shall remain in the country, and attend at court when called upon; but few would consent to engage absolutely to pay his debt for him. The proviso in 7 Vic. ch. 31, sec. 6, that the court might in its discretion order an *exoneretur* to be entered on the bail-piece, if the plaintiff should not examine the defendant on interrogatories within two terms after judgment, shews very clearly that all the legislature meant to afford the plaintiff was a reasonable opportunity to propose his interrogatories, and to have his debtor confined if he could be shewn to have acted fraudulently. This recognizance, we must notice judicially, was taken with no other view, and it can be made no other use of. When it was taken, imprisonment for the debt, unless there had been fraud, could not have been contemplated by the parties; and the recognizance cannot be used for enforcing it or any substitute for it. The proceeding which it had in view has been abolished by law; no such examination upon interrogatories could now take place—it would be extra-judicial. But we have not, therefore, the power to treat this recognizance as if it had contemplated an imprisonment, not with a view•to examination, but an imprisonment in satisfaction. The legislature has left the plaintiff, in suits that were pending, with a useless recognizance upon his hands, by putting an end to the practice with which it was inseparably connected, and they inadvertently omitted to provide for the inconveniences to which they would leave him exposed. We cannot meet the case by enlarging the undertaking of the bail, in order to make it produce the same effect to the plaintiff as if they had engaged that the defendant should be surrendered to be detained in execution.

I think, when the legislature directed that the court may enter an *exoneretur* if the plaintiff delays examining the defendant, thus giving to the court a discretion in that respect after hearing the parties, they shew plainly their intention that, as the bail had only been given in order to insure the opportunity for such examination, the plaintiff must be made to use the opportunity in a reasonable time, or lose the only benefit contemplated by the recognizance. What might be reasonable time they left to be judged of according to the facts that might be shewn in each case. When, from a change in the law, the defendant can never be examined, that new law, I think, by consequence, discharges the bail as clearly as they would have been discharged if the defendant had died. The substance and intention of the condition is, that the defendant shall attend and be examined, not merely that he shall attend on pretence that he is to be examined, when by law he cannot be. The giving notices by the plaintiff to the debtor and the bail, as set out in the declaration, were all nugatory acts, steps taken in the cause contrary to law, and which the defendant was not bound to attend to. The plaintiff, when he got judgment in November, 1845, had all the advantage of the old law which was restored on the repeal of the other, and could take out execution under it against the defendant's person. If he did so, and could not find him, and on that account seeks his remedy against the bail, he is seeking his remedy not because the defendant was not to be had to answer to interrogatories, but because he was not there to be imprisoned in satisfaction, which the bail never undertook he should be. The bail may have been willing to answer for the one, when they would not have answered for the other.

I am of opinion, that the necessary legal consequences of the repeal of the Act 7 Vic. ch. 31, was that the recognizances taken under it were of no use, except in regard to cases in which the debtor had been notified and had made default while the Act was still in force. The case of Hardy v. Hall et al., 2 Cameron, 60, in effect, I think, decides this. If the 7th Vic. ch. 31, had provided for the examination of the defendant before a particular tribunal, and the subsequent Act had abolished that tribunal, the effect would have been to discharge the bail from the recognizance as much as if the defendant had died, which would undoubtedly have discharged them; and the abolishing the proceeding is, in my judgment, the same in its effect. All that by the law, and by the recognizance itself, it was intended to secure by this recognizance, has now been made impossible by act of law; and it is attempted by this action to make the bail in consequence pay the money, as if they had undertaken to do so absolutely. And this injustice would follow, if we were to hold the action sustainable, that the plaintiff might decline to take out a *ca. sa.*, and yet collect the debt from the bail, who would have no power to surrender the defendant. With respect to the effect of the repeal of the 17th Vic. ch. 31, in putting an end to all further examinations upon interrogatories, in order to establish fraud, there can be no doubt upon that point—the judge could no longer make orders under that statute. If the former Act had directed the judge to make an order for the defendants' examination, and appointed a day, and if the recognizance had been framed accordingly, then I should think it clear that the judge could no longer make the order after the Act had been repealed, and the plaintiff would have lost all benefit from his recognizance; and if the judge had made the order it would be illegal, and the effect would have been the same. Taking the Act and recognizance as they are, the same reasoning and principle, I think, apply to them. I see it is stated in the declaration, that the notice to the defendant to appear on the 22nd December, (nine months after the Act was repealed, and the whole proceeding by examination abolished,) was served on him at his last place of abode, from which I infer, that he may have absconded after judgment was entered, or perhaps long before; and that plaintiff not being able to take him on a *ca. sa.*, which would have been then his plain course, has supposed that by calling upon him in his absence to attend and be examined, he would be able to fix the bail by his default; but that would be turning to one purpose the recoguizance taken for another; the bail never undertook that he would be present for the purpose of being imprisoned on a *ca. sa.*, but only that he would attend to be examined according to law on interrogatories or pay the money, and when the law no longer permitted the plaintiff to call upon him for that purpose, the defendant could not make default in that undertaking, and it was only in case he should fail in both conditions that the bail could become liable. It is true that the defendant might have gone before a judge and tendered himself for examination; but it would have been a mere idle intrusion. I think we are bound to say, that the performance of the condition had become impossible without the concurrence of any act or omission of the debtor. He would be justified in declining to comply with any notice served on him to appear and answer interrogatories, because the administering them would be contrary to law; and the intent and effect of the recognizance was only to make the bail liable if the defendant did not fulfil that particular condition. When the debtor is discharged, by matter which he could plead, his bail are discharged also. That the repeal of the statute need not be pleaded is clear, for we are bound to notice it. It is a change in the public law of the land, not a matter *in pais*, like the death of the debtor, which the court cannot judicially know, and which therefore the bail must plead. In Whitbread v. Brockhurst, 1 Br. Ch. Ca. 409, the Lord Chancellor observes with respect to a plea setting up the statute of frauds as a defence, "perhaps it would have been better to have demurred, for though the course "of the court has been to admit these pleas of the statute, I do not see the "reason of it, as it is a public statute."

The facts which give rise to this question are novel; they arise from the accidental omission of the legislature to save to the parties the power of proceeding under the repealed statute in cases then pending, or to make any other provision for such cases. We cannot expect to find English decisions bearing on the point; and as we have not all been able to concur in the same view of the legal consequences of the repeal of the statute, under which this recognizance was taken, we have endeavoured during our discussion to place the question in all its aspects. Among other things, we have considered that if neither these defendants, nor any one else, had become bail for the debtor, he must have gone to gaol, and the plaintiff would have had him then in custody at the time of the Act being repealed. Would he then have been entitled to be discharged? If, under the state of the law previous to the statute 7th Vic. chap 31, there had been no process of execution against the person of a debtor, and if that Act had first allowed an arrest, and that only for the purpose of insuring the debtor being forthcoming to answer interrogatories, then when that proceeding was abolished, all authority to detain him must of course have ceased, as his imprisonment under the facts as they stood would have been solely with a view to that proceeding. I am not prepared at present to say, that his discharge from imprisonment must not, at any rate, have followed the repeal of the Act, the plaintiff being left to sue out a *ca. sa.* against him under the revived law upon a proper affidavit; but admitting this to be otherwise, the plaintiff might then argue, that as the repeal of the Act of 1843, by reviving the old law, would have enabled him to detain the person of the debtor in satisfaction of his debt, he ought not to be placed in a worse situation in consequence of these defendants having saved him from imprisonment by becoming bail for him, and that the effect of the recognizance should therefore be to make them liable, because their principal has withdrawn. But this seems to me to be no sound legal deduction. The legislature, we may admit, ought to have taken care that the plaintiff did not suffer from having taken the peculiar kind of recognizance required by the statute which they were about to repeal; but their omission to provide for the case cannot have the effect of extending the liability of the bail beyond their undertaking, and surely nothing could be more unjust than that, because the legislature has changed the law, the bail should be treated as if they had bound themselves to pay the debt or surrender the debtor in execution, when they had only undertaken to pay the debt in case the debtor, being duly notified (which after the repeal of the Act he never could be) to appear in court to answer interrogatories, should fail to do so. It is not an imaginary difference, but a very substantial one; for a person, relying on the integrity of a friend who has been unfortunate, and not doubting that he will be at all times ready when notified to give an account, according to the truth, of his property and circumstances, might be quite willing to undertake for that on his behalf, though he might refuse to assume the responsibility of his remaining in the country, subject to the risk of being taken in execution, and imprisoned in satisfaction of the debt.

The decisions, that bail cannot plead the bankruptcy and certificate of the debtor in their discharge, do not appear to be applicable; for, in the first place, the matter of discharge does not arise there from the mere operation of the general law of the land, irrespective of anything done or omitted by the debtor—it arises from his insolvency; and, in the next place, as the court in Donnelly v. Dunn, 2 B. & P. 47, observes, the certificate is no legal defence, for the debtor may be rendered to prison notwithstanding, and may not choose to avail himself of his certificate. The Bankrupt Act merely enables him to procure his discharge on application, if he chooses to apply; the bail are not disabled from discharging the condition of their recognizance. Mr. Justice Buller in that case remarks, "that the bail must shew a legal impossibility to "perform the condition of the recognizance, or state something that will dis- "charge them." Whatever is a legal bar must of course discharge them. Now, how can it be said here that the debtor *neglected* to appear upon notice before a judge to answer interrogatories to be proposed to him? It was no *neglect* to decline attending for the purpose of a proceeding which had been placed out of the plaintiff's power by law. It was no default of the debtor to go where he pleased, after the Act was repealed. The bail had no power to restrain or prevent him; he was at liberty to do so by law, and in point of form the bail did not become liable in case *he did not attend* simply, though the breach is assigned in those words, but only in case, being notified, which must mean legally notified, he should refuse or neglect to attend, and he did neither. The case of Worlick v. Massey, Cro. Jac. 67, is a strong case to shew that it is the object and intended effect of a recognizance, according to the known course of proceedings and practice, which the court are to regard; and surely it would be departing from that principle if such an effect were to be given to this recognizance, as to make the bail liable for the debtor because the debtor did not render himself in execution, when at the time of their entering into the recognizance, a render in execution could not have been contemplated, either by the plaintiff or by the bail, because the law did not permit it. Under the law, as it stood before 7 Vic., the condition of the recognizance was, that the debtor should pay the debt, or render himself, or the bail would do it for him. It is in the same form again now; and if, while a recognizance in this form is in force, the legislature should pass an Act abolishing imprisonment for debt, and making no provision for cases pending, the effect of that would be that the debtor could not render himself, nor could the bail render him, because he could not be legally detained in custody; but I do not consider that in consequence the bail could be compelled to pay the debt. The Act of the legislature, preventing the defendant being taken in execution, would be as clear an impediment to his being rendered as his death would be; and the late Act of Parliament in this case is, in my opinion, as absolute a bar to any pro- ceedings under the statute which it repeals; the one would be an impossibility created by the act of God, the other an impossibility created by the law; they both stand on the same principle as to their legal effect in discharging the bail; they neither of them are in any degree occasioned by the act of the debtor, and neither is a contingency of such a kind as the bail can be con- sidered to have insured against.

The cases of the debtor becoming insolvent, or a lunatic, or being sent away as an alien, or becoming a peer, or member of the House of Commons, or being transported as a felon, all are very distinguishable. Those are changes in the personal condition of the debtor for whom the bail undertook, and they are risks against which the bail may with some reason be held to have insured the plaintiff. They shew that the plaintiff, by something personal that has occurred to the debtor, connected with his own conduct or *status*, has not that advantage of satisfaction from his person which by the law of the land he might have against other debtors, and which he was to have had against him. Of some of those the court has said (what cannot be said here), that they are risks for which the bail had undertaken : in others of those cases the court will relieve the bail upon their application, and upon their shewing that they have not been indemnified by the debtor, and have not had the means placed in their hands of paying the debt. In the case before us, the circumstance which ought to exonerate the bail, is a change in the public law of the land, abolishing the proceeding which the bail undertook the plaintiff should have the benefit of, so far as depended on the debtor being present to be the object of that proceeding. This is, in my opinion, as effectual a legal bar to the plaintiff's making any use of that recognizance, as if the statute had in express words made void the recognizance itself. Lord Coke, in his first Institute, 206, says, "a bond or recognizance is a thing in action and executory, whereof "no advantage can be taken until there be a default in the obligor; and there- "fore in all cases where a condition of a bond or recognizance is possible at the "time of the making the condition, and before the same can be performed, "the condition becomes impossible, by *the act of God or of the law*, or of the "obligee, then the obligation is saved." I think it is so here, and that defendants are entitled to judgment on the demurrer (a).

MACAULAY, J.—The principal objection is, that the statute under which the recognizance was given is repealed. It was repealed on the 29th of March, 1845, and though the dates in the declaration are all laid under a *videlicet*, it may be assumed that it was entered into before the repeal of the Act, and filed in the District Office before that period, but transmitted to the Home Office and enrolled afterwards, and that the judgment was obtained afterwards, and the notice to appear given afterwards. The question is, whether under such circumstances the recognizance is avoided. The defendants contend that it is, upon the ground, that by act of law, in the repeal of the Act, it became *impossible* for them to perform that part of the condition which undertook for the appearance of the debtor, and one argument is, that after the repeal of the Act, it was no longer in the defendants' power to take the debtor *nolens volens*, and surrender him or compel him to appear according to the notice alleged.

It is quite clear, that when entered into, the recognizance was duly authorized by a statute then in force, and it is not objected that the bail was not regularly entered, and the recognizance duly filed and enrolled, and while it remains in that state, I must look upon it as a recognizance, legal and valid, binding at

(a) Bac. Ab. Condition, N.

the time it was acknowledged, and that it has been adopted and recorded by the court, and constitutes thereby an obligation of the highest kind.

The repeal of the statute did not put an end to the recognizance necessarily so as to *discharge* the bail. If it did, the enrolment would be irregular, and still it is suffered to remain ; and there are cases in the books of recognizances not dissimilar in terms entered into apart from an arrest, or any statutes, supported when necessary by adequate consideration, not essential when it is of *record*, though it is here implied, being the enlargement of the debtor on bail.-- 1 Bing. N. R. 444, Atkinson v. Baynton ; Sayer, 186-7, Hesketh v. Gray ; 5 Co. 21-2, Laughter's Case ; Yel. 207, Rosse v. Pye ; T. Ray. 373, Topham v. Parnell.

The statute 2 Geo. IV. chap. 1, sec. 8, prescribed the form of affidavit to entitle a plaintiff to hold the defendant to bail. Sec. 11 provided that every recognizance of bail should be, that if the defendant should be condemned in the action, he should satisfy the condemnation money or render himself to the custody of the sheriff, &c., or that the bail should do it for him, being in substance the usual condition in like cases in England. 7 Vic. chap. 31, did not expressly repeal this Act, but superseded its provisions, and by sec. 1 required a stricter affidavit to justify a plaintiff in holding the defendant to bail, and by sec. 5 a different form of recognizance of bail was appointed, in effect that if the defendant should be condemned, &c., and should neglect or refuse to pay the condemnation money, *or* to appear in open court, or before any judge or commissioner of such court (when duly notified as therein directed) and there to answer such questions as should be prepounded to him, touching his lands, goods, &c.; *then* the bail should pay the costs and condemnation money for him. Sec. 6 provides for the examination and contingent commitment of the defendant for a period not exceeding a year, and for the entering of an *exoneretur* in case of unreasonable delay, or *after* the defendant shall have submitted to any such examination as aforesaid. The statute 8th Vic. chap. 48, sec. 1, repealed 7th Vic. chap. 31, and by sec. 44, provided for arrest and bail in civil cases, so far as the amount and form of affidavit to be made by the plaintiff were material, following in terms, as to the affidavit, the 7th Vic. chap. 31, sec. 1, except that the word "Upper Canada" is substituted for the "Province of Canada ;" no form of recognizance is given ; the consequence was, that upon the repeal of the 7th Vic. ch. 31, the 2nd Geo. IV. ch. 1, sec. 11, revived as to the recognizance of bail, and has been since followed. Now if a defendant was in close custody, for want of bail upon the aforesaid repeal, I do not see that he became thereupon supersedable and entitled to his unconditional discharge, but on the contrary, that he would be still continued in custody for want of bail, and could not then be enlarged without entering bail with the recognizance required by 2nd Geo. IV. ch. 1, sec. 11. So also, after judgment, he might be charged in execution without any additional or other affidavit than had been made and filed under 7th Vic. ch. 31, being in terms similar to that required by the repealing Act, 8th Vic. ch. 48, sec. 44. If so, it shews that the arrest continued with its consequences, so far changed only as it was affected by the change in the obligation of the bail. Of course the contract of bail already entered, could not be altered by construction so as to render it more onerous upon them, but the defendant having been lawfully delivered to bail, and being therefore lawfully in the constructive custody of his bail, I do not see why they might not have taken and surrendered their principal after the repeal of the Act, as well as before. If the defendant, being already in custody, would not be entitled to his discharge, neither would he be discharged from the implied custody of his bail, and if not, his bail might take and surrender him into close custody, and if this be so, it proves that the recognizance of bail was not put an end to, or the bail discharged, by the repeal of the 7th Vic. ch. 31.

It is true, the authority of the court, or of a judge, to examine, and (if deemed proper) to commit the defendant, under section 6, no longer existed; but I do not see that this rendered it impossible for the bail to perform their undertaking, that he should appear, when called for, to answer, &c. Had the Act continued, and the debtor, upon being brought into court by his bail, refused to answer, I do not think his contumacy would be a breach of the recognizance; the course, I think, would be for the court to commit him, under the 6th section, for contempt. The notice required by section 5 is equivalent to a *ca. sa.* under the former and present practice; and the appearance of the party, on his being brought into court by the bail in pursuance thereof, equivalent to a render in discharge, with this difference, that were the Act still in force, the court, or judge, would proceed to examine the party under section 6, and the effect of the undertaking might be, that the bail would continue responsible for his appearance day after day, or at any future period when notified afresh, unless they relieved themselves by a surrender; whereas, since the repeal of the Act, it would properly be the duty of the court, or a judge, to commit the defendant to custody, as upon a surrender of his bail, if prayed by them or by the plaintiff. At all events, there is nothing to prevent the defendant appearing, or being brought by the bail, before the court, or a judge, in compliance with their undertaking, when the plaintiff might resort to final process against him, if not entitled to a commitment upon a surrender of the bail. If the effect of the repeal was to discharge the bail, then it ought to follow that the plaintiff might, before judgment, proceed to issue an *alias ca. re.*, and re-arrest the defendant, without any new affidavit; that is, if being in close custody already, he could detain him there, and charge him in execution, without any further affidavit, as I think he might.

It is true, as a general rule, that a statute repealed is as if it had never existed; still there must be the qualification, that a contract entered into in pursuance of a statute, valid and binding at the time, would not be rescinded, as a contract, illegal when entered into, would not be set up by the repeal of the statute which made it illegal.

If performance was rendered really *impossible* by the repeal of the Act, it would, no doubt, be a good defence as a plea. Here the court is called upon to take judicial notice of the repeal, and that thereby it became impossible for the defendant to perform one of the two alternatives contained in the recognizance of bail. But for my part, I do not see the *impossibility*. If it cannot be fully and completely performed, the condition ought to be performed as nearly as possible, and the bail should do, and shew that they have done, all in their power to perform it; and I can perceive no insuperable difficulty in their doing it, so far as respects the appearance of the debtor, as required by the notice served. In what way he might be dealt with then is an ulterior consideration, and questions or difficulties upon that head cannot dispense with any effort to perform at all, or operate as an absolute discharge of the bail from doing anything. The recognizance was valid when entered into, and it is at present a record of this court, not vacated or set aside, and is at least entitled to as much force as a bond with a similar condition entered into at present would have, and though such a bond would be a deviation from the condition prescribed by the statute, I do not see that the condition would be void, as undertaking an impossibility. The present recognizance is a debt of record, and while it so remains, the condition must be performed as nearly and effectually as can be done. The bail have undertaken for the act of a stranger, and while the contract subsists everything must be performed that can be done towards compliance. This I take to be the principle of law applicable to contracts, and looking upon this as a contract of record, I do not perceive that performance has become quite impossible by the repeal of 7th Vic. chap. 31; on the contrary, it appears to me, it might be fully performed so far as the obligation of the bail goes, namely, that the defendant should appear before a judge of this court upon due notice in that behalf. Had he appeared, it seems to me at present, that since no examination under the statute could take place, and the party was not discharged from the arrest, but continued subject to and under it, he would have been liable to commitment in discharge of the bail, upon their prayer or upon the prayer of the plaintiff, unless he gave new bail, according to the altered terms required of bail since the repeal of 7th Vic. ch. 31. At all events, his appearance would shew him to be forthcoming within the jurisdiction of the court, and answerable to its ulterior process, which may not have been the case in this instance, notwithstanding the engagement of the bail that he should appear to answer the plaintiff when duly called for. If the repeal of the Act imposed any hardship on the bail, as if their responsibility became enhanced, or the risk greater, or they could no longer surrender the debtor, or if they could not compel his appearance, or ought to be exonerated from it by reason of any privilege or exemption which the repeal conferred upon the debtor, the defendants ought to have applied for an *exoneretur;* but although I at first thought that the proper course, a further consideration of the case has convinced me that there are great if not insuperable obstacles to relief even in that mode.

Had the Act continued still in force, and the defendants had made default, as they have done, I apprehend they would have had the same time and privileges in rendering their principal, even after service of process, as bail at present have, and if so, it follows that they might (notwithstanding the repeal) have so rendered their principal in their discharge in the present case, unless indeed he were discharged by virtue of the repeal, so that they could not render him; but I have already expressed my opinion that it did not discharge the debtor from the arrest. The question depends upon this consideration—if the debtor, being in custody for want of bail, did not become supersedable without bail, if the arrest and commitment remained good, and if he could only be enlarged by entering bail according to 2nd Geo. IV. chap. 1, sec. 11, and might be charged in execution without an additional affidavit, it follows that the bail were not discharged, and could only be relieved by surrender—performance of the recognizance—or by the entry of an *exoneretur*, by none of which have they attempted to relieve themselves.

JONES, J.—The statute under which the recognizance was taken, and upon which this action was brought, having been totally repealed before the commencement of the suit, the action cannot be supported, and the defendants must have judgment. It became impossible by the act of the law to comply with one of the alternatives of the recognizance. No judge, after the repeal of the law, could administer the interrogatories to the principal. The notice therefore to him to appear was, and such appearance, if the party had appeared, must have been a useless and nugatory proceeding. There was no undertaking unconditionally to pay the money by the defendants, but if this action can be maintained, it will have the effect of making the undertaking to pay unconditional, whereas they undertook to pay the money, or produce the principal, on notice, before a judge for examination. The law being repealed, no such examination could be had; it would be extra-judicial, and therefore the defendants are not liable on their recognizance. The case of Hardy v. Hall et al., 2 Cam. 276, shews that a recognizance of the bail is not forfeited by the non-payment of the money recovered by the judgment, unless the alternative condition in the recognizance was not complied with; and here it could not be complied with, by reason of the act of the law in repealing the statute. In Com. Dig. Condition, D. 1, it is said, "But if the condition of an obligation, "recognizance, &c., was possible at the making, and afterwards becomes "impossible by the act of God, of the law, or of the obligee himself, the "obligation shall he saved; so if a condition be in the disjunctive, and give "liberty to do one thing or another at his election, and the one part becomes "impossible."—T. Ray. 373; Cro. J. 67.

McLEAN, J., concurred in opinion with the Chief Justice and Mr. Justice Jones.

MACAULAY, J., *dissentiente.*

Per Cur.—Judgments for the defendants on demurrer.

CAMERON V. LOUNT.

Where to a declaration in trespass, containing two counts, charging two distinct trespasses in taking different goods at different times; the defendant justifies the two distinct trespasses under one writ—*Held*, plea good.

The justifying under a writ issued in May, 1845, a trespass charged to have been committed in September, 1843, though bad on special demurrer, from its seeming inconsistency, is not necessarily bad on general demurrer.

A replication, newly assigning a trespass different from *that* by the plea justified, when the plea justifies *all* the trespasses complained of, is bad on special demurrer.

The plaintiff declared in trespass. Venue, Home District.

1st Count. For that the defendant, on the 12th of September, 1845, in the said district, *vi et armis*, seized, took and carried away certain goods, chattels and cattle, the property of the plaintiff, to wit, two horses, &c., of the value of £100, *there then* found and being, and kept and detained the same, to wit, for two months, whereby the plaintiff was deprived of the use, &c.

2nd Count. For that the defendant, on the 1st September, 1843, *vi et armis*, in the said district, seized, took and carried away, certain other goods, chattels and cattle, the property of the plaintiff, to wit, two horses, &c., &c., value £100, and converted the same to his own use. Damages, £100.

3rd Plea. As to the declaration (except as to the force and arms, and whatever else is against the peace), that *before the times when*, &c., to wit, on the 1st of January, 1844, an action was pending in the Home District Court, to which the defendant and Mary Smith were plaintiffs, and the plaintiff was the defendant, in which action the plaintiff, to wit, on the 16th day of January, 1844, by a confession signed and sealed by him, confessed the said action and damages, to the amount laid in the declaration, besides the costs, and agreed thereby with the defendant and Mary Smith, that judgment might be entered up at any time, and thereby promised to pay the defendant and Mary Smith £17 2s. 4d., and interest from the 16th of January, and costs, being the true debt; and in default thereof, on or before the 16th of January, 1844, they should be at liberty to sue out execution upon the said judgment, so to be entered, &c., and upon any such execution, to levy the same and expenses, &c., and that he would not levy any writ of error, &c. That afterwards, to wit, on the 31st January, the defendant and Mary Smith entered judgment on such cognovit (the plaintiff having made default), in the said District Court, to wit, for £39 damages, in declaration mentioned, and costs £1 18s. 9d., making £40 18s. 9d., and upon such judgment, to wit, on the 21st of May, 1845, and after default, &c., *and* under *and in pursuance* of said cognovit, the defendant and Mary Smith sued out an *alias fi. fa.* to the Home Sheriff, to levy £40 18s. 9d., for damages and costs, as aforesaid, returnable the 9th of June, whereof the plaintiff was convicted, &c., which writ *afterwards*, and *before the return*, and before the alleged trespasses, was, *under* and in pursuance of the said cognovit, endorsed for £17 2s. 4d., and interest from the 16th of July, and £18s. 9d. for costs, and 20s. for that writ and a former writ of *fi. fa.*, and being so endorsed afterwards, and before the times, when, &c., to wit, on the day and year last aforesaid, was delivered to the sheriff to be executed under and by virtue of the said cognovit, *and judgment* entered thereon; and the said sheriff, after the delivery of the said writ, and before the return thereof, and under the same writ, seized and took down and carried away the *said* goods, chattels and cattle, in the said *declaration* mentioned, at *the said times*, &c., *quæ sunt eadem*, &c.

Replication, as to so much of the said 3rd plea as applied and was pleaded to the *first* count of the said declaration, and the trespasses therein set forth; that after the giving of the said cognovit and the entry of the said judgment, and issue of the said *alias fi. fa.*, a motion was made in the October or November Term of the said District Court, 1845, to set aside the said cognovit, the judgment, and the writ, for irregularity and *taliter processum*, &c.; that in December Term following the said judgment and all ulterior proceedings had thereon, and the writ of *vend. exp.* in the said 3rd plea named (*not named*) and the levy made by the said Home Sheriff, on the plaintiff's goods, &c., were set aside for irregularity.

And the plaintiff further says, that he brought his action not merely for the *said trespasses in the said first count mentioned*, and on the said third plea attempted to be justified, but also for that the defendant, on the *1st September*, 1843, before the giving of said cognovit, and before the said judgment, or the issue of the said *alias fi. fa.*, *and* on another and different occasion, *vi et armis*, seized, took, drove and carried away certain of the goods, &c., of the plaintiff, to wit, other two horses, &c., (enumerating them, as in the 2nd count), and converted them, &c., to his own use, which said trespass newly assigned is another and different trespass than the said trespass in the said 3rd plea mentioned. Verification.

Demurrer to replication to 3rd plea.

1st. Because it gives three answers to the said 3rd plea.
    1st. It assumes to confess and avoid the 3rd plea.
    2nd. It assumes that the 1st count contains more than one trespass.
    3rd. The new assignment refers to another trespass and is a departure.
2nd. That it is double.
3rd. It enlarges the plaintiff's cause of action.

The following grounds of demurrer were taken to the 3rd plea.

1st. That there was no averment that the cause of action, in which the plaintiff confessed judgment, was within the jurisdiction of the Home District Court.

2nd. That there was no allegation that the cognovit was taken through an attorney.

3rd. That it was not alleged out of what court the *alias fi. fa.* issued.

4th. That it was not shewn that the previous *fi. fa.* was returned or returnable, or what had been done thereon.

5th. That the delivery of the writ, as laid, 16th July, 1844, was long before judgment, or issue of such writ.

6th. That plea is repugnant and inconsistent.

7th. That it professes to answer the whole declaration, but only answers a part.

A. Wilson, for the demurrer, cited 2 A. & E. 365 ; 3 D. & R. 605 ; 8 M. & W. 136 ; 8 T. R. 127 ; 1 Wilson, 255 ; Viner's Abridge. Pl. 13 ; Willes, 688.

C. Durand, contra, cited Cro. Eliz. 812 ; 1 Arch, N. P. 391 ; 1 Saund. 300, note 6 ; 1 Saund. 299 ; 5 Bing. N. C. 554 ; 4 M. & W. 245 ; 2 Mod. 20 ; 1 Cowp. 18 ; 2 Wil. 5 ; 1 Ld. Ray. 80.

ROBINSON, C. J., delivered the judgment of the court.

The replication is to the third plea only, and is demurred to. The plaintiff, therefore, cannot on this demurrer raise any question about the sufficiency of the second plea, as he desires to do. The sufficiency of the third plea is to be considered ; many objections have been taken to it ; of course none can prevail unless the plea is bad in substance, as it is before us only on general demurrer. It professes to answer the whole declaration, which contains two counts, charging two distinct trespasses in taking different goods at different times; the first count charging a trespass in September, 1845, and the second count a trespass in September, 1843. The defendant may have known that there was but one act of trespass to be proved, and in that case he might have pleaded the general issue to the second count. But there might have been in fact two seizures made under the one writ, between its issuing and the return, and if there had been he would have two apparent trespasses to justify. In such cases it is usual, in order to avoid pleading a long justification to each, to aver that the trespasses complained of in the two counts are one and the same trespass; but this it seems is held not to be regular, and for good reasons I think; and if the defendant had so pleaded the plaintiff might have demurred, or he might have waived demurring and traversed that they were identical. The defendant took neither course, but has justified two distinct trespasses under one writ, as he well might, if they were in fact so committed. There is in this case, however, this repugnancy in the plea—it justifies under a *fi. fa.* issued in *May*, 1845, a trespass charged to have been committed in *September*, 1843. But it is not every repugnancy of this kind that will be fatal on general demurrer, because the parties in their evidence are at liberty to vary from the day laid. Here I think we must take it, that the *fi. fa.* must have issued after 1843, because by the terms of the cognovit, as set out, it could not legally issue till after July, 1844. But on the second count, the plaintiff might prove, for all we know, a trespass committed in 1845, after the writ, and therefore one to which the plea would apply. That being so, the repugnance is not fatal on general demurrer; though it would be good cause for special demurrer, on account merely of the seeming inconsistency. I do not see any objection pointed out that should prevail on general demurrer; it is plain on the plea that the execution issued on the judgment set out, and therefore must have emanated from the Home District Court, though it is not stated. The plea does sufficiently shew, that the action in the District Court was one of which that court could take cognizance, being for a debt, and for damages for not performing promises. The contradiction in dates, by an accidental reference to July, 1846, as "the "day *last aforesaid*," when that day was evidently not the one intended to be referred to, is immaterial on general demurrer; the repugnance is easy to be reconciled, and it is clear what is meant.

The replication is bad in our opinion. So far as it proposes to answer the first count it might, I apprehend, on several grounds that are not taken, have been demurred to specially; but it is clearly bad also on account of some of the exceptions taken; it proposes to new assign another trespass than *that* by the plea justified, as if the plea had justified but one, but the plea justifies *all* the trespasses complained of; and the replication therefore should have newly assigned a trespass which was not *any of those justified*. It assumes incorrectly that the plea can apply only to one trespass.

We do not consider the replication double; the plea had answered the several trespasses as it might do; the replication as to one of the trespasses admits that it was done by colour of the writ, but replies (not in good form), that the writ had been set aside; and so far as the plea had answered the other trespass by justifying under the writ, the plaintiff replies, that that trespass was committed on another occasion. That is only a single answer to the defence as it applies to each writ. The pleadings would be simplified by the defendant shaping his defence differently.

Per Cur.—Judgment for defendant, unless the plaintiff desires to amend, paying costs.

PETRIE V. TAYLOR.

Where the losing party has failed at the trial, from the omission of his attorney, to establish some legal right he might have shewn, the court will exercise their discretion in granting a new trial; they will not grant this indulgence where an expensive litigation would be protracted about a trifling matter.

One tenant in common may commit trespass, by expelling his co-tenant and taking the whole enjoyment of the estate wrongfully to himself.

Trespass *quare clausum fregit*.

The plaintiff complained, that defendant had broken and entered a brick-yard of his, and taken certain goods.

The defendant pleaded, first, not guilty.

Second, that one Foster and his wife, in right of the wife, were seized in their demesne as of freehold, for the natural life of the wife, who is still living, of and in the closes in the counts mentioned, and that being so seized, Foster, on, &c., demised the closes by indenture to the defendant for a year, and the defendant justified the entering and other injuries complained of under that demise.

He pleaded also, that the closes were not the closes of the plaintiff. The plaintiff replied, denying the demise.

At the trial it was proved, that the brick-yard was part of a lot of land which had belonged to one Canniffe deceased, and which he had devised to his wife for life, and after her death to his four daughters. The plaintiff had taken the brick-yard from a person who had rented it from Canniffe, in his lifetime, for a small sum, and Canniffe and his wife being both dead, the plaintiff wished to continue in possession of the premises; but the defendant having taken from Foster, husband of one of the four devisees, a lease for a year, entered upon the premises, and removed the materials which plaintiff had left there and some bricks, doing no unnecessary damage; nothing was converted by the defendant or injured.

The case was tried before the Chief Justice, who directed the jury that he thought the plea justifying under the demise from Foster was proved, and they found on that issue for the defendant, which barred the action.

Campbell, of Kingston, moved for a new trial on the law and evidence, and for misdirection, and on affidavits of surprise. He relied on Co. Litt. 200, a.

L. Wallbridge, of Belleville, shewed cause.—He cited 8 B. & C. 268; 8 T. R. 145.

ROBINSON, C. J., delivered the judgment of the court.

We have considered the evidence in this case, and it appears to my brothers, as it did to me upon the trial, that the defendant was entitled to succeed upon the second plea. The substance of the issue upon that plea was, whether Foster did make such a demise as was stated. The replication does not deny the seizin of Foster and his wife, which is set out in the inducement to the plea, but says that Foster made no such demise, which plea admits the seizin set out in the inducement. It was proved that Foster did make the demise pleaded. He and his wife had in fact a freehold interest in the *locus in quo*, or rather the wife had, which gave Foster the right to demise, and that demise gave the defendant the same right to possession, during the term which Foster had, in right of his wife, as one of several tenants, in common under the will. There is no doubt that any one of the daughters could have entered without being guilty of a trespass, for they all had an equal right to possession, and the defendant had the same right, claiming under one of them, or rather under the husband, while his term lasted. Undoubtedly one tenant in common may commit trespass by expelling his co-tenant, and taking the whole enjoyment wrongfully to himself; but the plaintiff shewed no estate or right whatever in himself, and stands as a mere stranger to the title; he cannot question the right of one of the tenants in common, or his lessee, to possess any part of the whole; the question of wrongful ouster of the other co-tenants, is a matter to be discussed among themselves. The plaintiff now files affidavits, setting forth that he could have shewn a legal right held by him under one of the other parties, but that from some misapprehension of his attorney he omitted to do so. This does not seem, however, a case for granting any extraordinary indulgence, in order to afford a second chance of recovering, for it would be protracting an expensive litigation about a trifling matter. The brick-yard was a very small piece of land, from which the clay had been mostly removed, and it had been usually let for five or six pounds a-year. The personal property which the plaintiff had on the ground had been carefully removed to the adjoining land without injury, and the plaintiff had got it. It seemed to me at the trial, that the verdict was consistent with the justice of the case, as well as with the law, and my brothers agree in that opinion.

Per Cur.—Rule discharged.

CROUSE V. PARK.

Interest made payable by a promissory note is part of the debt, and not merely damages for detaining the debt.

The plaintiff declared on seven promissory notes, all bearing interest from date, and amounting without interest to £155 5s. 7d.; and also on the common counts for £500, concluding by laying his damages at £500.

The defendant pleaded first, except as to the first seven counts (those on the promissory notes), and except as to £55 14s. 5d. on the other counts, *non-assumpsit*.

Second, to the whole declaration, except as to £211, parcel of the moneys therein mentioned, payment before action brought.

Third, and as to the £211, being the moneys in the first seven counts, and parcel of the moneys in the other counts, except as before mentioned, (that is in the first plea) *actio non*, because he now pays into court that sum, and denies that plaintiff had sustained damages beyond the £211, *in respect to the causes of action in the declaration mentioned, so far as they relate to the said sum of £211, parcel, &c.*, concluding with a verification and prayer of judgment, if plaintiff ought further to maintain his action.

The plaintiff demurred specially to the third plea, objecting that it offered the sum of £211 in satisfaction of the notes declared on in the first seven counts, and of £55 14s. 5d. claimed by the other counts; whereas the £211 only equals in amount the notes exclusive of interest, and the £55 14s. 5d.;

and also, because the plaintiff, paying money into court after action brought, has pleaded in bar of the action, and not of the further maintenance only.

A. Wilson, for the demurrer, cited 5 Jurist, 828 ; 8 M. & W. 228; 2 Dowl. & L. 81 ; Cro. Jac. 67 ; Cro. Eliz. 445, 52, 904.

Eccles, contra, referred to Watkins v. Nicolls, 1 Cam. Rep. page 473 ; Fortescue, 355.

ROBINSON, C. J., delivered the judgment of the court.

It is clear on the pleadings, that the defendant, by his first plea, admits £211 to have been due when the action was brought, which he pays into court, pleading in effect that it amounts to as much as will discharge the whole of the notes declared on in the seven counts, and also £55 14s. 5d. on account of the other counts; but it will not, because the £55 14s 5d. deducted from the £211, leaves exactly the amount of the promissory notes, exclusive of anything to be allowed for interest, and the notes are made payable on the face of them with interest from the date. The defendant therefore puts it to the court, whether the plaintiff has any right to recover for the interest, which the defendant has expressly contracted to pay. We cannot but see that he has, and it is repugnant to the record, so long as the defendant does not shew how the interest has been discharged, to aver, as the plea does, that the plaintiff has sustained no damages beyond the principal moneys. In Hudson v. Fawcett, 2 D. & L. Rep. 81, it is expressly held that interest made payable by a promissory note is part of the debt, and not merely damages for detaining the debt.

Per Cur.—Judgment for plaintiff on demurrer.

LESLIE V. DAVIDSON.

The plaintiff declares on two counts : 1st, On a promissory note ; 2nd, On an account stated. To the defendant's plea to the 1st count on the note, the plaintiff replies ; to which replication the defendant demurs ; the plaintiff then, to avoid the risk of the demurrer, entered a simple *nolle prosequi* to the 1st count.

Held, that the plaintiff might give the note in evidence to support the second count, on the account stated.

Semble: Such evidence would have been inadmissible, if the *nolle prosequi* had involved an express admission, as it sometimes does, that the plaintiff had no right of action on the note.

The plaintiff declared in this case on a promissory note made by the defendant to the plaintiff, 28th May, 1845, for £93 14s. 4d., payable in ninety days, adding a count upon an account stated.

The defendant pleaded to the first count, that the plaintiff obtained the note from him by fraud.

Secondly, that the note was made by him without consideration, and for the accommodation of the plaintiff.

To the second count he pleaded *non-asssumpsit*.

The plaintiff replied to the first plea, denying the fraud.

In answer to the second plea, he replied that "he received the note" from the defendant for a good and sufficient consideration.

The defendant demurred to the second replication, assigning for causes, that it did not state that the defendant *made* the note for a good consideration, nor for what consideration it was made, nor deny that it was for the accommodation of the plaintiff, as the plea alleged.

The plaintiff thereupon entered a *nolle prosequi* to the first count, the entry on the record being in these words, "that he freely here in court confesses "that he will not further prosecute his suit against the said defendant, in "respect of the said first count in the said declaration mentioned;" and at the trial he offered the note in evidence to support the count upon an account stated.

It was objected that it was not competent to him to do so, after having entered a *nolle prosequi* to the count on which the note was declared upon.

The plaintiff was allowed to take a verdict for the note and interest, with leave reserved to the defendant to move to enter a nonsuit, if the objection should be found entitled to prevail.

Eccles moved to enter a nonsuit accordingly. He contended that the plaintiff, by his *nolle prosequi* to the note, after the pleas that had been put in, admitted the note to be worth nothing; no use could afterwards be made of it.

Gorham shewed cause. He relied upon 3 Scott, N. R. 325; M. & M. 311.

ROBINSON, C. J., delivered the judgment of the court.

The bill of particulars attached to the record, claims only the money due upon the note, stating, as is usual, that the plaintiff will avail himself of the several counts in the declaration to support his claim for that amount; this in effect confined the plaintiff to the note, so that he could not at the trial be allowed to set up any other demand; and it would seem reasonable to hold, that where he has expressly relinquished by his *nolle prosequi* any right to recover in this action upon the *premises* in the first *count mentioned* (for it is so upon the record, though *promises* may have been the word intended to be understood), he should not be allowed to advance the *note* as his ground of action upon the account stated, any more than upon the count in which the note is declared upon. I should have no doubt that he would be thus precluded if the entry of the *nolle prosequi* had involved an express admission, as it sometimes does, that the plaintiff had no right of action on the note; as for instance, if the plaintiff had said that "inasmuch as he could not deny that "the note was made for his accommodation and not for value," or if he had confessed that the note had been paid, or that he had released the demand, &c., and upon that ground declared that he would not further prosecute. It would appear on the record, in such case, that the plaintiff had given up his claim upon the note, for a reason which destroys his right of action. We cannot say, certainly, that in this case, the plaintiff's abandoning his count upon the note, involves the admission that he has no right of action upon it. Upon a defence being pleaded which goes to the right, he simply enters a *nolle prosequi;* if the inference were inevitable, that he must mean to admit the truth of the plea pleaded, then it would be clear that he should not be allowed to recover on the note under the common count; but I cannot say that we should be warranted in so treating the *nolle prosequi*, for though I confess I think that ought to be the consequence, yet authority tends the other way. Mr. Chitty, in his Treatise on Pleading, lays it down as clear, that "a *nolle* "*prosequi* to one count does not preclude the plaintiff from proceeding at the "trial upon another count, which, although apparently for a different cause "'of action, is in reality founded on the demand which might have been "recovered upon the count which the plaintiff abandoned."—1 Chitt. Plead. 427, 603, note. The plaintiff may have entered a *nolle prosequi* merely because he apprehended that his replication was informal, and did not wish to incur the costs of arguing the demurrer; and at all events he merely gives up that count. He might, no doubt, after this bring another action upon the note; so he might at the trial have given up the first count, and yet produce the note as evidence to entitle him to a verdict on the second count; and this being so, there is no injustice done by allowing him to recover on the second count upon the note, as he did in this case at the trial, for by the *nolle prosequi* he has only abandoned the first count. If the defendant omitted to consider that the plaintiff was confined by his particulars, he might very naturally conclude, that he had no intention of attempting to recover on the note, but on some other demand; and if, acting on that impression, he came unprepared to substantiate the defence which he had pleaded to the first count, he might be allowed to have that opportunity yet afforded to him. But upon the mere question of practice, we do not find that the plaintiff was improperly permitted to recover as he has done. Those cases have clearly no application, in which for want of a proper stamp, or on account of a variance in setting out the note, the plaintiff has been prevented from recovery on the special count. There it is plain, that in the first case he cannot recover on the account stated by producing the note, but that in the second case he can; and the reasons are obvious. The note being unstamped is not admissible in evidence to support any count, but in the case of variance the difficulty can clearly not extend to the count on an account stated, because the true note, when produced in evidence, appears to be a different cause of action from that on which the plaintiff has failed to recover.

Per Cur.—Rule discharged. Postea to plaintiff.

HODGKINSON ET AL. V. BROWN.

The court will not grant a new trial to the plaintiff (complaining of the smallness of his verdict), on an affidavit that a witness was absent from the province at the time of the trial whom he might get for another trial, and by whom he could better make out his case.

This was an action of *assumpsit*, on a special agreement set forth in two counts, and on the common counts.

The defendant pleaded, first, to the first count, *non-assumpsit.*

Secondly, that the plaintiffs did not deliver wheat to him as they had in that count alleged.

To the second count similar pleas.

Non-assumpsit to the common counts, and set off.

The jury, under the evidence the plaintiffs gave at the trial (which appears in the judgment of the court, as delivered by the Chief Justice), rendered a verdict for a trifling amount in their favour.

Becher, of London, moved for a new trial against his own verdict, on account of the smallness of damages, upon an affidavit of the plaintiffs that there was a witness absent from the province whom they could get for another trial, and by whom they could better make out their case.

Wilson, of London, shewed cause.—If the witness was absent, the plaintiffs should have forborne to go to trial. No new trial can be granted on such a ground.

ROBINSON, C. J.—The first count states an agreement, which clearly was not proved, that plaintiffs had bound themselves to deliver a certain quantity of wheat at the defendant's mill, in return for which defendant agreed that he would, during the season of navigation in 1845, deliver to them certain specific quantities of flour, bran and shorts. There was no evidence whatever that plaintiffs were bound to deliver any wheat to defendant. The second count lays the agreement somewhat differently, but it is subject to the same exception, that there is really no proof of plaintiffs having stipulated to send any wheat to defendant to be ground, but merely that they had sent a large quantity, during the summer of 1845, to a mill which defendant owned in Malahide, but which he had leased to one Johnson for three years, from the 1st of January, 1845, that is, before any of the wheat was delivered. The effect of the mill being so leased of course would be, under ordinary circumstances, that the defendant, having no control over the mill, and not working it for his own benefit, could not be responsible for a proper quantity or any quantity of flour, &c., being returned for wheat that had been sent to the mill, while it was in the hands of his tenant. But the plaintiffs attempted to prove, that the defendant had personally agreed, in December, 1844, that *he* would deliver to them flour, bran and shorts, in certain proportions, for *whatever* quantity of wheat the plaintiffs should deliver at the mill in 1845. If they had proved that, still I think they would not have proved such an agreement as they had declared upon; but the only proof they gave of it was altogether inconclusive, and was not such as I think ought to have satisfied the jury that the defendant had entered into a positive agreement, that whether he should continue to hold the mill in his own hands or not, he was at all events to see that the plaintiffs should receive a certain specified proportion of flour, &c., for the wheat they might send. That Johnson had a regular written lease of the mill, and was working it for his own benefit, while all this wheat was brought to it, paying £75 a year rent to defendant, was clearly proved. Johnson had absconded, and the parties respectively intimated, that that alone has suggested the claim on the one hand and the denial on the other. Certainly, to charge the defendant upon an agreement not very likely to be made, requires distinct and positive evidence; and if the plaintiffs suffer from their great inattention in taking no writing, nor preserving evidence of any kind, of so special a contract, as they allege, they ought rather to bear the consequence, than expect a jury to support their claim on the kind of attempt at proof that was made on the trial. The case was very fairly given to the jury, on such a charge as left them at liberty to find for the plaintiffs, if they were satisfied that such an agreement as the plaintiffs allege was made. They found, however, against the plaintiffs in respect to the agreement, and gave them a verdict for three pounds nineteen shillings and four pence only, upon some small demand proved on the common counts. The plaintiffs now make affidavit, that there was a witness absent from the province whom they may get for another trial, and by whom they could better make out their case ; but except under very peculiar circumstances, this is never admitted as a ground for granting a new trial. The plaintiffs could have abstained from bringing the cause to trial until they could get the witness they speak of ; but having chosen to go to trial without him, we should not interpose by granting them a new trial when the verdict is already in their favour, in order to give them a chance of getting a better verdict.

Per Cur.—Rule discharged.

Bank of Montreal v. Humphries et al.

The plaintiffs sue on a promissory note, made by A., payable to B. or order, endorsed by B. to C., and by C. to the plaintiffs, who sue A. B. and C. jointly, under our statute.

The defendants plead usury, setting forth that the making of the note, and the endorsements by B. & C., were all without consideration ; that C. endorsed the note and delivered it to A., for A.'s accommodation, and in order to enable him to procure a loan ; that A. did make a corrupt agreement with D. for the loan of a sum of money on usurious interest, and gave him this note as security, and that D. afterwards endorsed and delivered the note to the plaintiffs, who gave him no consideration for the note, adding this special traverse, "without this, that the said C. endorsed the said note to the said "plaintiffs, as in the said declaration is alleged," and the plea concludes to the country.

Held, plea bad on special demurrer, as being repugnant, inconsistent and double.

The plaintiffs sued on a promissory note for £50, made by Humphries, payable to Kerr, or order, endorsed by Kerr to Reid, and by Reid to the plaintiffs, and they sued Humphries, Kerr, and Reid jointly under our statute.

The defendants pleaded usury, setting forth that the making of the note and the endorsements by Kerr and Reid were all without consideration; that Reid endorsed the note and delivered it to Humphries for Humphries' accommodation, and in order to enable him to procure a loan. That Humphries did make a corrupt contract with one Scott, for the loan of a sum of money on usurious interest, and gave him this note as security, and that Scott afterwards endorsed and delivered the note to the plaintiffs, who gave him no consideration for the note, adding this special traverse, "without this, that the said Reid "endorsed the said note to the said plaintiffs, as in the declaration is alleged ;" and the plea concluded to the country.

The plaintiffs demurred to this plea specially for duplicity, and for improperly concluding to the country.

Richards, for the demurrer.

J. H. Hagarty, contra.

ROBINSON, C. J., delivered the judgment of the court.

My brothers have had less difficulty than I have had in making up their minds on this plea, but I agree with them that the plea is bad on special demurrer. It traverses a material fact in the plaintiff's case, which at the same time it does in effect confess and avoid, and it is therefore repugnant and inconsistent, and it is double. The defendant fell into an error of which one can easily see the cause. This plea was clearly not intended to set up a double answer to the declaration. The defendant supposed he was resting his defence on the usury alone. His alleging want of consideration for the making and endorsing of the note, was not necessary to the extent to which he carried it for availing himself of the defence of usury. The fact that these plaintiffs were not *bona fide* holders for value, was all that could in that respect be material. As to the special traverse, the defendant seems to have felt, that as he had set up a case inconsistent with the fact of endorsement by Reid to the plaintiffs stated in the declaration, he must therefore traverse that endorsement. He does not mean by his plea to deny that the plaintiffs are the holders of the note, through endorsement from Reid, and as such entitled *prima facie* to sue upon it. The matter of inducement in his plea fully admits this; but he thought it necessary to deny that plaintiffs took the note by direct endorsement from Reid, which he takes to be the effect of the statement in the declaration, because if that was so, there could have been no such transaction with Scott, an intermediate endorser as his plea states, and the alleged usurious agreement could not have been made. But the traverse was clearly unnecessary, for the plaintiffs' declaration did not bind him to prove an endorsement by Reid directly to themselves. The statement would be supported on a trial by shewing that Reid endorsed the note; whether he did endorse it or not, that is, write his name upon it, is alone the substance of the issue, and that the traverse denied as explicitly as the defendant could have denied it by a plea, having that object only in view, and as they have indeed denied it in a separate plea. But in the same plea they admit it in their inducement, while they conclude by denying it. The plaintiffs' title clearly depends upon the fact of Reid having endorsed the note; the traverse cannot be held to be immaterial, and being material, it shuts out the plaintiffs from traversing the usury, which is new matter. There should have been no traverse of Reid's endorsement, and then the replication of *de injuria* would have thrown it upon the defendant to have proved his inducement, and the endorsement to Scott as part of it.

Per Cur.—Judgment for plaintiffs on demurrer.

IVES ET AL. V. CALVIN.

The Provincial Act 9 Vic. ch. 9, as well as the common law, authorize a person to make use of his own boat, *within the limits of a ferry*, in the pursuit of his business or pleasure, freely, and without any necessity of shewing the particular motives or occasions he may have for allowing any individual to pass in his boat, provided such person be not a *traveller*, and provided nothing be charged for carrying.

This was an action on the case brought by the plaintiffs, for the disturbance of a right of ferry granted by letters patent to the plaintiffs across the waters of the St. Lawrence, between Kingston and Garden Island, and between Garden Island and Wolfe Island.

The defendant lived on Garden Island, where he carried on a large business in loading and unloading vessels, rafting timber, and building and repairing vessels, employing a great number of hands, and it was plain from the evidence on the trial, that he had used his own boats at all times in carrying backwards and forwards, especially to and from Kingston, the members of his own family, his servants and labourers in his employment, and persons having business with him or visiting him on various pretences. The plaintiffs, while they did not admit that he had a right to use his own boats to this extent in derogation of their ferry, endeavoured to shew that he had gone even beyond that large use of them, and had allowed his boats to be employed in carrying persons from Long Island to Kingston, who were in no manner employed by him, and had no connection whatever with his business. For this they claimed damages, but not for this only, for they put it to the court at the trial: First, that if our statutes 8th Vic. ch. 50, and 9th Vic. ch. 19, gave a more extensive privilege to the owners of boats in this respect than could have been exercised at common law, yet this more extended privilege is only to be recognized with reference to summary proceedings under the 8th Vic. ch. 50, so that a party cannot be convicted before a magistrate for anything done that would come fairly within the exception stated in the statutes, but that when the owner of the ferry proceeds by action at common law, he can still claim a right of ferry as exclusive as the common law allows him. Secondly, they contended that the use which the defendant made of his boats, went beyond what either the common law or our statutes warranted. A good deal of evidence was given to shew on what occasions, and to what extent, the defendant had made use of his boats.

Verdict for the defendant.

Kirkpatrick, of Kingston, moved for a new trial, on the law and evidence and for misdirection. He relied upon Tripp v. Frank, 4 T. R. 666 ; 2 C. M. & R. 432.

Henderson, of Kingston, shewed cause. He cited 4 T. R. 666 ; 2 C. M. & R. 432 ; 9 Vic. ch. 9 ; 8 Vic. ch. 50, sec. 1 ; 3 Mod. 294.

ROBINSON, C. J., delivered the judgment of the court.

There was no dispute about the distance from either terminus to which it could be held to extend, and consequently no such point presented itself as was before the court in Tripp v. Frank, 4 T. R. 666, and Impey v. Field, 2 C. M. & R. 432 ; but the plaintiffs contended that they had been aggrieved by the defendant carrying over passengers in great numbers in his own boat, over the precise and undisputed line of their ferry.

It has been made clear enough that it was not a trifling or imaginary loss that the plaintiffs were complaining of, if they were in fact entitled to insist upon the defendant's servants, workmen or family, or the persons having business with the defendant at Garden Island, going backwards and forwards in the plaintiffs' ferry-boat. The fact was shewn to be, that the defendant's establishment contained nearly all that there is of population on Garden Island. If that establishment did not exist, the right of ferry as regarded Garden Island would at any rate be but of little value, and if the defendant were precluded from using his own boats, and were compelled to avail himself of the plaintiffs' ferry on all occasions, he would he exposed to an unreasonable, if not an intolerable burthen. It was natural, on the one hand, that the plaintiffs, paying a considerable rent to the government for the ferry, and being obliged to keep boats for the accommodation of the public, should look with jealousy on the extent to which the defendant claimed the right of using his own boats, even for his own purposes, and should desire to confine him within the narrowest limits. And on the other hand, it did appear to me at the trial, that the defendant, on his part, was only desirous of fairly using a privilege which he might sincerely suppose the law gave him, of using his own boats for his own purposes; that he did not desire to make a profit by carrying on, as it were, an illegal ferry for accommodating others, and by that means making a gain to himself; and that he was not actuated by any malicious motive of prejudicing the plaintiffs in regard to their right of ferry, which might lead him to interfere with their proper business for the purpose of injuring them. On the contrary, there was much to shew that the defendant was scrupulously careful not to go beyond what he claimed to be his right, and that he enjoined upon his servants not to carry over strangers in his boats, for hire or otherwise, and that he did not use his boats with any view of making it a source of profit, otherwise than by saving the expense of ferriage to himself and those employed by him. If he did go beyond the limits I have mentioned, it was in but very few instances. I believe only clearly in one, and I think he was shewn to have acted throughout in that spirit, that if he did what was illegal, it was unintentional, and that he only required to know clearly what the plaintiffs could properly insist upon, to insure his conforming to it. The one exception to which I allude, was his allowing his boat to go, not for profit, but as a favour, to take a number of the inhabitants of Long Island over to Kingston on a Sunday to attend church, their own boat, in which they had been for years in the habit of constantly crossing, being then undergoing repair in the defendant's yard. I told the jury that the patent, in the words of it, gave to the plaintiffs a right to ferry over travellers and their baggage; that these would be persons having generally no conveyance of their own; that *travellers*, in common parlance, meant persons not inhabiting in the vicinity, but coming from a distance, which construction would not include those employed by defendant on Garden Island, and merely going between that place and Kingston on their daily or ordinary business. I considered that, at common law, the defendant would be at liberty to use a boat for carrying backwards and forwards his own household and servants, or the labourers in his employment, and I could not see clearly that the right would not extend as well to persons labouring for him at Garden Island, by contract at shipbuilding or other work, as to persons hired at monthly or daily wages; for it might be an equal accommodation to him in the one case as in the other, by saving him an additional charge that might be made if the workmen were driven to go by the ferry. I further told the jury, that I regarded the late statute, 9th Vic. ch. 9, as speaking the sense and will of the legislature with regard to the use which all parties are to be allowed to make of their own boats, notwithstanding any right of ferry in another; that the preamble of that Act evinced that the legislature intended that the privilege was to be liberally accorded, and that in my opinion the principle, whatever it was, must prevail throughout, and not merely when the right to convict by summary proceedings was in question; that I thought a person owning a boat was entitled under the Act, at least, if not at common law, to carry his guests and visitors backwards and forwards, as well as his children or servants, and also persons resorting to him for the purposes of business, so long as he did not use his boat in this manner in order to make a profit of it, by taking a reward for ferrying, and so long as he did nothing for the malicious purpose of injuring the proprietor of the ferry, but acted *bona fide* in using his own boat for his own purposes, either of pleasure or of business. It appeared to me, and so I told the jury, that the allowing his boat to take the trip on the Sunday, to bring over many persons unconnected with himself in any way, who would perhaps have gone by the ferry if he had not lent his boat, was an act not sanctioned by the statute, and was an injury to the plaintiffs' right, though the defendant did it apparently with no view to profit. I explained to the jury that the taking no fee for ferrying did not alter the case, for that a person might by gratuitously passing persons over interfere more with the franchise of the ferry than by making them pay. The plaintiffs did not press for damages; they signified their object to be merely to establish their right, and that they would be content with a nominal verdict. The question therefore lay between a verdict for defendant, or a nominal verdict for the plaintiffs, which my charge did authorize the jury to give in respect of that particular instance of interference with the plaintiffs' ferry which I have described. Admitting that I was clearly right in holding that a verdict should or might be given on that ground, yet as the jury, not being misdirected to find for the defendant, did nevertheless find for him, I do not think this is a case in which a new trial should be granted. There was no evidence that the defendant has persevered in claiming a right so extensive as was exercised on that one occasion, and exercised then, as it seemed, from no bad motive. There is nothing to shew, therefore, that the granting a new trial is necessary in order to put an end to a continuing malpractice of that kind. In general we should not grant a new trial in a case of tort in order to enable a plaintiff to recover a nominal verdict, unless we see that a clear right is intended to be disputed. So far as this single instance is concerned, it may have been on the one side an unintentional transgression, as there was apparently no view to an illegal profit, and on the other side, the plaintiffs may be standing on an extreme right when they have no ground for apprehending a perseverance in anything wrong, after the right has been declared and understood. The preamble of our statute 9th Vic. ch. 9, sets out that the previous Act (8th Vic. ch. 50), "had been so construed as to prevent "parties from carrying *persons and goods* in their own boats and vessels, and "without hire or gain, or hope thereof, across waters in Upper Canada within "the limits of ferries, contrary to the true intent and meaning of the said "Act." I can only infer from this that the legislature did not understand or intend that people should be restrained in the use they might wish to make of their own boats, provided they did not set up in effect a rival ferry by carrying people for hire. If we can suppose a person using his own boat not *bona fide* for his own purposes, or merely to oblige others, but in order to put down or annoy the regular ferry, I should hope that we might feel ourselves authorized to hold that such acts, whether done for profit or not, would subject a party to an action in consequence of the illegal motive; but except in such a case, I am not prepared to say that the statute, or even the common law without aid from that statute, would not allow a person to make use of his own boat, within the limits of the ferry, in the pursuit of his business or pleasure freely, and without any necessity of shewing the particular motives or occasions he may have for allowing any individual to pass in his boat, provided such person is not a *traveller*, and provided nothing is charged for carrying. One finds little in text books upon the right of ferry, and few adjudged cases; none that lay down any principle as to the use persons may make of their own boats within the limits of a ferry. So far as my own observation has gone, I have always found that people residing on the banks of a water, over which there is a ferry, have assumed and been allowed to exercise without question the privilege of using their own boats for any purpose of business or pleasure, without inquiring whether those whom they allowed to occupy them were their servants or friends, or who they were, or what business they were upon, so long as it was not imagined that the person owning the boat was usurping the privilege of the ferry by carrying people for hire.

We are all of opinion that we cannot properly set aside the verdict, and that the rule must be discharged.

Per Cur.—Rule discharged.

SHERWOOD V. MOORE.

A surveyor cannot act independently of the provisions of the statute 5 Geo. III. ch. 13, and arbitrarily lay on one side the evidence which neighbours are ready to give, from their own knowledge, of the situation of original posts.

Trespass for *mesne* profits, on Lot 23, in the 1st concession of Montague. Two counts.

Pleas: first, not guilty;

And, secondly, that the closes were not the plaintiff's.

The trespass in the first count was laid on 1st March, 1839, charging expulsion of plaintiff, and keeping out for six years.

In the second count, the trespass is laid on 10th July, 1841, and expulsion and keeping out of plaintiff for five months.

The plaintiff put in the exemplification of judgment in ejectment entered 28th August, 1844.—Doe on the demise of this plaintiff against the casual ejector; demise laid 7th July, 8th Vic.; to hold for ten years; a writ of possession issued on the judgment 29th December, 1844, under which the plaintiff was put in possession, and defendant removed on the 23rd of January, 1845.

The question at the trial was merely one of boundary between the Lots 22, which the defendant owned, and 23.

The evidence shewed that the defendant, in 1841, had a survey made by one Campbell, a surveyor, and according to that survey he would be entitled to the premises in dispute; but the evidence was strong to shew that the post planted in the original survey stood twenty rods to the east of the boundary as fixed by Campbell's survey. The evidence of the post between 22 and 23 was explicit and positive; and Campbell was made aware while he was making his survey that there was such evidence, and that the neighbours could describe the position of the original posts from their own recollection of them, but he did not take their evidence, and acted on his own ideas of what the lines should be.

Mr. Justice McLean charged strongly in favour of the plaintiff, but the jury found for the defendant.

This was a second verdict on the same side, the court having granted a new trial, because the first was against evidence. There was clear proof of the actual possession having been for many years according to the limits which the plaintiff desired to abide by, till about 1840, when the defendant, relying upon a survey which had been made at his request by Campbell, a surveyor, took upon himself to enter upon and keep possession of about twenty rods in width of the land, which had before that been always considered to be and held as part of 23, and not of 22, as defendant claimed it to be.

Sherwood, Q. C., moved for a new trial, the verdict being contrary to evidence and the judge's charge.

Vankoughnet shewed cause; he cited 3 Bing, N. C., 892; 6 A. & E. 407; 12 L. J. 250; 12 A. & E. 631.

ROBINSON, C. J.—In such cases as a general principle, the burthen of proof surely lies upon the party disturbing the previously acknowledged boundaries. No doubt, if there had been an error in the possession as first taken, the defendant had a right by law to have the error corrected. and to have his possession conformable to the original survey. Then, whether by the alteration he has taken upon himself to make, by excluding the former possessor, he is departing from the original survey, or is in fact only conforming to it, was the whole question to be tried. This to be sure is an action for *mesne* profits, which the plaintiff brought only for the purpose of obtaining damages for the former alleged wrongful occupation, and for the costs of an ejectment, which, for whatever reason, the defendant did not oppose, but allowed him to recover without setting up a title against him. But though this action would not necessarily bring the title in question, the defendant has made it to do so expressly by the defence which he has placed upon the record. He seeks to throw the costs of the action in which the plaintiff recovered, upon him, on the ground that he ought not to have recovered, for that the land was not his. Then since the trial proceeded on that ground, it was incumbent upon the court and jury to see that the question of right between them was determined according to law. That necessarily calls attention to the statute 58th Geo. III. ch. 13, a just and salutary Act, as I think, and certainly a very important one, and one that is binding alike upon courts and juries, so long as the legislature allows it to remain in force. The learned judge who tried the cause was clear in his opinion, that the evidence taken in connection with enactments of the statute referred to, shewed the right to be with the plaintiff, as regarded the question of boundary, and he so stated to the jury. They nevertheless found for the defendant, as they had a perfect right to do, if it can be looked upon as a question turning merely upon the weight of evidence. But the parties in this cause had a right to have the provisions of the statute carried into effect? have they or have they not been set at nought and disregarded by the jury; It appears to me they have been, for certainly the evidence on the plaintiff's side was strong and clear to shew that the posts of the original survey, planted to mark the front angle of the plaintiff's lot, entitled him to what he claims, and that the defendant sets up a survey recently made at variance with these facts, but not made as the Act directs it shall be, for the surveyor took upon himself to act independently of the statute, and to lay on one side, arbitrarily as it seems to me, the evidence which the neighbours were ready to give, from their own knowledge of the situation of the original posts, and which they did give at the trial. Fortune, it is proved, made the first survey; and before any patent issued for the lot, Stegman, a surveyor, was sent to examine his survey. This evidence is too clear to be doubted, that the possession to which the defendant limited himself till lately, was according to the posts, and the only posts which had been known for forty years and more as the posts set to mark the angles in the original survey, and no evidence of any other posts upon this lot was given. Then when Mr. Campbell is called upon at this late day to make a survey, he proceeds as if there never had been any such posts, and measures between a post that was proved to him to have stood between 17 and 18, and a post between 23 and 24, in the opposite township of Wolfred, and dividing the space equally according to the number of lots, he assigns to this Lot 23 what really appear to be new boundaries. Now if there were in fact no traces of the original posts between Lots 24 and 18, then this mode of proceeding would have been one which he might properly have adopted under the statute; but if it can be allowed to Mr. Campbell the surveyor, upon anything that he himself stated, and after attending to what the other witnesses so positively proved, to lay aside all evidence of a former survey of the front of Lot 23, and to run out the lines as if no traces of posts had existed there, then it will follow, that notwithstanding the clear provisions of the statute of 1818, every proprietor of lands must hold his possession at the mercy of any new survey that it may suit the fancy of a surveyor employed by his next neighbour to make. I think it is the duty of this court to be careful that that confidence which the legislature intended all should repose in original boundaries, should be firmly upheld. It is true that although witnesses who have lived on and around this lot of land from the time of this survey, swore these posts to be the original posts intended to mark the front angles, yet Mr. Campbell, upon no very convincing reasons, appears resolved to treat them as not being planted by Stegman, but by Fortune, whose survey he says was erroneous, and was intended to be corrected by Stegman's, but there was no evidence whatever of any double set of posts having been set there, and it is impossible, I think, to read the evidence of all the respectable neighbours produced by the plaintiff, and at the same time believe that the posts they speak of were planted, and that although ascertained and known by Stegman to be erroneous, were nevertheless always suffered to remain there, and that the proprietor of Lot 22, for thirty years or more, was content to be governed by them, as if they were the correct and true boundaries. It is true, that after the base line of what was intended at first to form the first concession of Montague was run, the government resolved not to make that straight line the dividing line between Montague and Wolfred, but to allow the Rideau River to be the boundary between the two townships, and the patents do accordingly carry the lands on each side down the river. It may therefore be said truly, that the posts spoken of do not in fact mark the front angle of Lot 23, as it was granted, and the same may be said of the other lots in the concession. But the same objection may be made to the surveyor Campbell taking the post which he found between 17 and 18 as a corner post, for that was on the old base line and not at the front angle of the lot as afterwards settled. If that then is an objection to what the plaintiff contends for, it is in like manner an objection to the legality of the survey, by which the defendant seeks to displace the occupant of what was so long considered to be part of 23. In reason, however (and the remark would apply equally to both), the posts planted on the old base line (if no others were planted) should be the guide in regard to the width of the lot, and the side lines should be produced from them to the river, on the proper course, in order to find the front angles. The costs of the ejectment which the plaintiff claims in this action were only about £7; what damages could fairly be given besides for the occupation of the land in dispute, could not be precisely made out from the evidence given. But it is not contended, I believe, by the plaintiff, that the verdict which he is entitled to expect, should exceed £20. The defendant objects that the case is within the rule, which in general is strictly observed, that where there is no misdirection, the court will not grant a new trial on the evidence, when the amount claimed does not exceed £20. That rule does not, in my opinion, fairly apply under the circumstances of this case. It is not the fact of occupation, or the amount of damages, about which the evidence is doubtful, but the defendant has chosen to make this action, and not the action of ejectment that preceded it, the means of trying the title. I will not venture to assume that the verdict as rendered may not, in connection with the pleadings on the record, helped out as they may be by averments, be found to be conclusive upon the question of right; and at any rate, it must be for the interest of the parties, that since the question has been thus raised, it should, if possible, be brought to a final conclusion consistent with law and evidence upon this record, and not left to be agitated in other actions, on account of its being unsatisfactorily disposed of on the trial of this cause. I regret exceedingly the necessity of frequently interposing to set aside verdicts in the same action, but circumstances occasionally render it necessary, unless we can properly leave parties in questions of property to acquiesce in verdicts which we must at the same time admit to be contrary to law and fact. One of the last cases in which we could properly decline to grant a new trial (whatever might be our reluctance), is where a proprietor of land takes upon himself to disturb an old boundary, and to narrow his neighbour's possession upon the pretence of a new survey, which, when it is explained, turns out not to be in conformity to the express directions of the statute. A man, whose boundary is called in question, may be reasonably allowed to defend a possession which he has long peaceably enjoyed, by evidence which tends only to make out a strong probable case in favour of his possession, until a survey regularly made shall show it to be wrong, because there the burthen of the proof is on the side of the person attempting to disturb him. But when, as in this case, a person comes to change the existing state of things under colour of a new survey, the onus lies upon him to shew that the possession hitherto has been erroneously held. Probabilities in such a case are not what is required; he comes to correct an error, and must be regular himself, and in my opinion, no evidence of new survey should be attended to as deserving of any weight for such a purpose, unless it has been made as the statute prescribes; except perhaps in some case where the alleged error is so manifest that it can admit of no doubt, and can be detected by any other person as well as a surveyor. I have several times, in other cases, expressed such an opinion upon this point as I am now stating, and if we should not carry the law into effect according to such principles, then it appears to me we should be leaving the door open for endless litigation, for after we had allowed the possession to be changed in deference to one irregular survey, and not made as the Act requires, we might find ourselves obliged to allow it to be brought back again, or otherwise modified, in consequence of a survey made in strict compliance with the Act, and which must therefore necessarily prevail in the end.

MACAULAY, J., concurred.

JONES, J., being connected with the plaintiff, gave no judgment.

McLEAN, J., concurred.

Per Cur.—Rule absolute for a new trial.

ARMSTRONG V. SOMERVILLE.

By the usury laws, all securities which have been given *in furtherance* of an usurious transaction, with the knowledge of the person who took the security, are void.

The plaintiff declared in covenant on the following agreement:

For that whereas heretofore, to wit, on the twenty-fourth day of July, in the year of our Lord one thousand eight hundred and forty-five, by certain articles of agreement then made, concluded and agreed upon, between the defendant and the plaintiff, which said articles of agreement, sealed with the seals of the defendant and of the plaintiff respectively, the plaintiff now brings here into court, the date whereof is the same day and year aforesaid, it was agreed, by and between the said parties, in these words: "First, Thomas "Somerville, in consideration of a conveyance this day made to him by the "said Armstrong, of one acre of land in Louth, formerly occupied by Jacob "Flander, agrees to pay to B. Meredith, Esquire (meaning thereby, Bridge- "water Meredith, Esquire), the amount of a mortgage thereon, being fifty "pounds currency, due in November next, and does also agree to release the "said John Armstrong from a certain debt due by the said Armstrong to the "said Somerville, amounting to about fifty pounds, upon the said Armstrong "obtaining his wife's execution to her release of dower to the conveyance this "day made as aforesaid, which Armstrong hereby agrees to do." And although afterwards, to wit, on the said first day of November, and before the commencement of this suit, the said sum of fifty pounds so due upon the mortgage in the said covenant mentioned, did become due and payable, and although the said Armstrong, to wit, on the day and year first aforesaid, did procure his wife to execute the release of dower contained in the conveyance in the indenture herein declared upon mentioned, of all which the defendant then and there had notice; yet the defendant had not paid to the said Bridgewater Meredith the amount of the said mortgage, or any part thereof, but hath hitherto wholly neglected and refused, and still doth neglect and refuse, so to do, contrary to the said articles of agreement, and the said covenant of the defendant by him in that behalf made as aforesaid; and the plaintiff saith that he, the defendant, hath not kept with him the covenant so made between them as aforesaid, but hath broken the same, and to keep the same with the plaintiff the defendant hath hitherto wholly refused, and still doth refuse, to the damage of the plaintiff of one hundred pounds, and therefore he brings his suit.

The defendant pleaded that before the making of the said articles of agreement, and the mortgage in the said declaration mentioned, to wit, on the fourth day of November, in the year of our Lord one thousand eight hundred and forty-three, it was corruptly, and against the form of the statute in such case made and provided, agreed by and between the plaintiff and the said Bridgewater Meredith, that he the said Bridgewater Meredith should lend and advance to the plaintiff a certain sum of money, to wit, the sum of thirty-one pounds five shillings, and that the said Bridgewater Meredith should forbear and give day of payment of the said sum of thirty-one pounds five shillings, from the time of lending the same until the first day of November, in the year of our Lord one thousand eight hundred and forty-five; and that for the forbearing and giving day of payment of the said sum, he the plaintiff should pay to the said Bridgewater Meredith, on the said first day of November last aforesaid, more than lawful interest, that is to say the sum of twenty-six pounds five shillings of like lawful money, and that for the securing the repayment of the said sum of thirty-one pounds five shillings, on the said first day of November, in the year last aforesaid, the said plaintiff should execute and give to the said Bridgewater Meredith the mortgage in the said declaration mentioned; and it was also then further corruptly and against the said statute agreed upon between the said plaintiff and the said Bridgewater Meredith and the defendant aforesaid, for the purpose of better securing the repayment of the said sum of thirty-one pounds five shillings, together with the said sum of twenty-six pounds five shillings, to the said Bridgewater Meredith on the said first day of November, and for the purpose of evading the said statute, that the said defendant should make and execute the said articles of agreement in the said declaration mentioned; and the defendant saith that in pursuance of the said corrupt and unlawful agreement, he the defendant did afterwards, to wit, on the day and year aforesaid, make and execute the said articles of agreement in the said declaration mentioned, for the corrupt and unlawful purpose aforesaid; and that he the said Bridgewater Meredith did, to wit on the day and year aforesaid, for the corrupt and unlawful purpose aforesaid, lend and advance to the plaintiff the said sum of thirty-one pounds five shillings; and the defendant further saith, that the said sum of twenty-six pounds five shillings, so agreed to be paid by the said plaintiff to the said Bridgewater for such loan and forbearance, exceeds the rate of six pounds for the forbearance of one hundred pounds for a year, contrary to the statute in such case made and provided; and this the defendant is ready to verify, &c. General demurrer to plea.

W. H. Blake for the demurrer. He relied upon 7 Mod. 119 ; Cro. Jac. 33 ; 8 T. R. 390 ; 4 Esp. C. 11 ; 4 Q. B. R. 511.

H. Eccles, contra, relied upon 1 Cam. 357 ; Cro. Eliz. 643 ; 12 M. & W. 481.

ROBINSON, C. J., delivered the judgment of the court.

We have no doubt that the plea in this case does state such a usurious agreement as avoids the written contract sued upon. The very cases cited by the plaintiff from Cro. Jac. 33 ; 8 T. R. 390 ; Cro. El. 588 ; 2 Mod. 279 ; and 4 Q. B. R. 51, tend strongly to support the plea, for those cases turned upon the fact of the plaintiff being ignorant of any usurious transaction, and of the security sued upon not being given as a colourable shift devised to evade the statute, when the money was originally lent; whereas this plea distinctly states, that before the agreement which is sued upon was made, it was corruptly agreed between Meredith and *the plaintiff*, that Meredith should lend the plaintiff £31 5s., to be repaid on 1st Nov. 1845, and that the plaintiff should pay him £26 5s. by way of interest for the use of the £31 5s., from the 4th day of November, 1843, to the 1st day of November, 1845, which would be about seven times the legal rate of interest; that it was agreed that the plaintiff should give to Meredith the mortgage mentioned in the declaration: and that it was *then*, corruptly and against the statute, further agreed between the plaintiff and Meredith, and the defendant, that for the purpose of *better securing* the payment of the money lent, and interest, and *for the purpose of evading the statute*, the defendant should execute the agreement which is sued upon in this action. The plea then avers that in pursuance of such corrupt agreement, the defendant did execute the instrument sued upon. The plaintiff demurring generally, puts it to the court whether, admitting all these facts to be true, they constitute any defence; and nothing can be clearer than that they do.

The argument of the plaintiff is, that because there was no usury as between the plaintiff and the defendant, that is, because the defendant may, for all that appears, have received from the plaintiff a full consideration for undertaking to pay this mortgage, therefore he must pay the money to Meredith on the plaintiff's account, although he well knew it was a mere contrivance for evading the statute. This would be rendering the mortgage available in the hands of a lender for recovering usurious interest, merely by resorting to the easy and obvious device of having the payment made through the hands of a stranger.

Our statute, like the English statute, makes it usury to take more than legal interest "directly or indirectly," and how is it possible to deny that Meredith would be taking the usurious interest indirectly at least, if (as the plea states) he contrived for the very purpose of evading the statute, and by express agreement with the borrower, that he should receive his payment from a debtor of the borrower's, instead of from the borrower himself.

Mr. Sergeant Hawkins says "that all writings whatever, for the *strengthen-ing* of a usurious contract, are void" (a). And notwithstanding there is a difference between the language of our statute 51 Geo. III. chap. 9, and the English Statute 12 Anne, chap. 16, we have held that the intention and effect of both are the same as regards the making void securities. I refer to the case in this court of Boag v. Lewis et al., 1 Cam. 357; and there have been other decisions to the same effect.

As the court say in Button v. Downham, Cro. El. 643, "it is the corrupt "agreement confessed by the demurrer which makes it usury, and it is the "intent that makes it to be so, or not so."

The statute would be so easily evaded as to be merely a dead letter, if so palpable a shift as this must succeed: for upon the statements made in the plea, the security, though taken in the name of this plaintiff, is in effect for the benefit of Meredith; and, for all we know, if the court should sustain this action, they would be giving the aid of the law to carry the usurious contract into effect; for we must suppose that either this action is brought by Meredith in the plaintiff's name, as is the common case when a bail bond has

---

(a) Ch. 82, sec. 23.

been assigned, or that the plaintiff, as soon as he collects the money, will pay it over to Meredith, as he is bound to do by the agreement which he has admitted by the demurrer

The case of Harrison v. Hannell, 5 Taunt. 784, is undistinguishable from the present; the plaintiff there contended that the security was not void, because as between him and the defendant there was no usurious interests to be paid: but Gibbs, C. J., said, "The fallacy of the counsel's argument is, that he "supposes the objection to the plaintiff's recovering to be, that his contract "*with the defendant* is usurious; whereas the objection really arises from the "circumstance that these notes are *deposited* to enforce another contract which "was usurious; and the defence rests on this, not that more than five per "cent. is secured by these bills, but they are destined to enforce a contract "which is usurious. If a man lends a thousand pounds on usurious interest, "and gets from a third person a collateral security for eight hundred pounds "only without usurious interest, I hold that bond is void, not because it is "given for securing usurious interest, but because it is given for enforcing a "contract for usurious interest."

It is true, though the agreement here was to pay the lender, yet the undertaking was not directly to him, but to the borrower; but that can make no difference to him; it was the repayment to the lender of the very money lent with the usurious interest that was the express object of the agreement; nor can it make any difference whether the defendant in this case entered into the undertaking gratuitously and to oblige the borrower, or upon receiving a consideration from him of equal, or greater, or less amount. The intention of the law is, that a security shall not be enforced, whether in the name of the lender, or any other person for his use and by agreement with him, or by any device or contrivance whatever which the art of man can suggest, if such security has been given in furtherance of a usurious transaction with the knowledge of the person who took the security.

Per Cur.—Judgment for the defendant on demurrer.

EASTON AND JUDD, ASSIGNEES OF THE SHERIFF, v. JOHN LONGCHAMP, EDWARD LONGCHAMP, AND EDWARD PATTERSON.

The provision in 8 Vic. chap. 13, secs. 66, 58, 72, is retrospective as well as prospective.

Held, that the endorsement on the writ of execution being stated to be for a less sum than that mentioned in the judgment, is no ground of special demurrer.

Held also, that it is not necessary to aver in an action brought by the assignees of a bail bond, that the sheriff did not receive the money after the assignment of the bond; neither is it necessary to aver that the defendants had notice of the assignment.

The declaration stated a judgment recovered in *assumpsit*, by the plaintiffs, against the defendant J. Longchamp, in the Victoria District Court, to wit, on the 15th of September, A.D. 1843, in a cause of action within its jurisdiction, for £40 damages, and £2 4s. 6d. costs, as by the record thereof remaining in the said District Court at Belleville more fully appears; and that for having execution of the said judgment, afterwards, to wit, on the 2nd December, in the 9th Vic., duly sued and prosecuted according to law and under the statute 8 Vic., and by virtue of and according to the requirement of the 44th section of the said Act, out of the District Court of the Newcastle District, a writ of *ca. sa.* tested the first of November, 9 Vic., upon the said judgment so obtained as aforesaid, against the said John Longchamp, to the sheriff of the said Newcastle District, to take the said J. Longchamp to satisfy the plaintiffs for £40 17s. 6d., being an amount within its jurisdiction, and *part* of the damages, costs, and charges so as aforesaid recovered, returnable on the 16th of December then next endorsed for £40 8s. 11d., 9s. for interest, and interest from the 2nd December, 1845, and sheriff's fees, which writ afterwards, and before, &c., to wit, on the 4th December, 1845, was delivered to the said sheriff; that the said sheriff arrested the said J. Longchamp before the return thereof, to wit, on the 6th of December, 1845, and that *afterwards*, and before the return, to wit, on the same day, within his district, the said sheriff took bail of the said J. Longchamp for the limits.

The declaration then stated the bond from the defendants to the said sheriff for £60, reciting that the said J. Longchamp, then a prisoner under the said *ca. sa.*, at the suit of, &c., to satisfy the plaintiffs for £28 16s. 5d. and interest, &c., and *conditioned* that if the said J. Longchamp, arrested on the *ca. sa.* aforesaid, should remain within, and not depart from or without the limits of the said Newcastle District Gaol, then to be void, otherwise, &c.

It then alleged for breach, that the said J. Longchamp did depart from without the said limits, afterwards, to wit on the 26th January, 1846. It stated assignment to the plaintiffs, by means whereof, &c.

The defendants craved oyer of the said bond and condition, which were set out; the condition was, that if the said John Longchamp should remain within, and not depart from, or without the limits assigned to the said gaol; *or* if the defendants should indemnify and save harmless the said sheriff of, from and against all losses, costs, damages, and expenses which they might sustain for, or on account of, or by reason or by means of allowing the said John Longchamp to go at large on the said limits, then, to be void.

Demurrer to declaration:

First, because it is not alleged in what *term* the said judgment was recovered.

Second, because the allegation of the defendant J. Longchamp's conviction, and whether the judgment was still in force, are uncertain.

Third, that the statute did not authorize the issuing of the *ca. sa.*

Fourth, because it is not alleged that the said *ca. sa.* issued upon the said judgment.

Fifth, that the declaration shewed that it did not follow the judgment but varied in the amount, as if for *residue* after the levy of part.

Sixth, that the breach is bad, in not negativing payment to the sheriff *after* the assignment, or alleging that the defendants had notice of the assignment.

Seventh, that the plaintiffs have not alleged that the exemplification of judgment and affidavit according to the 44th section of the Act, were filed; and that the same were conditions precedent to the issuing of the said writ of *ca. sa.*, and should have been alleged.

J. Cockburn, of Cobourg, for the demurrer. He relied upon 8 M. & W. 319; 3 Dowl. 679.

Campbell, of Kingston, contra, cited 5 B. & Ad. 68; 1 Saund. 330, note 4.

ROBINSON, C. J., delivered the judgment of the court.

It is not necessary, in our opinion, that the judgment should be "expressly "averred to have been rendered in term time," though in this case the judgment was entered before the late District Court Act, which extends our 22nd rule, Easter, 5 Vic., to the District Courts. Thenceforward there can be no question, that stating the true day will be proper, whether it be in term or out of term, and so we think it is equally sufficient in respect to this district court judgment, entered before that rule was made applicable to the district courts.

The District Court Act, 2 Geo. IV. ch. 2, does appoint certain periods of sitting for the court, but it gives no names by which they can be designated, and stating the day according to the truth is sufficient; though before the late rules, the judgments of the superior courts must have been averred to have been entered in a certain term.

It is not necessary to aver that the judgment is still in force, and it is indeed stated here, that when the bond was assigned, which was long after the *ca. sa.* was taken out, the money remained unpaid (*a*).

The third objection is one of substance. In my opinion, the provision in 8 Vic. chap. 13, secs. 44, 58, 72, applies to past judgments as well as to future. It is reasonable to suppose that the legislature so intended, and the form of expression in the statute admits, I think, of that construction. "It shall be "lawful for the party recovering judgment," may receive a more extensive construction than such as would limit the provision to those "*who shall recover* "*judgment after the passing of the Act,*" as the "*party suing*" may be used with the intention to refer it to a party who has already sued. The 58th clause warrants the provision being so applied, and it is in advancement of justice, and to remedy a plain defect, and so the clause should have a liberal construction though it does affect the liberty of the subject, for it could not have been intended to have put some creditors, whose judgments were unsatisfied, on a different footing from others.

The fifth and sixth objections depend on one point, and are not, as we think, tenable. It is no objection in the mouth of the bail (two of the defendants) that the endorsement was for a less sum than that recovered by the judgment, and the other defendants having joined in demurring, his case must be governed by the same rule as theirs (*b*). But at any rate it is mere matter of practice, and there is nothing apparently erroneous.

The declaration shews no variance between the execution and the judgment, but merely a direction to levy less than they both authorized, which is a common case with executions when the judgment is for more than the true debt, as it often is. The debt may, for all we know, have been paid in part since judgment; all that can be said is, that the declaration does not explain

---

(*a*) 1 Saund. 330, note 4; Com. Dig. Pl. 2 W. 12.
(*b*) Moravia v. Sloper, Willes, 34.

why the writ was not endorsed for more, but it need not. The difference is in the defendant's favour, and furnishes him with no ground of exception.

As to the objection, that it ought to have been alleged that the sheriff did not receive the money after the assignment of the bond, the forms of declaration in such cases do not require it, nor can it be necessary; for payment to the sheriff after the assignment would be illegal, unless the defendants were ignorant of the assignment, in which case, if the defendants could rely upon the payment, they must set it up as matter of defence; neither is it any defect that notice of the assignment is not stated.—8 M. & W. 319.

Per Cur.—Judgment for plaintiffs on demurrer.

COOK ET AL. V. MAIR.

The plaintiffs declare in *assumpsit* for not paying a bill of exchange, which the defendant agreed to accept, payable at Montreal, on the 18th day of July, 1845, in consideration of the plaintiffs delivering to the defendant, at *St. Catharines*, 10,000 bushels of good, clean, merchantable fall wheat. The declaration avers the delivery of the said wheat to the defendant *at St. Catharines*, and that the defendant *accepted and received* the same. The defendant pleads, secondly, that the plaintiffs did not deliver *the said* 10,000 *bushels of wheat in the 1st count mentioned* to the defendant; and 3rdly, that the said 10,000 bushels of wheat *averred* to have been delivered by the plaintiffs to the defendant was not, nor is, good, clean, merchantable fall wheat, concluding with a verification. Demurrer to the 2nd plea, because it leaves it uncertain whether the defendant intends to object to the non-delivery of the wheat altogether, or to the non-delivery at the time or place mentioned in the declaration. Demurrer to 3rd plea, because it should have concluded to the country, and not with a verification, and because it was no answer to the 1st count. Several grounds of objection were taken to the sufficiency of the declaration.

Held, per Cur.—Declaration good on general demurrer. *Held,* also, 2nd plea good, and 3rd plea bad, on special demurrer.

Assumpsit for not paying a bill of exchange which defendant agreed to accept, payable at Montreal on the 18th July, 1845, in consideration of plaintiffs delivering at St. Catharines, 10,000 bushels of *good, clean, merchantable fall wheat.*

The declaration averred the delivery of the said wheat *at St. Catharines*, and that defendant *accepted the same.*

Common counts were added.

The defendant pleaded, 1st, *non-assumpsit.*

2nd, That plaintiffs did not deliver the said 10,000 bushels of wheat in the 1st count mentioned.

3rd, That the said 10,000 bushels of wheat averred to have been delivered by the plaintiff to defendant was not, nor is, good, clean, merchantable fall wheat, and concluded with a verification.

Demurrer to 2nd plea: That it left it uncertain whether the defendant intended to object to the non-delivery of the wheat altogether, or the non-delivery at the time or place mentioned in the declaration.

Demurrer to 3rd plea: That it should have concluded to the country and not with a verification, and that it was no answer to the 1st count.

Exceptions were taken to the 1st count on general demurrer—

That it is uncertain and double, inasmuch as it sets forth two separate and distinct contracts, and does not shew clearly upon which the plaintiffs are proceeding.

Also, that it is insufficient in not stating the delivery of *good, clean, merchantable fall wheat*, according to the express terms of the agreement.

Also, that there is no proper averment of the presentment of the draft, in the said 1st count to the defendant stated.

Also, for the insufficiency and uncertainty of the agreement set out in the said 1st count, and for want of a proper averment of non-performance by defendant.

Cameron, Sol.-Gen., for demurrer, relied upon Com. Dig. Pleader, C. 76.

Phillpotts, contra, relied upon 6 M. & G. 36.

ROBINSON, C. J.—With regard to the objections which have been taken to the declaration, it does appear sufficiently (on general demurrer) that the plaintiffs are suing on the agreement last set forth; that is, for not paying a bill drawn payable at Montreal, on the 18th of July, which can only refer to the last agreement. All that goes before is mere inducement: a relation of the transaction which led to the agreement last stated.

I think also, that upon general demurrer, we may intend the wheat to be such as the original agreement called for; the words "*the said*" as there used, can only mean wheat, such as had been before described, because no specific parcel of wheat had been spoken of. On special demurrer we might have found it necessary to hold otherwise. Wallis v. Scott, Stra. 88, is much in point, and supports the declaration against this objection. As to the want of any averment that the bill had been presented, the declaration should properly, I think, have contained a statement, that the plaintiffs had drawn a bill in their own favour, or in favour of some third party, and that it had been presented. It does, however, contain a statement, that defendant had notice of the bill which the plaintiffs did draw and *refused* to accept or pay it, and that the bill was protested; and this I think is sufficient, especially when the defendant has not demurred, but has pleaded over, resting his defence on other grounds, not denying the breach in not paying the bill of which he had due notice, but giving as an excuse for his alleged breach, that the plaintiffs had not done what entitled them to a performance on the defendant's part.

There is no ground, I think, on which we could properly hold the declaration bad in substance.

Then as regards the pleas, the second plea is objected to on the ground that it leaves it uncertain whether the defendant means to object to the non-delivery at the time or place mentioned in the declaration.

I do not see that it is liable to such an exception. The plaintiffs had agreed to deliver to the defendant 10,000 bushels of wheat at St. Catharines (not on or before any particular time as the contract is stated), for which the defendant was to pay the plaintiff's bill on him, for a certain sum, to be made payable on the 18th July following. The plaintiffs aver that they did deliver the said 10,000 bushels of wheat to the defendant at St. Catharines (not saying when), and that the defendant *then* accepted and received the same. The defendant pleads in his defence, that plaintiffs did not deliver the said 10,000 *bushels of wheat in the said first count mentioned* to the defendant.

This is certainly a full and direct denial of the plaintiffs' alleged performance of the condition precedent. If the defendant had added, "in *manner* and *form*," it could have made no difference as to the *time* of delivery in the issue raised, because the plaintiffs had stated no time. The only difference would have been, that he would then have more precisely met the plaintiffs' averment, not going beyond it in his denial; whereas now he has denied what the plaintiffs have affirmed, and something more. He says in effect, that the plaintiffs did not deliver the wheat at St. Catharines, *nor anywhere else.* To deny the delivery anywhere else than at St. Catharines was unnecessary, because a delivery elsewhere would have availed nothing to the plaintiffs, unless indeed the defendant accepted of the delivery, which the declaration states he did. But why should it make the plea bad? I can see no reason : as the court observed in a similar case, in Paine v. Emery, 2 Cr. M. & R. 306, "If the "party did not pay at all, he did not pay at the particular time and place. It "amounts therefore to a denial of what the plaintiffs had alleged and more."

If the plea had tendered an issue which would have called on the plaintiffs to shew performance of something which they had not agreed to do, it would have been bad, no doubt, as for instance, if the defendant had pleaded that the plaintiffs did not deliver the wheat at a particular place in St Catharines, as upon a certain wharf there. But the effect must be just the reverse of this, if it varies the issue at all. This plea, concluding, as it does, to the country, will either have the effect of letting the plaintiffs into proof of delivery of the wheat at any other place than St. Catharines, or it will not: if it will, then the effect of its being too large a traverse could tend only to the advantage of the plaintiffs themselves, and so would furnish no ground of exception to the plaintiffs (a). If it would not have the effect of making proof of delivery elsewhere than at St. Catharines sufficient for the plaintiffs' purpose, then it is wholly insignificant, and cannot affect the issue (b).

My opinion, at present is, that the plaintiffs must still prove a delivery at St. Catharines, for that is what the plaintiffs have averred in express terms; and the defendant denies that they have delivered the wheat at all, which is certainly a full and direct denial; wherefore proof of the affirmation rests with the plaintiffs, that is, they are to prove what they have affirmed, and nothing more or less. The substance of the issue then is, the delivery of the wheat at St. Catharines; *a delivery* elsewhere would not be *a delivery* according to *the intent*, and so could not prove what the defendant must be considered to have denied, when he pleaded that the plaintiffs had not delivered the wheat. In actions of replevin, the issue of *non cepit* is held to traverse the seizure at the place.

It would be absurd to suppose, that the defendant could mean by his plea to deny that the plaintiffs had delivered the wheat anywhere else than at St. Catharines, since a delivery at any other place would have signified nothing; it was at St. Catharines that they were bound to deliver it, and the defendant by denying the delivery, and concluding at once to the country, can only be taken to be denying that delivery which the plaintiffs had averred. The

---

(a) Com. Dig. Pl. 9, 16; 2 Lev. 81.   (b) 5 M. & W. 6.

plaintiffs on their side are perfectly formal in their allegation of performance; it cannot be denied that the plea directly and fully meets the averment, for it is impossible they can both be true; and there being thus a complete issue, the proof of the affirmative lies on the plaintiffs, who are to prove what they affirmed, namely, the delivery at St. Catharines.

The third plea, in my opinion, is bad, for it does not admit that the ten thousand bushels of wheat were delivered, nor any wheat, but states that the ten thousand bushels averred to have been delivered by the plaintiffs, were not, nor are, good, clean, merchantable fall wheat. Now, unless the wheat was in fact delivered, it is of no consequence what its quality was; and if the plea can be taken to admit the delivery as the plaintiffs have averred it, then it admits also, that the defendant had "accepted and received it;" and if he did accept the wheat, its quality could not afterwards be objected to unless upon some ground of latent fraud not here pleaded.

I think the defendant is entitled to judgment on the demurrer to the second plea, and the plaintiffs on the demurrer to the third plea.

MACAULAY, J.—I am of opinion that the declaration is good on general demurrer. The defendant undertook to pay any bill drawn on him at Montreal, and it is alleged that he had notice of its having been drawn payable there. The plaintiff has averred performance of all required of him by the terms of the contract, and the defendant not being entitled to have the bill presented to him for acceptance, being payable at a named day, or for payment, being bound to pay it without presentment as the drawer, it was incumbent upon him, according to his agreement, to pay it to the holder in Montreal. If unknown to him, he might, on receipt of notice that it had been drawn, have applied to the plaintiffs for the name and residence of the holder; and if not informed, the neglect or refusal might, if pleaded, have constituted a sufficient excuse for non-payment; but in the absence of any such defence, I consider the declaration sufficient.

The plea that the wheat delivered was not good merchantable fall wheat, is bad in substance; it is consistent with it that nine-tenths of it was of such quality, and the delivery and acceptance of the whole being averred, and not denied, any defect of quality is not pleadable in bar of the action for non-performance of the contract on the defendant's part. It would form but a partial failure of consideration undefined in amount, and unless admissible in reduction of damages, would form the proper subject of a cross action; besides, it having been alleged that the wheat delivered was accepted by the defendant, the matter pleaded without more (as want of opportunity to inspect, imposition or the like) is sufficient to excuse the defendant from the alleged breach of agreement on his part. As to the conclusion of this plea, the plea being in the negative, there was nothing asserted requiring proof on the defendant's part to be verified; the onus of the proof would have been on the plaintiff to shew that the wheat delivered was of the description promised.—6 M. & G. 36, n. (4); 7 M. & W. 274, Bodenham v. Hill.

If the plea traverses a material allegation of the declaration, expressed or necessarily implied, it should have strictly concluded to the country; if not, and it is questionable whether the matter traversed is impliedly alleged, it certainly is not expressly (a), there being a negative of new matter, though not necessary to have concluded with a verification, it does not seem demurrable, because it has so concluded (b); if it had been a good plea in the matter of it, I should have considered the conclusion unexceptionable.

I have felt much difficulty with the second plea; the plaintiff avers that he did deliver to the defendant the *said* ten thousand bushels of wheat at St. Catharines, and that the defendant (not saying *and there*) accepted and received the same.

The plea is, that the plaintiffs did not deliver the *said* ten thousand bushels of wheat, in the said first count mentioned, to the defendant, concluding to the country. The ground of demurrer to this plea is, that it is uncertain whether it intends to object the non-delivery of the wheat at all, or its non-delivery at the time and place mentioned in the declaration; and the question is, whether it puts in issue not only the fact of delivery, but such delivery at the place alleged. The *place* being material by the contract, the plaintiff, to entitle himself to recover, was bound to aver a delivery there, and must, if denied, prove it. The plea does not admit it, wherefore it does not appear by the defendant's confession, nor would a verdict, merely establishing the delivery of the wheat, shew it, unless by intendment, and the uncertainty on this head is made the ground of objection. It is said a traverse to the defendant's disadvantage is not demurrable (c); but this plea is not to his disadvantage, unless the effect of it is to render the plea immaterial, and to waive proof of delivery there. It is clear, that were it not material on the face of the declaration, the same plea would be a good denial of the delivery, and would not include the place, or put it in issue; a plea having that effect would, in such a case, be bad on special demurrer. A general denial of delivery is somewhat inconsistent with a denial restricted to a particular place, unless upon the principle, that delivery being the most material thing, must, when denied, be proved according to the allegation as to place when material; and when it is so, such a plea may be construed to include it in the traverse, or the plaintiff be restricted in proof to such place. Had it concluded with the usual words, *modo et forma*, it would undoubtedly have been good on the ground, that when time or place is material, a denial *modo et forma* includes them in the substance of the issue. The general issue in replevin shews this; there the plaintiff is obliged to name the place of taking in his declaration, and the plea of *non cepit modo et forma* traverses the taking at such place, and the plaintiff must prove both upon the trial (d). It is also clear, that when the *modo et forma* is mere form and immaterial, as when the plea expressly traverses the whole allegation material to be denied, and put in issue, without requiring any aid by implication from the *modo et forma* (as in Nevil v. Cook, 2 Lev. 5, where a demurrer to a plea, traversing the request for not concluding *modo et forma*, was overruled) its omission is not a ground of special demurrer; still, when it may be material to the substance of the issue, as in this case, I am not satisfied the objection is not valid, and it appears to me to have analogy to the case of Cuvillier v. Brown on demurrer, decided last term. The argument

---

(a) Str. 88. (b) Stephen's Pleading, 223, 225.
(c) Do v. Parmiton, 2 Lev. 61. (d) 6 Bing. 107; 1 Str. 507; Bull. N. P. 300.

that the objection would not be available on general demurrer, or would be cured by verdict, does not prove it to be insufficient cause of special demurrer. A resort to such an argument rather concludes it to be otherwise, and certainly the plea does not adhere to the usual form of traverse, where time or place is material, and involved in the substance of the issue. However, as the rest of the court are clear that the plea, without the *modo et forma*, puts in issue both the delivery and the place; and as I find no instance of a special demurrer for its omission being allowed, I am disposed, on the whole, to adopt that view, on the ground, that the delivery having been necessarily averred to have been at St. Catharines, the proof of the delivery is local, and the plaintiff is confined in evidence to the place so necessarily averred and material to be established, to entitle him to recover, and that therefore it is virtually, though not expressly, embraced in the traverse.

McLEAN, J.—The defendant was bound, by the agreement stated, to pay the bill referred to on the 18th of August, if the plaintiff delivered the 10,000 bushels of good, clean, merchantable fall wheat, at St. Catharines, but not otherwise. Plaintiff alleges the delivery of the said wheat at St. Catharines; and the word *said*, seems to me to refer to the quality as well as the quantity of wheat delivered. The defendant says he did not deliver the *said wheat*, in general terms, and puts himself upon the country as to that fact; but the plaintiff objects that the defendant should have been more particular, and should have alleged that the plaintiff did not deliver at St. Catharines. Now, when plaintiff alleges a delivery at St. Catharines, and defendant denies any delivery, I cannot understand why plaintiff cannot take issue on the fact of delivering as tendered by defendant. I do not see any uncertainty in the plea which can render it demurrable.

As to the 3rd plea, I think it ought to have concluded to the country, as it was a plain matter of fact, on which issue was tendered, which did not require any answer from plaintiff, and it does not answer the declaration; it does not deny that defendant *accepted* the *said* wheat, as alleged in the declaration, but merely attempts to put in issue the description and quality of the wheat; whereas, if it had been accepted by defendant, he could not afterwards object to it on that account. I think this plea is bad, for the reasons stated.

The defendant objects to the declaration on general demurrer, on the ground that the declaration contains a statement of two distinct contracts, and does not shew clearly upon which the plaintiff is proceeding; that it should have alleged the delivery of good, clean, merchantable fall wheat, according to the agreement; and that there is no averment of a presentment of the draft; for the insufficiency and uncertainty of the agreement set out in the 1st count, and for want of a proper averment of non-performance by defendant.

As to the first of these objections, I do not think there can be any doubt as to the contract sued on. The declaration states, perhaps unnecessarily, the whole agreement between the parties about the wheat, the failure of the first arrangement, and the subsequent promise to pay the bill of plaintiff at Montreal on a particular day, in consideration of plaintiff delivering the wheat at St. Catharines. The non-payment of the plaintiff's bill is clearly the ground of action, and special damage is laid, as arising from the defendant's breach of agreement. The averment of the defendant is, that the plaintiff delivered the *said wheat*, referring to the wheat mentioned in the first part of the declaration, and which is there stated to be "good, clean, merchantable fall wheat;" and, as I have already stated, I think the statement of delivery sufficient, the word "said" embracing as well the quantity as the quality of the wheat delivered.

It is further objected, that there is no averment of presentment of the bill for payment. I do not consider such averment necessary. Defendant, it is alleged, agreed to pay at Montreal, on a *particular day*, a bill to be drawn by plaintiff. Plaintiff alleges that he drew such bill, and that defendant had notice of it, but did not pay it. The non-payment and the notice of the bill being drawn are not denied by defendant, and it was not necessary it should have been presented to defendant for payment. If defendant had notice of it, he was bound by his agreement to go to the holder and to pay the amount. He admits by his manner of pleading that he did not do so, but he alleges as his reason that plaintiff did not deliver the said wheat, and then, that it was not good, clean, merchantable fall wheat. The only remaining objection is the want of a proper averment of non-performance by defendant. I do not, however, see any defect or informality in this respect; the promise and the non-fulfilment of it, and the injury arising by the default, seem to me to be explicitly stated, and not subject to the objections raised by defendant.

JONES, J., gave no judgment.

Per Cur.—Judgment for the defendant on the demurrer to the second plea, and for the plaintiffs on the demurrer to the third plea.

MONAGHAN V. FERGUSON ET AL.

Under the 44th sec. of the 7th Vic. ch. 29, the trustees of the public schools (and not the schoolmaster), should be made the plaintiffs in an action of trespass to the school house; unless at least it can be shewn, that the trustees have given the schoolmaster a particular interest in the building, beyond the mere liberty of occupying it during the day for the purpose of teaching.

Trespass *quare clausum fregit*, for breaking and entering a certain school house of the plaintiff, situate on Lot 17, in the 12th concession of London, making a noise and disturbance therein, breaking doors, &c.

And a second count for breaking and entering another school house of the plaintiff, and expelling him therefrom.

The defendant pleaded these pleas: first, not guilty.

Second, denial of plaintiff's property in the school house.

And third, denial of the plaintiff's possession of the school house.

The building in question was in fact a meeting house, belonging to the Methodist Society, and was vested in trustees by a deed, made in 1833, upon the understanding that it was to be occupied also as a school house, on the school trustees engaging to repair any damage done to the building in consequence of its being so used.

In 1845, there was some contest about the appointment of trustees to the public school, but the prevailing party appointed the plaintiff as their teacher, and he was allowed to occupy the building as a school house for some months. In the autumn, the trustees of the meeting house wished to do some repairs to it, and it appeared to be a matter of dispute between them and the school trustees, whether the school should continue to be kept there while the work was being done. At length, on the 2nd of December, the defendants went there together, at a time when the building was locked up, broke off the lock and took away the stove pipes; since which time, the plaintiff has not taught there.

It was objected at the trial, that the plaintiff, being a mere servant to the school trustees, could not bring trespass for the injury to the freehold.

The learned judge was of that opinion, and by consent a nonsuit was entered, with leave to the plaintiff to move the court to direct a verdict to be entered in his favour for £5, if he should be considered entitled to recover.

J. Duggan moved accordingly. He cited 1 E. R. 244; 5 B. & Ald. 600. The plaintiff had sufficient possession as against a mere wrong-doer; 5 Q. B. R. 139; 4 B. & C. 574.

Boulton shewed cause. The plaintiff was a mere servant, and had no interest in the estate or possession, except as a servant.

ROBINSON, C. J., delivered the judgment of the court.

We are of opinion, that this rule should be discharged; the 44th clause of the School Act, 7 Vic. ch. 29, gives the custody of the school house expressly to the trustees; we must therefore, we think, regard them as being in possession, and not the teacher employed by them, even if upon general principles the facts of this case might otherwise have enabled the teacher to sue. The teacher was absent when the alleged trespass was committed; the meeting house was locked up, the books or the furniture in it we are not to look upon as his, so as to give him a constructive possession. On the contrary, we think, the constructive possession was in the trustees under the law, which places the building in their keeping. The 44th clause of the Act defines very clearly what are the duties and position of the trustees, when it provides that they are first, "to have the custody and safe keeping of the common school house "for their district;" second "to contract with, and employ all teachers "within the same." This building, by the arrangement made with the trustees, was the common school house for the time, and since the law vests in the trustees the custody and safe keeping of it, they must be regarded as being for the time in possession, unless they had actually parted with the possession, which they certainly had not done by employing a person to teach in it, for that was the very purpose for which they held it. They might have given to their teacher that kind of interest in the building, beyond his mere liberty to occupy it during the day for the purpose of teaching, which would have constituted a tenancy, but nothing of that kind is shewn. If such a relation had existed, of course the tenant, and not the landlord, must have sued for the injury that is complained of here; but then, if the trustees had placed themselves in that position with regard to the school house, they would no longer have had the actual custody of the building as the law contemplates, for that implies the means of exercising an immediate control, power to prevent damage by instant interference, and a right to compel compensation for injuries done by others, in order that the trustees may effectually fulfil their trust of safe keeping: all of which are repugnant to the condition of a landlord. It appears to me, that the case of Wildbor v. Rainforth, 8 B. & C. 5, applies in principle to the present; there a pauper who had been allowed by the overseers of the poor to occupy a small tenement, went away leaving her children in the house; ten days afterwards the overseer entered and took possession, put locks on the doors, and removed the children to the workhouse; the pauper brought trespass against them, and the court held, "that she could not sue in trespass, for "she was not tenant of the premises, but was merely allowed to occupy them "by the parish officers; the occupation was in fact theirs." This, it is true, is not an action by the schoolmaster against the trustees, but neither can it be looked upon as an action against a mere stranger entering without colour of right. There had arisen a dispute about the premises; the trustees of the meeting house claimed a right to enter and make repairs; and if that was an infringement of any exclusive right of possession, the question lay between them and the school trustees, and not between them and their teacher.

Rule discharged.

DOE PERRY ET AL. v. HENDERSON.

Where A. has been twenty years in possession of land, paying no rent, and signing no written acknowledgment of title in another, such possession, whether it originate adversely to the claims of the true owner B., or with his permission, operates under the Statute of Limitations to extinguish the title of B., and to vest the title in A.

Held, that a verbal acknowledgment of title by A. in B., made during the twenty years, would not save the statute.

Held also, that A.'s acknowledgment in *writing* of a title in B., *after* the twenty years, could not have the effect of reviving a title which the twenty years' possession had extinguished.

Held also, that a judgment in ejectment recovered by B. against A. *after the twenty years had expired*, would not save the statute. *Aliter*, if recovered *within* the twenty years, and A. within the twenty years had *been dispossessed* upon such judgment.

Held also, that a conveyance by B. to A., within the twenty years, of a part of the lot in dispute, would not save the estate—his deed to A. being no written acknowledgment on the part of A. of B.'s title.

Held also, that the fact of A.'s paying the taxes by B.'s direction is no bar to the statute.

Held also, that A., commencing his possession by the permission of B., and upon a contract to purchase, B. must be held as in the *actual possession* of the land through his tenant at will A., and as being *dispossessed* at the end of the first year's tenancy; and that therefore the 17th section of our Provincial Statute of Limitations would apply so as to bring B. within its operation.

Semble, that if A. could be shewn to have been occupying the land as the mere servant or agent of B., during the twenty years, and not for his own use or benefit, the statute would not run.

Ejectment for Lot 9, in 5th concession of Sidney, the east half, one hundred acres, being the only part in question. The lessors of the plaintiff, Simeon and Daniel Perry, claimed under a conveyance, made to them in 1842, by their father Robert Perry, the brother and heir at law of Amoy Williams, to whom the land was granted by patent, in 1802.

The defendants endeavoured to shew title in themselves under a conveyance from Robert R. Perry, brother of the two lessors of the plaintiff, all these being the sons of Robert Perry, under whom the lessors of the plaintiff make title. The deed under which they claimed was made 11th March, 1846.

Both parties claimed under Robert Perry; his title therefore was not disputed; and the question at the trial was, whether his son Robert R. Perry, who conveyed to the defendants, had acquired a title by long possession under the Statute of Limitations; or rather, the more correct way of stating the question would be, whether the title of Robert Perry, the father, had not become extinguished by his suffering himself to be dispossessed for more than twenty years before he made the deed to his other sons, the lessors of the plaintiff.

To prove the long possession of Robert R. Perry to have been held under such circumstances as gave him a title and extinguished his father's, he was himself called as a witness; he was objected to on the ground that he had covenanted for title in his conveyance to the defendants, but that objection was removed by a release; and he was again objected to on the further ground that he was in actual possession of the premises as tenant to the defendants, and would therefore be liable to be dispossessed if these plaintiffs recovered.

In answer to this objection it was shewn, that the term of his tenancy would expire almost immediately (about six days after the trial), so that the verdict in this cause could not affect him, unless it could be supposed that he intended wrongfully to hold over. He was admitted, and upon his evidence and the other testimony in the cause, the defendants had a verdict.

Independently of the testimony of Robert R. Perry, it was proved by several disinterested witnesses, and was in fact not disputed on the argument, that he went into possession of the whole of this Lot No. 9 in 1818, and lived on it and cultivated it as his own from thence, without interruption, until the 18th of September, 1844, being twenty-six years; at which time he was dispossessed by the sheriff under a writ of *hab. fac. poss.*, issued upon a judgment in ejectment entered on 16th Feb., 1844.

The ejectment was brought on the demises of Simeon Perry and Daniel Perry, who are the lessors of the plaintiff in this action, and tried in October, 1843, when the jury gave a verdict for the plaintiffs. Robert R. Perry by some means got again into possession before he conveyed to the defendants. The plaintiffs relied much upon the effect of this recovery in ejectment against Robert R. Perry, as precluding him from again setting up a title under the Statute of Limitations. They contended that he could not now revert again to his possession as giving him a title; and that it must be assumed against him, that his possession before the ejectment had not been of that nature, that it could bar the person having the actual title, since it had been on the former occasion relied upon in vain. The origin and nature of that possession was fully gone into on the last trial before the Chief Justice, and much evidence was received respecting it. No attempt was made to shew that Robert R. Perry had, within the twenty years, given any acknowledgment in writing of Robert Perry's (his father's) title, or that he had paid him at any time any rent. It was clearly proved, quite apart from any evidence given by Robert

R. Perry, that in 1818, while his father was the proprietor of this lot, he, Robert R. Perry, had been allowed by his father to go upon it and to occupy it, not as a tenant, but for his own benefit; that his father gave him the west half (one hundred acres), and allowed him throughout the whole period to make the same use of the east half as of the west half, cultivating as much of that half as of the other. His father, who lived in another township, frequently visited his son while he was thus living upon the land, and was often heard to say, that he had given him the west half, and agreed to let him have the east half, upon the condition that he was to work for him a year, and pay him £25. In confirmation of this, the defendants produced in evidence a writing on a small piece of paper, apparently very old, not under seal, in these words:

"*Fredericksburg, 12th December, 1818.*
"This is to certify, that I do quit all my claim, right and title, to Lot No.
"9, in the fifth concession of Sidney, to my son Robert, in law or equity, and
"that he has paid me the sum of twenty-five pounds in work for the same.
"(Subscribed,)   ROBERT PERRY."

The genuineness of this writing was disputed; it was not given in evidence on the former trial, because, as it was alleged, it could not then be found, and had been discovered since; several witnesses swore that they were well acquainted with Robert Perry's handwriting, and believed the signature to be genuine; Robert Perry himself, however, denied that it was his signature, and there was no subscribing witness.

Alexander Campbell, of Kingston, moved for a new trial, on the ground of misdirection, and for the reception of illegal evidence, and also on the law and evidence.

Robert R. Perry, being the tenant of the defendant, and in actual possession of the lot in dispute, his evidence was inadmissible; he should have been rejected as an incompetent witness. If the plaintiffs recovered he could be dispossessed; he was therefore clearly interested in the verdict (*a*). It is admitted that Robert R. Perry was in possession for twenty years; but it is contended that the judgment recovered in ejectment by the lessors of the plaintiff against him, deprives him of the benefit of such possession, as conferring any title. Besides, the admissions that have been made by Robert R. Perry to his father, and to Ham, and his whole conduct during the twenty years' possession, created a new tenancy at will.—6 Jurist, 266. When R. R. Perry got the deed from his father for the west half of the lot, that also created a new tenancy.—3 A. & E. 63; 9 M. & W. 13; 5 Jurist, 170; 6 M. & W. Doe Crogan v. Edwards. And of course, a new tenancy being created within the twenty years, a new starting point for the commencement of the twenty years' possession has been gained, which will have the effect of saving the Statute of Limitations. He contended that from the reception of Robert R. Perry's evidence, and from proof being given of a tenancy at will having been created within the twenty years, the plaintiff should have a new trial.

Kenneth McKenzie, of Kingston, on the same side, relied on the 17th

---

(*a*) 6 B. 394; Bent v. Baker, 2 Smith's Leading Cases.

section of the Real Property Act, as preventing the operation of the statute with respect to the possession of Robert R. Perry. The father had never been "*dispossessed.*" There had been no "*discontinuance of his possession*" while entitled to the land; he merely said to his son, he might go upon the land and take care of it. Under these circumstances, the possession was the father's and not the son's. The son was the agent of the father; there was no *dispossession* therefore, and the Act did not apply. He also contended, that Robert R. Perry's acknowledgment of title in his father, to Ham, was sufficient under the statute, and would apply, though given after the twenty years' possession had created a perfect title.

Cameron, Sol.-Gen., shewed cause. He admitted Robert R. Perry was an incompetent witness, but as the verdict might stand wholly unaffected by the rejection of his evidence, the admission of his evidence was no ground for a new trial.—8 C. & P. 570; 3 M. & W. 527. He contended that the judgment in the former ejectment was not conclusive. A party might resort to his title, in a new action of ejectment, as much when it rested on possession only, as on a paper title.—8 E. R. 358; 7 M. & W. 593; 7 Bing. 346; 1 Ld. Raym. 741. A judgment in ejectment is clearly no estoppel. 2 M. & W. 294; 2 Smith's L. C.; 11 A. & E. 1008; 4 M. & G. 30; 8 M. & W. 643; Jurist, 815 (1846). The conversations of Robert R. Perry with his father, or with Ham, could not prevent the statute running. These were merely verbal acknowledgments of title; to save the statute, they must be in writing. So also the deed *from* the father to Robert R. Perry, was no acknowledgment in writing by Robert R. Perry of the title being in the father, consequently no new tenancy had been created within the twenty years to save the statute. As to the objection urged by the learned counsel Mr. McKenzie, it could not apply. The father was in possession as the patentee, through the son, as tenant at will. At the end of the year then, by the 19th sec. of our Statute of Limitations, the father would be dispossessed by the son continuing longer in possession; there was a dispossession therefore sufficient to satisfy the 17th clause of the Act. Upon the whole facts of the case, he felt satisfied that notwithstanding all the grounds of objection the title was in the defendants, and the court ought not to disturb the verdict.

D. B. Read, on the same side.—He fully concurred in the law, as laid down by the learned Solicitor-General, on all the points in the case except one. He would therefore refrain from directing the attention of the court to any of the points, but the one at which he held an opinion decidedly at variance with the admission made by his learned friend the Solicitor-General. He was strongly of opinion that the reception of Robert R. Perry's evidence was correct. If Robert R. Perry had been a tenant under a lease which was not to expire till a lengthened period after the verdict, he would have been no doubt incompetent, because he might have been dispossessed by the plaintiffs in ejectment; but as Robert R. Perry's tenancy was to expire in six days after the verdict, and therefore before any use could be made of the verdict for dispossessing him, he has no real interest in the suit, and his evidence was clearly admissible.

ROBINSON, C. J., delivered the judgment of the court.—I told the jury, that the case did not turn upon the writing, because, not being a deed for want of a seal, it could not transfer the estate, and all must depend on the defence set up under the Statute of Limitations. I wished the jury, nevertheless, to express their belief respecting the genuineness of the writing, because that might be a material fact in connection with the statute, so far as it might seem to shew the footing upon which Robert R. Perry had been let into possession; but the jury did not pronounce upon it, being told that the case rested upon the question of fact, whether Robert Perry had been more than twenty years out of possession; and finding it difficult, I suppose, (as I certainly did myself) to come to any certain conclusion upon the reality of the signature. On the one side they could scarcely suppose it possible that Robert Perry, apparently a respectable farmer of advanced age and unimpeached character, would wilfully swear falsely about a matter of this kind; on the other hand, several of his neighbours considered the signature to be his, and it certainly had no appearance of being a counterfeit signature, but was written in a natural unconstrained hand; and moreover, Robert Perry assigned as his reason for stating the signature to be forged, that he always put the addition of *junior* to his name at that time, because his father was then living. But in this he was mistaken, for it was shewn that to the deed which he had given to Robert R. Perry for the west half of the same lot, while his father was still living, he had signed his name, as in this case, without the addition of *junior.* After hearing all the evidence, I was inclined to believe that Robert Perry had signed this writing in 1818, and had forgotten it; but as the jury were unable to say conclusively whether it was genuine or not, we must suppose that they threw it out of the case. If the verdict had turned upon it (which it could not properly have done), and if Robert R. Perry was incompetent as a witness, then we ought not to let the verdict stand, because his evidence in support of the writing was positive and circumstantial, and ought in that case to be supposed to have had weight with the jury. It was only in this one respect that it was desirable that the jury should have been able to satisfy themselves of the truth of this paper, namely, that if Robert did in 1818 give a writing to that effect, although it could convey no interest for want of a seal, it would yet serve to shew clearly that he had allowed and intended Robert R. Perry to possess the land as owner, acknowledging that he had been paid for it in work, for if he did not mean by the words used in it that he had been paid in full, but only that he had received so much on account of whatever was to be paid, it would still have shewn that he was willing to look for the payment of the remainder as for any other debt, and did not wish to withhold, in the meantime, such title as an illiterate man might have thought it sufficient to give, the land being at that early day of comparatively small value. In that view of the case we should feel that the Statute of Limitations would not have an unjust effect, as it would only then be confirming what both parties really intended. But this consideration, after all, could not influence the legal decision of the case, because when the statute clearly applies, it must have its effect, whether it seems to us to operate justly or otherwise; so that I did not think at the trial, and do not now think, that the writing was of much moment one way or the other. It was plainly proved, that from the spring of 1818, for more than twenty-six years without interruption, Robert R. Perry had lived upon this Lot No. 9 as owner, with the knowledge and assent of the father, cultivating and using both halves of it alike. With respect to the west half, there had been no dispute, and in

1830, Robert Perry made a deed to his son of that hundred acres; why he did not before that time, or at that time, make him a deed of the east half did not certainly appear. On the part of the defendants it was accounted for by saying, that the deed of the one hundred acres was only obtained in 1830 as a matter of form, to enable Robert R. Perry to vote at an election, and was sufficient for this purpose: that he did not press for a deed of the other hundred acres on that occasion, because Robert Perry's second wife was opposed to his getting it, and it would have given rise to trouble in the family. However this may be, Robert R. Perry continued to possess the whole lot as before, paying the tax (which was trifling) on the whole lot, as he alleged by the desire of his father, and having his dwelling in fact on the east half, as one of the witnesses proved. There was evidently a misunderstanding between Robert R. Perry and his father about the east hundred acres; when it began did not appear, but there is no doubt that, whether justly or not, Robert Perry did not acknowledge the right of Robert R. Perry to the east half to stand on the same footing as his right to the west half. There was proof by his admission on the trial, that he did agree from the first to let him have that half; but his complaint was, that his son had not paid him for it as he had promised to do; that he was to have worked for him two years, and paid him one hundred dollars, or to have worked for him one year and to have paid him two hundred dollars; and that he had only laboured for him eleven months, and had paid no money. The son's account was, that his father only required him to labour for him one year with a team, which he had done, and when that was completed, his father gave him the small writing which I have already spoken of, observing that as he had no deed himself to shew, (claiming the land by inheritance from his sister,) no more formal conveyance from him was necessary. These were the opposing statements of father and son, both of them objected to on the trial as incompetent witnesses from interest, the son because he was living on the land in dispute at the time of the trial as tenant to the defendants, and moreover because (as it appeared in the progress of the trial) he had, on the 14th of April, 1840, made a mortgage of the whole lot to one John Reynolds, to secure a debt of £40, with covenants for title and for quiet enjoyment. The father was objected to, because, in the conveyance which he had made of the east half of the lot to the lessor of the plaintiff, he had given similar covenants. All that either of them swore to on this point, might, without prejudice to the case on either side, be rejected, for so far as it could be material, since the rigid rule laid down by the late Statute of Limitations, to know why the owner of an estate has suffered himself to be dispossessed for more than twenty years, the facts of the case were proved from their own admissions by a disinterested witness, Mr. Ham, who had heard their respective statements. From the evidence of this witness, it appeared about four years ago (two years before the recovery in ejectment in the action brought by these same lessors against Robert R. Perry) he was pressed by Robert R. Perry to advance him a sum of money, and in the course of their negotiation a reference was made to the father, Robert Perry, with a view to get him to take back the deed which he had given to Robert R. Perry in 1830, of the west half only, and to make a conveyance to him of the whole lot; that the father objected, stating that his son still owed him one hundred dollars, with twenty-four years' interest upon it; that the son did not deny this, and offered £50 if his father would make the deed, not speaking of having already received from him any writing for the lot. It seemed to the witness, that Robert Perry would have consented to take the £50 and make the deed; but when his son admitted that he had mortgaged the *whole lot* to John Reynolds, which is the mortgage I have described as being given in 1840, the father was angry that he had presumed to do so. The son attempted to excuse himself by saying, that he had at the time told Reynolds, that he had no right to the east half; but the father persisted in his refusal, giving that as his reason, and declined executing a deed which the witness at the request of Robert R. Perry had prepared, and taken up to him, for conveying the whole lot, as a substitute for the one which he had given in 1830 for the west half only. There is therefore clear evidence from a witness not excepted against, that in 1842, while Robert R. Perry was still living on the land, he acknowledged verbally that he was not the legal owner—that the title was in his father—that he had agreed to pay for the land now in dispute, in which case he would have been entitled to a conveyance, but that he had not paid for it; that he was then, in 1842, willing to pay what the father claimed—was anxious to obtain a title—pressed for it—and had a deed prepared and tendered to his father to sign. On the other hand, the father acknowledged what was clearly enough proved by other testimony on the trial, that his son had been allowed to live on the land continually, paying no rent for more than twenty-four years, but that he had required him about fifteen years ago to pay the taxes for him, which the son had done. So far as verbal admissions can be material, the case against Robert R. Perry was strengthened by the testimony of another witness, who swore that within a few months, while Robert R. Perry was again in possession of the land, (after he had been removed under the writ of *hab. fac. poss.*) he admitted to him unequivocally, that the east half of the lot was his father's, and that he had no objection to his father's having it, if he would remunerate him for the improvements he had made upon it, The negotiation which the witness Ham spoke of, was put an end to by Robert R. Perry, by writing a letter, in which he desired Mr. Ham not to make any further attempt to get his father to make the deed, and not to give notes, as had been spoken of, for the £50, "for that *he* had dis-"covered that there was a statute which would enable him to keep the land, "without thanks to his father." There was no account of anything further having passed between Robert R. Perry and his father respecting the land. Not long after this, as it seems, the father made the deed of the east half to his two younger sons, the lessors of the plaintiff, under which they now claim. Upon this deed they brought their ejectment soon after, and recovered against Robert R. Perry, who defended the action; and he was dispossessed by the sheriff as I have stated. He took advantage of an opportunity of getting quietly into possession again, and on 11th March, 1846, made the deed to the defendants, under which they now claim. Whether this conveyance, which Robert R. Perry seems to have been reluctant to make, was sustained by any valuable consideration or not, it is not important in this action to inquire. No creditor of Robert R. Perry is objecting to it as fraudulent, nor any subsequent purchaser from him for valuable consideration; and the question is not whether these defendants have an honest or legal title, but whether the plaintiffs, after what has been proved, can be allowed to sustain this ejectment. In point of fact, the mortgage for £40, which Robert R. Perry had given on the lot, seems to have been cancelled in the transaction; but whether he got anything substantial beyond that, is very doubtful. At the conclusion of the case, I told the jury that, in my view, the question of title turned wholly upon the Statute of Limitations; that the small paper writing alleged to have been given in 1818, could not, if it were proved to their satisfaction, confer any legal interest; that after having given it, Robert Perry's legal estate would continue in him as before. That the question was, whether before he made the deed to the plaintiff in November, 1842, his title had not been extinguished under the effect of our statute 4 Will. IV. chap. 1, by his having suffered himself to be dispossessed, or by discontinuing his possession and the receipt of the rents and profits for more than twenty years continually; no rent being paid to him during that period, or any written acknowledgment of his title given by the party in possession. I considered that if the writing dated 12th December, 1818, was in fact given by Robert Perry, it would have only the effect of creating from that time a new tenancy at will, and preventing any antecedent possession from being counted (if indeed it could have such an effect, when it professed to part with the whole interest). That supposing a tenancy at will to commence then, in a year after that the Statute of Limitations would begin to run, that is, from 12th December, 1819; and there is no question that Robert R. Perry continued in actual possession undisturbed till September, 1843. The twenty years in that case had expired on 12th December, 1839. The statute came into force 1st July, 1834, and assuming the possession of Robert R. Perry not to have been adverse at that time, the five years within which he might on that account have brought his ejectment, had expired on the 6th of March, 1839, being five years after the Act was passed. I told the jury, that the effect of the recovery in the former ejectment would be a fit matter to be discussed more deliberately; that for the present, I should hold that it made no difference in the case. That the verbal admissions of Robert R. Perry of his father's title, were unavailing, as well as the fact itself that his possession was not adverse, but permissive; that the origin of the possession in 1818, or before (that is, whether it was as tenant at will or upon a contract of purchase), was now immaterial. That the mortgage by Robert R. Perry, in April, 1840, could not, as I thought, have any legal effect; if it had been given before the twenty years were out, it might have put an end to the current tenancy at will, and given a new starting point as to time; but being given as it was after twenty years had run out, and also the five years from the passing of the statute, it could not revive the title of Robert Perry, which had been extinguished. The fact of the treaty about the title in 1842, could not have any legal effect, as it appeared to me, for the same reason; nor even the letter of Robert R. Perry, written to the witness Ham, which put an end to that treaty, even supposing it to amount to what would come within the statute, as a written acknowledgment of title, because it was after the period of twenty years, and not during it; that it was no acknowledgment in fact of a then existing title in his father, but an assertion of title in himself by virtue of the statute. I saw upon the whole case no clear ground upon which I could hold that the statute had not the effect of barring the ejectment and extinguishing the title of Robert Perry before 1842, when he conveyed to the lessors of the plaintiff, and I left the case to the jury with a direction to find for the defendants, if they were satisfied that Robert R. Perry had been in possession continually for twenty years before April, 1840, without paying any rent, or acknowledging in writing within that period Robert Perry's title; otherwise to find for the plaintiff. They found for the defendants, probably with some degree of that reluctance which, I confess, I felt in being compelled to give them that direction; for the justice and good conscience of the case seem to be against Robert R. Perry, if the witness Ham's evidence be correct, and I have no reason to doubt it is; and so far as equitable considerations could apply, the defendants do not seem to stand in any other situation than he would have stood if he had not transferred his right to them; they do not seem to have been *bona fide* purchasers for value. With respect to the grounds on which the plaintiffs have moved for a new trial. First, on the reception of illegal evidence; that refers to the witness Robert R. Perry, who, it is contended, was incompetent. If the objection were well founded, I think we could not set aside the verdict for that reason, for he proved nothing material to the case in the way in which it went to the jury. If the jury had been told that they were at liberty to decide according to the good conscience and equity of the case, setting aside the Statute of Limitations, then Robert R. Perry's testimony might be supposed to have had much influence upon the verdict, for he placed his own conduct in the matter, and his own right upon the merits, in a light much more favourable to himself than it would have stood upon the other evidence; but with respect to his possession for more than twenty years, and extending from 1818 at least down to 1843, the fact stood undisputed; it was amply proved by other evidence, and is not now denied; and it was upon that fact that the jury were told that the case must turn, taken in connection with the recovery in ejectment, the attempt to obtain a deed in 1842, the letter of Robert R. Perry, written about that time, and the mortgage given by him in April, 1840, if it should be found that they could control the effect of the Statute of Limitations; and these points in the case, as well as every other upon which an argument has been founded, stand just the same upon the evidence without his testimony, as with it; except indeed, so far as any stress may be supposed to have been laid by the jury upon his assertion, that he had paid in full for the land, and that his father, in 1818, gave him the writing which was produced. As to that, I can only say that his evidence on those points had no weight with me; and that I expressly directed the jury that it ought to have none with them; and that it is quite clear to us now, that if Robert R. Perry had not been called, or if all his evidence were struck out, it could have made no difference as to the verdict which it would have been proper for the jury to give, and we could not dispose of the case upon a different ground. As the objection has been raised, however, I must say that I do not see that it ought to have prevailed. If, at the time of the trial, Robert R. Perry had been in possession of the land in dispute, either as a trespasser holding indefinitely, or upon a lease which he could have expected to hold under for any length of time, he would have been clearly incompetent, because the effect of the recovery of the plaintiffs in ejectment, would be to enable them to disposses him in either case ; but his lease was to expire, as he said, in ten days, and before any use could be made of the verdict for dispossessing him. Unless we could assume that he meant to hold over wrongfully, he had no apparent interest. There was ground, I dare say, for surmising that there was a very good understanding between him and the defendants, and that he expected, and perhaps would get, further indulgence if they succeeded ; but that should only go to his credibility as tending to give him a bias. Objections to competency go upon stricter grounds, and must rest upon some clear principle ; no case upon the point has been cited, and probably none can be found, for it may not have happened in any other case that a witness when he was called, stood in such a situation as this witness described himself to be in, whether truly or untruly. After he had been examined, a further objection was taken to his evidence, on the ground that he had given a covenant for title in his mortgage to J. Reynolds, but as it appeared to me that that mortgage had fulfilled its purpose, and was in effect cancelled, and that he was no longer in a position to be sued on his covenant, I did not strike out his evidence, but gave it to the jury with the observation that it proved nothing material to the case which was not clearly proved by other evidence, and nothing material indeed that did not seem to be admitted. With respect to the objection raised in the course of the trial to the competency of Robert Perry the father as a witness, it is now of no consequence, because he was admitted, and the party who called him failed on the trial.

This case has been argued, both on the trial and on this motion against the verdict, as if it were one of great hardship upon the former proprietor of the land, or rather upon his sons, the lessors of the plaintiff, to whom he has conveyed it. That depends, as I have stated, in a great measure upon whether Robert Perry did really give such a writing in 1842 as was produced upon the trial. If he did, then it is evident that he was willing from that time to put his son Robert in full possession of the title, and to look to him for paying the consideration agreed upon, if indeed the instrument does not import upon the face of it, that it had been already all paid. If Robert Perry did not give any such writing, still if there was really a dispute between them on the fact of payment, then one could have little hesitation in saying, that this was one of those cases in which the Statute of Limitations must have been intended to apply, for as Robert R. Perry had been in possession of the estate, using it as his own for twenty-five or twenty-six years, it would be contrary to the avowed object of the legislature in quieting possession, if he must at the end of that time be liable to be turned out or not, according as he might be able to prove the payment of a disputed demand, from which any remedy in a court of law must have been barred many years before. But to state the case as the plaintiffs consider they have shewn it to be, we are to take it that there is in fact no dispute about the purchase money being unpaid ; that the father having in 1818, or before, kindly given to his son Robert the west half of the lot, allowed him to occupy also the east half, upon the understanding that if he paid a certain consideration for it he would make him a deed for that as well as for the other ; that the son continued to live upon the lot with that understanding, never paying the consideration for the east half, and all the time conscious that he had on that account no claim to a deed for it ; that his taking a deed from his father in 1830, for the west half, shews that he had then no right to a conveyance of more; and that there is no evidence for twelve years after, that he either expected or applied for a title; that in 1842, when he did endeavour to procure his father to sign a deed for the east half, he yielded at once to the objections made on account of his non-payment, and offered his notes for the money, and admitting that the title was still in his father, pressed him to convey. That he, or those to whom he has since taken it upon himself to sell, can now be suffered to turn round upon the father, and maintain that by virtue of the Statute of Limitations the land without any such conveyance has become his, and was in fact his all the time he was treating with his father as the owner of it, is exclaimed against as being too gross an injustice for the law to suffer.

Though it may often happen that legal principles and positive statutes which operate well in the greater number of instances will in some particular cases be attended with hardship, and though that is an inconvenience which must be borne where the rule or statute clearly applies, and cannot be allowed to sway the judgment of the court, yet it is always of use to attend to the operation of the rule or statute in the particular case, and to consider carefully the alleged circumstances of hardship, because the fact that the peremptory application of the rule will in any case produce hardship, should lead us generally to suspect that there may be some view of that case which may not at first strike us, but in which the law, as well as justice, requires that it should be viewed, and which if duly attended to would prevent any wrong being suffered. With regard to the statute 4 Will. IV., chap. 1, as it relates to the limitation of actions to try the right to real property, I confess I have always felt some degree of doubt whether the application in this country of the provisions which we have adopted from the English statute 3 & 4 Wm. IV. chap. 27, governed as it will be, while the law remains unaltered, by the decisions of English courts upon questions presented by that statute, may not produce more hardship and inconvenience than it will be reasonable to incur for the sake of enforcing a general rule for the quieting of possessions.

Without presuming to call in question the soundness of the English decisions upon the proper construction of the statute 3 & 4 Wm. IV., one cannot but be struck with the apparent inconsistency between the effect given to the statute under those decisions, and the explanations given by the real property commissioners who framed the Act, of the system which it was their intention to establish by their proposed new law. They speak throughout the report of *adverse* possession as the intended foundation of their law of limitations; they lay it down that "it is both reasonable and useful, *that enjoyment for a certain "period of time against all claimants* should be conclusive evidence of title," (page 39). Now, they could hardly have contemplated, that a man who was enjoying the use of an estate with the permission of the owner as a matter of favour, could be looked upon as enjoying "*again all claimants.*" When they proceed (page 40) to announce their measure, they say, "we propose that the "law should be rendered simple and consistent, by giving a uniform and "certain effect to *adverse enjoyment*," which they recommended should be done by abolishing real actions, and absolutely extinguishing the right after the twenty years' adverse enjoyment. "*Adverse possession* of land for a period "of twenty years, will then (they say) be *required to be*, and will be, a bar *to* "*all adverse claims;* and all the antiquated forms of proceeding, which are "now occasionally resorted to for the recovery of landed property, will give "way to ejectment." Then they notice (page 41), that if a chattel interest in land be claimed, an *adverse possession* of twenty years is an absolute bar, and that in courts of equity the rule is generally understood to be established, that after an "*adverse possession of twenty years*, no relief can be given," and they add, "so far the proposal *is no innovation.*" "We also think (they remark) "that continual claim, by which right of entry may be kept alive, beyond the "twenty years, should be abolished, and that within that time the claimant "must either redress his wrong by his own act in availing himself of an oppor- "tunity to take peaceable possession, or he must *call in the aid of law by* "*commencing his action.*"

Now it seems reasonable to remark, that a man who has allowed a friend or relation to occupy a lot of land as a matter of favour or of indulgence well understood between them, has *no wrong to redress* till he has been set at defiance; or in other words, till the possession, which was permissive, has, by a change of conduct in the occupant, become adverse. He has no occasion for the aid of the law, or for commencing an action, so long as the occupation is with his assent. The commissioners then discuss the allowance that ought to be made for disabilities, and they propose that no disability shall keep a claim alive for more than forty years. "We think (they say) that there should be a period "of *adverse possession*, after which all claims *against which the possession was* "*adverse*, shall be barred, notwithstanding any disabilities whatsoever." Now there is certainly in all this no intimation that the commissioners intended to propose a departure from the principle which had always been applied in acting on the old statute 21 Jac. I. ch. 16, namely, that it was only in the case of adverse possession, that the limitation was to operate; in other words, that a man was not to lose his estate on account of his omissions to pursue his remedy, when he had suffered no wrong, and was not conscious that he needed a remedy. But the commissioners in their lucid report come, a little afterwards (page 47), to the very point of what they wish to be understood to mean by "*adverse possession;*" and here, if anywhere, we should expect to see announced whatever change they intended to propose in the law, by attaching a new idea to that term. They treat the subject thus: "Great practical diffi- "culty (they say) has arisen in determining what is *adverse possession*, and "when it shall be considered to have begun. *This must generally be left as a* "*question of fact for a jury.* But there are some rules of law which absolutely "prevent the possession from being considered adverse, (when it is in fact so, "the commissioners mean), and the expediency of which is very questionable, "as they do not seem necessary for preserving rightful claims, and they greatly "impair the healing tendency of the Statute of Limitations. One of these "rules is, that a possession which began rightfully, cannot be considered as "having been wrongful; that is, *adverse* as against the rightful owner, by "being merely continued after the right of the party in possession has deter- "mined. It appears to us, that *it should be open to a jury to find* that *adverse* "possession began from the determination of the rightful estate of the party."

After reading these explanations, given by the commissioners of their views, one can hardly imagine that they were conscious that they were proposing enactments which, if adopted, were to have the effect of doing away thenceforward with all distinctions between adverse and non-adverse possession, and leaving nothing "*open* to the jury" upon the point. Yet, in Doe dem. Knight v. Nepean, 2 M. & W. 984, and several other cases, that has been determined to be the effect of the new Act.

I should have supposed that what the commissioners intended was, that the possession should in no case be absolutely presumed to have been non-adverse, merely because it had a rightful commencement; but that from the moment it became in fact adverse by the conduct of the occupant, it should be open to the jury to treat it according to the truth. They perhaps meant also, to throw, in all cases, the onus of proof that the occupation was permissive, upon the party suing after the twenty years; in other words, that whenever there had been no rent paid, and no written acknowledgment of title could be shewn, the occupation, during so long a period, should be presumed to have been adverse, till the contrary was shewn, to the satisfaction of the jury. But the court in England have not felt that they were at liberty so to construe the statute, as to leave the question of adverse or non-adverse possession open to the jury; and Mr. Sugden, in his learned work on the Law of Vendors, without objecting to the construction given to the Act by the Exchequer Chamber, in the case cited, remarks, "that the framers of the Act do not appear to "have followed out their own views, as contained in their report, but have "left the point of adverse possession to be settled by the *construction of the* "*Act*" (Sugden on Vendors, Vol. II. p. 349); and referring to what is now the acknowledged effect of the statute, he adds, "These provisions place landed "proprietors in danger of rapidly losing portions of their property, particularly "where they have allowed friends or dependants to occupy parts without the "payment of any rent. In many such cases the statute will be found to have "transferred the fee simple to the occupiers; where twenty years have not "already elapsed, written acknowledgments of title should be immediately "obtained from all such occupiers." Lord Denman, in a late case, observes that "in all such cases the statute operates as a parliamentary conveyance."

We can have no hesitation as to the propriety of giving full effect to the statute, and of deferring to the English decisions. It is incumbent upon us to do so in this case, to the same extent as in others; but it is important that these consequences of the Act 4 Will. IV. ch. 1, should be fully brought out and understood.

I have indeed already more than once alluded to them, and especially in a case decided during this term, of Doe dem. Ausman et al. v. Minthorn, though I did not there state them so fully as I thought it might be useful to do here.

In England, real estates are so much more valuable, and so much more circumspection is habitually used in dealing with them, that if there must be cases of hardship under the Act, they are not likely to be so numerous as in a country like this.

There it will not be found often to have happened, that the owner of land has allowed it to be occupied for more than twenty years by a person standing in an indefinite position, and paying him no rent; here that may, from various causes, have been allowed to happen much more frequently.

On the other hand, it must be considered that dormant claims upon landed property may require to be more strictly dealt with in a new country, where land is more freely passed from hand to hand ; and certainly, in most colonies, the tendency of legislation has been to shorten the period of limitation, and to favour the actual occupant. Whether it is reasonable, however, to pay so much respect to the twenty years' occupation, as to allow a person who has held, not in defiance of the real owner, but with his permission, to set it up as a title, after he has honestly retired from the possession, or after he has been dispossessed by a judgment at law, upon a trial of the merits, when the circumstances of his occupation have been shewn, is a matter for the consideration of the legislature. We have only to examine whether the statute, in the construction which it has received, admits of any such modifications.

In the case which we are now to dispose of, the fact of Robert R. Perry having been for more than twenty years in actual possession of the land in question, paying no rent, and giving no written acknowledgment of title, was clearly proved ; and feeling how desirable it is, that whatever questions the new Statute of Limitations is likely to give rise to shall be freely discussed, and determined as they arise, I was particular in requesting the jury explicitly to find for the defendant, if they took the same view of the evidence, upon the mere fact of occupation, as I did ; and the parties were given to understand, that any point which they had started at the trial, or which the evidence, upon a more mature consideration of it, might be found to present, should be regarded as open for discussion upon any motion that might be made against the verdict.

We have now, then, to consider the several matters which have been urged as grounds for preventing the twenty years' possession from operating as an extinguishment of Robert Perry's title : and, to give them their fullest effect, we may assume that Robert Perry had not received payment from his son, and had given him no assurance of a title, nor intended to give him any till he should be paid for the land.

1st. The origin of the possession was clearly not adverse, and the son was let in not to occupy as owner, but only upon the confidence that he would entitle himself to become owner at a future day.

That would not signify, if it be true (as I assumed at the trial) that Robert R. Perry being on the land twenty years, without paying rent or acknowledging title, would render it of no moment with what expectation, or with what assent, or under what agreement he went upon the land in the first instance. The decisions in England upon the statute 2 and 3 Will. IV., which is similar to ours, compel us so to hold.

If the title was all the time in the father, he should have taken some written acknowledgment, or brought his action before five years from the passing of the Act had expired. Not having done so, the son stood in the same situation as any other person entering upon a contract to purchase ; and it has been expressly adjudged, that if such intending purchaser be allowed to remain in possession twenty years, without making any payment or acknowledging the title of the owner in writing, he becomes himself the owner by the operation of the statute.

2ndly. Robert R. Perry has unequivocally acknowledged to several persons, in 1842 and since, that the land was his father's, and not his. The answer to that is, that all such verbal aknowledgments are made by the statute unavailing. If they were proved to have been made while the twenty years were running, they would not signify, because the statute expressly makes a written acknowledgment of title necessary. If made after the twenty years had run out, they could not overturn the title in his son, which the lapse of twenty years had the effect of creating, and could not revive the title of the father which had been extinguished.

There can be no clearer case than such as Mr. Sugden supposes, where a friend or relation has been suffered to occupy a place, as a favour, rent free; and yet, I think, we are compelled by the statute and the decisions upon it to say, that if the occupant had continually, during the twenty years and afterwards, verbally admitted that the land was not his, and that he was occupying it by permission, such admissions could not prevent the statute operating. I wish to guard, however, against expressing the opinion that there may not be an occupation by another, on behalf of the owner, as servant or agent, and not for the benefit of the occupier, which will not come within the statute. There seems to be no ground for raising that question here.—3 Ad. & Ell. 66; 3 Bing. N. C. 498; 2 Sugden, 349.

3rdly. As to the effect of the recovery in ejectment. It has been decided in England repeatedly, that a recovery in ejectment is no estoppel; and upon the second trial the same question is only brought a second time, as it may be in this form of action, before the court—that is, whether the title of Robert Perry has or has not been extinguished. Any other objection to his recovery might be insisted upon a second time, after a former judgment pronounced against his right; for repeated efforts may be made in successive actions to recover upon a title which has been adjudged invalid, until a court of equity thinks fit to interpose. If within the twenty years Robert Perry or his assignees had set up their title and recovered, and the possession had been changed, then of course the operation of the statute would have been prevented. But the judgment in this case was after the statute had taken effect; and we cannot hold that a person claiming to have had title conferred upon him by the statute may not defend himself under it a second time, because he has failed in a former action when he attempted the same defence. Of course Robert R. Perry's assignees can set up any defence which he could have done.

4thly. Robert R. Perry accepted a conveyance in 1830 for the west half only, which it is urged amounts to an admission that his father then owned that half; and that, as all was held by one title, it must be taken as an admission that he continued, after making that deed, to hold the half which he did not convey; but an admission, plain and unequivocal, by Robert R. Perry in 1830, that the land was not his, but his father's, and that he was living on it by his father's permission, or against his will, would signify nothing. The twenty years were suffered to run out without an acknowledgment in writing; and the taking in 1830 a deed from the father to the west half—saying nothing of the other half —cannot be strained into an acknowledgment in writing that the father owned the east half; and if it could, still the deed was not signed by Robert R. Perry, and is therefore no written acknowledgment by him.

5thly. Something was said in the argument on the effect of Robert R. Perry having paid the taxes by his father's direction; but that could be of no effect, unless as it might seem to place him in the situation of a mere agent of his father, and give that character to his occupation. It is clear, however, that he was in fact occupying for his own benefit, not as the servant or agent of his father; and his paying the taxes under such circumstances, is no more than what he ought to have done without any such direction. The tenant or occupant is *prima facie* liable to taxes; and there is no evidence that he was advancing them for his father, to be repaid, as an agent would be. If his father had made him a deed in 1818, he must have paid the taxes; and the insisting upon it that he should do so is a confirmation, so far as it goes, that his father threw upon him the liabilities of owner of the property.

6thly. The pressing for a deed in 1842, and the letter written by Robert R. Perry on that occasion, seem to me now, as they did at the trial, to be matter of evidence which cannot affect the title, because they took place some years after the twenty years had run out, and cannot undo the title which the statute had perfected by placing the parties back in such a position as they might have stood in before the twenty years had expired.

7thly. So, also, as to the mortgage given to Reynolds in 1840. If that had been given at any time during the period of twenty years, and while Robert R. Perry could have been regarded as tenant at will, it would, by putting an end to the tenancy at will, have brought the case within the principle of the decision in Doe dem. Bennett v. Turner, 7 M. & W. 226, and might have furnished ground for leaving to the jury to find a new tenancy at will created, which would have given a new starting point from whence to reckon the twenty years. This might have been the case, I mean, if the mortgage had been given before the statute 4 Will. IV. ch. 1, came into force. Since that statute any tenancy at will would be regarded as having ended at the expiration of the first year; and then any act, such as that of giving the mortgage, or an entry upon the premises by the right owner, as in Doe dem. Bennett v. Turner, would have no effect upon the relative position of the parties. But here the whole period of limitation must have run out in December, 1839, if not (as I apprehend it did) a year or two before; for I think Robert R. Perry had been some time in possession before December, 1818; and consequently the giving the mortgage could have no effect towards restoring the title of Robert Perry which the statute had extinguished—nothing but a conveyance to him, by the person entitled, could re-vest the estate in him. He stood, after the twenty years, as a stranger to the title. I find nothing whatever in the evidence that could be relied on for interrupting the tenancy at will between the time of Robert R. Perry first going into possession and the expiration of twenty years and more—nothing that could properly have been left to the jury, as a foundation on which they might find a new tenancy created at any time within the twenty years. Nothing particular was proved to have taken place between 1818 and 1840, except the giving a deed in 1830 for the west half. That might, one would suppose, have led to some understanding or arrangement between the parties in respect to the east half, shewing on what footing they then stood in regard to that half, or establishing some new relation between them in respect to it; but there was no evidence of any such arrangement or understanding.

One of the learned counsel for the plaintiff (Mr. McKenzie) argued this case upon a broad ground, under the statute, contending that upon what appeared in this case the period of limitation had never begun to run; for that Robert Perry, the patentee, had never been *dispossessed*, nor had *discontinued* any possession which he had ever held, or any receipt of rents or profits which he had at any time received. I have sometimes felt doubts, I confess (and in the case which we have given judgment in, this term, of Doe dem. Ausman et al. v. Minthorne, I have endeavoured to explain the grounds of them), whether the great change which the new Statute of Limitations introduced, by extinguishing the right, instead of merely barring the possessor's remedy, was meant to extend to other cases than those in which the owner had suffered himself to be ousted of an actual visible possession, or, as the Real Property Commissioners express it in one part of their report (page 47), "the occupation "of the soil;" or had discontinued the receipt of rents and profits, which, they say, must be looked upon as equivalent to the *occupation of the soil*— "since the person who is in receipt of them can do nothing more to establish " his right, and the person to whom they are denied is virtually *dispossessed*." Any such question must turn upon the construction to be placed upon the 17th section of our statute, which says, "That when the person claiming the land "shall, in respect of the estate or interest claimed, have been in possession, or "in the receipt of the profits of the land, or in receipt of the rent, and shall, "while entitled thereto, have been dispossessed, or have discontinued such "possession or receipt, then such right shall be deemed to have first accrued "at the time of such dispossession or discontinuance of possession, or at the "last time at which any such profits or rent were or was so received." And it seems to me that, even if we could hold that these words meant something more than that constructive possession which in the eye of the law the person seized of an estate in possession always has, so long as no one else is actually occupying the soil, holding it against him, yet in this case we cannot doubt that the statute applies, because it is not denied that Robert R. Perry did at the first occupy by permission of his father, and upon a contract to purchase. This made him tenant at will, as the court determined in Doe dem. Stanway v. Rock; and so an actual possession of the land by Robert Perry commenced through his tenant; and he must therefore be regarded as being *dispossessed* at the end of the first year's tenancy (a), according to the 19th clause, respecting tenants at will, which corresponds with the 7th section in the English Act.

I considered at the trial whether the provision in the 17th section, which is peculiar to our statute, and respects patentees of the crown, can be held to prevent the limitation from running in this case; but I think it cannot, because that modification of the statute was evidently intended to meet the case of intruders upon wild lands, of whose possession the patentee, if he had not hitherto occupied the land, may be supposed to be unconscious; but here the patentee had himself taken possession, when he placed his son on the land as an intended purchaser, and he knew from the first the footing on which his son was there, and must be supposed to have known the legal consequences attached to such possession.

Upon the whole case, I am of opinion that there is no valid ground on which we can hold otherwise than that the title of the lessors of the plaintiff was disproved, by reason of its being shewn that Robert Perry's interest in the land had been wholly extinguished, under the 37th clause of our statute, before he made the deed under which the lessors of the plaintiff claimed, and consequently that the verdict rendered for the defendants must stand.

Rule discharged.

(a) Sugden on Vendors, Vol. II. 349.

A DIGEST

OF

ALL THE REPORTED CASES

DECIDED IN THE

QUEENS' BENCH AND PRACTICE COURTS,

FROM HILARY TERM, 9 VIC., TO HILARY TERM, 10 VIC.

ACCOUNT STATED.

Evidence of. Sale of Lands. Statute of Frauds.] A defendant casually observing to a third party, in the presence of the plaintiff, that he had paid the whole price for his land, except a certain sum, without any further explanation of the circumstances, is not satisfactory evidence of an account stated. *Semble*, that if there had been satisfactory evidence of an account stated, the Statute of Frauds would not have applied, though the sum was due in respect of the sale of lands, Curtiss v. Flindall, 323.

ACTION.

Malicious Arrest. Liability of Parties. Forms of Action.] Where a debt is due to A. and B., and A. makes an affidavit to arrest the debtor, B. is not liable to an action for malicious arrest, unless it can be shewn that he participated in the malicious act, either of instructing or authorizing A. to do it, or by having some knowledge that it was done or intended, or by having afterwards adopted it by giving his assent thereto; though a writ of *capias* be set aside for irregularity, an action on the case will lie against the parties *suing out the same* maliciously. Trespass would be the proper form of action against the party *making the arrest*.—Cameron v. Playter et al., 138.

Against Sheriff for Surplus Money. Demand before Action Unnecessary.] In an action against a sheriff by an execution debtor, for the surplus of money remaining in his hands after satisfying a *fi. fa.*—no demand before action brought is necessary.—Ainslie v. Rapelje, Sheriff, 275.

Local Action. Change of Venue. Application, suggestion in Roll.] In a local action, it is irregular for the plaintiff, if he desires to try the cause in another district, to obtain an order to change the *venue*. The application should be to enter a suggestion on the roll to try the cause in another district. Doe dem. Crooks v. Cummings, 65.

Notice of, to Magistrate, must state place where injury complained of took place.] In the notice of the causes of action required to be served upon a magistrate, the place where the plaintiff was imprisoned must be correctly stated; the fact that the jury complained of took place in the same district, though not at the exact place named in the writ, will not make the variance less fatal. — Croukhite v. Sommerville, 129.

AFFIDAVIT.

Entitling of, Debts in.] Where there is a cause pending, the affidavit to hold to bail, must be entitled in that cause, otherwise the arrest will be set aside; and when more than one debt is mentioned in the affidavit, and the debts are not combined, and the aggregate stated, the affidavit must clearly express plaintiff's apprehension that defendant will leave the province with intent to defraud plaintiff of the *several* debts mentioned; any uncertainty as to which of the debts plaintiff apprehends he will be defrauded of, will be fatal.—Brown v. Palmer, 110.

Malicious motive. Conclusion of. Requisites of.] The conclusion of the affidavit of debt, negativing any vexatious or malicious motive, required by the statute 2 Geo. IV. ch. 1, sec. 8, is not necessary since the statute 8 Vic. ch. 48, sec. 44.— Lee et al. v. McClure, 39.

Commission, Entitling of.] *Semble:* That an affidavit, stating that a *commission* was duly taken, and not that *the evidence* was duly taken, in accordance with the literal wording of the statute, will nevertheless entitle the commission to be read. *Semble*, also, the affidavit need not be entitled in the cause.—McLeod v. Torrance, 146.

Jurat, Commissioner.] A commissioner administering an affidavit, need not state a designation of himself, as a commissioner.—Murphy v. Boulton, 177.

Plaintiff's Attorney, cannot be taken before.] During the *progress* of a cause, an affidavit to arrest the defendant cannot be taken before the plaintiff's attorney.--Burger v. Beamer et al., 170.

Ca. sa.: What sufficient degree of Deponent.] An affidavit, on which a *ca. sa.* is to be sued out, stating that the plaintiff hath good reason to believe that the defendant hath made some secret *and* fraudulent conveyance of his property, &c., and not some secret *or* fraudulent conveyance, is good under the statute.

Semble: Under our rule 2 Will. IV., it is not necessary in any case to state in an affidavit, of either the plaintiff or the defendant, the deponent's degree; certainly not where the affidavit is sworn in a foreign country.

Quære: Whether the defendant, having given bail to the limits, would not preclude him from taking a formal objection of this kind.—Ewing et al. v. Lockhart, 248.

AGENT.

Direction to. Compliance with. Countermand of. Pleadings.] Where in *assumpsit* for money had and received, the defendant pleaded that he had received the money as agent of the plaintiff, and had paid it over by his directions to a person to whom the plaintiff was indebted; and the plaintiff replied that he countermanded the direction before payment, to which the defendant rejoined, that before the countermand, or any notice thereof, he had given notice to the plaintiff's creditor that he held the money for his use, and the creditor had assented thereto, the rejoinder was held a good answer on demurrer. —Coates v. Lloyd, 51.

AGREEMENT.

Substitution of new Agreement. Original consideration imported into new.] While an agreement is open between the parties, and the time for performance has not arrived, a new agreement may be substituted for it, postponing the period for performance; and the original consideration will be regarded as being imported into such new agreement, and will be sufficient to support it.—Hurlburt v. Thomas, 258.

DIGEST OF CASES. 505

Cannot be declared on as a Promissory Note.] An agreement to do certain work, cannot be declared upon as a promissory note. The consideration for such agreement and breach must be properly averred. — Downs v. McNamara et al., 276.

ALIEN FRIENDS.

Not deprived of right to execution against lands of Debtor.] Alien friends residing in their proper country cannot, upon a summary application to this court, be deprived, under the words of the Statute 5 Geo. II., ch. 7, of their right to an execution against the lands of their debtor. *Semble*, the alienage should be pleaded in bar of execution.—Wood et al. v. Campbell, 269.

AMENDMENT.

Amended pleas. Time to reply.] *Quære*, has not a party eight days time to reply to amended pleas?—Playter v. Cameron, 129.

APPEAL.

From the District Court.] The court in *banc* will not overrule the opinion of the judge and jury in the District Court, on the question of weight of evidence in a trifling matter, especially when a new trial could not be granted without paying costs.—Harvey Fowler, Appellant, v. McDonald, Respondent, 385.

ARBITRATION.

Award. Calling in Umpire.] Where arbitrators disagree on some of the items of account referred to them, and during the investigation call in an umpire to give his opinion *on such items*, and subsequently adopt that opinion as their own, it is not necessary that the umpire should sign the award.—In the matter of Award, Cayley and McMullen, 124.

Objection to irregularity in conducting. Waiver of. Setting aside Award.] Where either party to an arbitration objects to what he conceives to be an irregularity in the mode of conducting the arbitration, as for instance against a certain person administering the oath to the witnesses, but still goes on and examines the witnesses and takes his chance of the award, he cannot afterwards be permitted on the same ground to impeach the award. Whenever a certain fact is relied on to set aside an award, that fact must be distinctly sworn to, and if denied, the denial is conclusive.—Slack v. McEathron, 184.

ARREST.

Second Writ.] A defendant discharged from an arrest cannot be detained in prison at the suit of the same plaintiff, upon a second writ issued upon an affidavit sworn while the defendant was in custody upon the first writ.—Barry v. Eccles, 112.

By Magistrate, illegal without summons.] Under the stat. 1 Vic. ch. 21, it is illegal in a magistrate to cause the arrest of a party, in *the first instance;* he must be first *summoned* before him.—Groukhite v. Sommerville, 129.

Prima facie Case. Exemplification of former Judgment.] In an action for malicious arrest without any probable cause of action, it is not sufficient to establish a *prima facie* case, that the plaintiff puts in at the trial the exemplification of the judgment in the former case, by which it appears that *a verdict* was rendered *for the defendant* in that action.—Sherwood v. O'Reilly, 4.

ASSAULT.

Arrest by private Person.] Where a man is himself assaulted by a person disturbing the peace in a public

2 Q   3 Q. B.

street, he may arrest the offender and take him to a peace officer, to answer for the breach of the peace. It need not be averred or proved that the party was taken to the nearest justice. —Forrester v. Clarke, 151.

ASSESSMENT.

Short notice of.] Where a defendant obtains time to plead on condition of taking short *notice of trial*, this condition does not compel him to take short notice of assessment; this further condition should be inserted in the rule. Wright v. McPherson et al., 145.

ASSUMPSIT.

Foreign Judgment. Impeachment of, for defect in, prior to judgment, under the general issue.] In *assumpsit* on a foreign judgment, the judgment cannot be impeached for any alleged defect in the proceedings prior to the judgment, under the general issue. The statute 7 Vic. ch. 16, is binding on the courts in Upper Canada, as well as upon the courts in Lower Canada.—McPherson et al. v. McMillan, 34.

Quære: If in *assumpsit* on a contract to carry goods safely, with an averment of total loss, and a plea that the goods were carried safely, and no evidence given to shew that any of the goods were lost, but only that the cask in which they were packed was injured, and some of the goods damaged, the plaintiff is entitled to recover anything, or more than nominal damages?—Hancock v. Bethune, 47.

Money had and received. Plea. Agent. Payment to third party, with Plaintiff's knowledge. Countermand. Rejoinder. Demurrer.] Where in *assumpsit* for money had and received, the defendant pleaded that he had received the money as the agent of the plaintiff, and had paid it over by his directions to a person to whom the plaintiff was indebted, and the plaintiff replied that he countermanded the direction before the payment; to which the defendant rejoined, that before the countermand or any notice thereof, he had given notice to the plaintiff's creditor that he held the money for his use, and the creditor had assented thereto, the rejoinder was held a good answer on demurrer.—Coates v. Lloyd, 51.

Work and Labour. Sealed Instrument. Independent Covenants. Nonsuit. Setting aside.] The plaintiff sued in *assumpsit* for work and labour, and at the trial put in a sealed instrument under which he had agreed to perform the work, by which it appeared that the defendant was bound to pay the price of the work at certain periods. The work was not done according to the contract, and the plaintiff consequently sued in *assumpsit;* but having been nonsuited at the trial, on the ground that the covenants were independent in the sealed instrument, and that he could sue for the money, although the work was not performed, the court set the nonsuit aside.—Barton v. Fisher, 75.

ATTACHMENT.

Costs. Over-holding Tenant. Order.] The court will not grant an attachment against an over-holding tenant, under 4 Will. IV. ch. 7, sec. 55, for the non-payment of costs, until an order to pay the costs has been first served upon the tenant, and a demand made. In re McLachlan, an over-holding tenant, 331.

On Irregular Rule. Motion to set aside.] The sheriff cannot be served with a rule to return a writ until the return day is past. Where an attachment has been issued on such an irregular rule, the proper course is to move to set aside the attachment, and not the irregular rule upon which the attachment has been founded.—The Queen v. Jarvis, 125.

ATTORNEY.

Costs of Client. Will not be ordered to pay, without express undertaking.] An attorney will not be ordered by the court to pay the costs due by his client to the opposite party, unless he has by himself, or by his agent expressly authorized in that behalf, positively engaged to do so.—Ross v. Calder, 180.

Client. Costs. Action for. Counsel Fees. Taxation. Allocatur.] The attorney is entitled to recover against his client fees paid to counsel conducting the case at the trial.

A client not having obtained a regular order for the taxation of his attorney's costs before the trial, will not be allowed, by producing the Master's allocatur at the trial, to dispute the items of his attorney's bill.—Brock et al. v. Bond, 349.

Assumpsit. Negligence. New Trial. Where a promissory note was given to an attorney, to get the amount of it secured, and the attorney subsequently said that he would pay the amount in a few days, and an action was subsequently brought against him for negligence in not *suing* the note, with a count for money had and received, the court held that neither count was supported by the evidence; and a verdict having been rendered for the plaintiff, a new trial was ordered without costs.—Drennan v. Boulton, One, &c., 72.

Liability for Negligence. Failure of Proof of Special Damage. Nominal Damages.] Where an attorney was retained to make an application to the court, to relieve a sheriff from an attachment, and the jury, in an action against the attorney for negligence in conducting the application, found that he was in fault: *Held*, that he was liable to nominal damages for such negligence, although all the grounds of special damage laid by the plaintiff failed.—McLeod v. Boulton, 84.

Writ of Trial to District Court.] Under the 51st and following clauses of 8 Vic. ch. 13, a writ of trial may go from the Queen's Bench to the judge of the District Court, in a case in which *an attorney* is the defendant. —The Bank of Montreal v. Burritt, 375.

AUCTION.

Sale at. Conditions. Deposit. Statute of Frauds. Resale. Loss on. Responsibility of First Purchaser.] Where at a sale by auction the defendant purchased goods, on the condition of furnishing endorsed notes for their amount, with the option of obtaining a discount of ten per cent. for cash, and that if the conditions were not complied with, the goods were to be resold at the risk of the purchaser, and after the sale the defendant paid £15 on account, but performed no other part of the conditions, and the plaintiff resold the goods at a loss: *Held*, that the part payment took the case out of the Statute of Frauds, so as to dispense with the necessity of proof of a written contract, and that such part payment could not be considered to deprive the plaintiff of the right to resell, and make the defendant responsible for the loss on the resale.—Furniss v. Sawers, 77.

AWARD.

Action on. Covenant.] Where a plaintiff has been awarded a certain sum of money, in accordance with the terms of an instrument under seal, for the non-payment of such award, the plaintiff should sue in covenant;

he cannot sue in *assumpsit*, unless some new consideration, apart from the written instrument, can be proved. The fact that a valuation took place a day later than at first agreed upon in the written instrument, makes no difference in the form of action that should be brought. —Tait et al. v. Atkinson, 152.

Construction of Submission] Where a case was referred to arbitration at *nisi prius*, under a rule of reference containing these words: "That the "costs of the said cause shall be "disposed of as follows: the costs on "the demurrer to be subject to the "judgment of the court on the issues "in law, upon which the arbitrators "are to assess the damages sustained "by the plaintiff; and the costs on "the issue in fact, and the costs on "the said reference, shall be in the "discretion of the said arbitrators," &c., and the award said nothing respecting the issues in law, and no damages were assessed thereupon: *Held*, that under this submission the award was good.—Masecar v. Chambers et al., 186.

Several Issues. Disposal of. Judgment on Award. Motion to set aside. Lapse of Time.] Where in trespass to personal property, and several pleas pleaded, verdict was taken for the plaintiff by consent, subject to be reduced on a verdict entered for the defendant, by the award of the arbitrators, and the arbitrators made their award, determining the cause in favour of the plaintiff, and that the verdict should be reduced to £7 10s., the court, after a lapse of two terms, refused to set aside the judgment entered on the award, on the ground that the award was void, as it did not dispose of the issues in the cause, and also held that the application was made too late.—Wood v. Moodie and Selden, 79.

BAIL.

Recognizance of. Filing in the Office of the Deputy Clerk of the Crown in the District wherein taken.] The plaintiff declares in debt on a recognizance of bail, and sets out in his declaration that the bail came before a commissioner in the Newcastle District, duly appointed according to the form of the statute in such case made and provided (2 Geo. IV. ch. 1, sec. 40); and then, after stating the condition of the recognizance, makes this averment, "as by "the record of the said recognizance, "still remaining in the said court, "fully appears:" *Held, per Cur.* (Macaulay, J., *dissentiente*), declaration bad on special demurrer, in not averring that the recognizance *was filed in the office of the Deputy Clerk of the Crown in the district in which it was taken*, as directed by the 40th section of the Act (2 Geo. IV. ch. 1). —Gillespie et al. v. Grant, 400.

BANKRUPTCY.

Bankrupt let in to plead. Certificate of, after Interlocutory Judgment staying Execution.] Though a certificate of bankruptcy be no discharge to the bankrupt till it be confirmed, an interlocutory judgment, entered up against him before the confirmation, will be set aside, to allow him to plead his certificate by way of *puis d'arreine* continuance; and if he omits to make such application, the court will still relieve him, by staying the execution of the *fi. fa.* on a proper application being made, after judgment shall have been obtained and execution issued.—Commercial Bank v. Culross et al.; Commercial Bank v. Newman et al., 176.

Execution. Commission. Portion of a Day. Priority of Writs.] A *fi. fa.*, at the suit of an execution creditor, placed in the sheriff's hands before a commission of bankruptcy against the debtor was sealed, but on the *same day* on which it was completed and delivered to the sheriff, has priority over the commission. Where goods are already in the custody of the law, a writ of *fi. fa.* at once attaches upon them without an actual seizure. In determining the priority of writs, the court will look to the portion of a day.—Beekman, Assignee of McKay, a Bankrupt, v. Jarvis, Sheriff, 280.

BOARD OF POLICE OF LONDON.

Power to establish a Market and appoint Fees.] Quære: Does the Act 3 Vic. ch. 31, give the Board of Police of London power to establish and regulate a market, and appoint fees to be taken thereat.—The Board of Police of London v. Talbot, 311.

BOND.

Breach of Condition.] In an action on a bond, for the breach of a condition assigned in the words used in the bond, "in not having duly rendered "all accounts which ought to have "been rendered," the plaintiff may recover whatever moneys the defendant ought to have received, though no money was in fact received by him.—Small v. Stanton, 148.

Separate agreement not sealed varying Condition—no Defence to Action on.] To an action upon a bond the defendant cannot set up as a defence separate agreement, not under seal, alleged to have been entered into *at the same time* with the making of the bond, varying the condition from that which the bond itself imports.—Cramer v. Hodgson, 174.

To the Crown. Co-Sureties. Benefit to one of Crown Process.] A. and B. enter, as co-sureties, into separate bonds to the crown for C.; C. becomes a defaulter. The crown proceeds by *sci. fa.* on each bond, and obtains a separate judgment against each surety. A. satisfies to the crown the judgment against himself; B. moves the court to be allowed, on paying the judgment against himself in full, to stand in the place of the crown, and to have the benefit of the crown process against his co-security on a moiety of the judgment: Held, that the court will not thus relieve B. from the effect of the judgment against himself; all that they could have done, would have been to allow him to proceed in the name of the crown, to enforce the judgment which had been obtained on *sci. fa.* against A., and this they could not now do, as it appeared the crown had already enforced that judgment.—The Queen v. Robert Land, 277.

Indemnity Bond to a Magistrate, not necessarily void. Declaration. Plea, Demurrer.] A party suspected of stealing a horse, is brought up on a warrant before a magistrate; he investigates the alleged larceny, and dismisses the charge.—The suspected individual pretends no right to the horse, and the magistrate after dismissing the charge restores the horse to its supposed owner (the party prosecuting), but before doing so takes a bond of indemnity from the owner. In an action brought upon this bond, the defendant pleads that the bond is void, relying upon its being contrary to the general policy of the law that a magistrate should take such a bond. The plaintiff demurs to the plea. *Held*, plea bad, as it does not shew any statute expressly prohibiting bonds of this description being taken and does not aver any corrupt purpose or undue motive on the part of the magistrate to whom it is given.—Ballard v. Pope, 317.

Indemnity, Assignment of Breach. Arrest of Judgment.] Where in debt on bond, conditioned to save the plaintiff harmless from all demands or suits regarding a certain sum of money, and to discharge all damages, costs and charges that might be recovered in respect thereof, the defendant pleaded *non-damnificatus*, and the plaintiff assigned two breaches, setting out a judgment for the said sum of money in the condition mentioned, not specifying any particular sum for which judgment had been recovered: *Held*, on motion in arrest of judgment, that the breaches were sufficiently assigned.— Powell v. Boulton, 19.

Condition. Plea. Demurrer.] Where the condition of a bond was to account for moneys received once in every six months, and the defendant pleaded that he did account, &c., according to the terms and true intent and meaning of the condition; the plea was held bad on special demurrer, because it did not expressly allege that the defendant accounted once in every six months.—Small v. Beasly, 40.

Arbitration Bond. One of two Partners cannot execute for both.] One of two partners cannot execute an arbitration bond in the partnership name, without the authority or consent of the other partner, so as to bind the other partner.—Baby v. Davenport, 54.

CA. SA.

Affidavit for.] An affidavit on which a *ca. sa.* is to be sued out stating that the plaintiff had good reason to believe that the defendant had made some secret *and* fraudulent conveyance of his property, and not some secret *or* fraudulent conveyance, is good under the statute.—Ewing et al. v. Lockhart, 248.

Amount in.] A *ca. sa.* commanding a sheriff to detain the defendant in custody until he should satisfy the plaintiff, without stating the amount of debt to be recovered, is void.—Henderson v. Perry et al., 252.

CASE.

Collision. Negligence of the Parties navigating injured Vessels.—7 Will. IV. ch. 22.] In order to enable the owners of a vessel that has been lost or injured by collision to recover damages for the injury, it must appear that the accident was not in any degree owing to the negligence, misconduct, or want of skill in those navigating such vessel, and that the provisions of our provincial statute, 7 Will. IV. ch. 22, have been, where they are applicable, properly observed. —Eberts et al. v. Smyth et al. 189.

Defamation. Charge of Felony in Foreign Country.] It is actionable to charge a man with having committed felony in a foreign country.—Smith v. Collins, 1.

Diverting Water of Stream. Common Right. Penning back.] A proprietor of land on a stream has a right to the use of the water flowing past him in its natural course, undiminished in quantity and quality; and nothing short of a grant or a twenty years' user (which presumes a grant) of the water in a particular way and for a special purpose, can entitle some one proprietor on a stream, in violation of this common right of all, *injuriously to divert or pen back* the waters from or upon proprietors living above or below him on the stream.

Where at the time of making a dam the plaintiff sustains no injury, but afterwards, having built a mill, he suffers real damages by the dam penning back the water upon the mill, he has no right of action against those who built the dam—he can only sue those who are *continuing* the dam at the time of the injury.—McLaren v. Cook et al., 299.

Fi. Fa. Injury to Goods. Reversionary Interest.] A. has a reversionary interest in goods leased to B.; the sheriff *seizes* the goods under a *fi. fa.*, against B., but does not sell or remove them. A. sues the sheriff for an alleged injury to his reversionary interest. *Held:* That if any trespass was committed by the seizure, B. should sue, and not A.—Henderson v. Moodie, Sheriff, 348.

CLERK OF ASSIZE.

Subpœna issued by. Attachment for disobeying.] The court in *banc* has no power to punish, by attachment, a witness disobeying a subpœna, issued at *nisi prius* by the clerk of assize.

Quære: Can the court at *nisi prius* punish a witness for contempt of its authority, in disobeying a subpœna. —The Queen v. Kerr, in suit, Bates v. O'Donohoe, 247.

THE COBOURG HARBOUR COMPANY.

Not liable for Goods left on the Wharf and lost.] The Cobourg Harbour Company are not wharfingers, because they have erected piers and wharves according to their charter, and are not therefore responsible for loss or damage sustained by persons whose goods have been left upon their wharves unstored. — Logan v. The Cobourg Harbour Company, 55.

COGNOVIT.

Additional Security.] A plaintiff giving time of payment to the defendant by accepting several promissory notes, to become due at distant days, may at the same time, as an additional security, take a cognovit for the whole amount of his debt, with power to issue execution thereon at any moment in his discretion.—Parker, Dunbar & Co. v. Henry C. Roberts, 114.

Restricted by verbal Agreement.] A verbal agreement, however, entered into between parties at the time of the cognovit being given, restricting such power, will be acted upon by the court.—*Idem.*

The fact that none of the notes had become due at the time of the cognovit being put in force, will not affect the judgment or execution on such cognovit.—*Idem.*

Style of.] When the plaintiffs are styled in the proceedings taken upon a cognovit in the same manner as they are named in the cognovit itself, the defendant, having recognized the plaintiff's name in his cognovit, cannot object that the Christian and surnames of the plaintiffs have not been used in the proceedings.—*Idem.*

COMMISSIONERS UNDER ACT OF PARLIAMENT.

Limited Power to demise. Demise beyond Power. Commissioners of the Midland District Turnpike Trust. Note for Rent. Extension of Time.] Commissioners appointed under an Act of Parliament limiting their powers with respect to demises, and to the collection and appropriation of rent when due, making a demise beyond the scope of these powers; the tenant is put into possession and enjoys his term; the commissioners, at the expiration of the term, take a promissory note from the tenant for the amount of rent, giving time for payment: *Held, per Cur.*, that the commissioners, by their clerk, could not sustain an action upon such note, upon two grounds: first, because the promise to pay the note arose upon an illegal consideration, viz., the illegal demise; and secondly, because the commissioners had no power, though the demise were legal, to give time of payment for rent already due. (The Chief Justice dissenting from the judgment of the court on both grounds.) — Ireland, Clerk to the Commissioners of the Midland District Turnpike Trust, v. Guess et al.

Demise by. Different from provisions in Act. Demurrer.] A. sues as clerk to commissioners exercising a public trust under an Act of Parliament (3 Vic. ch. 53), upon an alleged demise of tolls for a year, at a rent payable *every fortnight in advance;* the 27th section of that Act requiring the rent to be made payable *monthly,* the lease stated in the declaration is said to be subject to the provisions of the Act : Held, on demurrer to the declaration, that the plaintiff, as clerk to the commissioners, could not be permitted to recover on such a contract, because it is a contract substantially different from the one which the commissioners are expressly directed to make by the statute.—Ireland v. Noble, 235.

COMMISSION.

Affidavit of due taking.] *Semble:* that an affidavit stating that a *commission* was duly taken, and not that *the evidence* was duly taken in accordance with the literal wording of the statute, will nevertheless entitle the commission to be read. *Semble,* also, that an affidavit need not be entitled in the cause.—McLeod v. Torrance, 146.

COMMON COUNT.

Goods bargained and sold. Certain price must be proved.] To support the common count for goods *bargained and sold,* the plaintiff must prove a certain price agreed upon ; when this cannot be done, the declaration should contain a special count for not accepting.—Elvidge v. Richardson, 149.

COMMON SCHOOL ACT.

Appropriations under. Agreement by Trustees.] Under the Common School Act, 7 Vic. ch. 39, the trustees of any school district might make a valid agreement with the teacher of the school for the district, to give him the whole allowance appropriated for such school district for the year when the Act came into force, if the teacher served for three months.—Darby v. Earl, 6.

COMMON SCHOOLS.

A County Superintendent will be presumed to sign a Contract with a Teacher, only as approving the Appointment.] A county superintendent of common schools, signing, together with the trustees, a contract with a teacher, will be considered to have signed the same only as approving the appointment, and in pursuance of the direction of the statute, and not as a party contracting with the teacher.— Campbell v. Elliott et al., 241.

COMPUTATION OF TIME.

Fraction of a Day.] In determining the priority of writs, the court will look to the fraction of a day.—Beekman v. Jarvis, 280.

CONTRACT.

Joint. Verdict. Nonsuit. New Trial.] Plaintiffs charge defendants upon a joint contract ; one of the defendants allows judgment to go by default; the plaintiffs at the trial have a verdict against him, and elect to be nonsuited as to the other. *Held:* That the plaintiffs suing the defendants on a joint contract, could not have a verdict against one and be nonsuited as to the other ; and that the verdict must be set aside, and a new trial granted without costs.—Commercial Bank v. J. L. Hughes. Idem v. Idem, 361.

Deviation from. Objection. Verdict. New Trial.] When the defendant had ordered the plaintiffs to make for him some iron castings for a shop front, of a specified thickness, and the plaintiffs made them much thicker than the order, but the defendant allowed them to be put up in the building for which they had been made without objection, on a verdict for the plaintiffs for their full value, the court refused to grant a new trial.—Good et al. v. Harper, 67.

Deviation from Contract.] Defendants are taken by plaintiff to a quantity of timber already made upon the ground. Having seen the timber, they contract with the plaintiff to draw it out, and well and truly to deliver it to the plaintiff on the bank of a river. *Held:* that the timber cut in two by the defendants, to suit their convenience, and without the permission of the plaintiff, and drawn out to the river in that *altered state*, was not a delivery within the meaning of the contract.—Reynolds v. Shuter et al., 377.

Sale of Lands. Deceit. Statute of Frauds.] Before a defendant can be charged with deceit in a contract for the sale of land, he must be shewn to have entered into a contract such as is required by the Statute of Frauds, and to have clearly practised or intended the deceit alleged against him. —Irving v. Merygold, 172.

COSTS.

Certifying under Statute 4 Anne, ch. 16, sec. 5.] A judge will not certify under the statute 4 Anne, ch. 16, sec. 5, to protect a defendant against paying the costs of a plea which he knows is not true in itself, but which he pleads for a collateral purpose.— McLeod v. Torrance, 174.

Cost. Order. Attachment. Overholding Tenant.] The court will not grant an attachment against an overholding tenant, under 4 Will. IV. ch. 7, sec. 55, for the non-payment of costs, until an order to pay the cost has been first served upon the tenant and a demand made.—In re MacLachlan, an over-holding tenant, 331.

Counsel Fees. Attorney and Client. Action for Costs. Order for taxation. Disputing Bill.] The attorney is entitled to recover, against his client, fees paid to counsel conducting the case at the trial.

A client not having obtained a regular order for the taxation of his attorney's costs before the trial, will not be allowed by producing the master's allocatur at the trial, to dispute the items of his attorney's bill. —Brock et al. v. Bond, 349.

Separate action against Acceptor and Endorser of a Bill of Exchange. One not liable for the costs of the other. Restraining Execution.] Where the plaintiff commenced separate actions against the acceptor and endorsers of a bill of exchange, and the acceptor paid the amount of the claim against him, but without the costs, and judgment was entered and execution issued against him for their amount, and the costs of the suit against the endorsers, the court ordered the writ to be restrained to the costs against the acceptor alone.—Gillespie, Moffatt et al. v. Cameron, 45.

COVENANT.

Fraud. How pleaded.] To an action of covenant on a deed, the fraud, covin and misrepresentation of the plaintiff may be pleaded in general terms. *Quære:* Can a misrepresentation avoid a contract, without its being fraudulently made?—Lacey v. Spencer, 169.

Assignment of Breach. Plea Leave and License. By Deed or Writing. Plea need not shew.] The plaintiff in an action of covenant against the father of an apprentice, alleges as a breach that the apprentice unlawfully absented himself on a certain day, and from thence hitherto *remained and continued* absent from the service of the plaintiff. Plea, that the apprentice did absent and depart from the service of the plaintiff, by his leave and licence. *Held:* Sufficient without pleading a license to *continue* absent, as the plea only professed to answer the absenting himself from the plaintiff's service. *Held*, also: That the plea need not shew that the license to be absent was given by deed or in writing.—Black v. Stevenson, 160.

For Title. Plea that Defendant was seized. Onus of Proof.] In an action of covenant for title, where defendant pleads that he was seized, in the terms of the covenant, the onus of proof lies upon him. The plaintiff need not first give evidence of a breach, in order to entitle himself to a verdict.—Lemesurier v. Willard, 285.

Lands liable for Damages in.] Under the statute 5 Geo. II. ch. 7, real estate in the colonies is liable to satisfy a judgment *for damages in an action of covenant.*—Nugent v. Campbell et al., 301.

CUSTOMS.

Goods entered at a Port and accepted by the Collector, cannot be seized in another Port by another Collector, as having been undervalued.] Where goods subject to an *ad valorem* duty, have been entered at a port in this province upon the importer's own declaration of value, which the collector has accepted and acted upon, the same goods cannot be afterwards seized by the collector of another port on the ground of their having been undervalued upon their entry with the first collector.—The Queen v. Jagger & Garrison, 255.

DAMAGES.

Trespass for Seduction. Excessive Damages. New Trial.] In trespass for seduction the jury gave a verdict for the plaintiff with £200 damages, and the court refused to grant a new trial for excessive damages.—Ross v. Merritt, 60.

DEBT.

On judgment of the Court of Queen's Bench at Montreal. Want of Jurisdiction. Plea must shew. Mere denial insufficient. Demurrer.] In debt on judgment of the Court of Queen's Bench, at Montreal in Lower Canada, the defendant pleaded that the said court had no jurisdiction in the matter in which the judgment was rendered; and also, that the defendant was never served with any process whereby he could be, or was, notified or apprised that the action was commenced or was depending, and that the judgment was obtained without his knowledge, and contrary to reason and justice. The court held that both pleas were bad on demurrer.—McPherson et al. v. McMillan, 30.

DECEIT.

Contract for Sale of Lands. Statute of Frauds.] Before a defendant can be charged with deceit in a contract for the sale of land, he must be shewn to have entered into a contract such as is required by the Statute of Frauds, and to have clearly practised, or intended the deceit alleged against him.—Irving v. Merygold, 272.

DEED OF ASSIGNMENT.

Granting Part. Habendum.] Where the granting part of a deed of assignment transfers the *indenture* simply, and the habendum the *estate in the indenture*, the estate passes under the assignment.—Doe dem. Wood et al. v. Fox et al., 134.

DEED.

Sheriff's Deed not a mere "Release."] The deed given by the sheriff after the sale of lands under a *fi. fa.* whereby he conveys all the estate and interest of the debtor, is not to be considered as a mere "release" in the strict sense of the term.—Doe dem. Dissett v. McLeod, 297.

DE INJURIA.

Plea, that note was endorsed to plaintiff in fraud of the defendant. Discharge. Excuse.] The defendants plead that the note was endorsed to the plaintiff by the payee in fraud of the defendants, and without consideration, to deprive the defendant of a right of set-off, which he had at the time of the endorsement against the payee; the plaintiff replies "de injuria." Demurrer, that the replication is inapplicable, the plea being in discharge of the note: *Held*, replication good, the plea containing matter of excuse, and not matter of discharge. *Quære:* is not the plea double?—Rattray v. McDonald et al., 354.

DEVISE.

Fee simple. Contingency. Estate Tail.] A testator devises certain land to his daughter, to hold during her life, and afterwards to her heirs for ever, and then adds "should it so *happen* that my daughter shall not "have heirs," &c. : *Held*, that under these additional words the daughter takes only an estate tail.—Doe dem. Anderson et al. v. Fairfield, 140.

Several Trustees. Incapacity of One. Vesting of Estate. Illegal Trust. Charitable Uses.] Where lands are devised to A. B. and C. as trustees, and C. is incapable of taking, the estate may nevertheless vest in A. and B.—Doe dem. Vancott v. Read, 244.

The devise of an estate is not wholly void, because the estate has been charged, to *some extent*, with an illegal trust.—Ib.

Where trustees are directed, by a will, to dispose of an estate "as the "ministers of a certain church may see "fit," the devise is good, not being *necessarily* a devise to charitable uses. —Ib.

DISTRICT COURT.

Writ of Trial. Motion to set aside.] A motion to set aside proceedings under a writ of trial, in the District Court, when the irregularity is in the writ itself, and not in the subsequent proceedings, is bad.—Bank of Montreal v. Denison, 136.

Appeal from.] The court in *banc* will not overrule the opinion of the judge and jury in the District Court, on the question of weight of evidence in a trifling matter, especially when a new trial could not be granted without paying costs. Harvey Fowler, appellant, v. McDonald, respondent, 385.

Replevin. Jurisdiction. Plea Non Tenuit.] The plea of "non tenuit" to an action of replevin does not necessarily oust the District Court of its jurisdiction.

The mere fact of the plaintiff in his declaration in replevin stating the value of the goods distrained at a higher sum than £15, does not shew that the action could not have been brought in the District Court. The plaintiff, to entitle himself to Queen's Bench costs, must prove at the trial that the goods are really of greater value.

Macaulay, J., *dissentiente* upon this last point. — Wheeler v. Sime and Bain, 265.

DISTRESS.

Replication. Special Agreement.] To an avowry under a distress for rent, the plaintiff replied *rien in ar-*

riere, and also set out specially an agreement to be allowed to make certain repairs, and to deduct the amount thereof from the rent, which he averred he had done; this answer to the avowry is good, under either of the above pleas.—Wheeler v. Simc and Bain, 143.

Lease of Wharf and privileges. Vessels attached thereto not liable to Distress.] Where a wharf has been leased "with all the privileges thereto belonging," a vessel attached to the wharf by the usual fastenings cannot be distrained for rent.—Sanderson et al. v. The Kingston Marine Railway Company, 168.

EJECTMENT.

Declaration. Service of.] The service of a declaration in ejectment on the son of a tenant, on the premises, will not be allowed, unless it be shewn by affidavit that before the first day of term the tenant had knowledge of such service.—Doe ex. dem. Hunter et al. v. Roe, 127.

Second Action. Costs.] Where a party fails in his first action of ejectment, and then brings a second, the defendant cannot apply for the payment of costs of the first action till he has entered his appearance.—Doe Flanders et al. v. Roe, 127.

Deed to several Parties, Trustees, named, and to others not named. Presbyterian Church, Galt. A Devise by Trustees, as Grantors, not in their corporate capacity, good.] Where by deed of bargain and sale, land was conveyed to certain persons named as trustees, and "to others," not named, and their successors to hold to the persons as named, and "to others, "trustees as aforesaid, and their successors in office, in fee simple absolutely for ever, to the only proper use and behoof of the said (the persons named), and others trustees as afore- "said and their successors in office, for "ever, for the use of the minister of "the Presbyterian Church, Galt, in "connection with the Church of Scotland, and his successors in office in all "times coming, provided that such "minister shall be a member of the "Synod of Canada, in connection with "the Church of Scotland." *Held:* That no action will lie on a demise in the name of the Trustees of the Presbyterian Church at Galt, as in a corporate capacity; but that a demise might be laid by those named as grantees in the deed, though they were not in fact trustees as the deed assumed them to be.—Doe on the several demises of the Trustees of the Presbyterian Church in Galt in connection with the Church of Scotland, and of the Hon. William Dickson v. Bain, 198.

No Title in Defendant. Prima Facie Evidence.] In an action of ejectment against a defendant pretending no title in himself, *prima facie* evidence is sufficient to prove that a party through whom the lessor of the plaintiff claims is heir at law to the title; no express evidence of the fact is necessary, till the presumption in favour of the title has been repelled. —Doe dem. Sullivan v. Read, 293.

EVIDENCE.

Marriage. Reputation and Cohabitation. Prior Marriage.] Where a marriage in fact has been proved, evidence of reputation and cohabitation is not sufficient to establish a prior marriage.—Doe dem. Wheeler v. McWilliams, 165.

Promissory Note. Witness. Maker and Endorser.] In a joint action against the maker and endorsers of a promissory note under the statute, the maker is a good witness against the endorsers.—McLaren v. Muirhead et al., 50.

Former Action. Plea of. Onus of Proof.] Where in *assumpsit* the defendant pleaded that the plaintiff had impleaded him in a former action on the same promises, and that the defendant had in that action recovered judgment, to which the plaintiff replied that the action in which the judgment was recovered was not on the promises, it was held that the issue was on the defendant, and that he must prove the record of the former recovery.—O'Neil et al. v. Leight, 70.

Witness to Deed. Dispensing with Production of.] In order to dispense with the production of subscribing witnesses to a deed, it must be shewn that every reasonable inquiry has been made for them in the place where they were most likely to be found, and that they cannot be discovered. —Tylden v. Bullen, 10.

Parties to Note. Name of Firm signed by third Party.] A note signed A. & Co., by A. jun., *prima facie* imports that A. signs the note for the firm, and not as one of the firm.— Dowling v. Eastwood et al. 376.

Slander. Variance. Proof of Colloquium.] Where in an action for slander the declaration charged the defendant with saying of the plaintiff "he burnt Knox's barn," and the evidence was not that the defendant said simply, "he burnt Knox's barn," but that he added the words "because one of the girls would not marry him;" and no notice was taken of these latter words in the declaration. *Quære:* Would there not be a fatal variance between the words as laid and proved.

Where, by way of introduction, the declaration averred that the defendant, &c., "in a certain discourse which "he then and there had, of and con- "cerning the plaintiff, and of and "concerning a certain barn upon the "premises of the late Mrs. Knox, now "deceased, which had been burnt," spoke and published of and concerning the plaintiff, "and of and con- "cerning the said barn," the false and scandalous words following, &c., "he "burnt Knox's barn." *Held:* That mere proof of defendant's saying of the plaintiff, "he burnt Knox's barn," without proof of the colloquium respecting the burning of Mrs. Knox's barn, was insufficient. — Manly v. Corry, 380.

Secondary Evidence. Libel. Reading Libel. Notice to Produce.] A plaintiff charging a defendant with *publishing* a libellous pamphlet against him, is not entitled to have the alleged libellous matter read upon the production of evidence merely leading to the presumption that one or two pamphlets, seen in the defendant's hands, and delivered by him to others at their request, *but not produced at the trial,* and which, for all that appeared, had never been read, were in all respects identical in their contents with a pamphlet which somebody else, unconnected with the defendant, had been proved to publish.—(Jones, J., *dissentiente.*)

Before secondary evidence of the publication of a libellous pamphlet can be received, it must be shewn that notice to produce the identical pamphlet has been served; or that it has been either lost or destroyed.

Quære: When a declaration complaining of the publication of a libel contains but one count, can a plaintiff, having already given evidence of the publication of a certain pamphlet as the cause of action, be allowed to introduce evidence of another *and distinct* publication, the defendant being neither the author nor the printer of the libel charged?—McGrath v. Cox, 332.

Age. Declarations of Testator.— The declarations of a deceased testator respecting his age at the time of the execution of his will, are not admissible as evidence.—Doe dem. Stephens & Wife v. Ford, 352.

Promissory Note. Notice of Dishonour. Proof of service.] In order to charge the endorser of a promissory note, it is not necessary that the holder should prove the notice to have been absolutely received—if he shews that due diligence has been used in putting a letter into the post, though the post miscarry, that is sufficient. The fact that there is a post office in the township in which the endorser resides does not make it incumbent on the holder to direct his notice to that office, if there be a nearer office in an adjoining township, to which the endorser's letters are generally sent.—The Bank of Upper Canada v. Smith, 358.

Ejectment. Prima facie Evidence.] In an action of ejectment against a defendant pretending no title in himself, *prima facie* evidence is sufficient to prove that a party through whom the lessor of the plaintiff claims is heir at law to the title: no express evidence of the fact is necessary, till the presumption in favour of the title has been repelled.—Doe dem. Sullivan v. Read, 293.

Malicious arrest. Evidence. Prima facie case.] In an action for malicious arrest without any probable cause of action, it is not sufficient to establish a *prima facie* case, that the plaintiff puts in at the trial the exemplification of the judgment in the former case, by which it appears that a *verdict* was rendered for the *defendant* in that action.—Sherwood v. O'Reilly, 4.

EXECUTORS.

Control over Testator's Lands. Lands, Assets to satisfy Judgment.] Plaintiff declared in *indebitatus assumpsit*. The defendant pleaded *plene administravit*, except as to £20. The plaintiff replied, admitting that the defendant had not any goods or chattels, except, &c., yet that the testator died seized *of lands*, and that the said lands, &c., were, at the testator's death, and when suit brought, assets in the hands of the defendant, as executor, and liable to satisfy the *plaintiff's damages*. Demurrer to replication, on the ground that executor had no control over the lands, or could not as such executor dispose thereof: *Held*, replication good.—Seaton v. Taylor, Executor of Taylor, 302.

FERRY.

Right to use private Boat within limits of a Ferry.] The Provincial Act 9 Vic. ch. 9, as well as the common law, authorizes a person to use his own boat within the limits of a ferry, in the pursuit of his business or pleasure, freely and without any necessity of shewing the particular motives or occasions he may have for allowing any individual to pass in his boat, provided such person be not a traveller, and provided nothing be charged for carrying.—Ives et al v. Calvin, 464.

FI. FA.

Trespass q. c. f. Sheriff. Bill of Sale. Plea not possessed. Fraud. Judgment. Proof of.] *Semble:* that when the sheriff in a fi. fa. seizes goods in the possession of the debtor, and a third party claims them as his, under a bill of sale, which is impeached as being merely pretended and colourable, the sheriff, when sued in trespass for taking the goods, may, upon a plea that the goods are not the plaintiff's, contest his right on the ground of fraud, without proving the judgment; and the learned judge reporting that the non-production of the judgment was not objected to at the trial, the court would not afterwards entertain the objection. — Keeser v. McMartin, Sheriff, &c., et al., 327.

Direction of.] A writ of fi. fa. directed to no one, is void, and cannot be amended.—Wood et al. v. Campbell, 269.

Goods in Custody of the Law.] Where goods are already in the custody of the law, a writ of fi. fa. at once attaches upon them without an actual seizure. In determining the priority of writs, the court will look to the fraction of a day.

Priority of.] A fi. fa. at the suit of an execution creditor, placed in the sheriff's hands before a commission of bankruptcy against the debtor was sealed, but on the same day on which it was completed and delivered to the sheriff, has priority over the commission.—Beekman, Assignee, v. Jarvis, 280.

Against Land. Interest in possession may be sold, not mere right of Action.] The sheriff, under a fi. fa. against lands, can only sell the debtor's interest in possession, whatever that interest may be; he cannot sell the debtor's mere right of action, while a third party is in adverse possession of the land.—Doe on the several demises of Ausman and Montgomery v. Minthorne, 423.

FOREIGN JUDGMENT.

Jurisdiction of Court in which rendered. Cause of action within. Averment.] In an action upon a foreign judgment, rendered in an inferior court, it is not necessary to aver that the cause of action arose within the jurisdiction of that court.

Assumpsit. Plea. Notice of Proceedings. Demurrer.] Plaintiff declared in assumpsit on a foreign judgment against two defendants. Defendants pleaded that one of them had never been served with process, and had no notice whatever of the proceedings in the foreign court. *Held:* Plea bad, as setting up a matter of defence for both of the defendants which applied only to one of them.—Bacon v. McBean et al., 305.

FRAUD.

Plea of, may be General.] To an action of covenant on a deed, the fraud, covin and misrepresentation of the plaintiff, may be pleaded in general terms. *Quære:* Can a misrepresentation avoid a contract, without its being fraudulently made.—Lacy v. Spencer, 169.

GRANT.

Lands. For Rideau Canal. Improvident Grant.] *Quære:* Whether any grant, improvidently made by the crown, of lands set apart for the Rideau Canal before the passing of the late Act 7 Vic. ch. 11, would not be void at common law, if injurious to the canal, without the necessity of a proceeding by *scire facias* to repeal it?

Held: That lands which had been so granted before the passing of the Vesting Act, 7 Vic. ch. 11, but afterwards marked out and reserved by the Ordnance Department, as necessary for the canal, became again revested in the crown.—Doe dem. Malloch v. The Principal Officers of Her Majesty's Ordnance, 387.

HORSE RACE.

Liability of Proprietor of Racecourse for Purse run for. Entrance Money.] The proprietor of a racecourse is not responsible for the purse run for, unless upon clear proof of an express undertaking to that effect.

A winner at a horse race has no right to recover back his entrance money, because the purse has not been paid over to him.—Gates v. Tinning, 295.

INFORMATION.

Quo Warranto. Municipal Councillor.] An information in the nature *quo warranto* may issue, to shew cause by what authority a municipal councillor for any district in the province claims to be a member of such council.—In re Biggar, 144.

INTEREST.

Payable by Promissory Note. Debt, not damages.] Interest made payable by a promissory note is part of the debt, and not merely damages for detaining it.—Crouse v. Park, 458.

IRREGULARITY.

No Appearance. Waiver.] The plaintiff accepting plea, and giving notice of trial, cannot afterwards object that an appearance has not been entered for the defendant.—Doe ex dem. McLean v. McDonald, 126.

JUDGMENT.

Non Obstante Veredicto.] Neither the declaration nor replication in an action of trespass *quare clausum fregit* against a sheriff, charged as an injury "*the breaking of the outer door,*" and the plea justifying the trespass under a writ of fi. fa. on grounds sustained at the trial, contained no allegation "that *the outer door was open,*" the plaintiff cannot, because the plea does not contain such allegation, move for judgment *non obstante veredicto.*—Evans v. Kingsmill, Sheriff of Niagara, 118.

As in case of a Nonsuit. Affidavit.] In an application for judgment as in case of a nonsuit, for not proceeding to trial pursuant to notice, the affidavit on which such motion is made must shew that issue had been joined; or the record must be produced to shew that the similiter had been added by the officer of the court.—Price v. Brown, 127.

Nunc pro tunc. Interest.] Where a case had been pending for several terms on a motion for a new trial after a verdict for the plaintiff, the court refused, after discharging the rule for a new trial, to allow the plaintiff to enter judgment as of the term in which the motion was made, in order that he might obtain interest on his verdict, while the proceedings had been stayed by the motion for a new trial.—Powell v. Boulton, 53.

On Verdict subject to Reference.) The court will not allow judgment to be entered on a verdict subject to a reference, on account of the attempt to arbitrate having failed.—Gould v. Freeman, 270.

JUSTIFICATION.

Trespass. Fi. fa. Inconsistency in Dates.] The justifying under a writ, issued May, 1845, a trespass charged to have been committed in September, 1843, though bad on special demurrer, is not necessarily bad on general demurrer.—Cameron v. Lount, 453.

KINGSTON MARINE RAILWAY COMPANY.

May give and receive Promissory Notes. Declaration on. Consideration.] Under the Acts, 1 Vic. ch. 30, and 7 Vic. ch. 16, the Kingston Marine Railway Company may give and receive promissory notes in the course of transacting their legitimate business. In declaring upon such notes, the plaintiffs need not aver the consideration upon which they were received. The omission of the words "value received" in a note, or the fact that a note is made payable at a certain time after date, affords no inference that such notes were taken in violation of that clause of the Act of incorporation prohibiting the company from banking operations.—The Kingston Marine Railway Company v. Gunn, 368.

LANDLORD AND TENANT.

Trespass. Who may sue in. Conversion of Property.] Where premises have been let, and the tenant is in possession, the landlord has no right of action against a defendant for breaking and entering the said premises and pulling down the said fences, unless the defendant has at some other time removed the rails and converted them to his own use.—Bleeker v. Colman, 172.

Wrongful encroachment by Tenant. Twenty years. Title in Landlord.] Where the landlord places a tenant in possession of Lot No. 1, and the tenant knowingly encroaches on Lot No. 2, to which the agreement as between himself and the landlord gives him no right whatever. *Held:* That the tenant's occupation does not enure to create for the landlord a title to Lot 2, by means of a twenty years' possession of the lot.—Doe dem. Smith v. Leavens, 411.

LANDS.

Fi. fa. against. Interest in possession. Right of Action. Adverse possession.] The sheriff under a *fi. fa.* against lands, can only sell the debtor's interest in possession, whatever that interest may be; he cannot sell the debtor's mere right of action, while a third party is in adverse possession of the land. Doe Ausman et al. v. Minthorne, 423.

Assets in hands of Executor. Liable to satisfy Judgment.] Plaintiff declared in *indebitatus assumpsit.* The defendant pleaded *plene administravit,* except as to £20. The plaintiff replied, admitting that the defendant had not any goods or chattels except, &c., yet that the testator died seised *of lands,* and that said lands, &c., were at the testator's death, and when suit brought, assets in the hands of the defendant, as executor, and liable to satisfy the plaintiff's damages. Demurrer to replication, on the ground that executor had no control over the lands, or could not as such executor dispose thereof. *Held:* Replication good.—Seaton v. Taylor, executor of Taylor, 303.

Liable on a Judgment in Covenant.] Under the statute 5 Geo. II. ch. 7, real estate in the colonies is liable to satisfy a judgment for damages in an action of covenant. Nugent v. Campbell et al., 301.

Sheriff's Sale. Venditioni Exponas. Notice of Adjourned Sale.] It is not necessary, under the statute 43 Geo. III. ch. 1, that there should be a year between the date and return of a writ of *venditioni exponas* against lands. Any want of regularity in giving public notice of an adjourned sale under a *fi. fa.* will not invalidate the sale, where the debtor attended the sale, by his agent, and afterwards ratified what had been done.—Doe dem. Dissett v. McLeod, 297.

LEASE.

Tenant in Tail. Death of. Without Issue. Lease for Lives. Determination of Lease. Remainder-man's Acceptance of Rent.] Where a tenant in tail makes a lease for lives, and dies without issue, the lease is absolutely determined by his death, so that no acceptance of rent by him in remainder or revision can make it good. The acceptance by the remainder-man of a yearly nominal rent, is not a confirmation of the lease, especially where the party disclaims to hold as his tenant.—Doe dem. Graham v. Newton, 249.

LIBEL.

Presumption of Identity. Right to Read Libel on Secondary Evidence.

Notice to Produce.] A plaintiff charging a defendant with *publishing* a libellous pamphlet against him, is not entitled to have the alleged libellous matter read upon the production of evidence merely leading to the presumption that one or two pamphlets, seen in the defendant's hands, and delivered by him to others at their request, but not produced at the trial, and which, for all that appeared, had never been read, were in all respects identical in their contents with a pamphlet which somebody else, unconnected with the defendant, had been proved to publish. (Jones, J., *dissentiente.*) Before secondary evidence of the publication of a libellous pamphlet can be received, it must be shewn that notice to produce the identical pamphlet has been served; or that it has been either lost or destroyed.—McGrath v. Cox, 332.

LONDON BOARD OF POLICE OFFICE.

Power of.] *Quære:* Does the Act 3 Vic. ch. 31, give the Board of Police of London power to establish and regulate a market, and appoint fees to be taken thereat?—The Board of Police of London v. Talbot, 311.

MANDAMUS.

Commissioners of St. Lawrence Canal.] *Mandamus nisi* awarded to the Commissioners of the St. Lawrence Canal, to appoint an arbitrator to join in awarding upon an unsettled claim.—In re McNairn and Commissioners for the St. Lawrence Canal, 153.

MARINE POLICY.

Total Loss. Partial Loss. New Trial.] Where in an action on a marine policy the plaintiff recovered as for total loss, the facts only shewing a partial loss, which, however, was not so distinctly left to the jury, the court granted a new trial, without costs.—Davis v. The St. Lawrence Inland Marine Assurance Company, 18.

MARRIAGE.

Second Marriage. Proof of former Marriage. Reputation and Cohabitation insufficient.] Where a marriage in fact has been proved, evidence of reputation and cohabitation is not sufficient to establish a prior marriage.—Doe dem. Wheeler v. McWilliams, 165.

MESNE PROFITS.

Trespass. Several Issues. Verdict to one Issue. New Trial. Consent to Verdict.] Where in trespass for *mesne* profits, there were several issues joined, and at the trial a verdict was given for the defendants upon one issue clearly against evidence, the court granted a new trial to the plaintiff, unless the defendants consented to allow a verdict for the plaintiff to be entered on that issue. —Anderson v. Todd et al., 16.

MIDLAND DISTRICT TURNPIKE TRUST.

Power of Commissioners. Cannot take Promissory Notes for rent due, or give time of Payment. Power to Demise.] Commissioners appointed under an Act of Parliament limiting their powers with respect to demises, and to the collection and appropriation of rent when due, made a demise beyond the scope of these powers; the tenant is put into possession and enjoys his term; the commissioners at the expiration of the term take a promissory note from the tenant for the amount of rent, giving time for payment. *Held, per Cur:* That the commissioners, by the clerk, could not sustain an action upon such note, upon two grounds:—first, because the promise to pay arose upon an illegal consideration, viz.: the illegal demise; and secondly, because the commissioners had no power, though the demise were legal, to give time of payment for rent already due. (The Chief Justice dissenting from the judgment of the court on both grounds.)—Ireland, Clerk to the Commissioners of the Midland District Turnpike Trust v. Guess et al., 220.

Demise must correspond with the Provisions of the Act.] A. sues as clerk to commissioners exercising a public trust under an Act of Parliament (3 Vic. ch. 53), upon an alleged demise of tolls for a year, at a rent payable *every fortnight in advance;* the 27th section of that Act requiring the rent to be made payable *monthly;* the lease stated in the declaration is said to be subject to the provisions of the Act. *Held:* On demurrer to the declaration, that the plaintiff, as clerk to the commissioners, could not be permitted to recover on such a contract, because it is a contract substantially different from the one which the commissioners are expressly directed by the statute to make.—Idem v. Noble, 235.

MONUMENTS.

Surveyor. Original Costs.] A surveyor cannot act independently of the provisions of the statute 58 Geo. III. ch. 13, and arbitrarily lay on one side the evidence which neighbours are ready to give, from their own knowledge, of the situation of original posts.—Sherwood v. Moore, 468.

MUNICIPAL COUNCIL.

Information. Quo Warranto.] An information in the nature of a *quo warranto* may issue, to shew cause by what authority a municipal councillor for any district in the province claims to be a member of such council.—In re Biggar, 144.

NEW TRIAL.

Trespass for Seduction. Excessive Damages.] In trespass for seduction the jury gave a verdict for the plaintiff with £200 damages, and the court refused to grant a new trial for excessive damages.—Ross v. Merritt, 60.

Forgery. Promissory Note.] Where the defence intended to be urged by the endorser of a note was forgery, and they defended on that ground at the trial, and the plaintiff recovered, the court refused to grant a new trial.—McLaren v. Muirhead, 59.

Trespass q. c. f. Evidence. Admission of Evidence. Secondary Evidence.] Where in trespass *quare clausum fregit,* the plaintiff proved admissions of the defendant as to the title to the land in question, which should have been left to the jury, but the case rested upon the want of sufficient evidence to admit the testimony of the handwriting of the subscribing witnesses to the deed under which the plaintiff claimed, which the court decided against him, a new trial was granted with costs to abide the event.—Tylden v. Bullen, 10.

Incompetency of Witness, Objection to must be taken at Trial.] A party cannot obtain a new trial on the ground that an incompetent witness has been examined against him, unless he took the objection to his incompetency at the trial.—Doe dem. Sullivan v. Read, 293.

Want of Diligence in making out Case. Verdict Contrary to Evidence.] Where a losing party has been wanting in diligence to make out his case at the trial, the court will not, as a matter of course, relieve against the verdict, though it may appear contrary to evidence.—Doe dem. Wheeler v. McWilliams, 165.

Joint Contract. Verdict. Nonsuit.] Plaintiffs charge defendants upon a joint contract; one of the defendants allows judgment to go by default; the plaintiffs at the trial have a verdict against him, and elect to be nonsuited as to the other. *Held:* That the plaintiffs, suing the defendants on a joint contract, could not have a verdict against one, and be nonsuited against the other; and that the verdict must be set aside, and a new trial granted without costs.—Commercial Bank v. J. L. Hughes et al., 361.

Attorney. Negligence. Insufficient Evidence.] Where a promissory note was given to an attorney, to get the amount of it secured, and the attorney subsequently said that he would pay the amount in a few days, and an action was subsequently brought against him for negligence in not *suing* the note, with a count for money had and received, the court held that neither count was supported by the evidence; and a verdict having been rendered for the plaintiff, a new trial was ordered without costs. —Drennan v. Boulton, One, &c., 72.

Contract, Deviation from, Acquiescence in.] When the defendant had ordered the plaintiffs to make for him some iron castings for a shop front, of specified thickness, and the plaintiffs made them much thicker than the order, but the defendant allowed them to be put up in the building for which they had been made, without objection, on a verdict for the plaintiffs for their full value, the court refused to grant a new trial.—Good et al. v. Harper, 67.

Trespass. Mesne Profits. Several Issues. Verdict on one Issue. Contrary to Evidence. Consent to change Verdict.] Where in trespass for *mesne* profits there were several issues joined, and at the trial a verdict was found for the defendants upon one issue clearly against evidence, the court granted a new trial to the plaintiff, unless the defendants consented to allow a verdict to be entered upon that issue for the plaintiff. —Anderson v. Todd et al., 16.

Marine Policy. Total Loss. Partial Loss.] Where in an action on a marine policy, the plaintiff recovered as for a total loss, the facts only shewing a partial loss, which however were not so distinctly left to the jury, the court granted a new trial without costs.—Davis v. The St. Lawrence Inland Marine Assurance Company, 18.

Award. Submission. Withdrawal of some of the matters Submitted. Resubmission by Parol. Production of Bond. Objection. Justice.] Where in debt on award, the plaintiff declared reciting a submission by bond, and that under the bond the arbitrators had made an award upon one of the matters in difference, the other matters submitted having been by the consent of the parties withdrawn from their consideration, and that afterwards the others matters having been again submitted, the arbitrators made an award in favour of the plaintiff, and the defendants pleaded no such submission, and never indebted, and at the trial the plaintiff proved the parol submission, but did not produce the bond, and a point was reserved to the defendant to move upon that objection; the court, on motion for a new trial, (the verdict being in accordance with the justice of the case) refused to interfere.—Baby v. Davenport, 13.

Trover. Unsatisfactory Evidence.] Where in trover for a schooner there was a great deal of evidence of an unsatisfactory character as to the plaintiff's right to the vessel, and the defendant was not proved to have used or employed, but merely to have allowed the person who left her with him to take her away, and the jury found a verdict for the defendant, the court refused to grant a new trial. —Brown v. Allen, 57.

Ejectment. Weight of Evidence. Third Trial.] The court, under particular circumstances, declined to grant a third new trial in ejectment, though they thought the evidence strongly preponderated againt the verdict.—Doe ex dem. Harris and Wife v. Benson, 164.

Omission of Attorney.] Where the losing party has failed at the trial from the omission of his attorney to establish some legal right he might have shewn, the court will exercise their discretion in granting a new trial. They will not grant this indulgence, where an expensive litigation would be protracted about a trifling matter.—Petrie v. Taylor, 457.

Absence of Witness. Smallness of Damages.] The court will not grant a new trial to the plaintiff (complaining of the smallness of his verdict) on an affidavit that a witness was absent from the province at the time of trial, whom he might get for another trial, and by whom he could better make out his case.—Hodgkinson et al. v. Brown, 461.

Buying Pretended Title. Value of Land. Want of Evidence of.] In an action for the sale of land under 32 Henry VIII. ch. 9, the court will refuse a new trial merely on the ground that no direct evidence was given as to the value of the property; the situation and condition of the land having been proved, and the sum acknowledged to have been paid for the land in the deed by the defendant being considered as evidence of the value to go to the jury.—Baldwin qui tam v. Henderson, 287.

NOLLE PROSEQUI.

Declaration. Two Counts. Promissory Note, and Account Stated. Evidence.] The plaintiff declares on two counts: first, on a promissory note; secondly, on an account stated. To the defendant's plea to the first count on the note, the plaintiff replies; to which replication the defendant demurs. The plaintiff then, to avoid the risk of the demurrer, enters a simple *nolle prosequi* to the first count. *Held:* That plaintiff might give the note in evidence to support the second count, on the account stated.

Semble: Such evidence would have been inadmissible, if the *nolle prosequi* had involved an express admission, as it sometimes does, that the plaintiff had no right of action on the note.—Leslie v. Davidson, 459.

NONSUIT.

Assumpsit, Work and Labour. Sealed Instrument, Departure from Contract. In Defendant's Covenant.] The plaintiff sued in *assumpsit* for work and labour, and at the trial put in a sealed instrument under which he had agreed to perform the work, by which it appeared that the defendant was bound to pay the price of the work at certain stated periods; the work was not done according to the contract, and the plaintiff consequently sued in *assumpsit*, but having been nonsuited at the trial on the ground that the covenants in the sealed instrument were independent, and that he could sue for the money although the work was not performed, the court set the nonsuit aside.—Barton v. Fisher, 75.

Election to take. Motion against.] A plaintiff *requesting* a nonsuit rather than risk his case with a jury, cannot afterwards be allowed in *banc* to move against the nonsuit.—McGrath v. Cox, 332.

Judgment as in case of. Tampering with Witness. Peremptory Undertaking.] Where a witness attending the assizes on the part of the plaintiff, is seen to converse with the defendant, and afterwards shews an unwillingness to remain, and leaves the assizes, this fact will entitle the plaintiff to enter into the peremptory undertaking, upon a judgment being moved for by the defendant as in case of a nonsuit.—Bates v. O'Donohoe, 178.

OVERHOLDING TENANT.

4 Will. IV. ch. 1.] The 53rd and other clauses of the statute, 4 Will. IV. ch. 1, giving a summary remedy against overholding tenants, apply only to the cases of tenants whose terms have expired by lapse of time, not to those who, by alleged breaches of covenant, have forfeited their terms. —In Re Duncan McNab, Landlord, and Nathaniel Dunlop and Lucretia McKeever, 135.

Costs. Attachment. Profit.] The court will not grant an attachment against an overholding tenant, under 4 Will. IV. ch. 7, sec. 55, for the non-payment of costs, until an order to pay the costs has been first served upon the tenant, and a demand made. —In Re McLachlan, an Overholding Tenant, 331.

PARTNERSHIP.

Arbitration. Bond. One partner cannot execute for another without Authority.] One of two partners cannot execute an arbitration bond in the partnership name, without the authority or consent of the other partner, so as to bind the other partner. —Baby v. Davenport, 54.

PAYMENT.

One Sum. Several Counts.] Where a plea of payment of a certain sum is pleaded to two counts, without alleging how much of the said sum is to be paid on each count : *Held* good on demurrer.—Brown et al. v. Ross et al., 158.

Condition Precedent. Plea of Payment. Averment of Manner.] Where payment is to be a condition precedent, or a concurrent act, and is to be made in a certain manner, the plaintiff must aver a readiness to pay in the precise manner stipulated.— Tanner v. D'Everado et al., 154.

PLEADING.

False Imprisonment.] Where a man is himself assaulted by a person disturbing the peace in a public street, he may arrest the offender and take him to a peace officer, to answer for the breach of the peace. It need not be averred or proved that the party was taken to the nearest justice.— Forrester v. Clarke, 151.

Award. Action on.] Where a plaintiff has been awarded a certain sum of money in accordance with the terms of an instrument under seal, for the non-payment of such award the plaintiff should sue in covenant; he cannot sue in *assumpsit*, unless some new consideration apart from the written instrument can be proved. The fact that the valuation took place on a day later than at first agreed upon in the written instrument, makes no difference in the form of action that should be brought.— Tait et al. v. Atkinson, 152.

Puis d'arreine Continuance. Certificate of Bankruptcy.] Though a certificate of bankruptcy be no discharge to the bankrupt till it be confirmed, an interlocutory judgment entered up against him before the confirmation will be set aside, to allow him to plead his certificate by way of *puis d'arreine* continuance ; and if he omit to make such an application, the court will still relieve him by staying the execution of the *fi. fa.*, on a proper application being made after judgment shall have been obtained and execution issued.—Commercial Bank v. Culross et al., Commercial Bank v. Newman et al., 176.

Board of Police of London. Authority to erect a market, and make bylaws respecting Fees.] A., upon being appointed clerk of the market of the Board of Police of London, enters into a bond for the payment of a certain sum of money in compensation for the market tolls, which the Board allowed him to receive. Being sued on his bond for non-payment of the money, he pleads "that he discovered, after the execution of the bond, that the plaintiff had no legal authority to erect a market, or make bylaws respecting fees to be taken thereat;" he then avers that the plaintiffs had no such authority, and that on this account the bond is void. *Held*, plea bad in not shewing that no market was erected, or existed, and in not averring that fees were not in fact received by him. *Quære:* Does the Act 3 Vic. ch. 31, give the Board of Police of London power to establish and regulate a market, and appoint fees to be taken thereat.—The Board of Police of London v. Talbot, 311.

Indemnity Bond. Declaration on Plea. Demurrer.] A party suspected of stealing a horse is brought up on a warrant before a magistrate; he investigates the alleged larceny, and dismisses the charge. The suspected individual pretends no right to the horse, and the magistrate, after dismissing the charge, restores the horse to its supposed owner (the party prosecuting), but before doing so takes a bond of indemnity from the owner. In an action brought upon this bond, the defendant pleads that the bond is void, relying upon its being contrary to the general policy of the law that a magistrate should take such a bond. The plaintiff demurs to the plea. *Held*, plea bad, as it does not shew any statute expressly prohibiting bonds of this description being taken, and does not aver any corrupt purpose or undue motive on the part of the magistrate to whom it was given.—Ballard v. Pope, 317.

Recognizances of Bail. Filing in the Office of the Deputy Clerk of the Crown, in the District wherein taken. Declaration. Demurrer.] The plaintiff declares in debt on a recognizance of bail, and sets out in his declaration that the bail came before a *commissioner of the Newcastle District*, duly appointed to take recognizances of bail according to the form of the statute in such case made and provided (2 Geo. IV. ch. 1, sec. 40); and then, after stating the condition of the recognizance, makes this averment, "as by the record of the said recognizance, still remaining in the said court, fully appears." *Held*, per *Cur.* (Macaulay, J., *dissentiente*), declaration bad on special demurrer, in not averring that the recognizance *was filed in the Office of the Deputy Clerk of the Crown in the District in which it was taken*, as directed by the 40th section of the Act (2 Geo. IV. ch. 1.)—Gillespie et al. v. Grant, 400.

Assumpsit. Foreign Judgment. General Issue.] In *assumpsit* on a foreign judgment, the judgment cannot be impeached by any alleged defect in the proceedings prior to judgment under the general issue. The statute 7 Vic. ch. 16, is binding on the court in Upper Canada, as much as upon the Court of Lower Canada.—McPherson et al. v. McMillan, 34.

Money had and received. Agent. Plea. Payment to third party. Direction. Replication. Countermand. Rejoinder. Demurrer.] Where in *assumpsit* for money had and received, the defendant pleaded that he had received the money as agent of the plaintiff, and had paid it over by his directions to a person to whom the plaintiff was indebted; and the plaintiff replied that he countermanded the direction before payment, to which the defendant rejoined that before the countermand, or any notice thereof, he had given notice to the plaintiff's creditor that he held the money for

Indemnity Bond. Non-damnificatus. Assignment of Breach. Particular Sum. Arrest of Judgment.] Where in debt on bond, conditioned to save the plaintiff harmless from all demands or suits regarding a certain sum of money, and to discharge all damages, costs and charges that might be recovered in respect thereof, the defendant pleaded *non-damnificatus*, and the plaintiff assigned two breaches, setting out a judgment for the said sum of money in the condition mentioned, not specifying any particular sum for which judgment had been recovered. *Held*, on motion in arrest of judgment, that the breaches were sufficiently assigned. —Powell v. Boulton, 19.

Condition. Plea. Performance must be in words of the Condition. Special Demurrer.] Where the condition of a bond was to account for moneys received once in every six months, and the defendant pleaded that he did account, &c., according to the terms and true intent and meaning of the condition; the plea was held bad on special demurrer, because it did not expressly allege that the defendant accounted once in every six months.—Small v. Beasley, 40.

Goods bargained and sold. Common Count. Proof. Special Count.] To support the common count for goods bargained and sold, the plaintiff must prove a certain price agreed upon; when this cannot be done the declaration should contain a special count for not accepting.—Elvidge v. Richardson, 149.

Covenant. Fraud, &c. How pleaded.] To an action of covenant on a deed, the fraud, covin and misrepresentation of the plaintiff may be pleaded in general terms. *Quære:* Can a misrepresentation void a contract, without its being fraudulently made?—Lacey v. Spencer, 169.

Covenant. Assignment of Breach. Leave and License. Plea need not shew License to be in writing.] The plaintiff, in an action of covenant against the father of an apprentice, alleges as a breach that the apprentice unlawfully absented himself on a certain day, and from thence hitherto *remained and continued* absent from the service of the plaintiff. Plea, that the apprentice did absent and depart from the service of the plaintiff, by his leave and license. *Held:* Sufficient without pleading a license to *continue* absent, as the plea only professed to answer the absenting himself from the plaintiff's service. *Held* also: That the plea need not shew that the license to be absent was given by deed or in writing.—Black v. Stevenson, 160.

Judgment of the Court of Queen's Bench at Montreal. Plea denying Jurisdiction of Court. Must shew why it has not. Mere denial insufficient.] In debt on a judgment of the Court of Queen's Bench, at Montreal, in Lower Canada, the defendant pleaded that the said Court had no jurisdiction in the matter in which the judgment was rendered; and also, that the defendant was never served with any process whereby he could be, or was, notified or appraised that the action was commenced or was depending, and that the judgment was obtained without his knowledge, and contrary to reason and justice. The court held that both pleas were bad on demurrer.—McPherson et al. v. McMillan, 30.

Replevin. Avowry Distress for Rent. Replication. Rien in Arrear. Special Agreement.] To an avowry under a distress for rent, the plaintiff replied *rien* in arrear, and also set out specially an agreement to be allowed to make certain repairs, and to deduct the amount thereof from the rent, which he averred he had done; this answer to the avowry is good, under either of the above pleas. —Wheeler v. Sime and Bain, 143.

Plea, former Judgment. Onus of Proof.] Where in *assumpsit* the defendant pleaded that the plaintiff had impleaded him in a former action on the same promises, and that the defendant had in that action recovered judgment, to which the plaintiff replied that the action in which the judgment was recovered was not on the same promises, it was held that the issue was on the defendant, and that he must prove the record of the former recovery.—O'Neil et al. v. Leight, 70.

Slander. Variance Colloquium.] Where in an action for slander the declaration charged the defendant with saying of the plaintiff "he burnt Knox's barn," and the evidence was not that the defendant said simply, " he burnt Knox's barn," but that he added the words "because one of the girls would not marry him ;" and no notice was taken of these latter words in the declaration. *Quære:* Would there not be a fatal variance between the words as laid and proved.—Manly v. Corry, 380.

Where, by way of introduction, the declaration averred that the defendant, &c., "in a certain discourse which he then and there had, of and concerning the plaintiff, and of and concerning a certain barn upon the premises of the late Mrs. Knox, now deceased, which had been burnt," spoke and published of and concerning the plaintiff, "and of and concerning the said barn," the false and scandalous words following, &c., "he burnt Knox's barn." *Held:* That mere proof of defendant's saying of the plaintiff, "he burnt Knox's barn," without proof of the colloquium respecting the burning of Mrs. Knox's barn, was insufficient.—Manly v. Corry, 380.

Professing to answer too much. Demurrer. Fraud. De injuria. Discharge. Excuse.] The plaintiff sues defendant on two counts :—first, on a promissory note; secondly, on an account stated. The defendant pleads that he did not make the note *in the declaration mentioned.* Demurrer to plea. *Held:* Plea bad, as professing to answer the whole declaration, while it in fact answers to the first count only. The defendants plead secondly, that the note was endorsed to the plaintiff by the payee in fraud of the defendants, and without consideration, to deprive the defendant of a right of set-off, which he had at the time of the endorsement against the payee ; the plaintiff replies "*De injuria.*"—Demurrer, that the replication is inapplicable, the plea being in discharge of the note ; *Held:* Replication good, the plea containing matter of excuse, and not matter of discharge. *Quære:* is not the plea double ? Rattray v. McDonald et al., 354.

Trespass q. c. f. Fi. fa. Sheriff. Bill of Sale. Not possessed. Fraud. Judgment. Proof of.] *Semble:* That when the sheriff on a *fi. fa.* seizes goods in the possession of the debtor, and a third party claims them as his, under a bill of sale, which is impeached as being merely pretended and colourable, the sheriff, when sued in trespass for taking the goods, may, upon a plea that the goods are not the plaintiff's, contest his right on the ground of fraud without proving the judgment; and the learned judge reporting that the non-production of the judgment was not objected to at the trial, the court would not afterwards entertain the objection. — Keeser v. McMartin, Sheriff, &c., et al., 327.

Case. Injury to Goods. Reversionary Interest. In whom right of Action.] A. has a reversionary interest in goods leased to B. ; the sheriff seizes the goods under a *fi. fa.* against B., but does not sell or remove them.

A. sues the sheriff for an alleged injury to his reversionary interest. *Held:* That if any trespass was committed by the seizure, B. should sue, and not A.—Henderson v. Moodie, Sheriff, 348

Trespass. District Trespass. Justification under one Writ. Replication. Newly Assigning different Trespass.] Where to a declaration in trespass, containing two counts, charging two distinct trespasses, in taking different goods at different times; the defendant justifies the two distinct trespasses under one writ. *Held,* plea good.

The justifying under a writ issued in May, 1845, a trespass charged to have been committed in September, 1843, though bad on special demurrer, from its seeming inconsistency, is not necessarily bad on general demurrer.

A replication, newly assigning different trespass from that by the plea justified, when the plea justifies all the trespasses complained of, is bad on special demurrer.—Cameron v. Lount, 453.

Action on Foreign Judgment. Averment of Jurisdiction of Court in which Rendered.] In an action upon a foreign judgment, rendered in an inferior court, it is not necessary to aver that the cause of action arose within the jurisdiction of that court.—Prentiss v. Beemer, 270.

Assumpsit. Foreign Judgment. Plea, too extensive.] The plaintiff declared in *assumpsit* on a foreign judgment against two defendants. Defendants pleaded *that one of them* had never been served with process, and had no notice whatever of the proceedings in the foreign court. *Held:* Plea bad, as setting up a matter of defence for both of the defendants which applied only to one of them.—Bacon v. McBean et al., 305.

Plea answering too much.] A plea to a declaration on a promissory note, and account stated, that the defendant did not make the note in the first count mentioned, is bad on special demurrer, as attempting to offer an answer to the whole declaration.—Prout v. Howard, 38.

Trespass. Assault and Battery. Justifying. Molliter Manus Imposuit.]—Wherein trespass the plaintiff declared for an assault and battery and striking blows, whereby the plaintiff was greatly hurt, bruised and wounded, and the defendant justified the hurting, bruising and wounding, concluding "which are the same trespasses," &c. the plea was held good on special demurrer. The plaintiff declared in the several counts for an assault and battery, and beating and bruising and wounding, and the defendant justified the assault and battery by a plea of *molliter manus imposuit.* *Held,* sufficient.—McLeod v. Bell, 61.

Plea of payment. Professing to answer too much.] To a declaration consisting of several common counts, claiming under *one promise* upon all the counts, the sum of £500, and laying the damages at £200, the defendant pleads a plea of payment, "of £250 in full satisfaction and discharge of the *said promise in the said declaration mentioned,* and also of *all damages* sustained by the plaintiff by reason of the *non-performance of such promise.*" *Held:* Plea bad on special demurrer.—Thompson v. Armstrong, 153.

Distinct causes of Action. Plea. Not Guilty of Grievances. Uncertainty.] The plaintiff declares on two distinct causes of action; the defendant pleads "not guilty of the said supposed grievances." *Held:* Plea bad on special demurrer.—Ambridge v. Foster, 157.

Plea to Part. Form. Payment. Several Counts.] Where a defendant, having stated his defence to part of a declaration, then pleads as to another part, "and as to the said, &c.,

that," without using the words "he says." *Held:* Good on demurrer.

Where a plea of payment of a certain sum is pleaded to two counts, without alleging how much of the said sum is to be paid on each count. *Held:* Good on demurrer. — Brown et al. v. Ross et al., 158.

Common Counts. Plea. Special Agreement to accept a right of Preemption. Averment. Acceptance. Demurrer.] To an action on the common counts, the defendant A. pleads that it was agreed between the plaintiff B. and the defendant A., and a third party, C., that C. should sell to B. all the claim, title and right of pre-emption which C. had to certain land, and that C. should execute a deed at B.'s request to D., in satisfaction of B.'s claim : and then avers that C. did, by the procurement of A. at B.'s request, execute a deed to D. of *all* the title C. had to the land.— *Held:* Plea bad on demurrer in not averring that the defendant A. had a certain right and interest in the land, and of a certain value, and that his conveyance to D. was accepted in satisfaction.—Fralick v. Lafferty, 159.

Special Count. Plea. Confessing cause of Action. General Issue. Duplicity.] To a declaration upon a special count for dismissing the plaintiff, a schoolmaster, from his situation before the end of his term without probable cause, the defendant A. pleads, justifying the dismissal, but at the same time averring that B., another defendant, made the contract with the plaintiff, and that he, A., *specially approved* of the same. *Held:* Plea bad, in not confessing the cause of action, and as amounting to the general issue, and for being double. —Campbell v. Elliott et al., 167.

Special Assumpsit. Plea Non-performance. Uncertainty.] The plaintiff in his declaration charges the defendant with the non-performance of a certain contract; the defendant pleads, that the said contract was not duly performed by the said parties, to wit, the plaintiff and the defendant respectively, in manner, &c. *Held:* Plea bad, in leaving it uncertain which of the said parties had not performed the contract, and in what particular it had not been performed.—Jones v. Hamilton, 170.

Promissory Note. Plea, Fraud. No Consideration. Duplicity.] To an action by the payee against the maker of a note, the defendant pleaded that the note was obtained by fraud, *and* without consideration. *Held:* On special demurrer, plea bad for duplicity.—West v. Brown (J.Y.)

Promissory Note. Endorsees v. Endorser. Plea, Money in hand of Endorsees. Direction to retain. Statement of time necessary. Demurrer. Uncertainty.] Endorsees v. Endorser of a promissory note. The defendant pleads that *before* and *at* the time when the note became due, and at the time of the commencement of the suit, the plaintiffs, as bankers and agents, had in their hands divers sums of money of the maker of the note, amounting to £500, and were *then* indebted to the maker in that amount, and that the maker *then* directed the plaintiffs to retain to their own use the amount of the said note, out of the said moneys, which exceeded the amount of the said note, &c. Demurrer to plea. *Held:* Plea bad, in not averring the particular time when the direction was given.— Bank of U. C. v. Lewis, 325.

Trespass, for assault and false imprisonment. Justification. Plea—answering part, without confessing and avoiding the rest—Bad.] The plaintiff declares against the defendants in trespass for an assault, beating, bruising and ill-treating. A., one of the defendants, justifies, alleging that upon suspicion that plaintiff had stolen his goods, he laid his information before a justice of the peace of the Niagara District, who granted a warrant, directed *to the Constable of Thorold*, in the Niagara District, authorizing him to search the plaintiff's house at the township of Louth, in the said district, for the said goods; that B., another defendant, being *the constable of Thorold, in the said district*, at the request of A., searched the house, found the goods, and arrested the plaintiff at Louth, and at the request of A., carried her before a magistrate. Demurrer to plea.

Held: Plea bad, in assuming to answer the whole injury complained of, and yet not denying, nor confessing and avoiding the arrest. *Held* also: that the direction of the magistrate to the constable of Thorold, not naming him, to execute the warrant in the township of Louth, was good.

Quære: Whether, when a defendant is charged with arresting, bruising, beating and ill-treating the plaintiff, a justification of the *mere arrest* will be sufficient ?—Jones v. Ross et al., 328.

Trover. Plea not possessed. Time Material.] To an action of trover, the defendant pleads that the plaintiffs "were not lawfully possessed of the goods and chattels, &c., as of their own property, as in the second count alleged." Demurrer to plea. *Held:* Plea bad, in not shewing *at what time* the defendant means to allege the plaintiffs were not possessed—the words "*at the said time when*," &c., should have been added.—Cuvillier et al. v. Brown, 353.

Plea, professing to answer whole Declaration—Answer only to part—Bad. Negative Pregnant.] Endorsees against the endorsers of a note. The plaintiffs declare on two counts: first, on the note; secondly, on an account stated. The defendants plead that "they did not endorse the promissory note in the said first count of the said declaration mentioned" in manner and form, &c. Demurrer to plea.

Held: Plea bad on two grounds: 1st, because not being limited in the introductory part of it to the first count, it must be taken as pleaded to the whole declaration, and thus while professing to answer the whole, it in fact only answers the first count. 2nd, because in its mode of traversing the endorsement it contains a negative pregnant with the admission that one or two of three defendants did endorse.—Commercial Bank v. Reynolds et al., 360.

Promissory Note. Joint Endorsement. Joint liability. Excuse for Omission of Party liable. Presentment. Notice.] Endorsees sue the defendants separately, as payees and endorsers of a promissory note. The declaration avers a joint endorsement by the defendants—*a due presentment* and *notice*, and the liabilities of the defendants. Demurrer to declaration? first, Because presentment at a particular place is not averred: secondly, Because a joint liability is shewn on the face of the declaration, and no excuse for omitting the party jointly liable alleged: thirdly, because *due* notice is not alleged, or a special averment of notice, with time, &c. *Held:* Declaration good upon the first and second grounds, but bad on the third.—Commercial Bank v. Cameron, Idem v. Culver, 363.

Plea, inconsistent, repugnant, and double. Absque Hoc. Usury.] The plaintiffs sue on a promissory note made by A. payable to B. or order, endorsed by B. to C. and by C. to the plaintiffs, who sue A., B. and C. jointly, under our statute. The defendants pleaded usury, setting forth that the making of the note and the endorsement by B. and C. were all without consideration; that C. endorsed the note and delivered it to A. for B.'s accommodation, and in order to enable him to procure a loan; that A. did make a corrupt agreement with D. for the loan of a sum of money on usurious interest, and gave him his note as security; and that D. afterwards endorsed and delivered the note to the plaintiffs, who gave him no consideration for the note; adding this special traverse: "without this, that the said C. endorsed the said note to the said plaintiffs, as in the said declaration is alleged;" and the plea concludes to the country. *Held:* Plea bad, on special demurrer, as being repugnant, inconsistent and double.—Bank of Montreal v. Humphries et al., 463.

Endorsement of Writ. Bail Bond. Averments in Declaration. 8 Vic. ch. 13.] The provision in 8 Vic. ch. 13, secs. 44, 58, 72, is retrospective as well as prospective. *Held:* That the endorsement on the writ of execution being stated to be for a less sum than that mentioned in the judgment, is no ground of special demurrer.

Held also: That it is not necessary to aver, in an action brought by the assignees of a bail-bond, that the sheriff did not receive the money after the assignment of the bond; neither is it necessary to aver that the defendants had notice of the assignment. Easton et al., Assignees of the Sheriff, v. Longchamp et al., 475.

Assumpsit. Pleading. Conclusion to the Country. Verification. Demurrer.] The plaintiffs declare in *assumpsit*, for not paying a bill of exchange, which the defendant agreed to accept, payable at Montreal, on the 18th day of July, 1845, in consideration of the plaintiff's delivering to the defendant, at St. Catharines, 10,000 bushels of good, clean, merchantable fall wheat. The declaration avers the delivery of the said wheat to the defendant, at St. Catharines, and that the defendant accepted and received the same. The defendant pleads, secondly, that the plaintiffs did not deliver the *said* 10,000 *bushels of wheat*, in the said count mentioned, to the defendant; and, thirdly, that the said 10,000 bushels of wheat, averred to have been delivered by the plaintiffs to the defendant, was not nor is good, clean, merchantable fall wheat; concluding with a verification. Demurrer to the 2nd plea, because it leaves it uncertain whether the defendant intends to object to the non-delivery of the wheat altogether, or to the non-delivery at the time or place mentioned in the declaration. Demurrer to 3rd plea, because it should have concluded to the country, and not with a verification; and because it was no answer to the first count. Several grounds of objection were taken to the sufficiency of the declaration.

Held, per Cur: Declaration good, on general demurrer. *Held* also: Second plea good, and third plea bad, on special demurrer.—Cook et al. v. Mair, 478.

PRACTICE.

Time to plead. Short notice of Assessment.] When a defendant obtains time to plead on condition of taking short *notice of trial*, this condition does not compel him to take short notice of assessment. This further condition should be inserted in the rule.—Wright v. McPherson et al., 145.

Notice to appear, no year in, irregular.] Where the notice, endorsed on the copy of a *ca. re.* specifies no year for the appearance of the defendant, or when the service has been made by a person not duly authorized by the sheriff, the service of the *ca. re.* will be set aside.—Murphy v. Boulton, 177.

Special Demurrer, pointing out Defect in Pleading.] If an objection to a pleading is taken on special demurrer, it must distinctly point out the defect objected to.—Small v. Beasley, 40.

Prisoner. Time for declaring against. New Rules.] Where a defendant was committed to prison on a bailable writ, and afterwards and before the return day of the writ was released on bail, and on the return day of the writ entered special bail, he is not entitled, under the third new rule of the court, to be served with declaration before the end of the term then next after such arrest.—Glen v. Box, 182.

Judgment as in case of a Nonsuit. Peremptory Undertaking. Tampering with Witness.] When a witness attending the assizes, on the part of the plaintiff, is seen to converse with the defendant, and afterwards shews an unwillingness to remain and leaves the assizes, this fact will entitle the plaintiff to enter into the peremptory undertaking, upon a judgment being moved for by the defendant, as in case of a nonsuit.—Bates v. O'Donohoe, 178.

Reviving Rule Nisi.] The defendant, after a verdict in detinue for the plaintiff in 1s. damages, was granted a rule *nisi* for a new trial; but having obtained a certificate to deprive the plaintiff of costs, under 43 Elizabeth, he served a written notice on the plaintiff's attorney, that he did not intend to proceed upon the rule *nisi*, which accordingly was never taken out or served. Afterwards, the certificate to deprive the plaintiff of costs was rescinded, and the defendant then obtained a rule *nisi*, to revive the rule *nisi* that he had abandoned; but the court refused to make the rule absolute.—Davidson Administrator of Davidson v. Raddick, 82.

Irregularity. Waiver. Writ of Trial.] A defendant having appeared and examined evidence on an assessment of damages, which had been carried down to the District Court by a writ of trial, issued from the Queen's Bench under our statute 8 Vic. ch. 13, sec. 65, has by such appearance waived any irregularity in the prior proceedings in the Queen's Bench.—Small v. Beasley, 141.

Staying Proceedings. Fi. fa. Absence of Plaintiff.] Where the plaintiff had obtained judgment against the defendant ten years ago, and two or three years afterwards fled from the province, charged with a criminal offence, and a writ of execution was issued on the judgment, without any leave of the court or notice to the party, the court made a rule absolute to stay the proceedings.—Hobson v. Shand, 74.

Venue, order to change. Rule. Alteration of Record.] Though an order to change the venue has been granted and served, unless the venue is in fact changed by taking out the rule and making the alteration in the record, the plaintiff is at liberty to proceed to trial, according to the original venue.—Hornby v. Hornby, 274.

Variance in Deeds and oyer, in particulars not material to the action, how taken advantage of.] When a plaintiff, declaring upon a deed, sets it out untruly, but in a particular not material to the action which has been brought upon the deed, the defendant wishing to take advantage of the variance should plead *non est factum*. He cannot crave oyer and demur.—Boulton et al. v. Weller, 372.

Testatum Writs. Outer Districts. 8 Vic. ch. 36. Notice to appear.] Under the 8th sec. of the 8th Vic. ch. 36, the defendant, living in a district east of the Home District, is entitled to *twelve* days' notice to appear on a testatum writ issued from the Niagara District; the Niagara District, for the purposes of that Act, being held to be a district west of the Home District. —Graham v. Quinn, 183.

PRESBYTERIAN CHURCH, GALT.

Action in the Name of Trustees of. Demise.] Where by deed of bargain and sale, land was conveyed to certain persons named as trustees, and "to others," not named, and their successors, to hold to the persons as named, and "to others, trustees as aforesaid, and their successors in office, in fee simple absolutely for ever, to the only proper use and behoof of the said (the persons named), and others trustees as aforesaid and their successors in office, for ever, for the use of the minister of the Presbyterian Church, Galt, in connection with the Church of Scotland, and his successors in office in all times coming, provided that such minister shall be a member of the Synod of Canada, in connection with the Church of Scotland." *Held:* That no action will lie on a demise in the name of the trustees of the Presbyterian Church at Galt, as in a corporate capacity; but that a demise might be laid by those named as grantees in the deed, though they were not in fact trustees as the deed assumed them to be.—John Doe on the several demises of the trustees of the Presbyterian Church in Galt in connection with the Church of Scotland, and of the Hon. Wm. Dickson v. Bain, 198.

PRETENDED TITLE.

A vendor, in order to have the benefit of the exception under the statute 32 Henry VIII. ch. 9, must *really* and in *truth* claim under some person in possession a year before the bargain made: a mere pretended fraudulent claim, under a person of whom *in fact* the vendor knew nothing, and with whom he had *in truth* no privity, will not satisfy the statute.—Baldwin *qui tam* v. Henderson, 287.

PRISONER.

Special Bail. Declaration. New Rules.] Where a defendant was committed to prison on a bailable writ, and afterwards and before the return day of the writ was released on bail, and on the return day of the writ, entered special bail, he is not entitled, under the third new rule of our court, to be served with a declaration before the end of the term then next after the arrest.—Glenn v. Box.

PROMISSORY NOTE.

Notice of Non-payment. What sufficient Service.] In order to charge the endorser of a promissory note, it is not necessary that the holder should prove the notice to have been absolutely received. If he shews that due diligence has been used, in putting a letter into the post-office, though the post miscarry, that is sufficient. The fact that there is a post-office in the township in which the endorser resides, does not make it incumbent on the holder to direct his notice to that office, if there be a nearer office in an adjoining township, to which the endorser's letters are generally sent.—The Bank of Upper Canada v. Smith, 358.

Payable with interest.] Interest made payable by a promissory note, is part of the debt, and not merely damages for detaining the debt.—Crouse v. Park, 458.

Joint Action. Evidence.] In a joint action against the maker and endorsers of a promissory note, under the statute, the maker is a good witness against the endorsers.—McLaren v. Muirhead et al., 59.

Making of.] A note signed A. and Co., by A. jun. *prima facie* imports that A. signs the note for the firm, and not as one of the firm.—Dowling v. Eastwood et al., 376.

Notice of Dishonour.] The following notice of dishonour was held to be insufficient, the note having been endorsed by the defendant, in his own name, and not in the name of partners, to whom the notice was addressed, although the defendant was one of the firm: "Messrs. P. M. Grover & Co. —Gentlemen,—Take notice, that the promissory note of I. R. Benson, for £46 0s. 11d., on which you are endorser, due this day, remains unpaid. Therefore the holders look to you for payment thereof, as such endorsers." —The Bank of Montreal v. Grover, 27.

The following notice of dishonour was held sufficient: "Sir,—The note of A. B. for £50, at 90 days from 20th January, 1841, endorsed by you, and due this day, remains unpaid. You are therefore hereby notified that this bank looks to you for payment.

"Yours, &c.,
"For the Cashier.

"To Mr. J. Street."
—Bank of Upper Canada v. Street, 29.

Note not negotiable. Liability of Parties endorsing.] A party endorsing his name on the back of a note not negotiable, or if negotiable not endorsed by payee, cannot be sued as endorsee by the payee.— West v. Bown (Robert R.), 290.

Notice of Non-payment. Notarial Certificate. Law of Lower Canada.] It is not necessary to state, in the notice of non-payment to an endorser of a bill, that the holder looks to him for payment.

The certificate of a notary in Lower Canada, at the foot of the protest, that he had put a notice into the post, addressed to the endorser, is evidence of that fact, under the statute 7 Vic. ch. 4, sec. 2.

The law of Lower Canada, with respect to time of giving notice, is to govern, when the note was made payable and was presented there, though the endorser resides in Upper Canada. —Smith et al. v. Hall, 315.

"Due" notice must be averred.— Commercial Bank v. Cameron, Idem v. Culver, 363.

PROOF.

Onus of. Covenant for Title. Plea, Seisin. Proof on Defendant.] In an action on a covenant for title, where defendant pleads that he was seised, in the terms of the covenant, the onus of proof lies upon him; and plaintiff need not first give evidence of a breach, in order to entitle himself to a verdict.—Lemesurier v. Willard, 285.

PUBLIC SCHOOLS.

Trespass to. Trustees. Master. 7 Vic. ch. 29.] Under the 44th section of the 7 Vic. ch. 29, the trustees of the public schools (and not the schoolmaster) should be made the plaintiffs in an action of trespass to the school house; unless at least it can be shewn that the trustees have given the school-master a particular interest in the building, beyond the mere liberty of occupying it during the day for the purpose of teaching.—Monaghan v. Ferguson et al., 484.

RACE COURSE.

Liability of Proprietor for Purse. Entrance-Money.] The proprietor of a race-course is not responsible for the purse run for, unless upon clear proof of an express understanding to that effect. A winner at a horse-race has no right to recover back his entrance-money because the purse has not been paid over to him.—Gates v. Tinning, 295.

RATES.

Action to recover back. Money had and received. Voluntary Payment.] When an inhabitant of a corporate town, being overrated, pays the overrate to the collector, without at the time making any remonstrance, he cannot afterwards recover back such rate, in an action for money had and received.

Semble: If he voluntarily pay the overrate, even though protesting at the time of payment, he cannot recover it back.—Grantham v. The City of Toronto, 212.

RECOGNIZANCE.
Since the repeal of the Act 7 Vic. ch. 31, *Held:* That recognizances taken under its authority, are not binding upon the bail, except in regard to cases in which the debtor has been notified, and has made default while the Act was still in force.—(Macaulay, J., *dissentiente.*)—Macdonald v. Weeks et al. 441.

REFERENCE.
Verdict. Subject to. Judgment.] The court will not allow judgment to be entered on a verdict, taken subject to a reference, on account of the attempt to arbitrate having failed.—Gould v. Freeman, 270.

REGISTRAR.
Proof of Deed. Affidavit sworn before Commissioners.] Under the 7th clause of the new Registry Act, 9 Vic. ch. 34, the registrar of a county is bound to receive proof of deeds by affidavit sworn to before a commissioner of this court, as well where they are executed within the county as without.—In re Registrar of the County of York, 188.

RIDEAU CANAL.
Lands set apart for. Improvident Grant.] *Quære:* Whether any grant, improvidently made by the crown, of lands set apart for the Rideau Canal before the passing of the late Act, 7 Vic. chap. 11, would not be void at common law, if injurious to the canal, without the necessity of a proceeding by *scire facias* to repeal it?

Held: That the lands which had been so granted before the passing of the Vesting Act, 7 Vic. ch. 11, but afterwards marked out and reserved by the Ordnance Department as necessary for the canal, became again revested in the crown.—Doe dem. Malloch v. The Provincial Officers of Her Majesty's Ordnance, 387.

SEDUCTION.
Action for, will not lie where the Defendant has connection with the Seduced against her Will.] When a witness, being called to prove the plaintiff's case, persists in making a positive, though very improbable, statement disproving it, the court, in the absence of any other witness, will not allow the case to go to the jury.—Macaulay, J., *dubitante*) Vincent v. Sprague, 283.

SHERIFF.
In an action against a Sheriff, he cannot object to Jury, summoned by himself. Demand for surplus money before Action unnecessary.] It is no objection on the part of the Sheriff, in an action against him, that the jury have been summoned by himself, and not by the coroner. In an action against the sheriff, by an execution debtor, for the surplus money remaining in his hands after satisfying a *fi. fa.*, no demand before action brought is necessary. — Ainslie v. Rapelje, Sheriff, 275.

Fi. fa. False Return.] Where a creditor has placed his writ of *fi. fa.* in the sheriff's hands, and afterwards and before any actual seizure by the sheriff under the *fi. fa.*, and before the return-day of the writ, the goods of the debtor are seized under a commission of bankruptcy, and *nulla bona* returned to the *fi. fa.*, the sheriff is liable, in such return, to an action at the suit of the execution creditor.—Decatur v. Jarvis, Sheriff, 133.

SLANDER.
Charge of Felony in Foreign Country.] It is actionable to charge a man with having committed a felony in a foreign country.—Smith v. Collins, 1.

Of Title. Spoken in assertion of Right.] An action for slander of title cannot be maintained, where the alleged slander is spoken *bona fide* and in assertion of right.—Boulton et al. v. Shields, 21.

Action for. Demurrer to part of the words. Innuendo. Trade or occupation. Averment of, unnecessary.] A defendant will not be allowed, in an action of slander, to single out some of the words of a count, and demur to them as not being actionable, while the same count contains other words, uttered in the same conversation, which are clearly actionable.

Where a defendant charges the plaintiff with being a "public robber," and the plaintiff shews that the defendant used the expression in a mitigated sense, by an innuendo that "he the plaintiff had defrauded the public in his dealings with them," it is not necessary for the plaintiff to aver that he is in any office, trade, or employment in which he could have defrauded the public.—Taylor v. Carr, 306.—(Macaulay, J., *dissentiente* on both points.)

SPECIAL JURY.

Notice of Striking.] There must be four clear days' notice of striking a special jury. Therefore, a notice given, after 11 o'clock a.m. on Saturday, to strike a special jury at 11 a.m. on Tuesday, is not sufficient. But in this case, the verdict being for more than £300, and the defendant not having made any defence, because the judge at *nisi prius* would not try the cause by a special jury, considering the notice too late, the court granted a new trial, the defendant having made a strong affidavit of merits, and the amount of the verdict being ordered to be paid into court, to stand as a security for the plaintiff.
—John Bell, Surviving Partner of William Bell v. Flintoft, 122.

STATUTE OF FRAUDS.

Assumpsit. Account stated for Sale of Lands.] *Semble:* That when there is satisfactory evidence of an account stated, the Statute of Frauds will not apply, though the sum was due in respect of the sale of lands.—Curtiss v. Flindall, 323.

STATUTE OF LIMITATIONS.

Twenty Years' Possession. Adverse, or by permission. Acknowledgment of Title. Effect of. Judgment.] Where A. has been twenty years in possession paying no rent, and signing no written acknowledgment of title in another, such possession, whether it originate adversely to the claims of the true owner B., or with his permission, operates under the Statute of Limitations to extinguish the title of B., and to vest the title in A.

Held: That a verbal acknowledgment of title by A. in B., made during the twenty years, would not save the statute.

Held also: That A.'s acknowledgment in *writing* of a title in B. *after* the twenty years, could not have the effect of reviving a title which the twenty years' possession had extinguished.

Held also: That a judgment in ejectment recovered by B. against A., *after the twenty years had expired*, would not save the statute: *aliter* if recovered *within* the twenty years, and A. within the twenty years had been *dispossessed* upon such judgment.

Held also: That a conveyance by B. to A., within the twenty years, of a part of the lot in dispute, would not save the statute—his deed to A. being no written acknowledgment on the part of A. of B.'s title.

Held also: That the fact of A.'s paying the taxes by B.'s direction is no bar to the statute.

Held also: That A., commencing his possession by the permission of B., and upon a contract to purchase, B. must be held as in the *actual possession* of the land through his tenant at will A., and as being *dispossessed* at the end of the first year's tenancy, and that therefore the 17th section of our provincial Statute of Limitations would apply so as to bring B. within its operation.

Semble: That if A. could be shewn to have been occupying the land as the mere servant of B., during the twenty years, and not for his own use or benefit, the statute would not run.—Doe Perry et al. v. Henderson, 486.

Ejectment. Possession by Permission.] *Quære:* As to the effect of the Statute of Limitations, when the twenty years' possession has not been an adverse one; when a person has gone into possession with the consent of the plaintiff, as an act of kindness on his part, and has remained there under the same assent, paying no rent and acknowledging no title.—Doe dem. Smith v. Leavens, 411.

Land. Agreement to purchase. Conveyance to third party. Notice to quit. Ejectment. Judgment. Twenty years' Possession. Acknowledgment. Bar to Statute. Voluntary Restoration.] A., the owner of land, agrees to sell to B. B. goes into possession and fails in making his payments. A. then conveys the land to C., in B.'s presence, and apparently with the consent of B., who says that he will at once leave the place. B. nevertheless continues uninterruptedly in possession for more than twenty years, paying C. no rent, and making no written or other acknowledgment of C.'s title.

Held: That B.'s twenty years' possession, under these circumstances, gives him the legal title.

Held also: That a notice to quit, given by C. to B., within the twenty years, does not save C. from being barred by the statute.

Held also: That a judgment in ejectment, recovered by C. against B. within twenty years, but upon which B. had never been dispossessed, is no bar to the statute.

Quære? If B., in undisturbed possession for twenty years, voluntarily restores possession to C., can B. turn C. out again, by reverting to his title under the Act?—Doe dem. Ausman et al. v. Minthorne, 423.

Admission of Defendant.] A statement by a defendant, "that he did not think that he owed the money, and that if he did, the Statute of Limitations would prevent the recovery, but that he would give the plaintiff fifty dollars rather than have any trouble about it," is not sufficient to take the case out of the Statute of Limitations.—Spalding v. Parker, 66.

ST. LAWRENCE CANAL.

Mandamus. Commissioners of. Unsettled Claim. Arbitrator.] Mandamus nisi, awarded to the commissioners of the St. Lawrence Canal, to appoint an arbitrator to join in awarding upon an unsettled claim.—In re McNairn and Commissioners of St. Lawrence Canal, 153.

SUBPŒNA.

Witness, Time of attending as. Subpœna.] When a witness is subpœnaed to attend the assize, *on a particular day*, and not from *day to day*, he cannot be attached for disobedience to the subpœna, if he was present on that day, but went away afterwards.—In the matter of complaint, Rainville v. Powell, 128.

Issued by Court of Assize. Power of Court in Banc to attach for disobeying.] The court in *banc* has no power to punish by attachment a witness for disobeying a subpœna issued at *nisi prius*, by the clerk of assize.

Quære? Can the court at *nisi prius* punish a witness for contempt of its authority, in disobeying a subpœna?—The Queen v. Kerr, 247.

SURVEY.

Original Posts. Alteration of Survey by Government, previous to Grant. Patent, Description in. 50 Geo III. ch. 14.] In regard to a survey made before the 50th Geo. III. ch. 14, the provisions of that Act will not have the effect of *necessarily* confining the grantee to the land designated by the posts planted in the original survey, if the plan of survey had been altered by the government before the issuing of the patent, and before the passing of that statute. Therefore when the government had added to the ends of the several concessions a strip of land, which the surveyor had left unsurveyed, between his concessions and the adjoining townships, and, in consequence of such addition, had changed the numbering of the lots throughout the concession: *Held*, that the patent issued in accordance with such reformed survey, would cover the land which the government intended to be included within the boundaries expressed in the patent, though the number of lots would not correspond with the posts set by the surveyor—Doe dem. Talbot v. Paterson, 431.

SURVEYOR.

Original Posts. Evidence of Neighbours.] A surveyor cannot act independently of the provisions of the statute 58 Geo. III. ch. 13, and arbitrarily lay on one side the evidence which neighbours are ready to give, from their own knowledge of the situation of original posts.—Sherwood v. Moore, 468.

TENANT IN COMMON.

Trespass.] One tenant in common may commit trespass, by expelling his co-tenant, and taking the whole enjoyment of the estate wrongfully to himself.—Petrie v. Taylor, 457.

TENANT IN TAIL.

Lease for Lives. Death. Issue. Determination. Acceptance of Rent.] Where a tenant in tail makes a lease for lives, and dies without issue, the lease is absolutely determined by his death, so that no acceptance of rent by him in remainder or in reversion can make it good.

The acceptance by the remainderman of a yearly *nominal* rent, is not a confirmation of the lease, especially where the party disclaims to hold as his tenant.—Doe dem. Graham v. Newton, 249.

TENANT.

Occupation by, of Land not let by Landlord, for Twenty Years. Title, to land occupied by Encroachment.] Where the landlord places a tenant in possession of Lot No. 1, and the tenant knowingly encroaches on part of Lot No. 2, to which the agreement as between himself and the landlord gives him no right whatever. *Held:* That the tenant's occupation does not enure to create for the landlord a title to Lot 2, by means of a twenty years' possession of the lot.—Doe dem. Smith v. Leavens, 411.

TESTATUM WRIT.

Niagara District. 8 Vic. chap. 36. Notice to Appear.] Under the 8th section of the 8 Vic. ch. 36, the defendant, living in a district east of the Home District, is entitled to *twelve* days' notice, to appear on a testatum writ issued from the Niagara District: the Niagara District, for the purposes of that Act, being held to be a district west of the Home District. —Graham v. Quinn, 183.

TITLE.

Slander of. Spoken in assertion of Right. No Action.] An action for slander of title cannot be maintained, where the alleged slander is spoken *bona fide*, and in assertion of right.— Boulton et al. v. Shields, 21.

TOLL-GATES.

Tolls chargeable only once in twenty-four Hours.] A person passing a toll-gate more than once on the same day, could not, while the statute 3 Vic. ch. 53, was in force, be legally charged more than one toll in the twenty-four hours.

NOTE.—No further difficulty need be apprehended from the construction the court have given to this Act, as a recent proclamation from the government, founded upon an Act passed the last session of Parliament, has made express provision on the subject.— O'Hara v. Foley, 216.

TRESPASS.

Disputed Boundaries. Taking Possession against Protest. Right to sue for Trespass.] Plaintiff and defendant own adjoining lots of land ; they had a fence between them, supposed to be on the true division line ; a correct line is however run, and the defendant is found to be encroaching some acres on the plaintiff's land ; the plaintiff takes possession of the disputed piece of ground, though under a protest from the defendant, and cultivates it. When the crop is fit to cut, the defendant enters and takes it away. The plaintiff sues the defendant in trespass.

Held: That the plaintiff had such a possession as would enable him to maintain an action of trespass.— Gallagher v. Brown et al., 350.

Landlord and Tenant. Right of Action. Conversion of Property.]— Where premises have been let, and the tenant is in possession, the landlord has no right of action against a defendant for breaking and entering the said premises and pulling down the fences, unless the defendant has at some other time removed the rails and converted them to his own use. —Bleeker v. Colman, 172.

Quare clausum fregit against Sheriff. Outer door.] Neither the declaration nor replication in an action of trespass *quare clausum fregit* against a sheriff, charged as an injury, "*the breaking of the outer door,*" and the plea justifying the trespass under a writ of *fi. fa.*, on grounds sustained at the trial, contained no allegation that the "outer door was open," the plaintiff cannot, because the plea does not contain such allegation, move for judgment *non obstante veredicto.*— Evans v. Kingsmill, Sheriff of Niagara, 118.

TROVER.

Plea, not possessed. Averment of time material.] To an action of trover, the defendant pleads that the plaintiffs "were not lawfully possessed of the goods and chattels, &c., as of their own property, as in the 2nd count alleged." Demurrer to plea.

Held: Plea bad in not shewing *at what time* the defendant means to allege the plaintiffs were not possessed —the words "*at the said time when,*" &c., should have been added.—Cuvillier et al. v. Brown, 353.

Property. Unsatisfactory evidence of Ownership. New Trial.] Where in trover for a schooner there was a great deal of evidence of an unsatisfactory character, as to the plaintiff's right to the vessel, and the defendant was not proved to have used or employed but merely to have allowed the person who left her with him to take her away, and the jury found a verdict for the defendant, the court refused to grant a new trial.—Brown v. Allen, 57.

TRUST.

Trust. Devise of Estate on.] The devise of an estate is not wholly void because the estate has been charged to some extent with an illegal trust. —Doe dem. Vancott v. Read, 244.

Charitable uses.] Where trustees are directed by a will to dispose of an estate "as the ministers of a certain church may see fit," the devise is good, not *necessarily* being a devise to charitable uses.—Idem v. Idem, 244.

TRUSTEES.

Incapacity of one. Vesting of Estate.] Where lands are devised to A., B. and C. as trustees, and C. is incapable of taking, the estate may nevertheless vest in A. and B.—Doe dem. Vancott v. Read, 244.

USE AND OCCUPATION.

Proof of.] In an action for use and occupation, the plaintiff, proving a legal title to the premises and a mere naked possession by defendant, is entitled to a verdict. He need not go further, and prove an attornment or contract between himself and the defendant.—Price v. Lloyd, 120.

USURY.

Securities in furtherance of, Void.] By the usury laws, all securities which may have been given *in furtherance* of an usurious transaction, with the knowledge of the person who took the security, are void.—Armstrong v. Somerville, 472.

Promissory Note. Antecedent Debt. New Consideration.] A *bona fide* endorser, without notice, who takes a bill of exchange or note, in payment of an *antecedent debt*, and not upon a new consideration, given at the time by discount or otherwise, is not protected against the offence of usury by our Provincial Act, 7 Will. IV. ch. 57. There is no distinction in this respect, between the effect of our Act and of the British Act 58 Geo. III. ch. 93.

VARIANCE.

Oyer. Deeds. Non est factum. Demurrer.] When a plaintiff, declaring upon a deed, sets it out untruly, but in a particular not material to the action which has been brought upon the deed, the defendant wishing to take advantage of the variance, should plead *non est factum ;* he cannot crave oyer and demur.—Boulton et al. v. Miller, 372.

VENUE.

Local Action. Change of Application. Suggestion on Roll.] In a local action, it is irregular for the plaintiff, if he desires to try the cause in another district, to obtain an order to change the venue. The application should be to enter a suggestion on the roll, to try the cause in another district.—Doe dem. Crooks v. Cumming, 65.

Order to change. Taking out Rule. Alteration of Record.] Though an order to change the venue has been granted and served, unless the venue is in fact changed, by taking out the rule and making the alteration in the record, the plaintiff is at liberty to proceed to trial according to the original venue.—Hornby v. Hornby, 274.

VENDITIONI EXPONAS.

Against Lands.] It is not necessary, under the statute 43 Geo. III. ch. 1, that there should be a year between the date and return of a writ of *venditioni exponas* against lands.—Doe dem. Dissett v. McLeod, 297.

VERDICT.

Subject to Reference. Judgment.] The court will not allow judgment to be entered on a verdict, subject to a reference, on account of the attempt to arbitrate having failed.—Gould v. Freeman, 270.

WARRANT.

What sufficient direction of Search-Warrant.] Held, that the direction of the magistrates to the constable of Thorold—not naming him—to execute the warrant in the township of Louth, was good,—Jones v. Hornby, 274.

WATER-COURSES.

Right of User. Building Obstructions. Continuing Dam.] A proprietor of land on a stream has a right to the water flowing past him in its natural course, undiminished in quantity and quality; and nothing short of a grant or twenty years' use (which presumes a grant) of the water in a particular way and for a special purpose, can entitle some one proprietor on a stream, in violation of this right of all, injuriously to divert or pen back the water from or upon proprietors living above or below him on the stream.

When, at the time of making a dam, the plaintiff sustains no injury, but afterwards, having built a mill, he suffers real damage, by the dam penning back the water upon the mill, he has no right of action against those who built the dam; he can only sue those who are *continuing* the dam at the time of the inquiry.—McLaren v. Cook et al., 299.

WHARVES.

Distress for Rent. Vessels attached to Wharves not liable.] When a wharf has been leased, "with all the privileges thereto belonging," a vessel attached to the wharf with the usual fastenings, cannot be distrained for rent.—Sanderson et al. v. The Kingston Marine Railway Company, 168.

WITNESS.

Improbable Statement by Plaintiff's Witness disproving case. Without other Witness, Nonsuit.] When a witness, being called to prove the plaintiff's case, persists in making a positive though very improbable statement disproving it, the court, in the absence of any other witness, will not allow the case to go to the jury. — (Macaulay, J., *dubitante*)— Vincent v. Sprague, 283.

WRIT OF TRIAL.

Irregularity. Waiver.] A defendant, having appeared and examined evidence, on an assessment of damages which had been carried down to the District Court, by a writ of trial issued from the Court of Queen's Bench, under our statute, 8 Vic. ch. 13, sec. 55, has, by such appearance, waived any irregularity in the prior proceedings in the Queen's Bench.— Small v. Beasley, 141.

Irregularity. Notice of Motion. District Court.] The notice of motion to set aside a writ under the 54th clause of 8 Vic. ch. 13, must specify the day on which the party will apply. A motion to set aside proceedings under a writ of trial in the District Court, when the irregularity is in the writ itself, and not in the subsequent proceedings, is bad. — Bank of Montreal v. Denison, 156.

When an Attorney is Defendant.] Under the 51st and following clauses of 8 Vic. ch. 15, a writ of trial may go from the Queen's Bench to the judge of the District Court, in a case in which *an attorney* is the defendant. —The Bank of Montreal v. Burritt, 375.

END OF VOL. III.

www.ingramcontent.com/pod-product-compliance
Lightning Source LLC
Chambersburg PA
CBHW031942290426
44108CB00011B/647